Cana

Canadian Cultural Studies

A READER

Sourayan Mookerjea, Imre Szeman, and Gail Faurschou, eds.

Foreword by Fredric Jameson

DUKE UNIVERSITY PRESS   DURHAM AND LONDON   2009

Printed in the United States of America on acid-free paper ♾
Typeset in Quadraat by Keystone Typesetting, Inc.
Library of Congress Cataloging-in-Publication Data appear on the
last printed page of this book.
Duke University Press gratefully acknowledges the support of McMaster
University, which provided funds toward the production of this book.

CONTENTS

FREDRIC JAMESON Foreword, xi

Editors' Note, xv

Acknowledgments, xvii

SOURAYAN MOOKERJEA, IMRE SZEMAN, AND GAIL FAURSCHOU
Introduction
Between Empires: On Cultural Studies in Canada, 1

1. Canadian Cultural Theory: Origins

HAROLD INNIS A Plea for Time, 37

HAROLD INNIS The Military Implications of the American
Constitution, 54

MARSHALL MCLUHAN Canada as Counter-Environment, 71

MARSHALL MCLUHAN The Medium Is the Message, 87

PAUL-ÉMILE BORDUAS Refus Global, 100

NORTHROP FRYE Conclusion to the Literary History of Canada, 111

NORTHROP FRYE City of the End of Things, 129

GEORGE GRANT Canadian Fate and Imperialism, 145

GEORGE GRANT In Defence of North America, 160

FERNAND DUMONT Of a Hesitant Quebec, 173

HAROLD CARDINAL The Buckskin Curtain: The Indian-Problem
Problem, 200

ANTHONY WILDEN The Old Question, but Not the Old Answers, 210

2. Contemporary Canadian Cultural Studies

A. NATIONALISM AND CANADA, 229

IAN ANGUS The Social Identity of English Canada, 231

JOCELYN LÉTOURNEAU "Remembering (from) Where You're Going": Memory as Legacy and Inheritance, 248

ROB SHIELDS The True North Strong and Free, 276

KEVIN PASK Late Nationalism: The Case of Quebec, 289

MAURICE CHARLAND Technological Nationalism, 308

B. RACE, DIFFERENCE, AND MULTICULTURALISM, 325

HIMANI BANNERJI On the Dark Side of the Nation: Politics of Multiculturalism and the State of "Canada", 327

KATHARYNE MITCHELL In Whose Interest? Transnational Capital and the Production of Multiculturalism in Canada, 344

EVA MACKEY Postmodernism and Cultural Politics in a Multicultural Nation: Contests over Truth in the Into the Heart of Africa Controversy, 366

LEE MARACLE Another Side of Me, 383

KRISTINA FAGAN Tewatatha:wi: Aboriginal Nationalism in Taiaiake Alfred's Peace, Power, Righteousness: An Indigenous Manifesto, 390

LEN FINDLAY Always Indigenize! The Radical Humanities in the Postcolonial Canadian University, 405

C. MODERNITY AND CONTEMPORARY CULTURE, 423

STEPHEN CROCKER Hauled Kicking and Screaming into Modernity: Non-Synchronicity and Globalization in Post-War Newfoundland, 425

IOAN DAVIES Theorizing Toronto, 441

WILL STRAW Shifting Boundaries, Lines of Descent: Cultural Studies and Institutional Realignments, 457

JODY BERLAND Writing on the Border, 472

RICK GRUNEAU AND DAVID WHITSON Communities, Civic Boosterism, and Fans, 488

SERRA TINIC Global Vistas and Local Reflections: Negotiating Place and Identity in Vancouver Television, 501

3. Government Documents

Preface to Government Documents, 515

GOVERNMENT OF CANADA From the *Report of the Royal Commission on National Development in Arts, Letters and Sciences* (Massey Commission), 518

GOVERNMENT OF CANADA From the *Report of the Royal Commission on Bilingualism and Biculturalism* (Bi and Bi Commission), 533

GOVERNMENT OF CANADA From *Multiculturalism and the Government of Canada* (Canadian Government Pamphlet), 548

YVES LABERGE Afterword
Are Cultural Studies an Anglo-Saxon Paradigm? Reflections on Cultural Studies in Francophone Networks, 561

Contributors, 581

Index of Names, 585

FREDRIC JAMESON

Foreword

American cultural studies conventionally traces its origin back to the Birmingham Centre for Contemporary Cultural Studies, which pioneered new approaches to cultural and social life (primarily under the direction of Stuart Hall) in the 1970s. The development of cultural studies in the non-English-speaking world has been more belated and more rudimentary, partly owing to the late development in so many parts of the world of a commercial mass culture (as opposed to popular cultural traditions), so much of which was imported from the United States in the first place.

But it can be argued not only that cultural studies in the United States has known a second fundamental influence, less often noted than the British one, but also that the North American sphere includes a third, mostly invisible player. It is not generally realized that, alongside U.S. French departments (University of California–San Diego, Yale, Cornell, Columbia), the principal transmission circuits for continental theory, via British translations and the Birmingham Centre for Contemporary Cultural Studies, passed through eastern and western Canadian (and Australian) cultural studies, while Quebec became the principal New World center for semiotics (which can in this context be seen as another and very distinctive version of cultural studies and theory as such). Indeed, Canada is well placed to appreciate the emergence of a mass cultural society in the twentieth century, but with enough distance from it to take the more critical "outsider's view." Canadians have often enough (from John Kenneth Galbraith to Lorne Greene) tended to pass for Americans, unlike the more obvious immigrants from other, more heavily accented parts of the Commonwealth. They are indeed our cousins from the counter-revolutionary branch of the family, the Tories who fled north, the French who declined Benjamin Franklin's invitation to join the Union; and they have other characteristics that distinguish them from us: a fully achieved universal medical system, a functioning multiculturalism, a lowering of the decibel level of commercialism and pornography, genuine regional identities and real linguistic struggles, a socialist party (and maybe even a more representative party system), and, above all, a disinclination to endorse the policies of their competitive, aggressive cold war neighbor to the south. But they are also fully exposed to the unprotected blasts of the mass culture which is one of the fundamental exports of the United States and which Canada is under constant pressure to admit and be submerged by.

This experience constitutes a privileged dimension of Canadian cultural studies, but by no means its only one. Indeed, it might be said that the impulse behind Canada's first influence on nascent American cultural studies—the work of Marshall McLuhan—was sparked as much by the new technologies of the 1950s as by their appropriation by the American neighbor. Meanwhile, behind him, the figure of Harold Innis (always somewhat mysterious for the foreign observer) drew his insights from the originality of Canada's own navigational systems, rather than from anything on the other side of the border.

Today, however, even the problems that distinguish Canadian cultural studies (and to which the present collection offers a stimulating introduction)—problems of federalism, of multiple ethnicities, of the place of Quebec in a predominantly English-speaking country, of the future of Canada's social network in the force field of the market system, indeed the future of Canada's culture in the framework of the North American Free Trade Agreement—have all the universality of the exception, and dramatize many American abstract theoretical concerns in urgent and suggestive new ways.

Indeed, I would argue that the strength of Canadian theory lies precisely in its vulnerability, and in particular its openness to a variety of influences, not only from the United States, but also from Britain and, in the context of Quebec, from France. Immigration—from the Ukraine to Haiti, from Spain to Hong Kong—has created a remarkable cultural coexistence, whose varied components have a vested interest in the survival of the Canadian experiment, periodically threatened by Americanization. Meanwhile, in the immense land mass which is geographical Canada (in contrast to its modest population of some 33 million—not noticeably bigger than greater Shanghai), the stakes of the First Nations movement (including the Inuit and the Métis), and above all of the autonomy of the French-speaking province of Quebec, are higher and rather different from those of ethnic minorities in the United States.

For many people, urban life in Canada is reminiscent of an older

1930s-style urban life in the U.S., and it is not too much to invoke a kind of nostalgia of such Americans for Canada itself, as well as an anxiety about its possible subsumption by American big business and the free-market reforms of the last decades. But we are only beginning to recognize that to this still distinctive way of life corresponds a rich and distinctive intellectual ferment, to which the present volume may serve as an introduction. The cultural fear of Canadians has often been that, compared to the United States, but also to Europe, they have remained provincial. On the contrary: it is the United States itself which in its lack of curiosity about the outside world and its "blindness of the center" is preeminently provincial and parochial. Canadian cultural studies gives us the example of social and cultural analyses open to all the forces of the outside world: its theoretical and practical research may indeed serve to deprovincialize us and to help overcome the blindness of the center, that conviction of American exceptionalism which so often encourages the feeling that U.S. consumer culture and the market system are the final flowering of human nature as such.

EDITORS' NOTE

In an effort to maximize the number of perspectives and positions included in this collection, some of the essays have been edited for length. We have endeavoured to retain original punctuation, spellings, hyphenation, and capitalization, except where we have corrected internal inconsistencies or typographical errors. Throughout the volume, citations have been modified for consistency and to supply missing bibliographic information wherever possible. Editorial additions to the texts are enclosed in square brackets; editors' notes are identified as such.

ACKNOWLEDGMENTS

This book could not have been completed without the extraordinary work of Tim Kaposy, Alex Khasnabish, Nicholas Holm, Carolyn Veldstra, and, finally, Sarah Blacker, all of whom acted as editorial assistants at different points in the life of this project. Tim and Sarah in particular are to be thanked for their tireless efforts on its behalf. We would also like to thank Fredric Jameson for contributing a foreword to this volume. Those who know Fred know that he has a long interest in things Canadian; we're pleased to be able to have him involved in this volume, even if in a small way. Finally, this book benefited from the patience of Reynolds Smith at Duke University Press, who kept us going through inevitable delays and frustrations. Final work on this project was aided by research grants and fellowships from the Alexander von Humboldt Foundation (Szeman) and the Social Sciences and Humanities Research Council of Canada (Mookerjea).

Assistance with funding for permissions was provided by the Faculty of Arts, University of Alberta; the Office of the Vice-President, Research and International Affairs, McMaster University; the Department of English, McMaster University; and the Dean of Humanities, McMaster University. Thanks to all of these sources.

Every effort has been made to contact the copyright holders of the materials included in this volume. We are grateful for the permissions granted by authors and copyright holders, acknowledged in the notes section of individual chapters.

SOURAYAN MOOKERJEA, IMRE SZEMAN,

AND GAIL FAURSCHOU

Between Empires: On Cultural Studies in Canada

Canadian Cultural Studies?

Cultural studies has been established in Canada as field of scholarship and teaching for several decades. The Canadian academic system has historical ties to the United Kingdom, where cultural studies is typically thought to have been born; to the United States, where it lives out its mature, professionalized life; to other parts of the British Commonwealth, especially Australia, where university programs in cultural studies have long flourished; and, finally, to France, from which distinct ideas of cultural analysis have found their way into both Quebec and English Canadian universities. In addition, many scholars in Canada have trained abroad, or have been trained in Canada by scholars from the United States and the United Kingdom, who arrived in large numbers at the time of the expansion of the Canadian university system in the 1960s and 1970s.[1] Indeed, since Canadian scholars and students are plugged heavily into the U.S. academic circuit and its omnipresent popular culture machine, it would be strange for cultural studies, in all its anti-disciplinary indeterminacy, not to have found its way into Canada long before the beginning of the twenty-first century. Cultural studies is here and from the number of programs of study and research already in existence or in the process of being developed, it looks here to stay.

What might come as more of a surprise is the claim that what Canadians are doing with cultural studies—whether they are doing it in reference to Canadian themes and contexts, or with respect to other materials—is, first of all, unique and distinctive, and second, offers theoretical and analytic resources that can contribute significantly to the conceptualization and interpretation of issues at the heart of critical cultural analysis today, wherever this is done. Which is to say: not only does cultural studies exist in Canada as a disciplinary formation, Canadian cultural studies *matters* for issues and topics taken up in contemporary cultural, social, and political theory around the world. What we hope to do in this introduction is to show how and why this is the case by offering a critical pathway through the essays we have collected here.

Cultural studies' itinerary from the Centre for Contemporary Cultural Studies at Birmingham University to the present—that is, from the United Kingdom to Canada, retracing an earlier and even more vexed movement of bodies, narratives, and knowledges—can be recounted in a number of ways. One can try to understand the path traveled in terms of the expanding range of sites and topics brought under investigation—an expansion animated by a persistent slippage back and forth between popular culture and mass culture within critical analysis. Or one can lean more heavily on established (though finally unsatisfactory) scholarly habits and recall a familiar succession of "theoretical paradigms" moving, as in the ordering of some survey course, forward toward the present: the "linguistic turn" coming on the heels of existential and phenomenological Marxisms, and with it, the familiar faces of structuralism, poststructuralism, postcolonialism, and, finally, identity theories and the various feminisms, all of which culminate in a shift from "theory" to the more open-ended practice called "cultural studies." Or perhaps, as Stuart Hall and, especially, Fredric Jameson have each in his own way insisted, one can attempt to understand the historical conditions of possibility of theories and then attempt further to understand how the historical conditions of their intelligibility come to weigh on the debates and on the urgency of considering this or that site of study.[2]

For example, the postmodern problematic, so recently at the fore of our theoretical considerations, has just as quickly been transformed by events we have been living through into the even more bewildering problematic of globalization. It then becomes exceedingly difficult to tell any story about where cultural studies has been and where it is going. This difficulty moreover seems to be rooted in a paradox: with the emergence of the globalization problematic, the interdisciplinary aspirations of cultural studies find, on the one hand, a powerful impetus such that strategies of critique and modes of analyses that were worked out and elaborated in the humanities are all of a sudden confronted with the detailed attention and specialized questions of the social sciences. On the other hand, this very "transversal movement" (as Gilles Deleuze and Félix Guattari would say) across fields of knowledge makes it seem as though cultural studies itself has disappeared off the map, so unpronounceable are the questions we now feel the need to ask in the languages we presently know!

Even given these challenges and confusions, it is possible to find a conceptual thread that brings together the essays collected here. For it will be remembered that the novel situation that British cultural studies sought to understand was the transformations of everyday life wrought by the postwar reconstruction of Europe and, more specifically, the construction of the mass society of the spectacle. U.S. corporations and U.S. government agencies were active and obvious players in this construction, but it was the effects on the ground of resistance through ritual and style—new subcultural formations and marginalized expressive cultures that appeared as enigmatic displacements of national culture—that the British New Left sought to understand.

The Canadian situation runs parallel to the emergence of such cold war cultural formations, except for two significant and consequential differences. First, a characteristically neocolonial reorganization of the "national" economy was already well underway in Canada before the Second World War. Second, the questions raised by the rapid advances of new kinds of mass culture and mass media, and the deeper reach of commodification and urbanization, have in Canada involved the further complications of debates and disputes over always troubled ideas of national identity (though here the British situation has had echoes). For it has not merely been a matter of Canada's fate to be bound up "with the interplay of various world empires," as George Grant put it (see his essay "Canadian Fate and Imperialism" in this volume), nor a matter of Canada serving, as Marshall McLuhan argued (see "Canada as Counter-Environment," in this volume), as a counterenvironment for the singularity of American nationalism and the American superpower state in the global system today. Rather, our regional situation as a moon of Jupiter brings to life and works itself through a more enduring history involving a multitude of *nations* living under an imperially formed *state*. What is distinctive about the cultural studies work done in Canada is that it has had to think through the condensation of cultural-political dilemmas emerging out of late-capitalist postmodernization in terms of other longstanding political deadlocks. These dilemmas involve the conflicts and antagonisms of a multiplicity of collectivities standing on some common ground. To borrow and extend Étienne Balibar's argument, in Canada the Left confronts once more the modern dialectic of masses and classes but now in a situation in which the stakes—*of socialism or barbarism, as they used* to say—have been raised ominously.[3] Insofar as globalization can be said to involve the emergence of comparable situations around the world, this reader should thus prove useful to scholars working in national situations and local contexts well beyond the northern climes of Canada.

This is perhaps nowhere so clear as with respect to the contemporary status of the nation-state around the globe. While some voices in recent discussions of globalization and diaspora have assumed the obsolescence of nation-states (often by confusing their own ethical and political stance with facts on the ground), it is not difficult to grasp how both nations and states are still crucial features of a world being transformed by global flows. Indeed, developments of the past few years make this amply clear. For example, despite the economic necessity of immigrants for first-world economies, they are once again seen as threats to communities insistent on claiming the purity of national identifications. Proposed immigration exams in countries such as Denmark, Germany, and Switzerland foreground knowledge of high cultural canons and test for supposedly national cultural dispositions (say, tolerance with respect to difference);[4] to these cultural fences we can add the physical barriers erected between the United States and Mexico, Israel and Palestine, Spain and Morocco. The idea of national culture, too, is making a comeback. The 2005 UNESCO Convention on the Protection and Promotion of the Diversity of Cultural Expressions affirms all over again the need for nations to be able to foster and protect culture within their borders—not, of course, to support state sovereignty (the convention's real aim), but in the name of cultural diversity, tolerance, and social justice. Moreover, jingoistic and misogynist nationalisms (often connected to religious fundamentalisms) have been on the move everywhere, especially in the United States, Europe, the Arab world, India, China, and Japan. From this renewed attention to the nation spins out a web of issues at the heart of contemporary social, cultural, and political debates: racism, ethnicity, difference, identity, multiculturalism, the future of citizenship, the construction of new kinds of commons, of new modes of production, and the possibility and promise of new modes of cosmopolitan belonging.

The essays collected in this reader are relevant to many of these contemporary issues because the cultural and class contradictions of nationhood have long been at the center of cultural theory and public discourse in Canada. On the one hand, English-language cultural criticism has been forced to confront the dissolution of national-imperial "high" culture in the wake of the collapse of the British Empire. On the other, cultural critics and producers alike in Canada have needed to understand the new global politics of mass-popular culture as this emerged after the Second World War within the hegemonic formation of the capitalist world economy centered in the United States—a new, postmodern, American incorporated space that, while not formally an empire like that of the British, is nevertheless often nicknamed as such by Canadians, especially with regard to cultural matters. Consequently, Canadian cultural criticism characteristically engages with the connections between culture, politics, and nationhood. Poised between old and new, historical and metaphorical empires, and operating within the conditions of incomplete modernity and economic and cultural dependency, the specific context and situation of Canada has generated a body of cultural criticism and theory that offers unique insights into the dynamics of *both* center and periphery.

Like any number of middle powers, Canada participates actively in the capitalist world economy: it remains one of the larger economies in the world, is a member of the Group of Eight (G8), and for all the recent talk of China, remains the United States' largest trading partner—including being the biggest source for that most essential commodity of all, oil.[5] At the same time, despite its geographic size and because of its small population, its status in the geopolitical imaginary is more akin to Belgium or the Scandinavian countries than France or Germany: modern, democratic, left-leaning, safe and unremarkable enough to not usually be an object of realpolitik anxieties. And yet, even here there is a key feature of Canadian cultural history that is now more widely instructive. Like many small- or mid-power countries, Canada's national identity has always been intensely contested in ways that have had a determinate impact on the character of social, political, and cultural life in the country.

Historians conventionally fill out this story of precarious national unity and enduring conflict with reference to five main periods. The first of these is the long era of aboriginal civilizations on the continent, with ancient continuities running intact well beyond the arrival of the first transatlantic cod fisheries after John Cabot's voyages of 1497 and the emergence of the fur trade society of the sixteenth century. The second period begins with the founding of New France by Samuel de Champlain through the establishment of the Habitation (later, Acadia) in 1607 and the settlement of Quebec in 1608. New France remained primarily a fur trade society, its routes and portages of hybridization, of change and exchange, running from the Great Lakes through the Ohio River Valley as far south as the Gulf of Mexico, though agriculture and the fisheries also grew in importance during this time.

Throughout the eighteenth century, the struggle between England and France to supersede the Dutch in political and commercial supremacy in the post-1492 "world economy" intensified, and both New France and British North America were part of the chessboard of this imperial contest. In Europe, this rivalry culminated in the Seven Years' War (1756–63), but warfare had run hot and cold in North America from a much earlier period. A decisive moment of this conflict was the conquest of Quebec by the British in 1759 and the fall of Montreal in 1760. British attempts to control New France thereafter were immediately confronted by a rebellion of aboriginal nations of the Great Lakes region (Pontiac's Rebellion, 1763–66). Nevertheless, the establishment of a British government in Quebec by the Royal Proclamation of 1763 is usually said to begin the colonial period, the third era in usual accounts of Canadian history.

The royal proclamation instanced a radical beginning in another important way as well. Its assertion of the British crown's sovereignty over the former territorial claims of New France also acknowledged the national and territorial rights of the "Indians," an unprecedented and singular formulation of sovereignty that underlies both the constitutional concept of the treaty rights of aboriginal peoples today and the legal concept of aboriginal title, both of which have been crucial to First Nations' contemporary struggles. Moreover, the royal proclamation was soon supplemented by the Quebec Act of 1774, which restored French civil law and permitted Catholics to enter public service, two key accommodations offered to the defeated but still insurrectional Quebecois.

This period would also see the expansion and consolidation of the British settlements in Upper and Lower Canada (now Ontario and Quebec), New Brunswick, and Nova Scotia, through the arrival of Loyalist refugees from the American Revolution and, later, those dispossessed and displaced by the Industrial Revolution in Britain. While these British North American colonies were primarily agricultural societies organized around a staples economy serving the British Empire, the early decades of the nineteenth century leading up to Confederation in 1867 saw the beginnings of industrialization as well. In fact, economic and political crises in the island heartland of the Industrial Revolution traveled along the imperial routes of the world economy to the British North American colonies. In 1837–38, rebellions of small farmers against the anglophone mercantile oligarchy broke out in Lower Canada and spread to Upper Canada, as the agricultural crises of industrialization worsened across the imperial circuitry. Though these uprisings were eventually suppressed, they achieved one of their major objectives when responsible government was established throughout the British North American colonies between 1848 and 1855.

A fourth period in the conventional historical narrative begins with the bringing together of the two Canadas, New Brunswick, and Nova Scotia into a modern nation-state through confederation in 1867, which launches the era of nation-building proper. Thus, western expansion across the northern prairies, seeking to outrun the advance of the American frontier, becomes a matter of policy involving mass immigration and the construction of a transcontinental railway. Manitoba and the Northwest Territories were brought into confederation in 1870, as was British Columbia in 1871. In the east, Prince Edward Island would join the Confederation in 1873 and Newfoundland in 1949. (The most recent member of the Confederation is the high-Arctic Inuit territory of Nunavut, the northeastern half of the Northwest Territories, which joined in 1999.)

The fifth part of the narrative—the story of Canada in the twentieth century—can be told in a number of ways. For our purposes, we can conceive of this latest chapter as itself comprising three distinct eras, the first beginning with the world depression of 1873 and closing with the tumultuous decades spanning the First World War, the Great Depression of the 1930s, and the Second World War. During this period, industrialization, racialized class conflict, and urbanization all emerge as the horizon of the national future. So, too, does the incalculable fall into the economic and political orbit of the United States that comes to eventually sever postcolonial Canada's tether to the British Empire. The second period of the postwar boom and the new cold war is when the social trends associated with this new orbit assert themselves as the order of the day. American capital now dramatically overshadows British capital in the major sectors of the Canadian economy, especially the branch plant industries and resource extraction. Moreover, urbanization reaches a new threshold, as depopulation and unemployment afflict agricultural regions and the hinterlands in cycles of boom and bust.

A third era can then be said to begin sometime between the election of the *separatiste* Parti Quebecois to the government of Quebec for the first time in 1976 and the "patriation" of the Constitution from being an act of the British Parliament to becoming an act of the Parliament of Canada in 1982. It is in this era that the Parti Quebecois holds two referendums in Quebec (in 1980 and 1995) on the question of national autonomy and independence from Canada, the last one keeping Quebec in confederation by only the very slightest of margins. In this same period, aboriginal peoples launch a war of position on three fronts: against a paternalistic and repressive state, the ongoing destruction of the environment, and the extraction of contested resources by national and multinational corporations. It is also in this era that Canada officially adopts a multicultural national identity (in 1988) and enters a new free trade agreement with the United States (in 1989), deepening existing, regionally mediated class conflicts and creating new political fissures as well.

Such a brief overview of Canadian history already brings into the foreground the ways in which nationhood in Canada, as in many other postcolonial societies, has always been a contested construction. As a quintessentially modern mode of belonging, nationhood posits a peculiarly bourgeois form of legal and imaginary universality, limited by political borders and contradicted by institutions of domination and exclusion. Nationhood thus brings together the social relations of race, class, gender, and sexuality into their characteristic patterns of conflict. From a distance, Canada may seem to offer a peaceful model of a liberal democratic state, but is actually riven with divisions: the linguistic and cultural divide between French and English, between these postcolonial "nations" and the ones they colonized (First Nations, the Métis, and the Inuit),[6] and between strong regional identities ("the West," Newfoundland, the Maritimes), all complicated further by gendered class conflict— inevitable in a capital-intensive resource economy. As a wealthy country, however, Canada's conflicts are mostly "ameliorated" with various Band-Aids of crisis management. And yet, the Canadian passage *between empires* has also sowed the seeds of utopian possibilities. Popular and marginal movements have created cultural spaces and won political concessions that allow engagements with the politics of community, citizenship, and sovereignty in ways that many other people (even in the United States) can only dream of and look to longingly.

This reader therefore seeks to make legible a historical problematic that keeps demanding attention in the cultural studies work done in Canada. This problematic is defined by the historical transformation over the twentieth century of the terms and conditions for carrying out a national struggle for hegemony. As such, it also concerns the new and different ways the concept of "hegemony" has to then be thought about and understood. The passage from British tutelage to American dependency held enormous consequences for the strategies the Canadian national ruling class needed to devise in order to maintain their leadership in the face of "popular" and "marginal" social movements. Moreover, the latter have also been radically determined by Canada's passage from colony to dominion and then to a quasi-sovereign signatory of the North American Free Trade Agreement (1994). For this reason, most sustained programs of research in cultural studies in Canada sooner or later find themselves entangled in this problematic.

Since the primary postwar project of regional crisis management and national hegemony under the direction of the federal state has involved the Canadian ideology of multiculturalism, this cultural-political formation occupies a strategically prominent position in this problematic. While the Canadian state's official policy of multiculturalism has attracted the attention of scholars and policy makers from various quarters in recent years, it is less often noted how multiculturalism has been a particularly crucial site of contestation in Canada. As Himani Bannerji points out in her essay in this volume, "The Dark Side of the Nation," multiculturalism's immediate roots are to be found in a political compromise forged by Pierre Elliot Trudeau's Liberal government (1968–79) that would commit the alienated western provinces to a federalist project intended to contain and defuse Quebecois national liberation, which had gained self-confidence and class consciousness through the transformative experiences of the Quiet Revolution (see, in this collection, Paul Émile Borduas's manifesto, and essays by Fernand Dumont and Jocelyn Letourneau for an account of the fortunes of nationalism in Quebec). The Liberal government's initial device—a policy of official bilingualism and biculturalism that would institutionalize the myth of the two founding nations (England and France)—didn't fly. Multiculturalism was then offered to immigrant groups—for example, farmers from Eastern Europe—unrelieved from Anglo racism on the prairies, in order to secure bilingualism and thus also the narrative of the two founding nations. There was a further carrot of particular interest to the proprietors of resource extraction industries. The Liberal government's 1969 white paper *Statement on Indian Policy* proposed to strip aboriginal peoples of all their treaty rights and so present their land and labor power to white Canada on a platter in the name of assimilation and formal equality.[7] The aboriginal political leader Harold Cardinal raised the alarm in his eloquent and influential book *The Unjust Society* (1969, excerpted here). Aboriginal people, mobilizing themselves now as the First Nations, were able to block this move.[8] For these reasons, neither the Quebecois nor First Nations have ever really consented to the gradual redefinition of Canadian national identity from the British Dominion of Canada to multicultural Canada between 1962—when policies restricting nonwhite immigration were reformed—and 1988, when the Multiculturalism Act was proclaimed. Furthermore, as Bannerji's critique here argues, Canada's multiculturalism policy leaves intact the coordination of patriarchal power with class domination. The policy has been substituted for any meaningful and comprehensive antiracist and antisexist, popular and common program of social justice that would move us further along toward classlessness. Consequently, neither those who practice the kind of popular racism that is anti-immigration nor so-called visible minority immigrants can give their heart and soul over completely to this new project of multicultural national identity.

Canada moreover has long had to struggle with the difficulties of its proximity to the United States, the undisputed hegemon of the past century, and to contend with its empire of electronic signals and the economies-of-scale might of its cultural industries, well before the advent of satellite technologies. Whatever one might want to identify as a distinctly "Canadian" mass culture (with regard to music, media, urban lifestyle, etc.), if indeed there is any such thing, it ultimately circulates within the gravitational field of this postmodern "North American empire" so that older, local popular-cultural traditions and newer multicultural ones are all brought together into various contradictions of collective identity. It is for this reason that reflections on modernity and culture, the problems of cultural borrowing, and alternative political possibilities—or their lack—have been so rich and fruitful in Canada. The problems and consequences of the commodification of everyday life, of consumerism, alienation, and reification seem to be accessible to cultural critique in Canada, in the first instance, through questions of identity and belonging. Globalized *avant la lettre*, cultural theory in Canada has had to address its positioning at both the center and periphery in ways that speak directly to the cultural and social complexities of the current era.

The How and Why of This Reader

We will take up some of these issues again below in order to spell out more clearly our understanding of what we have here called a radical problematic of "passages between empires." Before we turn to that task, however, it is important to engage in some reflections on the construction and organization of this book. This collection brings together more recent work in Canadian cultural studies, especially by those contemporary figures who have had an impact on the constitution of cultural studies in Canada, with works by some key Canadian thinkers writing in the decades immediately following the Second World War. The figures whom we have located at the "origins" of Canadian cultural theory—Paul Émile Borduas, Harold Innis, Marshall McLuhan, Northrop Frye, Fernand Dumont, George Grant, Harold Cardinal, and Anthony Wilden—have each played a role in establishing the questions and issues that continue to frame cultural and social analysis in Canada. These include reflections on the problems and possibilities opened up by Canada's belated modernity; its problematic and incomplete nationalism; the relationship between technology, communication, and geography; and the fate of minority language communities and of indigenous identities, ideas, and ways of life. These originary figures of the immediate postwar period remain important to the constitution and self-understanding of contemporary intellectual formations: Innis, McLuhan, and Wilden to communications theory in Canada, Frye to Canadian literary studies, Grant and Innis to a left-nationalist tradition of critical political economy, Dumont and Borduas to Quebecois national and political culture, and Cardinal to native studies. However, as the essays in the second part of the book attest, cultural studies in Canada has become heterogeneous in a way that precludes the easy establishment of direct intellectual lineages. Those working in cultural studies in Canada since the 1980s draw as much (if not more) on work in critical race theory, feminist and queer theory, postcolonial studies, the work of the Birmingham Centre or the Frankfurt school, and the whole panoply of contemporary theory—from Jacques Derrida to Judith Butler, from Fredric Jameson to Gilles Deleuze—as on earlier Canadian theorists. The figures in the first part of the book remain essential to understanding cultural studies in Canada not because they together constitute a point of clear origin to which everything must refer, but because they offer some of the first and most influential attempts to map the links between space, culture, communication and the nation—a mapping materially and conceptually enabled by the complex space that is Canada.

The essays in the second part of this collection highlight contemporary work in cultural studies in Canada, including work on feminism; First Nations issues; culture and politics in Quebec; studies of race, nation, and multiculturalism; and explorations of the lived realities of urban and regional geographies in Canada. While a diversity of approaches and issues is taken up in these essays, they have for convenience been placed into three thematic groups that reflect key areas in which work in Canadian cultural studies has been carried out: (1) the trials and tribulations of nationalism and national culture; (2) race, difference, and multiculturalism; and (3) modernity and contemporary culture. It is on these issues, too, that cultural studies in Canada has perhaps the most to contribute conceptually to contemporary work being done in other zones and spaces, and across a range of disciplines. What is perhaps lost in the process are specialized examinations of Canadian cultural production (films, literature, television, fine and popular arts, music, and so on), which taken together might offer some overview of the contemporary Canadian cultural scene. But it should be emphasized that this collection is not meant to capture or articulate a specific vision of Canadian culture, so much as to reconstruct a problematic in relation to which a wide range of concepts and critical strategies have been developed in Canadian cultural studies to begin with.[9]

One of the aims of the collection is to open greater dialogue and debate across different modes of cultural analysis within Canada. These differences are not constituted by the typical range of various politico-theoretical solitudes (cultural studies vs. "traditional" academic approaches, Marxism vs. psychoanalysis, etc.). In Canada, they correspond to linguistic and social divides that have yet to be broached—and not just between anglophone and francophone academic cultures, but also between both of these and concepts and theories developed in First Nations writing.[10]

We would need to begin by recognizing that there is no easy translation from English Canadian cultural studies to the forms of cultural analysis currently being undertaken in Quebec. (See Yves Laberge's afterword in this collection for a discussion of these issues.) Though Quebec has a distinct and rich intellectual tradition, it does not at the moment count "cultural studies" as a part of it—at least not in the way that this practice, however heterogeneous, has come to be understood in the Anglo-American academy. "Études culturelles" sounds simply like "sciences humaines" in another guise: a general description of the activity of the humanities. Several decades ago, Fernand Dumont, whose work would be a seminal point of reference in any compilation of a Quebecois cultural studies (see his essay " Of a Hesitant Quebec" in this reader), suggested that social history has been the major intellectual movement to arise in Quebec after World War II, emerging out of that province's "Quiet Revolution."[11] Moreover, for some Quebecois writers such as the theorist Marcel Rioux, trends in the English Canadian intellectual world appear far too imitative of American developments. To some Quebecois intellectuals, English Canadian scholars, unless they are area specialists, appear not to know their own history and so seem to need to undergo a process of decolonization before hoping to effect the kind of intellectual rapprochement so desperately needed in Canadian letters.[12]

A similar point can be made with respect to First Nations writings. Certainly cultural studies and aboriginal cultural politics have had several encounters over the years. Perhaps the most prominent of these has been the critique of the appropriation of voice formulated by aboriginal artists and writers protesting the increasing commodification of aboriginal cultures in expanding global markets serving, ironically, the desire for an "authentically noncommodified experience." Aboriginal cultural critics thus have instigated a politics of cultural property as well as a politics of representation in museums and in the mass media. Despite these encounters, cultural studies in Canada and native studies programs of research have more often proceeded on parallel paths than in common formation.

Drawing on distinct archives and speaking from unique material and cultural formations, English Canadian, Quebecois, and First Nations forms of cultural analysis each contribute invaluable insights into the complexities of culture and hegemony, nation and community, within which all three groups are implicated. To give just two examples: the trauma of belated modernity that Northrop Frye describes in "City of the End of Things" is echoed in Borduas's manifesto, *Refus Global*, written two decades earlier, just as there are parallels worth considering in the defenses of particularity argued by George Grant in "Canadian Fate and Imperialism," Fernand Dumont in "Of a Hesitant Quebec," and Harold Cardinal in "The Buckskin Curtain." It is high time to begin to see how these different spaces and ways of thinking might critically encounter one another, even as it must also be seen as symptomatic that there isn't already a greater connection between these sites and spaces of cultural analysis.

Unlike in the United States—where cultural studies, despite its self-identity as a somewhat marginal academic practice, has established journals, has monographs published by prestigious university presses, and is taught on campuses across the country—cultural studies in Canada has endured a more subterranean existence. While the first university program in cultural studies was established at Trent University in 1978, it took a quarter of a century for the second to be established, at McMaster University. Hiring freezes in the public university system largely account for this break in institution building. The Canadian Association of Cultural Studies was founded in 2003, shortly after Canadian universities started recruiting in significant numbers once more.

In the intervening years, cultural studies was taken up and developed through other disciplinary routes. From the mid-1970s on, cultural studies taught in the Department of Sociology and the Graduate Programme in Social and Political Thought at York University (Toronto) attracted large numbers of graduate students and subsequently influenced many English Canadian academic programs and critical cultural projects. The interdisciplinary organization of the Graduate Programme in Social and Political Thought was particularly conducive to forging the early formation of cultural studies by bringing together the work of the Birmingham school, the Frankfurt school, a phenomenologically oriented sociology of the body, decolonization theory, and humanist and existentialist currents of Marxism and Fanonian psychoanalysis. The communications programs at Simon Fraser University (Vancouver), and at Concordia University and McGill University (both in Montreal), were also key sites of innovation, as was the Critical Pedagogy Group, active in the early 1980s, at the Ontario Institute for Studies in Education (Toronto). Some of the important sites and spaces in which critical ideas were developed and circulated have come and gone: journals (*Canadian Journal of Political and Social Thought* [1976–1991], the early Canadian years of *Telos*); independent presses; small magazines fusing art, culture, and politics (*Border/lines*, *Impulse*, *Public*, *Parallelogramme*, *Alphabet City*, *Parachute*, *Fuse*, *Rungh*); and seminar and lecture series (University of Toronto's International Summer Institute for Semiotic and Structural Studies, Culture Lab, Public Access, the artists' collective Basic Research, and the Institute for Humanities at Simon Fraser University's experimental public spheres: "The Body Project" and "Spectacular State: Fascism and the Modern Imagination"—all of which stimulated a proliferation of colloquia and festivals bringing together scholars, artists, activists, and publics in urban centres across the country). The precarious life of the field at times means that it can sometimes be a challenge for those interested in cultural studies in Canada to locate essays and hunt down articles. This collection aims to bring together materials that are at times difficult to find—including government documents of the kind that are included in the third part of this book.

The assembly of this collection is marked inevitably by ambivalences that are characteristic of both cultural studies in general and *Canadian* cultural studies more specifically. While it is true that the problematic of the nation cannot be passed over in silence in Canada, it is also the case that the production of a book that proposes to represent a national tradition of cultural studies will be controversial. We would be the first to recognize that discussion of a national style or mode of thinking is, for the most part, hopelessly archaic or misplaced—at its worst, an example of the kind of "ethnico-editorial parthenogenesis" that Pierre Bourdieu and Loïc Wacquant mock when they imagine a volume on "French Arab" or "German Turkish" cultural studies to follow those on British, Italian, and German cultural studies.[13] Any study of national culture today needs to track the links to structures of inequality and exclusion, to strategies of empowerment and disempowerment; and to discussions of the transnational condition of cultural studies at present.[14] For all this, however, the space of Canada within the global system is such that thinking which arises "here" and which tries to understand the precise historical constitution of this "here"—varied, multiple, contested—responds to problematics and formations that *are* different from what they are "elsewhere." Not utterly different, not without resemblances or connections: we are trying to create neither a canon of work *on* Canada nor one that reflects some deep Canadian essence. Rather, we have sought to make legible a problematic arising from particular historical formations in line with the very best critical impulses of cultural studies wherever it is practiced.

Between Empires, or, Always Already Globalization

What does it mean then to understand cultural studies in Canada as an exploration of the multiple passages *between empires*—an exploration that turns critically on the contradictions of national identity, difference and belonging, opportunity, and oppression? On the one hand, there is the formation of a state conditioned by both local and distant events; on the other, there are the multiple collective projects of national belonging with their conflicts and contradictions. It is in the unbridgeable gaps between nation building and state formation in Canada where the tasks of hegemonic struggle emerge historically.

In Canada, we can discern the cultural character of political struggle over state formation quite clearly in one of the decisive early moments of the process (in some accounts, these are foundational events). A politics of culture is evident in the strategy of colonization pursued by the British through the Royal Proclamation of 1763 shortly after the conquest of Quebec (1759–60), followed by its hasty reversal in the Quebec Act of 1774. The royal proclamation announced a policy of assimilation with respect to New France (replacing French civil law with British legal institutions, in a bid to attract immigrants from the thirteen colonies).

With Pontiac's Rebellion a spur, the royal proclamation moreover recognized the nationhood of aboriginal peoples and implied their territorial sovereignty around the Great Lakes region against encroachments from the thirteen colonies; a mere decade later, the Quebec Act asserted more unambiguously the British crown's sovereignty over this territory (as yet another strategy against encroachment, such that the Quebec Act served as one of the provocations of the American Revolution). However, the act also restored New France's seigneurial system and its religious and linguistic autonomy as a concession to the resistance that emerged in New France against the assimilatory measures of the royal proclamation.[15] A politics of cultural diversity can be traced back even earlier, as Richard Day argues, to the needs of the administrators of New France to seek alliances with various aboriginal nations in order to secure the fur trade and yet not lose *les habitants*—francophone peasants on the seigneurial estates—to the freedoms of *métissage*.[16]

After Confederation in 1867, the importation of old-world myths about ancient races naturally evolving into modern nation-states would have to erase both the emergent singularity of "place" and its actual history in order to mutate into our contemporary two founding nations narrative. A rhetoric of technological development then plays a crucial role in this hegemonic project of erasure (as Maurice Charland points out in this volume), demonstrating again the imperial imperatives involved in the formation of national hegemony, since the construction of the transcontinental Canadian Pacific Railway not only builds the nation and a national market but links the latter to an imperial one.

But it is the continual intrusion of struggles of class and gender into the politics of national identity that make apparent that the final horizon of "local" hegemony has long been a global one. The long-term conditions for economic growth and capitalist accumulation, as Marx pointed out, require an incessant reach into the far corners of the globe. Ruling classes of the Canadian state have had to place their fate first in the hands of British capital and then, ever increasingly, in those of American capital. For this reason, the Canadian state, and whatever stamp it has been able to put on national cultures and societies here, has been deeply comprador in character, running its domestic agenda with one eye riveted on imperatives coming from elsewhere.[17] From the racializing biopolitics of immigration—in particular the importation of British working- and lower-middle-class women to work as domestic servants and then become mothers of the nation during the nineteenth and first half of the twentieth centuries—to Canadian capital's current dependence on the cheapened labor of women and men throughout the world, our "Canadian" habits of consumption and high standard of living have ensured that national hegemony remains systematically connected to struggles taking place around the globe.

"Hegemony," of course, has been one of the key words of the intellectual project of cultural studies, if not its central enabling concept, ever since Stuart Hall's mobilization of Gramsci to understand the victories of Thatcherism. Critical voices, mindful of state expenditures on arms, have always objected that the dimensions of "consent" and "leadership" in hegemony applied only to a middle stratum made up of roughly 18 percent of the world's population, whereas for the remaining 82 percent, consent was neither sought nor given, as force sufficed. In recent years, there have been occasional calls to abandon the Gramscian problematic of "hegemony," from Tony Bennett's discontent with the alleged utopianism of attempts to join in wars of position from inside universities to Michael Hardt and Antonio Negri's diagnosis of the problematic's obsolescence.[18] Indeed, the currency in Canadian cultural studies of other seemingly alternative concepts such as "governmentality" (Foucault) and, most recently, "control society" (Deleuze) probably has much to do with the greater continental integration sealed by NAFTA and with the global reach of multinational corporations. For these developments would tip one's estimation of the balance between force and consent at work in the local run of things considerably in favor of the former, as the social changes we are living through are increasingly planned and administered privately, withdrawn from any public domain of consent. In any case, the problematic of passages between empires not only poses the problem of national hegemony in relation to a global horizon but directs us, self-reflexively, toward the historical limit of the concept as well.

Our account of our passages between empires will therefore emphasize each of these aspects of the radical problematic. But most important, we will need to construct a historical interpretation that connects popular and marginal social movements in Canada with the course of other struggles around the world. For it is these popular and marginal struggles that are the inescapable determinants of the reflections on culture, identity, history, and place in the essays we have collected together here. We begin first, in the section below, by considering a theoretical resource we have found helpful for this task of interpretation.

In the historical perspective elaborated by Giovanni Arrighi, Immanuel Wallerstein, and their colleagues in their seminal work *Antisystemic Movements*, we are invited to understand social movements in terms of their significance as cultural transformations that have reshaped the modern world system.[19] The daunting scale of their historiographical imagination—spanning the globe for over five hundred years of what Wallerstein calls "historical capitalism"—has been an important and productive theoretical breakthrough for many postcolonial ethnographers, historians, and theorists in cultural studies and beyond, insofar as this imagination radically breaks with the nation-state as the normal (and often unthought) "unit of analysis" for both theoretical and empirical work. In this way, their historiography also breaks with developmentalism, which assumes that modern history is the history of each nation-state running on its own head of steam, some far ahead, others trying to catch up, and yet others occasionally colliding with each other in war. Instead, these neo-Braudelians argue that our proper concern should be with what they call the "modern world system," which is defined in their technical language as a capitalist world economy. Consequently, the first misunderstanding that must immediately be dispelled is that we are being led here back to some kind of economic reductionism. Quite the contrary: the capitalist world economy of which they speak is understood precisely to be a historical system. Indeed, they offer us a hypothesis about the multiplicity of time. Following Braudel, they argue that to think historically we must be prepared to think in terms of at least three orders of time: the time of events, a time of conjunctures, and that of *la longue durée.*[20] Their endeavor to reformulate for us some of the problems posed by the matter of time moreover accords with the fundamental importance these historical sociologists give to agency and so to social struggles that, they argue, have transformed the modern world system even as it endures as a worldwide division of labor. This emphasis on agency and struggle then also makes their work relevant to the concerns of a tradition of cultural studies running from E. P. Thompson and Raymond Williams to Stuart Hall—in particular the debates over the idea of a "long revolution" and Hall's subsequent Gramscian correction of Althusser—while allowing us at the same time to move beyond the Eurocentric limits of much Birmingham theorizing.

We are now, in any case, able to consider what these authors mean by the phrase "antisystemic movement." Resistances and revolts throughout the world system have continually breathed life into a wide range of social movements that often endure beyond the punctual events that gave birth to them and that sometimes even give purpose, sense, courage, and direction to subsequent revolts and strategies of resistance. Despite all the diversity and locality of their immediate provocations and their immediate demands, the long-term historical significance of resistance and revolt in forging social movements and shaping modernity, as well as defining present possibilities, may be best grasped, so these authors argue, by understanding these movements to be partly conscious, partly confused participants in one of two "world revolutions." Arrighi and his colleagues name these revolutions after two dates that symbolize historical worldwide insurrection, plus or minus several decades: The first is the "world revolution of 1848," a "long revolution" out of which the Old Left emerged in both the core and periphery—the socialist, communist, anarchist movements and the decolonizing national liberation movements, as well as first-wave feminism. The second is the "world revolution of 1968," which stands, for them, as the defining conjuncture in which the new social movements emerge as subject positions around the world. Cultural studies, with its roots in the New Left, would on these terms be a legacy of the world revolution of 1968. There are two conceptual innovations in this theory of "world revolutions" that we first need to make clear. The symbolic dates "1848" and "1968" designate not only punctual events but such events understood from the perspective of la longue durée. They are "world revolutions" insofar as they designate conjunctural processes of becoming revolutionary. Thus the world revolution of 1848 would include with Europe's "1848" revolts and upheavals ranging from the Haitian Revolution of 1791 to the African national liberation struggles of the 1950s. While in terms of chronology these uprisings are certainly all distant from each other, with regard to "political time" they belong to the same conjunctural situation of systemwide struggles. Similarly, the world revolution of 1968 would include, with Paris and Berkeley, student protests in Mexico and Japan, and the Hungarian uprising of 1956, as well as identity and minority movements in both the northern and southern hemispheres. Consequently, the second conceptual innovation in this approach to rethinking the political then invites us to interpret national or local mobilizations relationally (and not merely Eurocentrically) with regard to protest and insurrection boiling around the globe.

But it is also important to understand that for Arrighi et al., both world revolutions were "antisystemic" in character; that is to say, they articulated and mobilized protest against a wide range of oppressions and injustices intensified by crises of accumulation and conflicts over the articulation of a worldwide division of labor. There is however also a crucial difference between them. The world revolution of 1848, they argue, was to an appreciable degree "successful," in effect and in the long run, but in a completely ambivalent and contradictory way. Indeed, during the formative period for British cultural studies (1945–68), political parties had achieved state power throughout much of the world in the name of the socialist, communist, and national liberation movements of 1848. This was the case not only with the socialist states of Eastern Europe, or the People's Republic of China, or with many of the new postcolonial states throughout the periphery, but also with the Keynesian welfare states of Western Europe and New Deal America, where key concessions to organized labor were the condition for continuing hegemony by the proprietors of capital. During this period, in a significant number of national situations, parties or coalitions ascended to state power claiming to represent the long-enduring mass movements that brought them there.

But the very condition of such "victories" of the Old Left of 1848 over the first half of the twentieth century—a reach into state power in order to achieve important parts of their agendas and not be wiped off the face of the earth—was also the condition of their failure: cooptation through the imperialist world interstate system. This is the contradiction they came to live. We now can identify the crucial difference between the two world revolutions—indeed why we need to think, historically, in terms of two world revolutions, which in turn can help us see our own situation anew.[21]

As Arrighi et al. argue, the world revolution of 1968—the insurrections and insurgencies spanning a decade or two on either side of that year—was a revolt against both the institutions of postwar capitalism and the blindness, errors, and collusions of the social movements of 1848—their failure, despite some prominent successes, on so many things. Once the immediate reverberations of these various "becomings revolutionary" subsided, the new social movements of 1968 continued their struggles in a conjuncture in which the cultural and political rules of the game in the world had changed dramatically from 1945 (as everyone now says), and in which U.S. hegemony, paramount in the interstate system between 1945 and 1973, entered a period of continual crisis (indeed, is even in decline, Wallerstein and others insist) which still persists.[22]

Passages Between

We can now place the story of the passage from British dominion to multicultural Canada into the wider global context of the seismic convulsions of decolonization that shattered the British Empire after the Second World War. First of all, the disintegration of the British Empire made U.S. hegemonic supremacy in the capitalist world system apparent to everyone. This supremacy rested not only on military capability. American supremacy was also based upon industrial productive capacity, as the United States towered over the rubble of war in rival centers of industrialization. But such industrial power is useless unless there is a steady supply of cheap input resources as well as substantial markets for its output. American hegemony in the first and third worlds involved securing each of these and so the "ethical project" undertaken by the U.S. state (as Gramsci would have put it) was to arrange the production of the appropriate subjectivities for the wider extension and deeper penetration of consumption. It has been the contradictory privilege of Canada to be all of these things at once: a primary source of material resources for the United States and a major consumer of both its goods and its ideologies of consumption. One of the outcomes of this close material and imaginative connection to the United States would be to leave postwar Canada without a clear cultural identity, even if desperately in need of one. At this point, the ruling elite in Canada undertook a long quest to reconstitute national hegemony in a time of transition marked symbolically by the end of the Second World War and by Indian independence from the British Raj in 1947. Multiculturalism can be understood as the overdetermined result of this search for an imaginary identity enabling the reconstitution of hegemony. Even with the Multiculturalism Act of 1988, however, hegemony remains precariously secured.

Canada's new multicultural identity nevertheless shares in the utopianism of the worldwide popular antiracism of the decolonization movements and their sympathizers in the post-Nuremberg era, as well as the utopianism of postwar Canadian social democracy generally. The latter's programs of social and political equality, and cultural reform, were more or less adopted—though in the face of bitter resistance from elite privilege—by successive postwar governments, culminating especially in those of Lester B. Pearson (1963–68) and Pierre Elliot Trudeau (1968–79). The rights of labor with respect to the legal recognition of trade unions and collective bargaining were achieved in 1944. With memories of the Great Depression still vivid, postwar governments in Canada then began toying with Keynesianism and the rudiments of a welfare state. Unemployment insurance, first introduced in 1941, was extended to cover almost the whole work force by the Unemployment Insurance Act of 1971. Similarly, old age pensions, welfare and social assistance, job creation and training programs were adopted piecemeal and expanded over the postwar decades. Universal health care was established, in a close vote, through the Medical Care Act of 1966. Such concessions with respect to the rights of labor as were secured in the Canadian welfare state were of one piece with the historic terms and conditions for continuing capitalist production outside the periphery, as Wallerstein and his colleagues point out, *in the face of resistance and revolt throughout the world system.*

In the Canadian context, the systemic temporalities of these global struggles have their own nonsynchronous local rhythms as well. The construction of the Canadian welfare state was thus not the fulfillment but rather the deferred and differing epilogue of the Rebellion of 1837–38 in Lower Canada (now Quebec), which was the eruption of "our" 1848, so to speak. But, first, we note the cooptation of the antisystemic protests of 1848. The ruling bloc appropriated key planks of the political platform of Canadian social democracy, as articulated by the New Democratic Party (formed in 1961 in a merger of the Commonwealth Cooperative Federation, the Canadian Labour Congress, and the New Party clubs). We have already noted that the Liberal Party, forming minority governments under the leadership of Pearson in 1963 and 1965, introduced the Canada Pension Plan and universal Medicare, along with a new national flag that dispensed with the Union Jack.

Along with the fall of the British Empire, the Quiet Revolution in Quebec was the second postwar earthquake to shake the Canadian state. With roots going back to the 1940s, particularly to the asbestos miners' strike of 1949 (and, indeed, ultimately to the Rebellion of 1838, as the prominent historian Gérard Bouchard has argued),[23] Quebeckers revolted against clerical authority in the decades following World War II. This cultural revolution was also a social revolution. With the electoral sweep into power in 1960 of the Liberal Party of Quebec led by Jean Lesage, after sixteen years of rule by the conservative Union Nationale, Quebecois society was mobilized in a rapid program of secularization and modernization. Led not only by a new class of urban professionals but in important respects by the trade union and women's movements as well, the revolution built the most extensive provincial welfare state in the Canadian confederation, nationalized the electricity industry, and completely reorganized and secularized education. Thus a significant antisystemic current had for some time been nurtured in Quebecois nationalism by the Quiet Revolution. Trudeau and his colleagues, Jean Marchand and Gerard Pelletier, all politicians formed by the deep social and cultural transformations of the Quiet Revolution, were brought into the Pearson cabinet precisely to manage and contain these developments.

The cooptation of the antisystemic protests of 1838 and 1848 by the ruling bloc was ultimately consolidated when Trudeau succeeded Pearson as prime minister in 1967. A new formation of Canadian nationalism found expression in Trudeau's 1968 campaign slogan "The Just Society." But the conjuncture of the "Just Society" also included two key symbolic elements of the antisystemic protests of 1968. This, indeed, is the historical significance of "Trudeaumania."[24] One considers here not only the Act of 1969, which decriminalized homosexuality, but also the establishment of the Royal Commission on the Status of Women in 1967. The first of these is an important but limited step. The second led to the formation of the Status of Women Directorate as a cabinet portfolio, as well as the autonomous National Action Committee for the Status of Women, an umbrella organization that has been crucial for a wide range of feminist mobilization. Indeed, the conjunction of 1848 and 1968 would appear to be not only a striking feature of Canadian national identity of the Trudeau era but also a distinctive feature of the first phase of second-wave feminism in Canada.

The Royal Commission on the Status of Women was a crucial cultural-political event of the conjuncture. The commission traveled the length and breadth of the country and, as it did so, turned into a major media event. Its importance as a counter–public sphere, as well as the reforms it was able to set in motion, points to the singularity of the political possibilities of this conjuncture. But at the time, the English Canadian and Quebecois women's movements were themselves singularly distinctive modes of radicalization, which is why the women's movement (whether one wants to speak of a "third wave" or not) has been the leading counterhegemonic force in the ideological positioning of cultural politics and in organizational practices among antisystemic protest movements in Canada and Quebec ever since. Jill Vickers, for example, has described the Canadian women's movement of this era, with its faith in Canadian political institutions, its popular front strategy, and its commitment to the welfare state, as a feminist "radical liberalism" in order to distinguish it from what she considers to be the more individualistic, middle-class orientation of American radical feminism with its uncritical acceptance of cold war antisocialism. Vickers sees this distinctiveness arising largely from the continuities between first-wave and second-wave mobilization in English Canada, made possible by peace movement organizations of the 1950s and 1960s such as the Congress of Canadian Women and Voice of Women but especially the links between the women's caucuses of the Co-operative Commonwealth Federation (CCF) and of the radical left "Waffle" movement within the New Democratic Party (NDP).[25]

In Quebec, the formation of the Fédération des Femmes du Quebec in 1966 and its participation in the National Action Committee on the Status of Women (NAC) until 1981 ensured not only a continuity with the first wave of feminist mobilization among rural women, especially in the 1940s and 1950s in organizations such as les Cercles des Fermières (founded in 1915) and the Union Catholique des Fermières (1945), but also, as Micheline Dumont has suggested, that a feminist front would be opened throughout the Quiet Revolution and within Quebecois nationalism thereafter.[26] These links between first-wave and second-wave feminism in both English Canada and Quebec, moreover, also enabled the two women's movements to work together in the wake of the royal commission and in the formation of the NAC. This opening in the state, however, was closed off again when Prime Minister Brian Mulroney's Conservatives (spearheading the Canadian version of Thatcher-Reagan neoliberalism) formed the government (1984–93). Nevertheless, these inroads have been the subject of continual debate in feminist scholarship in Canada as to whether what is, for some, at least partial inclusion is not, as others argue, mere cooptation.

In any case, these rhetorical turns in the language of rule need to be placed alongside three other strategies of crisis management that unfold over the subsequent decades. First, the abandonment of an assimilationist Indian policy is followed by constitutional recognition of Aboriginal Treaty Rights. Second, the Canadian Charter of Rights, which opened the door for making a wide range of equality and redress claims against the state through the courts, was proclaimed in 1982 (significantly, the right to unionize is not protected by the charter). Finally, these juridical reconfigurations of the state are then supplemented, as we have noted, with the state's cultural project of redefining national identity through the creation of a new national myth called multiculturalism.

All of these design changes in the engine of state power, taken together, allow us to observe an important feature of the character of hegemonic leadership attempted by the ruling elite, especially as this has been piloted by the Liberal Party, which has formed the government during most of this time. As we have noted, the attempt to suture together a hegemonic bloc in the postwar era "between empires" has involved not only the partial reach into state power by the movements of 1848 but also, and again only in part, by the antisystemic movements of 1968 as well. Indeed, it has sometimes seemed that the movements of 1968 in Canada have turned to the state with even higher expectations of being granted "inclusion" than anything the movements of 1848 ever hoped for. This resulted in a kind of hegemony in Canada that Alan Cairns describes as the "socially embedded state."[27] But such hegemony was as precarious and mercurial as Stuart Hall taught us it is likely to be. It is quite evident that the high water mark of the Keynesian welfare state has long passed in Canada. The neoliberal restructuring launched by Thatcher and Reagan reclaimed as much of the state for the Washington consensus in Canada as elsewhere. But the ease with which the Conservatives led by Brian Mulroney and then Jean Chrétien's Liberals (prime minister, 1993–2003) were able to carry out this agenda may be understood in light of the ideologically advanced positions of the 1968 critique of the political projects and cultural repertoires of 1848. The cynicism that frothed in the wake of 1968's "good utopian" denunciations of 1848's "bad utopianism"—1968's contempt for 1848's "simple faith" in the universal, for 1848's retreat from international solidarity to affirmations of the national-popular, for its commitment to planning and to the public sector—allowed hegemony to be reformed quickly around a rhetoric of "revolutionary" common sense regarding the inevitabilities of free trade, new technology, and globalization. The shift in the official discourse of multiculturalism from an emphasis on recognizing difference to an emphasis on tapping each individual's social capital illustrates in broad and rough strokes the nature of the change.

The key point that we then wish to make here is that one can discern, in the essays collected in this reader, lines of argument that not only articulate the critique of the movements of 1848 by 1968 but also, in various and original ways, critiques now directed against the cultural spaces of 1968 as well. This second order of negativity is neither programmatic nor even thematic, let alone a commonly affirmed position. Rather, it emerges in moments of sustained engagement and critical insight or when theoretical arguments are pushed to their limits. This is particularly the case in the works in the second part of the reader. But this kind of movement of critique can also be detected over what we consider to be the "threshold texts" for Canadian cultural studies presented in part 1. In different ways, Harold Innis, Northrop Frye, Marshall

McLuhan, Paul-Émile Borduas, George Grant, Fernand Dumont, Harold Cardinal, and Anthony Wilden all attempt to plumb the depths of their times and grasp the significance for Canadian society, culture, and identity of the fall of the British Empire and the rise of the American one.

Despite the diversity of their intellectual agendas, each of these threshold works makes intelligible in its own way a crisis of identity and hegemony, indeed the historical ruin of the "red ensign" (as the old flag prior to the red-and-white maple leaf design was called) Dominion of Canada. For one thing, nearly all of them search for a way to respond to Canada's economic dependence on, political subordination to, and cultural intimacy with the United States. In doing so, they furthermore point in various ways to a transformation of the Gramscian problematic of hegemony (and so perhaps beyond this concept). Consider, for example, the fundamental theme of Harold Innis's late research: what makes civilizations fall? Consider the force of his diagnosis of the space bias of industrialized communication, which makes clear its deepest connections to warmongering and foretells a mode of domination through all-pervasive spectacle that we now know only too well. Note, in this regard, Northrop Frye's account of Canadian literary history as a return from the wilderness garrison to transhistorical myth and the surprising conclusions he then draws about our arrival in a postnational world culture (albeit an Eurocentrically conceived one). Or recall the equally surprising resolution that myth provides to the historical dialectic of progress and alienation Frye rehearses in his 1967 centennial essay where again our postnational transcendence is a matter of taking up the geopolitical identity of the cold war "West." Consider, for that matter, Marshall McLuhan's account of the new Canadian cold war role of being an "anti-environment"—a "hidden ground for big powers"—and his probing of multiple borderlines diverging from the Distant Early Warning (DEW) line, which accompanies his announcement of the birth of a brave new American world environment, extended in the cool, acoustic space surrounding a now Lilliputian globe. Finally, think of the inevitable force of Fernand Dumont's question—"Why should our children not simply be American?"—posed in his sympathetic critique of Quebecois nationalism, which he defends by arguing that only collective values allow us to face the choices such a world environment presents to us.

Overall, we can track through these threshold texts a trajectory of critique that forges a new space of negativity—perhaps most openly in George Grant's uncompromising opposition to liberal discourse and in his consequent confession to an even "profounder alienation" than his interlocuters in the Canadian New Left. We also encounter it, though from a completely different perspective, in Harold Cardinal's reclamation of a politics of the treaties that would, if they could ever serve as a foundation of our collective existence, take Canadian society well beyond the geopolitical flanks of "the West."

With Anthony Wilden too we seem to step completely through to our own side of the threshold. We find already cogently articulated in this early work from Wilden's oeuvre nearly all of the major themes that have animated cultural studies from the 1980s on: not only the decentering of the subject into a signifier of the other but also the more urgent and perplexing question underlying this famous theoretical result—how do we understand the articulation of sexism, racism, and other modes of domination with class exploitation? Anticipating us again, Wilden connects these differences in domination not to the universal structure of mediation as such (perhaps the theoretical move par excellence of the semiotically oriented sixty-eighters) but rather to the historical problematic and project of decolonization, arguing that this is where English Canadians share a common ground with the national liberation movements of the First Nations and the Quebecois.

In this trajectory, the positions of 1968—which opposed themselves to the unholy alliance between the capitalist world economy (and thus Anglo-American hegemony) and the movements of 1848—themselves become the targets of critique, especially as the cultural politics of 1968 increasingly finds accommodation with the state and eventually slides into merely trying to square the vicious circles of liberal discourse. This, we want to suggest, is the animating inner struggle of much of the substantial argument of the essays found in part 2.

Attempts to think not only with 1968 but also against it are forcefully articulated in Himani Bannerji's thoroughgoing critique of Charles Taylor's "politics of difference," especially with regard to her insistence on the everyday lived relations of rule through which domination and exploitation connect systematically. This new negativity can also be discerned in Eva Mackey's critique of the dissembling knowledge claims of reified postmodern cultural theory as she tracks them in play through the course of a particular cultural-political conflict over the Royal Ontario Museum's exhibition "Into the Heart of Africa." As postmodern cultural theory is imported to serve as an auratic discourse of distinction in the exhibition with little regard for the local vernacular, it collapses into sheer ideology, Mackey shows us, in the face of community protest.

A trajectory of critique of the conjunction of 1848 and 1968 in Canada is evident as well in Katharyne Mitchell's rediscovery of the immanence of class politics within the racialized aesthetic politics of house construction in Vancouver during the 1990s. At that time, Lower Mainland (Vancouver) real estate served as insurance for investment capital seeking safe havens from uncertainty surrounding the transfer of power in Hong Kong in 1997. Her analysis of the contradictions arising from these global flows takes her well beyond 1968's paradigm of keywords: "culture," "power," "exclusion," "petit recit," and "difference." In this way, Mitchell's critique helps us see how the conjunction of 1848 and 1968 prepared the ground for what we would come to call the neoliberal agenda.

Lee Maracle's feminist critique of the American Indian Movement (AIM) and her attempt to remake an aboriginal communism may also be considered to move in a similar direction. "We are now paralyzed with fear at cultural innovation," writes Maracle, and, with this diagnosis, sweeps aside a discursive ontology of cultural difference to confront history: "The basis for this fear is the inequitable relations inherent in colonialism." Something provocatively nonconformist can also be heard in Len Findlay's exhortation to "Always Indigenize!," uttered in the face of Geoffrey Hartman's conservative recuperation of deconstruction. Findlay here takes up the unfinished project of decolonization in his sketch of a "good instrumentality" for an indigenized humanities. With respect to English studies specifically, Findlay offers a "vision" and a "conspiracy" that would radicalize the linguistic turn further by historicizing-indigenizing language by recovering its materiality in social reproduction rather than the physics of the signifier. It is, after all, the historical fate of the world's many Englishes to serve as a "compliantly technocratic, multinational corporate instrument." Full recognition of the strategic implications of English's status as a world language takes us well beyond the usual epistemological and ontological problems that get rehearsed on the question of language and requires any proposals for a politics of knowledge to understand how English language competence now mediates class reproduction globally. Issues such as these prompt Findlay to suggest that an indigenized, anglophone cultural studies attend to the resistances of linguistic impurity to find the idioms of a good pedagogic instrumentality.[28]

Ian Angus's critical reconsideration of the legacy of Canadian left nationalism seems to be yet another dimension of this emergent negative space. After left nationalism's dismissal by a line of cultural criticism that descends from Frye and McLuhan, Angus does not seek to return to its venerable ideological-political positions but rather to find a new point of departure in the era of NAFTA. This kind of attention to historical passages seems to be a characteristic feature of many of these works. Rob Shields's study of the place myth of the "True North, Strong and Free," for example, brings the very mythic imagination celebrated by Frye back into history and politics in order to critically describe the ways it is set to work. Jocelyn Létourneau may also be said to be trying to do something not so different in his chapter from A History for the Future: Rewriting Memory and Identity in Quebec. Examining the transformation of Quebecois history into collective myth in the classroom, Létourneau refuses the mode of narrative remembering crafted by 1968's nationalist historiography and argues for a more future-oriented engagement with history through the active memory figured in his trope for culture: "remembering (from) where you're going."

As a working hypothesis that we are formulating for the consideration of our colleagues, we want to suggest that this inchoate space of negativity traced by the strategies of critique in the essays in part 2 involve the following features: speaking in the dialects of difference and fragment, they nevertheless insist upon examining the everyday social relations of rule in which inequalities are always systematically organized to serve strategies of capital accumulation. In this regard, they immerse themselves in their sites of intervention deeply enough to avoid having to depend on easy reified distinctions between the cultural, the social, the economic, and the political, finding instead the movements and processes by which events become the fault lines of conjunctures.

Our hypothesis regarding our passages between empires has, we believe, the following virtues: this problematic opens a strategy of reading contemporary and past work on cultural politics in relation to the history of social movements on the left, locally and globally. It furthermore allows us to investigate the enduring significance of national situations —always in the plural in our case—of collective projects of nationhood (and especially their ways of mystifying or resisting relations of domination and exploitation) without either necessarily committing ourselves to a nationalist position, on the one hand, or precluding critical and tactical engagements altogether on the other. Much writing on culture and politics in Canada is forced by the historical articulation of racism to nationalism, on the one hand, and the multiplicity of "our" conflicting claims to nationhood, on the other, to adopt this kind of critical distance from such claims without then assuming the historical obsolescence of nation-states.

Be that as it may, the essays in this reader can then at least help us better understand how cultural studies anywhere must search in the multitude of passages that keep historical capitalism from ever becoming identical to itself, if we desire to construct a cultural common for our politics of liberation.

Notes

1. Those universities most commonly associated with cultural studies in Canada were all founded in this period: York University (Toronto, 1959), Trent University (Peterborough, Ontario, 1963), Simon Fraser University (Vancouver, 1965), Concordia University (Montreal, 1974). The countercultural and radical identity of these universities was established in contrast to the more traditional universities in each of the major cities: York against the University of Toronto, Simon Fraser against the University of British Columbia, and Concordia against McGill. The creation of these new universities, with all new faculty, provided a unique opening for the articulation of countercultural ideas and ideals in Canada, including those of the British New Left. The programs that emerged from the first generation of faculty at these universities continue to play an important role in intellectual life in Canada: social and political thought at York, cultural studies at Trent, and communications studies at both Simon Fraser and Concordia.

2. Fredric Jameson, *The Ideologies of Theory* (Minneapolis: University of Minnesota Press, 1988), 2:178–208, and passim. Stuart Hall, "Gramsci's Relevance for the Study of Race and Ethnicity," *Journal of Communication Inquiry* 10.2 (Summer 1986): 5–27.

3. Étienne Balibar, *Masses, Classes, Ideas: Studies on Politics and Philosophy before and after Marx*, trans. James Swenson (New York: Routledge, 1994), 142–49.

4. See, for example, Hans Gumbrecht, "Taking the Immigrant Test," *Sign and Sight: Arts, Essays, Ideas from Germany*, March 15, 2006, http://www.signandsight.com/features/646.html (accessed March 22, 2006).

5. Total trade between Canada and the United States in 2005 was $499.29 billion; between the United States and China, $285.30 billion (U.S. dollars; U.S. Census Bureau figures). See http://www.census.gov/foreign-trade/top/dst/2005/12/balance.html (accessed May 31, 2006).

6. First Nations, the Métis, and the Inuit are the three officially recognized groupings of aboriginal peoples in Canada. The name "First Nations" is sometimes used to include all aboriginal peoples in Canada, but, confusingly, also to constitute all those indigenous groups other than those who are Métis—descendants of marriages of Ojibway, Cree, Menominee, and Saulteaux aboriginals with French Canadian or Celtic settlers—or Inuit, the indigenous peoples of the Arctic regions.

7. Government of Canada, "Statement on Indian Policy," white paper, cat. no. R32 2469, 1969 (Ottawa: Queen's Printer, 1969).

8. Harold Cardinal, *The Unjust Society* (Edmonton: Hurtig, 1969).

9. In his overview of Canadian debates in film criticism, Bart Testa identifies a "con-

sensual moralism" that underlies the analysis of film in Canada. This moralism has a twofold character that is familiar to anyone engaged in research on Canadian topics. First, criticism is prescriptive, focusing more on what the film should have "done" as opposed to what it is in fact "doing"; second, there is an insistence on the need for Canadian cultural products to actively participate in the constitution of Canadian identity. Michael Dorland has gone even further. He argues that "consensual moralism" forms "the *sine qua non* of cultural production in Canada, the basis on which it received critical attention, articulation in the public sphere and, last, but not least, subsidy by the state. . . . It has been the primary medium through which the discourses of Canadian cultural production were to be publicly conducted and given institutional form." This is one of the major reasons why a straightforward survey of Canadian cultural criticism would be less rewarding than one that looks at the constitution of theoretical forms and concepts, such as the conditions that give rise to the dominance of consensual moralism. See Bart Testa, "In Grierson's Shadow," *Literary Review of Canada* (November 1994): 9–12, and "The Escape from Docu-Drama," *Literary Review of Canada* (December 1994): 17–22; and Michael Dorland, "Changing Theorizations of Cultural Production in Canada and Quebec," *Journal of Canadian Studies* 31 (1996–97): 178–94.

10. In her assessment of Jonathan Kertzer's *Worrying the Nation: Imagining a National Literature in Canada*, Sylvia Söderlind argues that "there is something fundamentally missing when—in an age when the concept of the nation is more than ever at issue—one writes a history in which 'nation' is the structuring principle without mentioning the role Quebec has played in English-Canadian thinking about the nation" (674). This kind of deliberate blind spot remains in place across the disciplines in Canada. There is often a frank admission by anglophone thinkers of the need to make greater connections to developments in Quebec, followed by a deferral of such a project to some (unspecified) later date. Sylvia Söderlind, "Ghost-National Arguments," *University of Toronto Quarterly* 75 (2006): 673–92.

11. Fernand Dumont, *The Vigil of Quebec*, trans. Sheila Fischman and Richard Howard (Toronto: University of Toronto Press, 1974), 19.

12. Susan Crean and Marcel Rioux, *Two Nations: An Essay on the Culture and Politics of Canada and Quebec in a World of American Pre-eminence* (Toronto: James Lorimer, 1983), 98–99.

13. Pierre Bourdieu and Loïc Wacquant, "On the Cunning of Imperialist Reason," *Theory, Culture and Society* 16 (1999): 41–58.

14. For an overview, see Imre Szeman, "Cultural Studies and the Transnational," in *New Cultural Studies: Adventures in Theory*, ed. Gary Hall and Claire Birchall (Edinburgh: University of Edinburgh Press, 2006), 200–218.

15. See Anthony Hall, *The American Empire and the Fourth World* (Montreal: McGill-Queen's University Press, 2003) for an extensive discussion of the historical and contemporary cultural-political significance of the Royal Proclamation of 1763.

16. Scholars and cultural producers in Canada have reclaimed the term *métissage* from its earlier meaning of "mixed blood" to work as a critical metaphor for transformation, creativity, and hybridity in the production of culture, narrative, and identity, as well as a name for a strategy of antiracist critical pedagogy.

17. For an assessment of the similarities of the cultural politics of Canada and developing nations (such as Brazil), see Imre Szeman, "Literature on the Periphery of Capitalism, *Ilha do Desterro* (Brazil) 40 (2001): 25–42.

18. Tony Bennett, "Out in the Open: Reflections on the History and Practice of Cultural Studies," *Cultural Studies* 10.1 (1996): 133–53; Michael Hardt and Antonio Negri, *Empire* (Cambridge, Mass.: Harvard University Press, 2000). For more recent takes on Gramsci, see Peter Ives, *Gramsci's Politics of Language* (Toronto: University of Toronto Press, 2004), and Richard Day, *Gramsci Is Dead: Anarchist Currents in the Newest Social Movements* (Toronto: Between the Lines, 2005).

19. Giovanni Arrighi, Terence K. Hopkins, and Immanuel Wallerstein, eds., *Antisystemic Movements* (London: Verso, 1989). See also Wallerstein, *Historical Capitalism with Capitalist Civilization* (London: Verso, 1983).

20. Immanuel Wallerstein, *The Essential Wallerstein* (New York: New Press, 2000), esp. 160–69; and Fernand Braudel, "History and the Social Sciences: The *longue durée*," in *Economy and Society in Early Modern Europe*, ed. P. Burke (reprint, London: Routledge and Kegan Paul, 2006), 11–42.

21. The theory of world revolutions and antisystemic movements presents a hypothesis for historical interpretation. However, the theory is not meant to include every kind of political struggle nor all political movements but rather only those that may be understood to be "antisystemic" in the sense discussed here. Consequently, how this or that specific case may be interpreted is a matter of considerable debate in the literature, especially in the cases of historical and contemporary religious fundamentalist movements, and racist movements, as well as conflicts between ruling classes and factions and peasant movements of the past. See Giovanni Arrighi, "Hegemony and Anti-Systemic Movements," in *The Modern World System in the Longue Durée*, ed. Immanuel Wallerstein (Boulder, Colo.: Paradigm Publishers, 2004); Thomas Reifer, ed., *Globalization, Hegemony and Power: Anti-systemic Movements and the Global System* (Boulder, Colo.: Paradigm Publishers, 2004); Samir Amin, Giovanni Arrighi, et al., *Transforming the Revolution: Social Movements and the World-System* (New York: Monthly Review Press, 1990).

22. See for example Giovanni Arrighi, "Hegemony Unravelling," *New Left Review* 32 (2005): 23–80, and *New Left Review* 33 (2005): 83–116; David Harvey, *The New Imperialism* (Oxford: Oxford University Press, 2003); Neil Smith, *The Endgame of Globalization* (New York: Routledge, 2005); and Immanuel Wallerstein, "The Curve of American Power," *New Left Review* 40 (2006): 77–94. For a different approach to the same issues, see Gérard Duménil and Dominique Lévy, *Capital Resurgent: Roots of the Neoliberal Revolution*, trans. Derek Jeffers (Cambridge, Mass.: Harvard University Press, 2004).

23. Gérard Bouchard, "L'histoire comparée des collectivités neuves. Esquisse d'étude comparée," *Recherches sociographiques* 39 (1998): 219–48. Cited in Jocelyn Létourneau, *A History for the Future: Rewriting Memory and Identity in Quebec*, trans. Phyllis Aronoff and Howard Scott (Montreal: McGill-Queen's University Press, 2004).

24. "Trudeaumania" refers to the social and cultural euphoria (partially media-generated) which accompanied the emergence of Pierre Trudeau onto the public scene after his successful run for the political leadership of the Liberal Party in 1967, through his

election as prime minister in 1968, and up to his marriage in 1971. The reasons for Trudeaumania—so called because the crowds of young people swarming him at public appearances recalled Beatlemania—are complex, but have to do with Trudeau's appeal to the media and ease with the emerging youth culture (inviting, for instance, John Lennon and Yoko Ono to Parliament Hill), as well as the fact that for many at the moment of Canada's centenary Trudeau came to symbolize the modern maturity of the nation itself: a bachelor prime minister, a cosmopolitan intellectual with excellent command of French and English, owner of a Mercedes, and so on.

25. Jill Vickers, "The Intellectual Origins of the Women's Movements in Canada," in *Challenging Times: The Women's Movement in Canada and the United States*, ed. Constance Backhouse and David H. Flaherty (Montreal: McGill-Queen's University Press, 1992), 39–60.

26. Micheline Dumont, "The Origins of the Women's Movement in Quebec," in *Challenging Times: The Women's Movement in Canada and the United States*, ed. Constance Backhouse and David H. Flaherty (Montreal: McGill-Queen's University Press, 1992), 72–89.

27. Alain Cairns, *Reconfigurations: Canadian Citizenship and Constitutional Change* (Toronto: McLelland and Stewart, 1995), 35–61.

28. Findlay and his colleagues Marie Battiste and Lynne Bell are currently undertaking a groundbreaking research project that aims to construct an alternative, indigenized humanities. For further information see the Web site of the Postcolonial University at the University of Saskatchewan: http://www.usask.ca/education/postcolonial/ (accessed October 3, 2005).

I

Canadian Cultural Theory:

Origins

HAROLD INNIS
A Plea for Time

Harold Innis was born in 1894 in the farming community of Otterville in southwestern Ontario. He attended McMaster University, then located in Toronto, and took preparatory courses for law, among which he found history and political economy particularly interesting. He graduated during World War I, served in the Signal Corps, and was wounded. Upon returning to Canada and finishing his M.A. thesis (titled "The Returned Soldier"), Innis enrolled in law school at the University of Chicago but took courses in political economy, eventually completing a doctorate in economics. His major works of economic history begin with his dissertation, published as *A History of the Canadian Pacific Railway* (1923), followed by the classic *The Fur Trade in Canada* (1930) and *The Cod Fisheries: A History of an International Economy* (1940). Innis develops and elaborates his influential "staples thesis" of uneven, center-dependent marginal historical development during this period. His work on media and communications began in the early 1940s, when he started to rework the key insights of his staples thesis in light of his recognition of the centrality of the social relations of communication to modern industry. Innis was able to complete three books that present his research over the 1940s—*Empire and Communication* (1950), *The Bias of Communication* (1951), and *Changing Concepts of Time* (1952)—before dying of cancer in 1952.

Innis was also the chairman (1945–46) of the Social Science Research Council of Canada. He taught political economy at the University of Toronto. Though Innis never considered himself to be a Marxist, his work was hugely influential for the development of a mostly Marxist-oriented critical political economy tradition of scholarship, which sustained the political movement of left nationalism from the 1960s through the 1980s.

I must plead the bias of my special interest in the title of this paper. Economic historians and indeed all historians assume a time factor and their assumptions reflect the attitude towards time of the period in which they write. History in the modern sense is about four centuries old[1] but the word has taken on meanings which are apt to check a concern with facts other than those of immediate interest and its content is apt to reflect an interest in immediate facts such as is suggested by the words "all history proves." As a result history tends to repeat itself but in the changing accents of the period in which it is written. History is threatened on the one hand by its obsession with the present and on the other by the charge of antiquarianism. Economic history is in a particularly exposed position as is evident in the tendency to separate it from economics or to regard it as a basis of support for economics. "Knowledge of the past is at all times needed only to serve the present and the future, not to enfeeble the present or to tear the roots out of the vigorous powers of life for the future" (Nietzsche). The danger that knowledge of the past[2] may be neglected to the point that it ceases to serve the present and the future—perhaps an undue obsession with the immediate—supports my concern about the disappearance of an interest in time.

Perhaps the exposed position of economic history may strengthen the urge to discover a solution of the difficulty, particularly as it becomes imperative to attempt to estimate the significance of the attitude towards time in an analysis of economic change. The economic historian must consider the role of time or the attitude towards time in periods which he attempts to study, and he may contribute to an escape from antiquarianism, from present-mindedness, and from the bogeys of stagnation and maturity. It is impossible for him to avoid the bias of the period in which he writes but he can point to its dangers by attempting to appraise the character of the time concept.

It has been pointed out that astronomical time is only one of several concepts. Social time, for example, has been described as qualitatively differentiated according to the beliefs and customs common to a group and as not continuous but subject to interruptions of actual dates.[3] It is influenced by language which constrains and fixes prevalent concepts and modes of thought. It has been argued by Marcel Granet that the Chinese are not equipped to note concepts or to present doctrines discursively. The word does not fix a notion with a definite degree of abstraction or generality but evokes an indefinite complex of particular images. It is completely unsuited to formal precision.[4] Neither time nor space is abstractly conceived; time proceeds by cycles and is round; space is square.[5]

The linear concept of time was made effective as a result of humanistic studies in the Renaissance. When Gregory XIII imposed the Julian calendar on the Catholic world in 1582 Joseph Justus Scaliger following his edition of Manilius (1579) published the *De emendatione temporum* and later his *Thesaurus temporum* (1606) "probably the most learned book in the world."[6] With his work he developed an appreciation of the ancient world as a whole and introduced a conception of the unity of history at variance with the attitude of the church. While Scaliger assisted in wresting control over time from the church he contributed to the historical tradition of philosophy until Descartes with his emphasis on mathematics and his unhistorical temper succeeded in liberating philosophy from history. The ideal of mathematical sciences dominated the seventeenth century. It was not until the Enlightenment that the historical world was conquered and until Herder and romanticism that the primacy of history over philosophy and science was established. Historicism was almost entirely a product of the nineteenth century.[7] In geology the precise date of the earth's formation advanced by Bishop Ussher was destroyed. "The weary series of accommodations of Genesis to geology was beginning."[8] In archaeology a knowledge of earlier civilizations implied a vast extension of time. In the hands of Darwin the historical approach penetrated biology and provided a new dimension of thought for science. In astronomy time was extended to infinity. Laws of real nature became historical laws. Even in mathematics arithmetic escaped from its bondage to geometry and algebra as "the science of pure time or order in progression" (Sir William Hamilton) came into its own.

I have attempted to show elsewhere[9] that in Western civilization a stable society is dependent on an appreciation of a proper balance between the concepts of space and time. We are concerned with control not only over vast areas of space but also over vast stretches of time. We must appraise civilization in relation to its territory and in relation to its duration. The character of the medium of communication tends to create a bias in civilization favourable to an over-emphasis on the time concept or on the space concept and only at rare intervals are the biases offset by the influence of another medium and stability achieved. Dependence on clay in Sumerian civilization was offset by dependence on stone in Babylon and a long period of relative stability followed in the reign of the Kassites. The power of the oral tradition in Greece which checked the bias of a written medium supported a brief period of cultural activity such as has never been equalled. Dependence on the papyrus roll and use of the alphabet in the bureaucracy of the Roman Empire was offset by dependence on parchment codex in the church and a balance was maintained in the Byzantine Empire until 1453. "Church and Army are serving order through the power of discipline and through hierarchical arrangement"

(Metternich).[10] On the other hand in the West the bias of the parchment codex became evident in the absolute dominance of the church and supported a monopoly which invited competition from paper as a new medium. After the introduction of paper and the printing press, religious monopoly was followed by monopolies of vernaculars in modern states. A monopoly of time was followed by a monopoly of space. A brief survey of outstanding problems of time will perhaps assist in enabling us to understand more clearly the limitations of our civilization.

The pervasive character of the time concept makes it difficult to appreciate its nature and difficult to suggest its conservative influence. The division of the day into 24 hours, of the hour into 60 minutes, and of the minute into 60 seconds suggests that a sexagesimal system prevailed in which the arrangement was worked out and this carries us immediately into Babylonian history.[11] The influence persists in systems of measurement and more obviously, for example, in Great Britain where the monetary system is sexagesimal. The advantages of the sexagesimal system are evident in calculations which permit evasion of the problem of handling fractions and have been exploited effectively in the development of aviation with its demands for rapid calculation.

In a system of agriculture dependent on irrigation the measurement of time becomes important in predicting periods of floods and the important dates of the year, seed-time and harvest. A concern with time was reflected in the importance of religion and in the choice of days on which festivals might be celebrated. The selection of holy days necessitated devices by which they could be indicated and violation of them could be avoided.[12] Dependence on the moon for the measurement of time meant exposure to irregularities such as have persisted in the means of determining the dates for Easter. Sumerian priesthoods apparently worked out a system for correcting the year by the adjustment of lunar months but the difficulties may have contributed to the success of Semitic kings with an interest in the sun, and enabled them to acquire control over the calendar and to make necessary adjustments of time over the extended territory under their control.[13] With control over time kings began the system of reckoning in terms of their reigns; our present statutes defy Anno Domini and date from the accession of the king in whose reign they are enacted. Control over time by monarchies, on the other hand, in addition to the human limitations of dynastic and military power, was limited by the continuity of priesthoods and the effectiveness of an ecclesiastical hierarchy.

In Egypt the power of the absolute monarchy reflected in the monumental architecture of the pyramids and in sculpture was offset by the power of the priesthood based on a complex system of writing and the use of papyrus. The emphasis of a civilization on means of extending its duration as in Egypt accompanied by reliance on permanence gives that civilization a prominent position in periods such as the present when time is of little significance. In Babylonia the power of the priesthood was dependent in part on a mastery of complex cuneiform writing on clay tablets, and an increasing power of the monarchy on the creation of new and elaborate capitals emphasizing sculpture and architecture. Relative stability was gradually established over a long period by compromises between political and religious power.

The limited possibility of political organizations expanding their control over space incidental to the control of priesthoods in their monopolies of knowledge over time facilitated the development of marginal organizations such as those of the Jews in Palestine. The marginal relation to cultures with monopolies of complex systems of writing favoured the development of relatively simple systems of writing such as emerged in the alphabet of the Phoenicians and the Aramaeans. In these marginal cultures religious organization emphasized a system of writing in sharp contrast with those of Egypt and Babylonia, and in compensation for lack of success in political organization with control over space built up an elaborate hierarchy with control over time. The latter emphasized the sacred character of writing and drew on the resources of Egyptian and Babylonian civilizations to an extent obvious to students of the Old Testament.

Contact with barbarians on the north shore of the Mediterranean with older civilizations was followed by the emergence of Greek civilization. An emphasis on problems of space incidental to a concern with conquest of territory was evident in the Homeric poems developed in the oral tradition. Geometry with its bias toward measurement and space imposed restrictions on a concern with time. The spread of money economy strengthened an interest in numbers and arithmetic and in turn mystery religions in conflict with the established Apollonic religion. The flexibility of an oral tradition enabled the Greeks to work out a balance between the demands of concepts of space and time in a city state. In the reforms of Cleisthenes control over time was wrested from religion and placed at the disposal of the state. The results of a balanced society were evident in the defeat of the Persians and the flowering of Greek culture in the fifth century. But such a balance was not long maintained.[14]

A balanced civilization in its concern with the problems of duration or time and of extent in space is faced with several difficulties. Systems of government concerned with problems of duration have been defeated in part by biology, when dynasties fail to provide a continued stream of governing capacity, and by technology,[15] when invaders are able to exploit improvements in the methods of warfare at the expense of peoples who have neglected them. Writing as a means of communication provides a system of administration of territory for the conquerors and in religion a system of continuity but in turn tends to develop monopolies of complexity which check an interest in industrial technology and encourage new invaders. A balanced concern with space or extent of territory and duration or time appears to depend on a dual arrangement in which the church is subordinate to the state and ensures that the mobilization of the intellectual resources of the civilization concerned, by religion or by the state will be at the disposal of both and that they will be used in planning for a calculated future in relation to the government of territory of definite extent. If social stratification is too rigid and social advancement is denied to active individuals as it is in plutocracies a transpersonal power structure will be threatened with revolt.[16]

It is beyond the bounds of this paper to enumerate the inventions for the measurement of time or to suggest their implications in the various developments of modern industrialism. It is concerned with the change in attitudes toward time preceding the modern obsession with present-mindedness, which suggests that the balance between time and space has been seriously disturbed with disastrous consequences to Western civilization. Lack of interest in problems of duration in Western civilization suggests that the bias of paper and printing has persisted in a concern with space. The state has been interested in the enlargement of territories and the imposition of cultural uniformity on its peoples, and, losing touch with the problems of time, has been willing to engage in wars to carry out immediate objectives. Printing has emphasized vernaculars and divisions between states based on language without implying a concern with time. The effects of division have been evident in development of the book, the pamphlet, and the newspaper and in the growth of regionalism as new monopolies have been built up. The revolt of the American colonies, division between north and south, and extension westward of the United States have been to an important extent a result of the spread of the printing industry. In the British Empire, the growth of autonomy and independence among members of the Commonwealth may be attributed in part to the same development. In Europe division between languages has been accentuated by varying rates of development of the printing industry. Technological change in printing under constitutional protection of freedom of the press in the United States has supported rapid growth of the newspaper industry. Its spread to Anglo-Saxon countries has sharpened the division between English and languages spoken in other areas and in turn contributed to the outbreak of the First World War. Not only has the press accentuated the importance of the English language in relation to other languages, it has also created divisions between classes within English-speaking countries. Emphasis on literacy and compulsory education has meant concentration on magazines and books with general appeal and widened the gap between the artist concerned with improvement of his craft and the writer concerned with the widest market. The writing of history is distorted by an interest in sensationalism and war. The library catalogue reflects an obsession of commercialism with special topics, events, periods, and individuals, to mention only the names of Lincoln, Napoleon, Churchill, Roosevelt, and others.

Large-scale production of newsprint made from wood in the second half of the nineteenth century supported large-scale development of newspaper plants and a demand for effective devices for widening markets for newspapers. The excitement and sensationalism of the South African War in Great Britain and of the Spanish-American War in the United States were not unrelated to the demands of large newspapers for markets. Emergence of the comics[17] coincided with the struggle for circulation between Hearst and Pulitzer in New York. Increased newspaper circulation supported a demand for advertising and for new methods of marketing, notably the department store. The type of news essential to an increase in circulation, to an increase in advertising, and to an increase in the sale of news was necessarily that which catered to excitement. A prevailing interest in orgies and excitement was harnessed in the interests of trade. The necessity for excitement and sensationalism had serious implications for the development of a consistent policy in foreign affairs which became increasingly the source of news. The reports of MacGahan, an American newspaper man, on Turkish activities were seized upon by Gladstone and led to the defeat of Disraeli.[18] The activity of W. T. Stead in the *Pall Mall Gazette* was an important factor in the fiasco of Gordon's expedition to Egypt. While it would be fatal to accept the views of journalists as to their power over events it is perhaps safe to say that Northcliffe played an important role in shifting the interest of Great Britain from Germany to France and in policy leading to the outbreak of the First World War.

Technological advance in the production of newspapers accompanied the development of metropolitan centres. In the period of western expansion "all these interests bring the newspaper; the newspaper starts up politics, and a railroad."[19] A large number of small centres were gradually dwarfed by the rise of large cities. In turn the opinion of large centres was reflected in their newspapers and in an emphasis on differences. "No," said Mr. Dooley, "They've got to print what's different."[20] Large centres became sources of news for distribution through press associations and in turn press associations became competitive with an emphasis on types of news which were mutually exclusive. The United Press became a competitor of the International News Service (Hearst) and of the Associated Press. The limitations of news as a basis of a steady circulation led to the development of features and in particular the comics and photography. Improvements in the reproduction of photographs coincided with the development of the cinema. News and the cinema complemented each other in the emphasis on instability. As a result of the struggle between various regions or metropolitan centres political stability was difficult to achieve. "It is one of the peculiar weaknesses of our political system that our strongest men cannot be kept very long in Congress."[21] While Congress was weakened the power of the president was strengthened. Theodore Roosevelt appealed to the mass psychology of the middle class and significantly gave the press a permanent room in the White House.[22] Oswald Garrison Villard claimed that "Theodore Roosevelt did more to corrupt the press than anyone else."[23]

The steadying influence of the book as a product of sustained intellectual effort was destroyed by new developments in periodicals and newspapers. As early as 1831 Lamartine would write: "Le livre arrive trop tard; le seul livre possible dès aujourd'hui, c'est un journal." The effect of instability on international affairs has been described by Moltke: "It is no longer the ambition of princes; it is the moods of the people, the discomfort in the face of interior conditions, the doings of parties, particularly of their leaders, which endanger peace."[24] The Western community was atomized by the pulverizing effects of the application of machine industry to communication. J. G. Bennett is said to have replied to someone charging him with inconsistency in the *New York Herald*, "I bring the paper out every day." He was consistent in inconsistency. "Advertisement dwells [in] a one-day world."[25]

Philosophy and religions reflected the general change. In the words of *Punch*: "It was the gradually extended use of the printing press that dragged the obscure horrors of political economy into the full light of day: and in the western countries of Europe the new sect became rampant." Hedonism gained in importance through the work of Bentham. Keynes has described his early belief by stating that he belonged to the first generation to throw hedonism out the window and to escape from the Benthamite tradition. " . . . I do now regard that as the worm which has been gnawing at the insides of modern civilization and is responsible for its present moral decay. We used to regard the Christians as the enemy, because they appeared as the representatives of tradition, convention and hocus-pocus. In truth it was the Benthamite calculus, based on an over-valuation of the economic criterion, which was destroying the quality of the popular Ideal. Moreover, it was this escape from Bentham, joined with the unsurpassable individualism of our philosophy, which has served to protect the whole lot of us from the final *reductio ad absurdum* of Benthamism known as Marxism."[26] But Keynes was to conclude "we carried the individualism of our individuals too far" and thus to bear further testimony to the atomization of society. In religion "the new interest in the future and the progress of the race" unconsciously under-mined "the old interest in a life beyond the grave; and it has dissolved the blighting doctrine of the radical corruption of man."[27] We should remind ourselves of Dean Inge's remarks that popular religion follows the en-slavement of philosophy to superstition. The philosophies of Hegel, Comte, and Darwin became enslaved to the superstition of progress. In the corruption of political science confident predictions, irritating and incapable of refutation, replaced discussion of right and wrong.[28] Econo-mists (the Physiocrats) "believed in the future progress of society towards a state of happiness through the increase of opulence which would itself depend on the growth of justice and 'liberty'; and they insisted on the importance of the increase and diffusion of knowledge."[29] The monopoly of knowledge which emerged with technological advances in the printing industry and insistence on freedom of the press checked this development.

The Treaty of Versailles recognized the impact of printing by accept-ing the principle of the rights of self-determination and destroyed large political organizations such as the Austrian Empire. Communication based on the eye in terms of printing and photography had developed a monopoly which threatened to destroy Western civilization first in war and then in peace. This monopoly emphasized individualism and in turn instability and created illusions in catchwords such as democracy, free-dom of the press, and freedom of speech.

The disastrous effect of the monopoly of communication based on the eye hastened the development of a competitive type of communica-tion based on the ear, in the radio and in the linking of sound to the cinema and to television. Printed material gave way in effectiveness to the broadcast and to the loud speaker.[30] Political leaders were able to appeal directly to constituents and to build up a pressure of public opinion on legislatures. In 1924, Al Smith, Governor of the State of New York, appealed directly by radio to the people and secured the passage of legislation threatened by Republican opposition. President F. D. Roosevelt exploited the radio as Theodore Roosevelt had exploited the press. He was concerned to have the opposition of newspapers in order that he might exploit their antagonism. It is scarcely necessary to elaborate on his success with the new medium.

In Europe an appeal to the ear made it possible to destroy the results of the Treaty of Versailles as registered in the political map based on self-determination. The rise of Hitler to power was facilitated by the use of the loud speaker and the radio. By the spoken language he could appeal to minority groups and to minority nations. Germans in Czechoslovakia could be reached by radio as could Germans in Austria. Political boundaries related to the demands of the printing industry disappeared with the new instrument of communication. The spoken language provided a new base for the exploitation of nationalism and a far more effective device for appealing to larger numbers. Illiteracy was no longer a serious barrier.

The effects of new media of communication evident in the outbreak of the Second World War were intensified during the progress of the war. They were used by the armed forces in the immediate prosecution of the war and in propaganda both at home and against the enemy. In Germany moving pictures of battles were taken[31] and shown in theatres almost immediately afterwards. The German people were given an impression of realism which compelled them to believe in the superiority of German arms; realism became not only most convincing but also with the collapse of the German front most disastrous. In some sense the problem of the German people is the problem of Western civilization. As modern developments in communication have made for greater realism they have made for greater possibilities of delusion. "It is curious to see scientific teaching used everywhere as a means to stifle all freedom of investigation in moral questions under a dead weight of facts. Materialism is the auxiliary doctrine of every tyranny, whether of the one or of the masses."[32] We are under the spell of Whitehead's fallacy of misplaced concreteness. The shell and pea game of the country fair has been magnified and elevated to a universal level.

The printing industry had been characterized by decentralization and regionalism such as had marked the division of the Western world in nationalism and the division and instability incidental to regions within nations. The radio appealed to vast areas, overcame the division between classes in its escape from literacy, and favoured centralization and bureaucracy. A single individual could appeal at one time to vast numbers of people speaking the same language and indirectly, though with less effect, through interpreters to numbers speaking other languages. Division was drawn along new lines based on language but within language units centralization and coherence became conspicuous. Stability within language units became more evident and instability between language units more dangerous.

The influence of mechanization on the printing industry had been evident in the increasing importance of the ephemeral. Superficiality became essential to meet the various demands of larger numbers of people and was developed as an art by those compelled to meet the demands. The radio accentuated the importance of the ephemeral and of the superficial. In the cinema and the broadcast it became necessary to search for entertainment and amusement. "Radio . . . has done more than its share to debase our intellectual standards."[33] The demands of the new media were imposed on the older media, the newspaper and the book. With these powerful developments time was destroyed and it became increasingly difficult to achieve continuity or to ask for a consideration of the future. An old maxim, "sixty diamond minutes set in a golden hour," illustrates the impact of commercialism on time. We would do well to remember the words of George Gissing: "Time is money—says the vulgarest saw known to any age or people. Turn it round about, and you get a precious truth—money is time."[34]

These tendencies reflect a concern with information. They are supported by the textbook industry and other industries which might be described as information industries. Information is provided in vast quantities in libraries, encylopaedias, and books. It is disseminated in universities by the new media of communication including moving pictures, loud speakers, with radio and television in the offing. Staff and students are tested in their ability to disseminate and receive information. Ingenious devices, questionnaires, intelligence tests are used to tell the student where he belongs and the student thus selected proceeds to apply similar devices to members of the staff.

Under these circumstances we can begin to appreciate the remarks of an Oxford don who said after solving a very difficult problem in mathematics, "Thank God no one can use that." There must be few university subjects which can claim immunity or few universities which will refrain from pleading that their courses are useful for some reason or other.[35] The blight of lying and subterfuge in the interests of budgets has fallen over universities, and pleas are made on the grounds that the universities are valuable because they keep the country safe from socialism, they help the farmers and industry, they help in measures of defence. Now of course they do no such thing and when such topics are mentioned you and I are able to detect the odour of dead fish. Culture is not concerned with these questions. It is designed to train the individual to decide how much information he needs and how little he needs, to give him a sense of balance and proportion, and to protect him from the fanatic who tells him that Canada will be lost to the Russians unless he knows more geography or more history or more economics or more science. Culture is concerned with the capacity of the individual to appraise problems in terms of space and time and with enabling him to take the proper steps at the right time. It is at this point that the tragedy of modern culture has arisen as inventions in commercialism have destroyed a sense of time.

It is significant that Keynes should have said that in the long run we are all dead and that we have little other interest than that of living for the immediate future. Planning is a word to be used for short periods—for long periods it is suspect and with it the planner. The dilemma has been aptly described by Polanyi, "laissez-faire was planned, planning is not." The results have been evident in the demand for wholesale government activity during periods of intense difficulty. The luxury of the business cycle has been replaced by concerted measures directed toward the welfare state and full employment. Limited experience with the problem has involved expenditures on a large scale on armaments.

The trend towards centralization which has accompanied the development of a new medium of communication in the radio has compelled planning to a limited extent in other directions. Conservation of natural resources, government ownership of railways and hydro-electric power, for example in Canada and by TVA in the United States, and flood control are illustrations of a growing concern with the problems of time but in the main are the result of acute emergencies of the present. Concern with the position of Western civilization in the year 2000 is unthinkable. An interest in 1984 is only found in the satirist or the utopian and is not applicable to North America. Attempts have been made to estimate population at late dates or the reserves of power or mineral resources but always with an emphasis on the resources of science and with reservations determined by income tax procedure, financial policy, or other expedients. Obsession with present-mindedness precludes speculation in terms of duration and time.

Concern of the state with the weakening and destruction of monopolies over time has been supported by appeals to science whether in an emphasis on equilibrium suggested by the interest of the United States in a balanced constitution following Newtonian mathematics or in an emphasis on growth, competition, and survival of the fittest of Darwin. Attempts to escape from the eye of the state have been frustrated by succession duties, corporation laws, and anti-combine legislation. The demands of technology for continuity have been met by rapid expansion of the principle of limited liability and devices such as long-term leases guaranteeing duration but these have provided a base for active state intervention in income taxes. Little is known of the extent to which large corporations have blocked out the utilization of future resources other than in matters of general policy. A grasping price policy sacrifices indefinite possibilities of growth. A monopolist seeks expanding business at a reasonable profit rather than the utmost immediate profit.[36] Organization of markets and exchanges facilitates the determination of predictions and the working-out of calculations which in turn have their effect on immediate production as an attempt to provide continuity and stability, but limitations progressively increased as evident in business cycles and their destruction of time rigidities. The monopoly of equilibrium was ultimately destroyed in the great depression and gave way to the beginnings of the monopoly of a centralized state. The disappearance of time monopolies facilitated the rapid extension of control by the state and the development of new religions evident in fascism, communism, and our way of life.

The general restiveness inherent in an obsession with time has led to various attempts to restore concepts of community such as have appeared in earlier civilizations. The Middle Ages have appeared attractive to economic historians, guild socialists, and philosophers, particularly those interested in St. Thomas Aquinas. "The cultivation of form for its own sake is equally typical of Romanticism and Classicism when they are mutually exclusive, the Romantic cultivating form in detachment from actuality, the Classicist in subservience to tradition" (Fausset).[37] It is possible that we have become paralyzed to the extent that an interest in duration is impossible or that only under the pressure of extreme urgency can we be induced to recognize the problem. Reluctance to appraise the Byzantine Empire may in part be a result of paralysis reinforced by a distaste for any discussion of possible precursors of Russian government. But the concern of the Byzantine Empire in the Greek tradition was with form, with space and time. The sense of community built up by the Greeks assumed a concern with time in continuity and not in "a series of independent instantaneous flashes" (Keynes) such as appealed to the Romans and Western Christianity. "Immediacy of presentment was an inevitable enemy to construction. The elementary, passionate elements of the soul gave birth to utterances that would tend to be disconnected and uneven, as is the rhythm of emotion itself."[38] There was a "parallel emergence, in all the arts, of a movement away from a need which, whether in the ascendant or not, was always felt and honoured: the craving for some sort of continuity in form."[39] The effort to achieve continuity in form implies independence from the pressure of schools and fashions and modes of expression.

The results of developments in communication are reflected in the time philosophy of Bergson, Einstein, Whitehead, Alexander, and Russell. In Bergson we have glorification of the life of the moment, with no reference beyond itself and no absolute or universal value.[40] The modern "clerks" "consider everything only as it exists in time, that is as it constitutes a succession of particular states, a 'becoming,' a 'history,' and never as it presents a state of permanence beyond time under this succession of distinct cases." William James wrote: "That the philosophers since Socrates should have contended as to which should most scorn the knowledge of the particular and should most adore knowledge of the general, is something which passes understanding. For, after all, must not the most honourable knowledge be the knowledge of the most valuable realities! And is there a valuable reality which is not concrete and individual."[41] The form of mind from Plato to Kant which hallowed existence beyond change is proclaimed decadent. This contemporary attitude leads to the discouragement of all exercise of the will or the belief in individual power. The sense power and the instinct for freedom have proved too costly and been replaced by the sham independence of democracy.[42] The political realization of democracy invariably encourages the hypnotist.[43] The behaviourist and the psychological tester have their way. In the words of one of them: "Great will be our good fortune if the lesson in human engineering which the war has taught us is carried over, directly and effectively, into our civil institutions and activities" (C. S. Yoakum).[44] Such tactlessness and offence to our good sense is becoming a professional hazard to psychologists. The essence of living in the moment and for the moment is to banish all individual continuity.[45] What Spengler has called the Faustian West is a result of living mentally and historically and is in contrast with other important civilizations which are "ahistoric." The enmity to Greek antiquity arises from the fact that its mind was ahistorical and without perspective.[46] In art classical man was in love with plastic whereas Faustian man is in love with music.[47] Sculpture has been sacrificed to music.[48]

The separation and separate treatment of the senses of sight and touch have produced both subjective disunity and external disunity.[49] We must somehow escape on the one hand from our obsession with the moment and on the other hand from our obsession with history. In freeing ourselves from time and attempting a balance between the demands of time and space we can develop conditions favourable to an interest in cultural activity.

It is sufficient for the purpose of this paper if attention can be drawn on the occasion of the 150th anniversary of a university on this continent to the role of the university in Western civilization. Anniversaries remind us of the significance of time. Though multiples of decades are misleading measures as the uniform retiring age of 65 is inhuman in its disrespect of biological differences they draw attention to a neglected factor. The university is probably older than Hellenistic civilization and has reflected the characteristics of the civilization in which it flourished, but in its association with religion and political organization it has been concerned with problems of time as well as of space.

Notes

Originally published as "A Plea for Time," in *The Bias of Communication*, by Harold Innis. Copyright © University of Toronto Press 1951. Reprinted with permission of the publisher. This paper was first presented by Innis at the University of New Brunswick in 1950.

1. The use of the letters A.D. and B.C. apparently dates from the eighteenth century. Hellenic rationalism might be said to have persisted for 700 years and to have been obscured for 1,200 years. " . . . the longest period of consecutive time in human history on which we can found inductions is, upon the whole, a period of intellectual and moral darkness." Julien Benda, *The Great Betrayal*, trans. Richard Aldington (London: Routledge, 1928), 159.

2. History "threatens to degenerate from a broad survey of great periods and movements of human society into vast and countless accumulations of insignificant facts, sterile knowledge, and frivolous antiquarianism" (Money in 1878). Emery Neff, *The Poetry of History* (New York: Columbia University Press, 1947), 193.

3. P. A. Sorokin and R. K. Merton, "Social Time: A Methodological and Functional Analysis," *American Journal of Sociology* 42 (1936–67).

4. "In general, the rigidity of the Japanese planning and the tendency to abandon the object when their plans did not go according to schedule are thought to have been largely due to the cumbersome and imprecise nature of their language, which rendered it extremely difficult to improvise by means of signaled communication" (Winston Churchill).

5. R. K. Merton, "The Sociology of Knowledge," in *Twentieth Century Sociology*, ed. G. Gurvich and W. E. Moore (New York: The Philosophical Library, 1945), 387–88.

6. H. W. Garrod, *Scholarship, Its Meaning and Value* (Cambridge: University Press, 1946), 42.

7. Ernst Cassirer, *The Problem of Knowledge: Philosophy, Science, and History since Hegel*, trans. W. H. Woglom and C. W. Hendel (New Haven, Conn.: Yale University Press, 1950), 170–73.

8. Leslie Stephen, *History of English Thought in the Eighteenth Century* (London: Smith, Elder, 1876), 458.

9. *Empire and Communications* (Oxford: Clarendon, 1950).

10. Cited by Alfred Vagts, *A History of Militarism* (New York: W. W. Norton, 1937), 16.

11. See J. T. Shotwell, "The Discovery of Time," *Journal of Philosophy, Psychology, and Scientific Methods* (1915): 198–206, 254–316. It is argued that mathematics made the use of time possible. See F. Thureau-Dangin, "Sketch of a History of the Sexagesimal System," *Osiris* 7. The Sumerian system was developed by crossing the numbers 10 and 6. Babylonian science was weak in geometry whereas the Greek science was strong. The Greeks learned the sexagesimal system through astronomy and discovered the Hindu system with a zero.

12. J. T. Shotwell, *An Introduction to the History of History* (New York: Columbia University Press, 1922), 43–44.

13. The calendar was apparently organized by Marduk and was under the control of the ruler of Mesopotamia. Frankfort et al., *The Intellectual Adventure of Ancient Man* (Chicago: University of Chicago Press, 1957), 181.

14. A new concern with time was evident in Herodotus who presented a history "that neither the deeds of men may fade from memory by lapse of time, or the mighty and marvelous works wrought partly by the Hellenes, partly by the Barbarians, may lose their renown." See also Thucydides' reason for writing history.

15. See Benjamin Farrington, *Head and Hand in Ancient Greece: Four Studies in the Social Relations of Thought* (London: Watts, 1947).

16. N. S. Timasheff, *An Introduction to the Sociology of Law* (Cambridge, Mass.: Harvard University Committee on Research in the Social Sciences, 1939), 207.

17. Coulton Waugh, *The Comics* (New York: Macmillan, 1947).

18. Archibald Forbes, *Souvenirs of Some Continents* (London: Macmillan, 1894).

19. Matthew Josephson, *The Robber Barons: The Great American Capitalists, 1861–1901* (New York: Harcourt, Brace, 1934), 27.

20. Cited by L. M. Salmon, *The Newspaper and the Historian* (New York: Oxford University Press, 1923), 29.

21. Brand Whitlock, *Forty Years of It* (New York: D. Appleton, 1925), 157.

22. Matthew Josephson, *The President Makers, 1896–1919* (New York: Harcourt, Brace, 1940), 145.

23. Oswald Garrison Villard, *Fighting Years: Memoirs of a Liberal Editor* (New York: Harcourt, Brace, 1939), 151.

24. Vagts, *A History of Militarism*, 173.

25. Wyndham Lewis, *Time and Western Man* (London: Chatto and Windus, 1927), 28.

26. John Maynard Keynes, *Two Memoirs* (London: R. Hart-Davis, 1949), 96–97.

27. J. B. Bury, *A History of Freedom of Thought* (London: Greenwood, 1928), 227.

28. W. R. Inge, *Diary of a Dean, St. Paul's 1911–1934* (London: Macmillan, 1950), 193–98.

29. J. B. Bury, *The Idea of Progress: An Inquiry into Its Origin and Growth* (London: Clarendon, 1920), 175.

30. William Albig, *Public Opinion* (New York: McGraw-Hill, 1939), 220.

31. Siegfried Kracauer, *From Caligari to Hitler* (Princeton, N.J.: Princeton University Press, 1947), 297–98. "The camera's possibility of choosing and presenting but one aspect of reality invites it to the worst kinds of deceit." *The Journals of André Gide*, trans. Justin O'Brien IV (New York: A. A. Knopf, 1951), 91.

32. Henri-Frédéric Amiel, *Amiel's Journal: The Journal intime of Henri-Frédéric Amiel*, trans. Mrs. Humphrey Ward (London: Macmillan, 1885).

33. Ilka Chase, *Past Imperfect* (New York: Doubleday, Doran, 1942), 236. For a reference to the breathtaking feats of tightrope walking to avoid any possible offence by major networks see ibid., 234.

34. George Gissing, *The Private Papers of Henry Ryecroft* (London: Arden Library, 1914), 287.

35. For example, the teaching that "intellectual activity is worthy of esteem to the extent that it is practical and to that extent alone . . . the man who loves science for its fruits commits the worst of blasphemies against that divinity." Benda, *The Great Betrayal*, 121. The scholar's defeat "begins from the very moment when he claims to be practical." Ibid., 151.

36. J. M. Clark, *Alternative to Serfdom* (New York: A. A. Knopf, 1948), 65.

37. E. E. Kellett, *Fashion in Literature* (London: G. Routledge, 1931), 282.

38. Louis Cazamian, *Criticism in the Making* (New York: Macmillan, 1929), 72.

39. Ibid., 64.

40. Lewis, *Time and Western Man*, 27.

41. Benda, *The Great Betrayal*, 78–80.

42. Lewis, *Time and Western Man*, 316.

43. Ibid., 42.

44. Cited in ibid., 342.

45. Ibid., 29.

46. Ibid., 285.

47. Ibid., 295.

48. Ibid., 299.

49. Ibid., 419. For a discussion of the effects of printing on music see Constant Lambert, *Music Ho! A Study of Music in Decline* (London: Faber and Faber, 1934).

HAROLD INNIS

The Military Implications of the American Constitution

I

This paper is an attempt to understand the policies of the United States. In Canada we are under particular obligations to attempt such an understanding in our own interests as well as in the interests of the rest of the world. The difficulties involved in any country's understanding itself, particularly a country with a complex unstable history, are overwhelming and the most penetrating studies of the United States have been made by de Tocqueville, a Frenchman, and by Lord Bryce, an Englishman. A Canadian is too close to make an effective study but he has the most to gain from it. He is handicapped by tradition especially in English-speaking Canada, evident in the pervasive influence of those who left the United States after the American Revolution, namely the United Empire Loyalists, and by language in French-speaking Canada. The writer of this paper can scarcely pretend to the necessary objectivity, nor, I suspect, can most of his readers. Nevertheless we must do our best.

Whatever our view about the American Revolution we must agree that it was achieved by a resort to arms against Great Britain. To the British it may have been a war of little consequence; we remember the remarks of an Englishman who when told that in the War of 1812 the British forces had burned Washington said he thought he had died in bed. To Americans the achievement was a result of desperate struggle. Revolutions leave unalterable scars and nations which have been burned over by them have exhibited the most chauvinistic brand of nationalism and crowd-patriotism.[1] These nations have developed highly depersonalized social relationships, political structures, and ideals and their counsels are determined most of all by spasms of crowd propaganda. "Public policy sits on the doorstep of every man's personal conscience. The citizen in us eats up the man."[2] The founders of the American Constitution appear to have recognized the danger by framing an instrument which put limits on the number of things concerning which a majority could encroach on the position of the individual.[3] But the extent of such protection has varied and declined with improvements in the technology of communication and the increasing powers of the executive, as Senator McCarthy has conspicuously shown.

Washington and his successors in the nineteenth century renounced an interest in Europe but steadily expanded their influence in the Americas following the increase in demand for new land on which to raise cotton. The demand implied steady expansion westward, in the south, and, in order to maintain a balance, in the north. In the south expansion was at the expense of the French empire, notably in Jefferson's administration when Louisiana was bought from Napoleon, and in the north at the expense of the British empire when Lewis and Clark were sent on a journey of exploration to the northwest and when John Jacob Astor established Astoria on the Columbia River. Later expansion in the south was safeguarded in the Monroe Doctrine, enunciated in 1823, which warned European powers to keep their hands off South America and was directed to the absorption of Texas, California, and other states at the expense of the Spanish empire and of Mexico. The remnants of a crumbling Spanish empire were finally taken over after the explosion of the *Maine* in Cuba ("Remember the *Maine*") and when Puerto Rico and the Philippines became American possessions. Expansion in the south to some extent intensified and to some extent eased the pressure on the British empire in the north. The line was eventually tightened to the present Canadian border and Alaska, "Seward's icebox," was purchased from Russia in 1867. These developments remind us of Disraeli's comment when Poland had been partitioned by European powers at a meeting at breakfast, "What will they have for lunch?"

II

The outbreak of the American Revolution marked a return to ideological warfare such as had largely disappeared in England after the Civil War.[4] Democratic nationalism and the mass army became the new basis of warfare.[5] George Washington, an officer in the British army in the Seven Years' War against the French, had gained experience which gave him the leadership of the Revolutionary Army. The immediate significance of the

Revolution was evident in the position of this soldier from Virginia. A mass army could not be built up under a New England general.[6] As a result of success in arms he secured not only independence for the colonies but also a stable federal government. He presided over the Convention and was asked to take the chief position in the new government. An interest in western lands was not unrelated to his sympathy with the Federalists in their proposal for a strong central government with "powers competent to all general purposes," words included in a letter from him to Hamilton in 1783.[7] His sympathies found reflection in the views of delegates concerned about the dangers implicit in the radical character of state constitutions written by revolutionary legislatures. "Our chief danger rises from the democratic parts of our constitutions" (Edmund Randolph of Virginia to the Convention).[8] Conservatism and an emphasis on the theory of divided powers led to provisions strengthening the executive power, such as those making the President Commander-in-Chief of the Army and Navy and giving him control over patronage. The Secretaries of State and War were made responsible to the President alone and, with the exception of the Treasury Department, the precedent was followed in the establishment of new Cabinet posts. The President became a focus of executive power. The influence and character of Washington finally left their impression on the United States as he secured Virginia's acceptance of the Constitution in 1787 and gave leadership to the other states which followed.

In the work of establishing a nation, the influence and prestige of the first President left an indelible impression on the operation of government. However, Washington's efforts to secure the advice of the Senate as a sort of privy council were met with distrust. The decision of the Senate to receive reports of Cabinet ministers in writing and to exclude them from its meetings drove the Cabinet into the position of being the President's council. As a further guarantee against presidential interference, in Congress a system of committees was emphasized in which members were protected by secrecy from any group including the press.

John Adams, the second President (1797–1801), whose election implied a recognition of the role of New England in the Revolution and its aftermath, inherited the task of maintaining the prestige of the office, but he found it difficult to maintain the delicate balance between New England and the South, in the face of the power of Alexander Hamilton as a representative of industrial and commercial interests in the middle states. At Hamilton's insistence, Washington had agreed to call out the militia of four states to put down the Whisky Rebellion in 1794. In 1798 Hamilton advised his friends in the government to prepare for war with

France, and Congress planned for a large emergency army and an increase in the regular army. Under his influence Washington agreed to head the army and by virtue of his prestige could insist on choosing his generals. Strife between Adams and Hamilton was followed by defeat of the former for a second term and by a weakening of the Federalist position.

In opposition to the centralizing tendencies of the Constitution, Jefferson (1801–1809) led a group whose views were reflected in the Declaration of Independence and the Articles of Confederation. He emphasized the position of the land, the small farmer, and the labourer against banking and the commercial interests. On his trip up the Hudson with Madison in 1791 he laid the foundations for the "longest-lived, the most incongruous, and the most effective political alliance in American history: the alliance of southern agrarians and northern city bosses."[9] In contrast with the Federalists who insisted that survival depended on the sword, Jefferson stated: "I hope no American will ever lose sight of the essential policy of interdicting in the seas and territories of both Americas, the ferocious and sanguinary contests of Europe." "Our first and fundamental maxim should be, never to entangle ourselves in the broils of Europe."[10] As a representative of the South, and in spite of his statement that "our peculiar security is in the possession of a written Constitution," he accepted the annexation of Louisiana and acquired the port of New Orleans without asking the question of constitutional propriety. To an alliance between the city bosses of New York and the South, he added the West.

After Jefferson's two terms, Madison, also a native of Virginia, became President (1809–17) and acquired additional territory. On April 14, 1812, Congress formally divided West Florida at the Pearl River, annexing the western half to the new state of Louisiana, and, a month later, the eastern half to the Mississippi Territory. In 1813 the American army forced the Spanish garrison at Mobile to surrender and took possession. Henry Clay and the Committee on Foreign Affairs persuaded Congress to declare war on Great Britain on June 18, 1812. "The conquest of Canada is in your power." "This war, the measures which preceded it, and the mode of carrying it on, were all undeniably Southern and Western policy, and not the policy of the commercial states" (Josiah Quincy).[11] On December 5, 1814, Madison recommended liberal spending on the Army and the Navy and the establishment of military academies.

Following the two terms of Madison, Monroe, again a native of Virginia, and an officer in the Revolutionary Army, became President (1817–

25). The decline of the Federalist party meant that there was no official opposition, and also no party discipline. The President was thus left without any device to secure cohesion in Congress. In the House of Representatives, for example, an Army bill, opposed by the President and the Secretary of War, was "carried notwithstanding many defects in the details of the bill by an overwhelming majority."[12] In 1822 Monroe recognized the independence of the Latin American republics which had been part of the Spanish empire, and, on the insistence of John Quincy Adams, included in his statement of the Monroe Doctrine on December 2, 1823, a protest against the encroachment of Russians in the northwest.

The success of the War of 1812 and the re-election of Monroe in 1820 finally destroyed the Federalist party as a political factor. Decline in prestige and power of the congressional caucus opened the way for a free fight in 1824; New England influence was once more reflected in the election of John Quincy Adams, who like his father, John Adams, served only for one term (1825–29).

His successor, Andrew Jackson (1829–37), a native of South Carolina, had suffered at the hands of the British in the Revolutionary War. In the War of 1812 he had led western militiamen against the Indians of Georgia and Alabama and destroyed British troops under General Sir Edward Pakenham in New Orleans. In 1817 he pursued marauding Indians into Spanish territory, marched to Pensacola, and removed the Spanish governor. After his invasion of Florida he became military governor. As a national figure and a popular hero he introduced a system of military organization to national politics. Beginning in 1825 he built up a national political machine. A small, divided, virulent, and undisciplined[13] press which had contributed to the disappearance of the Federalist party and a monopolistic Washington press were replaced by an organized party press designed to provide discipline and propaganda. The National Intelligencer,[14] the organ of Jefferson, Madison, Monroe, and J. Q. Adams, had been the oracle of war sentiment before and after 1812 and had a wide circulation for daily, semi-weekly, and weekly editions.[15] In opposition, Jackson and his followers established media to maintain a close contact with voters. After his election the United States Telegraph and the Washington Globe became administrative mouthpieces for partisan purposes.[16] Rewards were offered to strengthen the morale of the troops; "no plunder no pay." Political organizers in state politics such as Van Buren at Albany were brought to the national stage. In 1832 at the time of the nomination of Jackson for a second term, a system of nominating conventions was introduced in which a two-thirds rule was invoked to protect the position of the South. The news value of the system became evident in the emergence of the presidential candidate as the chief consideration of politics. Under Jackson and his successor, Van Buren (1837–41), a representative of New York State, campaign techniques were elaborated. Veto messages, written up by journalistic members of the Kitchen Cabinet for popular consumption, had a wide distribution. The difficulties of the system became evident when attempts were made to meet the demands of regional groups. The Tariff of Abominations, and the opposition to Vice-President Calhoun of South Carolina in the nullification controversy, made the latter a defender of state rights and led to the enactment of the Force Act by which the President was given authority to call out the Army and Navy to enforce laws of Congress. The dragon's teeth of secession were sown.

J. K. Polk (1845–49), a native of North Carolina, the first dark horse ever nominated for the presidency, aggressively pressed for settlement of the Oregon boundary dispute under the slogan "Fifty-Four Forty or Fight" and secured recognition of a boundary in 1846. This aggressiveness was designed to increase the number of states in the north, to parallel the increase in the south with the addition of Texas and the acquisition of New Mexico and California. Americans in California took a hint from Polk and declared an independent state. Polk ordered General Zachary Taylor to occupy the left bank of the Rio Grande; at length the exasperating Mexicans committed an overt act, which was followed by a brief successful war. In 1847, in "the spot" resolutions, Lincoln took an active part in attacking Polk, and to a resolution of Congress thanking General Taylor, secured the addition of a rider that the war had been started by Polk "unnecessarily and unconstitutionally."[17] Polk[18] was accused by the Whigs of forcing a war to extend the institution of slavery. Opposition to the aggressiveness of the south in the interests of new territory became more vocal through the activities of Lincoln and organs such as the *Chicago Tribune.*

The long struggle between the North and South was drawing to a close as the North was no longer able to offset southern influence by such tactics as nominating generals for President. These tactics had been to an extent self-defeating since military power was reinforced by recognition of heroes in elections to the presidency. The Whig party[19] was replaced by the Republican party supported by the free soil movement. The plantation system led to the acquisition of Indian and Mexican lands. The spoils of Mexico were poisoning the political system—each addition of territory accentuated the rivalry between North and South.

The gold rush in California precipitated a more intense struggle for control over the first transcontinental railway. Jefferson Davis, Secretary of War under Pierce, a native of New Hampshire and a minor national hero at Buena Vista, insisted on a Pacific railway along the Mexican border linking California to the Gulf states and opening the trade of Asia to the plantation society. In the north, on the other hand, Stephen Douglas of Illinois demanded a route through Nebraska.

At the end of the Civil War a national army had emerged to serve a national state. The President and executive were supreme above the states. Washington became the significant capital and state governments became less important. The South was invited to join a vastly different union than that she had left, but in turn the war had created a solid and a different South from the one which had left the union. Ideological warfare had been carried to great lengths. The North imposed a peace more bitter than war. The Republican party, as a result of the costs of civil war and victory, became a sacred cause to New England, the farmers of the Middle West, veterans concerned with pensions, and negroes. Andrew Johnson (1865–69) was finally disregarded as President. In spite of the Constitution, the President was deprived of control of the Army and governments in the South which had been elected in 1865 were replaced in 1867 by military rule with the whole area divided into five military districts each under a major general. Grant, trained as a general, became the head of an executive which had been built up by a skilful politician but which had deteriorated under Johnson who followed the precedent of vice-presidents in reversing policy. Like Jefferson Davis, Grant carried the dominating qualities of a soldier into the administration of civil affairs (1869–77). He was thwarted in his ambition to annex San Domingo in the south by Sumner, chairman of the Foreign Relations Committee of the Senate, who long served as a focus of northern bitterness, following the savage physical attack on him by Brooks of South Carolina on the floor of the Senate,[20] and who insisted on the acquisition[21] of Canada to the north.

With the aggressive support of Union veterans of the Grand Army of the Republic, Hayes, a brigadier general under Sheridan, was elected to the presidency by a narrow margin in 1876 (1877–81). In his fight with the Senate, the telegraph became an effective instrument in the mobilization of public opinion. He acquired control of the appointive power and "the long domination of the executive by the Congress was at an end" (H. J. Eckenrode). Grant had been unable to restore the South to white rule because of the Army and the bitterness following the war but under

Hayes, as a result of the cohesiveness of white southerners in the Demo-cratic party, the retreat of the North from the South was begun. It was finally ended in 1894 and the negro was left a third-class citizen, legally free, but deprived of his vote. On the other hand Hayes began the unfor-tunate precedent of using his power over federal troops to break strikes in West Virginia, Pennsylvania, and Maryland.

As a nominee of the Democratic party reflecting the demands of the West for monetary reform, Bryan was defeated by W. J. McKinley (1897–1901) who had served as a private, and was a brevet major at the end of the Civil War. The war mania, developed over the Venezuela dispute, persisted and led to demands for war with Spain. This Congress declared in April, 1898. "McKinley had in part given in to public pressure, for fear of disrupting his party and losing the autumn elections.[22] From the Rio Grande to the Arctic Ocean there should be but one flag and one coun-try!" was the cry of Henry Cabot Lodge. Regarding the Philippines, Mc-Kinley decided that "there was nothing left for us to do but take them all, and to educate and uplift and civilize and Christianize them," a process involving a long period of hostilities with the Filipinos.[23] The Hawaiian Islands were annexed, partly because they would be needed to defend the Philippines. In the peace treaty Puerto Rico was ceded by Spain.

During the war in Cuba, Theodore Roosevelt, God's gift to news-papermen, who had raised the Rough Riders, and, with the assistance of Richard Harding Davis as war correspondent, secured important space on the front pages of newspapers, became a centre of attention.[24] He was elected Governor of New York State, became Vice-President in McKin-ley's second term, and President (1901–1909) on the latter's assassina-tion. This was attributed to an incendiary press, particularly the writings of Bierce and the Hearst papers, which supported the Democratic party.[25] Such was the background for a belief in power for the central govern-ment; "I achieved results only by appealing over the heads of the Senate and House leaders to the people, who were the masters of both of us."[26] Cleveland gave out messages on Sunday evenings[27] to get more space in the Monday papers and Roosevelt exploited the practice following the development of Sunday papers by making important statements on Sun-day and compelling the dull Monday papers to feature them.[28] He pre-pared speeches well ahead of time in order that they could be distributed to all newspapers before public delivery and the expenses of telegraph-ing them be avoided.[29] The interest of newspapers in his activities was a result of his sense of news, and of his concern with trust busting, which implied defeat of the International Paper Company as a trust, and lower prices of newsprint. "I took the canal zone and let Congress debate." Panama had "a most just and proper revolution."[30] In spite of Congress he sent the United States fleet to the Pacific to impress the Japanese. Under pressure from Roosevelt the Canadian claim in the Alaska boundary dispute had been sacrificed.[31] Regarding the appointment of judges to the Supreme Court, Roosevelt wrote: "he [a judge of the Court] is not in my judgment fitted for the position unless he is a party man, a constructive statesman. . . ."[32] His position was summed up in his statement: " . . . I did greatly broaden the use of executive power."[33]

The disastrous results of the bitter aftermath of the Civil War, shown as late as in the uncomfortable position of President Wilson and the attitude of the Republican party toward the peace treaty, were ultimately evident in the successive readjustments of the terms of peace, in the collapse of 1929, and the election of President F. D. Roosevelt, formerly Governor of New York. He exploited to the full the systematic efforts of Theodore Roosevelt to rid the name of association with the aristocracy.[34] Extensive control over patronage, the advantage of radio in appealing to the people over the head of Congress, and the disciplined support of labour enabled him to dominate the party until his death and enabled the party to dominate Congress to the present. "The radio . . . the supreme test for a presidential candidate" was Roosevelt's "only means of full and free access to the people."[35] He was extremely sensitive to public opinion especially the opinion of religious groups.[36] The picture changed from one of a little-regarded presidential office and a supreme legislative branch under Harding, Coolidge, and Hoover and the strong position of business interests represented by lobbies; to one featuring a strong executive and a vast patronage to executive agencies.[37] In 1938 enormous relief funds were shifted toward preparation of armaments.[38] Even the Supreme Court which, as Chief Justice Hughes remarked, says what the Constitution is, generally sympathetic to the legislative branch of government, after a bitter struggle[39] became more sympathetic to the executive. Finally the transfer of the Bureau of the Budget from the Treasury Department gave the President access to all activities of the government.

The disequilibrium created by a press protected by the Bill of Rights had its effects in the Spanish American War, in the development of trial by newspaper, and in the hysteria after the First World War. Holmes wrote "when twenty years ago a vague tremor went over the earth and the word socialism began to be heard, I thought and I still think that fear was translated into doctrines that had no proper place in the Constitution or the common law." The effects of this hysteria were registered in the influence of the press on legislatures and on the Supreme Court (notable dissents only prove its strength). As a result power shifted increasingly to the executive and involved reliance of the executive on force. In the words of Brooks Adams: "Democracy in America has conspicuously, and decisively failed in the collective administration of common public property."

The power of the President in his control over patronage and party was not only enhanced by the radio but also by military considerations. The importance of the military factor strengthened the possibilities of leadership by a single person with power to intervene in war in spite of public opinion and of Congress. He was compelled to exercise wide discretion to lead or to force Congress to recognize and to accept his power and position. The position of the Democratic party and the President in the First World War, and in the Second World War, particularly as a result of the radio which widened the gap between the executive and the legislative branches, made it necessary to rely on important intermediaries—House in the case of President Wilson and Hopkins in the case of President F. D. Roosevelt.[40] In Great Britain by way of contrast the Prime Minister had the support of coalition and of Parliament. The solidity of the parliamentary tradition made it possible to defeat and to re-elect Churchill whereas the continued dominance of the Democratic party, while facilitating the transfer of power from Roosevelt to Truman, meant that changes could only be made in personnel, including members of the Cabinet. Americans were amazed at the necessity of Churchill's maintaining constant touch with the British Cabinet in drawing up the Atlantic Charter in Newfoundland in contrast with the independence of Roosevelt.

In the conduct of foreign affairs, a lack of continuity,[41] incidental to the importance of individuals, and in spite of the encouragement given to careermen in the Rogers Act of 1924,[42] was in strong contrast with the continuity evident in Great Britain and in Russia. This made for less attention to Europe, especially since the importance of interests in Latin America meant greater concern with ministers from these countries, particularly as they were men of ability and industry.[43] Difficulties in conducting negotiations with English representatives were evident at Bretton Woods, Washington, and Savannah. English negotiators were constantly faced by Americans with the statement that they could not get that through Congress. The judgment of American negotiators as to the political tolerance of Congress and of public opinion became a determining consideration.

The conflict between Cavalier and Roundhead, between absolute monarchy and absolute parliament, in England was transferred to North America. The southern colonies established at an earlier date reflected the influence of aristocratic organization and the northern colonies the influence of Puritan organization. The demands of the northern colonies for independence with relation to trade were paralleled by demands of the southern colonies for independence in relation to land. Before 1861 all but two of fifteen administrations represented the Democratic party and of the thirteen nine were served by southern presidents. The Jefferson revolution from 1800 to 1860 was followed by Republican policy from 1860 to 1932.[44]

The dominance of representation from the South and especially Virginia, and of representation from the Army in the period prior to the Civil War, was a reflection of the dynamic power of the plantation system and its demand for more and better land. The weakness of the Spanish, Indians, and Mexicans made it possible for an aggressive government to steadily expand its territory to the west. Expansion of territory to the southwest gave an impetus to parallel expansion to the northwest to be accomplished with an occasional extension of territory at the expense of the British, for example in Maine and Oregon, and at the expense of the Russians on the north Pacific coast. In the race for land to the west and with its disappearance, the South attempted to expand territory for the slave trade along the northern border of the southern states. The friction eventually led to the outbreak of civil war or the war between the states.

With the end of the Civil War presidents were elected from the North and were again largely representative of the successful northern army. The aggressiveness of the North was checked by growing nationalism in Canada evident in controversies, over the fisheries centring around the Washington Treaty, the Alaska boundary dispute, and the reciprocity treaty of 1911. It took new forms in a continuation of the war against Spain and was effective in the addition of new territory.

Broadening of the powers of the executive such as those boasted about by Theodore Roosevelt and the improvement of communication notably in radio strengthened the position of the President. Control over vast sums following the depression and continued during the war enabled the President to control the party. The seven principles of politics, five loaves and two fishes, were handled more effectively. Patronage and assistance in elections were distributed in accordance with the record of the roll calls in Congress.[45] In the election of presidents directly by majority vote was registered the importance of the middle class urban vote, especially of New York, and the election of senators, following the abolition of election by caucus,[46] two from each state representing predominantly a rural middle class, increased the possibilities of friction.[47] The House of Representatives also reflected the influence of the urban vote but its size left it exposed to vicious partisan and predatory interests and to manipulation under stupid rules such as prevailed under Cannon and after 1925 under the Longworth Snell Tilson triumvirate.[48] It has been described as the greatest organized inferiority complex in the world.

With the tendency toward increased power in the executive and the increasing importance of urban centres the policy of parties is less dependent on a single figure in the presidency. Family names will probably persist as a factor in the selection of President—to mention Harrison, Roosevelt, and Taft—and the dangers of assassination[49] will be checked by strengthening of the secret service. Formerly vice-presidents were selected as representatives of a defeated minority within the party and were consequently in a weak position when they rose to the presidency.[50]

The President cognizant of his power must be constantly alert to the implication of policy for voting strength. In foreign policy the results have been evident in several directions. Timing has been carefully worked out in relation to voting or rather voting has been carefully planned in relation to time. A rigid time arrangement compels an emphasis on maneuverability or the settlement of issues when the effects will be most evident in relation to votes. Mr. Truman immediately before the election in 1948 decided to recognize Palestine and to strengthen the position of the Democratic party in New York State of which Mr. Dewey was Governor. A period of tension and war enormously increases the executive power. The opposition is prevented on the large vague grounds of security and military secrecy from discussing effectively the most crucial element of policy. During the war Republicans were appointed to the Cabinet and bi-partisan responsibility in foreign affairs was assumed. The argument about swapping horses in midstream has proved difficult to answer. It might be answered by nominating a general, let us say Eisenhower, but West Point has never produced good politicians, and he may be content with actually having more power than the President. F. D. Roosevelt, with a personal interest in the Navy, left Army experts with much greater freedom of decision.[51] Such freedom, however, tends to throw the President into the hands of the armed forces. The two-thirds rule regarding treaties in the Senate has been effective in checking the foreign policy of presidents and has been exploited by German, Russian, and Clan-na-Gail delegations,[52] but it has been of little avail with the development of the United Nations and the power of armed force. Indeed the Senate has shown considerable readiness at the demands of the party to co-operate with armed forces.

In the twentieth century the enormous development of industry accentuated by war has greatly enhanced the problems of the executive. Use of the blockade and the threat of blockade has increased dependence on domestic industries. "An all-round increase in armed forces" has been necessary "to mitigate unemployment." We must have "war to solve unemployment in order to ensure against internal anarchy, instead of war solely to protect employment (ordered life) against external aggression." "The dependence on war has become even more vital to our economic system than the dependence of war on industry." "Should an enemy not exist he will have to be created."[53] "A war cannot be carried on without atrocity stories for the home market."[54]

These remarks have been made by one who does not pretend to understand the United States and who cannot appraise the significance of the party struggle as part of the domestic scene. But we are required in the interests of peace to make every effort to understand the effects not only of the actions of the United States but also of our own actions. We have never had the courage of Yugoslavia in relation to Russia and we have never produced a Tito. We have responded to the demands of the United States sometimes with enthusiasm and sometimes under protest. Members of the British Commonwealth struck back against the Hawley-Smoot tariff in the Ottawa Agreements. But we have been a part of the North American continent. The enormous increase in the production of wheat on this continent in the last century was directly related to the Russian revolution, the rise of agrarianism in Germany, of higher tariffs in France and of marked adjustments in England. Germany imposed a tariff on sugar to secure independence in supplies of sugar, drove down the prices of cane sugar, contributed to the outbreak of revolt in the Spanish American colonies, and enabled the United States to take full advantage of the break-up of the Spanish empire.[55] The immigration quota of American legislation in 1924 accentuated the population problems of Italy and contributed to fascism. The silver purchase agreement of 1934 and the consequent destruction of the Chinese monetary system were related to the revolution in China. The protectionist policy of North America and the difficulties of penetrating the American market compel the United States to export dollars and at the same time make it difficult for other countries to acquire dollars. As a result there is resort to enormous expenditure on armament. In the words of the late Carl Becker, what we didn't know hurt us a lot.

A written constitution with its divisive nature established by the Declaration of Independence and the Constitution, centralization under Washington and Adams, decentralization from Jefferson to Lincoln, and centralization after Lincoln, first under the Republican party and later the Democratic party, so that at one time there has been a weakening of the power of the executive and at another a strengthening of that power depending largely on the dominant medium of communication, stand in sharp contrast with the unwritten constitution of Great Britain and the undivided power of the Prime Minister responsible to Parliament. In the United States parties are "devoted to the search for compromise between sectional, class, and business groups" and are "frankly uninterested in logical programs or 'eternal' principles."[56] The practice of representation from party rather than regions characteristic of Great Britain finds no expression in the United States.[57] "The most profound of American political thinkers saw in the perpetual search for compromise between selfish interests the basic principle of free government." In the words of Calhoun, "the negative power . . . makes the constitution, and the positive . . . makes the government. The one is the power of acting; and the other the power of preventing or arresting action. The two, combined, make constitutional government."[58] The emphasis on negation, the constant fear of Leviathan, of the encroaching state, has been offset by the promotion of strong government by war and industrial revolution.[59] Under the American Constitution reliance on force has become increasingly necessary whereas under the British, following the brief period in which Parliament was dominated by Cromwell and the army and the period in which the Duke of Wellington was Prime Minister, force has been increasingly subjected to the authority of Parliament. A general as Prime Minister of England would be unthinkable, though the influence of the army and navy are not to be disregarded, whereas in the United States a general as President has been regarded almost as a rule. Ostrogorski has quoted the remark that God looks after little children, drunken men, and the United States. I hope it will not be thought blasphemous if I express the wish that He take an occasional glance in the direction of the rest of us.

Notes

Originally published as "The Military Implications of the American Constitution," in *The Strategy of Culture*, by Harold Innis. Reprinted with permission of the Estate of Harold Innis. This essay was first presented by Innis in New York City on December 6, 1951.

1. E. D. Martin, *The Behavior of Crowds: A Psychological Study* (New York: Harper, 1920), 223.

2. Ibid., 248.

3. Ibid., 249. "The most certain test by which we judge whether a country is really free, is the amount of security enjoyed by minorities." "By liberty I mean the assurance that every man shall be protected in doing what he believes his duty, against the influence of authority and majorities, custom and opinion. . . . It is bad to be oppressed by a minority, but it is worse to be oppressed by a majority." (Lord Acton.) See Sir John Pollock, Bt., *Time's Chariot* (London: Murray, 1950), 166–67.

4. J. F. C. Fuller, *Armament and History* (London: Eyre and Spottiswoode, 1946), 101.

5. Ibid., 109.

6. Herbert Agar, *The United States: The Presidents, the Parties and the Constitution* (London: Eyre and Spottiswoode, 1950), 28. "For it is a fact, that more than one third of their general officers have been inn-keepers, and have been chiefly indebted to that circumstance for such rank. Because by that public, but inferior station, their principles and persons became more generally known." Smyth; cited by Kittredge, *The Old Farmer and His Almanack* (Cambridge, Mass.: Harvard University Press, 1920), 264.

7. Agar, *The United States*, 37.

8. Ibid., 45.

9. Ibid., 88.

10. Washington, of course, in his Farewell Address had said, "It is our true policy to steer clear of permanent alliances with any portion of the foreign world, so far, I mean, as we are now at liberty to do it."

11. Agar, *The United States*, 174.

12. Ibid., 200.

13. James Cheetham, an exile from England after the Manchester riots in 1798, attempted in the *American Citizen*, a daily sponsored by Clinton, to break the power of Aaron Burr in New York. William Duane, editor of the powerful Jeffersonian paper, the *Aurora*, because of a bitter grudge against Madison and Gallatin who refused to give him a job contributed to the defeat of the Navigation Act of Gallatin and hastened the outbreak of war.

14. This had been the *Independent Gazetteer* of Philadelphia under Joseph Gales, a son of the editor and proprietor of the *Sheffield Register*, who had left England following a charge of sedition in 1795. It was purchased by S. H. Smith in 1800 and moved to Washington.

15. A. K. McClure, *Recollections of Half a Century* (Salem: Salem Press Company, 1902), 37–39.

16. J. E. Pollard, *The Presidents and the Press* (New York: Macmillan, 1937), 147.

17. See R. S. Harper, *Lincoln and the Press* (New York: McGraw-Hill, 1951), 9.

18. T. W. Barnes, *Memoir of Thurlow Weed* (Boston: Houghton Mifflin, 1884), 172.

19. The Whigs failed to capture the popular vote. Daniel Webster was alleged to have said that they should "come down into the forum and take the people by the hand," words which were printed innumerable times in the largest type in Democratic newspapers. Governor J. A. Clifford, on the other hand, imprudently called the Democrats "poor in character and meager in numbers." Charles Taber Congdon, *Reminiscences of a Journalist* (Boston: James R. Osgood, 1880), 60.

20. See Congdon, *Reminiscences of a Journalist*, 253.

21. *The Education of Henry Adams: An Autobiography* (Boston: Constable, 1918), 275.

22. Agar, *The United States*, 624.

23. Ibid., 625.

24. Commenting on Roosevelt's Rough Riders, Mr. Dooley wrote: " 'Tis 'Th' Biography iv a Hero be Wan who Knows.' . . . If I was him I'd call th' book 'Alone in Cubia.' " Elmer Ellis, *Mr. Dooley's America* (New York: A. A. Knopf, 1941), 145.

25. W. H. J. Abbott, *Watching the World Go By* (Boston: Little, Brown, 1933), 139.

26. Agar, *The United States*, 639.

27. Pollard, *The Presidents and the Press*, 511.

28. Abbott, *The United States*, 244.

29. Oscar King Davis, *Released for Publication: Some Inside Political History of Theodore Roosevelt and His Times, 1898–1918* (Boston: Houghton Mifflin, 1925), 102.

30. Agar, *The United States*, 650.

31. Ibid., 626.

32. Ibid., 644.

33. Ibid., 638.

34. E. C. Bentley, *Those Days* (London: Constable, 1940), 198.

35. R. E. Sherwood, *Roosevelt and Hopkins* (New York: Harper, 1950), 184, 186–67. Every word in his speeches was judged not by appearance in print but by effectiveness over the radio and careful attention was given to accurate timing in relation to the number of words and the rate of delivery (217, 297). It is significant that before the radio no pre-eminent orator ever succeeded in reaching the presidency. A. K. McClure, *Our Presidents and How We Make Them* (New York: Harper, 1900), 88. It might also be noted that Blaine and Tilden were the only men who managed their own campaigns for the presidency and that both were defeated. Ibid., 312.

36. Sherwood, *Roosevelt and Hopkins*, 384.

37. R. G. Tugwell, "The New Deal: The Decline of Government," *Western Political Quarterly*, June 1951, 295–312. For a study of the conflict between presidential and congressional authority over the administration see C. S. Hyneman, *Bureaucracy in a Democracy* (New York: Harper, 1950).

38. Sherwood, *Roosevelt and Hopkins*, 101.

39. J. Alsop and T. Catledge, *The 168 Days* (New York: Doubleday, Doran, 1938).

40. Sherwood, *Roosevelt and Hopkins*, 931–93. Ickes complained in 1940 that Hopkins had "never even attended a county meeting and wouldn't know how to get into one.

Now here he is taking over a national convention. It's disgraceful." J. A. Farley, *Jim Farley's Story: The Roosevelt Years* (New York: Whittlesey House, 1948), 297.

41. The diplomatic corps was an adjunct of the spoils system and the football of politicians. See J. D. Whelpley, *American Public Opinion* (New York: Chapman and Hall, 1914), 113, 121.

42. See Drew Pearson and R. S. Allen, *Washington Merry-Go-Round* (New York: H. Liveright, 1931), 140.

43. Ibid., 30, 46.

44. McClure, *Our Presidents and How We Make Them*, 21.

45. George Michael, *Handout* (New York: G. P. Putnam's Sons, 1935), 73.

46. For a criticism of the direct primary see C. J. Stackpole, *Behind the Scenes with a Newspaperman: Fifty Years in the Life of an Editor* (Philadelphia: J. B. Lippincott, 1927).

47. A. N. Holcombe, *The Middle Classes in American Politics* (Cambridge, Mass.: Harvard University Press, 1940), 104.

48. Pearson and Allen, *Washington Merry-Go-Round*, 217–19.

49. The influence of anarchism and the Colt revolver on the disappearance of apparent dictatorships in business and in governments has never been given careful study. See Emma Goldman, *Living My Life* (New York: A. A. Knopf, 1934).

50. H. L. Stoddard, *As I Knew Them: Presidents and Politicians from Grant to Coolidge* (New York: Harper, 1927), 123.

51. Churchill exercised much greater control over the army. See Sherwood, *Roosevelt and Hopkins*, 246.

52. Count Cassini, a Russian minister, and Von Holheben, a German minister, appealed successfully through the press to the Senate against presidential policy. *The Education of Henry Adams*, 375.

53. Fuller, *Armament and History*, 164–65.

54. Bentley, *Those Days*, 184.

55. See Brooks Adams, *America's Economic Supremacy* (New York: Macmillan, 1900), 36–41.

56. Agar, *The United States*, vii.

57. The fathers were particularly concerned to avoid the borough system of England. "State law and custom have practically established that a representative must be a resident of the district from which he is elected." See D. A. S. Alexander, *History and Procedure of the House of Representatives* (Boston: Houghton Mifflin, 1916), 5. As a result the mobility of the ablest individuals has been checked, whereas in England parties have been much more effective in attracting and securing the election of the ablest individuals irrespective of residence.

58. Agar, *The United States*, vii.

59. Ibid., xiii.

Canada as Counter-Environment

Marshall McLuhan was born in Edmonton in 1911. He studied engineering and English literature at the University of Manitoba (B.A. 1933, M.A. 1934) and literature at Cambridge University (M.A. 1940, Ph.D. 1942). McLuhan converted to Catholicism in 1937. At Cambridge, he studied under I. A. Richards and F. R. Leavis. McLuhan's first book, *The Mechanical Bride* (1951), is one of the inaugural studies of popular culture that appeared at mid-century, a few years before Roland Barthes's *Mythologies* (1957) and Richard Hoggart's *Uses of Literacy* (1961). Subsequent books such as *The Gutenberg Galaxy* (1962) and especially *Understanding Media* (1964) are pathbreaking works whose influence on the subsequent development of North Atlantic cultural theory (especially the work of Guy Debord, Jean Baudrillard, Fredric Jameson, Anthony Wilden, and Arthur Kroker) is only beginning to be charted. (See, for example, Gary Genosko's study *McLuhan and Baudrillard: Masters of Implosion*, 1999.) Though sympathetic, McLuhan's distance from the New Left and then the appropriation of his image by the dotcom hype machine may have lessened interest in his work among cultural studies scholars, but his influence on Canadian media artists has been considerable. Other major book projects by McLuhan are (with Q. Fiore) *The Medium Is the Massage* (1967), *War and Peace in the Global Village* (1968), *Culture Is Our Business* (1970), and *The Global Village* (1989). McLuhan taught at Saint Louis University from 1937 to 1944 and at St. Michael's College, University of Toronto, from 1946 to 1979. He founded the Centre for Culture and Technology at the University of Toronto in 1963. McLuhan died in Toronto in 1980.

Canadians and Americans share something very precious: a sense of the last frontier. The Canadian North has replaced the American West. That primeval woodland, that vast wilderness is there, from Banff to Newfoundland, giving all North Americans a spatial habitation Europeans do not know. For two centuries, at least, the frontier has taught us how to go out alone.

As it did for nineteenth-century plainsmen, going out to be alone raises the ultimate question: who am I? We remove ourselves from the anonymity of the crowd. Standing on the edge of the Grand Canyon or a glacial tundra, we are swept with a sense of immensity, a feeling of awe, which—for most of us—is swiftly followed by a prayer and thanksgiving. For those breaking the Oregon Trail, the wilderness was a red-clawed menace. Today we reclaim and repossess ourselves in forest and glen and take stock, once again, of our individual worth.[1]

We have tried to demonstrate how video-related technologies, taking advantage of left-hemisphere overload, will implode our inner sensibilities, destroying a previous imbalance between the hemispheres. But more than that, these technologies will invade our inner peace, occupying our every waking moment. We will need a place to hide.

Earlier in the century, Charlie Chaplin seemed to find a partial answer. He was the overburdened European turned inside out. In the time of Dickens, English coketowns allowed no man to be idle. But as soon as the immigrant left Ellis Island, he discovered a marvelous thing about America: he was free to do anything and go anywhere he liked. He might have been Huck Finn exploring the mighty Mississippi. You will remember that Huck told Tom Sawyer that loafing, carefully pushed to its limits, defined the meaning of independence. As he and the slave Jim floated down the river they could carelessly lose their goals and objectives. Loafing could reveal your true self because you are "dropping out" to be alone. Chaplin, like Huck, epitomized the transformation of loafing. Spiffy, elegant in bowler, cane, and morning coat, he became a footloose knight of the road.

Carefree individuality, though, is foreign to the European. He doesn't find privacy in the great outdoors but in the crowd itself. He spends his lifetime learning the strategies and uses of the social mask. Like the legendary Heidelberg prince, he must wear a tribal and corporate mask in the same way he does his uniform. Fixed economic and social rank obsolesces nonchalance from the moment of birth. And release can only be obtained briefly in a *Fasching* or Mardi Gras. The European habitually goes out to be social and comes home to be alone. The American and Canadian do exactly the reverse.

But electronic technologies have begun to shake the distinction between inner and outer space, by blurring the difference between being here or there. The first hint of this condition came with the telephone. By increasing the speed of the private voice, it retrieved telepathy and gave everyone the feeling of being everywhere at once. After teleconferencing is established, the picturephone will be reintroduced, taking the user outside for public inspection whether he or she is ready or not.

As the border is gradually erased between inner and outer space, between the aggressive extroversion of the marketplace and the easy sociability of the home, North Americans will need another refuge, a place where nostalgia, for example, could serve as a link with the stability of times gone by. If a U.S. citizen so chose, Canada could become an enormous psychic theme park; something like a Hollywood set that simultaneously links the past with the present, the city with the wilderness. The Province of Quebec seems to have anticipated this role with its recent advertising slogan, "Foreign yet Near." The calculated ambivalence of the Canadian is a most efficient way of maintaining a low profile, as a receptive ground for other people's fantasies.

In the nineteenth century the Germans were expert at the art of discovery, that is, deciding what effect they wanted and working back step-by-step to uncover the starting point of the thing to be discovered. In a similar way, the Canadians are masters of what Bertrand Russell has called the twentieth century's highest achievement: the technique of suspended judgment. Canadians experiment with technology from all over the world, but rarely adopt any technical stratagem broadly. For example, in their current examinations of teletext, Canadian telephonic engineers will test both U.S. Telidon and British Ceefax, with a side nod to Gallic Antiope, while resisting AT&T's efforts to standardize all teletext transmission equipment.

Canadians are always waiting for the latest model without making a commitment to what is available here and now. As the United States careens toward its rendezvous with the unified effects of combined video technologies, it might steadily keep its eyes on the rear-view mirror—as indeed all other previous cultures have done in terms of the introduction of new technical artifacts—to see how the Canadians sidestep the impact of these new media, keeping a sort of stasis in place so characteristic of the northern ability to juggle fierce separatism and regionalisms without cataclysmic finality.

A border is not a connection but an interval of resonance, and such gaps abound in the land of the DEW line. The DEW line itself (Distant Early Warning system), installed by the United States in the Canadian North to keep this continent aware of activities in Russia, points up a major Canadian role in the twentieth century—the role of hidden ground for big powers. Since the United States has become a world environment, Canada has become the anti-environment that renders the United States more acceptable and intelligible to many small countries of the world; anti-environments are indispensable for making an environment understandable.

Canada has no goals or directions, yet shares so much of the American character and experience that the role of dialogue and liaison has become entirely natural to Canadians wherever they are. Sharing the American way without commitment to American goals or responsibilities makes the Canadian intellectually detached and observant as an interpreter of the American destiny.

In the age of the electronic information environment the big nations of the First World are losing both their identities and goals. France, Germany, England, and the United States are nations whose identities and goals were shaped by the rise of the self- regulating markets of the nineteenth century, markets whose quantitative equilibrium has been obsolesced by the dominance of the new world of instant information. As software information becomes the prime factor in politics and industry, the First World inevitably is minus the situation which has given meaning and relevance to its drive for mere quantity. New images of identity based on quality of life are forming in a world where suddenly *small is beautiful* and centralism is felt to be a disease.

In this new world the decentralized and soft-focus image of the flexible Canadian identity appears to great advantage. Canadians, who never got "delivery" on their first national identity image in the nineteenth century, are the people who learned how to live without the bold accents of the national "egotrippers" of other lands. Today they are even more suited to the Third World tone and temper as the Third World takes over the abandoned goals of the First World. Sharing many characteristics of the Third World, Canada mediates easily between the First and Third Worlds.

If there are 250,000 unnamed lakes in Ontario alone, there is an even larger problem of toponymy in tracing the Canadian language. Morton Bloomfield, a professor of English at Harvard University and a Canadian by birth, surfaced one of the many hidden borderlines that interlace the Canadian psyche when he explored the character of Canadian English, a subject neglected by both Canadian and American scholars. In "Canadian English and Its Relation to Eighteenth-Century American Speech," he noted: "The probable explanation for this neglect lies in the fact that most American investigators, ignorant of Canadian history, are under the impression that Canadian English, as undoubtedly is the case with Australian, South African, and Newfoundland English, is a direct offshoot of British English and therefore does not belong to their field of inquiry. It is, however, necessary to know the history of a country before one can know the history of its language."[2] Bloomfield pointed out that in The American Language, H. L. Mencken shared the widespread illusion that American English conquered the British English of Canada, whereas Canadian English had been American from the time of the American Revolution: "After 1776, however, the situation changed and a large increase in population occurred, entirely owing to the movement north of many Tories or Loyalists who wished, or were forced, to leave the United States because of the American Revolutionary War. They carried with them, as a matter of course, the language spoken in the Thirteen Colonies at the time."[3] Without any self-consciousness English Canadians enjoy the advantages of a dual language. Canada is linguistically in the same relation to the United States as America is to England. Stephen Leacock humorously varied the theme: "In Canada we have enough to do keeping up with the two spoken languages without trying to invent slang, so we just go right ahead and use English for literature, Scotch for sermons and American for conversation."[4] Another psychological borderline shared by Canadians and Americans is a legacy of their nineteenth-century war on the empty wilderness, as indicated in Lord Durham's Report on the Affairs of British North America (1839): "The provision which in Europe, the State makes for the protection of its citizens against foreign enemies, is in America required for what a French writer has beautifully and accurately called; the 'war with the wilderness.' The defence of an important fortress, or the maintenance of a sufficient army or navy in exposed posts, is not more a matter of common concern to the European, than is the construction of the great communications to the American settler; and the State, very naturally, takes on itself the making of the works, which are matters of concern to all alike."[5] It would be strange indeed if the population of North America had not developed characteristic attitudes to the spaces experienced here. A century of war on the wilderness made customary the habit of going outside to confront and explore the wilderness and of going inside to be social and secure. Going outside involved energy and effort and struggle in frontier conditions that called for initiative amidst solitude. Thus, Margaret Atwood notes in her critical study, Survival: "The war against Nature assumed that Nature was hostile to begin with; man could fight and lose, or he could fight and win. If he won he would be rewarded: he could conquer and enslave Nature, and, in practical terms, exploit her resources."[6]

Atwood's study of Canadian writers reveals a frontier trauma, yet one that is not uniquely Canadian. Twain's *The Adventures of Huckleberry Finn*, Whitman's *Leaves of Grass*, Thoreau's *Walden*, and Melville's *Moby Dick* record new attitudes to both inner and outer space; spaces that had to be explored rather than inhabited. Here, then, is the immediate effect of continental space: to seem to be a land that has been explored but never lived in. The Oriental comment is not without good grounds: "You Westerners are always getting ready to live!" Expressed in Whitman's "Song of the Broad-Axe" and C. C. Moore's " 'Twas the Night Before Christmas" ("The stockings were hung by the chimney with care") lie the two psychic poles of the special North American feeling for space—the outer space for aggressive extroversion and the inner space for cozy sociability and security amidst dangers.[7] On the borderline between these areas of aggression and hospitality Hawthorne and Henry James etched their psychic adventures and "the complex fate" of being a North American. "It's a complex fate, being an American," James wrote, "and one of the responsibilities it entails is fighting against a superstitious valuation of Europe."[8] To become cultured in America while resisting European values became a major theme in Hawthorne and James. Neither thought to consider the hidden physical polarities of this continuing conflict.

The mutual feeling for space in Canada and the United States is totally different from that of any other part of the world. In England or France or India people go outside to be social and go inside to be private or alone. By contrast, even at picnics and camping holidays and barbecues North Americans carry the frontier with them, just as their cars, their most cherished form of privacy, are designed for special effects of quiet enclosure. Where a European thinks of "a room of one's own," the North American depends upon the car to provide the private space for work and thought. Typically, one can see *through* an American car when driving, but one cannot see *into* the car when standing. The reverse is true of a European car; one can see into it but not through it when on the road.

Since we are seeking to delineate some of the Canadian borderlines, it is natural that those psychologically shared with the United States are the areas of maximal interplay and subtle interpenetration. One mythic borderline Canada shares with the United States springs from the heroic deeds of Paul Bunyan and Babe, the Big Blue Ox. It is generally accepted that Paul Bunyan was an American logger of the 1840s and 1850s. The folk art of the tall story is dear to the frontier, that world of the resonant interval where public amplification proliferates. These tall stories are often called in to calm the ardor of those who delight in exaggeration. The Paul Bunyan man can retort with a story of the huge pines in his territory which he began to notch with Paul. After notching for an hour or more, they went round the tree and found two Irishmen who had been chopping at the same tree for three years, including Sundays. Paul is a frontier or borderline figure who is a continent-striding image. Newfoundland poet E. J. Pratt had a special gift for the gigantic in verse as in his *Witches' Brew* and *The Cachalot*. The frontier poet or novelist will feel "the call of the wild" rather than the lure of the parlor or even the pub. As Thoreau wrote in *Walden*: "I have never found the companion so companionable as solitude."[9]

The frontier is naturally an abrasive and rebarbative area which generates grievance, the formula for humor. Thus the first major Canadian literary character was Sam Slick, the Yankee clock-maker. The frontier abounds in figures of fun-writing like Stephen Leacock, Canada's Mark Twain.

Hugh Kenner looked into the borderline matter in his essay "The Case of the Missing Face." He begins his quest for the missing face of Canadian culture with an observation of Chester Duncan: "Our well-known Canadian laconicism is not always concealed wisdom, but a kind of . . . between-ness. We are continually on the verge of something but we don't quite get there. We haven't discovered what we are or where we're going and therefore we haven't much to say."[10] Duncan found the key with "between-ness," the world of the interval, the borderline, the interface of worlds and situations. It may well be that Canadians misconceive their role and opportunities and feel the misguided urge to follow the trendy ways of those less fortunately placed. The interface is where the action is. No need to move or follow, but only to tune the perceptions on the spot.

Harold Innis, the Canadian pioneer historian of economics and communication, imaginatively used the interface, or borderline situation, to present a new world of economic and cultural change by studying the interplay between man's artifacts and the environments created by old and new technologies. By investigating social effects as contours of changing technology, Innis did what Plato and Aristotle failed to do. He discovered from the alphabet onward, the great vortices of power at the interface of cultural frontiers. He recovered for the West the world of entelechies and formal causality long buried by the logicians and teachers of applied knowledge; and he did this by looking carefully at the immediate situation created by staples and the action of the Canadian cultural borderline on which he was located.

Looking for the missing face of Canada, Kenner feels Canadians have been beguiled into nonentity by the appeal of the big, tough "wilderness-tamers" and our urge to identify with "rock, rapids, wilderness and virgin (but exploitable) forest." But Kenner gave up just when the trail was promising. Yes, the Canadian, as North American, answers the call of the wild and goes out into the wilderness to "invite his soul," but unlike the rest of mankind, he goes out with a merely private face (and also a private voice). Whereas the Frenchman or the Russian or the Irishman records the defeats and miseries (as well as the joys and successes) of his life on his countenance, the North American keeps his face to himself and "scrubs" it daily.[11]

Somewhat in the manner of Dorian Gray, the real picture of the individual life is hidden away for private judgment rather than public inspection. On the other hand, the extrovert who goes outside to be a lonely fighter and explorer is not an extrovert at home. Charlie Chaplin's pictures of the lonely tramp never take us inside an American home, thereby ignoring the hidden ground of his lonely figure of the Little Tramp. Chaplin was an Englishman who never understood America, but he gave Europeans what they still view as American documentaries.

Equally as fascinated and confused as Chaplin, W. H. Auden shared the bafflement of Henry James about the missing face in North America:

> So much countenance and so little face. (Henry James) Every European visitor to the United States is struck by the comparative rarity of what he would call a face, by the frequency of men and women who look like elderly babies. If he stays in the States for any length of time, he will learn that this cannot be put down to a lack of sensibility—the American feels the joys and sufferings of human life as keenly as anybody else. The only plausible explanation I can find lies in his different attitude to the past. To have a face, in the European sense of the word, it would seem that one must not only enjoy and suffer but also desire to preserve the memory of even the most humiliating and unpleasant experiences of the past.

> More than any other people, perhaps, the Americans obey the scriptural injunction: "Let the dead bury their dead."

> When I consider others I can easily believe that their bodies express their personalities and that the two are inseparable. But it is impossible for me not to feel that my body is other than I, that I inhabit it like a house, and that my face is a mask which, with or without my consent, conceals my real nature from others.

It is impossible consciously to approach a mirror without composing or "making" a special face, and if we catch sight of our reflection unawares we rarely recognize ourselves. I cannot read my face in the mirror because I am already obvious to myself.

The image of myself which I try to create in my own mind in order that I may love myself is very different from the image which I try to create in the minds of others in order that they may love me.[12]

Auden is here speaking of a psychic dichotomy alien to North Americans. "The case of the missing face," however, has a simple solution from one point of view, since the North American, in poetry, art, and life, tends to substitute the face of nature for the human countenance.

Like Wordsworth and Thoreau North Americans spend their time scanning the environmental mystery, taking spins in the country instead of spinning thoughts at home. The North American goes to the movies or theater to be alone with his date, whereas Europeans go to enjoy the audience. The North American excludes advertisements from his cinema and theater, while Europeans find no violation of their privacy from ads in places of public entertainment. Europeans, on the other hand, exclude ads from radio and television in their homes; but since there is little or no privacy in the North American home, ads are tolerated, if only because we go elsewhere for privacy.

It is by an encounter with the hidden contours of one's own psyches and society that group identity gradually develops. That Canada has had no great blood-letting such as the American Civil War, may have retarded the growth of a strong national identity, reminding Canadians that only the bloody-minded could seriously wish to obtain a group identity by such violence.

The 1976 strike of Canadian air pilots and controllers over the bilingual issue at airports clearly marks another of the vivid borderlines of Canadian interface and abrasion. The French language is a cultural border and vortex of energy that has roots in the beginnings of Canada as a territory cherished by both French and English settlers. The new technology of air travel projects an ancient quarrel in a new dramatic medium. The drama of the civilian air controllers resonates with the events of 1759 and the fall of Quebec City. The repercussions of that event affect all of North America today. Donald Creighton discerns the action on both sides of the border in the opening sentence of The Empire of the St. Lawrence:

When, in the course of a September day in 1759, the British made themselves the real masters of the rock of Quebec, an event of apparently unique importance occurred in the history of Canada. There followed rapidly the collapse of French power in North America and the transference of the sovereignty of Canada to Great Britain; and these acts in the history of the northern half of the continent may well appear decisive and definitive above all others. In fact, for France and England, the crisis of 1759 and 1760 was a climax of conclusive finality. But colonial America, as well as imperial Europe, had been deeply concerned in the long struggle in the new continent; and for colonial America the conquest of New France had another and a more uncertain meaning. For Europe the conquest was the conclusion of a drama; for America it was merely the curtain of an act. On the one hand, it meant the final retirement of France from the politics of northern North America; on the other, it meant the regrouping of Americans and the reorganization of American economies.[13]

The Fall of Quebec (1759) and the Peace of Paris (1763) created the same psychic border for French Canada as the Civil War defeat did in the mind of the American South. The defeat stimulated the feeling of an historical present that was absent in the victors. "For many French Canadians," writes Ramsay Cook in The Maple Leaf Forever, "the past, and especially the conquest, has always been part of the present." He continues with the words of Canon Groulx:

History, dare I say it, and with no intention of paradox, is that which is most alive; the past, is that which is most present. Or in Esdras Minville's revealing remark about "we who continue history, who are history itself." This attitude toward history which makes the past part of the present is not, of course, uniquely French Canadian. It bears a marked similarity to the comment of a distinguished Mexican philosopher concerning Hispanic America. "The past, if it is not completely assimilated, always makes itself felt in the present," Leopoldo Zea has written, "Hispanic America continued to be a continent without a history because the past was always present. And if it had a history, it was not a conscious history. Hispanic America refused to consider as part of its history a past which it had not made." Is it not the failure to "assimilate" the Conquest, to make it French-Canadian history, that explains the endless attempts to interpret it?[14]

These hidden borders in men's minds are the great vortices of energy and power that can spiral and erupt anywhere; and it is not for lack of such vortices that the Canadian identity is obscure. Rather, there are so many that they have been dissipated and smothered in consumerism and affluence. The vast new borders of electronic energy and information created by radio and television have set up world frontiers and interfaces among all countries on a new scale that alters all pre-existing forms of culture and nationalism. The superhuman scale of these electric "software" vortices has created the Third World with its threat to the old industrial world of "hardware."

On the occasion of Queen Elizabeth's visit to the White House to congratulate the United States on its bicentennial, the president proposed that the dignity of the occasion might be enhanced by reading aloud the Declaration of Independence. So much for subliminal wisdom, even though a G. K. Chesterton might well have found in this much food for transcendental meditation. The historian Kenneth McNaught observes: "It is sometimes said that Americans are benevolently uninformed about Canada while Canadians are malevolently well-informed about the U.S."[15] McNaught is here pointing to one of the great borderline features of the Canadian, namely, his opportunities to "take over" the United States intellectually in the same way Alexis de Tocqueville did earlier. Is it not significant that Tocqueville was unable to see the French situation with the same clarity that he brought to the United States? France was driving to the extremes of specialism and centralism under the fragmenting pressure of print technology, creating the matrix for Napoleon while Tocqueville was enjoying the naiveté of Americans whose politics were the first to be founded on the printed word.

In the same way, Canadians repine in the shadow of the American quest for identity, saying "Me too!" while ignoring the anguish of the American struggle to find out "who are we?" Kenneth McNaught cites the American historian C. Vann Woodward to underline the plight of fellow borderliners: "How many of us have experienced a feeling of being really Canadian only during our first trip abroad? I suspect that this feeling flows from the fact that we have always been self-confident without really understanding it."[16]

Many Canadians had their first vivid experience of national identity while watching the Russian teams play the Canadians at their own game of hockey. The Russians gave them a very bad time by playing a close style of hockey that the Canadians had developed in the 1930s and forgotten in the 1940s. It was in the earlier period that the Canadians sent their coaches to Russia to teach the game. Here was surely an admirable example of the borderline case in full interface. Canadian participation in past wars, whether in 1812 or 1914 or after, has never been on a scale to enable them to identify with the total operation. With hockey the scale is right but the personnel is confusing. In the Olympics the American hockey team consists mostly of Canadians. The jet plane knows no geographic borders with the result that hockey is played by Canadians in American arenas as an American sport. There is enough psychic and social overlap to make both American baseball and Canadian hockey acceptable dramatizations of the competitive drives and skills of both countries.

Related and comparable in scope to the gap of the missing face of North America is the case of the missing voice. If going outside to be alone forbids the assuming of a culturally acquired countenance, the same inhibition extends to "putting on" the North American voice. When we go outside, we use only a private voice and avoid the cultivation of an educated or modulated tone. One might even suggest that the absence of class barriers in North America owes more to its refusal to assume a group or class speech than to its political convictions or institutions.

When a Bill Buckley Jr. tilts his head and intones on television, he is clowning. Any American who tried to do seriously what the British public schoolboy is taught to do publicly would be run out of town on a rail. The North American hesitation to "put on" a public voice or a face is also a block to the artist and writer in "putting on" an audience for his work. Going out to be alone is antithetical to the role of the artist who must invent an image that will sting or intrigue a public to encounter his challenge. For the artist has to upset his audience by making them aware of their automatism or their own inadequacy in their daily lives. Where mere survival exhausts the creative energies as on our borderline, few have the daring to confront their public with an aesthetic vision.

There is a great new TV borderline in North America which endangers many established features of our lives, including our assumed right to use only the private voice out-of-doors. The TV generation has begun to "put on" a peer group or tribal dialect which could send us "Upstairs or Downstairs" in our sleep. The fact that the great vortex of interface between inside and outside in North America has gone unnoted by historians and psychologists for two centuries and more, is testimony to the vast subliminal energies that are outside our consciousness.

Canada is a land of multiple borderlines, psychic, social, and geographic. Canada has the longest coastline in the world, a coastline which represents the frontier for Europe on one side and the Orient on the other side. T. S. Eliot was very conscious of the "up-dating" power of frontiers. Commenting on this in regard to Mark Twain and the Mississippi on whose shores he was born, Eliot states: " . . . I am very well satisfied with having been born in St. Louis: in fact, I think I was fortunate to have been born here, rather than in Boston, or New York, or London."[17] Within the city itself, he was conscious of borderlines. Mentioning the boundaries of the city, he says: " . . . the utmost outskirts of which touched on Forest Park, terminus of the Olive Street streetcars, and to me, as a child, the beginning of the Wild West." Eliot is especially concerned with the effects of borderlines on language and literature, seeing in Mark Twain: " . . . one of those writers, of whom there are not a great many in any literature, who have discovered a new way of writing, valid not only for themselves but for others. I should place him, in this respect, even with Dryden and Swift, as one of those rare writers who have brought their language up to date, and in so doing, 'purified the dialect of the tribe.' "[18]

Eliot sees the frontier as an area of transformation and purgation, a character which belongs to frontiers and borderlines in many other places. Frederick J. Turner wrote a celebrated piece "The Significance of the Frontier in American History," noting that "again on the frontier," "this perennial rebirth, this fluidity of American life, this expansion westward with its new opportunities, its continuous touch with the simplicity of primitive society, furnish the forces dominating American character."[19]

The Canadian borderline (as well as the numerous frontiers within Canadian borders) shares many of the features that Turner observes concerning the frontier in American history. He sees it as reacting on Europe as well as being the door for the entry of Europeans. In saying that the frontier is "the line of most rapid and effective Americanization" he is pointing to one of the major features of the Canadian borderline where the process of Canadianization also takes place.[20] A frontier, or borderline, is the space between two worlds, constituting a kind of double plot or action that the poet W. B. Yeats discovered to be the archetypal formula for producing "the emotion of multitude" or the sense of universality. In his essay "The Emotion of Multitude" Yeats explains and illustrates how in poetry and in art, the alignment of two actions without interconnection performs a kind of magical change in the interacting components. What may be banal and commonplace situations, merely by their confrontation and interface, are changed into something very important.

The borderline of interface between cowboys and Indians captured the imagination not only of Europeans, but of Orientals as well. Even today affluent Germans and Japanese dress up in the costumes of cowboys and Indians and mount their horses to play the games of the Wild West. This frontier, to them exotic, has always been a major part of the Canadian experience. The old frontier had been the melting pot for the immigrant, while today it continues as the melting pot of the affluent. Suburban Canada camps and cottages in the North.

Borderlines, as such, are a form of political "ecumenism," the meeting place of diverse worlds and conditions. One of the most important manifestations of Canadian ecumenism on the Canadian borderline is the interface between the common law tradition (oral) and the American Roman law (written). There have been no studies of this very rich situation, but then there have been no studies of how the oral traditions of the Southern states are the creative foundations of American jazz and rock music. Borderlines [give] cosmopolitan character to Canada.

One of the more picturesque borderlines in Canadian life is its royal commissions which serve as mobile interdisciplinary and intercultural seminars, constituting a kind of "grass roots" tradition in Canada. In search of hyperbole, only a Canadian can say: "As Canadian as a Royal Commission!" There is an outré hyperbole of even more local significance: "As Canadian as Diefenbaker's French!" John Diefenbaker would have been delighted to know that he had become a cultural frontier!

Yes, Canada is a land of multiple borderlines, of which Canadians have probed very few. These multiple borderlines constitute a low profile identity, since, like the territory, they have to cover a lot of ground. The positive advantage of a low profile in the electronic age would be difficult to exaggerate. Electronic information now encompasses the entire planet, forming another hidden borderline or frontier whose action has been to rob many countries of their former identities. In the case of the First World, the Fourth World of electronic information dims down nationalism and private identities, whereas in its encounter with the Third World of India, China, and Africa, the new electric information environment has the effect of depriving these people of their group identities. The borderline is an area of spiraling repetition and replay, both of inputs and feedback, both of interlace and interface, an area of "double ends joined," of rebirth and metamorphosis.

Canada's 5000-mile borderline is unfortified and has the effect of keeping Canadians in a perpetual philosophic mood which nourishes flexibility in the absence of strong commitments or definite goals. By contrast, the United States, with heavy commitments and sharply defined objectives, is not in a good position to be philosophic or cool or flexible. Canada's borderline encourages the expenditure on communication of what might otherwise be spent on armament and fortification. The Canadian Broadcasting Corporation and the National Film Board are examples of federally sponsored communication rather than fortification. At the same time, Canadians have instant access to all American radio and television which, experienced in the alien milieu of Canada, feeds the philosophic attitude of comparison and contrast and critical judgment. The majority of Canadians are very grateful for the free use of American news and entertainment on the air, and for the princely hospitality and neighborly dialogue on the ground.

The advantages of having no sharply defined national or private identity in Canada appear in the general situation where lands long blessed by strong identities are now bewildered by the growing preformation and porousness of their identity image in this electronic age. The low-profile Canadian, having learned to live without such strongly marked characteristics, begins to experience a security and self-confidence that are absent from the big-power situation. In the electronic age centralism becomes impossible when all services are available everywhere. Canada has never been able to centralize because of its size and small population.

The national unity which Canadians sought by the railway "hardware" now proves to be irrelevant under electronic conditions which yet create an inclusive consciousness. For Canada a federal or inclusive consciousness is an inevitable condition of size and speed of intercommunication. This inclusiveness, however, is not the same as the nineteenth-century idea of national unity; rather, it is that state of political ecumenism that has already been mentioned as the result of multiple borderlines.

In order to have a high-profile identity nationally and politically, it is necessary to have sharp and few political and cultural borders. From 1870 onward Germany strove for a high-profile identity, within its multiple borders. In the industrial age this drive toward centralized and intense identity imagery seemed to be part of competitive commerce. Today, when the old industrial hardware is obsolescent; we can see that the Canadian condition of low-profile identity and multiple borders approaches the ideal pattern of electronic living.

Notes

Originally published as "Canada as Counter-Environment," in *The Global Village*, by Marshall McLuhan and Bruce R. Powers. Copyright © Corinne McLuhan and Bruce R. Powers. Reprinted with permission of Oxford University Press.

1. Gertrude Stein: "In the United States there is more space where nobody is than where anybody is. That is what makes America what it is." This was quoted in the official bicentennial gift to the people of the United States, *Between Friends/Entre Amis* (Toronto: McClelland and Stewart, 1976), 4, 24.

2. Morton W. Bloomfield, "Canadian English and Its Relation to Eighteenth-Century American Speech," *Journal of English and Germanic Philology* 47 (1948): 59.

3. Ibid., 60.

4. Stephen Leacock, *How to Write* (New York: Dodd, Mead, 1943), 119.

5. Lord Durham, *Report on the Affairs of British North America* (Oxford: Clarendon, 1912), 2:91.

6. Margaret Atwood, *Survival: A Thematic Guide to Canadian Literature* (Toronto: Anansi, 1972), 60.

7. Walt Whitman, *Leaves of Grass* (New York: Oxford University Press, 1990), 148; Clement Clarke Moore, *'Twas the Night Before Christmas* (New York: Houghton Mifflin, 1912), 2.

8. Henry James, *The Letters of Henry James*, ed. Percy Lubbock (New York: Charles Scribner's Sons, 1920), 13.

9. Henry David Thoreau, *Walden: Or, Life in the Woods* (New York: Dodd, Mead, 1946), 113.

10. Hugh Kenner, "The Case of the Missing Face," in *Our Sense of Identity*, ed. Malcolm Mackenzie Ross (Toronto: Ryerson Press, 1954), 203–8.

11. Ibid., 203.

12. W. H. Auden, *The Dyer's Hand, and Other Essays* (New York: Random House, 1962), 103–4.

13. Donald Creighton, *The Empire of the St. Lawrence* (Toronto: Macmillan of Canada, 1956), 1.

14. Ramsay Cook, *The Maple Leaf Forever: Essays on Nationalism and Politics in Canada* (Toronto: Macmillan of Canada, 1971), 111–12.

15. Kenneth McNaught, "Canadian Independence, Too, Was Won in the 1770s," *The Toronto Star*, July 1, 1976, C3.

16. Ibid.

17. T. S. Eliot, *To Criticize the Critic* (London: Faber and Faber, 1965), 45.

18. Ibid.

19. Frederick Turner, "The Significance of the Frontier in American History," in *The Frontier in American History* (New York: Holt, 1920), 2–3.

20. Ibid., 3–4.

MARSHALL MCLUHAN

The Medium Is the Message

In a culture like ours, long accustomed to splitting and dividing all
things as a means of control, it is sometimes a bit of a shock to be
reminded that, in operational and practical fact, the medium is the message. This is merely to say that the personal and social consequences of
any medium—that is, of any extension of ourselves—result from the new
scale that is introduced into our affairs by each extension of ourselves, or
by any new technology. Thus, with automation, for example, the new
patterns of human association tend to eliminate jobs, it is true. That is
the negative result. Positively, automation creates roles for people, which
is to say depth of involvement in their work and human association that
our preceding mechanical technology had destroyed. Many people
would be disposed to say that it was not the machine, but what one did
with the machine, that was its meaning or message. In terms of the ways
in which the machine altered our relations to one another and to ourselves, it mattered not in the least whether it turned out cornflakes or
Cadillacs. The restructuring of human work and association was shaped
by the technique of fragmentation that is the essence of machine technology. The essence of automation technology is the opposite. It is integral and decentralist in depth, just as the machine was fragmentary,
centralist, and superficial in its patterning of human relationships.

The instance of the electric light may prove illuminating in this connection. The electric light is pure information. It is a medium without a
message, as it were, unless it is used to spell out some verbal ad or name.
This fact, characteristic of all media, means that the "content" of any
medium is always another medium. The content of writing is speech, just
as the written word is the content of print, and print is the content of the
telegraph. If it is asked, "What is the content of speech?," it is necessary to
say, "It is an actual process of thought, which is in itself nonverbal." An
abstract painting represents direct manifestation of creative thought pro-

cesses as they might appear in computer designs. What we are considering here, however, are the psychic and social consequences of the designs or patterns as they amplify or accelerate existing processes. For the "message" of any medium or technology is the change of scale or pace or pattern that it introduces into human affairs. The railway did not introduce movement or transportation or wheel or road into human society, but it accelerated and enlarged the scale of previous human functions, creating totally new kinds of cities and new kinds of work and leisure. This happened whether the railway functioned in a tropical or a northern environment, and is quite independent of the freight or content of the railway medium. The airplane, on the other hand, by accelerating the rate of transportation, tends to dissolve the railway form of city, politics, and association, quite independently of what the airplane is used for.

Let us return to the electric light. Whether the light is being used for brain surgery or night baseball is a matter of indifference. It could be argued that these activities are in some way the "content" of the electric light, since they could not exist without the electric light. This fact merely underlines the point that "the medium is the message" because it is the medium that shapes and controls the scale and form of human association and action. The content or uses of such media are as diverse as they are ineffectual in shaping the form of human association. Indeed, it is only too typical that the "content" of any medium blinds us to the character of the medium. It is only today that industries have become aware of the various kinds of business in which they are engaged. When IBM discovered that it was not in the business of making office equipment or business machines, but that it was in the business of processing information, then it began to navigate with clear vision. The General Electric Company makes a considerable portion of its profits from electric light bulbs and lighting systems. It has not yet discovered that, quite as much as AT&T, it is in the business of moving information.

The electric light escapes attention as a communication medium just because it has no "content." And this makes it an invaluable instance of how people fail to study media at all. For it is not till the electric light is used to spell out some brand name that it is noticed as a medium. Then it is not the light but the "content" (or what is really another medium) that is noticed. The message of the electric light is like the message of electric power in industry, totally radical, pervasive, and decentralized. For electric light and power are separate from their uses, yet they eliminate time and space factors in human association exactly as do radio, telegraph, telephone, and TV, creating involvement in depth.

A fairly complete handbook for studying the extensions of man could be made up from selections from Shakespeare. Some might quibble about whether or not he was referring to TV in these familiar lines from *Romeo and Juliet*: "But soft! what light through yonder window breaks? It speaks, and yet says nothing." In *Othello*, which, as much as *King Lear*, is concerned with the torment of people transformed by illusions, there are these lines that bespeak Shakespeare's intuition of the transforming powers of new media:

> Is there not charms
> By which the property of youth and maidhood
> May be abus'd? Have you not read Roderigo,
> Of some such thing?

In Shakespeare's *Troilus and Cressida*, which is almost completely devoted to both a psychic and social study of communication, Shakespeare states his awareness that true social and political navigation depend upon anticipating the consequences of innovation:

> The providence that's in a watchful state
> Knows almost every grain of Plutus' gold,
> Finds bottom in the uncomprehensive deeps,
> Keeps place with thought, and almost like the gods
> Does thoughts unveil in their dumb cradles.

The increasing awareness of the action of media, quite independently of their "content" or programming, was indicated in the annoyed and anonymous stanza:

> In modern thought, (if not in fact)
> Nothing is that doesn't act,
> So that is reckoned wisdom which
> Describes the scratch but not the itch.

The same kind of total, configurational awareness that reveals why the medium is socially the message has occurred in the most recent and radical medical theories. In his *Stress of Life*, Hans Selye tells of the dismay of a research colleague on hearing of Selye's theory: "When he saw me thus launched on yet another enraptured description of what I had observed in animals treated with this or that impure, toxic material, he looked at me with desperately sad eyes and said in obvious despair: 'But Selye, try to realize what you are doing before it is too late! You have now decided to spend your entire life studying the pharmacology of dirt!' "[1]

As Selye deals with the total environmental situation in his "stress" theory of disease, so the latest approach to media study considers not only the "content" but the medium and the cultural matrix within which the particular medium operates. The older unawareness of the psychic and social effects of media can be illustrated from almost any of the conventional pronouncements.

In accepting an honorary degree from the University of Notre Dame a few years ago, General David Sarnoff made this statement: "We are too prone to make technological instruments the scapegoats for the sins of those who wield them. The products of modern science are not in themselves good or bad; it is the way they are used that determines their value." That is the voice of the current somnambulism. Suppose we were to say, "Apple pie is in itself neither good nor bad; it is the way it is used that determines its value." Or, "The small-pox virus is in itself neither good nor bad; it is the way it is used that determines its value." Again, "Firearms are in themselves neither good nor bad; it is the way they are used that determines their value." That is, if the slugs reach the right people firearms are good. If the TV tube fires the right ammunition at the right people it is good. I am not being perverse. There is simply nothing in the Sarnoff statement that will bear scrutiny, for it ignores the nature of the medium, of any and all media, in the true Narcissus style of one hypnotized by the amputation and extension of his own being in a new technical form. General Sarnoff went on to explain his attitude to the technology of print, saying it was true that print caused much trash to circulate, but it had also disseminated the Bible and the thoughts of seers and philosophers. It has never occurred to General Sarnoff that any technology could do anything but *add* on to what we already are.

Such economists as Robert Theobald, W. W. Rostow, and John Kenneth Galbraith have been explaining for years how it is that "classical economics" cannot explain change or growth. And the paradox of mechanization is that although it is itself the cause of maximal growth and change, the principle of mechanization excludes the very possibility of growth or the understanding of change. For mechanization is achieved by fragmentation of any process and by putting the fragmented parts in a series. Yet, as David Hume showed in the eighteenth century, there is no principle of causality in a mere sequence. That one thing follows another accounts for nothing. Nothing follows from following, except change. So the greatest of all reversals occurred with electricity, that ended sequence by making things instant. With instant speed the causes of things began to emerge to awareness again, as they had not done with things in sequence and in concatenation accordingly. Instead of asking which came first, the chicken or the egg, it suddenly seemed that a chicken was an egg's idea for getting more eggs.

Just before an airplane breaks the sound barrier, sound waves become visible on the wings of the plane. The sudden visibility of sound just as sound ends is an apt instance of that great pattern of being that reveals new and opposite forms just as the earlier forms reach their peak performance. Mechanization was never so vividly fragmented or sequential as in the birth of the movies, the moment that translated us beyond mechanism into the world of growth and organic interrelation. The movie, by sheer speeding up the mechanical, carried us from the world of creative configuration and structure. The message of the movie medium is that of transition from lineal connections to configurations. It is the transition that produced the now quite correct observation: "If it works, it's obsolete." When electric speed further takes over from mechanical movie sequences, then the lines of force in structures and in media become loud and clear. We return to the inclusive form of the icon.

To a highly literate and mechanized culture the movie appeared as a world of triumphant illusions and dreams that money could buy. It was at this moment of the movie that cubism occurred, and it has been described by E. H. Gombrich (Art and Illusion) as "the most radical attempt to stamp out ambiguity and to enforce one reading of the picture—that of a man-made construction, a colored canvas."[2] For cubism substitutes all facets of an object simultaneously for the "point of view" or facet of perspective illusion. Instead of the specialized illusion of the third dimension on canvas, cubism sets up an interplay of planes and contradiction or dramatic conflict of patterns, lights, textures that "drives home the message" by involvement. This is held by many to be an exercise in painting, not in illusion.

In other words, cubism, by giving the inside and outside, the top, bottom, back, and front and the rest, in two dimensions, drops the illusion of perspective in favor of instant sensory awareness of the whole. Cubism, by seizing on instant total awareness, suddenly announced that *the medium is the message*. Is it not evident that the moment that sequence yields to the simultaneous, one is in the world of the structure and of configuration? Is that not what has happened in physics as in painting, poetry, and in communication? Specialized segments of attention have shifted to total field, and we can now say, "The medium is the message" quite naturally. Before the electric speed and total field, it was not obvious that the medium is the message. The message, it seemed, was the "content," as people used to ask what a painting was *about*. Yet they never thought to ask what a melody was about, nor what a house or a dress was about. In such matters, people retained some sense of the whole pattern, of form and function as a unity. But in the electric age this integral idea of structure and configuration has become so prevalent that educational theory has taken up the matter. Instead of working with specialized "problems" in arithmetic, the structural approach now follows the lines of force in the field of number and has small children meditating about number theory and "sets."

Cardinal Newman said of Napoleon, "He understood the grammar of gunpowder." Napoleon had paid some attention to other media as well, especially the semaphore telegraph that gave him a great advantage over his enemies. He is on record for saying that "Three hostile newspapers are more to be feared than a thousand bayonets."

Alexis de Tocqueville was the first to master the grammar of print and typography. He was thus able to read off the message of coming change in France and America as if he were reading aloud from a text that had been handed to him. In fact, the nineteenth century in France and in America was just such an open book to de Tocqueville because he had learned the grammar of print. So he, also, knew when that grammar did not apply. He was asked why he did not write a book on England, since he knew and admired England. He replied:

> One would have to have an unusual degree of philosophical folly to believe oneself able to judge England in six months. A year always seemed to me too short a time in which to appreciate the United States properly, and it is much easier to acquire clear and precise notions about the American Union than about Great Britain. In America all laws derive in a sense from the same line of thought. The whole of society, so to speak, is founded upon a single fact; everything springs from a simple principle. One could compare America to a forest pierced by a multitude of straight roads all converging on the same point. One has only to find the center and everything is revealed at a glance. But in England the paths run criss-cross, and it is only by traveling down each one of them that one can build up a picture of the whole.

De Tocqueville, in earlier work on the French Revolution, had explained how it was the printed word that, achieving cultural saturation in the eighteenth century, had homogenized the French nation. Frenchmen were the same kind of people from north to south. The typographic principles of uniformity, continuity, and lineality had overlaid the complexities of ancient feudal and oral society. The Revolution was carried out by the new literati and lawyers.

In England, however, such was the power of the ancient oral traditions of common law, backed by the medieval institution of Parliament, that no uniformity or continuity of the new visual print culture could take complete hold. The result was that the most important event in English history has never taken place; namely, the English Revolution on the lines of the French Revolution. The American Revolution had no medieval legal institutions to discard or to root out, apart from monarchy. And many have held that the American Presidency has become very much more personal and monarchical than any European monarch ever could be.

De Tocqueville's contrast between England and America is clearly based on the fact of typography and of print culture creating uniformity and continuity. England, he says, has rejected this principle and clung to the dynamic or oral common-law tradition. Hence the discontinuity and unpredictable quality of English culture. The grammar of print cannot help to construe the message of oral and nonwritten culture and institutions. The English aristocracy was properly classified as barbarian by Matthew Arnold because its power and status had nothing to do with literacy or with the cultural forms of typography. Said the Duke of Gloucester to Edward Gibbon upon the publication of his *Decline and Fall*: "Another damned fat book, eh, Mr. Gibbon? Scribble, scribble, scribble, eh, Mr. Gibbon?" De Tocqueville was a highly literate aristocrat who was quite able to be detached from the values and assumptions of typography. That is why he alone understood the grammar of typography. And it is only on those terms, standing aside from any structure or medium, that its principles and lines of force can be discerned. For any medium has the power of imposing its own assumption on the unwary. Prediction and control consist in avoiding this subliminal state of Narcissus trance. But the greatest aid to this end is simply in knowing that the spell can occur immediately upon contact, as in the first bars of a melody.

A Passage to India by E. M. Forster is a dramatic study of the inability of oral and intuitive oriental culture to meet with the rational, visual European patterns of experience. "Rational," of course, has for the West long meant "uniform and continuous and sequential." In other words, we have confused reason with literacy, and rationalism with a single technology. Thus in the electric age man seems to the conventional West to become irrational. In Forster's novel the moment of truth and dislocation from the typographic trance of the West comes in the Malabar

Caves. Adela Quested's reasoning powers cannot cope with the total inclusive field of resonance that is India. After the Caves: "Life went on as usual, but had no consequences, that is to say, sounds did not echo nor thought develop. Everything seemed cut off at its root and therefore infected with illusion."

A Passage to India (the phrase is from Whitman, who saw America headed Eastward) is a parable of Western man in the electric age, and is only incidentally related to Europe or the Orient. The ultimate conflict between sight and sound, between written and oral kinds of perception and organization of existence is upon us. Since understanding stops action, as Nietzsche observed, we can moderate the fierceness of this conflict by understanding the media that extend us and raise these wars within and without us.

Detribalization by literacy and its traumatic effects on tribal man is the theme of a book by the psychiatrist J. C. Carothers, The African Mind in Health and Disease. Much of his material appeared in an article in Psychiatry magazine, November, 1959: "The Culture, Psychiatry, and the Written Word."[3] Again, it is electric speed that has revealed the lines of force operating from Western technology in the remotest areas of bush, savannah, and desert. One example is the Bedouin with his battery radio on board the camel. Submerging natives with floods of concepts for which nothing has prepared them is the normal action of all of our technology. But with electric media Western man himself experiences exactly the same inundation as the remote native. We are no more prepared to encounter radio and TV in our literate milieu than the native of Ghana is able to cope with the literacy that takes him out of his collective tribal world and beaches him in individual isolation. We are as numb in our new electric world as the native involved in our literate and mechanical culture.

Electric speed mingles the cultures of prehistory with the dregs of industrial marketeers, the nonliterate with semiliterate and the postliterate. Mental breakdown of varying degrees is the very common result of uprooting and inundation with new information and endless new patterns of information. Wyndham Lewis made this a theme of his group of novels called The Human Age. The first of these, The Childermass, is concerned precisely with accelerated media change as a kind of massacre of the innocents. In our own world as we become more aware of the effects of technology on psychic formation and manifestation, we are losing all confidence in our right to assign guilt. Ancient prehistoric societies regard violent crime as pathetic. The killer is regarded as we do a cancer victim. "How terrible it must be to feel like that," they say. J. M. Synge took up this idea very effectively in his *Playboy of the Western World*.

If the criminal appears as a nonconformist who is unable to meet the demand of technology that we behave in uniform and continuous patterns, literate man is quite inclined to see others who cannot conform as somewhat pathetic. Especially the child, the cripple, the woman, and the colored person appear in a world of visual and typographic technology as victims of injustice. On the other hand, in a culture that assigns roles instead of jobs to people, the dwarf, the skew, the child create their own spaces. They are not expected to fit into some uniform and repeatable niche that is not their size anyway. Consider the phrase "It's a man's world." As a quantitative observation endlessly repeated from within a homogenized culture, this phrase refers to the men in such a culture who have to be homogenized Dagwoods in order to belong at all. It is in our I.Q. testing that we have produced the greatest flood of misbegotten standards. Unaware of our typographic cultural bias, our testers assume that uniform and continuous habits are a sign of intelligence, thus eliminating the ear man and the tactile man.

C. P. Snow, reviewing a book of A. L. Rowse on *Appeasement* and the road to Munich, describes the top level of British brains and experience in the 1930s. "Their I.Q.'s were much higher than usual among political bosses. Why were they such a disaster?" The view of Rowse, Snow approves: "They would not listen to warnings because they did not wish to hear."[4] Being anti-Red made it impossible for them to read the message of Hitler. But their failure was as nothing compared to our present one. The American stake in literacy as a technology or uniformity applied to every level of education, government, industry, and social life is totally threatened by the electric technology. The threat of Stalin or Hitler was external. The electric technology is within the gates, and we are numb, deaf, blind, and mute about its encounter with the Gutenberg technology, on and through which the American way of life was formed. It is, however, no time to suggest strategies when the threat has not even been acknowledged to exist. I am in the position of Louis Pasteur telling doctors that their greatest enemy was quite invisible, and quite unrecognized by them. Our conventional response to all media, namely that it is how they are used that counts, is the numb stance of the technological idiot. For the "content" of a medium is like the juicy piece of meat carried by the burglar to distract the watchdog of the mind. The effect of the medium is made strong and intense just because it is given another medium as "content." The content of a movie is a novel or a play or an opera. The effect of the movie form is not related to its program content. The "content" of writing or print is speech, but the reader is almost entirely unaware either of print or of speech.

Arnold Toynbee is innocent of any understanding of media as they have shaped history, but he is full of examples that the student of media can use. At one moment he can seriously suggest that adult education, such as the Workers Educational Association in Britain, is a useful counterforce to the popular press. Toynbee considers that although all of the oriental societies have in our time accepted the industrial technology and its political consequences: "On the cultural plane, however, there is no uniform corresponding tendency."[5] This is like the voice of the literate man, floundering in a milieu of ads, who boasts, "Personally, I pay no attention to ads." The spiritual and cultural reservations that the oriental peoples may have toward our technology will avail them not at all. The effects of technology do not occur at the level of opinions or concepts, but alter sense ratios or patterns of perception steadily and without any resistance. The serious artist is the only person able to encounter technology with impunity, just because he is an expert aware of the changes in sense perception.

The operation of the money medium in seventeenth century Japan had effects not unlike the operation of typography in the West. The penetration of the money economy, wrote G. B. Sansom, "caused a slow but irresistible revolution, culminating in the breakdown of feudal government and the resumption of intercourse with foreign countries after more than two hundred years of seclusion."[6] Money has reorganized the sense life of peoples just because it is an *extension* of our sense lives. This change does not depend upon approval or disapproval of those living in the society.

Arnold Toynbee made one approach to the transforming power of media in his concept of "etherialization," which he holds to be the principle of progressive simplification and efficency in any organization or technology. Typically, he is ignoring the *effect* of the challenge of these forms upon the response of our senses. He imagines that it is the response of our opinions that is relevant to the effect of media and technology in society, a "point of view" that is plainly the result of the typographic spell. For the man in a literate and homogenized society ceases to be sensitive to the diverse and discontinuous life of forms. He acquires the illusion of the third dimension and the "private point of view" as part of his Narcissus fixation, and is quite shut off from Blake's awareness or that of the Psalmist, that we become what we behold.

Today when we want to get our bearings in our own culture, and have need to stand aside from the bias and pressure exerted by any technical form of human expression, we have only to visit a society where that particular form has not been felt, or a historical period in which it was unknown. Professor Wilbur Schramm made such a tactical move in studying *Television in the Lives of Our Children*. He found areas where TV had not penetrated at all and ran some tests. Since he had made no study of the peculiar nature of the TV image, his tests were of "content" preferences, viewing time, and vocabulary counts. In a word, his approach to the problem was a literary one, albeit unconsciously so. Consequently, he had nothing to report. Had his methods been employed in 1500 A.D. to discover the effects of the printed book in the lives of children or adults, he could have found out nothing of the changes in human and social psychology resulting from typography. Print created individualism and nationalism in the sixteenth century. Program and "content" analysis offer no clues to the magic of these media or to their subliminal charge.

Leonard Doob, in his report *Communication in Africa*, tells of one African who took great pains to listen each evening to the BBC news, even though he could understand nothing of it. Just to be in the presence of those sounds at 7 P.M. each day was important for him. His attitude to speech was like ours to melody—the resonant intonation was meaning enough. In the seventeenth century our ancestors still shared this native's attitude to the forms of media, as is plain in the following sentiment of the Frenchman Bernard Lam expressed in *The Art of Speaking*: " 'Tis an effect of the Wisdom of God, who created Man to be happy, that whatever is useful to his conversation (way of life) is agreeable to him . . . because all victual that conduces to nourishment is relishable, whereas other things that cannot be as simulated and be turned into our substance are insipid. A Discourse cannot be pleasant to the Hearer that is not easie to the Speaker; nor can it be easily pronounced unless it be heard with delight."[7] Here is an equilibrium theory of human diet and expression such as even now we are only striving to work out again for media after centuries of fragmentation and specialism.

Pope Pius XII was deeply concerned that there be serious study of the media today. On February 17, 1950, he said: "It is not an exaggeration to say that the future of modern society and the stability of its inner life depend in large part on the maintenance of an equilibrium between the strength of the techniques of communication and the capacity of the individual's own reaction."

Failure in this respect has for centuries been typical and total for mankind. Subliminal and docile acceptance of media impact has made them prisons without walls for their human users. As A. J. Liebling remarked in his book *The Press*, a man is not free if he cannot see where he is going, even if he has a gun to help him get there. For each of the media is also a powerful weapon with which to clobber other media and other groups. The result is that the present age has been one of multiple civil wars that are not limited to the world of art and entertainment. In *War and Human Progress*, Professor J. U. Nef declared: "The total wars of our time have been the result of a series of intellectual mistakes . . ."

If the formative power in the media are the media themselves, that raises a host of large matters that can only be mentioned here, although they deserve volumes. Namely, that technological media are staples or natural resources, exactly as are coal and cotton and oil. Anybody will concede that society whose economy is dependent upon one or two major staples like cotton, or grain, or lumber, or fish, or cattle is going to have some obvious social patterns of organization as a result. Stress on a few major staples creates extreme instability in the economy but great endurance in the population. The pathos and humor of the American South are embedded in such an economy of limited staples. For a society configured by reliance on a few commodities accepts them as a social bond quite as much as the metropolis does the press. Cotton and oil, like radio and TV, become "fixed charges" on the entire psychic life of the community. And this pervasive fact creates the unique cultural flavor of any society. It pays through the nose and in its other senses for each staple that shapes its life.

That our human senses, of which any media are extensions, are also fixed charges on our personal energies, and that they also configure the awareness and experience of each one of us, may be perceived in another connection mentioned by the psychologist C. G. Jung: "Every Roman was surrounded by slaves. The slave and his psychology flooded ancient Italy, and every Roman became inwardly, and of course unwittingly, a slave. Because living constantly in the atmosphere of slaves, he became infected through the unconscious with their psychology. No one can shield himself from such an influence."[8]

Notes

Originally published as "The Medium Is the Message," in *Understanding Media: The Extensions of Man*. Copyright © Marshall McLuhan. Reprinted with permission of The Massachusetts Institute of Technology Press.

1. Hans Selye, *The Stress of Life* (New York: McGraw-Hill, 1956), 28.

2. E. H. Gombrich, *Art and Illusion* (Princeton, N.J.: Princeton University Press, 1960), 238.

3. J. C. Carothers, *The African Mind in Health and Disease* (Geneva: World Health Organization, 1953); "The Culture, Psychiatry, and the Written Word," *Psychiatry* (November 1959): 307–20.

4. C. P. Snow, review of A. L. Rowse's *Appeasement*, "Englishmen of Power and Place on the Road that Led to Munich," *New York Times Book Review*, December 24, 1961.

5. Arnold J. Toynbee, *A Study of History*, vol. 7, ed. D. C. Somervell (New York: Oxford University Press, 1952), 267.

6. G. B. Sansom, *Japan* (Stanford, Calif.: Stanford University Press, 1952), 471.

7. Bernard Lamy, *The Art of Speaking* (London, 1696). [This book is reproduced in its entirety in John T. Harwood, *The Rhetoric of Thomas Hobbes and Bernard Lamy* (Carbondale: Southern Illinois University Press, 1986). The quotation can be found on page 255. —Eds.]

8. C. G. Jung, *Contributions to Analytical Psychology* (London: Lund Humphries, 1928), 173.

PAUL-ÉMILE BORDUAS

TRANSLATED BY RAY ELLENWOOD

Refus Global

Paul-Émile Borduas (1905–60) was one of the most important Canadian artists of the twentieth century. Apprenticed to Ozias Leduc, another prominent Canadian artist who lived in the same village, St. Hilaire, Quebec, he earned a degree at the School of Fine Arts in Montreal in 1927. In 1928, he left Montreal for Paris, where he held positions teaching design, painting, and art history. He returned home in 1930. Under the influence of surrealism and psychoanalysis (which traveled to Montreal with Parisians fleeing the German invasion of France), in 1941, Borduas began producing the abstract paintings for which he is world-renowned. In 1946, he was included in a show of Canadian abstract art with a number of other artists, including Jean-Paul Riopelle. These artists came to be known as Les Automatistes as a result of the importance of surrealism for their work.

Refus Global has been described as "far and away the most important text in the history of Canadian art and a signal event in the history of Québec" (Douglas Fetherling). Published in 1948 as a collective manifesto signed by Borduas and fifteen younger artists in Les Automatistes, its impact on Quebecois society went well beyond what one might expect from a document of which only four hundred copies were produced (and only half of which were sold). Relentlessly attacking the social conservatism of Quebecois society and the power of the Catholic Church in social and cultural affairs, *Refus Global* helped to inaugurate the Quiet Revolution that would reshape life in Quebec. The scandal generated by the manifesto cost Borduas his teaching position at the École du Meuble. Borduas left Canada in 1953 and lived in New York and then Paris, where he died in 1960. Examples of Borduas's work are included in major collections around the world.

The following text is the lead manifesto—one of nine texts by various authors—that appeared under the collective title *Refus Global*, first published in a full English edition in 1985.

We are the offspring of modest French-Canadian families, working-class or petit-bourgeois, French and Catholic from the day we set foot on these shores, steadfast out of resistance to the conqueror, out of stubborn attachment to the past, out of sentimental pleasure and pride, and other drives.

As early as 1760, this colony was cast behind slick walls of fear (the normal refuge of defeated peoples) and abandoned there, for the first time. Our leaders sailed away, or sold themselves to the highest bidder, as they have done ever since, whenever they had the chance.

We are a small and humble people clutching the skirts of priests who've become sole guardians of faith, knowledge, truth, and our national heritage; and we have been shielded from the perilous evolution of thought going on all around us, by well-intentioned but misguided educators who distorted the great facts of history whenever they found it impractical to keep us totally ignorant.

A small and humble people grown from a Jansenist colony, isolated, defeated, we were powerless to defend ourselves against invasion by all the religious orders of France and Navarre, carrying with them the pomp and privilege of a Catholic Church badly mauled in Europe, rushing to establish themselves in this land blessed by fear-the-mother-of-wisdom. Since then, our institutions of learning, past masters of obscurantism, heirs to automatic, infallible papal authority, have never lacked means to organize a monopolistic reign of selective memory, static reason, paralyzing intention.

Nonetheless, our small and humble people was able to multiply in the generosity of flesh (if not spirit), just north of an immense, youthful, vibrant America, golden-hearted but morally simian; and we were bewitched, intimidated, our confidence destroyed by memories of European masterpieces, disdainful of the authentic creations of our own oppressed classes.

Our destiny seemed fixed forever.

But revolutions and distant wars broke the binding spell, opened intellectual blockades.

A few uncontrollable pearly drops oozed through the walls.

Political struggles turned bitter. The clergy made unhoped-for blunders.

Rebellions followed, then an execution or two. The first few angry breaks occurred between clergy and faithful.

Slowly the breach grew wider, came together, widened once more.

Individuals began traveling abroad, with Paris the center of attraction. Too distant in time and space, too lively for our timid souls, it was usually just an excuse for a vacation spent catching up on a belated sexual education or gaining the facile assurance that comes from a trip to France, all the better to manipulate crowds back home. For example, with very few exceptions, the conduct of our medical doctors (well-traveled or not) has been scandalous (of-course-we-have-to-pay-for-those-long-hours-of-study!).

Revolutionary works, if we could ever get our hands on them, seemed like the bitter fruit of a bunch of eccentrics. Academic works impressed our stunted judgments much more.

Occasionally one of those many voyages actually caused an awakening.

Unmentionable things could not be kept out forever. Banned books circulated widely, bringing a little relief and hope.

Fuzzy intellects began to clear, stimulated by contact with the *poètes maudits* who were not monsters, but dared to express loudly and clearly those things which the most unfortunate among us stifled out of shame and a fear of being swallowed alive. These poets shed some light by their example. They were first to acknowledge the anxieties of a modern world as painfully lost as a babe in the woods. The answers they brought were disturbing, incisive, fresh, altogether different from the tired old refrains heard in this land of Quebec and in seminaries the world over.

The bounds of our dreams were changed forever.

The thick, tattered curtains of our horizons suddenly fell, and we were left dizzy.

Shame at our hopeless bondage gave way to pride in a liberty that could be won with vigorous struggle.

To hell with holy water and the French-Canadian tuque!

Whatever they once gave, they were now taking back again, a thousandfold.

We reached beyond Christianity to touch the burning brotherhood of humanity, on which the Church had become a closed door.

And fear in its many forms no longer ruled the land.

Let me describe that fear, with the insane hope of expunging it from memory:

> fear of prejudice—of public opinion—of persecution—of general re-
> probation
> fear of being alone without God or a society that inevitably isolates us
> fear of ourselves—of our brothers—of poverty
> fear of the established order—of absurd laws
> fear of fresh relations
> fear of the surrational
> fear of internal drives
> fear of opening the floodgates of our faith in man—in the society of
> the future
> fear of anything that might trigger a transforming love
> blue fear—red fear—white fear: links in our chain.

We were moving out of the reign of debilitating fear into the reign of anguish.

Only a stone man could have remained indifferent, faced with a pathetic nation resolutely pretending to be happy in a cruelly extravagant psychological reflex—a cellophane undershirt covering the poignant despair of our times. (How could anyone not scream, reading the news of that horrible collection of lamp shades made of tattooed skin stripped from wretched prisoners at the request of an elegant lady; or stifle a moan at the endless lists of concentration-camp torments? Who would not be chilled to the bone at descriptions of Spanish jails, gratuitous reprisals, cold-blooded revenge?) In front of the cruel lucidity of science, how could anyone suppress a shudder?

And now, after the reign of overpowering mental anguish comes the reign of nausea.

Faced by man's apparent inability to right wrongs, by the futility of our efforts, by the vanity of our past hopes, we have grown sick.

For centuries, the generous artifacts of poetic inspiration have been doomed to fail, socially. They have been violently spurned, beyond the pale of a society which then tried to exploit them, distorting them forever through absorption and false assimilation.

For centuries, magnificent revolutions, their breasts gorged with life, have been crushed after one brief moment of delirious hope, scarcely interrupting a relentless downward slide:

The French revolutions
The Russian Revolution
The Spanish Revolution

aborted in international confusion despite the impotent hopes of countless simple souls throughout the world.

Once again, death triumphant over generosity.

How could we not feel nauseous in the face of rewards handed out for brutal cruelty, to liars, counterfeits, makers of still-born artifacts, to hair-splitters, tired self-servers, manipulators, to the false prophets of humanity, the foulers of springwater?

How could we not feel nauseous in the face of our own cowardice, impotence, fragility and bewilderment?

In the face of our own disastrous loves. . . . Confronted by the fact that cherished illusions will always win out over objective mysteries.

Since man alone has this talent for causing misery to others, where can the secret of such a skill be found, if not in our zeal to defend a civilization that governs the fates of powerful nations?

The United States, Russia, England, France, Germany, Italy, and Spain; sharp-fanged heirs to the same Ten Commandments, a common gospel.

The religion of Christ has dominated the world. Look what we've done with it: sister religions have taken to step-sister exploitation.

If you want to abolish the specific forms of competition for raw materials, prestige, and authority, they will heartily agree. It doesn't matter to them which nation is most powerful. Give the upper hand to whomever you like, pick anyone you want to rule the world, you'll still have the same basic structure, perhaps with a few minor changes in detail.

Christian civilization has reached the end of its tether. The next world war will see its collapse as any possibility of international competition is destroyed.

Its cadaverous condition will strike even tight-shut eyes.

A decomposition begun in the sixteenth century will turn even the toughest stomachs.

A loathsome exploitation, effectively maintained for centuries at the cost of the best things in life, will be exposed at last to a multitude of victims, docile slaves whose eagerness to defend their servitude has been in direct proportion to their wretchedness.

The torture will end.

Christian decadence in its collapse will drag down all the peoples and classes it has touched, from first to last, top to bottom.

The nadir of its disgrace will correspond inversely to the heights of the thirteenth century.

In the thirteenth century, when the first stage of moral evolution had gone as far as it could, intuition gave way to reason. Gradually, calculated acts replaced acts of faith. Exploitation began in the heart of the church with the self-serving use of emotions which were already there, but petrified; it began with the rational study of scriptures for the sake of maintaining a supremacy gained originally through spontaneity.

In the name of maximum productivity, rational exploitation gradually spread to everything society did.

Faith took refuge in the heart of the masses, becoming the last hope for revenge, the final compensation. But even there, hope lost its edge.

Among the elite, mathematics took the place of metaphysical speculations now seen as useless.

Observation became more important than transfiguration.

Scientific method showed us that progress was imminent in the short term. Decadence became pleasant and necessary, encouraging the birth of versatile machines capable of dizzying speeds. It allowed us to strait-jacket mighty rivers as a prelude to the willful destruction of our planet. Our scientific instruments gave us astonishing ways of investigating and controlling things that were too small, too fast, too vibrant, too slow or too immense for us. Reason allowed us to conquer the world; a world in which we have lost our unity.

The struggle between psychic and rational powers is near paroxysm.

Through systematically controlled material progress—the privilege of the affluent—we were able, with the help of the Church (and later without it), to evolve politically. But we have not been able to renew our basic sensitivity, our subconscious; nor have we allowed the full emotional evolution of the masses, which is all that could have gotten us out of our deep Christian rut.

A society born in faith will perish by that two-edged sword of reason: INTENTION.

Our collective moral strength has regressed steadily into a purely individual and sentimental one, and thus we have woven a lining for an already impressive screen of abstract knowledge behind which society hides, quietly devouring its ill-gotten gains.

It took the last two wars to bring us to this absurd condition. The horror of the third will be decisive. The zero hour of total sacrifice is at hand.

European rats are already trying to build bridges for a headlong rush across the Atlantic. But a wave of events will break over the greedy, the glutted, the opulent, the smug, the blind, and the deaf.

They will be tossed without mercy.

A new collective hope will be born.

We must make ready to meet it with exceptional clear-sightedness, bound together anonymously by a renewed faith in the future, in the community of the future.

Magic spoils, magically wrested from the unknown, lie ready for our use, collected by all true poets. The transforming powers of this booty are as great as the violent reactions it once provoked, as great as its resistance to later attempts at assimilation. After more than two centuries, Sade still can't be found in our bookstores, and Isidore Ducasse, dead for over a hundred years of revolution and carnage, is still too potent for flabby contemporary minds, however much they've grown used to filth and corruption.

All the objects in this treasure-hoard have proven themselves immune to our society. They remain an incorruptible, perceptible legacy for tomorrow. They were spontaneously ordained outside of civilization and in opposition to it. For them to become active (on the social level) today's drives must be set free.

Until that happens, our duty is plain.

We must break with the conventions of society once and for all, and reject its utilitarian spirit. We must refuse to function knowingly at less than our physical and mental potential; refuse to close our eyes to vice and fraud perpetrated in the name of knowledge or favors or due respect. We refuse to be confined to the barracks of plastic arts—it's a fortress, but easy enough to avoid. We refuse to keep silent. Do what you want with us, but you must hear us out. We will not accept your fame or attendant honors. They are the stigmata of shame, silliness, and servility. We refuse to serve, or to be used for such purposes. We reject all forms of INTENTION, the two-edged, perilous sword of REASON. Down with both of them, back they go!

> MAKE WAY FOR MAGIC! MAKE WAY FOR OBJECTIVE MYSTERIES!
> MAKE WAY FOR LOVE!
> MAKE WAY FOR INTERNAL DRIVES!

Set against and balancing this total refusal is our complete responsibility.

The self-serving act remains attached to its author—it is stillborn.

Acts of passion break free because they are inherently dynamic.

Gladly we accept full responsibility for tomorrow. Let rational effort turn backward and concern itself with disengaging the present from the limbo of the past.

Our passions are shaping the future spontaneously, unpredictably, compulsively.

We are forced to accept the past along with our birth, but there is nothing sacred about it. We don't owe the past a thing.

It is naive and unhealthy to look at people and events in history through a magnifying glass of fame, exaggerating their virtues to the point where they seem unattainable by modern man. Of course they show qualities beyond the reach of slick, academic counterfeits, but the same may be said whenever a man follows the most basic drives of his nature; whenever he consents to be a new man in a new age (which is the definition of all men for all time).

Enough brutal assassination of the present and future under repeated clubbings from the past.

We have done enough if we turn back to yesterday in order to extricate the drives of today. At best, tomorrow can never be anything more than the unforeseeable consequence of today.

No use worrying until it comes.

A Final Squaring of Accounts

The Establishment resents our dedication to a cause, our anxious outbursts, our excesses. They see them as an insult to their indolence, their smugness, their fine sense of the good things in life (real life, full of generous hope and love, having been smothered under habit).

Friends of the status quo suspect us of preaching "Revolution." Friends of the "Revolution" call us mere rebels, saying we "protest against the established order, but our desire is only to transform, not change it."

Very delicately put, but we think we understand.

It's a matter of class.

We are credited with the naive intention of wanting to "transform" society by replacing the men in power with others just like them. So obviously, why change at all?

But they're not the right class! As if a change of class meant a change of civilization, change of desires, change of hope.

They dedicate themselves (on a fixed salary, plus a cost-of-living allowance) to organizing the proletariat; and more power to them. The trouble is, once victoriously ensconced, they'll want more than their present meagre wages. Always on the backs of that same proletariat and always in the time-honored way, they will demand supplementary adjustments and long-term renewals with no questions asked.

We agree, nonetheless, that they are part of a long historical tradition. Salvation will only come after exploitation to great excess.

They will be that excess.

They will be so in the normal course of things, with no need of anyone in particular. And the feast will be sumptuous. We have refused, in advance, to take part.

Therein lies our "guilty abstention."

You can keep your spoils, rational and premeditated like everything else on the warm bosom of decadence. We'll settle for unpredictable passion; we'll settle for total risk through global refusal.

(We can't help the fact that various social classes have succeeded each other in governing the people, and all inevitably fell into decadence. Nor can we help it if history teaches that only a full development of our faculties, followed by a complete renewal of our emotional wellsprings, can take us out of this dead end, onto the open road leading toward a civilization impatient to be born.)

Those in power, and those with aspirations, would all love to grant our every wish, if only we would measure out our activities in coffee spoons and help pave the way for their schemes of distortion.

To win the day, we have to pull our caps over our eyes, plug our ears, roll up our sleeves, and wade into the pack, clearing a path left and right.

If we're going to be cynics, we'd like to do it spontaneously and without malice aforethought.

Kind souls are apt to smile at the limited financial success of our collective exhibitions, charmed to think they're the first to notice how poorly our works sell.

It is no vain hope of getting rich that causes us to go on mounting one exhibition after another. We know there's a world of difference between us and the wealthy. They don't like playing with fire.

In the past, any sales in that direction have come about through unintentional misunderstandings.

We believe this text will help avoid any future confusion.

If our activities seem feverish, it is because we feel the urgent need for solidarity with others.

And in that regard, our success has been explosive.

Yesterday we were alone and irresolute.

Today a group exists, with deep and courageous ramifications, some of them already spreading beyond our borders.

We must share the glorious responsibility of conserving the precious treasure we are heir to. It too is part of a long historical tradition.

Our relationship to its artifacts must be constantly renewed, challenged, called into question. This is an impalpable, demanding relationship which requires the vital forces of action.

The treasure I speak of is the poetic stock, the emotional fountain of youth from which future centuries will drink. It can only be transmitted if it is TRANSFORMED. Otherwise, it is distorted.

Let those moved by the spirit of this adventure join us.

Within a foreseeable future, men will cast off their useless chains. They will realize their full, individual potential according to the unpredictable, necessary order of spontaneity—in splendid anarchy.

Until then, we will not rest or falter. Hand in hand with others thirsting for a better life, no matter how long it takes, regardless of support or persecution, we will joyfully respond to a savage need for liberation.

Paul-Émile Borduas

Magdeleine ARBOUR, Marcel BARBEAU, Bruno CORMIER, Claude GAUVREAU, Pierre GAUVREAU, Muriel GUILBAULT, Marcelle FERRON-HAMELIN, Fernand LEDUC, Thérèse LEDUC, Jean-Paul MOUSSEAU, Maurice PERRON, Louis RENAUD, Françoise RIOPELLE, Jean-Paul RIOPELLE, Françoise SULLIVAN

Note

Originally published as "Refus Global," in *Refus Global*, by Paul-Émile Borduas. Copyright © Exile Editions 1985. Reprinted with permission of the publisher.

NORTHROP FRYE

Conclusion to the *Literary History of Canada*

Northrop Frye was born in Sherbrooke, Quebec, in 1912 and grew up in Moncton, New Brunswick. He studied history and philosophy at the University of Toronto, receiving in 1933 a B.A. from Victoria College, where he would eventually teach (from 1939 until his death in 1991). Frye also studied theology at Emmanuel College and was ordained as a minister of the United Church of Canada in 1936. Frye's study of the poetry of William Blake, *Fearful Symmetry* (1947), was acclaimed internationally and his reputation as one of the foremost literary critics of his day was established by his classic work *Anatomy of Criticism* (1957). Important books such as *The Educated Imagination* (1963), *The Modern Century* (1967), *The Bush Garden* (1971), *Divisions on a Ground* (1982), as well as the ninety-four essays, reviews (from the *University of Toronto Quarterly* and *Canadian Forum*), and speeches in the twelfth volume of his *Collected Works* (2003) evidence Frye's deep critical engagement with Canadian literature and culture. Frye is widely regarded as one of the major forces that ensured the success of Canadian literary studies in Canadian universities as well as that of the range of other public institutional supports that emerged over the 1960s, making the remarkable flowering of contemporary Canadian literature possible. Frye was made Companion of the Order of Canada in 1972 and was awarded the Royal Society of Canada's Lorne Pierce Medal. His book *Northrop Frye on Shakespeare* (1986) won the Governor General's Medal for nonfiction. The Government of Canada honored him posthumously by issuing a postage stamp with his image in 2000.

I

It is much easier to see what literature is trying to do when we are studying a literature that has not quite done it. If no Canadian author pulls us away from the Canadian context toward the centre of literary experience itself, then at every point we remain aware of his social and historical setting. The conception of what is literary has to be greatly broadened for such a literature. The literary, in Canada, is often only an incidental quality of writings which, like those of many of the early explorers, are as innocent of literary intention as a mating loon. Even when it is literature in its orthodox genres of poetry and fiction, it is more significantly studied as a part of Canadian life than as a part of an autonomous world of literature.

So far from merely admitting or conceding this, the editors[1] have gone out of their way to emphasize it. We have asked for chapters on political, historical, religious, scholarly, philosophical, scientific, and other non-literary writing, to show how the verbal imagination operates as a ferment in all cultural life. We have included the writings of foreigners, of travellers, of immigrants, of emigrants—even of emigrants whose most articulate literary emotion was their thankfulness at getting the hell out of Canada. The reader of this book, even if he is not Canadian or much interested in Canadian literature as such, may still learn a good deal about the literary imagination as a force and function of life generally. For here another often deplored fact also becomes an advantage: that many Canadian cultural phenomena are not peculiarly Canadian at all, but are typical of their wider North American and Western contexts.

This book is a collection of essays in cultural history, and of the general principles of cultural history we still know relatively little. It is, of course, closely related to political and to economic history, but it is a separate and definable subject in itself. Like other kinds of history, it has its own themes of exploration, settlement, and development, but these themes relate to a social *imagination* that explores and settles and develops, and the imagination has its own rhythms of growth as well as its own modes of expression. It is obvious that Canadian literature, whatever its inherent merits, is an indispensable aid to the knowledge of Canada. It records what the Canadian imagination has reacted to, and it tells us things about this environment that nothing else will tell us. By examining this imagination as the authors of this book have tried to do, as an ingredient in Canadian verbal culture generally, a relatively small and low-lying cultural development is studied in all its dimensions. There is far too much Canadian writing for this book not to become, in places, something of a catalogue; but the outlines of the structure are clear. Fortunately, the bulk of Canadian non-literary writing, even today, has not yet declined into the state of sodden specialization in which the readable has become the impure.

I stress our ignorance of the laws and conditions of cultural history for an obvious reason. The question: why has there been no Canadian writer of classic proportions? may naturally be asked. At any rate it often has been. Our authors realize that it is better to deal with what is there than to raise speculations about why something else is not there. But it is clear that the question haunts their minds. And we know so little about cultural history that we not only cannot answer such a question, but we do not even know whether or not it is a real question. The notion, doubtless of romantic origin, that "genius" is a certain quantum that an individual is born with, as he might be born with red hair, is still around, but mainly as a folktale motif in fiction, like the story of Finch in the Jalna books.[2] "Genius" is as much, and as essentially, a matter of social context as it is of individual character. We do not know what the social conditions are that produce great literature, or even whether there is any causal relation at all. If there is, there is no reason to suppose that they are good conditions, or conditions that we should try to reproduce. The notion that the literature one admires must have been nourished by something admirable in the social environment is persistent, but has never been justified by evidence. One can still find books on Shakespeare that profess to make his achievement more plausible by talking about a "background" of social euphoria produced by the defeat of the Armada, the discovery of America a century before, and the conviction that Queen Elizabeth was a wonderful woman. There is a general sense of filler about such speculations, and when similar arguments are given in a negative form to explain the absence of a Shakespeare in Canada they are no more convincing. Puritan inhibitions, pioneer life, "an age too late, cold climate, or years"—these may be important as factors or conditions of Canadian culture, helping us to characterize its qualities. To suggest that any of them is a negative cause of its merit is to say much more than anyone knows.

One theme which runs all through this book is the obvious and unquenchable desire of the Canadian cultural public to identify itself through its literature. Canada is not a bad environment for the author, as far as recognition goes: in fact the recognition may even hamper his development by making him prematurely self-conscious. Scholarships, prizes, university posts, await the dedicated writer: there are so many medals offered for literary achievement that a modern Canadian Dryden might well be moved to write a satire on medals, except that if he did he would promptly be awarded the medal for satire and humour. Publishers take an active responsibility for native literature, even poetry; a fair proportion of the books bought by Canadian readers are by Canadian writers; the CBC [Canadian Broadcasting Corporation] and other media help to employ some writers and publicize others. The efforts made at intervals to boost or hard-sell Canadian literature, by asserting that it is much better than it actually is, may look silly enough in retrospect, but they were also, in part, efforts to create a cultural community, and the aim deserves more sympathy than the means. Canada has two languages and two literatures, and every statement made in a book like this about "Canadian literature" employs the figure of speech known as synecdoche, putting a part for the whole. Every such statement implies a parallel or contrasting statement about French-Canadian literature. The advantages of having a national culture based on two languages are in some respects very great, but of course they are for the most part potential. The difficulties, if more superficial, are also more actual and more obvious.

Some of the seminal facts about the origins of Canadian culture are set down with great clarity near the beginning of this book. Canada began, says Mr. Galloway, as an obstacle, blocking the way to the treasures of the East, to be explored only in the hope of finding a passage through it. English Canada continued to be that long after what is now the United States had become a defined part of the Western world. One reason for this is obvious from the map. American culture was, down to about 1900, mainly a culture of the Atlantic seaboard, with a western frontier that moved irregularly but steadily back until it reached the other coast. The Revolution did not essentially change the cultural unity of the English-speaking community of the North Atlantic that had London and Edinburgh on one side of it and Boston and Philadelphia on the other. But Canada has, for all practical purposes, no Atlantic seaboard. The traveller from Europe edges into it like a tiny Jonah entering an inconceivably large whale, slipping past the Straits of Belle Isle into the Gulf of St. Lawrence, where five Canadian provinces surround him, for the most part invisible. Then he goes up the St. Lawrence and the inhabited country comes into view, mainly a French-speaking country, with its own cultural traditions. To enter the United States is a matter of crossing an ocean; to enter Canada is a matter of being silently swallowed by an alien continent.

It is an unforgettable and intimidating experience to enter Canada in this way. But the experience initiates one into that gigantic east-to-west thrust which, as Mr. Kilbourn notes, historians regard as the axis of Canadian development, the "Laurentian" movement that makes the growth of Canada geographically credible. This drive to the west has attracted to itself nearly everything that is heroic and romantic in the Canadian tradition. The original impetus begins in Europe, for English

Canada in the British Isles, hence though adventurous it is also a conservative force, and naturally tends to preserve its colonial link with its starting-point. Once the Canadian has settled down in the country, however, he then becomes aware of the longitudinal dimension, the southward pull toward the richer and more glamorous American cities, some of which, such as Boston for the Maritimes and Minneapolis for the eastern prairies, are almost Canadian capitals. This is the axis of another kind of Canadian mentality, more critical and analytic, more inclined to see Canada as an unnatural and politically quixotic aggregate of disparate northern extensions of American culture—"seven fishing-rods tied together by the ends," as Goldwin Smith, quoted by Mr. Windsor, puts it. Mr. Kilbourn illustrates the contrast in his account of the styles, attitudes, and literary genres of Creighton and Underhill.[3]

The simultaneous influence of two larger nations speaking the same language has been practically beneficial to English Canada, but theoretically confusing. It is often suggested that Canada's identity is to be found in some *via media*, or *via mediocris*, between the other two. This has the disadvantage that the British and American cultures have to be defined as extremes. Haliburton seems to have believed that the ideal for Nova Scotia would be a combination of American energy and British social structure, but such a chimera, or synthetic monster, is hard to achieve in practice.[4] It is simpler merely to notice the alternating current in the Canadian mind, as reflected in its writing, between two moods, one romantic, traditional and idealistic, the other shrewd, observant and humorous. Canada in its attitude to Britain tends to be more royalist than the Queen, in the sense that it is more attracted to it as a symbol of tradition than as a fellow-nation. The Canadian attitude to the United States is typically that of a smaller country to a much bigger neighbour, sharing in its material civilization but anxious to keep clear of the huge mass movements that drive a great imperial power. The United States, being founded on a revolution and a written constitution, has introduced a deductive or *a priori* pattern into its cultural life that tends to define an American way of life and mark it off from anti-American heresies. Canada, having a seat on the sidelines of the American Revolution, adheres more to the inductive and the expedient. The Canadian genius for compromise is reflected in the existence of Canada itself.

The most obvious tension in the Canadian literary situation is in the use of language. Here, first of all, a traditional standard English collides with the need for a North American vocabulary and phrasing. Mr. Scargill and Mr. Klinck have studied this in the work of Mrs. Moodie and

Mrs. Traill.[5] As long as the North American speaker feels that he belongs in a minority, the European speech will impose a standard of correctness. This is to a considerable extent still true of French in Canada, with its campaigns against "joual" and the like.[6] But as Americans began to outnumber the British, Canada tended in practice to fall in with the American developments, though a good deal of Canadian theory is still Anglophile. A much more complicated cultural tension arises from the impact of the sophisticated on the primitive, and vice versa. The most dramatic example, and one I have given elsewhere, is that of Duncan Campbell Scott, working in the Department of Indian Affairs in Ottawa.[7] He writes of a starving squaw baiting a fish-hook with her own flesh, and he writes of the music of Debussy and the poetry of Henry Vaughan. In English literature we have to go back to Anglo-Saxon times to encounter so incongruous a collision of cultures.

Cultural history, we said, has its own rhythms. It is possible that one of these rhythms is very like an organic rhythm; that there must be a period, of a certain magnitude, as Aristotle would say, in which a social imagination can take root and establish a tradition. American literature had this period, in the northeastern part of the country, between the Revolution and the Civil War. Canada never had it. English Canada was first a part of the wilderness, then a part of North America and the British Empire, then a part of the world. But it has gone through these revolutions too quickly for a tradition of writing to be founded on any one of them. Canadian writers are, even now, still trying to assimilate a Canadian environment at a time when new techniques of communication, many of which, like television, constitute a verbal market, are annihilating the boundaries of that environment. This foreshortening of Canadian history, if it really does have any relevance to Canadian culture, would account for many features of it: its fixation on its own past, its penchant for old-fashioned literary techniques, its preoccupation with the theme of strangled articulateness. It seems to me that Canadian sensibility has been profoundly disturbed, not so much by our famous problem of identity, important as that is, as by a series of paradoxes in what confronts that identity. It is less perplexed by the question "Who am I?" than by some such riddle as "Where is here?"

Mr. Bailey, writing of the early Maritimes, warns us not to read the "mystique of Canadianism" back into the pre-Confederation period. Haliburton, for instance, was a Nova Scotian, a Bluenose: the word "Canadian" to him would have summoned up the figure of someone who spoke mainly French and whose enthusiasm for Haliburton's own political ideals would have been extremely tepid. The mystique of Canadianism was, as several chapters in this book make clear, specifically the cultural accompaniment of Confederation and the imperialistic mood that followed it. But it came so suddenly after the pioneer period that it was still full of wilderness. To feel "Canadian" was to feel part of a no-man's-land with huge rivers, lakes, and islands that very few Canadians had ever seen. "From sea to sea, and from the river unto the ends of the earth"—if Canada is not an island, the phrasing is still in the etymological sense isolating. One wonders if any other national consciousness has had so large an amount of the unknown, the unrealized, the humanly undigested, so built into it. Rupert Brooke, quoted by Mrs. Waterston, speaks of the "unseizable virginity" of the Canadian landscape. What is important here, for our purposes, is the position of the frontier in the Canadian imagination. In the United States one could choose to move out to the frontier or to retreat from it back to the seaboard. The tensions built up by such migrations have fascinated many American novelists and historians. In the Canadas, even in the Maritimes, the frontier was all around one, a part and a condition of one's whole imaginative being. The frontier was primarily what separated the Canadian, physically or mentally, from Great Britain, from the United States, and, even more important, from other Canadian communities. Such a frontier was the immediate datum of his imagination, the thing that had be dealt with first.

After the Northwest passage failed to materialize, Canada became a colony in the mercantilist sense, treated by others less like a society than as a place to look for things. French, English, Americans plunged into it to carry off its supplies of furs, minerals, and pulpwood, aware only of their immediate objectives. From time to time recruiting officers searched the farms and villages to carry young men off to death in a European dynastic quarrel. The travellers reviewed by Mrs. Waterston visit Canada much as they would visit a zoo: even when their eyes momentarily focus on the natives they are still thinking primarily of how their own sensibility is going to react to what it sees. Mrs. Waterston speaks of a feature of Canadian life that has been noted by writers from Susanna Moodie onward: "the paradox of vast empty spaces plus lack of privacy," without defences against the prying or avaricious eye. The resentment expressed against this in Canada seems to have taken political rather than literary forms: this may be partly because Canadians have learned from their imaginative experience to look at each other in much the same way: "as objects, even as obstacles," to quote Miss Macpherson on a Canadian autobiography.

It is not much wonder if Canada developed with the bewilderment of a neglected child, preoccupied with trying to define its own identity, alternately bumptious and diffident about its own achievements. Adolescent dreams of glory haunt the Canadian consciousness (and unconsciousness), some naïve and some sophisticated. In the naïve area are the predictions that the twentieth century belongs to Canada, that our cities will become much bigger than they ought to be, or, like Edmonton and Vancouver, "gateways" to somewhere else, reconstructed Northwest passages. The more sophisticated usually take the form of a Messianic complex about Canadian culture, for Canadian culture, no less than Alberta, has always been "next year country." The myth of the hero brought up in the forest retreat, awaiting the moment when his giant strength will be fully grown and he can emerge into the world, informs a good deal of Canadian criticism down to our own time.

Certain features of life in a new country that are bound to handicap its writers are obvious enough. The difficulties of drama, which depends on a theatre and consequently on a highly organized urban life, are set out by Mr. Tait. Here the foreshortening of historical development has been particularly cruel, as drama was strangled by the movie just as it was getting started as a popular medium. Other literary genres have similar difficulties. Culture is born in leisure and an awareness of standards, and pioneer conditions tend to make energetic and uncritical work an end in itself, to preach a gospel of social unconsciousness, which lingers long after the pioneer conditions have disappeared. The impressive achievements of such a society are likely to be technological. It is in the inarticulate part of communication, railways and bridges and canals and highways, that Canada, one of whose symbols is the taciturn beaver, has shown its real strength. Again, Canadian culture, and literature in particular, has felt the force of what may be called Emerson's law. Emerson remarks in his journals that in a provincial society it is extremely easy to reach the highest level of cultivation, extremely difficult to take one step beyond that. In surveying Canadian poetry and fiction, we feel constantly that all the energy has been absorbed in meeting a standard, a self-defeating enterprise because real standards can only be established, not met. Such writing is academic in the pejorative sense of that term, an imitation of a prescribed model, second-rate in conception, not merely in execution. It is natural that academic writing of this kind should develop where literature is a social prestige symbol, as Mr. Cogswell says. However, it is not the handicaps of Canadian writers but the distinctive features that appear in spite of them which are the main concern of this book, and so of its conclusion.

II

The sense of probing into the distance, of fixing the eyes on the skyline, is something that Canadian sensibility has inherited from the *voyageurs*. A vast country sparsely inhabited naturally depends on its modes of transportation, whether canoe, railway, or the driving and riding "circuits" of the judge, the Methodist preacher, or the Yankee peddler. The feeling of nomadic movement over great distances persists even into the age of the aeroplane, in a country where writers can hardly meet one other without a social organization that provides travel grants. Pratt's poetry is full of his fascination with means of communication, not simply the physical means of great ships and locomotives, though he is one of the best of all poets on such subjects, but with communication as message, with radar and asdic and wireless signals, and, in his war poems, with the power of rhetoric over fighting men.[8] What is perhaps the most comprehensive structure of ideas yet made by a Canadian thinker, the structure embodied in [Harold] Innis's *Bias of Communication*, is concerned with the same theme, and a disciple of Innis, Marshall McLuhan, continues to emphasize the unity of communication, as a complex containing both verbal and non-verbal factors, and warns us against making unreal divisions within it. Perhaps it is not too fanciful to see this need for continuity in the Canadian attitude to time as well as space, in its preoccupation with its own history (the motto of the Province of Quebec is *je me souviens*) and its relentless cultural stock-takings and self-inventories. The Burkean sense of society as a continuum— consistent with the pragmatic and conservative outlook of Canadians—is strong and begins early. Mr. Irving quotes an expression of it in Mc-Culloch,[9] and another quotation shows that it was one of the most deeply held ideas of Brett. As I write, the centennial of Confederation in 1967 looms up before the country with the moral urgency of a Day of Atonement: I use a Jewish metaphor because there is something Hebraic about the Canadian tendency to read its conquest of a promised land, its Maccabean victories of 1812, its struggle for the central fortress on the hill at Quebec, as oracles of a future. It is doubtless only an accident that the theme of one of the most passionate and intense of all Canadian novels, A. M. Klein's *The Second Scroll*, is Zionism.

Civilization in Canada, as elsewhere, has advanced geometrically across the country, throwing down the long parallel lines of the railways, dividing up the farm lands into chessboards of square-mile sections and concession-line roads. There is little adaptation to nature: in both architecture and arrangement, Canadian cities and villages express rather an arrogant abstraction, the conquest of nature by an intelligence that does not love it. The word conquest suggests something military, as it should —one thinks of General Braddock, preferring to have his army annihilated rather than fight the natural man on his own asymmetrical ground. There are some features of this generally North American phenomenon that have a particular emphasis in Canada. It has been remarked—Mr. Kilbourn quotes Creighton on the subject—that Canadian expansion westward had a tight grip of authority over it that American expansion, with its outlaws and sheriffs and vigilantes and the like, did not have in the same measure. America moved from the back country to the wild west; Canada moved from a New France held down by British military occupation to a northwest patrolled by mounted police. Canada has not had, strictly speaking, an Indian war: there has been much less of the "another redskin bit the dust" feeling in our historical imagination, and only Riel remains to haunt the later period of it, though he is a formidable figure enough, rather like what a combination of John Brown and Vanzetti would be in the American conscience. Otherwise, the conquest, for the last two centuries, has been mainly of the unconscious forces of nature, personified by the dragon of the Lake Superior rocks in Pratt's *Towards the Last Spike*: "On the North Shore a reptile lay asleep— / A hybrid that the myths might have conceived, / But not delivered."

Yet the conquest of nature has its own perils for the imagination, in a country where the winters are so cold and where conditions of life have so often been bleak and comfortless, where even the mosquitoes have been described, Mr. Klinck tells us, as "mementoes of the fall." I have long been impressed in Canadian poetry by a tone of deep terror in regard to nature, a theme to which we shall return. It is not a terror of the dangers or discomforts or even the mysteries of nature, but a terror of the soul at something that these things manifest. The human mind has nothing but human and moral values to cling to if it is to preserve its integrity or even its sanity, yet the vast unconsciousness of nature in front of it seems an unanswerable denial of those values. I notice that a sharp-witted Methodist preacher quoted by Mr. Cogswell speaks of the "shutting out of the whole moral creation" in the loneliness of the forests.

If we put together a few of these impressions, we may get some approach to characterizing the way in which the Canadian imagination has developed in its literature. Small and isolated communities surrounded with a physical or psychological "frontier," separated from one another and from their American and British cultural sources: communities that provide all that their members have in the way of distinctively human values, and that are compelled to feel a great respect for the law and order that holds them together, yet confronted with a huge, unthinking, menacing, and formidable physical setting—such communities are bound to develop what we may provisionally call a garrison mentality. In the earliest maps of the country the only inhabited centres are forts, and that remains true of the cultural maps for a much later time. Frances Brooke, in her eighteenth-century *Emily Montague*, wrote of what was literally a garrison; novelists of our day studying the impact of Montreal on Westmount write of a psychological one.

A garrison is a closely knit and beleaguered society, and its moral and social values are unquestionable. In a perilous enterprise one does not discuss causes or motives: one is either a fighter or a deserter. Here again we may turn to Pratt, with his infallible instinct for what is central in the Canadian imagination. The societies in Pratt's poems are always tense and tight groups engaged in war, rescue, martyrdom, or crisis, and the moral values expressed are simply those of that group. In such a society the terror is not for the common enemy, even when the enemy is or seems victorious, as in the extermination of the Jesuit missionaries or the crew of Franklin (a great Canadian theme, well described in this book by Mr. Hopwood, that Pratt pondered but never completed).[10] The real terror comes when the individual feels himself becoming an individual, pulling away from the group, losing the sense of driving power that the group gives him, aware of a conflict within himself far subtler than the struggle of morality against evil. It is much easier to multiply garrisons, and when that happens, something anti-cultural comes into Canadian life, a dominating herd-mind in which nothing original can grow. The intensity of the sectarian divisiveness in Canadian towns, both religious and political, is an example: what such groups represent, of course, vis-à-vis one another, is "two solitudes," the death of communication and dialogue. Separatism, whether English or French, is culturally the most sterile of all creeds. But at present I am concerned rather with a more creative side of the garrison mentality, one that has had positive effects on our intellectual life.

They were so certain of their moral values, says Mr. Cogswell, a little sadly, speaking of the early Maritime writers. Right was white, wrong black, and nothing else counted or even existed. He goes on to point out that such certainty invariably produces a sub-literary rhetoric. Or, as Yeats would say, we make rhetoric out of quarrels with one another, poetry out of the quarrel with ourselves. To use words, for any other purpose than straight description or command, is a form of play, a manifestation of *homo ludens*. But there are two forms of play, the contest and the construct. The editorial writer attacking the Family Compact, the preacher demolishing imaginary atheists with the argument of design, are using words aggressively, in theses that imply antitheses. Ideas are weapons; one seeks the verbal *coup de grace*, the irrefutable refutation. Such a use of words is congenial enough to the earlier Canadian community: all the evidence, including the evidence of this book, points to a highly articulate and argumentative society in nineteenth-century Canada. Mr. MacLure remarks on the fact that scholarship in Canada has so often been written with more conviction and authority, and has attracted wider recognition, than the literature itself. There are historical reasons for this, apart from the fact, which will become clearer as we go on, that scholarly writing is more easily attached to its central tradition.

Mr. Watt's very important chapter on the literature of protest isolates another rhetorical tradition. In the nineteenth century the common assumption that nature had revealed the truth of progress, and that it was the duty of reason to accommodate that truth to mankind, could be either a conservative or a radical view. But in either case it was a revolutionary doctrine, introducing the conception of change as the key to the social process. In those whom Mr. Watt calls proletarian social Darwinists, and who represented "the unholy fusion of secularism, science and social discontent," there was a strong tendency to regard literature as a product and a symbol of a ruling-class mentality, with, as we have tried to indicate, some justification. Hence radicals tended either to hope that "the literature of the future will be the powerful ally of Democracy and Labour Reform," or to assume that serious thought and action would bypass the creative writer entirely, building a scientific socialism and leaving him to his Utopian dreams.

The radicalism of the period up to the Russian Revolution was, from a later point of view, largely undifferentiated. A labour magazine could regard Ignatius Donnelly, with his anti-Semitic and other crank views, as an advanced thinker equally with William Morris and Edward Bellamy. Similarly, even today, in Western Canadian elections, a protest vote may go Social Credit or NDP [New Democratic Party] without much regard to the difference in political philosophy between these parties. The depression introduced a dialectic into Canadian social thought which profoundly affected its literature. In Mr. Watt's striking phrase, "the Depression was like an intense magnetic field that deflected the courses of all the poets who went through it." In this period there were, of course, the inevitable Marxist manifestos, assuring the writer that only social significance, as understood by Marxism, would bring vitality to his work. The New Frontier, a far-left journal of that period referred to several times in this book, shows an uneasy sense on the part of its contributors that this literary elixir of youth might have to be mixed with various other potions, not all favourable to the creative process: attending endless meetings, organizing, agitating, marching, demonstrating, or joining the Spanish Loyalists. It is easy for the critic to point out the fallacy of judging the merit of literature by its subject matter, but these arguments over the role of "propaganda" were genuine and serious moral conflicts. Besides helping to shape the argument of such novels as [Frederick Philip] Grove's The Master of the Mill and [Morley] Callaghan's They Shall Inherit the Earth, they raised the fundamental issue of the role of the creative mind in society, and by doing so helped to give a maturity and depth to Canadian writing which is a permanent part of its heritage.

It is not surprising, given this background, that the belief in the inspiration of literature by social significance continued to be an active force long after it had ceased to be attached to any specifically Marxist or other political programmes. It is still strong in the Preview group in the forties, and in their immediate successors, though the best of them have developed in different directions. The theme of social realism is at its most attractive, and least theoretical, in the poetry of [Raymond] Souster. The existentialist movement, with its emphasis on the self-determination of social attitudes, seems to have had very little direct influence in Canada: Mr. Beattie's comment on the absence of the existential in Pratt suggests that this lack of influence may be significant.

During the last decade or so a kind of social Freudianism has been taking shape, mainly in the United States, as a democratic counterpart of Marxism. Here society is seen as controlled by certain anxieties, real or imaginary, which are designed to repress or sublimate human impulses toward a greater freedom. These impulses include the creative and the sexual, which are closely linked. The enemy of the poet is not the capitalist but the "square," or representative of repressive morality. The advantage of this attitude is that it preserves the position of rebellion against society for the poet, without imposing on him any specific social obligations. This movement has had a rather limited development in Canada, somewhat surprisingly considering how easy a target the square is in Canada: it has influenced [Irving] Layton and many younger Montreal poets, but has not affected fiction to any great degree, though there may be something of it in [Mordecai] Richler. It ignores the old political alignments: the Communists are usually regarded as Puritanic and repressive equally with the bourgeoisie, and a recent poem of Layton's contrasts the social hypocrisy in Canada with contemporary Spain. Thus it represents to some extent a return to the undifferentiated radicalism of a century before, though no longer in a political context.

As the centre of Canadian life moves from the fortress to the metropolis, the garrison mentality changes correspondingly. It begins as an expression of the moral values generally accepted in the group as a whole, and then, as society gets more complicated and more in control of its environment, it becomes more of a revolutionary garrison within a metropolitan society. But though it changes from a defence of to an attack on what society accepts as conventional standards, the literature it produces, at every stage, tends to be rhetorical, an illustration or allegory of certain social attitudes. These attitudes help to unify the mind of the writer by externalizing his enemy, the enemy being the anti-creative elements in life as he sees life. To approach these elements in a less rhetorical way would introduce the theme of self-conflict, a more perilous but ultimately more rewarding theme. The conflict involved is between the poetic impulse to construct and the rhetorical impulse to assert, and the victory of the former is the sign of the maturing of the writer.

To go on with this absorbing subject would take us into another book: *A Literary Criticism of Canada*, let us say. Here we can only refer the reader to Mr. Beattie's able guidance and sum up the present argument emblematically, with two famous primitive American paintings. One is "Historical Monument of the American Republic," by Erastus Salisbury Field. Painted in 1876 for the centennial of the Revolution, it is an encyclopaedic portrayal of events in American history, against a background of soaring towers, with clouds around their spires, and connected by railway bridges. It is a prophetic vision of the skyscraper cities of the future, of the tremendous technological will to power of our time and the civilization it has built, a civilization now gradually imposing a uniformity of culture and habits of life all over the globe. Because the United States is the most powerful centre of this civilization, we often say, when referring to its uniformity, that the world is becoming Americanized. But of course America itself is being Americanized in this sense, and the uniformity imposed on New Delhi and Singapore, or on Toronto and Vancouver, is no greater than that imposed on New Orleans or Baltimore. A nation so huge and so productive, however, is deeply committed to this growing technological uniformity, even though many tendencies may pull in other directions. Canada has participated to the full in the wars, economic expansions, technological achievements, and internal stresses of the modern world. Canadians seem well adjusted to the new world of technology and very efficient at handling it. Yet in the Canadian imagination there are deep reservations to this world as an end of life in itself, and the political separation of Canada has helped to emphasize these reservations in its literature. English Canada began with the influx of defeated Tories after the American Revolution, and so, in its literature, with a strong anti-revolutionary bias. The Canadian radicalism that developed in opposition to Loyalism was not a revival of the American revolutionary spirit, but a quite different movement, which had something in common with the Toryism it opposed: one thinks of the Tory and radical elements in the social vision of William Cobbett, who also finds a place in the Canadian record. A revolutionary tradition is liable to two defects: to an undervaluing of history and an impatience with law, and we have seen how unusually strong the Canadian attachment to law and history has been. The attitude to things American represented by Haliburton is not, on the whole, hostile: it would be better described as non-committal, as when Sam Slick speaks of a Fourth of July as "a splendid spectacle; fifteen millions of freemen and three millions of slaves a-celebratin' the birthday of liberty." The strong romantic tradition in Canadian literature has much to do with its original conservatism. When more radical expressions begin to creep into Canadian writing, as in the poetry of Alexander McLachlan, there is still much less of the assumption that freedom and national independence are the same thing, or that the mercantilist Whiggery which won the American Revolution is necessarily the only emancipating force in the world. In some Canadian writers of our own time—I think particularly of Earle Birney's *Trial of a City* and the poetry of F. R. Scott—there is an opposition, not to the democratic but to the oligarchic tendencies in North American civilization, not to liberal but to laissez-faire political doctrine. Perhaps it is a little easier to see these distinctions from the vantage-point of a smaller country, even one which has, in its material culture, made the "American way of life" its own.

The other painting is the much earlier "The Peaceable Kingdom," by Edward Hicks, painted around 1830. Here, in the background, is a treaty between the Indians and the Quaker settlers under Penn. In the foreground is a group of animals, lions, tigers, bears, oxen, illustrating the prophecy of Isaiah about the recovery of innocence in nature. Like the animals of the Douanier Rousseau, they stare past us with a serenity that transcends consciousness. It is a pictorial emblem of what Grove's narrator was trying to find under the surface of America: the reconciliation of man with man and of man with nature: the mood of Thoreau's Walden retreat, of Emily Dickinson's garden, of Huckleberry Finn's raft, of the elegies of Whitman, whose reaction to Canada is also recorded in this book. This mood is closer to the haunting vision of a serenity that is both human and natural which we have been struggling to identify in the Canadian tradition. If we had to characterize a distinctive emphasis in that tradition, we might call it a quest for the peaceable kingdom.

The writers of the last decade, at least, have begun to write in a world which is post-Canadian, as it is post-American, post-British, and post everything except the world itself. There are no provinces in the empire of aeroplane and television, and no physical separation from the centres of culture, such as they are. Sensibility is no longer dependent on a specific environment or even on sense experience itself. A remark of Mr. Beattie's about Robert Finch illustrates a tendency which is affecting literature as well as painting: "the interplay of sense impressions is so complicated, and so exhilarating, that the reader receives no sense impression at all." Marshall McLuhan speaks of the world as reduced to a single gigantic primitive village, where everything has the same kind of immediacy. He speaks of the fears that so many intellectuals have of such a world, and remarks amiably: "Terror is the normal state of any oral society, for in it everything affects everything all the time." The Canadian spirit, to personify it as a single being dwelling in the country from the early voyages to the present, might well, reading this sentence, feel that this was where he came in. In other words, new conditions give the old ones a new importance, as what vanishes in one form reappears in another. The moment that the peaceable kingdom has been completely obliterated by its rival is the moment when it comes into the foreground again, as the eternal frontier, the first thing that the writer's imagination must deal with. Pratt's "The Truant," already referred to, foreshadows the poetry of the future, when physical nature has retreated to outer space and only individual and society are left as effective factors in the imagination. But the central conflict, and the moods in which it is fought out, are still unchanged.

One gets very tired, in old-fashioned biographies, of the dubious embryology that examines a poet's ancestry and wonders if a tendency to fantasy in him could be the result of an Irish great-grandmother. A reader may feel the same unreality in efforts to attach Canadian writers to a tradition made up of earlier writers whom they may not have read or greatly admired. I have felt this myself whenever I have written about Canadian literature. Yet I keep coming back to the feeling that there does seem to be such a thing as an imaginative continuum, and that writers are conditioned in their attitudes by their predecessors, or by the cultural climate of their predecessors, whether there is conscious influence or not. Again, nothing can give a writer's experience and sensitivity any form except the study of literature itself. In this study, the great classics, "monuments of its own magnificence," and the best contemporaries have an obvious priority. The more such monuments or such contemporaries there are in a writer's particular cultural traditions, the more fortunate he is; but he needs those traditions in any case. He needs them most of all when what faces him seems so new as to threaten his identity. For present and future writers in Canada and their readers, what is important in Canadian literature, beyond the merits of the individual works in it, is the inheritance of the entire enterprise. The writers featured in this book have identified the habits and attitudes of the country, as Fraser and Mackenzie have identified its rivers.[11] They have also left an imaginative legacy of dignity and of high courage.

Notes

Originally published as "Conclusion," in Literary History of Canada, edited by Carl F. Klinck. Copyright © University of Toronto Press 1965. Reprinted with permission of the publisher.

All notes to this chapter are by the editors.

1. Carl F. Klinck, Alfred G. Bailey, Claude Bissell, Roy Daniells, Desmond Pacey, and Northrop Frye, editors of Literary History of Canada: Canadian Literature in English (Toronto: University of Toronto Press, 1965). The references throughout that take the form of "Mr. Galloway," "Mrs. Macpherson," "Mr. Bailey," and so on are to authors of sections of the Literary History.

2. The reference here is to a series of novels written by the Canadian writer Mazo de la Roche between 1927 and 1958. The character of Finch in Finch's Fortune (1932) is usually assumed to be based on the novelist herself.

3. Donald G. Creighton (1902–79) and Frank Underhill (1885–1971), prominent mid-century Canadian historians.

4. Thomas Haliburton (1796–1865), a major nineteenth-century Canadian writer.

5. Susanna Moodie (1803–85) and Catherine Parr Traill (1802–99), sisters and au-

thors, whose books (Traill's *The Backwoods of Canada* [1836] and Moodie's *Roughing it in the Bush* [1852]) detailing everyday life in nineteenth-century Canada remain important to understanding the period.

6. "Joual" is the name for informal, working-class French Canadian speech.

7. Duncan Campbell Scott (1862–1947), a Canadian writer known for his poems about aboriginal peoples and nature. The reference here is to his role as head of the Department of Indian Affairs (1913–32). During Scott's tenure, it became mandatory for aboriginal children to attend Canada's residential school system, designed to "solve" the Indian "problem" by stripping aboriginal peoples of their culture and language. The conditions in the residential schools were extremely violent and dangerous. Peter Bryce's *The Story of a National Crime* (1922) reported mortality rates at western Canadian residential schools at 35 to 60 percent over a five-year period. See John Milloy, *A National Crime: The Canadian Government and the Residential School System* (Winnipeg: University of Manitoba Press, 1999).

8. E. J. Pratt (1882–1964), Canadian poet, recipient of the Governor General's Award for poetry in 1937, 1940, and 1952.

9. Thomas McCulloch, author of the first major work of Canadian humor, *The Stepsure Letters* (1821–22).

10. Name of an expedition led by Sir John Franklin to discover the Northwest Passage through the Canadian Arctic. The Franklin expedition set out in 1845; in 1846 the expedition became ice-locked, leading to the death of all involved.

11. The Fraser and Mackenzie are two of Canada's major rivers, named after explorers Simon Fraser (1776–1862) and Sir Alexander MacKenzie (1764–1820) respectively.

City of the End of Things

The Whidden Lectures have been a distinguished series, and anyone attempting to continue them must feel a sense of responsibility. For me, the responsibility is specific: I have been asked to keep in mind the fact that I shall be speaking to a Canadian audience in the Centennial year of Confederation. I have kept it in mind, and the first thing that it produced there was what I hope is a sense of proportion. The centenary of Confederation is a private celebration, a family party, in what is still a relatively small country in a very big world. One most reassuring quality in Canadians, and the one which, I find, chiefly makes them liked and respected abroad, when they are, is a certain unpretentiousness, a cheerful willingness to concede the immense importance of the non-Canadian part of the human race. It is appropriate to a Canadian audience, then, to put our centenary into some kind of perspective. For the majority of people in North America, the most important thing that happened in 1867 was the purchase of Alaska from Russia by the United States. For the majority of people in the orbit of British traditions, the most important thing that happened in 1867 was the passing of the Second Reform Bill, the measure that Disraeli called "a leap in the dark," but which was really the first major effort to make the Mother of Parliaments represent the people instead of an oligarchy. For a great number, very probably the majority, of people in the world today, the most important thing that happened in 1867, anywhere, was the publication of the first volume of *Das Kapital* by Karl Marx, the only part of the book actually published by Marx himself. It was this event, of course, that helped among other things to make the purchase of Alaska so significant: another example of the principle that life imitates literature, in the broad sense, and not the other way round. There is a still bigger majority to be considered, the majority of the dead. In the year 1867, Thomas Hardy wrote a poem called "1967," in which he remarks that the best thing he can say about that year is the fact that he is not going to live to see it.

My own primary interests are in literary and educational culture. What I should like to discuss with you here is not Canadian culture in itself, but the context of that culture in the world of the last century. One reason for my wanting to talk about the world that Canada is in rather than about Canada is that I should like to bypass some common assumptions about Canadian culture which we are bound to hear repeated a good deal in the course of this year. There is, for instance, the assumption that Canada has, in its progress from colony to nation, grown and matured like an individual: that to be colonial means to be immature, and to be national means to be grown-up. A colony or a province, we are told, produced a naive, imitative, and prudish culture; now that we have become a nation, we should start producing sophisticated, original, and spontaneous culture. (I dislike using "sophisticated" in an approving sense, but it does seem to be an accepted term for a kind of knowledgeability that responds to culture with the minimum of anxieties.) If we fail to produce a fully mature culture, the argument usually runs, it must be because we are still colonial or provincial in our attitude, and the best thing our critics and creators can do is to keep reminding us of this. If a Canadian painter or poet gets some recognition, he is soon giving interviews asserting that Canadian society is hypocritical, culturally constipated, and sexually inhibited. This might be thought a mere cliché, indicating that originality is a highly specialized gift, but it seems to have advanced in Canada to the place of an obligatory ritual. Some time ago, when a Canadian play opened in Paris, a reviewer, himself a Canadian, remarked sardonically: "Comme c'est canadien! Comme c'est pur!" I should add that this comment was incorporated by the Canadian publisher as a part of his blurb.

Analogies between the actual growth of an individual and the supposed growth of a society may be illuminating, but they must always be, like all analogies, open to fresh examination. The analogy is a particularly tricky form of rhetoric when it becomes the basis of an argument rather than merely a figure of speech. Certainly every society produces a type of culture which is roughly characteristic of itself. A provincial society has a provincial culture; a metropolitan society has a metropolitan culture. A provincial society will produce a phenomenon like the tea party described in F. R. Scott's well-known satire, "The Canadian Authors Meet." A metropolitan society would turn the tea party into a cocktail party, and the conversation would be louder, faster, more knowing, and cleverer at rationalizing its pretentiousness and egotism. But its poets would not necessarily be of any more lasting value than Mr. Scott's Miss Crotchet, though they might be less naive. It is true that relatively few if any of the world's greatest geniuses have been born in Canada, although a remarkable British painter and writer, Wyndham Lewis, went so far as to get himself born on a ship off Canadian shores, and developed an appropriately sea-sick view of Canada in later life. But we do not know enough about what social conditions produce great or even good writers to connect a lack of celebrated birth-places with the moral quality of Canadian civilization.

Another aspect of the same assumption is more subtle and pervasive. It is widely believed, or assumed, that Canada's destiny, culturally and historically, finds its fulfilment in being a nation, and that nationality is essential to identity. It seems to me, on the other hand, quite clear that we are moving towards a post-national world, and that Canada has moved further in that direction than most of the smaller nations. What is important about the last century, in this country, is not that we have been a nation for a hundred years, but that we have had a hundred years in which to make the transition from a pre-national to a post-national consciousness. The so-called emergent nations, such countries as Nigeria or Indonesia, have not been so fortunate: for them, the tensions of federalism and separatism, of middle-class and working-class interests, of xenophobia and adjustment to the larger world, have all come in one great rush. Canada has so far been able to avoid both this kind of chaos and the violence that goes with the development of a vast imperial complex like the U.S.A. or the U.S.S.R. The Canadian sense of proportion that I mentioned is especially valuable now, as helping us to adopt an attitude consistent with the world it is actually in. My present task, I think, is neither to eulogize nor to elegize Canadian nationality, neither to celebrate its survival nor to lament its passage, but to consider what kinds of social context are appropriate for a world in which the nation is rapidly ceasing to be the real defining unit of society.

We begin, then, with the conception of a "modern" world, which began to take shape a century ago and now provides the context for Canadian existence, and consequently for our Centennial. A century ago Canada was a nation in the world, but not wholly of it: the major cultural and political developments of Western Europe, still the main centre of the historical stage, were little known or understood in Canada, and the Canadian reaction even to such closer events as the American Civil War was largely negative. Today, Canada is too much a part of the world to be thought of as a nation in it. We have our undefended border with the United States, so celebrated in Canadian oratory, only because it is not a real boundary line at all: the real boundary line, one of the most heavily defended in the world, runs through the north of the country, separating a bourgeois sphere of control from a Marxist one.

Culturally, the primary fact about the modern world, or at least about our "Western" and "democratic" part of it, is that it is probably the first civilization in history that has attempted to study itself objectively, to become aware of the presuppositions underlying its behaviour, to understand its relation to previous history and to see whether its future could in some measure be controlled by its own will. This self-consciousness has created a sharp cultural dialectic in society, an intellectual antagonism between two mental attitudes. On one side are those who struggle for an active and conscious relation to their time, who study what is happening in the world, survey the conditions of life that seem most likely to occur, and try to acquire some sense of what can be done to build up from those conditions a way of life that is at least self-respecting. On the other side are those who adopt a passive and negative attitude, responding to the daily news and similar stimuli, aware of what is going on but making no effort to understand either the underlying causes or the future possibilities. The theatre of this conflict in attitudes is formed by the creative and the communicating arts. The creative arts are almost entirely on the active side: they mean nothing, or infinitely less, to a passive response. The subject matter of contemporary literature being its own time, the passive and uncritical attitude is seen as its most dangerous enemy. Many aspects of contemporary literature—its ironic tone, its emphasis on anxiety and absurdity, its queasy apocalyptic forebodings—derive from this situation.

The communicating arts, including the so-called mass media, are a mixture of things. Some of them are arts in their own right, like the film. Some are or include different techniques of presenting the arts we already have, like television. Some are not arts, but present analogies to techniques in the arts which the arts may enrich themselves by employing, as the newspaper may influence collage in painting or the field theory of composition in poetry. Some are applied arts, where the appeal is no longer disinterested, as it normally is in the creative arts proper. Thus, propaganda is an interested use of the literary techniques of rhetoric. As usual, there are deficiencies in vocabulary: there are no words that really convey the intellectual and moral contrast of the active and passive attitudes to culture. The phrase "mass culture" conveys emotional overtones of passivity: it suggests someone eating peanuts at a baseball game, and thereby contrasting himself to someone eating canapés at the opening of a sculpture exhibition. The trouble with this picture is that the former is probably part of a better educated audience, in the sense that he is likely to know more about baseball than his counterpart knows about sculpture. Hence his attitude to his chosen area of culture may well be the more active of the two. And just as there can be an active response to mass culture, so there can be passive responses to the highbrow arts. These range from "why can't the artist make his work mean something to the ordinary man?" to the significant syntax of the student's question: "Why is this considered a good poem?" The words advertising and propaganda come closest to suggesting a communication deliberately imposed and passively received. They represent respectively the communicating interests of the two major areas of society, the economic and the political. Recently these two conceptions have begun to merge into the single category of "public relations."

One very obvious feature of our age is the speeding up of process: it is an age of revolution and metamorphosis, where one lives through changes that formerly took centuries in a matter of a few years. In a world where dynasties rise and fall at much the same rate as women's hemlines, the dynasty and the hemline look much alike in importance, and get much the same amount of featuring in the news. Thus the progression of events is two-dimensional; a child's drawing reflecting an eye that observes without seeing depth, and even the effort to see depth has still to deal with the whole surface. Some new groupings result: for example, what used to be called the trivial or ephemeral takes on a function of *symbolizing* the significant. A new art of divination or augury has developed, in which the underlying trends of the contemporary world are interpreted by vogues and fashions in dress, speech or entertainment. Thus, if there appears a vogue for white lipstick among certain groups of young women, that may represent a new impersonality in sexual relationship, a parody of white supremacy, the dramatization of a death-wish, or the social projection of the clown archetype. Any number may play, but the game is a somewhat self-defeating one, without much power of sustaining its own interest. For even the effort to identify something in the passing show has the effect of dating it, as whatever is sufficiently formed to be recognized has already receded into the past.

It is not surprising if some people should be frustrated by the effort to keep riding up and down the manic-depressive roller-coaster of fashion, of what's in and what's out, what is U and what non-U, what is hip and what is square, what is corny and what is camp. There are perhaps not as many of these unhappy people as our newspapers and magazines suggest there are: in any case, what is important is not this group, if it exists, but the general sense, in our society, of the panic of change. The variety of things that occur in the world, combined with the relentless continuity of their appearance day after day, impresses us with the sense of a process going by a little too fast for our minds to focus on anything in it.

Some time ago, the department of English in a Canadian university decided to offer a course in twentieth-century poetry. It was discovered that there were two attitudes in the department towards that subject: there were those who felt that twentieth-century poetry had begun with Eliot's The Waste Land in 1922, and those who felt that most of the best of it had already been written by that time. There also appeared to be some correlation between these two views and the age groups of those who held them. Finally, a compromise was reached: two courses were offered, one called Modern Poetry and the other Contemporary Poetry. But even the contemporary course would need now to be supplemented by a third course in the post-contemporary, and perhaps a fourth in current happenings. In the pictorial arts the fashion-parade of isms is much faster: I hear of painters, even in Canada, who have frantically changed their styles completely three or four times in a few years, as collectors demanded first abstract expressionism, then pop art, then pornography, then hardedge, selling off their previous purchases as soon as the new vogue took hold. There is a medieval legend of the Wild Hunt, in which souls of the dead had to keep marching to nowhere all day and all night at top speed. Anyone who dropped out of line from exhaustion instantly crumbled to dust. This seems a parable of a type of consciousness frequent in the modern world, obsessed by a compulsion to keep up, reduced to despair by the steadily increasing speed of the total movement. It is a type of consciousness which I shall call the alienation of progress.

Alienation and progress are two central elements in the mythology of our day, and both words have been extensively used and misused. The conception of alienation was originally a religious one, and perhaps that is still the context in which it makes most sense. In religion, the person aware of sin feels alienated, not necessarily from society, but from the presence of God, and it is in this feeling of alienation that the religious life begins. The conception is clearest in evangelical thinkers in the Lutheran tradition like Bunyan, who see alienation of this kind as the beginning of a psychological revolution. Once one becomes aware of being in sin and under the wrath of God, one realizes that one's master is the devil, the prince of this world, and that treason and rebellion against this master is the first requirement of the new life.

A secularized use of the idea appears in the early work of Marx, where alienation describes the feeling of the worker who is cheated out of most of the fruit of his labour by exploitation. He is unable to participate in society to the extent that, as a worker, he should, because his status in society has been artificially degraded. In this context the alienated are those who have been dispossessed by their masters, and who therefore recognize their masters as their enemies, as Christian did Apollyon. In our day those who are alienated in Marx's sense are, for example, the Negro, whose status is also arbitrarily degraded, or those who are in actual want and misery. The Negro, looking at the selfishness and panic in white eyes, realizes that while what he has to fight is ultimately a state of mind, still his enemies also include people who have got themselves identified with this state of mind. Thus his enemies, again, are those who believe themselves his masters or natural superiors. Apart from such special situations, not many in the Western democracies today believe that a specific social act, such as expropriating a propertied class, would end alienation in the modern world.

The reason is that in a society like ours, a society of the accepted and adequately fed, the conception of alienation becomes psychological. In other words it becomes the devil again, for the devil normally comes to those who have everything and are bored with it, like Faust. The root of this aspect of alienation is the sense that man has lost control, if he ever had it, over his own destiny. The master or tyrant is still an enemy, but not an enemy that anyone can fight. Theoretically, the world is divided into democracies and peoples' republics: actually, there has never been a time when man felt less sense of participation in the really fateful decisions that affect his life and his death. The central symbol of this is of course the overkill bomb, as presented in such works as *Dr. Strangelove*, the fact that the survival of humanity itself may depend on a freak accident. In a world where the tyrant-enemy can be recognized, even defined, and yet cannot be projected on anything or anybody, he remains part of ourselves, or more precisely of our own death-wish, a cancer that gradually disintegrates the sense of community. We may try to persuade ourselves that the complete destruction of Communism (or, on their side, of capitalist imperialism) would also destroy alienation. But an instant of genuine reflection would soon tell us that all such external enemies could disappear from the earth tomorrow and leave us exactly where we were before.

The conception of progress grew up in the nineteenth century around a number of images and ideas. The basis of the conception is the fact that science, in contrast to the arts, develops and advances, with the work of each generation adding to that of its predecessor. Science bears the practical fruit of technology, and technology has created, in the modern world, a new consciousness of time. Man has doubtless always experienced time in the same way, dragged backwards from a receding past into an unknown future. But the quickening of the pace of news, with telegraph and submarine cable, helped to dramatize a sense of a world in visible motion, with every day bringing new scenes and episodes of a passing show. It was as though the ticking of a clock had become not merely audible but obsessive, like the tell-tale heart in Poe. The first reactions to the new sensation—for it was more of a sensation than a conception—were exhilarating, as all swift movement is for a time. The prestige of the myth of progress developed a number of value-assumptions: the dynamic is better than the static, process better than product, the organic and vital better than the mechanical and fixed, and so on. We still have these value-assumptions, and no doubt they are useful, though like other assumptions we should be aware that we have them. And yet there was an underlying tendency to alienation in the conception of progress itself. In swift movement we are dependent on a vehicle and not on ourselves, and the proportion of exhilaration to apprehensiveness depends on whether we are driving it or merely riding in it. All progressive machines turn out to be things ridden in, with an unknown driver.

Whatever is progressive develops a certain autonomy, and the reactions to it consequently divide: some feel that it will bring about vast improvements in life by itself, others are more concerned with the loss of human control over it. An example of such a progressive machine was the self-regulating market of laissez faire. The late Karl Polanyi has described, in The Great Transformation, how this market dominated the political and economic structure of Western Europe, breaking down the sense of national identity and replacing it with a uniform contractual relationship of management and labour. The autonomous market took out a ninety-nine year lease on the world from 1815 to 1914, and kept "peace" for the whole of that time. By peace I mean the kind of peace that we have had ourselves since 1945: practically continuous warfare somewhere or other, but with no single war becoming large enough to destroy the overall economic structure, or the major political structures dependent on it. And yet what the autonomous market created in modern consciousness was, even when optimistic, the feeling that Polanyi has finely described as "an uncritical reliance on the alleged self-healing virtues of unconscious growth." That is, the belief in social progress was transferred from the human will to the autonomous social force. Similar conceptions of autonomous mass movement and historical process dominate much of our social thinking today. In Communist theology the historical process occupies much the same position that the Holy Spirit does in Christianity: an omnipotent power that co-operates with the human will but is not dependent on it.

Even earlier than the rise of the market, the feeling that man could achieve a better society than the one he was in by a sufficiently resolute act had done much to inspire the American and more particularly the French revolutions, as well as a number of optimistic progressive visions of history like that of Condorcet. Here the ideal society is associated with a not too remote future. Here too there are underlying paradoxes. If we ask what we are progressing to, the only conceivable goal is greater stability, something more orderly and predictable than what we have now. After all, the only thing we can imagine which is better than what we have now is an ensured and constant supply of the best that we do have: economic security, peace, equal status in the protection of law, the appeal of the will to reason, and the like. Progress thus assumes that the dynamic is better than the stable and unchanging, yet it moves toward a greater stability. One famous progressive thinker, John Stuart Mill, had a nervous breakdown when he realized that he did not want to see his goals achieved, but merely wished to act as though he did. What was progress yesterday may seem today like heading straight for a prison of arrested development, like the societies of insects. In the year 1888 Edward Bellamy published *Looking Backward*, a vision of a collectivized future which profoundly inspired the progressive thinkers of that day, and had a social effect such as few works of literature have ever had. Today it impresses us in exactly the opposite way, as a most sinister blueprint for a totalitarian state.

A more serious consequence is that under a theory of progress present means have constantly to be sacrificed to future ends, and we do not know the future well enough to know whether those ends will be achieved or not. All we actually know is that we are damaging the present. Thus the assumption that progress is necessarily headed in a good or benevolent direction becomes more and more clearly an unjustified assumption. As early as Malthus the conception of sinister progress had made its appearance, the vision of a world moving onward to a goal of too many people without enough to eat. When it is proposed to deface a city by, say, turning park lots into parking lots, the rationalization given is usually the cliché "you can't stop progress." Here it is not even pretended that progress is anything beneficent: it is simply a juggernaut, or symbol of alienation. And in history the continued sacrificing of a visible present to an invisible future becomes with increasing clarity a kind of Moloch-worship. Some of the most horrible notions that have ever entered the human mind have been "progressive" notions: massacring farmers to get a more efficient agricultural system, exterminating Jews to achieve a "solution" of the "Jewish question," letting a calculated number of people starve to regulate food prices. The element of continuity in progress suggests that the only practicable action is continuous with what we are already doing: if, for instance, we are engaged in a war, it is practicable to go on with the war, and only visionary to stop it.

Hence, for most thoughtful people progress has lost most of its original sense of a favourable value-judgement and has become simply progression, towards a goal more likely to be a disaster than an improvement. Taking thought for the morrow, we are told on good authority, is a dangerous practice. In proportion as the confidence in progress has declined, its relation to individual experience has become clearer. That is, progress is a social projection of the individual's sense of the passing of time. But the individual, as such, is not progressing to anything except his own death. Hence, the collapse of belief in progress reinforces the sense of anxiety which is rooted in the consciousness of death. Alienation and anxiety become the same thing, caused by a new intensity in the awareness of the movement of time, as it ticks our lives away day after day. This intensifying of the sense of time also, as we have just seen, dislocates it: the centre of attention becomes the future, and the emotional relation to the future becomes one of dread and uncertainty. The future is the point at which "it is later than you think" becomes "too late." Modern fiction has constantly dealt, during the last century, with characters struggling toward some act of consciousness or self-awareness that would be a gateway to real life. But the great majority of treatments of this theme are ironic: the act is not made, or is made too late, or is a paralyzing awareness with no result except self-contempt, or is perverted into illusion. We notice that when the tone is less ironic and more hopeful about the nature and capacities of man, as it is for instance in Camus's La Peste, it is usually in a context of physical emergency where there is a definite enemy to fight.

Even in theory progress is as likely to lead to the uniform and the monotonous as to the individual and varied. If we look at the civilization around us, the evidence for uniformity is as obvious and oppressive as the evidence for the rapid change toward it. The basis of this uniformity is technological, but the rooted social institutions of the past—home, school, church—can also only be adapted to a nomadic society by an expanding uniform pattern. Whatever the advantages of this situation, we have also to consider the consequences of the world's becoming increasingly what in geology is called a *peneplain*, a monotonous surface worn down to a dead level by continued erosion. We are not far into the nineteenth century before we become aware of a different element both in consciousness and in the physical appearance of society. This is a new geometrical perspective, already beginning in the eighteenth century, which is scaled, not to the human body, but increasingly to the mechanical extensions of the body. It is particularly in America, of course, that this perspective is most noticeable: Washington, laid out by L'Enfant in 1800, is already in the age of the automobile. This mechanical perspective is mainly the result of the spreading of the city and its technology over more and more of its natural environment. The railway is the earliest and still one of the most dramatic examples of the creation of a new kind of landscape, one which imposes geometrical shapes on the countryside. The prophet Isaiah sees the coming of the Messiah as symbolized by a highway which exalts valleys and depresses mountains, making the crooked straight and the rough places plain. But, as so often happens, the prophecy appears to have been fulfilled in the wrong context.

The role of communications media in the modern world is a subject that Professor Marshall McLuhan has made so much his own that it would be almost a discourtesy not to refer to him in a lecture which covers many of his themes. The McLuhan cult, or more accurately the McLuhan rumour, is the latest of the illusions of progress: it tells us that a number of new media are about to bring in a new form of civilization all by themselves, merely by existing. Because of this we should not, in staring at a television set, wonder if we are wasting our time and develop guilt feelings accordingly: we should feel that we are evolving a new mode of apprehension. What is important about the television set is not the quality of what it exudes, which is only content, but the fact that it is there, the end of a tube with a vortical suction which "involves" the viewer. This is not all of what a serious and most original writer is trying to say, yet Professor McLuhan lends himself partly to this interpretation by throwing so many of his insights into a deterministic form. He would connect the alienation of progress with the habit of forcing a hypnotized eye to travel over thousands of miles of type, in what is so accurately called the pursuit of knowledge. But apparently he would see the Gutenberg syndrome as a cause of the alienation of progress, and not simply as one of its effects. Determinism of this kind, like the determinism which derives Confederation from the railway, is a plausible but over-simplified form of rhetoric.

Similarly, with the principle of the identity of medium and message, which means one thing when the response is active, and quite another when the response is passive. On the active level it is an ideal formulation which strictly applies only to the arts, and to a fully active response to the arts. It would be true to say that painting, for example, had no "message" except the medium of painting itself. On the passive level it is an ironic formulation in which the differences among the media flatten out. The "coolness" of television is much more obvious in the privacy of a middle-class home than it is when turned on full blast in the next room of a jerrybuilt hotel. All forms of communication, from transistors to atom bombs, are equally hot when someone else's finger is on the button. Thus the primary determining quality of the medium comes from the social motive for using it and not from the medium itself. Media can only follow the direction of the human will that created them, and a study of the social direction of that will, or what Innis called the bias of communication, is a major, prior, and separate problem.

Technology cannot of itself bring about an increase in human freedom, for technological developments threaten the structure of society, and society develops a proportionate number of restrictions to contain them. The automobile increases the speed and freedom of individual movement, and thereby brings a proportionate increase in police authority, with its complication of laws and penalties. In proportion, as the production of retail goods becomes more efficient, the quality of craftsmanship and design decreases. The aeroplane facilitates travel, and therefore regiments travel: a modern traveller, processed through an immigration shed, might think ruefully of the contrast with Sterne, traveling wide to France in the eighteenth century, suddenly remembering that Britain was at war with France, and that consequently he would need his passport. The same principle affects science itself. The notion that science, left to itself, is bound to evolve more and more of the truth about the world is another illusion, for science can never exist outside a society, and that society, whether deliberately or unconsciously, directs its course. Still, the importance of keeping science "free," i.e., unconsciously rather than deliberately directed, is immense. In the Soviet Union, and increasingly in America as well, science is allowed to develop "freely" so that the political power can hijack its technological by-products. But this means a steady pressure on science to develop in the direction useful to that power: target-knowledge, as the Nazis called it. I am not saying that there are no answers to these questions: I am saying that no improvement in the human situation can take place independently of the human will to improve, and that confidence in automatic or impersonal improvement is always misplaced.

In earlier times, the sense of alienation and anxiety was normally projected as the fear of hell, the "too late" existence awaiting those who, as Dante's Virgil says, had never come alive. In our day this fear is attached, not to another world following this one, but to the future of our own world. The first half of the modern century was still full of progressive optimism: an unparalleled number of Utopias, or visions of a stabilized future, were written, and universal prosperity was widely predicted, partly because most of the people being exploited in the main centres of culture were well out of sight in Asia or Africa. After the midway point of 1917 there came an abrupt change. Spengler's *Decline of the West* appeared in Germany the next year. Here it is said that history consists of cultural developments which rise, mature, and decline like organisms. After they have exhausted their creative possibilities, they turn into "civilizations." The arts give place to technology and engineering; vast cities spread over the landscape, inhabited by uprooted masses of people, and dictatorships and annihilation wars become the course of history. A Classical "culture" entered this stage with Alexander, and, later, the rise of Rome. The Western world entered it with Napoleon, and is now in the stage corresponding to that of the Punic Wars, with the great world states fighting it out for supremacy. Spengler is often dismissed as "fatalistic" today, but his paralleling of our historical situation with earlier periods, especially that of the Roman Empire, and his point that our technology could be part of a decline as easily as it could be part of an advance, are conceptions that we all accept now, whether we realize it or not, as something which is inseparably part of our perspective.

The progressive belief suffered a rude set-back in America in the crash of 1929; it was adopted by the Soviet Union as part of its revolutionary world-view, but is gradually fading out even there, much as the expectation of the end of the world faded out of early Christian thought. In our day the Utopia has been succeeded by what is being called, by analogy, the "dystopia," the nightmare of the future. H. G. Wells is a good example of a writer who built all his hopes around the myth of progress, in which the role of saviour was played by a self-evolving science. His last publication, however, *The Mind at the End of its Tether* (1940), carried all the furious bitterness of an outraged idealism. Orwell's 1984 is a better known dystopia, and perhaps comes as close as any book to being the definitive *Inferno* of our time. It is a particularly searching study because of the way in which it illustrates how so many aspects of culture, including science, technology, history, and language, would operate in their demonic or perverted forms. The conception of progress took off originally from eighteenth-century discussions about the natural society, where the progressive view was urged by Bolingbroke and Rousseau and the opposite one by Swift and Burke. According to Rousseau, the natural and reasonable society of the future was buried underneath the accumulated injustices and absurdities of civilization, and all man had to do was to release it by revolution. Writers of our day have mostly reverted to the view of Swift's *Gulliver's Travels*, that slavery is to man at least as natural a state as freedom: this is the central insight of one of the most penetrating stories of our time, William Golding's *Lord of the Flies*, and is certainly implied, if not expressed, in Aldous Huxley's *Brave New World* and many similar works.

It is natural that many people should turn from the vision of such a world to some illusion or distracting fiction that seems to afford a more intelligible environment. Nationalism is or can be a distracting fiction of this kind. The nation, economically considered, is a form of private enterprise, a competing business in the world's market; hence, for most people, nationality comes to their attention chiefly through inconvenience—customs duties, income taxes, and the like. But it also may provide some sense of a protected place. It can't happen here, we may say, deliberately forgetting that the distinction between here and there has ceased to exist. It is significant that intense nationalism or regionalism today is a product either of resistance to or of disillusionment with progress. Progress, when optimistic, always promises some form of exodus from history as we know it, some emergence on to a new plateau of life. Thus the Marxist revolution promised deliverance from history as history had previously been, a series of class struggles. But just as there are neurotic individuals who cannot get beyond some blocking point in their emotional past, so there are neurotic social groups who feel a compulsion to return to a previous point in history, as Mississippi keeps fighting the Civil War over again, and some separatists in Quebec the British Conquest.

However, one wonders whether, in an emergency, this compulsion to return to the same point, the compulsion of Quixote to fight over again the battles he found in his books, is not universal in our world. In ordinary life, the democratic and communist societies see each other as dystopias, their inhabitants hysterical and brainwashed by propaganda, identifying their future with what is really their destruction. Perhaps both sides, as Blake would say, become what they behold: in any case seeing tendencies to tyranny only on the other side is mere hypocrisy. The Nuremberg trials laid down the principle that man remains a free agent even in the worst of tyrannies, and is not only morally but legally responsible for resisting orders that outrage the conscience of mankind. The Americans took an active part in prosecuting these trials, but when America itself stumbled into the lemming-march horror of Vietnam the principle was forgotten and the same excuses and defiances reappeared.

All the social nightmares of our day seem to focus on some unending and inescapable form of mob rule. The most permanent kind of mob rule is not anarchy, nor is it the dictatorship that regularizes anarchy, nor even the imposed police state depicted by Orwell. It is rather the self-policing state, the society incapable of formulating an articulate criticism of itself and of developing a will to act in its light. This is a condition that we are closer to, on this continent, than we are to dictatorship. In such a society the conception of progress would reappear as a donkey's carrot, as the new freedom we shall have as soon as some regrettable temporary necessity is out of the way. No one would notice that the necessities never come to an end, because the communications media would have destroyed the memory.

The idea of progress, we said, is not really that of man progressing, but of man releasing forces that will progress by themselves. The root of the idea is the fact that science progressively develops its conception of the world. Science is a vision of nature which perceives the elements in nature that correspond to the reason and the sense of structure in the scientist's mind. If we look at our natural environment with different eyes, with emotion or desire or trying to see in it things that answer other needs than those of the reason, nature seems a vast unthinking indifference, with no evidence of meaning or purpose. In proportion as we have lost confidence in progress, the scientific vision of nature has tended to separate from a more imaginative and emotional one which regards nature or the human environment as absurd or meaningless. The absurd is now one of the central elements in the contemporary myth, along with alienation and anxiety, and has extended from man's feeling about nature to his feeling about his own society. For society, like nature, has the power of life and death over us, yet has no real claim on our deeper loyalties. The absurdity of power is clearer in a democratic society, where we are deprived of the comforting illusions that surround royalty. In a democracy no one pretends to identify the real form of society either with the machinery of business or with the machinery of government. But in that case where is the society to be found to which we do owe loyalty?

I have tried to indicate the outlines of the picture that contemporary imagination has drawn of its world, a jigsaw-puzzle picture in which the Canada of 1967 is one of the pieces. It is a picture mainly of disillusionment and fear, and helps to explain why our feelings about our Centennial are more uneasy than they are jubilant. In the twentieth century, most anniversaries, including the annual disseminating neurosis of Christmas, are touched with foreboding. I noticed this early in life, for my twenty-first birthday was spent at the Chicago World's Fair of 1933, entitled "A Century of Progress," where the crowds were much more preoccupied with worrying about the depression than with celebrating what had led to it. And yet this picture, as I have tried also to explain, is the picture that the contemporary imagination draws of itself in a mirror. Looking into the mirror is the active mind which struggles for consistency and continuity of outlook, which preserves its memory of its past and clarifies its view of the present. Staring back at it is the frozen reflection of that mind, which has lost its sense of continuity by projecting it on some mechanical social process, and has found that it has also lost its dignity, its freedom, its creative power, and its sense of the present, with nothing left except a fearful apprehension of the future. The mind in the mirror, like the characters in Beckett, cannot move on its own initiative. But the more repugnant we find this reflection, the less likely we are to make the error of Narcissus, and identify ourselves with it. I want now to discuss the active role that the arts, more particularly literature, have taken in forming the contemporary imagination, which has given us this picture. The picture itself reflects anxiety, and as long as man is capable of anxiety he is capable of passing through it to a genuine human destiny.

Note

Originally published as "City of the End of Things," chapter 1 of *The Modern Century*, new ed., by Northrop Frye. Copyright © Oxford University Press Canada 1991. Reprinted with permission of the publisher.

Canadian Fate and Imperialism

George Parkin Grant was born in Toronto in 1918 to a family prominent in Canadian education. Grant studied history at Queen's University, graduating in 1939. Winning a Rhodes scholarship enabled him to enroll in law at Balliol College, Oxford, shortly after the Second World War began. His understanding of the meaningless carnage of the First World War made Grant a pacifist, so the war against fascism posed a moral dilemma for him. His solution was to join the Air Raid Precaution Service in 1940. This put Grant at the center of the London Blitz, and his post at Stayner's Arch near the London Docks suffered a direct hit on February 17, 1941. More than three hundred people under his care were killed or seriously wounded. Grant would later describe this event as his first "primal experience," which came to inform his philosophical attitude of an "agnostic" Christian Platonism.

Grant returned to Toronto in 1942 to convalesce after contracting tuberculosis. From 1943 to 1945, Grant was active in the Canadian Association of Adult Education, as its national secretary, where he worked with progressive Catholic and communist colleagues. The CAAE, in some ways a forerunner of the Council of Canadians, sought to organize and educate a broad citizens' coalition that would enable Canadians radicalized by the Depression to have a voice in the shaping of public and foreign policy. During this time, Grant was a regular contributor to the CAAE's magazine *Food for Thought* and he wrote extensively for its CBC radio program, *Citizens' Forum*. Later, over the 1950s and 1960s, Grant remained deeply involved in broadcasting, delivering many lectures on the CBC Talks Department program *University of the Air* and appearing on the CBC television programs *Fighting Words* and *Architects of Modern Thought*. Grant returned to Balliol College in 1945 to study theology and was awarded a D.Phil. degree in 1950 for his dissertation, "The Concept of Nature and Supernature in the Theology of John Oman." Grant taught philosophy at Dalhousie University in Halifax from 1947 to 1961, when he moved to McMaster University, where he taught until 1980. He then returned once more to Dalhousie. Grant died in Halifax in 1988. His major works are *Philosophy in the Mass Age* (1960); "An Ethic of Community," published in *Social Purpose for Canada* (1961), a book issued to coincide with the founding of the

New Democratic Party; *Lament for a Nation* (1965); *Technology and Empire* (1969); *English Speaking Justice* (1974); and *Technology and Justice* (1986). The social, cultural, political, and philosophical positions Grant articulates over this body of writing are radically singular. Though a Red Tory conservative on many issues—he opposed women's access to safe, legal abortions—his work refuses easy pigeonholing. Left nationalists were never able to fully dispense with him. Moreover, Grant's works have been very important for a number of contemporary cultural studies theorists.

To use the language of fate is to assert that all human beings come into a world they did not choose and live their lives within a universe they did not make. If one speaks in this way, one is often accused either of being pessimistic or of holding a tragic view of life. Neither of these accusations is correct. To say that one holds a tragic view of life would be to follow Nietzsche in thinking that Dionysian tragedy was a higher stance than that of Socrates; I do not think this. And the words "optimistic" and "pessimistic" are surely most accurately used, following Leibniz, to describe what one thinks about the nature of things, whether the world is good or not. It is quite possible to use the word "fate," and to think that "nature" is good, and not contradict oneself. It is in my opinion a sensible way to talk about events, though obviously it is far from the liberal dogmas within which most people are taught to think.

A central aspect of the fate of being a Canadian is that our very existing has at all times been bound up with the interplay of various world empires. One can better understand what it is to be Canadian if one understands that interplay. As no serious person is interested in history simply as antiquarianism but only as it illumines one's search for a good in a here and now, let me set the problem in its most contemporary form—Vietnam. What our fate is today becomes most evident in the light of Vietnam. It is clear that in that country the American empire has been demolishing a people, rather than allowing them to live outside the American orbit.

The Americans are forced to that ferocious demolition because they have chosen to draw the line against the Chinese empire in a country where nationalism and communism have been in large measure identified. How does this affect Canadians? On the one hand, many Canadians, whether their moral traditions come from Judaism, Christianity, the liberal enlightenment or a mixture, are not yet so empty that they can take lightly the destruction of a people—even in the case of Asians. On the other hand, the vast majority of Canadians are a product of western civilization and live entirely within the forms and assumptions of that enterprise. Today the enterprise of western civilization finds its spearhead in the American empire. In that sense our very lives are inevitably bound up in the meeting of that empire with the rest of the world, and the movements of war which draw the limits in that meeting. The depth of that common destiny with the Americans is shown in the fact that many Canadians who are forced to admit the sheer evil of what is being done in Vietnam say at the same time that we have no choice but to stand with the Americans as the pillar of western civilization. Beyond this kind of talk is of course the fact that this society is above all a machine for greed, and our branch plant industry is making a packet out of the demolition of Vietnam.

Our involvement is much deeper than the immediate profits of particular wars. Our very form of life depends on our membership in the western industrial empire which is centred in the U.S.A. and which stretches out in its hegemony into parts of Western Europe and which controls South America and much of Africa and Asia. Somewhere in the minds of nearly all Canadians there is the recognition that our present form of life depends on our place as second class members of that system. By "second class" I do not imply a low status, because there are a large number of classes within it. It is much nicer to be a Canadian than a Brazilian or a Venezuelan, or for that matter an Englishman.

Indeed our involvement in the American empire goes deeper than a simple economic and political basis; it depends on the very faith that gives meaning and purpose to the lives of western men. To most Canadians, as public beings, the central cause of motion in their souls is the belief in progress through technique, and that faith is identified with the power and leadership of the English-speaking empire in the world.

This then is why our present fate can be seen with such clarity in the glaring light of Vietnam. The very substance of our lives is bound up with the western empire and its destiny, just at a time when that empire uses increasingly ferocious means to maintain its hegemony. The earlier catastrophes and mass crimes of the age of progress could be interpreted as originating entirely with other peoples, the Germans, or the Russians. They could be seen as the perverse products of western ideology—national socialism or communism. This can no longer be said. What is being done in Vietnam is being done by the English-speaking empire and in the name of liberal democracy.

Not only in our present but in our origins, Canada was made by western empires. We were a product of two northwestern empires as they moved out in that strange expansion of Europe around the world. It is essential to emphasize that they were northwestern. Hegel's language is here the clearest. He speaks of the "germanische Geist," and in using those words he does not mean the German spirit. He means geographically those European lands whose rivers flow into the North Atlantic. He means the particular secularising Christianity which characterized those lands. He understands that the dominant spirit of the modern age is no longer in the Mediterranean peoples, but has passed northward and westward to the Abendland.

If one is to understand Canada one must understand the history of those empires—and not simply in terms of what they did, but in terms of the spirit which drove them to such enormous motion. If one is to pick the society where modernity first makes its appearance in a more than individual way, one must pick England. To understand English modernity one must look above all at that unique meeting of Calvinist Protestantism and the new secular spirit of the Renaissance. That secular spirit can be seen in the new physical science whose origins we identify with Galileo, and in the new moral science of Machiavelli. It was the liberals' superficial interpretation of what we call the Renaissance to see such thinkers as a return to the Greeks, when they were a profound turning away from the ancients. The role of Calvinism in making possible the capitalism which has shaped the western world has been described by Weber.[1] He sees with great clarity how Calvinism provided the necessary ethic for capitalism; what he does not understand is that deeper movement of the mind in which the Puritans were open to the new physical and moral science in a way the older Christianity was not. You can see this acceptance taking place in the seventeenth century. At the end of the sixteenth century, Shakespeare writes: "to set the murderous Machiavell' to school." But during the seventeenth century, Bacon, Hobbes and Locke have achieved the terrible task of making Machiavelli widely respectable, and the new secular, moral and physical science is particularly welcomed by the Protestants. The union of the new secularism and Protestantism brought forth the first great wave of social modernity in England and its empire.

These days when we are told in North America that capitalism is conservative, we should remember that capitalism was the great dissolvent of the traditional virtues and that its greatest philosophers, Hobbes and Locke, Smith and Hume, were Britishers. In the appeal to capitalism as the tradition it is forgotten that the capitalist philosophers dissolved all ideas of the sacred as standing in the way of the emancipation of greed. For example, the criticism of any knowable teleology by Hume not only helped to liberate men to the new natural science, but also liberated them from knowledge of any purposes which transcended the economically rational. It is not surprising that North America was won by the English empire rather than the French. It is enough to read John Nef's book about the differing uses of iron in England and France in the seventeenth century. Despite the work of Henri IV, Richelieu and Colbert, France was not to the same degree an initiator of capitalism and modernity. The French who were left as an enclave on the shores of the St. Lawrence came from an earlier tradition, before France had initiated the second great wave of modernity with Rousseau and the French Revolution. What is so endearing about the young French Canadians revolting against their tradition is that they sometimes write as if Voltaire's *Candide* had come off the press last week instead of two hundred years ago. One's enchantment is however limited by the knowledge that their awakening to modernity, which seems to them an expression of independence, in fact leaves them wide open to conquest by a modernity which at its very heart is destructive of indigenous traditions. Of course, many stylish French Canadian liberals are quite clear that their espousal of the modern does not consistently include any serious interest in the continuance of their own traditions, including even language.

Although the English who conquered North America were of a more modern tradition than the French left in their enclave, it must be remembered that there was always a strong losing party in all the great public events in which modernity put its stamp on English society. Progressivist historians do not write much about the losers of history, because belief in progress often implies the base assumption that to lose is to have failed to grasp the evolving truth. Nevertheless, the losers existed and they are worth reading now that we see what kind of society the winners have made. We can read what Hooker wrote against the Puritans and the society they would build. Above all, the views of the losing party can be found in the greatest of English prose stylists. Swift was a comic genius because he understood with clarity that the victory of the Whigs was not simply a passing political event, but involved new intellectual assumptions. In the quarrel between the ancients and the moderns, Swift knew why he accepted the ancients against the new moral science of Hobbes and Locke.

Though the empire of the English was the chief of the early driving forces towards modernity, many traditions from before the age of progress remained alive in parts of English society, and some of these existed in an inchoate way in the early English-speaking peoples of this country. It would be balderdash to imply that the early English-speaking leaders of Canada had a firm tradition like their French compatriots, or that they were in any sense people who resisted modernity with the clarity of Swift. Most of the educated among the Loyalists were that extraordinary concoction, straight Locke with a dash of Anglicanism. They were above all a product of the English empire, and the victory of modernity had long since been decided in favour of the Whigs. What can be fairly said, however, is that they were not so given over to modernity as were the leaders of the U.S., particularly insofar as the Americans had incorporated in their revolution a mixture of Locke with elements of Rousseau. The fact that the Canadians had consciously refused the break with their particular past meant that they had some roots with tradition, even though that tradition was the most modern in Europe up till the eighteenth century. Indeed, when one reads the speeches of those founders whom we celebrated in 1967, one is aware of their continual suspicion of the foundations of the American republic, and of their desire to build a political society with a clearer and firmer doctrine of the common good than that at the heart of the liberal democracy to the south. (One would never know this from what one reads about our founders in our liberal text books.)

Nevertheless, having asserted these differences, what is far more important is to repeat that the English empire was a dominant source of modernity. The early Canadian settlers may have wanted to be different from the Americans in detail but not in any substantial way which questioned that modernity. I emphasize this for a personal reason. A couple of years ago I wrote a book about the dissolution of Canadian sovereignty. These days when psychologising is the chief method for neutralising disagreeable opinions, my psyche was interpreted as harking back in nostalgia to the British empire and old fashioned Canada. This was the explanation of why I did not think that the general tendencies of modern society were liable to produce human excellence. In this era when the homogenising power of technology is almost unlimited, I do regret the disappearance of indigenous traditions, including my own. It is true that no particularism can adequately incarnate the good. But is it not also true that only through some particular roots, however partial, can human beings first grasp what is good and it is the juice of such roots which for most men sustain their partaking in a more universal good? Still, regret, however ironical, is not an adequate stance for living and is an impossible stance for philosophy. Conservatism is a practical stance; it must be transcended to reach philosophy. What I said in that book was that the belief that human excellence is promoted by the homogenising and universalising power of technology is the dominant doctrine of modern liberalism, and that that doctrine must undermine all particularisms and that English-speaking Canada as a particular is wide open to that doctrine.

In the nineteenth century the European empires modernised themselves. Nearly all those aspects of their cultures from before the age of progress disappeared. The fact that England came into that century with a vast empire (despite its loss of the American colonies), and as the pioneer of industrialism, meant that it started with an enormous advantage over the other modernising empires. In some ways it was this sense of advantage and unquestioned power which made it indifferent to immediate political control in Canada. But after 1870 industrial and imperial competition was the order of the day and England threw itself into the wild scramble for more possessions and greater imperial control to counter the growing strength of its European rivals. The imperialism of the last half of the nineteenth century is modern man (man as Hobbes has said he is) realising his potentialities. The culmination of that European process was the war of 1914.

Canada, as always, was involved in the general western fate. Just read how English-speaking Canadians from all areas and all economic classes went off to that war hopefully and honestly believing that they were thereby guaranteeing freedom and justice in the world. Loyalty to Britain and loyalty to liberal capitalist democracy was identified with loyalty to freedom and justice. For example, I have met people from Cape Breton who were so cut off from the general world in 1914 that they thought that Queen Victoria was still reigning and took for granted it was their duty to fight for her. When one thinks what that war was in fact being fought about, and the slaughter of decent men of decent motive which ensued, the imagination boggles. As that war spelled out the implicit violence of the West, it also spelled out Canadian fate.

First, it killed many of the best English-speaking Canadians and left the survivors cynical and tired. I once asked a man of that generation why it was that between the wars of 1914 and 1939 Canada was allowed to slip into the slough of despond in which its national hope was frittered away to the U.S. by Mackenzie King and the Liberal party.[2] He answered graphically: "We had our guts shot away in France." The energy of that generation was drained away in that conflict so that those who returned did not have the vitality for public care, but retreated into the private world of money making. Canada's survival has always required the victory of political courage over immediate and individual economic advantage.

Secondly, English-speaking Canadians in the name of that brutal struggle between empires forced French-speaking Canadians to take part in a way which they knew not to be theirs. If Canada were to exist, English and French-speaking peoples had to have sufficient trust to choose to be together rather than to be Americans. The forcing of the French by fanatics such as Sam Hughes and the culmination of that process in the election of 1917 meant that the French Canadians saw themselves threatened more by English-speaking Canadians than by the deeper threat to the south. Mackenzie King's stand in the election of 1917 must be taken to his political credit, and God knows he needs credit somewhere.[3] In saying that, however, one must remember that between the two great wars King and the Liberal party kept the flames of that hostility alive in Quebec so that they could take the full political benefit from it.

The third great effect of that war in Canada was due to the policies of the ruling classes in Great Britain. In the face of the competition from other European empires, the British ruling classes acted as if their only hope of continuing power was to put their fate into the hands of the American empire. That process is epitomized in the career of Winston Churchill. High rhetoric about partnership among the English-speaking peoples has been used about this process. It cannot, however, cover the fact that Great Britain's chief status in the world today is to do useful jobs for its masters and to be paid for so doing by the support of the pound and the freedom to provide entertainers and entertainment for the empire as a whole. The American empire may be having its diffi-culties with France and Germany, but it does not have them with Great Britain. Leaving aside the complex question of whether this status was the best that the English could achieve in the circumstances, it is clear that its effect on the possibility of Canada being a nation has been large. The elimination of Great Britain as an independent source of civilisation in the English-speaking world greatly increased the pull of English-speaking Canadians to an identity with the centre of that world in the United States. It is an ambiguity of present Canada that some serious French Canadians now turn to France for support against the English-speaking technological sea. They so turn just as English-speaking Cana-dians can no longer turn to Great Britain for alternative forms of life to those which press from the south. This present turning is ambiguous because for so long English-speaking Canadians were told by French Canadians that we were not properly Canadian because of our connection with Great Britain. English-speaking Canadians now lean on similar criticism when the great general is welcomed in Quebec.[4]

The supremacy of the American empire in the western world was important for Canada not only in the geographic and economic senses that our nation had to try to exist in the very presence of the empire, but in the much profounder sense that the dominance of the United States is identified with the unequivocal victory of the progressive spirit in the West. The older empires had some residual traditions from before the age of progress—the French more, the British less. The United States is the only society that has none. The American supremacy is identified with the belief that questions of human good are to be solved by technology, that the most important human activity is the pursuit of those sciences which issue in the conquest of human and non-human nature. Anybody who is in university today, and knows where he is, knows both that these are the ends for which the university exists and that the universities are becoming almost the chief institutions of our system.

The gradual victory of the progressive spirit has taken place in interdependence with an enormous expansion of the western peoples into the rest of the world. The era of modern thought has been the era of western imperialism. Imperialism, like war, is coeval with human existence. But the increasingly externalised view of human life which is the very nature of the progressive spirit has given and will continue to give an enormous impetus to imperialism. As the classical philosophers said, man cannot help but imitate in action his vision of the nature of things. The dominant tendency of the western world has been to divide history from nature and to consider history as dynamic and nature controllable as externality. Therefore, modern men have been extremely violent in their dealings with other men and other beings. Liberal doctrine does not prepare us for this violence because of its identification of technology with evolution, and the identification of evolution with movement of the race to higher and higher morality. Such a doctrine could not understand that an expanding technological society is going to be an imperialist society even when it is run by governments who talk and sometimes act the language of welfare both domestically and internationally. Among advanced liberals, this failure was compounded by the naïve account in

Marxism of imperialism as simply a product of late capitalism. In the case of the American empire, the vulgarity of the analysis can be seen in the assessments of the presidency of F. D. Roosevelt. The "right" wing has accused him of being soft about American interests at Yalta; the "left" wing has seen him as a lover of humanity whose untimely death prevented him from stopping the cold war and building a world based on the principles of the United Nations. In fact, under his presidency, the U.S. at last moved fully into the imperial role for which its dominant classes had been preparing since John Hay. Our modern way of looking at the world hides from us the reality of many political things; but about nothing is it more obscuring than the inevitable relation between dynamic technology and imperialism.

Of course, what has happened in our immediate era is that the nonwestern nations have taken on western means both technical and ideological, as the only way to preserve themselves against the West. They now move from being simply the sufferers of western dynamism to having an active imperialist role of their own. Indeed Russian and Chinese imperialism present an undoubted challenge to the West. There is equal distortion in the rhetoric of those who see the American empire as the sole source of violence in the world and in the rhetoric of those who see an essentially peaceful western world defending itself against communism. Modern imperialism—with all its ideological and technical resources—may have been invented in the West, but it is not now confined to it.

To live in a world of these violent empires, and in a satellite of the greatest of them, presents complex problems of morality. These problems may be stated thus. In human life there must always be place for love of the good and love of one's own. Love of the good is man's highest end, but it is of the nature of things that we come to know and to love what is good by first meeting it in that which is our own—this particular body, this family, these friends, this woman, this part of the world, this set of traditions, this country, this civilisation. At the simplest level of one's own body, it is clear that one has to love it yet pass beyond concentration on it. To grow up properly is not to be alienated from one's own body; but an adult who does not pay reverence to anything beyond his own body is a narcissist, and not a full human being. In many parts of our lives the two loves need never be in conflict. In loving our friends we are also loving the good. But sometimes the conflict becomes open. An obvious case in our era is those Germans who had to oppose their own country in the name of the good. I have known many noble Jewish and Christian Germans who were torn apart because no country but Germany could really be their own, yet they could no longer love it because of their love of the good.

This is why the present happenings in Vietnam are particularly terrible for Canadians. What is being done there is being done by a society which is in some deep way our own. It is being done by a society which more than any other carries the destiny of the West, and Canadians belong inevitably to that destiny. Canada could only continue to be if we could hold some alternative social vision to that of the great republic. Yet such an alternative would have had to come out of the same stream— western culture. Indeed our failure to find such an alternative is bound up with the very homogenising path of western history. So we are left with the fact. As the U.S. becomes daily more our own, so does the Vietnam war.

The majority of North Americans do not seem to believe that love of their own and love of the good are exposed to stringent conflict in Vietnam. They assume that the structure of our society is essentially good, that it requires to be defended against aggression, and that it is against aggression that the American troops are engaged in Vietnam. They are either not much concerned with the actual history of the conflict, or else have been convinced by propaganda that there is a gallant country, South Vietnam, which is defending itself from aggression with American help. When a more explicit ideology is sought, the position becomes divided at one particular point. Are we to fear the Vietnamese and beyond them the Chinese because they are non-western, or because they are communist? Is it the old Europocentric fear of the Asian hordes under Asian tyranny as a threat to the freedom and right which belong essentially to the West? Or is it because the Asians have taken on communism that they are to be feared? It is not easy to hold these two positions together for the reason that Marxism is an advanced product of the West which appealed to British industry, French revolutionary ideas and German philosophy. Of course many people in North America no longer appeal to any ideology beyond our affluence. They take the line that it's either them or us, and this position is wrapped up in Darwinian packaging which says that any means are permissible that allow us to protect our own.

For a minority, the events in Vietnam must help to push them over that great divide where one can no longer love one's own—where indeed it almost ceases to be one's own. Vietnam is a glaring searchlight exposing the very structure of the imperial society. Even if hopefully the violence there should ease off, the searchlight has still been cast on the structure. We can never be as we were, because what has been done has been done. Some could see the structure of that society before the last years, but Vietnam has been for many the means to a clearer analysis. It has had this result because here are obvious facts which cannot be accounted for within the usual liberal description by which the society is legitimised to its own members and to the world.

Many liberals who do not find the events in Vietnam easy to stomach sometimes talk as if what were happening there were some kind of accident—if only that Texan had not got into the White House, etc., etc. Such a way of thinking is worthy only of journalists. Let us suppose that the American ruling class (through either of its political instruments) comes to see more clearly what a tactical error it has made in Vietnam and allows the war to tail off. It still governs the most powerful empire in the history of the world. It may learn to carry out its policies (e.g., in South America) more effectively and without such open brutalities. But it will have to have its Vietnams if the occasions demand, and we will have to be part of them. A profounder liberal criticism is made by those who say that the health of the western empire is shown by the extent of dissent against war. They maintain that only the traditions of the West make such dissent possible and that that possibility shows us the essential goodness of liberal society. This argument turns on a judgement of fact—an extremely difficult one. Does this dissent in the West present a real alternative of action, or is it simply froth on the surface which is necessary to the system itself as a safety valve? I am not sure. I lean to the position that dissent on major questions of policy is impotent and that the western system has in truth achieved what Michels called "the bureaucratising of dissent."[5]

The word "alienation" has become a cliché to be thrown about in journalistic chitchat. Surely the deepest alienation must be when the civilisation one inhabits no longer claims one's loyalty. It is a rational alienation, and therefore not to be overcome by opting out of the system through such methods as LSD and speed. The ecstasy therein offered is just another package which one buys from the system and which keeps people quiet. Indeed the depth of the alienation is seen in the ambiguity of the words "one's own." To repeat, the events in Vietnam push one towards that divide where one can no longer love one's own—to the point where the civilization almost ceases to be one's own. Yet it is impossible to give up the word "almost." Think of being the parent or the child of a concentration camp guard. One would want to say: "This person is not my own," and yet one could not. The facts of birth are inescapable. So are the very facts of belonging to the civilisation that has made one. It is this inevitability which leads to the degree of alienation and disgust which some people feel in the present situation.

There is a distinction between those who in their alienation find political hope in loyalty to one of the other empires, and those who cannot find such an alternative. Sartre, for example, takes part in politics, but he takes part in it as seeking the victory of the eastern empires, and is able to do so because of the freedom granted him in the western world. Which of these two positions is more adequate turns on the following question of fact: whether the qualities common to technological empires are more fundamental than their differences. This is not the place to discuss that extremely difficult question. It is clear, however, that the person who says "no" to his own and cannot substitute a hope in some other empire is in a position of much profounder alienation than those who can put their political trust elsewhere.

A similar difference in alienation will be found between those who place expectation in changing our society by reform or revolution and those who do not. Those, such as myself, who think that the drive for radical change in this society tends only to harden the very directions the society is already taking, and who think of the source of revolutionary fervour as arising finally from a further extension of the very modernity which has brought us where we are, inevitably find it more difficult to know how to live in this society than those who have expectations from radical activity.

Some people, particularly some of the young, will say that I have used a lot of words about the obvious. They may say that they have known since they began to think that this society is quite absurd and that sanity requires one to be either indifferent or hostile to it. Why write so long about what is so evident? However, finding that one is hostile or indifferent to a society may be a necessary discovery, but it is always an emasculating one. Man is by nature a political animal and to know that citizenship is an impossibility is to be cut off from one of the highest forms of life. To retreat from loyalty to one's own has the exhilaration of rebellion, but rebellion cannot be the basis for a whole life. Like all civilisations the West is based on a great religion—the religion of progress. This is the belief that the conquest of human and non-human nature will give existence meaning. Western civilisation is now universal so that this religion is nearly everywhere dominant. To question the dominant world religion is indeed to invite an alienation far greater than the simply political.

Nothing here written implies that the increasingly difficult job of preserving what is left of Canadian sovereignty is not worth the efforts of practical men. However disgraceful has been our complicity in the Vietnam War, however disgusting the wealth we have made from munitions for that war, one must still be glad that Canadian forces are not fighting there. This is due to what little sovereignty we still possess. So equally our non-involvement in the imperial adventures elsewhere will continue to depend on the possible maintenance of some waning sovereignty. But what lies behind the small practical question of Canadian nationalism is the larger context of the fate of western civilisation. By that fate I mean not merely the relations of our massive empire to the rest of the world, but even more the kind of existence which is becoming universal in advanced technological societies. What is worth doing in the midst of this barren twilight is the incredibly difficult question.

Notes

Originally published as "Canadian Fate and Imperialism," in *Technology and Empire*, by George Grant. Copyright © George Grant. Reprinted with permission of House of Anansi Press, Toronto.
1. This question is discussed at greater length in the first essay of this volume. [Here Grant refers to the first essay in his own book, *Technology and Empire*. The present text is the third essay from that volume. The first essay, "In Defense of North America," appears as the next selection in this reader.—Eds.] Prof. G. E. Wilson has rightly pointed out to me that in emphasizing the importance of the English in this history, I have underestimated the importance of the Dutch.
2. William Lyon Mackenzie King (1874–1950), tenth and longest-serving prime minister of Canada (1921–26, 1926–30, 1935–48).—Eds.
3. The reference here is to the forced conscription of French Canadians (the 1917 Conscription Crisis) by Sir Samuel Hughes, Canadian minister of militia and defense during World War I.—Eds.
4. The reference here is to the general and French president Charles de Gaulle, whose visit to the World Exposition in Montreal in 1967 stirred controversy. While speaking to a large crowd gathered at Montreal's City Hall on July 24, de Gaulle shouted, "Vive le Québec libre!" (Long live free Quebec!). De Gaulle's support for Quebec's sovereignty movement was made even clearer when he left Canada without conducting an official state visit to Ottawa, returning to France from Montreal.—Eds.
5. Since this was written some of the evidence is in. Clearly the dissent over the war in the U.S. had some effect on some decisions. It was not only the difficulty of winning

the war which convinced the ruling class that the enterprise was a mistake, but also that too many of the influential young were being alienated from the purposes of the society by it. The dissent made this clear. No ruling class could afford to neglect such a circumstance particularly when its society was faced at the same time by a major racial crisis. But it would be wrong to carry the consequences too far. The Democratic party was punished by losing the presidency—but not by the dissenters, rather by the settled and unsettled bourgeois. Dissent was able to expose the folly of defending the imperial interests in such a misguided way in Vietnam. But it cannot be effective in turning the U.S. from its course as a great imperial power.

GEORGE GRANT

In Defence of North America

To exist as a North American is an amazing and enthralling fate. As in every historical condition, some not only have to live their fate, but also to let it come to be thought. What we have built and become in so short a time calls forth amazement in the face of its novelty, an amazement which leads to that thinking. Yet the very dynamism of the novelty enthralls us to inhibit that thinking.

It is not necessary to take sides in the argument between the ancients and moderns as to what is novelty, to recognize that we live in novelty of some kind. Western technical achievement has shaped a different civilisation from any previous, and we North Americans are the most advanced in that achievement. This achievement is not something simply external to us, as so many people envision it. It is not merely an external environment which we make and choose to use as we want—a playground in which we are able to do more and more, an orchard where we can always pick variegated fruit. It moulds us in what we are, not only at the heart of our animality in the propagation and continuance of our species, but in our actions and thoughts and imaginings. Its pursuit has become our dominant activity and that dominance fashions both the public and private realms. Through that achievement we have become the heartland of the wealthiest and most powerful empire that has yet been. We can exert our influence over a greater extent of the globe and take a greater tribute of wealth than any previously. Despite our limitations and miscalculations, we have more compelling means than any previous for putting the brand of our civilisation deeply into the flesh of others.

To have become so quickly the imperial centre of an increasingly realised technological civilisation would be bewildering for any human beings, but for North Americans particularly so. From our beginnings there has been an ambiguity for us as to who we are. To the Asians as they suffer from us, we must appear the latest wave of dominating Europeans who spread their ways around the world, claiming that those ways were not simply another civilisation, but the highest so far, and whose claim was justified in the fact of power, namely that it could only be countered by Asians who accepted the very forms which threatened them. To the Europeans also we appear spawned by themselves: the children of some low-class servants who once dared to leave the household and who now surprisingly appear as powerful and dominating neighbours masquerading as gentry, whose threat can only be minimised by teaching them a little culture. They express contempt of us as a society barren of anything but the drive to technology; yet their contempt is too obviously permeated with envy to be taken as pure.

In one sense both the Asians and Europeans are correct. Except for the community of the children of the slaves and the few Indians we have allowed just to survive, we are indeed Europeans. Imperially we turn out to the rest of the world bringing the apogee of what Europeans first invented, technological civilisation. Our first ways, in terms of which we met the new land, came with us from Europe and we have always used our continuing contact with the unfolding of that civilisation. To this day many of our shallow intellectual streams are kept flowing by their rain. It was exiled Europeans with the new physical theory who provided us with our first uses of atomic energy. Our new social science may fit us so perfectly as to seem indigenous; but behind Parsons is Weber, behind Skinner, Pavlov, behind social work and psychiatry, Freud. Even in seeking some hope against the inhuman imperial system and some less sterile ground of political morality than a liberalism become the end of ideology, many of the most beautiful young turn for their humanism to so European a thinker as Marcuse. In a field as un-American as theology, the continually changing ripples of thought, by which the professionals hope to revive a dying faith, originate from some stone dropped by a European thinker.

Yet those who know themselves to be North Americans know they are not Europeans. The platitude cannot be too often stated that the U.S. is the only society which has no history (truly its own) from before the age of progress. English-speaking Canadians, such as myself, have despised and feared the Americans for the account of freedom in which their independence was expressed, and have resented that other traditions of the English-speaking world should have collapsed before the victory of that spirit; but we are still enfolded with the Americans in the deep sharing of having crossed the ocean and conquered the new land. All of us who came made some break in that coming. The break was not only the giving up of the old and the settled, but the entering into the majestic continent which could not be ours in the way that the old had been. It could not be ours in the old way because the making of it ours did not go back before the beginning of conscious memory. The roots of some communities in eastern North America go back far in continuous love for their place, but none of us can be called autochthonous, because in all there is some consciousness of making the land our own. It could not be ours also because the very intractability, immensity and extremes of the new land required that its meeting with mastering Europeans be a battle of subjugation. And after that battle we had no long history of living with the land before the arrival of the new forms of conquest which came with industrialism.

That conquering relation to place has left its mark within us. When we go into the Rockies we may have the sense that gods are there. But if so, they cannot manifest themselves to us as ours. They are the gods of another race, and we cannot know them because of what we are, and what we did. There can be nothing immemorial for us except the environment as object. Even our cities have been encampments on the road to economic mastery.

[. . .]

The fact that such men[1] have so often been the shock troops of the English-speaking world's mastery of human and non-human nature lay not simply in the absence of a doctrine of nature into which vacuum came the Hobbesian account of nature (so that when revelation was gone all that was left was that account) but also in the positive content of their extraordinary form of Christianity. The absence of natural theology and liturgical comforts left the lonely soul face to face with the transcendent (and therefore elusive) will of God. This will had to be sought and served not through our contemplations but directly through our practice. From the solitude and uncertainty of that position came the responsibility which could find no rest. That unappeasable responsibility gave an extraordinary sense of the self as radical freedom so paradoxically experienced within the predestinarian theological context. The external world was unimportant and indeterminate stuff (even when it was our own bodies) as compared with the soul's ambiguous encounter with the transcendent. What did the body matter; it was an instrument to be brought into submission so that it could serve this restless righteousness. Where the ordinary Catholic might restrain the body within a corporatively ordained tradition of a liturgy rhythmic in its changes between control and release, the Protestant had solitary responsibility all the time to impose the restraint. When one contemplates the conquest of nature by technology one must remember that that conquest had to include our own bodies. Calvinism provided the determined and organised men and women who could rule the mastered world. The punishment they inflicted on non-human nature, they had first inflicted on themselves.

Now when from that primal has come forth what is present before us; when the victory over the land leaves most of us in metropoloi, where widely spread consumption vies with confusion and squalor; when the emancipation of greed turns out from its victories on this continent to feed imperially on the resources of the world; when those resources cushion an immense majority who think they are free in pluralism, but in fact live in a monistic vulgarity in which nobility and wisdom have been exchanged for a pale belief in progress, alternating with boredom and weariness of spirit; when the disciplined among us drive to an unlimited technological future, in which technical reason has become so universal that it has closed down on openness and awe, questioning and listening; when Protestant subjectivity remains authentic only where it is least appropriate, in the moodiness of our art and sexuality, and where public religion has become an unimportant litany of objectified self-righteousness necessary for the more anal of our managers; one must remember now the hope, the stringency and nobility of that primal encounter. The land was almost indomitable. The intense seasons of the continental heartland needed a people who whatever else were not flaccid. And these people not only forced commodities from the land, but built public and private institutions of freedom and flexibility and endurance. Even when we fear General Motors or ridicule our immersion in the means of mobility, we must not forget that the gasoline engine was a need-filled fate for those who had to live in such winters and across such distances. The Marxists who have described the conquest of the continent as an example of capitalist rape miss the substance of those events, as an incarnation of hope and equality which the settlers had not found in Europe. Whatever the vulgarity of mass industrialism, however empty our talk of democracy, it must not be forgotten that in that primal there was the expectation of a new independence in which each would be free for self-legislation, and for communal legislation. Despite the exclusion of the African, despite the struggles of the later immigrant groups, the faith and institutions of that primal encounter were great enough to bring into themselves countless alien traditions and make these loyal to that spirit.

To know that parents had to force the instincts of their children to the service of pioneering control; to have seen the pained and unrelenting faces of the women; to know, even in one's flesh and dreams, the results of generations of the mechanising of the body; to see all around one the excesses and follies now necessary to people who can win back the body only through sexuality, must not be to forget what was necessary and what was heroic in that conquest.

Now when Calvinism and the pioneering moment have both gone, that primal still shapes us. It shapes us above all as the omnipresence of that practicality which trusts in technology to create the rationalised kingdom of man. Other men, communists and national socialists, have also seen that now is the moment when man is at last master of the planet, but our origins have left us with a driving practical optimism which fitted us to welcome an unlimited modernity. We have had a practical optimism which had discarded awe and was able to hold back anguish and so produce those crisp rationalised managers, who are the first necessity of the kingdom of man. Those uncontemplative, and un-flinching wills, without which technological society cannot exist, were shaped from the crucible of pioneering Protestant liberalism. And still among many, secularised Christianity maintains itself in the rhetoric of good will and democratic possibilities and in the belief that universal technical education can be kind, etcetera, etcetera. Santayana's remark that there is a difference between Catholic and Protestant atheism ap-plies equally to liberalism; ours is filled with the remnantal echoes of Calvinism. Our belief in progress may not be as religiously defined as the Marxist, but it has a freedom and flexibility about it which puts nothing theoretical in the way of our drive towards it (or in other words as the clever now say, it is the end of ideology). In short our very primal allowed us to give open welcome to the core of the twentieth century—the un-limited mastery of men by men.

It may be argued that other later arrivals from Europe have so placed their stamp on North America as to have changed in essence what could come from that primal. But obvious facts about the power of Catholi-cism in our politics, or the influence of Jews in communications and intellectual life, or the unexpected power for continuance shown by ethnic communities, mean only that recent traditions have coloured the central current of the American dream. The effectiveness of Catholics in politics remains long after its origins in urban immigrant needs, but from the very beginning successful Catholic politicians have been par-ticularly dutiful towards institutions, customs and rhetoric which had been made by others before their arrival, and made from traditions utterly different from their own. In so far as Catholic contemplation ever crossed the ocean, it has been peripheral. Today when Catholics desiring to embrace the modern open themselves directly to the public liberalism, it looks as if even the few poor remnants of contemplation will die. For all the closeness of Jews to the American dream, it would be degrading to Judaism to say that it has been able to express its riches in American culture when the chief public contribution of Jews has been the packaged entertainment of Broadway and Hollywood, the shallow coteries of intellectual New York. As for pluralism, differences in the technological state are able to exist only in private activities: how we eat; how we mate; how we practise ceremonies. Some like pizza, some like steaks; some like girls, some like boys; some like synagogue, some like the mass. But we all do it in churches, motels, restaurants indistinguishable from the Atlantic to the Pacific.

Even as the fissures in the system become apparent, leading its enemies to underestimate its ability to be the leader in modernity, our primal spirit still partially survives to give our society its continuing dynamism. The ruthlessness and banal callousness of what has been done in Vietnam might lead one to see North American events as solely self-interested nihilism of a greedy technological empire. But such an interpretation would not be sufficient to the reality. It must be remembered that the exigencies of imperialism have to be justified to the public (particularly to the second-order managers) under the banner of freedom and a liberating modernisation. When they cannot there is widespread protest of a kind that never existed during the European depredations in the non-European world. The Vietnam war is disliked not only because it is obviously a tactical blunder; nor only because most of us are "last men" too comfortable to fight for the imperial power that buttresses that comfort; nor, simplistically, is it that television filters some of the ferocity to our living rooms; but also because the central dream still publicly holds, that North America stands for the future of hope, a people of good will bringing the liberation of progress to the world. The exigencies of violence necessary to our empire will increasingly make mockery of the rhetoric of that dream. The lineaments of our imperialism are less and less able to be dressed up in the language of liberal idealism to make them seem more than the affluence and power of the northern hemisphere. Nevertheless, as of now, the belief that America is the moral leader of the world through modernisation still sustains even the most banal and ruthless of our managers.

At home the ruling managers move "towards the year 2000." It might seem here that the practical primal has become no more than the unalloyed drive to technological mastery for its own sake. It is this interpretation which allows certain Europeans to consider us a wasteland with nothing seriously human amongst us but that self-propelling will to technology. But this interpretation underestimates the very effectiveness of North America in the world, in its forgetting that it is men who make that drive. What makes the drive to technology so strong is that it is carried on by men who still identify what they are doing with the liberation of mankind. Our ruling managers are able to do what they do just because among sufficient of them technology and liberalism support each other as identified. It is this identification which makes our drive to technology still more dynamic than the nihilistic will to will which is emptied of all conceptions of purpose. It may be (to use the indicative would be claiming to have grasped the very heart of what is) that this drive to practicality moves to become little more than a will to mastery governing the vacuous masses. But that is not yet how we understand our present. The identification in our practicality of masterful interference and the building of a human world still filters through the manifold structures of managerial and scientific elites to be the governing faith of the society. All political arguments within the system, the squalls on the surface of the ocean (for example that about the rights of property in relation to the common good, between the freedom for some and the freedom for all) take place within the common framework that the highest good is North America moving forward in expansionist practicality. To think outside this faith is to make oneself a stranger to the public realm.

Indeed the technological society is not for most North Americans, at least at the level of consciousness, a "terra incognita" into which we must move with hesitation, moderation and in wonder, but a comprehended promised land which we have discovered by the use of calculating reason and which we can ever more completely inherit by the continued use of calculation. Man has at last come of age in the evolutionary process, has taken his fate into his own hands and is freeing himself for happiness against the old necessities of hunger and disease and overwork, and the consequent oppressions and repressions. The conditions of nature—that "otherness"—which so long enslaved us, when they appeared as a series of unknown forces, are now at last beginning to be understood in their workings so that they can serve our freedom. The era of our planetary domination dawns; and beyond that? That this is obviously good can be seen in the fact that we are able to do what we never could and prevent what we have never before prevented. Existence is easier, freer and more exciting. We have within our grasp the conquest of the problem of work-energy; the ability to keep ourselves functioning well through long spans of life and above all the overcoming of old prejudices and the discovery of new experiences, so that we will be able to run our societies with fewer oppressive authorities and repressive taboos.

To such comprehension the technological society is only in detail a terra incognita, as in its rushing change new problems arise which cannot always be predicted in advance. We therefore require the clearest minds to predict by understanding those which are on the horizon and to sort them out by calculation with courage. As we move "towards the year 2000" we need all the institutes of urban studies and of race relations, all the centres of economic development and psychological adjustment we can get. We will have to see how cities need not set affluence and squalor, private competence and public disorganization against each other; how all can reach a level of educational competence to inherit the hope; how the young can be shown purpose in the midst of enormous bureaucracies; how banality need not be incumbent on mass culture; how neuroses and psychoses, which are so immediately destructive when power is great, can be overcome by new understandings of psychology and sociology, etcetera, etcetera. Add to these the international problems of how underdeveloped countries can be brought to share in the new possibilities by accepting the conditions of modernisation, how the greed of already modern societies does not hold the others in slavery, how mass breeding with modern medicine does not overwhelm them and us before modernisation can be accomplished, above all how the new military techniques do not explode us all before we have reached an internationalism appropriate to the age of reason. But these are difficulties of detail, requiring our best calculation to avoid, but not vitiating intrinsically the vision of the technological society as a supreme step in our liberation. Behind them lies the comprehension of this great experiment in the minds of our dominant majority as self-evidently good, that for which man has struggled in evolution since his origins in pain and chance, ignorance and taboo.[2]

Indeed the loud differences in the public world—what in a simpler-minded nineteenth-century Europe could be described as the divisions between left and right—are carried on within this fundamental faith. The directors of General Motors and the followers of Professor Marcuse sail down the same river in different boats. This is not to say anything as jejune as to deny the obvious fact that our technological society develops within a state capitalist framework and that that will have significant effect on what we are and what we will become, particularly in relation to other technological societies developed under other structures. But amid the conflict of public ideologies it is well to remember that all live within a common horizon. Those of the "right," who stand by the freedoms of the individual to hold property and for firmer enforcement of our present laws, seem to have hesitation about some of the consequences of modernity, but they do not doubt the central fact of the North American dream—progress through technological advance. It may be indeed that, like most of us, the "right" want it both ways. They want to maintain certain moral customs, freedoms of property and even racial rights which are not in fact compatible with advancing technological civilisation. Be that as it may, the North American "right" believes firmly in technical advance. Indeed its claim is that in the past the mixture of individualism and public order it has espoused has been responsible for the triumphs of technique in our society.[3]

Equally those of the "left" who have condemned our social arrangements and worked most actively to change them have based their condemnation in both the 1930s and 1960s on some species of Marxism. This is to appeal to the redemptive possibilities of technology and to deny contemplation in the name of changing the world. Indeed domestic Marxists have been able as a minority to concentrate on the libertarian and Utopian expectations in their doctrines because unlike the Marxists of the East they could leave the requirements of public order to others. But, however libertarian the notions of the new left, they are always thought within the control of nature achieved by modern techniques. The liberation of human beings assumes the ease of an environment where nature has already been conquered. For example, at the libertarian height of Professor Marcuse's writings (*Eros and Civilization*), he maintains that men having achieved freedom against a constraining nature can now live in the liberation of a polymorphous sexuality. The orgiastic gnosticism there preached always assumes that the possibilities of liberation depend on the maintenance of our high degrees of conquest. Having first conquered nature we can now enjoy her. His later *One Dimensional Man* is sadder in its expectations from our present situation, but technology is still simplistically described and blessed, as long as it is mixed with the pursuit of art, kind sexuality and a dash of Whiteheadian metaphysics.

Even the root and branch condemnation of the system by some of the politicised young assumes the opportunities for widespread instant satisfaction which are only possible in terms of the modern achievements. They want both high standards of spontaneous democracy and the egalitarian benefits accruing from technique. But have not the very forms of the bureaucratic institutions been developed as necessary for producing those benefits? Can the benefits exist without the stifling institutions? Can such institutions exist as participatory democracies? To say yes to these questions with any degree of awareness requires the recognition of the fact that the admired spontaneity of freedom is made feasible by the conquering of the spontaneity of nature. In this sense their rejection of their society is not root and branch. They share, with those who appear to them as enemies, the deeper assumptions which have made the technological society.

Indeed the fact that progress in techniques is the horizon for us is seen even in the humane stance of those who seek some overreaching vision of human good in terms of which the use of particular techniques might be decided. Who would deny that there are many North Americans who accept the obvious benefits of modern technique but who also desire to maintain firm social judgement about each particular method in the light of some decent vision of human good? Such judgements are widely attempted in obvious cases, such as military techniques, where most men still ask whether certain employments can ever serve good. (This is even so in a continent whose government is the only one so far to have used nuclear weapons in warfare.) At a less obvious level, there are still many who ask questions about particular techniques of government planning and their potency for tyranny. Beyond this again there are a smaller number who raise questions about new biochemical methods and their relation to the propagation of the race. As the possible harm from any new technique is less evident, the number of questioners get fewer. This position is the obvious one by which a multitude of sensible and responsible people try to come to terms with immediate exigencies. Nevertheless, the grave difficulty of thinking a position in which technique is beheld within a horizon greater than itself, stems from the very nature of our primal, and must be recognized.

That difficulty is present for us because of the following fact: when we seek to elucidate the standards of human good (or in contemporary language "the values") by which particular techniques can be judged, we do so within modern ways of thought and belief. But from the very beginnings of modern thought the new natural science and the new moral science developed together in mutual interdependence so that the fundamental assumptions of each were formulated in the light of the other. Modern thought is in that sense a unified fate for us. The belief in the mastering knowledge of human and non-human beings arose together with the very way we conceive our humanity as an Archimedean freedom outside nature, so that we can creatively will to shape the world to our values. The decent bureaucrats, the concerned thinkers and the thoughtful citizens as much conceive their task as creatively willing to shape the world to their values as do the corporate despots, the motivations experts and the manipulative politicians. The moral discourse of "values" and "freedom" is not independent of the will to technology, but a language fashioned in the same forge together with the will to technology. To try to think them separately is to move more deeply into their common origin.

Moreover, when we use this language of "freedom" and "values" to ask seriously what substantive "values" our freedom should create, it is clear that such values cannot be discovered in "nature" because in the light of modern science nature is objectively conceived as indifferent to value. (Every sophomore who studies philosophy in the English-speaking world is able to disprove "the naturalistic fallacy," namely, that statements about what ought to be cannot be inferred solely from statements about what is.) Where then does our freedom to create values find its content? When that belief in freedom expresses itself seriously (that is politically and not simply as a doctrine of individual fulfilment) the content of man's freedom becomes the actualising of freedom for all men. The purpose of action becomes the building of the universal and homogenous state—the society in which all men are free and equal and increasingly able to realise their concrete individuality. Indeed this is the governing goal of ethical striving, as much in the modernising east as in the west. Despite the continuing power in North America of the right of individuals to highly comfortable and dominating self-preservation through the control of property, and in the communist bloc the continuing exaltation of the general will against all individual and national rights, the rival empires agree in their public testimonies as to what is the goal of human striving.

Such a goal of moral striving is (it must be repeated) inextricably bound up with the pursuit of those sciences which issue in the mastery of human and non-human nature. The drive to the overcoming of chance which has been the motive force behind the developers of modern technique did not come to be accidentally, as a clever way of dealing with the external world, but as one part of a way of thought about the whole and what is worth doing in it. At the same time the goal of freedom was formulated within the light of this potential overcoming of chance. Today this unity between the overcoming and the goal is increasingly actualised in the situations of the contemporary world. As we push towards the goal we envisage, our need of technology for its realisation becomes ever more pressing. If all men are to become free and equal within the enormous institutions necessary to technology, then the overcoming of chance must be more and more rigorously pursued and applied—particularly that overcoming of chance among human beings which we expect through the development of the modern social sciences.

The difficulty then of those who seek substantive values by which to judge particular techniques is that they must generally think of such values within the massive assumptions of modern thought. Indeed even to think "values" at all is to be within such assumptions. But the goal of modern moral striving—the building of free and equal human beings— leads inevitably back to a trust in the expansion of that very technology we are attempting to judge. The unfolding of modern society has not only required the criticism of all older standards of human excellence, but has also at its heart that trust in the overcoming of chance which leads us back to judge every human situation as being solvable in terms of technology. As moderns we have no standards by which to judge particular techniques, except standards welling up with our faith in technical expansion. To describe this situation as a difficulty implies that it is no inevitable historicist predicament. It is to say that its overcoming could only be achieved by living in the full light of its presence.

Indeed the situation of liberalism in which it is increasingly difficult for our freedom to have any content by which to judge techniques except in their own terms is present in all advanced industrial countries. But it is particularly pressing for us because our tradition of liberalism was moulded from practicality. Because the encounter of the land with the Protestants was the primal for us, we never inherited much that was at the heart of western Europe. This is not to express the foolish position that we are a species of Europeans-minus. It is clear that in our existing here we have become something which is more than European—something which by their lack of it Europeans find difficult to understand. Be that as it may, it is also clear that the very nature of the primal for us meant that we did not bring with us from Europe the tradition of contemplation. To say *contemplation* "tout court" is to speak as if we lacked some activity which the Ford Foundation could make good by proper grants to the proper organisations. To say *philosophy* rather than contemplation might be to identify what is absent for us with an academic study which is pursued here under that name. Nevertheless, it may perhaps be said negatively that what has been absent for us is the affirmation of a possible apprehension of the world beyond that as a field of objects considered as pragmata—an apprehension present not only in its height as "theory" but as the undergirding of our loves and friendships, of our arts and reverences, and indeed as the setting for our dealing with the objects of the human and non-human world. Perhaps we are lacking the recognition that our response to the whole should not most deeply be that of doing, nor even that of terror and anguish, but that of wondering or marveling at what is, being amazed or astonished by it, or perhaps best, in a discarded English usage, admiring it; and that such a stance, as beyond all bargains and conveniences, is the only source from which purposes may be manifest to us for our necessary calculating.

Notes

Originally published as "In Defence of North America," in *Technology and Empire*, by George Grant. Copyright © George Grant. Reprinted with permission of House of Anansi Press, Toronto.

1. The "men" to whom Grant refers are John Locke, Benjamin Franklin, and other thinkers who bent Protestant ethos toward a modern view of the world—Locke by making Thomas Hobbes's view of nature "acceptable to a still pious bourgeoisie," and Franklin through the "practical drive of his science," which nevertheless maintained "public virtues." See Grant, "In Defense of North America," in *Technology and Empire* (Toronto: Anansi, 1969), 22–23.—Eds.

2. As is true of all faiths, this dominating modern faith has many different expressions of itself. Some of these formulations put forward a rather low and superficial view of what it is to be human, for example those of Daniel Bell or Marion Levy in the U.S. or that of Edmund Leach in the U.K. These formulations must not lead to the Hermeneutical error of judging the truth of the faith from the crassness of a particular formulation. This would be as fair as judging the truth of Christianity from the writings of its most foolish theologians. The same modern faith has been expounded thoughtfully by many; by liberals, both positivist or existentialist, by Marxists, by Christians and by Jews.

3. I use the term "right" because I have written elsewhere of the impossibility of political conservatism in an era committed to rapid technological advance. See *Lament for a Nation* (Princeton, N.J.: Van Nostrand, 1965), 66–67. The absurdity of the journalistic use of the word "conservative" was seen in the reporting of the recent invasion of Czechoslovakia when the term "conservative" was widely applied to the pro-Russian Czech communist leaders.

FERNAND DUMONT

TRANSLATED BY SHEILA FISCHMAN AND RICHARD HOWARD

Of a Hesitant Quebec

Fernand Dumont (1927–97) is one of the most important intellectuals to emerge from Quebec. A major figure in the field of sociology, Dumont published over twenty books during his career, including academic works, poetry (L'ange du matin [1952], La part de l'ombre [1996]), and his memoirs (Récit d'une immigration [1997]). He received an M.A. from Laval University, a Ph.D. in sociology from the Sorbonne (1967), and a second Ph.D. in theology from Laval (1987). Dumont was appointed a professor at Laval in 1955 and spent his career at the university.

Dumont wrote on a wide range of subjects, including sociology, theology and religion, culture, literature, education, and even economics (his La dialectique de l'objet économique [1970] includes a preface by Lucien Goldmann). However, the complex situation of Quebec society was a special focus of his work. Some of these works include the multivolume collective project Idéologies au Canada français (1971–81), La vigile du Québec, Octobre 1970 (1971), and Genèse de la société québécoise (1993). The excerpts here are taken from the English translation of La vigile du Québec, which addresses the political and social fallout of the 1970 October Crisis.

Dumont was the founding president of the Institut Québécois de Recherche sur la Culture (1979–90). He is an officer of the Order of Quebec (1992).

At first sight, we ought to make some kind of survey of the history of French Canada, either to trace out a particular route taken by freedom or to map or describe the obstacles in its way.[1] In doing this in so little space, one could only reveal one's prejudices and pin down with a handful of vague historical reminiscences the more or less arbitrary choices we are now making. On the other hand, it is not at all clear that we have to involve the past in any debate on freedom. I have the strong impression that, for many men of action among us, the appeal to history seems a useless detour. They are all the more entitled to this reaction in that, apart from national political action defined in terms of very formal democracy, our historiography conjures up scarcely any real capability to inspire action among people of today.

I would like, then, to raise the anterior question. Why is our history connected with our present activity, and does our history bring to us the very basis of our struggle for liberty? Or, if you wish, what purpose can our history serve for those members of our society in some sector of our collective life who are trying to instill there certain values, spiritual or economic, intellectual or political, and whose work must feature the promotion of liberty as one of the supreme values? To find an answer we shall have to make a brief detour.

In broad sectors of French Canada we are seeing a ferment of liberty. At the personal level, each person gets along with freedom: he makes a coherent adventure of it or else a discontinuous chain of caprice. Yet as soon as liberty is experienced inside a commitment, as soon as it is to be installed in collectivities and institutions, we are looking for social movements and organizations able to uphold their real aims of liberation.

In the present state of our collectivity, what are these social movements and organizations? They might be classified into four main groups:

1. The trade union movement must occupy a place of privilege. It was certainly born of problems specific to our milieu, those we refer to habitually when we speak of industrialization. Here it takes on polyvalent functions: given our society's deficiencies, the union movement was led to give a voice to those who, though not workers, were unsatisfied with the conditions of social and political stagnation. That helped make the trade union movement a characteristic element of our collective life. Moreover, it has no *official* source in any of our traditions: it would not be difficult to show that nationalism—that of Henri Bourassa,[2] for example —failed for a long time to recognize the unique quality of the trade union phenomenon. And the polyvalence we spoke of has limits: the union movement is too far from some social situations to give everyone a concrete rootedness. For some of us who are intellectuals, is not scoring the worker's struggles with rhetoric the substitute for a spiritual tradition that does not exist, or that we are not aware of in our own fields?

2. There are other associations, old or new, seeking coherent objectives. If we compare our milieu in this regard to others (American society, for instance), we realize that voluntary associations are relatively rare here. No doubt we are still tied to neighbourhood and family relations: we use a good many traditional patterns that make us think it inappropriate to invent new ones.

3. Opposition political parties or movements are looking for a very formal kind of democracy, in other words for a liberty whose content is poorly defined. In this connection many ask the question, "Democracy—what for?" They then inevitably challenge the special significance of our milieu and its traditional values.

4. A few rare socialist currents are emerging hesitantly. One does not belittle them by noting that the great part of our population does not consider them their own and sees them as a kind of import. It seems incontrovertible that socialism has not been given the kind of colouring here that would let it put down roots. It seems impossible—even more impossible than in the union movement—to locate traditional sources for a Quebec kind of socialism. It would be superficial, in fact, to couple our old nineteenth-century political or religious liberalism to it.

This very brief inventory leads me to the formulation of some provisional suggestions. We have now and will have in the future more institutions that can serve as arenas for the exercise of freedom. Some of these institutions are intimately connected in their origins with our problems (unions, voluntary associations, etc.), while others have been borrowed from foreign versions of more universal problems: such is the case with socialism. This does not mean, of course, that socialist institutions do not relate to our own situation. What is lacking in the ideologies and organizations offering a collective exercise in liberty is that men from our milieu cannot achieve self-recognition in them. We lack a clear image of ourselves in the light of liberty; we have no definition of liberty that can be absorbed by the society we are forming. Here we are far removed from episodic struggles for civil rights, but we are on a plane that is just as comprehensible, where talk of day-to-day liberty calls us jointly and severally to produce a definition of the collectivity where the struggle takes place, as well as a definition of the values to bring forward in the circumstances.

This is what each of us must have when he sets out to grope for the points of contact between his desire for commitment and history as it is taking place. At the same time, we may be isolating the malaise of a society that is failing to escape its own stagnation, despite the action of militants from milieux of the working-class, agriculture, the co-operative movement, certain areas of political action, or the university: for that society does not find self-recognition in this activity, nor can it find a formula to express its own self-awareness.

Where are we to find this definition of ourselves? Or rather how are we to invent it in unison with the groups in which we are involved?

It will not be in any immediacy of action, in any event. For then we would produce only a series of airy-fairy ideologies, such as exist among us now anyhow. Men who live by the moment always elude our own present in the most distressingly abstract manner; if it were possible for us to find our identity in these "immediate" labels, we would no doubt have done so in the years since they were first available.

In one sense the struggle for liberty means innovation, installing in the environment, near or distant, the values that are believed for themselves and liked also because they are new. The latter characteristic explains why so many of us talk about the "fad for novelty." The fad certainly exists, especially because here it finds no concrete pegs and so must become a kind of daydream. But we should remember too that novelty is inherent to values. Whether they be religious, political, or economic, values go beyond the immediate and the possible; he who has not heard the call to go beyond what is happening is not a bearer of values. Every struggle for values includes the struggle for liberty. In this sense, it is appropriate to refer to "our master the future."

But the future is not concrete. Utopia is made up from present and past. The "rational being," as our philosophy professors used appropriately to tell us, is made up of pieces borrowed from the real being. Counting only on visions of the future to justify the choices of today plunges us into the very abstractness we are attacking. We are too free of our anticipation for the future for it to appear as a collective image of society. A certain kind of Marxism very effectively illustrates the tyranny of obligatory images of the future. In our everyday commitments the "rational beings" must remain personal productions—as in poetry.

This leaves us with only one way to find what we are looking for, and that is to imagine a certain drawing back from immediacy while at the same time remaining within the continuation of life-experience. Such an approach would give meaning to a collective sharing in the goals of the future, and yet not amount to propaganda. We are left with our past. The history of our ancestors is solid ground for deciding what we are. The past, like the future, enables us to test this feeling of the possible which is inherent in values. But in the past this test is a concrete one, going to the core of events, without much possibility of escape from the collectivity into pseudo-Platonic universes. What we all feel deeply nostalgic about, both at times of doubt and at moments of exaltation, is that there is in our past a history of liberty. Without that invigorating self-knowledge which comes from it, our commitment can be only a delicate and uncertain personal aim or a search for opportunities. Such commitment is vacant and available like the liberty without content which waits every day for the morning paper before deciding what to be indignant about.

To grasp the profound importance of this history of liberty, it would be necessary to have felt something that does not occur very often in French Canada: how history leaps up at moments of crisis, when the immediate, the present, seizes one by the throat. One feels then the need for a certain distance, the need to retrieve a feeling of brotherhood with those who, in the past, foreshadowed our present fight. When France collapsed in 1940, the spirit of 1789, 1830, and the Commune were revived with a new, young face. The collectivities were then feeling what each of us feels when, in hard times, we look avidly for the continuity of our past, the reasons why our choices and our confusion are not arbitrary. "I write," said Bernanos, from his exile in Brazil and from the chaos of a conquered France, "I write for the child that I was."

We have never lacked historians. Half of French-Canadian literature is made up of historical works or novels inspired by our past. Our poetry itself, that traditional channel of liberty, has long been based on historical themes. However, our history often seems like an initial obstacle in the way of liberty, like the wrappings of an embalmed mummy from which we have to be disentangled. Some people have the impression that they are free when they cast off this weight of the past. Why is there this contradiction—our need for history and our oppression by it?

The demands of a history of liberty run up against a long-standing French-Canadian historiography with a unilateral interpretative bias. The stress on the 1760 conquest, an essential point in the explanation of our history and one that exasperates some of our historians today, is not a recent thing. It has inspired all our Canadian history textbooks and goes back to our first great historian. François-Xavier Garneau, moreover, had taken it from a European French historian, Augustin Thierry. When we look for our past, we find ourselves faced with a tradition of our historians, rather than a national tradition. Despite everything, whether Garneau borrowed the central pattern of his historical vision or not, the idea of the conquest appears to have arisen in response to the situation of his period, to the crucial problems being raised by his contemporaries. The anecdote claiming that he decided to write our history in response to an insult from an English-language colleague may be only a legend, but it is an excellent mythic representation of the period. For the bourgeois elite of which Garneau was a marginal member, history meant the history of the *nation*, the only true French-Canadian community.

But this community has fallen apart since the nineteenth century. Our environment has become industrialized. The towns have taken on a new look. A working class has arisen for whom the traditional deification of the peasant made very little sense. Imagine one of today's militant workers who, having acquired some historical awareness, might look for the memory of those of old who had fought battles like his own. In libraries or in Canadian history textbooks for the period that saw the rise of our proletariat, he would find information on the defence of "separate schools."

So we grew incapable of asking new questions of the past. Our state of evolution remained essentially that of the men of 1840, despite the steady accumulation of footnotes. It bears repeating that our society, mores, and problems are changing, and the gap widens between our self-definition as passed on by exasperated historians or textbooks which never change and what we have become by the shaping of events and the new urban environment. I see in this the basic secret of our collective malaise whenever we think about liberty. To be able to respond to new situations, our version of liberty finds it necessary to repudiate the past because it has become a burden, a thing that can be analysed and discussed from the outside, as though it did not belong to the consciousness of each one of us. This quality has been accentuated in recent years by some of our historians. The traditional treatment of the conquest has become a real childhood trauma: hence the pessimistic nature of this point of view. Through a kind of psychological corollary that is almost unavoidable, this history-as-thing is deterministic; "The historian is a seismography," in the words of one of our finest scholars. And here we are trapped when we try to know ourselves.

Our historiography has not completely pulled out of this tradition, taken in the anthropologist's sense. There is the persistent image of a "golden age," in this case the French regime; the idea of a determining factor, unique and almost inevitable, the conquest of 1760; a unilateral definition of the collectivity as a community, a nation. A tradition that is archaic and collective in this sense cannot be truly alive in an urbanized and industrial society. If it survives, it is more or less as conformism, as an element foreign to what is lived. Historiography is not a substitute for tradition; it is its heir. It cannot be unilateral. In terms of the variety of situations, history must ask many questions, from many points of view. Max Weber stated it thus: "The principles of the cultural sciences will continue to change in the future without limit, so long as a sclerosis of the life of the mind does not cause humanity, as in China, to lose the habit of asking new questions of a life that is inexhaustible."

Our historiography should be psychoanalysed, so to speak. If we really want to read in our history about the progress of freedom, about spiritual traditions rather than a sociological tradition, the historian himself must find his own freedom again to face the past; and he must recognize, at the source of what he considers as the crucial events, the choices made by groups and historians before him.

The conquest is indeed a central event, but only if our history is taken solely as the development of a nation. Depending on whether we decide to read the past in terms of different kinds of solidarity—political, religious, workers'—other events will seem equally decisive.

In 1809, Denis-Benjamin Viger took a stand in the first French-Canadian political pamphlet against the tyranny of the French regime, and spoke the language of British liberty; some of our historians are no doubt ready to see him as a "collaborator."[3] In the text where Burke is so frequently evoked, I am tempted to see the discovery of a political community, the feeling of a civic responsibility for which I do not see the equivalent or even the possibility under the French regime. When I learn (not in the textbooks, obviously) that in 1775 a number of peasants were sensitive to the clamour for independence coming from the land to the south, I doubt very much whether those anonymous people were concerned merely with la revanche des berceaux and the preservation of our folklore. The 1837 adventure, the working out by French Canadians of the idea of Canadian independence, the already subtle thinking of the first militant workers from the international unions at the end of the last century—all that tends to make me think that our country has not been barren for liberty and that all the groups now struggling for certain values can find ancestors in our past. From a related viewpoint, it seems to me that one of the crucial tasks for our contemporary historiography would be to explore our recent past, say from 1875 to the present, when our milieu really stopped being "traditional" and when a working class was born that, simply by existing, constitutes the greatest challenge to the national community. I do not make this statement to fill some kind of intellectual void in that universe of works about which we intellectuals think above all, alienated as we are somewhat by our trade and the bibliographies that it implies, but to fill a spiritual void, the distance between what we have been and what we are.

I do not reject the interpretation of our history in terms of a national past; I am willing to accept this along with other readings. A history of Canada conceived in a polyvalent fashion would not make our past appear as the nightmare of an interminable dying; it would present various faces of liberty. Those who, in the present, do not work on a plan of action that is strictly patriotic would then no longer be rootless in their compatriots' eyes and their own.

Some may say that I ascribe too much importance to books about the past. However, only the historian can psychoanalyse our unhappy consciousness and found our choices on integrity. The nation must become the nation of all. For this to be true, for the worker as well as the intellectual to find self-recognition in a common destiny and a common choice, it is no longer the *Anglais* but our class system that we must attack. Here as elsewhere, nationalism has concealed the problems of social inequality too long for us not to find, in this struggle for a deeper sense of community, worthy tasks for man and the countenance of a native land that has at last become contemporary with ourselves.

Is There a Future for the French Canadian?

For the moment, there is still a French Canadian.[4] He is difficult to isolate and define—slightly more so, no doubt, than the American or the Frenchman. But it is enough to travel in the Beauce or Charlevoix and even in certain sections of our big cities to recognize this singular being, and to feel one's own heart leap in that unmistakable way. Is there a point in this curious variety of human fauna continuing to exist? That is the real question, the most trivial and the stupidest; but I am surprised not to hear it more often in those debates that exhaust our emotional and intellectual energies. The questions leading up to it are always a trifle simplistic, but I may be allowed just the same to pause at one of them.

One thing seems certain to me: the nationalist language and aims that have guided our thinking on these problems are largely out of date. A normal man could not recognize himself in the cultural, religious, economic, and political syntheses that only yesterday covered over all the deficiencies and dreams of the French Canadian. Between the federal minister, Jean Marchand, and some village politician who still sounds off the old nationalistic slogans, clearly the former is right from the outset. When Mr. Marchand emphasizes that we are in the era of technology which, basically, recognizes no frontier, he gives me a useful reminder of the obvious.

But he brakes the development of his reasoning too rapidly. In this universal perspective I do not see what makes him stop at the Canadian border. Why should our children not simply be American? It is a serious question, and we have asked it here in every generation for over a century. As far as I am concerned, I do not feel any absolute opposition to the United States: their industrial power astonishes me, some of their universities inspire the greatest admiration in me, their literature interests me infinitely more than what comes from here or from Toronto. Of course, the American policy in Vietnam disgusts me, but Canada's policy does not seem to me to contain anything very original either. Frankly, to pass from the universality of a technological society's demands to the need to build a Canada in opposition to the United States seems a flagrant contradiction to me, and the ultimate in regionalist timidity. I do not see why we should not be content simply to shift the barriers, nor do I see anything that places Canada, as such, at serious variance with the United States or any need for the creation of a new nationalism. And so here we are, back at the question of a French Canada that no longer exists and a Canada that has not yet come into being. This is very disturbing for those who, like me, are at the mid-point of their lives.

I feel obliged to come back to the primary question of French Canada. People have made a lot of fuss about industrialization and urbanization in Quebec. We have heard how these changes have challenged the traditional modes of living and thinking, as do the ideologies in which we found the argument for our collective existence. The educational revolution now in progress will, perhaps, be equally important; in any case, it further extends, and in the same direction, a radical transformation of our milieu. If we have survived as a people, it is above all because of the isolation in which the mass of the people have been kept. In the days after the conquest, the seignorial system separated us from our Anglo-Saxon neighbour. Afterwards, our country-dwellers lived on the fringe of the North American world. It was also the period when Quebec City considered itself "the Athens of North America": this enraged Olivar Asselin, but reassured the others. Furthermore our collective ignorance preserved us. Even when we emigrated to the towns, our proletarian contingents were cooped up in neighbourhoods and in occupations where a more or less bastard but still distinctive language and mores were kept up. We should not speak too harshly of joual: it has been and is the most faithful companion and the most unbeatable evidence of our survival.

If the revolution in education succeeds, all that will quickly be disposed of. People will be better educated and there will be more technicians. But will they find normal working conditions in Quebec? And what is more important, will they perceive a rationale in the survival of the French-Canadian type? I would bet the American empire would have a stronger attraction. And any improvement in the quality of our language would not be enough to slow down the movement. Language goes back to something else besides itself; it is the echo of a collectivity that is worthy of expression, that feels in it an irresistible urge and an irreplaceable joy.

Something of the same sort might be foreseen for intellectuals; those who, by definition, examine values. Until recently our elites found their food for thought in our difficulties themselves, as well as an easy way to justify not becoming attached to the more universal anguish and problems of the period. We made a vocation of doing our thinking strictly among ourselves. Some of us are already trying to work from other perspectives: those of science, of philosophy, of the world that is being created. Some of us have dreamed of going off to work more peacefully somewhere else, of not getting caught every morning in the local morass opened to us by the front page of the paper, of not floundering around ever again in the philosophy of such-and-such a provincial *député* or the political science of some eminent representative of federalism.

Not so very long ago, very few of us had the choice. However, we know that in the fields of big business and of scientific research many have emigrated in body or mind. From now on the possibility will be open to more and more French Canadians. Some will rejoice: "each must count for one," they tell us in those speeches where they can still stir up the old nationalism. But is this not a dangerous delusion? No nation is viable unless the group itself gives the individual the idea of basically belonging. France's future would be seriously jeopardized in our view if each Frenchman, at a certain point in his life, had to make a conscious choice in her favour. It will soon be that way here for all those who have picked up, along with their education, the ability to uproot themselves.

What has been truly decisive in the Quiet Revolution, in fact, was referable to culture: there was educational reform but there were also assorted dreams, the desire for new attitudes. The very formal ideologies where we had found our identity rapidly faded. Catholicism, for example, ceased to be the framework of our nationality. Many believers, of whom I am one, were delighted; we believe that pluralism is a happy conquest. But where are we now to find that certain unanimity without which no nation can exist? We have reached a point where we must find another collective project. Is it possible? That is the whole question, and constitutional arguments are meaningful only in relation to it. Time is pressing. We should already have some concrete achievements. The revolution in the schools seems to have been achieved. But where are our definitive choices in the areas of the economy, planning, development, scientific research? We are too quickly reduced to confused questionings that are translated immediately into narrowly political ideological conflicts.

Finally, at the bottom of it all there is a problem of conscience that has not been elucidated. I would like to say quite simply how I see the problem.

At the end of an article on the destiny of our whole civilization, Paul Ricoeur wrote: "We must be progressive in politics and archaic in poetry." I will comment in my fashion on these opposing and complementary notions. In theory, there could be no true politics from now on unless focused along the development tracks of contemporary industrial societies: everywhere the boldest planning and development procedures are to be put to work and national barriers are illusory except for reasons purely and simply out of the dictates of strategy and competition. But technology and planning by themselves could not identify collective ideals or reasons for living. Raising the standard of living is not even a primary criterion, either for individuals or for the collectivity. The wish to restrict oneself to supplying everyone with a certain security and an appropriate income is a direct continuation of the old liberalism. We assume that the individual has the capacity to select his own values, but this faculty does not exist if it cannot find support in a certain consensus with other people. This consensus is archaic in two ways: it appeals to forms of interdependence that have slowly been created by history; it has its roots in the deepest layers of the conscience where essential values and symbols are at work. Archaism and progressivism: that is the point of contact of poetry and technology, of love and the family budget, of values and planning. And equally, of national feelings and politics. Loyalty to the nation falls into the realm of the archaic, but as only one element of it, and probably not the most important. The loyalty issue is nonetheless one of the most easily accessible ways in which the community of values can define itself as the opposite of the organizations.

In this context, I for one believe in the virtue of small nations, where common values have the opportunity to sink deep roots. The desire to create a Canadian nation means attempting to put together an archaism, which is clearly absurd. There remains Canadian politics. I have trouble seeing what it adds to our destitution faced with the American mastodon. Nor can I see how this would create a bigger window on to the international scene for Quebec.

If I tend to lean towards the separatist solution, it is paradoxically in reaction to any kind of narrow nationalism, whether it comes from

Quebec City or Ottawa. Quebec should avoid any useless detours and assert as quickly as possible its presence in the world. The flowering of our own still timid cultural values requires lots of air. The fertility of our own archaism is not found in opposition to English Canada or even to the Americans: it goes by way of Paris, Brussels, Algiers, Rabat, Tunis, through a geographical network where I do not see a place for Ottawa. If the Minister for External Affairs sees in this the incontrovertible dissolution of our federal ties, as he declared recently, I am sorry for him. But I can only ask myself, once again, what cultural ties bind us to Winnipeg or Toronto in so direct a manner that we should have to come to an agreement in order to define what our cultural growth has in common with that of France and Tunisia. After all, Canada is only one hundred years old, and I would like to emphasize this for any federalist thinker who leaps from the nineteenth century to the twenty-first.

Canada and the United States: An Ominous Proximity

Three-fifths of Canada's production is at present under foreign control.[5] This is unique among all the industrialized nations. The United States plays an enormous role in this economic dependence. In 1964, Canada's total debt to other nations was $32.8 billion, if we include short-term foreign investments and certain other liabilities. By 1967 this debt had reached $36 billion, of which $30 billion was in the form of long-term investments.

American investment in Canada is not, of course, a new phenomenon. It was already considerable at the beginning of the century, but so were British interests at that time. During the thirties America's share was approximately $5 billion. With the Second World War Canada reached a new and crucial stage in its industrialization and in its subjection to the United States. Its trade deficit became dangerously accentuated. In a courageous speech that created quite a stir, Mr. Walter Gordon voiced his alarm: "From 1958 to 1962 we had unused resources and a high rate of unemployment here. However, we continued to contract foreign debts and to sell Canadian companies in order to pay for our imports. This made no sense. In fact, we were importing unemployment." And we are continuing to do so.

Moreover, a large portion of Canadian savings are invested in the United States: approximately three-quarters, we are told. Even Quebec, an industrialized province whose revenue is considerably lower than Ontario's, exports a great deal of capital. Stock-market investments and the draining of our savings by American insurance companies are obviously factors here.

An article in the December 1963 issue of *Fortune* magazine recognized quite casually that Canada is "a country that American companies consider as an extension of their domestic market." The same statement could be broadly applied in the area of culture. Canada is experiencing a serious lack of highly qualified researchers and technicians. But for some time we have been sending a good number to the United States. No doubt we must invoke the deficiencies of Canada's science policy, and those of the provinces. But, with very rare exceptions, the large American companies with branches in Canada have been very careful to establish their own large research centres. An extension of American territory, perhaps, but a marginal zone, the first to be affected by unemployment that begins in the parent company in the neighbouring republic and the last to profit from the resources of research.

We have been denouncing the invasion of our universities by American textbooks for a long time now, particularly in Quebec. Is there any need to stress the importance of this phenomenon? A discipline does not yield up its secrets in a given language through a kind of transparency; in the social sciences especially, it is a way of seeing things, the reflection of a particular educational system, a certain general ideological climate that will set its mark on the student forever. The war was a decisive factor in this regard, as it was for the economy. Cut off from France and England, French-Canadian and English-Canadian students had to turn towards the United States for the foreign study that normally climaxes a program of post-graduate studies. Some came back thinking that science is American and with a complete scorn for the traditions and progress of European research. This tendency has been reversed, it is true, at least among French Canadians: in some disciplines the change in attitude has been profound and study sessions in France are increasing in number. But at the same time the American influence is making itself more insidious. Publishing houses establish branches in Quebec; American textbooks are translated, most often into very dubious French. Intensive training programs are given in Quebec, in Montreal, in English Canada, and they are all controlled directly by American universities. Last year, one of the latter even proposed the establishment in French Canada of a series of courses for training kindergarten teachers.

One suspects that the American influence is more obvious and more complex in our day-to-day life. The influence of American civilization on our mores is very uneven. It is clearly felt in the mass media, but this is not a specifically Canadian phenomenon, as the Europeans know very well. In Canada more than elsewhere we must try to distinguish what comes from American culture from what is simply a sign, done up in American packaging, of the new phase of the technological civilization in which the whole world is involved. There are still parts of Canada where flourishing signs of an indigenous culture can be found. One has only to spend an evening dining in a Toronto home to see ample evidence of this and to sense the Britishness of the surroundings and attitudes. This is even more true of the French Canadians, whom I know infinitely better: just to spend a few days in a small town or in the countryside is to realize right away that a unique culture exists there and is holding its own, almost without realizing it, in its daily routine. But these traditions are threatened on all sides. They are not deep-rooted over all Canadian territory: the western part of the country (with the exception of British Columbia) is more American than English. With the revolution now going on here in the field of education and the rapid climb in the level of instruction, Quebec seems likely to become more open to the influence of American culture.

Any attempt to make a diagnosis of American hegemony soon leads back to Canada's own internal problems.

The serious deficiencies in Canadian economic policy must be brought in question. But it is necessary first of all to recognize that the context is not very favourable. American capital has not simply invaded the country. It has put at its service what we may call the economic elite of Canada. The latter is still sometimes English in day-to-day life, but its interests and ideologies are generally only the echo of American capitalism. In a number of cases this elite participates only superficially in the meetings of directors who get their basic orientation from the neighbouring country. But because of ostensibly Canadian associations, this elite helps form public opinion. No less serious is the preponderance of American labour unions in Canada: at least three-quarters of Canadian union members belong to organizations that take their orders from across the border. Not long ago, the director of an independent union expressed his concern over this question to one of the Canadians in charge of an American union affiliate. The reply was that this independence was "an attempt to divide the labour movement and to stir up antagonism towards the Americans."

As for the Canadian government, it has been very timid. It did try, in 1963, to intervene in the key sector of the automobile industry. The Drury plan proposed, through various customs regulations, to re-establish a balance between the export and import of automobiles and parts. The

American Secretary of Commerce immediately protested and threatened reprisals. However, some progress has been made since then in the Canadian automobile industry. Some action has been taken. What is still needed is the imposition of an infinitely more severe policy. We could exercise a stronger control over foreign companies; European countries have shown how this can be done. Canada's vast natural resources, which are so attractive to foreign companies, are a powerful bargaining point. It goes without saying that further efforts have to be made to diversify the import of capital and the countries where Canadian investments are being directed. It would be necessary to go even further, following a pattern of which Quebec has already given an illustration. In order to check to some extent the flight of capital abroad, the provincial government established a pension fund that makes it possible to pull together considerable amounts of capital; in addition, the government proposed to finance independent companies in co-operation with private interests. If similar measures were intensified and combined with the import of non-American capital to finance industrial development, we might then be on the way towards a valid reaction against the economic grip of the United States. But the remedy would have to be tied irretrievably to socialist political planning. Canada is still very far from that.

It must be said that Canada does not form an integrated whole. It contains four distinct economic regions whose interests are often contradictory. The provinces are frequently in disagreement with the federal government; power is badly distributed. From the straight viewpoint of effective economic policy, Canada has to be remade.

And that is not the end of it. Culturally the country has never been so divided. For a long time now the British majority has more or less tolerated the strong French-Canadian minority. This condescension has been accompanied by day-to-day persecution: Canada has never really been the bicultural country it has at times claimed to be. The French province of Quebec, which has been engaged in a spectacular renewal for a number of years, is demanding a redefinition of its status within Confederation. Relations between it and the central government and between French and English Canadians are acutely tense. The threat of secession is felt more and more distinctly. The problem of American supremacy is presented in a new context: it is not inaccurate to say that Quebec holds the key to the future of Canada. The defenders of capitalism do not deny it. A certain French-Canadian cabinet minister in Ottawa likes reminding his compatriots of the American menace whenever they are attracted to independence. To this they are tempted to reply that the federal government has not yet been able to supply a remedy for this threat. Moreover, a good many French Canadians have very little desire to serve as hostages against the United States.

In any event, there are numerous advocates of Quebec independence who do not restrict themselves to the problems of their nation and who recognize the international scope of their position. They are looking for cultural reasons, for a fatherland, to justify their not being American. They are seeking to renew their own profound ties with France, and they devoutly hope that English Canadians will do the same for their own British heritage. There are some who understand, too, that although bonds with Europe need to be tightened, Quebec's calling, like that of the rest of Canada, is tied to the North American continent. But this is only apparently a paradox: some form of independence for Quebec is perhaps a necessary precondition for negotiation among the diverse people north of the United States who have not so far found a genuine way to co-operate and effectively check the hold of their neighbour.

One hundred years ago the Canadian Confederation was constructed in opposition to the United States. It was done hastily, with compromises that have meant that one of the partners paid too high a price. Moreover, this political structure is not adapted to present economic requirements and to the new challenges presented by our powerful neighbour. The Canadian adventure is sometimes compared to the one pursued in Europe by the countries of the Treaty of Rome. The basic intent is the same and it is a valid one. But in various ways its achievement responds to different conditions. Just as the European nations, assured of their mutual autonomy, must move more quickly towards some unified political structures, so must Canada dissolve the artificial, improvised structure that gives it apparent unity, in order to rebuild a fresh assemblage of the nations that compose it.

True it is that the roads are many and varied which lead, north of the United States, in Europe, and elsewhere, to the inevitable community of peoples.

Tasks Before the Nationalist

Let us stop to consider some current criticism.[6] At first sight, our nationalist associations have no future, and this is a statement one often hears made. Until fairly recently, so the claim goes, they did excellent work, but now they are out of date. For a long time they were active in the general area of social problems; however, in the past few years a number of new organizations with specific objectives have appeared. What purpose can a national association serve in a minor supporting role? Again, like many Quebecois, these associations have come to the independentist choice. There is now in existence a political party that is supposed to unite all our energies to follow this course. Why duplicate this party in an association with the same objectives but less real political effectiveness?

We must get beyond these two objections. They are related to more radical questions that broaden them to include the whole issue of nationalism.

Our national associations have been stripped of the various social functions they used to perform, but so has nationalism itself. Not so long ago nationalists willingly fought to get Quebec society to be more concerned with economics. Today, nationalism is being challenged in the name of those same concerns and impugned in the name of the future as well. Do nations still have meaning in societies increasingly submitted to imperatives that flow across the old boundaries and the old national individualities? Are they not, rather, vain survivals, useless fossils that bear witness to the past while we are apparently entering the post-industrial age?

We have noted that the advent of the Parti Quebecois seems to rob all national associations of meaning. Yet the independentist option carries with it a far broader challenge to nationalism itself. For is independence not the completion and consequently the outgrowing of nationalism? A people submissive to largely foreign political structures cannot rely, to shore up their integrity, on a spontaneous feeling about their own identity. They must be tirelessly on the alert for ideologies and social movements that recall their reasons for going on, that rally their energies in threatening periods of history. Briefly, people in such a position need nationalism. And our own have not varied from this universal law. Yet from the moment we decide to gain independence, the old substitutes for deficient political structures cease to have any rationale, or soon will do so. "Give us a state," say some, "and we will stop being nationalists."

Nationalism and a new society, nationalism and independence: here are the two great themes we will have to keep firmly before us in our thought and action over the years to come.

For a long time nationalism was based on survival. To many people this preoccupation has overshadowed the individual importance of other values, religious ones for example, and the practical nature of certain requirements, especially in the areas of economics and politics. The nation had become the rallying point of a doctrine, of a system that took in all our great social objectives. Obsession with survival made us put together, under the cover of national concerns, "our language, our institutions, our laws." We had lost sight to some extent of the diversity and the dynamism peculiar to each of these areas of reality. The old synthesis is disintegrating; we want to speak French without thinking constantly of the nation to be saved; we have learned that the logic of institutions and of rights is concerned not only with ethnic groups but with social classes as well.

For some years now, we have been talking a great deal about "neo-nationalism." One does not have to be much of a scholar to realize that in fact today's nationalism is no longer that of the past. In many cases, especially for people in their forties, it has been defined in opposition to the old nationalism. National fervour has often reappeared as a result of other commitments, socialist ones for example. We can observe conversions of this kind every day, and they are often very astounding. The content of this neo-nationalism is still indistinct, as are the loyalties it groups together. We must clarify this in the years to come.

The first, most urgent need is to demystify the economy.

Let there be no misunderstanding. We are not opposed to bread and butter in principle, or even to a Saturday beer. And we all agree too about creating more jobs. Economic growth is obviously one of the priorities, and we have been given a very timely reminder that before we make prophecies about our post-industrial future we should first of all make certain of the development of our secondary sector. Where all that is concerned it seems to me that there is perfect agreement.

The obscurity of the economy lies elsewhere.

First of all, the term "economy" is highly elastic. It denotes labour, capital, raw materials, markets, and many other things of the kind. But it also refers, and here we are in new territory, to general purposes, to powers that have been acquired or that are to be won, to domination and dependence. We must unravel all that just a bit, so that when people tell us about the imperatives of growth they will not try to persuade us at the same time of economic necessities in the strict sense, and of the eternal legitimacy of the powers currently profiting by them. It is a very widespread practice to place an accent on the economy which, on the pretext of necessary progress, guarantees weapons to the forces of conservatism.

Some people think it is sufficient to evoke the "flight of investments" to silence everybody on the subject of justice or independence. Like most Quebecois I condemn violence and bombs. But I am no less worried by the perverse uses the established disorder makes of terrorism. A politician declared after a bomb had exploded in Westmount, "One thing is certain, these events are going to have an effect on investment in Quebec." We have been hearing this for months, several times a day. Are we going to vegetate from now on beneath the terrorism of investment? We find it repugnant when our English neighbours live in fear of being blown up, but it seems no healthier to me that we have reached the point where we panic every time we see a Brinks truck at an intersection or get up in the middle of the night to scan the heavens for signs of a possible investment slump. This economic blackmail will finally wear out the last bits of that resilience that gives communities their strength and, in particular, their economic vitality. There is a possible recourse against this blackmail: a vast mass-education campaign on just those economic matters. Our businessmen who demand the teaching of more economics in the schools would agree completely with such a project. Besides, this need is not peculiar to us: in our modern societies, all responsible citizens need a high level of knowledge of this kind. It is even more necessary for the poor who have long been kept outside the decision-making processes and for whom the economy is a frightening mystery that the powerful handle with ease.

A different kind of obscurity, but one which implies the same ambiguity I have just mentioned, is the never-ending insistence on the primary importance of the economy. There are many examples of this, but I shall choose one at random. On May 27, 1969, Mr. J. B. Porteous, outgoing president of the Montreal Board of Trade, addressed that organization. His remarks were reported in *Le Devoir* on May 28: "He maintained that for a certain period of time it will be necessary to put aside any decision concerning language and education in Quebec and deal rather with boosting the province's economy." And he went even further: "According to Mr. Porteous, we cannot consider the spread of language, religion, and culture until Quebec's economic survival has been assured." It is a little as though you told someone you would like to see working harder that in order to do so he must forget, for the moment, the very reasons why he is working: his love for his wife and children, his faith, his highest motives for living. Would he work any harder? The same is true of communities. Does starting them on the road to progress consist in having them put aside the very values that could urge them into the paths of economic growth?

Now we are coming to the essential point. Today, confronting the problems that face all societies, even the most advanced, how do we see the basic problem of economic policy?

Let us listen for a moment to the advice of Mr. Porteous and silence, temporarily, the nationalist voices. Let us listen to the greatest economists of our day. What do they say?

First, they say that the enormous resources technology has put at our disposal oblige us to make more long-term plans, taking into account a more widespread range of variables. Then, that if our means of forecasting are refined, we will be faced with choices technology by itself could not make for us. More than ever, men must formulate projects in which their values are embodied. Not only individual values, as the old liberalism of the eighteenth and nineteenth centuries would have had it, but values with a collective appeal, that represent agreement and approval by human groups on a common lifestyle. Will these plans and agreements penetrate the isolated consciousness by magic? Will they be the synthesis of the so-called universal values—given, as it is often claimed, that in the planetary age particularisms are nothing but an obstacle?

I am skipping over the fact that those who plead for the universal sometimes speak, in another connection, of a necessary "Canadian nationalism," as I want to get right down to the basic question: are nations the essential foci for working out these values, these plans required by the new varieties of technology and development? In the last analysis what we have to know is whether nationalism is the opposite of humanism or one of its indispensable component parts.

Lest I be accused of building up philosophical points that lead subtly back to my own options, I will turn to a contemporary philosopher from abroad. To my knowledge Pierre Thévenaz has never spoken of nationalism; he has reflected deeply on humanism, however, and on the rationales for its regionalization. He has wondered, for example, why the Western nations have given pride of place to the Greeks and Romans in their concept of humanity and in the education of their children. He knew that the West has been discovering in other civilizations values that are different from but just as rich as our own, and he asked why we should not combine all these values. Why continue to refer to our own particular past? Let us first hear what he says about this: "We seem to be advancing an ideal of not stopping with any human type, of not choosing any as our own, of never shutting ourselves off in order not to lose any human possibility, of never concluding for fear of excluding. The humanist attitude can thus become an undefined curiosity, an infinite enquiry into mankind. We accumulate all the riches of humanity: are we liable to suffer from an embarrassment of riches, which is another form of interior poverty? By remaining open to all, will we not drift into a posture of dilettantism that receives humanity, greets it, samples it, but, lacking the support of a personal vocation that would be an exclusive commitment, sinks into inconsistency or breaks up in eclecticism? Does not being a man mean choosing, excluding, concluding, closing oneself to certain possibilities that are not his own; does it not mean judging, that is to say evaluating, measuring according to one's own standard?"[7]

At least, it will be said, this giddy faculty of welcoming everything excludes fanaticism. Do not those who decide on an irrevocable attachment to one particular bit of ground and its values risk being dogmatic? I do not deny it. But here is Thévenaz's next comment: "The dogmatic intellect is one that remains unaware of its own situation in the world. . . . The achievement of self-awareness means consciousness of the condition or conditions one must recognize as one's own. If humanism is awareness of the human and rejection of all that is doctrinaire, we find in one single integral act, the act of awareness, both the way to all that is human and, at the same time, our situation, our firm position in relation to it. . . . Humanist universalism will not thus appear as the obliteration of differences between men in the name of the universal, but as the highlighting of those particular contingencies in which the universal is manifested."[8]

In the same way, the nation is the focus and the token of an identity. It is not alone in playing this role; at another level, the West exercises it too. These particularisms are not the negation of a planetary humanism. Those who speak of "national prejudices" are never completely wrong, but they often contribute to an obscurant mystification of the sort we detected in the economy: they confuse the closing into the self, which is a denial of the universal, with the self-awareness which is the condition of attaining it.

Since we have defined ourselves as Quebecois a new responsibility has become ours: that of entering into a new kind of dialogue with other Quebecois who are not French-speaking. In this respect, it should be unnecessary to recall that the election of 1970 was a dangerous lesson and left us a no less dangerous temptation. It brought to light a rigid division that must cause pain not only to advocates of independence but also to any man graced with a little intelligence and feeling.

We are not going to hand over our future under pressure of a blackmail that is added to and sometimes mixed with those already cited. But neither must we work in isolation. For a small people like ours, the duty of welcome and assembly is a hard one. But it must be undertaken in terms of our lives' justification, as the highest proof that liberty is turned towards others. We must look patiently for interlocutors. I think of a young Anglais who went campaigning from door to door among his compatriots for the Parti Quebecois. I had a long talk with him during the campaign: anything but assimilated, Anglo-Saxon to his fingertips and prodigiously proud of the fact; anxious as well to share our values, to help construct a common home here for us all. He is certainly not unique. We must try particularly to reach the young people in our English-language colleges and universities. Not to persuade them to become faithful copies of ourselves, but to invite them to take part in our project, leaving it to them to bring their own colours and intentions.

I move on straight away to a second task. In our struggle for independence this is a traditional nationalist concern that we have quite naturally left in the shadows and which the independentists have tended to abandon to those nationalists who have remained faithful to Confederation. I am referring to our French-language brothers in the other Canadian provinces. They are already taking advantage of the new challenges we are throwing out and some of them confess it in secret. But they also feel bitterness towards us. The Estates-General showed this not long ago and, though I was not present at the sessions and was able to follow them only in the papers, I believe I understand those reactions.

Here again it is normal for a political party to urge the pace. But the nation must not be identified with a party nor should it be confused with a state. We must start anew, beginning with our options and the present situation, to consider this old problem.

I will go even further. Even if we decide to leave Confederation we cannot be indifferent to the fate of what is at present called Canada. Our common destiny will always be closely linked, whether we want it so or not, to that of the people who surround us. We can make any hypothesis we want about the possibility of an association between Quebec and the rest of Canada: hypotheses will not take on concrete form and be translated into reality unless we erect them not only in terms of ourselves but in terms of others as well.

Our Culture: Between Past and Future

How can we evaluate the development of our culture during the past decade?[9] What new challenges confront it? In connection with such questions we can only put forward here some hypotheses for reflection. Therefore I shall not draw up another balance sheet of our intellectual production over the past ten years, or even of educational reform. They have both been done often enough in books or periodicals. But I wonder to what extent, in these various attempts, we have succeeded in working out a new cultural debate. What changes have we made, in the meaning of our collective utterance? Into what new dilemmas have we thus been led? Asking all these questions will remind us that when a people want to transform their culture they will soon find themselves saying things other than those proposed at the outset.

The so-called Quiet Revolution is too often alluded to chiefly in terms of its political aspects. These were important, it is true. But as is frequently the case in such circumstances, they were largely inspired by what was already happening in our cultural life. I will go even further: the Quiet Revolution was itself essentially a cultural revolution. The major economic and political changes have yet to take place.

How then, in the years before 1960, did the advocates of progress, the leftists of that day, see the problem of change in our community? Broadly speaking, for them it was a matter of breaking once and for all with our traditional attitudes, developing the ability to set off in channels neighbouring peoples had taken well before we did. In the same way, it was necessary to break down the old monolithic culture and make pluralists of ourselves. Finally, and still as a corollary, we had to stop being obsessed by ideological speculation and get down to the concrete realities.

This new discussion, this new self-awareness, meant defining our collective conversion in rather formal terms. Proposing more progressive attitudes, promoting pluralism, denouncing ideologies in the name of the *concrete*: all that was not very precise in terms of the new values a changing culture had to represent. The discussion was effective, however: it gave direction to the earliest phases of the Quiet Revolution. We moved on, in various fields, to write off or to catch up. Educational reform is perhaps the most obvious illustration. Thinking of this kind was inevitable and moreover necessary to bring about a break. Yet this new cultural debate called for fresh values. Only a few reformers of the sixties have maintained their tireless advocacy of those ideals of a progress justified only in terms of formal freedom. Thus their solid statements of 1960 have become paradoxically a strange kind of abstraction.

In fact, various sectors of the population have witnessed, not an outright rejection of yesterday's arguments, but rather a profound transmutation. The themes and values of other times are still there, though in different settings: this is true whether you are looking at a Gilles Vigneault or at a René Lévesque. A bottomless rift seemed necessarily to separate the young generation of the sixties and those of past centuries.

Where we might have expected the age of the prophets of reason we have seen the emergence of the "bards" of the North Shore. Where we expected a cosmopolitan pluralism, we have seen the resurgence of the old fleur-de-lys banner, seized by young hands and waving in its thousands. Some will say that we are still repeating old forms of nostalgia. This is true in a sense. But what is its significance?

Radical breaks occurring in the history of cultures never take the form of a total winding up followed by a fresh departure. This can be verified in Quebec. In a sense—and we have often failed to recognize this—that old argument contained its own transcendence. For example, from Garneau to Groulx, from the latter to Fregault, to Seguin or Brunet, there is continuity of tradition, but also testing of an inner logic, of potential schism. There is a certain affinity between the poetry of the soil and Savard's *Menaud*, but there is also illumination from within: the masterpiece is not of another origin; it is an old story that finally, in its very despair, reveals what it had long concealed. After studying the Jesuit review *Relations* for the period from the 1940s to 1960, my students were surprised at the ease it displayed in assimilating events: the Quiet Revolution was all there in rough draft.

We could give many more examples, and further expose the criteria employed by the older consciousness in changing to survive. It may be enough to suggest that in periods of profound crisis the old debate stood for continuity while still exploring what was implicit in itself. What the old debate had kept in its depths rises again to the surface. The old problems, purposes long repressed, are seeking expression. The demonstrations against Bill 63 brought together suddenly, in the light of day, deep desires for survival that had never before related all their hope and all their despair. Many of the suggestions I heard during the sessions of the Commission on the Laity and the Church seem to me to have brought into the open what were for a long time simply private and veiled confidences. If I may be permitted an analogy with psychoanalysis, one could speak of a sort of lifting of the censorship exercised, on the surface at least, by our culture of yesteryear.

We know what the end result was. Never before have a people so long imprisoned in silence and so reticent in speech expressed themselves so fluently, in so many ways, and with such happiness. Poetry and religion came together there, passing by way of politics which itself became a kind of poetry. For better or for worse.

All that shows the limits of any really new cultural discussion a people want to hold. What, in fact, have we been "doing since 1960"? Was it simply a case of a minority, having survived by an oversight of history, remembering its reasons for existing? Was it the heady celebration of a society about to pass into a more silent agony? Did we produce a vocalization that would serve as ultimate alibi for the impossibility of assuming our own destiny? In fact we can no longer escape a more concentrated suffering than we have ever known in our history: despite the enthusiasm poured into it, have the last ten years been anything more than a cultural revolution? Are we a people who, by reason of the fatal forces at work on us, can accomplish no more than a change in language, thus in the end admitting the impotence already inscribed in our history?

For ten years we have been closed within the circle of culture. Our literature has gained an astonishing impetus. Young people fill the schools. Our civil servants, frequently turning competent, keep making diagnoses and making them well. Intellectuals abound; they are everywhere, in the CEGEPs [collèges d'enseignement general et professionnel], the universities, newspapers, television. The people of Saint-Jérôme and Saint-Roch, Cabano and Saint-Paulin, are beginning to talk as well. Is this a vast classroom revolt that we have produced? For a century the word was left to us as our domain. After preserving it for a long time, we are finally using it. But have we done no more than better explore from top to bottom the prison that was ours for so long? It may be that we have only gone deeper into our ancestral house, this time into rooms we abandoned a long time ago.

To look farther into the coming years, our speech and culture should expand into other areas where at first sight they seem to have no business. In this confined circle where we often place our culture, we are not yet really ourselves. Even among the extreme leftists, there are accents that, although new, are not completely local ones. We still define ourselves by superficial comparisons. "Colonization," "social design," "revolution" or, in another perspective, "social order," "just society," "economic development"—all these terms, like the French that is heard in our colleges, have the odour of imported languages. I can see traces of it in the narrower field of my own discipline, sociology. When we speak with young intellectuals, we often have the feeling that they are repeating, with adjustment and variation, what the foreign schools and fashions have been saying for some time. In many cases you are constantly distracted; you look for the father behind the one speaking to you—the absent and foreign father for whom the native son on duty, previous holder of a grant from the Canada Council or the Quebec Ministry of Education, is but the local representative.

I do not reject foreign influences: this will be easily accepted. But our cultural debate will have no basis unless it issues first from ourselves; if it is defined also in terms of its effect outside the close circle of our society. For example, we talk a lot about coordinating research in our universities. We should begin by ceasing to imitate what is done elsewhere with considerably ampler means. Populous and wealthy societies dispense culture as generously as napalm. Smaller societies are left with the resource of astuteness in which noble words have a chance to fix themselves on the more profound questions that get barely a pause from the big schemes and teams. I mean that we must commit ourselves more in our ties with the United States and France. And we must not lose sight of the priority of the United States. If our research does not go into the cultural life of our neighbours as a new challenge, how can we but console ourselves with being some kind of continental relay station for French civilization?

Reduced to its narrowest limits, our cultural problem has then become openly what it has always been implicitly: a problem of communication, in the sense however that it no longer applies to reception difficulties, but more to those of emission. Our economic problem, another traditional one, arises from similar difficulties in communication. The economist Jean-Luc Migue has produced some fundamental writings on that subject. There is no more to say about the backward mentality of our French-Canadian businessmen, in charge of small industries without a future, torn between the desire to stay within the family circle and the desire to give in to foreign powers, keeping only the vain glory of those visible powers the local elites still hold in esteem. Could it be otherwise? In every area, for two centuries, we have been cut off from channels of communication. Are not the subsidies the federal Department of Regional Expansion gives to American businesses that want to set up shop here not like the invitations given by intellectuals to foreign academics? By what route will we manage to unite our tools of economic growth and the broader decision-making processes, manage to push ourselves in as contributors of originality in a wider arena? The question is the same for our poetry, our fiction, our scientific research. In 1970 we are more aware that a people, no matter how small, can only speak to make themselves better understood by others.

In Quebec, a people have survived like an extraordinary paradox. Such a paradox is not unraveled by a borrowed speech or an economic policy copied from our neighbours. Elsewhere, the young are protesting against the "consumer society. " What they want to say is: "We are protesting against a kind of contamination of the economy and of our culture that makes it hard to distinguish between poetry and gadgets, between improved conditions and the promotion of capitalism, between the meaning of life and the meaning of power." In Quebec, we have been denouncing these confusions for centuries, more intensively during the past ten years, in our society itself. Will we elicit from it an original model for economic and cultural development? It seems undeniable to me that we must now put together these two aims, which have for a long time been foreign to each other. In the years to come, that will require a language where once more, this time more closely than before, the past will be mingled with the imperatives of the future.

Notes

Originally published as "Of a Hesistant Quebec," in *The Vigil of Quebec*, by Fernand Dumont. Copyright © University of Toronto Press 1974. Reprinted with permission of the publisher.

1. [The author's notes give the original provenance or publication history of each section of this chapter, prior to their collection in the 1971 book *La vigile du Québec*.—Eds.] This paper consists of a lecture given to the annual meeting of the Canadian Institute on Public Affairs in September 1959 under the title "Does Freedom Have a Past and Future in French Canada?" to which has been added a brief extract from a 1958 article. It will be noted that many of the hopes I expressed have been realized since that time, but it seems to me that our historical awareness is still characterized by traits that I pointed out in 1959. [The 1958 article Dumont refers to is likely "De quelques obstacles à la prise de conscience chez le Canadiens français," published in *La crise de conscience du Canada français* (Montreal: Canadian Institute of Public Affairs, 1957), 20–26.—Eds.]

2. Henri Bourassa (1868–1952), Quebecois political leader, member of Parliament, and founder (in 1910) of the newspaper *Le Devoir*.

3. *Considérations sur les effets qu'ont produit en Canada, la conservation des établissements du pays* (Montreal: Chez James Brown, 1809), 38–39.

4. Article published in the special issue of *Le Devoir* commemorating the Centennial of Canadian Confederation (June 30, 1967, supplement 1 14, 4) and reprinted in the journal *Esprit* (July–August 1969): 30–35.

5. Article commissioned for *Le Monde Diplomatique* (September 1967), 4.

6. Lecture given to the Congrès des Sociétés Nationales du Québec, June 1970.

7. Pierre Thévenaz, *L'homme et sa raison* (Neuchâtel: Éditions de la Baconnière, 1956), 1:28.

8. Ibid., 35–36.

9. From *Maintenant* 100 (November 1970): 290–92.

HAROLD CARDINAL

The Buckskin Curtain:
The Indian-Problem Problem

Harold Cardinal was born in 1945 in the Cree First Nations Reserve at Sucker Creek in northern Alberta. As a young man Cardinal was involved in the arduous grassroots Indian political mobilization that resulted in the formation of political organizations at the provincial level. The history of this postwar aboriginal militancy is recounted in Cardinal's first book, The Unjust Society (1969), written when he was still in his early twenties. The Unjust Society was a reply to both Prime Minister Pierre Trudeau's 1968 campaign slogan "The Just Society" and his government's new "Indian policy" as presented by his minister of Indian affairs, Jean Chrétien, in a now infamous ministerial white paper. The new policy was to extinguish the rights of aboriginal people as these are enshrined in the various treaties between the First Nations and the Crown, dismantle the Department of Indian Affairs, and transfer all governmental responsibility for aboriginal affairs to the provinces in the name of formal equality. The Unjust Society diagnosed this policy of assimilation as tantamount to cultural, political, and economic genocide.

The impact of this book was far-reaching, profoundly changing the way many newcomers to Canada understood their relationship to aboriginal peoples. It also had a significant effect on the way the state was to subsequently address aboriginal issues. The book established the principle that the "spirit and intent of the treaties" must be the central and unavoidable point of departure for any further nation-to-nation negotiation, a position First Nations organizations have consistently advanced against the state's maneuvering ever since. A crucial aspect of the treaties is their protection of collective rights. For these reasons, the historian Wes Pue argues that The Unjust Society made one of the most important contributions to political philosophy of the twentieth century. Indeed, few books in Canada have been as consequential in reshaping public culture. The Unjust Society deserves greater consideration as an exemplary cultural-political event, and its significance for the future of cultural studies in Canada deserves careful reflection and historical study. The Unjust Society also thrust

Cardinal further into the demands of political activism. As the president of the Indian Association of Alberta, he was a key figure in the formation of the National Indian Brotherhood, forerunner of the Assembly of First Nations, which he served as its vice-chief during the 1980s, when the Canadian Constitution was being repatriated.

The lessons of this period of militancy inform his second book, *The Rebirth of Canada's Indians* (1977). Cardinal was central to the formation of the Prairie Treaty Nations Alliance and was appointed by his colleagues as a Treaty 8 negotiator. The deadlocks he encountered in those negotiations prompted a long period of study with elders. At this time, Cardinal also studied law at the University of Saskatchewan and at Harvard University; he was was granted a doctorate in law from the University of British Columbia (2005). He subsequently served as the chief of the Sucker Creek Band. The fruits of his studies in this later period of his life appeared as *Treaty Elders of Saskatchewan: Our Dream Is That Our Peoples Will One Day Be Clearly Recognized as Nations* (2000, with Walter Hildebrandt). He was also the Indigenous Scholar in Residence at the University of Alberta's Law School and the recipient of the National Aboriginal Achievement Award in 2001. Harold Cardinal died in 2005.

The history of Canada's Indians is a shameful chronicle of the white man's disinterest, his deliberate trampling of Indian rights and his repeated betrayal of our trust. Generations of Indians have grown up behind a buckskin curtain of indifference, ignorance and, all too often, plain bigotry. Now, at a time when our fellow Canadians consider the promise of the Just Society, once more the Indians of Canada are betrayed by a programme which offers nothing better than cultural genocide.

The new Indian policy promulgated by Prime Minister Pierre Elliott Trudeau's government, under the auspices of the Honourable Jean Chrétien, minister of Indian Affairs and Northern Development, and Deputy Minister John A. MacDonald, and presented in June 1969 is a thinly disguised programme of extermination through assimilation. For the Indian to survive, says the government in effect, he must become a good little brown white man. The Americans to the south of us used to have a saying: "The only good Indian is a dead Indian." The MacDonald-Chrétien doctrine would amend this but slightly to, "The only good Indian is a non-Indian."

The federal government, instead of acknowledging its legal and moral responsibilities to the Indians of Canada and honouring the treaties that the Indians signed in good faith, now proposes to wash its hands of Indians entirely, passing the buck to the provincial governments.

Small wonder that in 1969, in the one hundred and second year of Canadian confederation, the native people of Canada look back on generations of accumulated frustration under conditions which can only be described as colonial, brutal and tyrannical, and look to the future with the gravest of doubts. Torrents of words have been spoken and written about Indians since the arrival of the white man on the North American continent. Endless columns of statistics have been compiled. Countless programmes have been prepared for Indians by non-Indians. Faced with society's general indifference and a massive accumulation of misdirected, often insincere efforts, the greatest mistake the Indian has made has been to remain so long silent.

As an Indian writing about a situation I am living and experiencing in common with thousands of our people it is my hope that this book will open the eyes of the Canadian public to its shame. In these pages I hope to cut through bureaucratic doubletalk to show what it means to be an Indian in Canada. I intend to document the betrayals of our trust, to show step by step how a dictatorial bureaucracy has eroded our rights, atrophied our culture and robbed us of simple human dignity. I will expose the ignorance and bigotry that has impeded our progress, the eighty years of educational neglect that have hobbled our young people for generations, the gutless politicians who have knowingly watched us sink in the quicksands of apathy and despair and have failed to extend a hand.

I hope to point a path to radical change that will admit the Indian with restored pride to his rightful place in the Canadian heritage, that will enable the Indian in Canada at long last to realize his dreams and aspirations and find his place in Canadian society. I will challenge our fellow Canadians to help us; I will warn them of the alternatives.

I challenge the Honourable Mr. Trudeau and the Honourable Mr. Chrétien to reexamine their unfortunate policy, to offer the Indians of Canada hope instead of despair, freedom instead of frustration, life in the Just Society instead of cultural annihilation.

It sometimes seems to Indians that Canada shows more interest in preserving its rare whooping cranes than its Indians. And Canada, the Indian notes, does not ask its cranes to become Canada geese. It just wants to preserve them as whooping cranes. Indians hold no grudge against the big, beautiful, nearly extinct birds, but we would like to know how they managed their deal. Whooping cranes can remain whooping cranes, but Indians are to become brown white men. The contrast in the situation is an insult to our people. Indians have aspirations, hopes and dreams, but becoming white men is not one of them.

We listen when Canadian political leaders talk endlessly about strength in diversity for Canada, but we understand they are talking primarily about the French Canadian fact in Canada. Canadian Indians feel, along with other minorities, that there is a purpose and a place for us in a Canada which accepts and encourages diversified human resources. We like the idea of a Canada where all cultures are encouraged to develop in harmony with one another, to become part of the great mosaic. We are impatient for the day when other Canadians will accord the Indian the recognition implied in this vision of Canada.

The vast majority of our people are committed to the concept of Canadian unity and to the concept of participation in that unity. The Indians of Canada surely have as great a commitment to Canada, if not a greater one, than even the most patriotic-sounding political leaders. More truly than it can be said of anyone else, it is upon this land that our heritage, our past and our identity originates.

We invite our white brothers to realize and acknowledge that the Indian in Canada has already made a considerable contribution to the greatness of our country, that the Indian has played a significant role in Canadian history. Our people look on with concern when the Canadian government talks about "the two founding peoples" without giving recognition to the role played by the Indian even before the founding of a nation-state known as Canada.

Positive steps by the government to fulfill its treaty obligations represent one aspiration common to all Indians. It was for this reason that our people were encouraged by Prime Minister Trudeau's call for the creation of the Just Society. This brief, dazzling flare of hope, however, quickly fizzled when Mr. Trudeau publicly announced that the federal government was not prepared to guarantee aboriginal rights and that the Canadian government considered the Indian treaties an anomaly not to be tolerated in the Just Society.

We will not trust the government with our futures any longer. Now they must listen to and learn from us.

"As Long as the Rivers Run . . ." with Forked Tongue

To the Indians of Canada, the treaties represent an Indian Magna Carta. The treaties are important to us, because we entered into these negotiations with faith, with hope for a better life with honour. We have survived for over a century on little but that hope. Did the white man enter into them with something less in mind? Or have the heirs of the men who signed in honour somehow disavowed the obligation passed down to them? The Indians entered into the treaty negotiations as honourable men who came to deal as equals with the Queen's representatives. Our leaders of that time thought they were dealing with an equally honourable people. Our leaders pledged themselves, their people and their heirs to honour what was done then.

Our leaders mistakenly thought they were dealing with an honourable people who would do no less than the Indians were doing—bind themselves, bind their people and bind their heirs to honourable contracts.

Our people talked with the government representatives, not as beggars pleading for handouts, but as men with something to offer in return for rights they expected. To our people, this was the beginning of a contractual relationship whereby the representatives of the Queen would have lasting responsibilities to the Indian people in return for the valuable lands that were ceded to them.

The treaties were the way in which the white people legitimized in the eyes of the world their presence in our country. It was an attempt to settle the terms of occupancy on a just basis, legally and morally to extinguish the legitimate claims of our people to title to the land in our country. There never has been any doubt in the minds of our people that the land in Canada belonged to them. Nor can there have been any doubt in the mind of the government or in the minds of the white people about who owned the land, for it was upon the basis of white recognition of Indian rights that the treaties were negotiated. Otherwise, there could have been nothing to negotiate, no need for treaties. In the language of the Cree Indians, the Indian reserves are known as the land that we kept for ourselves or the land that we did not give to the government. In our language, skun-gun.

When one party to an agreement continually, ruthlessly breaks that agreement whenever it suits his purpose, the other partner cannot forever be expected to believe protestations of faith that accompany the next peace offering. In our society, a man who did not keep his part of a fair bargain, a man who used tricks and shady deals to wriggle out of commitments, a man who continually spoke with a forked tongue became known as a crook. Indians do not deal with cheats.

Mr. Chrétien says, "Get rid of the Indian Act. Treat Indians as any other Canadians." Mr. Trudeau says, "Forget the treaties. Let Indians become Canadians." This is the Just Society? To the Indian people, there can be no justice, no just society, until their rights are restored. Nor can there be any faith in Mr. Trudeau, Mr. Chrétien, the government, in white society until our rights are protected by lasting, equitable legislation.

As far as we are concerned our treaty rights represent a sacred, honourable agreement between ourselves and the Canadian government that cannot be unilaterally abrogated by the government at the whim of one of its leaders unless that government is prepared to give us back title to our country.

Our rights are too valuable to surrender to Gallic or any other kind of rhetoric, too valuable to be sold for pieces of gold. Words change; the value of money fluctuates, may even disappear; our land will not disappear.

We cannot give up our rights without destroying ourselves as people. If our rights are meaningless, if it is inconceivable that our society have treaties with the white society even though those treaties were signed by honourable men on both sides, in good faith, long before the present government decided to tear them up as worthless scraps of paper, then we as a people are meaningless. We cannot and will not accept this. We know that as long as we fight for our rights we will survive. If we surrender, we die.

By and large, the articles of all written treaties between the Indians of Canada and the government of Canada must be considered misleading because they omitted substantial portions of what was promised verbally to the Indian. Additionally, they carry key phrases that are not precise, or they state that certain things were ceded that, in actual fact, were never considered or granted by the Indians who signed the treaties. Nevertheless, the government, although not willing even to begin to honour its side of the partnership, holds Indians to the strictest letter of the treaties. According to government interpretation, the following outline represents the sum total of its commitment to the Indians involved in one particular, but typical treaty.

Under Treaty Six, the Indians involved (the Plain and Wood Cree tribes in Saskatchewan and Alberta) surrendered land comprising an approximate area of 121,000 square miles. Concerning land, written reports of the treaty make the following commitment: "And Her Majesty, the Queen, hereby agrees and undertakes to lay aside reserves for farming lands, due respect being had to lands at present cultivated by the said Indians, and other reserves for the benefit of the said Indians, to be administered and dealt with for them by Her Majesty's Government of the Dominion of Canada; provided all such reserves shall not exceed in all one square mile for each family of five or in that proportion for larger or smaller families. . . . The Chief Superintendent of Indian Affairs shall depute and send a suitable person to determine and set apart the reserves for each band, after consulting with the Indians thereof as to the locality which may be found to be most suitable for them."

In the field of education, Treaty Six states: "Her Majesty agrees to maintain schools for instruction in such reserves hereby made as to Her Government of the Dominion of Canada may deem advisable, whenever the Indians of the reserve shall desire it."

The government also promised under treaty to give the Indians "the right to pursue their avocations of hunting and fishing throughout the tract surrendered as here into for described, subject to such regulations as may from time to time be made by Her Government of Her Dominion of Canada." The formal statement on aboriginal rights also outlines hunting restrictions in areas of settlement, mining or lumbering.

Surprisingly, many non-Indian people believe that the Indians receive all the money they need from the government throughout the year. In the Prairie provinces, the Indians were promised that the government would "pay to each Indian person the sum of $5.00 per head yearly."

In order to assist the Indians to make a beginning in farming, the government made the following commitment: "four hoes for every family actually cultivating; also, two spades per family aforesaid; one plough for every three families as aforesaid; one harrow for every three families as aforesaid; two scythes and one whetstone, and two hay forks and two reaping hooks, for every family aforesaid and also two axes; and also one crosscut saw, one hand-saw, one pit-saw, the necessary files, one grindstone and one auger for each band; and also for each chief for the use of his band, one chest of ordinary carpenter's tools; also, for each band, enough of wheat, barley, potatoes and oats to plant the land actually broken up for cultivation by such band; also for each band four oxen, one bull and six cows; also, one boar and two sows and one handmill when any band shall raise sufficient grain therefor."

Recognition of leadership was given: chiefs were to be paid an "annual salary of twenty-five dollars per annum and each subordinate officer, not exceeding four for each band, shall receive fifteen dollars per annum . . . ; shall receive once every three years a suitable suit of clothing and each chief shall receive in recognition of the closing of the treaty a suitable flag and medal and also as soon as convenient, one horse, harness and wagon."

The promise of medical care was contained in the following phrase: "A medicine chest shall be kept at the house of each Indian agent for the use and benefit of the Indians at the directions of such agent."

Under Treaty Six, welfare or social assistance was promised under the phrase, "In the event hereafter of the Indians comprised within this treaty being overtaken by any pestilence or by a general famine, the

Queen, on being satisfied and certified thereof by Her Indian agent or agents will grant to the Indians assistance of such character and to such extent as Her Chief Superintendent of Indian Affairs [the minister] shall deem necessary and sufficient to relieve the Indians from the calamity that shall have befallen them."

These pledges are typical, if not all-inclusive, of the promises that were made to the Indians by the government, although the cautionary phrase, "Her Majesty reserves the right to deal with . . . ," appearing commonly throughout the treaty, would have alerted a more sophisticated people to possible loopholes and pitfalls. There are many other aspects of the written treaties that are questionable. Generally, the treaties are outstanding for what they do not say rather than what they do say.

In spite of their admissions and omissions the treaties are doubly significant and important because they represent or imply principles that are intrinsically part of the concept of justice and respect for other men's property. They have a symbolic importance to Indians that cannot be ignored.

The Manitoba Indian Brotherhood, under its progressive and capable president, David Courchene, made the following observations about the treaties during their regional consultation meetings in December 1968. "From reading these treaties it is apparent that:

1. The officials representing the Government full well knew the value of the land requested to be ceded to the Crown;
2. . . . they were aware that the Indian was not able to communicate with them;
3. . . . the Indian had no counsel;
4. . . . the Indian was impressed by the pomp and ceremony and the authority of the officials;
5. . . . they [the officials] were dealing with uneducated people;
6. . . . the respect and ceremony with which the officials were dealing with the Indians lulled the Indians into a passive mood;
7. . . . a father image was being advanced by the authorities;
8. . . . the Indians, although it is alleged were explained the terms of the Treaties, really did not know or understand fully the meaning and implications;
9. . . . the alleged consideration that was being advanced by the Government to the Indians in exchange for the ceded land was not totally appreciated by the Indians, nor could they understand the concept of binding their heirs and executors, administrators and assigns to these documents;

10. . . . forever and a day it will be obvious to all who read the said Treaties and the history of their making, that the officials of Her Majesty the Queen committed a legal fraud in a very sophisticated manner upon unsophisticated, unsuspecting, illiterate, uninformed natives."

Manitoba's Indians, taking for the first time a hard look at the past, said, "These treaties must be renegotiated." Their study of the past pointed the way to the future.

We can brook no argument that the treaties are not relevant to the present.

"The terms of the treaties," insisted the Manitoba Indian Brotherhood, "must be extended and interpreted in light of present social and economic standards. To renegotiate the treaties does not necessarily mean to rewrite the treaties, nor does it mean to repudiate the treaties."

It was recognized at the Manitoba meeting that the importance of the treaties lies in the recognition and acceptance of the true spirit of the treaties rather than studied adherence to archaic phraseology.

The brotherhood noted: "A promise by the Government and a carrying out of that promise to give economic and financial assistance to the Indian so that he may better be able to advance his economic position in the community, would be a carrying out of one of the terms of the treaties. A promise and a carrying out of that promise by the Government that every child will have the right to a full education with all facilities made available to him for that purpose, is a carrying out of one of the terms of the treaties. A guarantee that every Indian will have full and adequate and immediate medical treatment as and when required, is a carrying out of one of the terms of those treaties.

"To renegotiate those treaties means to reach agreement, to carry out the full meaning and intent of the promises given by the representatives of the Queen, as interpreted, and as understood by the Indians. To successfully renegotiate those treaties is to bring about a legal commitment by the Government that the true intent and tenure of those treaties will be carried out."

The Indian people cannot be blamed for feeling that not until the sun ceases to shine, the rivers cease to flow and the grasses to grow or, wonder of wonders, the government decides to honour its treaties, will the white man cease to speak with forked tongue.

When the Curtain Comes Down:
Cultural Renaissance or Civil Disorder?

The Indian has reached the end of an era. The things that we hold sacred, the things that we believe in have been repudiated by the federal government. But we will not be silenced again, left behind to be absorbed conveniently into the wretched fringes of a society that institutionalizes wretchedness. The Buckskin Curtain is coming down.

The Indian, and with him the larger Canadian society, faces two alternatives—a future in which the Indian may realize his potential through the provision of the essential resources which are rightfully his, or a future where frustrations are deepened by a continued state of deprivation leading to chaos and civil disorder.

Many factors, some of them still beyond his control, will influence the Indian's choice. His choice will not be an answer to the question of who he is; that can never change. Rather, his choice will lie in how he decides to protect and build his sense of identity; his choice hinges upon his definition of the role he will play in modern society.

The Indian must have from the federal government immediate recognition of all Indian rights for the reestablishment, review and renewal of all existing Indian treaties. The negotiations for this must be undertaken in a new and different spirit by both sides. The treaties must be maintained. The treaties must be reinterpreted in light of needs that exist today. Such interpretation and application of the treaties by the Canadian government will help bring all generations of Indians together with a common sense of positive purpose. This is not a concept that should be strange to the government. The treaties differ little from the way the government deals with corporations or corporate bodies, and for that matter all segments of Canadian society, except Indians and possibly the poor of Canada.

Note

Originally published as "The Buckskin Curtain: The Indian-Problem Problem," in *The Unjust Society*, by Harold Cardinal. Copyright © Douglas and McIntyre Ltd. 1999. Reprinted with permission of the publisher.

ANTHONY WILDEN

The Old Question, but Not the Old Answers

Anthony (Tony) Wilden (b. 1935) taught communication theory at the School of Communication, Simon Fraser University. His first book, *The Language of the Self* (1968), translated and introduced the work of Jacques Lacan to anglophone North America. Other pathbreaking publications such as *System and Structure: Essays in Communication and Exchange* (1972), *The Imaginary Canadian* (1980), *The Rules Are No Game: The Strategy of Communication* (1986), and *Man and Woman, War and Peace: The Strategist's Companion* (1987) make Wilden's oeuvre one of the most innovative and important contributions to cultural and communication theory in Canada following in the wake of Innis and McLuhan.

Since our governments still call themselves "democratic," we may find there the beginnings of a ground to stand on and from which to defend ourselves and each other. We can begin by standing firm on the question of our civil liberties and our democratic rights. This is already happening, in any case. As we can see from the new kinds of books and histories being published in Canada in the 1970s, as well as from the various groups and protests springing up in different parts of Canada even in the past year or so, many Canadians are already agreed on the question of making democracy safe for the citizens and residents of Canada.

Of course, our problems in this country go far beyond the relatively simple question of democracy. Few people would suggest that introducing democratic government to Canada—and insisting that executive groups at all levels be *representative* of the grass roots, from whom they derive their power, and fully *responsible* to them—will solve the very serious difficulties we now face. Democracy alone cannot solve the problems of our economic exploitation, the destruction of our natural environment, the theft of our national resources (including our sources of energy), our perennial unemployment, inflation, confiscatory interest rates, the constant attacks on Canadian labor, the regressive taxation, the racism, the sexism, and the growing and ever more concentrated power of business in Canada.

But trying to solve huge problems all at once is not the point of our coming together to demand our rights as persons under the traditions of capitalist democracy. One point of the demand for democratic rights is that if we succeed, we may just be able to live a little more securely than we have been; and that alone is reason enough. And just because we choose to make a beginning there does not mean that this is where the process will end.

There is a much deeper and more important reason for making such a stand. Practically by definition, colonized peoples are inexperienced peoples. Colonization ensures that they are misinformed about each other and about the rest of the world. As a diverse and still relatively insulated people, we Canadians are inexperienced in working together, in learning from each other, in understanding the deeper social and economic issues which would unite us once we realized that they involve our common fate. We are too used to the anti-Canadian tradition of divide-and-rule in this country—but the only people who can do anything to change that situation are Canadians concerned with the long-range survival of Canada and its people.

We are not talking about a "one-time" solution to a "one-time" problem. Not at all. We are talking about a process, a long process of change that no one but ourselves can set going. Part of this process involves finding out about each other, about who wants what, about which priorities different groups and different regions regard as essential, and about who can be depended on to do what in this or that particular circumstance. In other words, what happens and what does not happen in this country is going to depend on the process of our mutual political education.

All these issues and concerns keep returning us to the major symptom of the real situation of Canadians in the modern world: the social, historical, and economic question of Canadian identity.

Why Is This Question So Important?

Why is the question of Canadian identity of such strategic importance in Canadian political consciousness and in our political and economic future?

We all have many different and distinct identities (identities in relation to others, for identity is always a relation). In various contexts, we have many distinct *levels* of identity as well: race, class, color, creed, sex, national origin, family background, region, and birthplace—and so on. Every person is made up of this complicated network of relationships to different contexts, and many more besides. Real identities are essential to the social individuality that makes us unique persons (as distinct from the imaginary individualism that makes us into alienated objects). Real identities—real relations to real contexts—are what help to define for each of us the ground of our existence in all these many contexts.

But if we are lacking the real identity which arises in the shared and collective relationship of *nationhood* (not nationalism in the sense of chauvinism and jingoism), then where on earth do we stand, as Canadians, in a world in which nations still exist as powerful collectivities? Where do we Canadians stand in a world in which most oppression and exploitation (whatever may be said about multinational corporations) still has national, as well as transnational, characteristics? Not on our own feet, that's for sure, but more than likely under someone else's.

"Nationhood" is still considered a dirty word in Canada, however, especially—and obviously—by our colonizers and by their "Canadian" collaborators. It is a forbidden word to them because the shared sense of nationhood provides the colonized with a special kind of unity and strength, a unity with which a people can resist the divide-and-rule of the colonizing interests.

There is in the common misunderstanding of the importance of national identity a misunderstanding of the actual processes of history—as distinct from the way we might like history to be. Because Canada is a neocolony of the United States, there is no truly international relationship between the people of Canada and the people of the United States. And even if the relationship between the working classes (for example) of both countries was a relationship between the working classes of two nations, this would not make labor transnational in the continental context, as capital is, and always has been.

For as long as Canada remains a colony of the United States, then American workers, brothers and sisters of ours as they may be, are nevertheless benefiting every day from the surplus value produced by Canadian workers in the resource industries, just as they benefit from the manufacture of the goods that we, in our mercantile subordination as a colony, are obliged to import from the United States.

The plain fact is that "internationalism"[1] refers to a relationship between two or more nations, each with control over its economy and its national territory. How then can such a term be applied to us, in any proper sense, when the country called Canada is not yet a nation?

There is also another problem here. Our major colonizers, the British and the Americans, are of course cultural and ideological colonizers, besides whatever else they are. This ideological colonization affects many different aspects of life in Canada, and many aspects of the ordinary spectrum of political positions and beliefs. The result is that most of the political positions taken by different groups in this country have been historically derived from the politics of colonization, the politics of colonizers, rather than from the politics of the colonized. Neither the British nor the Americans look upon Canada as the foreign country that it is; and their attitudes to Canada and Canadians are all too often infected with an imperial paternalism, both conscious and unconscious.

The result is that we have to face these colonial attitudes almost everywhere we look, colonial attitudes that most Canadians have been brought up with for so long that we too often take them upon ourselves, as if they were our own. The internalization, by the colonized, of the attitudes of the colonizers is a complicated and contradictory process, and one that it will be necessary to return to and to analyze in more detail. But what should be pointed out is that, in spite of all that we can and do learn from the French, American, and British political traditions, and especially from their radical traditions, we can learn very little from them about modern colonization and neocolonization as it is experienced by the colonized countries.

The politics of the colonizers are so deeply impressed upon most Canadians—and so much a part of the acceptance of the imaginary superiorities drummed into Anglo Canadians and repeatedly carried into the country by British and American immigrants—that few political positions in English-speaking Canada are immune from their unconsciously anti-Canadian ignorance. ("Ignorance, like knowledge," observed the Swedish sociologist, Gunnar Myrdal, "is purposefully directed.")

From this kind of ignorance there arises the inappropriate tendency to treat Canada as just another "industrialized" and "independent" country, rather than as the colony it actually is—a colony, moreover, which for the last twenty years at least has been progressively de-industrialized and de-developed by its colonial masters, by those whose control over industrial technology and research and development in Canada continues to increase.[2]

The struggles of the Canadian working class cannot fully be analyzed or understood solely from a perspective which is derived from the struggles of the working classes in the countries of the imperial powers. The same applies to the situation of the native Canadians colonized by the colonized; as also to the situation of the Québécois, as also to the situation of women in Canada. By the same token, the dominant class in Canada, allied as it is with enormously powerful foreign interests, has to be understood and treated differently from the way in which its apparent counterparts would be in Britain or the United States (or France, for that matter).

A significant part of politics in Canada thus still exists in a subordinate relationship to politics in Britain and in the United States. This is a colonial relationship; and it will remain as one just so long as we fail to treat the Canadian reality and the dominant Canadian consciousness as a colonized reality and as a colonized consciousness.

Common Ground

We can learn a great deal from the experience of Blacks, Chicanos, and Puerto-Ricans in the United States—except that their domestic colonization is not quite the same as our colonization from outside; because those born in any of the fifty states also bear the national identity of Americans. All of us can learn from the labor movement and the women's movement—except that national identity is not the issue here.

Who then do we turn to in order to become aware of the crucial importance of nationhood to Canada? I suggest we turn to the peoples we have most in common with, the peoples of the third-world—to their successes and their failures. To the Algerian War of Independence against the French; to China's victory over Japan; to Nicaragua; to the Vietnamese Wars of Independence against the Chinese, the French, the Japanese, the British, the French again, and eventually against the Americans and their colonial troops (e.g., the South Koreans). Whatever the failings—indeed, because of the failings—we have much to learn from them, just as we can learn from third-world countries protecting their present and their future by forming raw-materials cartels.

What we learn very quickly from the experiences of other colonized countries is that a colonized people, if they are to set out on the thorny and heady path of decolonization, have no choice whatsoever about nationhood.

A colonized people must unite on the common ground of their national identity and their national territory if they are ever to attain any significant measure of control over their own destiny.

This is in any case part of the message of the latest demand for independence and for control over resources and development from within the national territory of Canada: the Déné Declaration of 1975, reproduced as Item 1.

This declaration by the Déné Nation of the Northwest Territories was adopted by the General Assembly of the Indian Brotherhood and Métis Association of the North West Territories at Fort Simpson in July, 1975, and thence communicated to the United Nations. (These territories do not have provincial status; they are subject to the Federal government and "Indian Affairs"; their "government" in the territory is dominated by a white minority). The Declaration was also published in *The Canadian Forum* (November, 1976). Perhaps needless to say, the policy of the Federal government in regard to land settlements (and the pipelines and oil exploration they are holding up) is to offer seemingly large settlements in bits and pieces for parts and parcels in different areas—the predictable divide-and-rule.

Item 1: The Déné Declaration

We the Déné of the [North West Territories] insist on the right to be regarded by ourselves and the world as a nation.

Our struggle is for the recognition of the Déné Nation by the Government and people of Canada and the peoples and governments of the world.

As once Europe was the exclusive homeland of the European peoples, Africa the exclusive homeland of the African peoples, the New World, North and South America, was the exclusive homeland of Aboriginal peoples of the New World, the Amerindian and Inuit.

The New World like other parts of the world has suffered the experience of colonialism and imperialism. Other peoples have occupied the land—often with force—and foreign governments have imposed themselves on our people. Ancient civilizations and ways of life have been destroyed.

Colonialism and imperialism is now dead or dying. Recent years have witnessed the birth of new nations or rebirth of old nations out of the ashes of colonialism.

As Europe is the place where you will find European countries with European governments for European peoples, now also you will find in Africa and Asia the existence of African and Asian countries with African and Asian governments for the African and Asian peoples.

The African and Asian peoples—the peoples of the Third World— have fought for and won the right to self-determination, the right to recognition as distinct peoples and the recognition of themselves as nations.

But in the New World the native peoples have not fared so well. Even in countries in South America where the Native peoples are the vast majority of the population there is not one country which has an Amerindian government for the Amerindian peoples.

Nowhere in the New World have the Native peoples won the right to self-determination and the right to recognition by the world as a distinct people and as Nations.

While the Native people of Canada are a minority in their homeland, the Native people of the [North West Territories], the Déné and the Inuit, are a majority of the population of the NWT.

The Déné find themselves as part of a country. That country is Canada. But the government of Canada is not the government of the Déné. The government of the NWT is not the government of the Déné. These governments were not the choice of the Déné, these were imposed upon the Déné.

What we the Déné are struggling for is the recognition of the Déné Nation by the governments and peoples of the world.

And while there are realities we are forced to submit to, such as the existence of a country called Canada, we insist on the right to self-determination as a distinct people and the recognition of the Déné Nation.

We the Déné are part of the Fourth World. And as the peoples and Nations of the world have come to recognize the existence and rights of those peoples who make up the Third World the day must come and will come when the nations of the Fourth World will come to be recognized and respected. The challenge to the Déné and the world is to find the way for the recognition of the Déné Nation.

Our plea to the world is to help us in our struggle to find a place in the world community where we can exercise our right to self-determination as a distinct people and as a nation.

What we seek then is independence and self-determination within the country of Canada. This is what we mean when we call for a just land settlement for the Déné Nation.

Imaginary Oppositions and Real Conflicts

The question we are working our way toward answering here is the so-called "Canadian question," the "question of Canadian identity."[3] We

Canadians are a colonized people, but our colonization has been a more complex and less barbaric process than elsewhere in the world—and we don't relish talking about it very much. Hence, the real question: "Who is the dominant Other for Canadians?" requires some more groundwork before we can hope to answer it adequately, and in a non-paranoid way.

However real and necessary the hierarchical conflict between a "self" (or a collectivity) and an alienating Other (or Others) may actually be— and for any and all oppressed peoples, it is indeed a real and necessary struggle—we must nevertheless remain aware that if this struggle is defined in primarily Imaginary terms, then it will take on the unhelpful characteristics of a dualistic opposition between Imaginary images. The relation will then be played out as a single-level mirror-relationship— and, as a result, the subordinate will have already lost the struggle before it began. Consider what often happens in a "man-to-man"—or "woman-to-man"—argument with one's boss, for instance.

The struggle will have been lost because it will have been expressed and fought as an opposition which is a simple attempt to "negate" the dominating Other. In relations of oppression and exploitation, however, the subordinate is the one who is "negated" by the Other—and not in theory, but in body and soul and in person. One primary characteristic of the relation to dominant or dominating Others is that although the mediation of an oppressive Other can in principle and in practice be *overcome* in various ways when necessary; dominant Others cannot be "*negated*," except in a generally pathological sense, and in any case, not "from below." (Try "negating" American capital—any kind of capital— in Canada, for example.)

In the real world supported and maintained by real labor, and where words may also be forms of violence, potential and actual, we learned from the civil rights movement that one white person's "Nigger!" does incalculable damage to the "self-concept" of the black, whereas one thousand or one million blacks responding to an original white assault by means of "Honkie!" has no necessary or significant effect on the white at all. (It may result in guilt, of course, but guilt cannot be trusted. Neither can it form a real basis for political action.) Such "negation" and "counter-negation" cannot under state and private capitalism be reciprocal or symmetrical because the white collectivity represents a dominant and dominating Other for the black, as Frantz Fanon, for one, pointed out in his Black Skin, White Masks in 1952.

The parasitical ignorance of the dominant in these matters is alone a problem quite serious enough. It becomes even more awesome and dangerous to human well-being in its effects when those who are the targets of these real and Imaginary objectifications are so overwhelmed by the insidious power and the daily insistence of these violences that they come unconsciously to believe them to be true. The result will ordinarily be that they will match their objectification by the Other with an objectification of themselves, by themselves. They will tend to match their stereotyping by the Other with an unconscious collusion in the stereotyped roles laid out for them. They will match the hatred expressed by the representatives of the Other with self-hatred, and with a hatred of others like themselves. The violence coming from the representatives of the Other will be turned partly inward, against themselves, and partly outward, against each other, and partly downward (if possible), against others in even worse situations than they are.

This *internalization* of the Other's attitudes and behavior, this unconscious *collusion* with the representatives of the Other, this Other-induced "inferiority complex," this *oscillation*[4] between being (and behaving) as the Other commands and demands and *not* being (or behaving) in conformity with the desire of the Other—this, for the colonized, is the major ideological battleground, both personal and collective.

Dominances and Dependencies

In terms of race, the white collectivity represents real and alienating Others for the non-white—just as in Canada, in terms of one aspect of our internal colonial economics, the Anglos and all their kin represent the oppressive Others for the French, the "Canayen," the Québécois.[5] In these examples, amongst many others, the male, the white, or the Anglo participate in various and often overlapping systems of systematic domination, each system of oppression being identifiable in terms of the particular group of human beings that are its major targets. These systems of oppression are so complex and so interwoven with each other; however, that those who are the targets of oppression in one system— French-Canadian males, for example—may be the oppressors in another —their relation to Canadian women, for example, where Canadian males of whatever national origin link arms in that almost universal "brotherhood of man" we know as male imperialism.

These various forms of systematic alienation include oppression by class, of course—for just as male imperialism cuts across the boundaries of race and class, so also do class relations cut across some of the boundaries of sex and race.

One result of such systematic oppression in our society is a collective delusion, a collectively-shared denial of reality, a collective refusal to recognize the actual state of affairs. This is a delusion of the dominators, the delusion of autonomy which seeks to have us believe that in terms of race and sex, we males, we whites, and we Anglos do not have to answer for the meaning of our existence to anyone in any way whatsoever. This delusion is in its essence just one more version of the ideology of "genetic superiority" in our society. It allows us to forget that every aspect of our dominance and domination in the social hierarchy is dependent on its being paid for by the physical, emotional, and mental labor of those who have been obliged, by economic coercion and ideological cunning, to be the more oppressed of the oppressed at this time in history.

The delusion of autonomy—the illusion of the imperialist—is not shared by the non-white, by the woman, or by the Québécois, however, for they necessarily understand the reality of social relations in a much more fundamental way than those who dominate them do. Not that this understanding may not be distorted by the Imaginary, as indeed it often is. The point is rather that the imperialist—male, white, or Anglo—has been brought up in an "instrumental" relationship to the world and to others, a relationship that fails to recognize the parasitical dependency of the exploiter on those he exploits. Like the capitalist, the male, the white, and the Anglo are trained to relate to others primarily as objects to be manipulated by their practice of instrumentality. Not so the non-white, the woman, or the Québécois, however, for within the contexts defined by their exploiters, they have been brought up with an overtly recognized relational perspective on their reality—a perspective which is defined by their existence-in-relation to the alienating or oppressive Other. In these three contexts of "whiteness," "maleness," and "Angloness," their existence has been made by history and by economic realities into an overt and subordinate dependency in relation to the Other—into a function of the existence of the white, the male, and the Anglo as others who stand as representatives of the Others.

We hardly need wonder then, about the source of one common male-Anglo attitude to Quebec, an attitude often mimicked by dominant French Canadians who have "gone over to the English." This is the "liberal" and oh, so understanding attitude which paternalistically grants to French Canada the "female" role in the Canadian political and economic household.

Indeed, this use of "accepted" and therefore almost "invisible" metaphors of male imperialism to obscure from people other kinds of domination and exploitation goes further yet—and so easily, because male imperialism is so "natural" (to men). The same metaphors are characteristic of the way the media discuss the roles of the provincial governments in Canada, notably when they get invited out (to another conference) by the federal government, the conferences that often precede another unilateral escalation of the power of the federal government.

The colony of Canada itself, as well as its people, is often represented to the world in words and images as a woman. However, unlike the warlike Britannia! on British coins; unlike the powerful Victorian image of the "Widow of Windsor," Queen Victoria; and unlike the French Liberty!—the Amazonian with the Greek nose often represented as leading the sans-culottes in the storming of the Bastille in 1789 (her sister looks out over New York harbor)—unlike all these powerful female figures from other traditions, our Imaginary "Miss Canada" is quite often represented as a "sweet young thing" wandering around in her shift.

Nationhood and Individuality

In order to distinguish between real national identity and the Imaginary identities entangled in bourgeois nationalism, chauvinism, and jingoism, we find it necessary to use the word "nationhood" and also to redefine it. We know that as long as the debate about Canada's quest for nationhood is coded or mediated by the concept of the State (consistently confused with "the nation") and by the concept of nationalism as they are predominantly used in Canada today, then practically nothing worthwhile, and little that is new, can be said. But if we communicate *about* the *kind* of communication associated with the national question in Canada, if we step out of the confusion and the irrelevance of many of the messages, and direct our attention to the context of their sources, then we are properly addressing ourselves to the level of the code: to the code of the Other which is still mediating and dominating the issue in Canada, as it has traditionally done.

Just as we distinguish Imaginary nationalism from real nationhood, so also we distinguish Imaginary individualism from real individuality. Nationalism in the sense of chauvinism tends to exhibit the same Imaginary values as individualism does: atomism, divisiveness, unconstrained competition, paranoia about *others*, and associated forms of pathological behavior. Chauvinism is moreover predominantly an "either/or" relationship to other nations, just as individualism is to other individuals. In contrast, nationhood, like individuality, is a "both-and" relationship. What predominates here is not atomism, but relationship; not divisiveness, but connectedness; not competition, but cooperation; not paranoia, but realism.

This realism, however, obliges us to understand that we may be forced into "either/or" situations by dominating Others—as in the question of the foreign powers who are pillaging Canada of its natural resources, for instance. And because of the dominance of "either/or" values and behavior under capitalism, we may well have to call upon our nationhood and our individuality to resist these Others—they will not go away just because someone has "a better idea" of what is to be done than these Others and their collaborators in Canada do.

We should be careful also not to misunderstand the distinction between individualism and individuality. The dominance of "either/or" values and modes of thinking in our present society sets up an Imaginary opposite for "individualism": i.e., "collectivism." One almost automatic and misguided response to any critique of individualism, then, will be the assumption that any statement implying that individualism is A Bad Thing must *also* be implying that its Imaginary opposite, "collectivism," is A Good Thing—and the term "collectivism" is a code-word in the dominant ideology for totalitarianism.

Another misguided response, by means of an Imaginary "either/or" opposite, to the critique of individualism is to assume that individualism is a "negative" which can only be replaced by its "positive," i.e., by its Imaginary mirror-image. Thus, if individualism is seen to represent aggressiveness, then "aggressiveness" will become a supposed "either" in an Imaginary "either/or" duality. The dominant way of thinking about such relationships will imply that it can be replaced only by its supposed opposite—and this "or" in the Imaginary equation will be passive or pacifist.

In reality, individuality is neither of these Imaginary opposites, aggressiveness or passivity. Individuality is, however, *assertive*; and this assertiveness is born in relations of cooperation which are the grounds of its special strength. Like nationhood, at one level, and political consciousness, at another, individuality is a self *and* other relationship. But when the Other declares war on this cooperative relationship, when the Other defines itself by its behavior as an enemy, then individuality fights back.

It is not dominance, as such, or mediation by the Other, as such, which results in alienation in the dehumanizing sense. The problem is not the Other, it is the dominating Other; the problem is not mediation, it is alienating and oppressive mediation.

The human and social identity through which we come to live and feel our relational individuality as persons in society is a result of mediation. The Imaginary and alienated identities of (economic and psychological) individualism under state and private capitalism are also the products of mediation, but of a different kind of mediation—mediation by the machines that rule our lives in particular, and especially as this fundamental alienation is experienced by those who directly tend those machines.

Whereas (competitive) individualism is generated by the divisive mediation of dominating Others, social individuality is a function of mediation by what may generally be called "*Otherness*," the social world of Otherness. Many of us are quite unused to considering ourselves and our relation to other people in these terms; the following examples should help to deal with some aspects of the confusions about Otherness (confusions which might be called, in the Imaginary, the "Robinson Crusoe Complex").

Critics of the dominant ideology over the past one hundred years have insisted that "being human" in the proper sense of the term always means "being a social being." "Being human" is not an inborn, or innate, or genetic trait; only the propensity to be human forms part of our genetic make-up. Therefore, "wolf-children" and the like are not human beings in the proper sense (although we do of course treat them as such). They are human organisms. An organism is a member of a species (biological level of organization). A human being is a member of a society as well (socioeconomic level of organization). The "wolf-child" thus becomes a human (social) being only when brought into the human family of society, where the "Otherness" the child experiences is primarily a social and human Otherness, rather than simply a biological and animal one.

Another problem similarly related to the ideology of individualism in our society involves the understanding of mediation. Because in our ordinary experience a "mediator" arrives on the scene "after the event" in "business disputes" (strikes, lockouts, and so on), we tend to think of mediation as a conscious, highly visible, personally-represented, rather legalistic, and "surface structure" process. We confuse the least significant kind of mediation, represented in the person of an "arbitrator," with the profoundly unconscious mediation, and levels of mediation, at the level of the "deep structures" or the codes in our society.

In reality, long before the visible mediator or arbitrator appears on the scene in a dispute between "business" and "labor," the relations between worker and worker are already mediated by the present power of capital to constrain workers to compete with each other (for jobs, for promotions, and so on). Similarly, but at a different level in the overall system of conflict, the relations between a group of workers (or a union) and a business firm (or conglomerate) are already mediated by the presently effective power of business-in-general to subject workers to the constraint of "competing" with the very "business" which presently controls the workers' means of livelihood. This last is a form of relationship mediated by dominating Others in which no individual worker, no individual union, can ever win. Viewed as "competition," this hierarchical conflict between labor and capital is Imaginary. Viewed—and lived—as alienation, this conflict between the subordinate and the dominant in the workplace is of course entirely Real.

However, it is not the structure of mediation as such which creates the problem of alienation, for mediation is universal in human experience.

Rather it is the distortion and perversion of this structure by the Other, the twisted substructures created by oppression, and the alienating *contents* imposed on the *form* of this structure by those with the (relative) power to do so—these are the realities which are responsible for the dehumanizing mediation by dominating Others that almost all of us experience.

The result, of course, is to reinforce our fictional mosaic of individualism, our "social atomism"—for when oppression by the Other is predominant in our lived experience, then we will tend to reject recognition of any form of mediation in our lives as oppressive, lock, stock, and barrel.

Imaginary Identity, Positive and Negative

Most Canadians are brought up in the home and in the school in a tissue of contradictions about American people, American capital, and supposedly "American" ideas. Too often these contradictions involve an introverted feeling of inferiority to the American giant, a feeling of inferiority which is hammered on by many of our politicians, by many media personalities, and by Canadian quislings from various walks of life. This is felt and experienced as violence. But recognizing the real source of this violence is dangerous; and attempting to turn it back on its actual sources is psychological suicide—for the individual. The violence from above is turned inward, against the individual victim; the violence is turned outward, against others in the same situation; the violence is turned downward, against those less empowered to fight back. The violence of the colonizers against the colony is thus turned by the colonized against each other.

Most of us are brought up to feel predominantly "anti-American." Others of us are trained to be "pro-American." Still others switch back and forth, at different times or at different levels, between the two opposed poles of this Imaginary relation.

Moreover, as often as not, "anti-American" is taken to mean "pro-British," while "pro-American" is assumed to mean "anti-British." It makes little difference whether in our identification *with* or *against* the projected Other (the Imaginary American) our Imaginary relationship is predominantly positive (collusion) or predominantly negative (opposition). In both, cases, the quality called "Canadian" is being defined as subordinate to the quality called "American." The Imaginary code of "national identity" that is being (unconsciously) used in this pathological relation to the dominant and dominating Other is a code constructed out of whatever it is that "American" comes to stand for in any particular time or place.

The same is of course true when the Imaginary Others we are "for" or "against" include the other two major colonizers of Canadians, the British or the French.

A third position, however, transcends the dualism and one-dimensionality of the Imaginary relation. It does not depend on the symmetry of *either* "American" or "not-American" (and so on). This position and perspective, this position of political recognition, is one that can take all of the Imaginary positions into account and put them in their place. It goes beyond our Imaginary "identity of opposites"—or opposition of Imaginary identities—with the United States (and other nations). It is a way of communicating about our relation to our colonizers, providing that relation with the real context which can lay open its hidden significance.

This third position—the contextual position this essay seeks to speak from—is a position based on our actual history as Canadians, on our actual Canadian present, and on our real hopes for the future as a nation.

This is a position and a perspective which allows us to take whatever we need from wherever we find it from whatever tradition. It allows us to borrow from any number of traditions—besides the Canadian and Inuit and Amerindian traditions—and to transform them in whatever ways we find most fruitful and most useful. It is the position not of Canadian chauvinism, not of anti-American bourgeois nationalism, not of pro-American or pro-British or pro-French anti-Canadianism, but the position and the perspective of Canadian nationhood.

Notes

Originally published as "The Old Question, but Not the Old Answers," in *The Imaginary Canadian*, by Tony Wilden. Copyright © Pulp Press 1980. Reprinted with permission of the publisher.

1. On this topic, see for example the articles on "international" unions in Canada by R. B. Morris, and by R. Howard and Jack Scott, in *Capitalism and the National Question in Canada*, ed. Gary Teeple (Toronto: University of Toronto Press, 1972).

2. Canada has always been permitted by its colonial masters to export imperialism into other colonies (e.g., into the Caribbean and South America). Canadian and British-Canadian banks have often helped to prepare the way, and other capitalists from Canada have ridden into these countries on the coat tails of British and American imperialism. As we did for the Americans in their attempt to colonize Vietnam, Canada has often acted as the agent of imperial interests around the world. As a result, it is easy to confuse our subordinate role in these activities with "Canadian imperialism," so-called. The common tendency is to think that a country is *either* a colony *or* an imperialist power. If Canada is in certain ways less colonized than, say, Jamaica or Brazil, this does not mean that Canada is *not* colonized. The fact is that Canada is *predominantly* a colony, at the same time as Canadian businesses and governments collaborate with the dominant imperial powers in the world-wide imperial system. On this topic, see the analysis by Red Star Collective (*Canada: Imperialist Power or Economic Colony*, Pamphlet No. 1, March 1977).

3. The excerpts that follow are from chapter 7 of Wilden's *The Imaginary Canadian* (Vancouver: Pulp Press, 1980).—Eds.

4. On the topic of oscillation between paradoxical alternatives, see Wilden and Wilson, "The Double Bind: Logic, Magic, and Economics" (1976). In the terms of colonial identity, two major oscillations for Canadians are those between "(not) being French" and "(not) being English"; and between "(not) being British" and "(not) being American."

5. "Canayen" is a derogatory slang word used in Quebec to refer to those French Canadians who have accepted and acquiesced to colonization by English Canadians. It is also used by some Métis to distinguish themselves from English "Canadians" and French "Canadiens," that is, those born in France.—Eds.

II

Contemporary Canadian

Cultural Studies

A

Nationalism and Canada

IAN ANGUS

The Social Identity of English Canada

Ian Angus (b. 1949) is a professor of humanities at Simon Fraser University, where he has taught since 1992. He completed a B.A. and M.A. in philosophy at the University of Waterloo and a Ph.D. in social and political thought at York University in 1980. He is the author and editor of numerous books, the most recent of which are *A Border Within: National Identity, Cultural Plurality, and Wilderness* (1997), *(Dis)figurations: Discourse/Critique/Ethics* (2000), *Primal Scenes of Communication: Communication, Consumerism, and Social Movements* (2000), and *Emergent Publics: An Essay on Social Movements and Democracy* (2001).

The discourse of English Canadian left-nationalism was the key component of the self-expression of English Canada in the period of permeable Fordism from the end of the Second World War to the beginning of the Canada-U.S. Free Trade Agreement in 1989. In retrospect, it may be regarded as English Canada's self-expression even though its mode of identification, correlative to the historic bloc predominant in the period, was the federal government. In any case, it never made inroads either in Quebec or in Aboriginal politics and could not really be expected to do so. There were two main components to this left-nationalist discourse: an analysis of the historical reasons for the continued dependency that characterized the Canadian economy and an argument for the necessity of cultural autonomy, both intrinsically (as the key aspect of the expression of national identity) and strategically (as a condition for gaining control of the economy). While the political-economic and cultural components of left-nationalism were inseparable within the analysis, its impact on Canadian society (its Liberal domestication, one might say) was such as to propose the assertion of cultural autonomy without fundamentally altering the conditions of economic dependency. The argument for cultural autonomy influenced Canadian cultural institutions and policy, whereas the power to put the economic analysis into practice was never gained. I want to sketch the main contours of left-nationalism and its social effect in order to suggest that the conditions which gave rise to it have now fundamentally altered and that it can be seen as a sign of a historical period which has come to an end.

The two main axes of left-nationalism were the historical diagnosis of the Canadian economy as "dependent industrialization" as a result of the successive colonial relations of Canada to France, Britain, and the United States developed in the staple theory of Harold Innis and the lament for the failure of Canadian cultural autonomy by George Grant. These two axes constituted left-nationalism as an interdisciplinary intellectual space focused on the topic of Canada in relation to the usual division of academic specialization in the university structure—English, sociology, political science, geography, philosophy, and so forth. The third axis was usually supplied by the individual researcher or writer. Sometimes it was a set of interests formed within one of the academic specializations, such as English literature. An investigation would then focus on the issues raised by the history of Canadian literature in relation to a country that has been, and is, economically dependent in the context of a project of self-assertion of national identity.

Canadian Studies departments at Canadian universities were constructed by collecting scholars from different disciplines and bringing them into relation through the addition of these two axes, which they then had in common. However, it is important to note that the third axis need not necessarily be a university-based specialization. It might be, for example, the concern of union organizers to promote the interests of workers, of local librarians or historical societies to develop and disseminate knowledge about their area, of regions and localities far from federal power to account for their marginalized condition, and so forth. Left-nationalism was an intellectual discourse with a political orientation that connected academic inquiry with a wider political project which could involve Canadian society as a whole. It was a case of intellectual leadership in Gramsci's sense (not solely, but often importantly, university-based)— the articulation of a world-view with a goal of social transformation that appealed to a coalition of the currently less powerful groups in Canadian society. This intellectual leadership was not confined to the universities. It also embraced union leaders and researchers, some politicians (mostly in the New Democratic Party), community activists, and other radicals oriented to various issues. They are all intellectuals in Gramsci's sense: they articulate and propagate the ideas central to an emerging world-view.

The two main intellectual figures in the left-nationalist discourse were

Harold Innis and George Grant. Innis and Grant were continuous reference points for discussions within left-nationalism and also for more polemical debates with opposing political forces.[1] This does not mean that the works of Innis and Grant were accepted uncritically within left-nationalism, but rather that they became axes in relation to which criticism, empirical research, and theoretical development could be situated. Innis's classic analysis of Canada's staple economy centred on the dependency of a society developed through a colonial relation between peripheral colony and imperial centre. In the well-known conclusion to The Fur Trade in Canada he wrote: "The economic history of Canada has been dominated by the discrepancy between the centre and the margin of western civilization. Energy has been directed toward the exploitation of staple products and the tendency has been cumulative. The raw material supplied to the mother country stimulated manufactures of the finished product and also of the products which were in demand in the colony. ... The general tendencies in the industrial areas of western civilization, especially in the United States and Great Britain, have had a pronounced effect on Canada's export of staples."[2]

Here were all the basic components of the staple theory of Canadian economic dependency: a centre-periphery colonial relation, an underdeveloped manufacturing sector in the colony, the significance of transportation and communication links, and cultural continuity with Western civilization. Development of Innis's staple theory proceeded in a number of directions. To mention a few: a cleavage between commercial-financial and industrial sectors of the capitalist class was investigated by R. T. Naylor;[3] Melville Watkins pointed to the consequences of the high degree of foreign (United States) ownership for the export of resource-generated capital, over-concentration of resources in the export sector, and the failure to develop renewable forms of industry, that he called the "staple trap";[4] Wallace Clement investigated unequal development of regions within Canada by successive waves of staple extraction.[5] The political issue of the relation between the industrial working class and farmers was a prominent theme because of its immediate political implications.[6] Even Marxists who contended that the internal class formation of Canada was more important than foreign ownership and dependency felt obliged to argue their position as a critique of Innis,[7] but more thorough and influential was the attempt to reconcile Innis's ground-breaking empirical account of Canadian economic history with Marxist analysis. The point here is not to catalogue all of these developments and certainly not to enter into the debates between them; it is rather to indicate how the staple theory provided an axis for reference, research, and critique that tied such developments to the overall discourse of left-nationalism and its political project even as Innis's work was expanded, criticized, and surpassed in many specific respects.

George Grant's lament for the failure to achieve cultural autonomy was similarly used as a continuing reference within left-nationalism. In 1945 he had published a pamphlet that defended Canada's continuing membership in the Commonwealth and the maintenance of the British connection. It sounded a theme that persisted throughout his life's work: that the independence of Canada from the United States presupposed the notion that, even though we share language and cultural background with that country, some different way of life was—or ought to be—pursued here. Grant argued, "The meaning and significance of Canada as a nation is that on the northern half of this continent a sovereign state has been created, friendly to the U.S.A., but essentially different."[8] The American empire, he suggested, was based exclusively on the principle of the freedom of the individual. He defined the difference of Canada as based in the British tradition of effecting "a compromise between the two extremes of liberty and order" and a Canadian as "the blending of the best of the ancient civilization of western Europe with its maturity and integrity, with the best of North American life."[9] Here are, in germ, the main political themes of Grant's work: the definition of the United States (at least in the post-1945 period) as an empire, the description of its culture as based exclusively on the liberal doctrine of individual freedom, the defence of the greater European connection in Canada as the result of a non-revolutionary tradition and the heritage of Loyalism, the search for a principle of Canadian difference, and the definition of this difference through a communitarian stress on social order.

The appropriation of Grant's work within left-nationalism was always controversial. His own Toryism and Platonism, not to mention the influence of Leo Strauss, also led to more traditionally conservative interpretations. Left-nationalism revoked in one major way the formation of his work. It rejected, in the final analysis, the standpoint of lament. Certainly, a rhetoric of lament has strong overtones in left-nationalism insofar as it uncovers the historic failure of Canadian government to provide the policies that might lead the country from a cycle of dependence towards an independent economic and cultural existence. The emphasis on the "preservation" of our historical cultures has been a significant rhetorical form within which left-nationalism has articulated its prospective world-view in relation to the past. One might say that the main rhetorical form of left-nationalism is a lament for the failure adequately to preserve the past and an argument that such preservation requires a radical reorientation in the future. It is a vision of a Loyalist, Tory past and a socialist future. To call it a rhetorical form is to say that it goes far beyond specific arguments and analyses. It is a thought structure, or a form for the elaboration and presentation of ideas, which is often present even when virtually invisible and which derives more from the discourse of left-nationalism as a whole than from any one component. The influence of Grant on left-nationalism is through his provision of this rhetorical form of lament, as well as many of the specific themes of its vision of cultural autonomy.

However, left-nationalism was bound to reject this standpoint as the final word—as perhaps Grant himself did when faced with pressing political issues.[10] Lament, in the left-nationalist version, was relegated to covering only the story *up until now*. The other half of the story was oriented to the possibility of independence in the future, which was contingent on its most characteristic rhetorical component—as with any engaged political movement—the necessity for decision in the present. The present as endangered and as the locus for radical decision is the primary rhetorical form of left-nationalism. It has this characteristic in common with Marxism, which is the formative-rhetorical basis for the Marxist-nationalist synthesis (as opposed to the thematic basis, which is the analysis of the intersection of class and nation). Thus left-nationalism devalues Grant's rhetoric of lament in order to replace it with a rhetoric of a decisive present. In an influential collection entitled *Canada Ltd.: The Political Economy of Dependency*, Melville Watkins oriented his argument for Canadian socialism around a reassessment (in 1973) of Grant's book. He took issue with Grant's claim that socialism is impossible in Canada's current context and thereby turned the lament into a call for a new socialist and nationalist party.[11] In addition, consider the closing lines of a more recent essay by Mel Hurtig. "In conclusion, there can be no question that George Grant was a prophet. But so far his followers have failed—not because they are in the minority, but because they have used the wrong tactics. It remains to be seen whether or not they can learn from the bitter lessons of 1988. They have one last chance."[12] It is quite a move to interpret a lament as prophecy! Left-nationalism must always position itself one step before the end and point to "one last chance." Thus it cannot really indulge in lament from first to last, as perhaps Grant himself as a living and acting individual could not. The revoking of lament was the condition for his inclusion as an axis of left-nationalist discourse, and it explains the impossibility of entirely capturing his legacy within that discourse.

Within left-nationalist discourse, Harold Innis and George Grant are thus rather more than the names of two major Canadian thinkers: they are the symbols for two of its axes. They are the integrating conditions whereby the interests of specific researchers and activists became incorporated into the discourse by being placed within a common space. Moreover, these two axes, though they deal with economic dependency and the project of cultural autonomy, are not simply different; they bear important relationships to each other. For example, Harold Innis also referred to American imperialism, Loyalism, and Canadian autonomy, even though his work was not mainly about cultural issues.[13] Also, Grant's conception of culture was primarily an anthropological sense of everyday practices and routines and only secondarily that of scholarship and the arts; as reflected in his tendency to use the term "civilization" rather than "culture." In this sense, culture encompasses political economy and is not counterposed to material life. Grant often referred to political events symbolically, in the sense that they were not simply single events but condensed the meaning of larger turning points in the way of life of a people. This was the way he treated the 1963 defeat of John Diefenbaker in Lament for a Nation.

In sum, the works of Innis and Grant became almost canonical within left-nationalism—not in a static sense, but as the condition for the elaboration and development of the discourse in a way that held it close to the practical concerns of Canadian society and that articulated a project of its political transformation.

There were thus good reasons to suppose that an integration of Innis's dependency theory and Grant's cultural vision could be made meaningful within left-nationalism. These two axes provided the references whereby specific studies and activities could be integrated into a larger national project. But there was another component too, which relates to the rhetoric of "decision in the present" that marked the appropriation of Grant's lament. The three axes of left-nationalism had to be put together in such a way that its focus on the nation could be connected to the "left" character of the synthesis. This core, which enabled the construction of the discourse, concerned the status of the national capitalist class and its relationship to the project of nation building. The most characteristic tendency of left-nationalism was to argue that the Canadian bourgeoisie was thoroughly compromised by its dependent role. Jim Laxer wrote in Canada Ltd., "Canada's dependency is a function not of geography and technology but of the nature of Canada's capitalist class. . . . At no stage have native Canadian industrialists who profited from the production and sale of manufactured goods dominated Canadian capitalism. . . . Dependency has shaped the character of Canadian capitalism and has created a capitalist class that has needed continued dependency for its continued well-being."[14] This straightforward statement was open to considerable discussion and debate. It was argued by Daniel Drache, for example, in an echo of Innis's claim that Canada had moved "from colony to nation to colony," that bourgeois nationalism had been a factor but that now it was a "spent force."[15] The core of the integration of the discourse of left-nationalism was, of course, argued almost incessantly. It was the focus on this issue that defined left-nationalism as such. This is a consequence of a "discourse" that it defines through the intersection of axes a centre of concern which is open to continuous debate. Whatever the nuances of the specific analysis, the political conclusion was that nationalism had ceased to be (or never was) a bourgeois force in Canada and that it could become a factor in the politics of the working class, and perhaps a coalition of all subaltern classes.

This core defines left-nationalism "proper," that is, its clearest and most explicit form. Through this delineation it can be distinguished from two closely related analyses on either side, as it were, of the core. There was a Marxist argument that the Canadian state operated in the interests of a nationalist capitalist class, a class that often had imperialist interests and was thus in principle no different from those of other countries. Nationalism, on this argument, contained no possibility of being connected to the political aspirations of working and subaltern classes. At its extreme this argument rejected the discourse of left-nationalism entirely except insofar as it was oriented to political opposition to the policies of the U.S. government. One characteristic text argued, "Canada is not moving towards colonial status in the American empire; it is moving towards a greater imperial role in the world imperialist system."[16] If critics could depart from the "nationalist" side of the analysis on one hand, they could just as well depart from the "left" side as well. Non-left-nationalists such as Mel Hurtig accepted the argument against American ownership and dependency, but posed the question in this way: "Who should be in charge of society—the community or big corporations?"[17] There is a populist note in this appeal to be sure, though its undifferentiated concept of the community leaves a lot unsaid. A considerable overlap with left-nationalism is possible depending on one's interpretation of this point.

The core of left-nationalism was therefore the argument that the capitalist class had no (further) interest in nationalism and that a certain version of popular nationalism could become the political vehicle of the subaltern classes. Radiating from this core were the axes of the discourse. With this definition of the discourse of left-nationalism it is possible to clarify its practical effect on Canadian society. Simply put, the account of economic dependency was thoroughly documented, but did not have significant impact on Canadian society or policy. The Foreign Investment Review Board, possibly the only real institutional consequence to which one could point, was set up by the Liberal Party under nationalist pressure in the 1970s and never had any teeth to repatriate the economy. Rather, it presided over the continued takeover and reorganization of the national economy by international forces. On the other hand, the argument for cultural autonomy had some effect. Perhaps this severing of the left-nationalist discourse was the basis for the later pervasive polarization in English Canadian intellectual life between political economy and cultural approaches to social and political thought. This separation and opposition is by no means necessary, but it becomes unavoidable when political economy is interpreted reductionistically and culture is defined in opposition to economy.[18] The remnants of the left-nationalist synthesis and its social effects are deeper and more widespread in English Canadian intellectual life than is normally appreciated, especially in a time when all of this might appear to be merely ancient history.[19] I will briefly explore two examples of the limited success of the argument for cultural autonomy.

The first example I want to consider is the foundation and growth of the Association for Canadian Studies, mainly within tertiary education (universities and community colleges) but also with some impact on earlier and adult education, public libraries, and publications such as magazines. In 1969 Robin Mathews and James Steele published The Struggle for Canadian Universities, a report that documented the high numbers of American professors teaching in Canadian universities and the consequent lack of attention given to Canadian issues and themes. The report was careful to clarify that "there should be a large number of foreign scholars in Canadian universities at all times," and it focused attention on the fact that the overwhelming majority of foreign scholars were from the United States and on the difficulties encountered by qualified Canadians in finding positions.[20] Despite this important clarification, this document and its surrounding circumstances created controversy throughout higher education in Canada, controversy that went beyond the persons involved (or not having the chance to be involved) in teaching to the content of what was taught. In particular, attention was directed to the minimal Canadian content and preponderance of American world-views, ideologies, and histories, especially in the social sciences and humanities. One result of the controversy was the incorporation of an analysis of the universities into a rapidly developing left-nationalist analysis of Canadian society. As Ian Lumsden, the editor of the influential 1970 volume *Close the 49th Parallel: The Americanization of Canada*, put it, "The reversal of the Americanization of Canada can come about only through the substitution of a new world-view among its people in place of their addiction to the 'American way of life' and their adherence to the values perpetuated by the North American bourgeoisie. These values are diffused through a wide variety of cultural, educational, and social institutions."[21] The ignorance of Canada fostered by Canadian educational institutions was diagnosed as part of a process of cultural domination that accompanied and legitimated Canadian economic dependency on American capitalism and imperialism. While this analysis was hotly debated, defined, and extended within left-nationalist circles, it came to have an influence on the many university people who would not have defined themselves as left-nationalists and on many in the society at large.

In 1972 the Commission on Canadian Studies was formed by the Association of Universities and Colleges of Canada. It produced a report entitled *To Know Ourselves*, which is widely recognized as the intellectual legitimation for the Association for Canadian Studies and for Canadian Studies in educational institutions generally. The Symons Report, as it is generally known, in its chapter on "The Rationale for Canadian Studies," carefully separated the concern for Canadian Studies from nationalism, national unity, and other issues of sovereignty, but it argued that our differences from the United States are important and must be studied in order for us to come to grips with our own problems. The root issue was defined in the following way: "it is impossible to attempt to deal with problems unless our attempts are built on the strongest foundation of self-knowledge; as Northrop Frye has suggested, a citizen's primary duty is 'to try to know what should be changed in his society and what should be preserved'—a responsibility that we cannot begin to discharge until, as citizens, we *know* our country."[22] This was a weaker form of the left-nationalist rationale, purged of references to imperialism and nationalism and legitimated with reference to English Canada's most internationally known scholar, which could be accepted by a much wider public. The Association for Canadian Studies was formed in 1973 and has had a continuing influence on the agenda of Canadian universities, though it has never displaced the traditional academic disciplines or disciplinary-based scholarly organizations from their dominant position. A recent (1996) report on the current state of Canadian Studies, known as the Cameron Report, points out that the relation between Canadian Studies and what it calls the "national unity rationale" is loose: "To teach about Canada's historical experience and its social and economic life is not necessarily to reinforce identification with Canada."[23] The practice and rationale for Canadian Studies seems to have watered down considerably its original legitimation to the point where it appears divorced from any political project at all. This increasing divergence from the left-national-ist discourse that presided over its institution is the basis for what Row-land Lorimer has called the bland character of these reports and the "narrow line of development" that Canadian Studies has taken.[24] In the end, it has tended to accommodate itself increasingly to the dictates of established university structure rather than engage in the reconstruction of a national-popular collective will.

My second example is the rich cultural-policy discourse that emerged in Canada with the Massey Commission in the 1950s and continued until the exemption of cultural industries from the Free Trade Agreement (article 2005). The condition for this limited success of left-nationalism was a *separation of culture from political economy* that was not only not a part of its own internal discourse, but was explicitly denied by left-national-ism itself. The cultural-policy discourse that has emerged in Canada is tied to the intervention in culture by the Canadian federal state. It can be called a "discourse" in the same sense as left-nationalism, though it is of a more limited scope. Its justification is the argument that cultural indus-tries are special insofar as they are concerned with the formation of the identities of Canadians and therefore that they need to be regulated in a manner distinct from other industries. The success of this argument has created a federal cultural-policy discourse with institutional, economic, and regulatory dimensions. The separation of culture from political economy should be more accurately formulated as a separation of cul-tural industries from the political economy as a whole through an argu-ment concerning their specialness based upon the issue of Canadian identity. In other words, political economy is discussed, but only the political economy of cultural industries. This special status is conferred upon these industries by the extraction of the argument for cultural autonomy from the discourse of left-nationalism.

The cultural-policy discourse is structured through three axes[25] that create a "slide" between the terms such that they become, for all practical purposes, equivalent within the discourse. In other words, each term elicits all the connotations and effects of the others, to which it becomes pragmatically equivalent by the structuring of the discourse. The cultural-policy discourse compresses three cultural oppositions, each of which becomes an axis for the discourse: Canada versus the United States, high versus low culture, public versus private ownership. These terms are structured so that the first of each of the pairs becomes practically equivalent to the others, as does the second of each of the pairs. Thus it is suggested that the United States produces low, or popular, culture through private ownership of the media. This is the polemical object that the discourse constructs. Paul Litt has documented the equation of American influence with mass commercial culture in the Massey Report and connected it to the influence of Canada's cultural elite in government circles. It was entirely overlooked that mass culture critique was also largely imported from the U.S. and that American high culture was not regarded as a baleful influence.[26] Thus an equivalence is constructed between Canada, high culture, and government intervention that justifies government regulation of cultural industries in Canada and makes it difficult, though not exactly impossible, to argue against.

This slide between terms affected even the most perspicacious critics. Harold Innis, in his commentary on the Massey Report, concluded by claiming, "We can only survive by taking persistent action at strategic points against American imperialism in all its attractive guises. By attempting constructive efforts to explore the cultural possibilities of various media of communication and to develop them along lines free from commercialism, Canadians might make a contribution to the cultural life of the United States by releasing it from dependence on the sale of tobacco and other commodities."[27] Notice the equation of commercialism with the United States and the slide towards the worst "low" example of tobacco sales, whereas Canada is equated with the enlightening possibility, not its low actuality, of constructive efforts free of commercialism. Any argument against this policy of federal government regulation preferred by the discourse will tend to be conflated towards the polemical object. Margaret Prang concluded her study of the origin of public broadcasting in this way, "As in earlier Canadian enterprises there was no commitment to public ownership in principle, but once convinced that the choice lay between 'the State or the United States,' most Canadians of the thirties had a ready answer."[28] This attitude accounts for the success of the cultural-policy discourse in Canadian public life until recent times. It seemed essential to protecting (not developing or changing) Canadian identity and thus required no action oriented to redressing the issue of economic dependency, either of Canada on the U.S. or between unequal economic groups within the country. In this way the left-nationalist argument for cultural autonomy became the federal cultural-policy discourse.

This discourse incorporates a three-way *reductionism* from a comprehensive anthropological concept of culture as a "way of life" (Wittgenstein) with "a characteristic style" (Husserl) that incorporates a "structure of feeling" (Williams) utilized in left-nationalist discourse to a more limited domain. Each of these reductions produces a significant *silence* within cultural-policy discourse because of the systematic non-investigation of relevant aspects of Canadian culture to which they lead. First, the concept of culture utilized in the cultural-policy discourse is reduced to industrially produced culture. Thus the significance of the marginalization of autonomous *cultural production in everyday life* by commercially organized processes is left uninvestigated. Second, the concept of *public intervention* in culture is reduced to government regulation, specifically by the federal government. The conflation of widespread public discussion and debate with government regulation leaves uninvestigated the conditions for a well-functioning and democratically organized public sphere. Third, it cannot help but promote a notion of Canadian culture as uniform because of its emphasis on industrial production and federal government regulation.

These two examples are intended to illustrate the limited success that the left-nationalist discourse has had as the self-expression of English Canada in the period of permeable Fordism. They are, of course, not the only possible ones. Nor is this a comprehensive evaluation of the effect of left-nationalism as a whole. However, they do show the extent to which the project of cultural autonomy has had a certain efficacy as a result of the institutionalization of the project of self-knowledge of national identity. Moreover, they indicate the price of this success—the precise character of its limitation. The project of self-knowledge has been cut off from any national vision addressing issues of economic dependency by being narrowed to a conception of culture as dealing solely with the federal regulation of scholarly, artistic, or media expressions separately from their relation to the popular practices and feelings that constitute the national-popular collective will."[29] As a consequence, the discourse of cultural autonomy has become severed from the analysis of dependency in left-nationalism. It is this focus on dependency that could be the bridge between the legacy of left-nationalism and the other critiques of domination proposed by contemporary social movements. To date, this bridge remains unconstructed. The point thus far is only that its construction is not impossible, but has only come to appear so because of the precise character of the limited impact of left-nationalism on English Canadian society.

A Plurality of Dependencies

The discourse of left-nationalism was tied to a historical period whose demise can be indicated, though not fully explained, by reference to the new era of continental integration inaugurated by the FTA [Free Trade Agreement] and NAFTA. There have always been movements for economic and sometimes political union with the United States within Canada, but this time they have come at a moment and achieved a success that has changed the context in which one can speak of English Canadian identity or nationhood.

Left-nationalism was a discourse that attempted to reform the national-popular collective will in Canada. It linked together nation and class as an oppositional force in an era in which multinational, or transnational, corporations had become the leading economic force. Transnational corporations, it was argued, were really mainly American corporations extending beyond their borders into a multinational context to dominate the political economy of Canada. This contemporary situation was given historical explanation through an Innisian analysis of the colonial dependency of a staple-producing economy. The staple trap documented by Innis was such an essential part of Canadian history that it had an influence, or perhaps was independently discovered, even among analysts who would be more likely to insist on class factors over national concerns.

Class analysis of Canadian society required an explanation of the historic weakness of the capitalist class, and this was provided by colonial dependence based on staple extraction and failed industrialization. This explanation, however, obscured the new forces that were at work in the global economy, which have since come to fruition in the phenomenon known as globalization. In the interim a significant portion of the Canadian capitalist class initiated, through the Conservative Party, the process of formal economic integration of a free trade zone in North America through a bilateral agreement with the United States, which has since expanded to include Mexico and will soon expand further to encompass South American countries and potentially all of the Americas. In this context the core argument of left-nationalism that transnational corporations are really American ones has been undermined by several factors: the willingness of "American" transnationals to abandon the United States if it suits their interests, the growth of "Canadian" transnationals that operate outside of Canada, and the decreasing percentage of foreign ownership of the Canadian economy. In other words, globalization refers to a genuinely transnational economic environment dominated by large corporations that are increasingly gaining leverage over nation-states and whose influence cannot therefore be theorized as the influence of one nation-state over another.

Does this development mean that there has been an end to dependency? Dependency theory was oriented to the dependency of nations and was concerned with the use of the dependent nation-state in the interests of a foreign capitalist class operating through its own nation-state. It was concerned to construct a counter-hegemonic national-popular collective will to use the nation-state to steer domestic industry for the benefit of all citizens. This formulation has been surpassed by the globalization of the economy, in which dependency between nation-states does not play a central role in the analysis. But this does not mean that all forms of dependency have been eliminated, that the Canadian economy is independent of the American one, nor does it reduce the commercial dependency on American markets or cultural domination by U.S. media industries.[30] Further, it does not mean that the Canadian economy as a whole has escaped the staple trap. British Columbia is still exporting raw lumber and importing furniture and other finished wood products. This historic pattern remains pervasive throughout the Canadian economy. Globalization does mean, however, that it is impossible to describe adequately the dynamics of domination in the global economy mainly through the category of the nation-state—or, more exactly, through the nation-state as the main social actor in the interests of nationally based, but internationally operating capital—as does dependency theory. As Resnick has argued, "It was only when American imperialism began to weaken internationally in the 1960s that English Canadian sentiment began to shift, and that anti-imperialism, or simply anti-Americanism, became a potent force."[31] In this sense, left-nationalism can be seen as a transitory phenomenon between the years of full-fledged American hegemony and globalization.

The end of left-nationalism (as a dependency critique of Canadian society) does not mean the end of dependency as such. Rather, it implies a recognition of the multiple forms of dependency that exist in contemporary society and requires that each be analysed in terms of the *specific linkage* that ties it to the system as a whole. Second, it answers a nagging question that Marxist critics often put to Innisian dependency theory, that it implied that Canada is essentially a Third World country with problems of dependency equivalent to those of Latin America, for example.[32] Third, it directs attention to the plurality of new social movements that have arisen to criticize the multiple forms of dependency in a contemporary context. It resists the tendency to want to reduce the plurality of such movements (and their diverse critiques of contemporary society) to an underlying unity that is common both to left-nationalism and Marxism, whether the underlying unity be thought of as that of a dependent nation or as a central, and universal, class. Thus the issue of dependency is not dead, even though the moment of left-nationalism has passed. Dependency has become more diffuse and plural. It is no longer linked only to the nation-state but also to the various new definitions of dependency that are being invented by social movements. The analysis of dependency throughout society must become more extensive, not less. The end of left-nationalism with the end of the era of permeable Fordism means that social identities have become loosened from their arrangement under national identity. The nation does not seem to be able to play the key role assigned to it by dependency theory any longer.

Notes

Originally published as "The Social Identity of English Canada," in *A Border Within: National Identity, Cultural Plurality, and Wilderness*, by Ian Angus. Copyright © McGill-Queen's University Press 1997. Reprinted with permission of the publisher.

1. Jill McCalla Vickers has shown through a citation analysis that Innis and Grant were by far the most cited authors in Canadian Studies publications: see "Liberating Theory in Canadian Studies," in *Canada: Theoretical Discourse / Discours théoriques*, ed. Terry Goldie, Carmen Lambert, and Rowland Lorimer (Montreal: Association for Canadian Studies, 1994), 356, 360.

2. Harold Innis, "Conclusion from *The Fur Trade in Canada*," in *A Passion for Identity*, ed. David Taras, Beverly Rasporich, and Eli Mandel (Scarborough: Nelson Canada, 1993), 18–19.

3. The original essay, which was then elaborated in further works, was R. T. Naylor, "The Rise and Fall of the Third Commercial Empire of the St. Lawrence," in *Capitalism and the National Question in Canada*, ed. Gary Teeple (Toronto: University of Toronto Press, 1972).

4. Melville Watkins, "A Staple Theory of Economic Growth," *Canadian Journal of Eco-*

nomics and Political Science 19 (1963): 150–52; and "The Staple Theory Revisited," Journal of Canadian Studies 12 (1977): 86.

5. Wallace Clement, "Regionalism as Unequal Development: Class and Region in Canada," Canadian Issues / Thèmes canadiens 5 (1983): 68–80.

6. See, for example, Wallace Clement, The Challenge of Class Analysis (Ottawa: Carleton University Press, 1991), 26, 186ff.; Leo A. Johnson, "The Development of Class in Canada in the Twentieth Century," in Capitalism and the National Question in Canada, ed. Teeple; and "Independent Commodity Production: Mode of Production or Capitalist Class Formation," Studies in Political Economy 6 (1981): 93–112; Gordon Laxer, Open for Business: The Roots of Foreign Ownership in Canada (Toronto: Oxford University Press, 1989).

7. For example, Leo Panitch, "Dependency and Class in Canadian Political Economy," and David McNally, "Staple Theory as Commodity Fetishism: Marx, Innis and Canadian Political Economy," both in Studies in Political Economy 6 (1981): 7–33 and 35–63, respectively.

8. George Grant, The Empire: Yes or No? (Toronto: Ryerson Press, 1945), 21.

9. Ibid., 31, 29. It is important to note that Grant, for all of his argument for the British connection, maintained a significant place in his thinking for Canada as formed by the meeting of British and French civilizations. This commitment was maintained throughout his life. He argued in 1945 and later that the survival of French Canadian culture in Canada was due to the British connection. See ibid., 23.

10. Grant always took responding adequately to the exigencies of political action as significant for living the good life. In this he was rare among contemporary philosophers. In the 1970 preface to a reissue of Lament for a Nation, after rejecting several criticisms that he regarded as superficial, he referred to the "serious criticism" that his language of inevitability might produce despair in the reader (xi) and went on to discuss it in detail.

11. Melville Watkins, "Contradictions and Alternatives in Canada's Future," in Canada Ltd.: The Political Economy of Dependency, ed. Robert M. Laxer (Toronto: McClelland and Stewart, 1973).

12. Mel Hurtig, "One Last Chance: The Legacy of Lament for a Nation," in By Loving Our Own: George Grant and the Legacy of Lament for a Nation (Ottawa: Carleton University Press, 1990), 56.

13. See especially the essay "Great Britain, the United States and Canada," in Changing Concepts of Time (Toronto: University of Toronto Press, 1952).

14. Jim Laxer, "Introduction to the Political Economy of Canada," in Canada Ltd., ed. Laxer.

15. D. Drache, "The Canadian Bourgeoisie and Its National Consciousness," in Close the 49th Parallel: The Americanization of Canada, ed. Ian Lumsden (Toronto: University of Toronto Press, 1970), 21.

16. Steve Moore and Debi Wells, Imperialism and the National Question in Canada (Toronto: Between the Lines, 1975), 11. See also Panitch, "Dependency and Class."

17. Mel Hurtig, A New and Better Canada (Toronto: Stoddart, 1992), 67.

18. Consider the example of Donald Creighton in this respect. His polemic against the Royal Commission on Bilingualism and Biculturalism argued that it "grotesquely

exaggerated the importance of language and culture" by separating culture from "political, economic and financial relations." See "The Myth of Biculturalism," in *Towards the Discovery of Canada* (Toronto: Macmillan, 1972), 257.

19. The peculiarly stubborn character of the polarization between political economic and cultural approaches to social and political thought in English Canada was driven home to me when I began teaching in the United States and co-edited a collection of essays on American cultural politics. There was very little discussion, even in its critical reception, of the inclusion of representatives of both groups. The introduction to the volume, which attempted to show the historical and theoretical basis for their integration, did not provoke any polarizing counter-arguments. The U.S. intellectual left was, by way of contrast, much more preoccupied with the hegemonic success of the Reagan-Bush right. See Ian Angus and Sut Jhally, eds., *Cultural Politics in Contemporary America* (New York: Routledge, 1989).

20. Robin Matthews and James Steele, eds., *The Struggle for Canadian Universities* (Toronto: New Press, 1969), 1.

21. Ian Lumsden, "Imperialism and Canadian Intellectuals," in *Close the 49th Parallel*, 327.

22. *The Symons Report* (Toronto: Book and Periodical Development Council, 1978), 19–20.

23. David Cameron, *Taking Stock: Canadian Studies in the Nineties* (Montreal: Association for Canadian Studies, 1996), 31–32.

24. Rowland Lorimer, "A Personalized Review [of the Cameron Report]," *ACS Bulletin AEC* 18 (1996): 15.

25. One cannot help but notice the fact that there are three axes in this example as there were in the previous example of left-nationalist discourse. I do not want to engage in any general statement as to how many axes are necessary to the constitution of a discourse. I believe, as stated above, that *at least* three are required for any reasonably complex discourse. Perhaps I have not investigated thoroughly enough to find a fourth. In any case, I do not want to be accused of being a closet Hegelian, or Christian, because my two examples have three axes. I do not see anything necessary about the number.

26. Paul Litt, "The Massey Commission, Americanization, and Canadian Cultural Nationalism," *Queen's Quarterly* 98 (1991).

27. Harold Innis, "The Strategy of Culture," in *Changing Concepts of Time*, 20.

28. Margaret Prang, "The Origins of Public Broadcasting in Canada," *Canadian Historical Review* 46 (1965): 31.

29. This reduction in the concept of culture, often taken even further to refer only to mass media, is the basis for the suggestion that Canada's domination by American mass media does not pose any problems for the survival of the nation. See Richard Collins, "National Culture: A Contradiction in Terms?" *Canadian Journal of Communication* 16.2 (1991): 199–224.

30. See the responses by Jorge Niosi and John Warnock to Philip Resnick's essay "The Maturing of Canadian Capitalism" in *Our Generation* 15.3 (1983): 11–14: Niosi and Warnock, "Two Responses on Canadian Capitalism," *Our Generation* 15.4 (1983): 51–58.

31. Philip Resnick, *The Land of Cain: Class and Nationalism in English Canada, 1945–1975* (Vancouver: New Star Books, 1977), 202.

32. Panitch, "Dependency and Class."

JOCELYN LÉTOURNEAU

TRANSLATED BY PHYLLIS ARONOFF AND HOWARD SCOTT

"Remembering (from) Where You're Going": Memory as Legacy and Inheritance

Jocelyn Létourneau (b. 1956) obtained an M.A. from the University of Toronto and a Ph.D. from Laval University. He is currently the Canada Research Chair in the History and Political Economy of Contemporary Quebec at Laval University. He served as the director of the Centre Interuniversitaire d'Études sur les Lettres, les Arts et les Traditions (CELAT) from 1990 to 1994. His research focuses on the problems of interpretation in Quebecois historiography, on the role of intellectuals in contemporary society, and on Canada-Quebec relations. His book *A History for the Future: Rewriting Memory and Identity in Quebec* (*Passer à l'avenir: Histoire, mémoire, identité dans le Québec d'aujourd'hui*) was awarded the Prix Spirale de L'Essai in 2001. He was elected as member of the Royal Society of Canada in the humanities and social sciences in 2004. His major books include *Le coffre à outils du chercheur débutant: Guide d'initiation au travail intellectuel* (1989; 2005), *Le Québec, les Québécois: Un parcours historique* (2004), *Passer à l'avenir: Histoire, mémoire, identité dans le Québec d'aujourd'hui* (2000), and *Les années sans guide: Le Canada à l'ère de l'économie migrante* (1996). Létourneau's sympathetic yet critical engagement with towering post–Quiet Revolution social historians such as Fernand Dumont and Gérard Bouchard breaks new ground, placing his work at the center of current debates in Quebec over the contemporary trajectories of Quebecois identity, the fate of nationalism, and Quebec's place in Confederation.

In the mid-1990s, during a major discussion of Quebec's public education system,[1] many citizens asked for improvements in the teaching of history in the province. Recognizing the merits of this request, Jean Garon, then minister of education, set up a task force and gave its president, historian Jacques Lacoursière, a mandate to report on the issue and make recommendations for change.

Seven months later, the Task Force on the Teaching of History submitted its report to the minister. In keeping with its mandate, the report, entitled *Learning from the Past*,[2] presented broad reflections on (1) how history was taught in Quebec, (2) the curriculum that should be compulsory at each level of education, and (3) the objectives and content of a modified curriculum. These delicate and controversial issues, especially the last one, go to the heart of a fundamental and unavoidable question that preoccupies all societies in which the past is subject to debate—which is certainly the case in Quebec: *What* history, for *what* present and, especially, for *what* future?[3]

Not surprisingly, reactions to the report were many and varied, ranging from positive to harshly critical. To some observers, the report was an insult to the memory, history, and destiny of the Quebec people, as some recommendations—particularly those related to curriculum content—appeared to deny the centrality of the French fact in the construction of the representation of Quebec society.[4]

To others, the report—out of political correctness, conviction, wisdom, or sensitivity, or all of them combined—opened the door to a reappraisal of the narrative of Quebec's past featuring the heirs of Lord Durham on one side and those of Cartier, Montcalm, Papineau, and company on the other, eternal protagonists in an ongoing and seemingly never-ending struggle.[5]

To still others, the value of the report was more prosaic. In recommending an increase in the number of history courses at all levels of education and calling for substantial improvements in teacher training, the task force was calling for an end to the creeping marginalization of history in children's education—and the government listened![6]—thus paving the way to increased job possibilities for people with degrees in history and greater respect and enhanced social status for teachers. Finally, the report placed history at the centre of civic education, which was a boon to those concerned with broadening citizenship education through the study of history. It is easy to understand the enthusiastic welcome the report received from people who were likely to benefit from its recommendations.

It is not my intention in this chapter to reassess the recommendations of the Lacoursière committee or its appraisal of the teaching of history in Quebec. What interests me is of a different nature, probably more crucial. The problem that concerns me, and for my examination of which the *Report of the Task Force on the Teaching of History* provides an ideal pretext, is the relationship of Quebeckers of French-Canadian heritage to their past, a past seen as one of ordeals and sacrifices requiring an undying memory and necessitating reparation or redemption. It is through the memory of a difficult, sometimes tragic past that the relationship of *these* Quebeckers to the world, to "others," and to themselves is generally mediated.[7]

But we are living now. What is to be done with this historical despair which has been erected into a collective memory that still influences all thought about the future? How should the memory of the past be projected into the present and the future? How should we behave toward our ancestors and, especially, how should we honour their legacy while creating a viable horizon for the future? How can we build the future without forgetting the past but also without allowing ourselves to get bogged down in it?

Quebec historians and intellectuals in general have dealt little with these questions,[8] perhaps because anything related to memory and to forgetting—we will come back, at some length, to this difficult word—is extremely sensitive in this society that is constantly grappling with the inspiration, and sometimes the constraint, of its motto.[9]

Such questions should not, however, frighten those who look ahead to tomorrow. However thorny, they are unavoidable for anyone who seeks a way out of the aporias of a collective memory and history that have cast a discouraging shadow on the future. They should serve as inspiration to rise ever higher.

The Duty of Memory

The *Report of the Task Force on the Teaching of History* was not merely a technical document for bureaucrats anxious for diagnoses and prescriptions. In some of its recommendations, it touched on the subject of the collective identity of Quebeckers of French-Canadian heritage, and did so in at least two ways.

It did so, first of all, insofar as it subtly yet clearly backtracked on the necessity of dissociating history from patriotic preaching, which one might have thought—mistakenly, it seems—had been accepted since the Parent Report in the 1960s.[10] Clearly, while the study of history is decisive in the acquisition of civic consciousness and a conscious identity, it is above all, as Fernand Dumont has already stated, "a way of reminding man of his freedom to read his history and also to make it."[11] A word of warning to the patriots of *québécitude* . . .

The second way in which the task force addressed the question of Quebec identity was to propose that the presence of the cultural communities, the Native peoples, and the anglophone community be taken into account to a greater extent in the teaching of history, and that students be encouraged to be more open to world realities. Convinced of the need for a reorientation of the history curriculum, the task force urged the Ministry of Education to recognize in the new history curriculum that Quebec has long been a pluralistic society and to modify the great collective narrative accordingly, that is, to give the cultural communities an equitable place with respect to the role they have played in the province's history.

The authors also expressed a desire, apparently in accordance with the concerns and needs of the community, that in the core curriculum in history, including the (national) history of Quebec, the past be investigated in other ways than by applying the usual canonical frameworks of the history of Western civilization, the history of men, the history of the francophone community, political history, and so forth.

The report did not go any further, but many observers, clearly ill at ease with these positions, read between the lines and found flaws in the spirit and the letter of the document. They concluded that, in proposing to modify the accepted narrative of Quebec history, the Lacoursière committee was creating the conditions for the deconstruction and dissolution of that narrative, promoting an unacceptable revisionism, and ignoring a fundamental and founding truth of the national history of Quebec, namely, that it is a tumultuous saga dominated by the conflictual relationship between anglophones and francophones. As if the entire process of the establishment of Quebec society could be reduced to the national question.

These same observers made a second point, which was that the Lacoursière committee, in endorsing the idea of the Quebec collectivity's cultural pluralism, was relegating Quebec's francophones to a secondary role in their own history and their own society, an unacceptable and politically suicidal position, they argued, because to deny that Quebec, by virtue of its francophone majority, constitutes a full-fledged nation meant not only rejecting an objective reality but also diluting Quebec identity within the Canadian mosaic, ignoring the historical upheavals of a people, a "majority treated as a marginal minority," and the ultimate ignominy, impugning the right of a people to exist for itself and to call itself by its own name, its historical name.[12] Hence, probably, the title of a disapproving article by Josée Legault—"Histoire d'exister" (A matter of existence)[13]—which unleashed an avalanche of criticism of the report, but also some replies to those who were disappointed.

To Legault and her ilk, the phrase "histoire d'exister" had many meanings—meanings, obviously, that the Lacoursière committee failed to state or to stress enough. She therefore felt it necessary to publicly scold the authors of the report for their oversights or—it comes to the same thing in this case—their supposed refusal to address the specific situation of Quebeckers of French-Canadian heritage with respect to history and memory. This specific situation was recalled bluntly by André Turmel, a professor of sociology at Laval University, in an article—on an issue that does not interest us here—in which he harshly condemned an academic colleague, Marc Angenot, for exceeding the limits of polemic foolishness when Angenot wrote an emotional text accusing (francophone) Quebec intellectuals of a nationalist bias.[14]

Turmel's argument, which is typical of the kind of sermon that is frequently found in Quebec political discourse,[15] deserves to be quoted at length:

> It seems to me that the dyed-in-the-wool intellectuals of federalism, who include you and your friends, have tackled the formidable task of giving the handful of diehard believers—business people, Anglos, the Native peoples, barons of the cultural communities, and Ottawa feds —the selling points and the logic they so sorely lack. But it is five minutes to midnight. . . .
>
> What separates us radically from you is memory. Better yet, the duty of memory. We remember, among other things, the expulsion of the Acadians, the 92 Resolutions of 1834, the twelve men hanged in 1838, the Act of Union of 1840, the hanging of Riel in 1885, the abolition of French-language schools in Manitoba in 1890, conscription, Asbestos, Gordon, the unilateral repatriation in 1982, Meech, and what was said to Rene Lévesque when electricity was nationalized: "Do you think that you people can manage Shawinigan?" We have that memory within us and we remain faithful to those men and women who wanted to build a society that would be different from triumphal Americanness. The rule of law that we have known is not the most democratic.
>
> That is perhaps why the "Quebec democracy" that you so nastily caricature "grants" the rights of the people. A people that has not lost its memory.

In this excerpt, things are stated explicitly, and more bluntly than elsewhere. In order to exist now and in the future, Quebeckers have a duty to remember their sorrows, to bear in their turn the suffering of their ancestors, an immemorial suffering branded with the stigmata of so many tragic events. As if the past for French Canadians and francophone Quebeckers consisted of nothing but impediments. As if the "national story" of this community can be expressed only in terms of sorrows and grievances.

And what is more, Quebeckers cannot escape this legacy of adversity and contempt except by re-founding the Quebec people as a sovereign nation, transforming the historical nature of their relationship with others. It seems there is one thing that is impossible for Quebeckers to forget, and that is their having been the victims of the other. Not to acknowledge and deal with this fact that structures the narrative of the self yesterday, today, and tomorrow is to knowingly provoke in the body of the collective subject that terrible disease inherent in the political correctness and revisionism of our time, an alienating, self-negating amnesia, a refusal to recognize oneself and speak oneself as one was, as one is, and it would appear, if nothing changes, as one will be—which means a hopeless loser, a prisoner of the pathetic words "until the next time. . . ."[16]

The Weariness of the Inconsolable Mourner

Are Quebeckers eternally in mourning or trying to escape from the injunction to remember—"Je me souviens" (I remember)—that defines their relationship to the world? What is to be done with this motto on all the licence plates reminding people that they must remember what they are so as not to fall into that post-modern dialectic in which, as Victor-Lévy Beaulieu reminded us ironically, "we begin to discover what we are at the moment we forget it"?[17]

Jacques Godbout has tackled this issue in his documentary film Le sort de l'Amérique, which I will return to later. He portrays the dilemma in which he finds himself, caught between the weighty legacy of memory from his dying father ("Don't forget, Jacques, the English burned our farms and our homes") and the puny historical memory of his children and grandchildren ("My kids and grandchildren don't give a damn about the Plains. They're playing Nintendo. They don't think about the English, the French, who fired when. . . ."). He is pessimistic about the future memory of his family and seems to feel completely defenceless facing the drama of memory being played out: "Yet the Plains of Abraham have become a myth . . . the founding myth of Canada, since both generals [Wolfe and Montcalm] died there. There are two heroes. One doesn't dominate the other. The Anglo-French tension makes the country. If it disappears because we forgot our history what will happen?"[18]

At the end of his film, Godbout, as we might have suspected, has not found an answer; he has rejected the accepted credo. This will enrage his adversaries but will nevertheless by *default* free tomorrow's field of memory from subservience to that of yesterday.

The challenge Quebeckers have to meet now is not to opt for a memory based on resignation or contempt for the past. The challenge is to distinguish what in the past should be "re-acknowledged" and what should be "de-acknowledged" in the name of the values and contexts of the present. As regards memory, contemporaries should keep their eyes on the future. Failing that, they remain eternally in mourning, incapable of extricating themselves from the echoes of the past, so weighed down by the past that they are soon unable to envision new solutions to the histories that they, as the custodians of a legacy of memory, have a duty to take on for posterity, eternally.

It is this obligation of custodianship and fidelity, a duty of heirs to ancestors, to the past, and perhaps to their expected destiny, that I would now like to address. I will attempt to show in what way and to what extent it is constraining. Essentially, I will tackle the question of how to remember while forgetting, and how to forget while remembering, keeping in mind that in the end the tension between old and new must be resolved in favour of the future. In order to enable the heirs to advance and to live, the past must be a springboard and a source of motivation. Above all, the memory of the past must make itself felt in a positive way, or it will become a crushing burden or source of paralyzing resentment. The role of memory, we often forget, is to enrich experience, not to delay action.

The Art of Inheriting

Who has not heard the universal dictum "Those who forget the past are doomed to repeat it"? It seems indisputable and full of wisdom, but has it ever occurred to anyone that its opposite might be equally true: those who remember the past are doomed to repeat it? In fact, both the rejection of the past and its total remembrance are for contemporary people, the heirs of a previous world, unsatisfactory ways of accepting and acknowledging what has been.

Rejecting the past gives rise to a destructive anonymity and creates the conditions for a drifting of the subject into an alienating nowhere. While the cosmopolitan utopia of not being anywhere, of always being else-where, in transit between two free zones, is the object of an intoxicating quest by the new "globalists," it must be acknowledged that, for the vast majority of people, the idea of being a "citizen of the world" or the "ultimate mutant of human evolution," that is, of having a limitless sense of territorial and historical belonging, is impossible and even frightening. To interact with significant others remains a heartening prospect for many people afraid to confront the anxieties of the inner quest, the confusion of the universe, and the uncertainty of the future without references or paths.

For most people, unlimited space and infinite time are anonymous references, evoking absence and solitude, a desert, rather than presence and completeness, a justification for existing and a possibility of being. For them, remembering the past—or, what amounts to the same thing, feeling a connection or relationship to a continuity, a historical and territorial place that is *situated* and *inhabited*—offers freedom from insig-nificance and banality. It gives them the impression of having been chosen, that is, of having emerged from indifference and obscurity. If remembering the past is for the subject a source of completeness with others, a process of integration of the self, and a way of finding meaning, the rejection of the past is actually impracticable since it leads to the reduction and impoverishment of the person, which is a tragedy.

As has been said time and time again, you have to be a citizen of somewhere for travel to have meaning, you have to possess a homeland to put otherness into perspective. The moral is clear: you must be con-scious of where you come from in order to avoid disappearing in the reel of human destiny, to escape self-negation and desolation. "Freedom needs a world," as Alain Finkielkraut said in a recent book.[19]

This said, it would be wrong to think that remembering the past is only liberating. On the contrary, when it leads to the ancestors' domina-tion of the world of the living, it can obscure the self.

What is to be done, then, with a motto as powerfully suggestive as the one that marks Quebec identity: "Je me souviens"? Accept it as a solemn command of the forefathers, or get rid of it as a burdensome inheri-tance? What is the nature of the connection that should be established with ancestors in order both to respect their memory and to win a very personal place in the evolution of things? How can heirs shape their sense of history and situate themselves in relation to a specific continuity of memory without jeopardizing the possibility of exploring new territo-ries of identity?

There are no simple answers to these universal and eternal questions. There are, however, a few propositions that seem to me reasonable and helpful in organizing the present while dealing with the apparent dissonance between the forces of the past and those of the future. I say "dealing with," because the process of reflection that leads to the organization sought, that ultimately provides the form and the substance of the historical consciousness of living, thinking subjects, requires in the end that a choice be made. It is not possible to both embrace and reject the past; one has to go beyond the aporia by framing the problem differently. The following proposition is interesting from this point of view: "To honour one's ancestors is to be accountable to the future."

The appeal of this proposition is clear. For the heirs, there is no question of shutting themselves up in the universe of the unforgettable evoked in the injunction to remember, which takes over the future and obliterates it. The burden of memory on the lives of the descendants and on their horizon of expectation would be an insurmountable constraint on their present and immediate future. It is impossible from any point of view to envisage a legacy with such an annihilating effect on the future. The heirs have their lives before them. If they want to be the responsible custodians of a heritage for which they are indebted to their ancestors, a heritage that contributes objectively,[20] if not positively, to defining their identity, the fact remains that their historical mission—if it is still possible to use this language of transcendence which is rejected these days—is to renew the community so as to find their way and their meaning. Without this effort of renewal, the future is condemned to being nothing but an eternal return, as if caught in the trap of a founding imperative. To live, it is necessary to free oneself from the past, which does not mean repudiating what has been or despising the recognition ancestors are due. But it is important to be critical of tradition and hence of one's heritage, which is never carved in stone.

By "be critical," I mean, in sympathy with the descendants' cause and in order to build an open future, to reflectively distance oneself from the constraints knowingly or unintentionally created by ancestors. As Fernand Dumont aptly wrote, although in the context of a different argument: "We may see the traces of the past as testimony with which we feel solidarity without necessarily identifying fully with it, testimony which we in turn will provide; if we reject these traces, it is not because they did not exist but because they contradict the values we have chosen for the conduct of our lives."[21] In other words, the commitment to tradition and continuity, so that everything is not just the ephemeral moment, depends first of all on the search for meaning, the goals, and the refusals of the living. In a reversal of memory in favour of the future, it is the ancestors who must show solidarity with the goals of contemporary people, and not the opposite.

This idea of solidarity in favour of the descendants needs to be clarified. In my mind, solidarity here implies the mutual responsibility of ancestors and heirs, based on a kind of intergenerational friendship, hospitality, and generosity. Far be it from me to say that descendants have total licence and may if they please get rid of some previous presence, making a kind of tabula rasa of the past; that would be throwing out the baby with the bathwater. In practice, heirs have the extremely heavy responsibility of making their legacy bear fruit, that is, of capitalizing on their ancestors' contribution in order to increase the accumulated benefits of goodness. I am talking here about goodness in the sense of what is enriching, what is favourable to human development, what opens up the horizon rather than closes it, what is admirable and illuminates the darkness. Every generation produces its share of goodness and harm. The responsibility of heirs is precisely to exploit the capital of goodness accumulated by the ancestors, to make it the point of departure for their own specific quest, and to strive in their turn to increase it for the benefit of their descendants. In the operation of converting the accumulated capital into new capital of goodness—an operation that is based on a process of critical reflection and that leads necessarily to difficult questions of collective ethics—there are losses and gains of meaning.

While it is clear that meaning is at least in part passed on from generation to generation—that is, that the heritage of the past objectively marks the present even when it is not subjectively adopted by the descendants—this meaning is nevertheless itself transformed to meet new needs, unforeseeable by the ancestors, that arise in building the present. This transformation is crucial. It is the essence of intergenerational transmission, the ultimate purpose of which is the advancement of humanity. Clearly, while heirs can be very close to their forebears and draw on their values and actions, their questions and decisions are nevertheless determined by the realities of the present, insofar as they can grasp its complexity while trying not to obscure the future (too much). Hence the idea that love for ancestors should be the heirs' consciousness in relation to what is to come.

The responsibility of ancestors is dual. They must, of course, produce goodness rather than harm—a difficult challenge, given the uncertainties and complexities of real life. They must also be able to "die," that is, to refrain from ending the history in which they themselves are actors. Ancestors are obliged to leave the heirs to engage with their own destiny.[22] They must envisage their death as a moment of redemption or liberation. This is what we are taught by certain dogmas whose wisdom we have misused. Death is redemption and liberation because it allows the future to actually take place without being mortgaged by the past. In a sense, death is a gift of the self for the benefit of posterity, justice before life and for the benefit of life. Death can mean, depending on the situation, the end of suffering and the release of the survivors from the sorrows of the past, or the sowing of the seeds of the future with the goodness achieved during one's lifetime. Unless it is liberating, death is meaningless and inconsequential—as life may have been before it—or, what is much more serious, it usurps the future.

And herein lies, in part, the tragedy of Quebeckers of French-Canadian heritage as a community of memory and history. Inspired by their great intellectuals—the melancholy scholars and poets of an apparently failed or constantly postponed re-founding of their people[23]—they tend to remember the mistakes they have made, the pain caused them, what they did not do, or what they could have done, rather than emphasize what they did or are doing that is right and good.[24] In practice, these Quebeckers carry their past like a cross. For them, despite what many historians are now telling them loud and clear,[25] the past is a breeding ground of painful, depressing memories rather than a pretext for positive remembering. Worse still, Quebeckers of French-Canadian heritage maintain this obsession by perceiving their progress as a prelude to disaster rather than a sign of success.[26] Stuck in an inconsolable sadness resulting from their supposed situation as "failed rebels,"[27] they are unable, or barely able, to escape from the imaginary of a victim and the mentality of a person owed a debt. To grow up, they have been told and are still being told, you have to suffer. Between their "old" identity as French-Canadians and their supposed new identity as Quebeckers shaped by this heritage, there are as many continuities as ruptures, if not more. That is why the past, rather than being a source of motivation and hope, remains for most of them a place of intolerable alienation that requires reparation.

The past, the product of the action of ancestors, is a capital that contemporaries must place themselves in a position to exploit, a heritage they must use as a base from which to go forward to colonize the future. As Fernand Dumont also said, "It is important to discern what in the past deserves to be re-acknowledged [and, I would add, what deserves to be 'de-acknowledged'] in the name of the values of the present."[28] Otherwise, memory becomes nostalgia or resentment, or, worse, it gives rise to impediments.

The terms *re-acknowledged* and *de-acknowledged* are important here because they imply that memory (the past re-acknowledged) is the active, conscious, and therefore selective, remembering of what has been in order to extend its positive impact and favour the primacy of good (or good effects) over bad (harmful effects) in building the future. In the case of forgetting (the past de-acknowledged), the liberating amnesia consists less in ignoring, repudiating, or erasing what has been than in deactivating the bad (or the seeds of harm) so as to grant amnesty to what has been, liberate oneself from one's enduring furies, and free the future from what could prevent it from blossoming in a "renewal."

It cannot be overemphasized that choice in relation to memory is unavoidably a matter of collective morality and political culture and is carried out in keeping with the stakes and challenges of the present. This process of choice is also known as the work of mourning, which comprises selection, internalization, reappropriation, and updating of the past. It is the transformation of the past into a heritage of hope. Through the transformation of the past into memory, the work of mourning ensures the survival of positive values projected into the future. In practice, mourning is nothing less than an act of re-foundation and regeneration that makes it possible to move on to other things. The work of mourning is neither discharge nor renunciation, but rather the production of meaning, in favour of life and the future.

It should be understood that the motivation for choice in relation to memory is not to reduce the past to silence, but to draw from it a capital on which to build the future, honestly taking into account the situation of the contemporaries. Without the quest for positive values, the present remains inexorably in the shadow of a past that exudes sombre memories. There are memories that leave the heirs powerless, that, like vampires, suck the life out of the future, memories that kill contemporaries' passion and ambition. The past should never be allowed to limit or extinguish the future for the descendants. One does not redesign a house to accommodate an inherited object. Rather the object, placed in its new context, is reinvested with a meaning that will perpetuate the presence of yesterday in the creation of tomorrow. The same is true when one inherits an entire house: if that house is not renovated, it quickly becomes a coffin for its inhabitants unless there is a renewal; time causes the structure to disintegrate, beginning a cumulative process of deterioration. Renovation is not a betrayal of the past; it is an updating of the old in keeping with the challenges and constraints of the present. It is what allows the old to endure. The stakes of today should determine the uses of the old. Unless it is reclaimed for the present, the old dies forever, which is deplorable. With no past, the present risks falling into "absense." But if the past outweighs the present, it can lead to a vicious circle of repetition. As great thinkers have repeated ad nauseam, there is an art of inheriting that consists in updating what is transmitted, conserving it while modifying it. It is on this condition alone that heritage contributes to freedom.[29]

Hence the proposition that history and memory must be both recognition and distance; I mean that the relationship of heirs to the(ir) past can only be one of relative emancipation. Without this salutary emancipation, which is a duty as important as that of respect for ancestors, the descendants remain prisoners of an unforgettable heritage that weighs on their destiny like a mantle of lead. While the heirs are decisively marked by the actions of ancestors, history cannot take the place of being for them. In practice, moreover, societies develop through the heirs' insatiable (re)conquest of the past. It is through this liberation from the past as a result of critical reflection by the heirs on the actions of their ancestors that society creates the conditions for transcending itself and advancing through future human action, and that it is able to give rise to new events that mark its evolution in time. In and through the actions of the heirs, society emancipates itself from a memory that would otherwise crush it.

The perspective of "Je me souviens," as it is often exploited in public debate in Quebec by those anxious to remind supposed amnesiacs of their "duty of memory," offers heirs a disheartening option for the future, an option as senseless as the pure and simple forgetting expressed in "Je m'en vais" (I'm leaving), which a young, politically depressed (former) Quebecker, Hélène Jutras, proclaimed in the public arena, provoking strong reactions in the community.[30]

The positions taken by Legault and Turmel, described above, were indeed discouraging, not in relation to some other position that would be objectively more correct—the assessment of the opposing arguments is not what interests me here—but because they involve the total reification of the idea of the *unforgettable* as the matrix of collective meaning, the legacy to be transmitted, and the horizon toward which to project oneself. This same dependency, this same subjugation to an undying past is evident in the following words by Serge Cantin: "Ultimately, I would say that in Quebec one does not choose to be a nationalist: one is a nationalist by necessity, the necessity dictated by the future of one's self in a nation to which one knows one belongs and to which one acknowledges a debt, a nation one would have to be blind or in bad faith to claim is not threatened. Hence we are nationalists too, let us not be afraid of the word, out of duty: the duty the dead impose on the living to 'reappropriate something of what they have felt in order to make somewhat intelligible what they have experienced,' in Fernand Dumont's marvellous words."[31]

Such a perspective is clearly unacceptable for the descendants, who have an obligation to keep the possibility of choice open—the fundamental choice that I spoke of above and that I consider to be the very expression of the historical consciousness of the thinking subject—and to struggle to maintain control of it. It is by "remembering (from) where they are going" that the heirs can best reconcile the past and future dimensions of their present.

Despite the apparent ambiguity of this expression, it implies a clear position with respect to identity: the past cannot be that place we inhabit eternally, where we conceive the future and take refuge from the assault of the complexity and uncertainty of the present. On the contrary, the past must constantly be redeemed through action and questioning in the present so as to build an open future.

"Remembering (from) where you're going" means precisely undertaking this operation of questioning and redemption. It means taking on the work of mourning as one who grieves, not as one who is aggrieved. It means no longer stirring up the sediment of losses and instead transforming the consciousness of those losses into a source of creativity. "Remembering (from) where you're going" means finding ways to think about the past while binding its wounds; it means seeking in the past the impetus to go beyond the old torments rather than constantly coming back to them. "Remembering (from) where you're going" means re-articulating the historicity of subjects and communities around a structuring principle of collective action, the principle of memory as recognition and distance. It is in the tension between recognition and distance that the heirs' place of memory—and of identity as well—is to be found, with and against their ancestors, a place of memory that testifies to the place of man himself in the duality of his consciousness, irremediably divided between the past whose continuity he ensures and the horizon that calls to him indefinitely, between a presence that cannot fulfill him and an absence he strives inescapably to fill.[32]

It is possible, even necessary, to disobey the appeals and summonses of the past. What is more, historical consciousness is the inevitable product of a choice by contemporaries. And it is perhaps the fundamental vocation of the historian—in addition to illuminating the extraordinarily complex material of the past through scholarly work—to stimulate, harmonize, and enrich with rigour, subtlety, and hope the process of reflection that leads to this (re-)founding choice that has the potential to be emancipating and redeeming.[33] At least, that is what I am proposing.

The historian's main mandate, it is widely felt, is to prevent man from drifting senselessly, by reminding him of his origins. This reminder is needed so that he may avoid being absorbed in and by the uncertainty of the future. Without this saving reminder, man is considered powerless. He not only lacks the impetus to move forward, but becomes the unfortunate victim of oblivion, the Minotaur of lost souls. Without full historical consciousness, man is recognized to be unconscious. He drowns in the waters of the Lethe. He develops in a state of amnesia, which leads inevitably to uncertainty and the loss of the capacity for reflection. As a result, he can only repeat his blunders, following the siren songs of the ephemeral and getting drunk on senseless exiles.

Without historical consciousness, people are no better than lobotomized animals. Fernand Dumont said as much in his classic article on the social function of history, published in 1969; he was fundamentally concerned by the ravages resulting from the hold of technocratic ideology over collective historical references and social ties. Most of the authors of briefs to the Estates General on Education or the Task Force on the Teaching of History, sharing the same concern and using a fashionable cliché, also spoke of the need for the study of history in order to fight the spectre of irreparable forgetting and to regenerate consciousness—patriotic or civic, depending on the individual—particularly in young people.

But what if the study of history, instead of encouraging people to remember the past without any obligation to think about their heritage, gave them the means to rise above the past by playing dialectically, in a constructive way, with what is unsaid and what is remembered?[34]

There are times when the surplus of memory finally makes one believe in the end of things, drying up hope instead of generating it, and weakening the individual and collective capacity to project oneself into the future. To some extent, this is the situation now in Quebec. It is wrong to think that people in general, and young people in particular—I am talking here about Quebeckers of French-Canadian heritage—are ignorant of their history. On the contrary, they know it quite well, in the sense that they have grasped the central principle and the main framework of *one* narrative of Quebec and Quebeckers, namely the one of a people with a tragic destiny, a people that was for a long time backward, oppressed by the clergy and by the English, and that has succeeded in part in averting the terrible fate looming over it by re-founding itself through the Quiet Revolution, a great collective move forward.

It is quite possible, I readily admit, that a large majority of people, perhaps more young people than their elders—but this remains to be seen—know nothing more than this of their collective history, especially if they are asked specific questions, for example, to place events or individuals in context or locate them on a timeline. There are abundant examples of anachronisms and basic mistakes, some funny, some discouraging.[35] But this is not a fundamental problem of collective amnesia due to absence of historical knowledge. The "absence of memory" diagnosed by many experts wanting to hear precise answers to factual questions is quite simply a result of false expectations concerning the historical knowledge the general public is likely to assimilate. People obviously know what the (francophone) Quebec collectivity considers to be the heritage of memory that should be passed on to current and future generations.

While it is difficult to know to what extent people actually identify with this memory and draw on it practically or politically, it must nonetheless be acknowledged that its substance is widely accepted. This may be seen in the following quotes from essays by undergraduate students in history who were given the following task: "Describe the history of Quebec from the mid-19th century to the present as you know or remember it. You may structure your text as you wish, emphasizing the elements you consider important, regardless of how the history of Quebec is generally presented."[36]

> To me, the history of Quebec is a succession of struggles for recognition as a society. The history of Quebec is a beautiful saga that takes place over almost three centuries.
>
> However, since the mid-19th century, the only important fact, in my view, is the importance of wars. Even though they are representative of society throughout the world and the perpetual struggle between "good guys and bad guys," you also have to see in them the struggle of Francos and Anglos that has being going on forever.

I see the history of Quebec as a constant rivalry between anglophones and francophones. . . . I would like to emphasize the fact that the history of Quebec as I see it is one of anglophone dominance over the Quebecois, both economically and politically. Of respect for the Americans, in World War I, by the Quebecois, who were simple farmers and were led by the Catholic Church. In short, the Quebecois have always been dominated by another people and have been hesitant to take charge of their own country.

I have very few actual memories with regard to the history of Quebec, obviously. The perception I have always had—and that I still have a little, in spite of information from courses on the history of Canada—is one of a people that was backward, rather uneducated, dominated by fear of the all-powerful clergy, and that managed to stay more or less stable until 1960.

I see the Quiet Revolution as our awakening—the "springtime" of our people (much more than 1837–1838)—which brought Quebec into the world. I know that this is a little bit inaccurate, that changes take place over time and that they began well before 1960, but I have always had the perception that 1960–1966 was a crucial time. After that, the development continued at a varying rate, depending on the conditions. . . . Finally, I have always—perhaps this is because of my teachers—seen Canada as an endless war between French and English.

The history of Quebec has always focused more on political than social history. It is the history of the struggle of francophones for survival in an anglophone world. The entire social history revolves around that. It is a struggle against assimilation, a struggle for provincial autonomy. Economically, Quebec has been somewhat behind Ontario. An economy in which agriculture is very important.

Urbanization took place gradually in Quebec. The Québécois were poor. Many Québécois went into exile in the United States. The economy was controlled by the anglophones. Gradually, the Québécois have asserted themselves and have got rid of their complexes. With the Quiet Revolution, the Québécois opened up to the world and Quebec society modernized and got in step with the rest of the world.

The history of Quebec is in my opinion based on domination by the British or the English here. It is the history of English-French competition based on trade and profits. . . . To me, the history of Quebec is only about wood, fish, or furs. It is a people that has never been able to stand up and make its demands loud and clear. I would not go so far as to say that we are not fated for success, but our ambitions sometimes seem to make us feel that. We have not done anything major to distinguish ourselves. The history of Quebec does not really have any story to tell, we are too young a people. One day, perhaps, other generations will have something to learn about besides Indians, wood, fish, and furs.

My perception of Quebec has for a long time been based on courses I have taken as well as common-sense information. The Quebec franco-phone was marked by various aspects of life. Religion appears very important to me, it marked the daily lives of rural people, their way of think-ing (their submission to the Church and to Anglo-Saxon interests). The rural nature of francophones also prevented them for a long time from having an industrial mentality, it was only after the [Second] World War and with the Quiet Revolution that their values quickly changed.

In these excerpts, of which I could have included an infinite number, the students demonstrate not the slightest uncertainty, but rather con-siderable assurance concerning their knowledge. I will try to identify the key ideas:

- Young Quebeckers of French-Canadian heritage know that the des-tiny community they belong to, whose heritage they, "tomorrow's ancestors," must carry on—as was hinted to them in a famous document[37]—has been difficult. Their fate was decided long ago: they are part of the procession of the oppressed. They are the descendants of a lineage that has had to face terrible calamities in 1759, 1763, 1774, 1837–38, 1840, 1867, 1917, 1942, 1982, 1990, 2001—with more to come.[38]
- These students also know that the people whose dependents and trustees they are was for a long time in the grip of a kind of "evil beast," the "two-headed other," the first head of which was "the other within"—the clergy, Duplessis, traditionalists, federalists, etc.—and the second, "the other outside"—the English, foreign capital, the federal government, sometimes Americans, etc. For-tunately, thanks to the period known as the Quiet Revolution, this people has succeeded, at least in part, in emancipating itself, mod-ernizing, and thinking it might find a way to exist without being under trusteeship to others.

- These young people know, finally, that the culmination of the great Quebec journey in history will be when the will to exist without being under trusteeship leads to a decision by the community to free itself from the grip of the "two-headed other."

What more can we ask? It seems that (young) Quebeckers of French-Canadian heritage actually identify with what some, who take pride in this, would probably call their "tabarnaco" history, a kind of modern, decolonized version of the ideology of la survivance.[39] This is the narrative that primarily fuels their collective identity.[40] In fact, their memory is precise in that it is simple, focused, and assured. And that is certainly a problem, if not a failure, in terms of a memory for the future.

Contrary to the claims of the preachers worried about the survival of the French fact in Quebec, there is no lack of memory, but rather an excess of memory—or, at least, the abuse of a memory. This situation hampers discussion of the idea of some new beginning, with or without (English) Canada, in continuity with or against "our" past. What the (francophone) Quebec collectivity—like the (English) Canadian collectivity, for that matter—needs at the present time is air to ventilate, broaden, or defocus its accepted memory.[41]

While it is true that memory—more than just time, which has no moral meaning or purpose—heals wounds, perhaps we will have to learn also to forget, that is, to think of history in terms of mourning and possibly healing the wounds it leaves. There is nothing far-fetched about this idea. According to traditional wisdom, forgetting, far from the negation of remembering, is the most perfect form of remembering, and its ultimate transcendence.[42] An interesting paradox. But what is meant here by forgetting still has to be defined.

In my understanding, forgetting does not have any negative connotation, nor does it constitute a refusal. Forgetting is not a way of repressing or annihilating the past or of silencing the memory that could be born from it. It is, rather, the culmination of mourning, which, turned into forgiveness, opens a universe of the future, of possibility and understanding, based on the recollection of the good in the past rather than the harm. In this sense, forgetting is a transition, a transformation. Similarly, the concepts of mourning and forgiveness do not here mean abandonment, loss, omission, amputation, renunciation, abdication, or anything like that, but rather a predisposition to a regenerative new beginning. This desire for a new beginning is justified in a way that seems legitimate to me—the past cannot be changed, so why get bogged down in it?

What is at stake—and this is the challenge for the heirs—is precisely to go beyond the condition of their ancestors. The past cannot be set up as master, or it becomes hell. Nor, as Emmanuel Lévinas says, does it allow us to focus the present moment through images from memory, or the future through foretastes or promises. Like forgiveness or indulgence, probably, the past is useful only to enable contemporaries to lift themselves up. The fact that the past has been painful and that it still bears the marks of accumulated injuries does not change the moral obligation to distance oneself from it so that the wounds can heal. In some cases, this distancing process also demands that the lesion not be sutured but that its potential for scarring or catharsis be explored. As Sören Kierkegaard said, we should not be afraid to leave the wounds of possibility open in order to regenerate bruised bodies. To which I might add that hope should be at the beginning of history and of the memory of the past.

In this delicate, complex, subtle—even, because of the uncertainty involved, dramatic—transformation, through mourning, of wounds into possibility and of memory into regenerative consciousness, historians are called on to play an irreplaceable role as brokers, bringing together their qualities as scholars and their responsibilities as citizens in the enterprise of regeneration. For this reason, I see the historian as an educator and a "relay runner," someone who in keeping with rules and procedures, professional ethics, critical judgment, and faith in the future takes part in the process of transmission.

Historians, as those most qualified to ensure the past's effective fulfillment in the present with ethical and scholarly rigour, are also the ones who can best reconcile the apparent contradiction that exists between the loss and the gain of meaning in the evolution of things and the succession of generations. In my view, historians are not really the guardians of the past, the vestal virgins of time. They are the ones who transmit memory, who, based on the irreducible, teeming factuality of the past, present the panoply of possible paths to the future. Historians are the ones whose role is to "pass on the past" in a history that is not only the result of critical reflection by contemporaries, with and against the ancestors, but also a herald of the future and of hope.

What should at all times guide historians in their quest for meaning in the present-past is respect for the extraordinary complexity of the facts and the need to create the conditions for an open, better future. Their role inevitably takes them to the heart of problems of collective morality: as scholars and initiators of democratic debate, they have to work in favour of the good over the bad, by which I mean in favour of hope over pain, and of deliverance over animosity.

Through their work of writing the past as history, historians must strive to open the future as wide as possible. They have to create conditions such that the concept of fixity never prevails. They must remind contemporaries that the past only in part determines the horizon of their choices and that those choices constitute their freedom to make their history both in continuity with and against their ancestors. The ultimate role of historians, which gives fundamental meaning to their scholarly and civic activity, is to constantly encourage the men and women of their time to ask themselves not what they must remember in order to be, but what it means, in light of the experience of the past, to be what they are now.

It should be noted that these two questions entail very different responsibilities for heirs as subjects. The first question ("What must I remember in order to be now?") attaches them to a memory on which they must remain dependent, perhaps without wanting to, so that in order to exist socially as beings within a continuity of time, they must fulfill the duty of memory. Their mandate is clear: it is to nurture their ancestors, who, in a peculiar reversal of perspective, become their descendants. The second question ("Who am I by virtue of my past?") leads heirs as subjects, as participants in present and future collective life, to place their lives in the context of a movement in which they have a stake and which they are urged to build in the present, together with others, drawing more or less on the actions of their predecessors. In this perspective, they are or are not nurtured by their ancestors, who take their places once again—quite rightly, I would say—as forebears.

It should be understood that being a link in a chain does not mean being chained to the succession of previous determinations, but rather playing one's part in the ongoing enterprise, made up of gains and losses, additions and deletions, of building the world. Similarly, in this scenario the past does not appear as the pretext for an irrefutable, compact, exclusive demonstration of the events leading to the present—the present enlisted to serve the logic and the burdens of what has gone before. Rather, the past reveals itself as an unlimited universe of values created and tested by the ancestors, a universe in which contemporaries can draw inspiration, though not lessons or recipes, to soothe the unbearable anxiety arising from their lightness of being.

It is in these common values, a sort of transcendental "precipitate" of human action in time, that people of today can, as historical actors responsible for the evolution of their world—one can always make a liberating history of what the world has made of us—discover the common aspirations that motivate them to raise themselves ever higher.

For a History of the Future

History is the work of producing meaning that is indissociable from an ethical reflection on remembering. The role of historians is to remind heirs that they have a duty to "re-member (from) where they are going," and that the only demand that comes to them from the past is the obligation of mediation in the future.

Through the narratives they create, the inventive resources of which surmount all obstacles and justify all hopes, historians are situated at the centre of a paradoxical convergence that is essential to the continuity of the world—and that, according to Hegel, is the very engine of historicity—between the impossibility and the inevitability of forgetting and forgiveness. Such is the responsibility that falls to them.

There is an infinite dialogue—but not a relationship of causality, much less teleology—between past, present, and future. I would suggest that the heirs know this, without always exercising their right to freedom. Very often, it is their predecessors who, associating their time on earth with a certain finitude of history, mistakenly believe they hold the key to the fate of the heirs.

If there is, as it is said, a crisis in the transmission of history, it perhaps has less to do with the refusal of heirs to situate themselves in relation to a certain continuity and a certain tradition than with their hesitation to acknowledge an unsatisfactory heritage of memory that is incompatible with their political imaginary. In this perspective, the problem of the heirs is not to ensure the continuity of the past, but rather to understand the history of the forebears and to carry on their memory.

Indeed, for what future do we remember?

Notes

Originally published as " 'Remembering (from) Where You're Going': Memory as Legacy and Inheritance," in *A History for the Future*, by Jocelyn Létourneau. Copyright © McGill-Queen's University Press 2004. Reprinted with permission of the publisher.
1. In April 1995, thirty years after the publication of the report of the Royal Commission of Inquiry on Education in the Province of Quebec (Parent Report), the government of Quebec established the Estates General on Education to review and update the achievements of that very important commission of inquiry which revolutionized

the education system in Quebec in the 1960s. The purpose of the Estates General was to give (back) a voice to groups and individuals and allow them to express their ideas on the problems and possible reforms of the province's education system.

2. Quebec, Ministère de L'Éducation, *Learning from the Past: Report of the Task Force on the Teaching of History* (Quebec City: Ministère de L'Éducation, May 1996).

3. In a little book published in the mid-1980s, French historian Marc Ferro pointed out that this preoccupation with history exists in all societies in the world: *L'histoire sous surveillance. Science et conscience de l'histoire* (Paris: Calmann-Lévy, 1985). See also his *The Use and Abuse of History, or, How the Past Is Taught* (London: Routledge and Kegan Paul, 1984), translation of *Comment on raconte l'histoire aux enfants à travers le monde entier* (Paris: Payot, 1981).

4. Josée Legault, "Histoire d'exister," *Le Devoir*, July 17, 1996; Béatrice Richard, "Se souvenir et devenir, ou oublier et disparaître?" *Le Devoir*, August 25, 1996; Louis Comellier, "Comment peut-on être Québécois pure laine?" *Le Devoir*, September 7–8, 1996; Jean-Marc Léger, "L'histoire nationale révisée a l'aune du multiculturalisme," *Bulletin d'histoire politique* 5.1 (Fall 1996): 59–63; Marc-Aimé Guérin, *La faillite de l' enseignement de l'histoire (au Québec)* (Montreal: Guerin, 1996).

5. Jacques Dagneau, "Une vision dépassée de l'histoire. Réponse a Josée Legault," *Le Devoir*, July 29, 1996; Gonzalo Arriaga and Éric Normandeau, "Vous avez dit 'québécitude'? Réponse à Louis Cornellier," *Le Devoir*, August 28–29, 1996.

6. Since the beginning of the 1980s, the teaching of history in Quebec had been almost non-existent in elementary school, and in high school consisted of only two compulsory courses, one in general history (in the second year) and the other in national history (in the fourth year), as well as an elective course on twentieth-century history (in the fifth year). In keeping with the recommendations of the Task Force on the Teaching of History, students in the first two years of elementary school will have at least three hours of compulsory instruction in the social sciences each week; in the second and third years of elementary school, this will increase to five hours of weekly instruction. In high school, one history course will be compulsory each year, making a total of five courses in high school. At the college level, finally, students in pre-university education will be required to take one history course.

7. The use of the word *generally* is deliberate, because this is not always the case. In fact, sometimes, the relationship francophone Quebeckers of French-Canadian heritage establish with the world and with themselves as a community draws on a more positive view of their condition and a more glorious memory of their past. This said, francophone Quebeckers remain fundamentally stuck in a kind of dialectic of past and present for which they find no solution in either politics or memory, and which may be expressed in terms of three dilemmas: to open up to the other while avoiding losing themselves; to express their emancipation while remembering their alienation; to redefine the group identity without concealing its historical attributes. On this subject, see J. Létourneau and J. Ruel, "Nous autres les Québécois. Topiques du discours franco-québécois sur Soi et sur L'Autre dans les mémoires déposés devant la Commission sur l'avenir politique et constitutionnel du Quebec," in *Mots, représentations. Enjeux dans les contacts interethniques et interculturels*, ed. Khadiya-Toulah Fall, Daniel

Simeoni, and Georges Vignaux (Ottawa: Presses de l'Université d'Ottawa, 1994), 283–307.

8. The collective memory of francophone Quebeckers of French-Canadian heritage has been extensively studied and its central themes traced and associated with the formation of the group identity. There has also been increasing interest in the gaps and shadowy zones in that memory, which is making it possible to slowly bring to light the repressed aspects of the identity. But, at least until now, the question of how it is possible to forget while remembering, that is, how to live with the memory of the past without being obliterated by its stamp and its burden, has been practically untouched. One exception to this general silence, which I will comment on later, is Gérard Bouchard, La nation québécoise au futur et au passé (Montreal: VLB, 1999).

9. I would like to remind the reader that Quebec's motto, which has appeared on the licence plates of all vehicles registered in Quebec since 1976, is "Je me souviens" (the title of this article is a play on words on this expression). Although it has been used as a slogan since 1883, it was only in 1939 that it appeared officially under the province's coat of arms. Attributed to Eugène-Étienne Taché, the designer of the legislative building in Quebec City, the phrase "Je me souviens" remains largely enigmatic. It is a quotation from the first line of a poem that, for some people, expresses the ambivalent allegiance of the Canadians with respect to France and Great Britain, and which reads: "Je me souviens d'être né sous le lis et d'avoir grandi sous la rose" ["I remember having been born under the lily and growing up under the rose"]. For others, who are perhaps more pragmatic and realistic, this slogan simply expresses Taché's personal views on the history of Quebec as a distinct province in confederation. On the anecdotal history of Quebec's motto, see Gaston Deschênes, Les symboles d'identité québécoise (Quebec City: Assemblée Nationale, 1990).

10. It is obviously deplorable that history as it is taught in Quebec schools has never broken its ties with the political and national concerns of many people involved in education, but the fact is that this tendency is universal. History, as Marc Ferro points out, is everywhere "under scrutiny."

11. "La fonction sociale de l'histoire," Histoire Sociale 4 (November 1969): 16. Since I will be in continual dialogue with Dumont in this book, it is essential that I give some indication of his enduring importance in Quebec's intellectual landscape despite his death in May 1997. A professor of sociology at Laval University, poet, man of action, and leading intellectual in Quebec for more than thirty years, Fernand Dumont was a major thinker on Quebec identity and one of the important theorists of culture in the international francophone world. Author of an outstanding body of work, he has written some genuine classics, including Le lieu de l'homme (1968), Le sort de la culture (1987), and Genèse de la société québécoise (1993). To get a sense of Dumont's importance, see Jean-François Warren, Un supplément d'âme. Les intentions primordiales de Fernand Dumont (Quebec City: Presses de L'Université Laval, 1998); Serge Cantin, ed., Fernand Dumont, un temoin de l'homme (Montreal: L'Hexagone, 2000); "Memoire de Fernand Dumont," ed. Jean-Philippe Warren and Simon Langlois, special issue of Recherches sociographiques 42.2 (2001); "Présence et pertinence de Fernand Dumont," ed. Serge Cantin and Stéphane Stapinsky, special issue of the Bulletin d'histoire politique 9.1 (Fall 2000).

12. In defence of the authors of the report, it should be pointed out that their position with respect to the designation of Quebec as a culturally plural society was amply supported by the briefs submitted to the commission.

13. Josée Legault was an advisor to Premier Bernard Landry. She had previously been a columnist for Le Devoir and the Montreal Gazette. Associated with the radical wing of the Parti Québécois, she has often taken strong positions on questions concerning the future of Quebec. She has written several books, including L'invention d'une minorité. Les Anglo-Québecois (Montreal: Boreal, 1992).

14. André Turmel, "Le devoir de mémoire," Le Devoir, June 28, 1996. Turmel was replying to an article by Marc Angenot ("50% des voix plus une," Le Devoir, June 13, 1996), in which the author had harshly criticized what he felt was a deplorable complicity between francophone Quebec intellectuals, including journalists, and the political leadership, particularly sovereignists. (Angenot's counter-thrust to his critics was "La 'démocratie à la québécoise'. Les intellectuels nationalistes et la pensée unique," Le Devoir, July 19, 1996). In his review of the original French version of this book, Angenot again turned to the question of the relationship of the (francophone) Quebec intellectual to the "Quebec nation," but took a less categorical position. The calm debate between him and myself may be read in Spirale 180 (September–October 2001): 14–17.

15. This "memoriogram," a veritable memo of predetermined memory, has been used countless times to reply to someone who has "offended" or to bolster a rather uncertain historical consciousness with facts and dates. There is, for example, then minister Bernard Landry's rejoinder to Lise Thibault (who was about to become lieutenant governor of Quebec) following the honourable lady's declaration concerning the good fortune of Quebeckers to have been under the sovereignty of England rather than of France: "To say that is to forget all the attempts at assimilation by the British Crown and its agents. It is to forget the patriotes of 1837, the violent confrontations, and the hangings and exiles. It is to forget the Act of Union, which forced Quebec to unite with Ontario when Ontario was in debt, putting us in debt at the same time. The Act of Union by which they made us lose our majority by merging with a larger entity. It is to forget the Durham Report. It is to forget the decision of the Privy Council that amputated Labrador from Quebec." And the minister recommended that Her Excellency "refresh her memory, go back to her history books and devote her free time to reading Brunet, Séguin, Lacoursière, Vaugeois, Lamarche, and others"; reported by Pierre O'Neil, "Le bienfait de la conquête anglaise," Le Devoir, January 25–26, 1997. The chronological reminder by the Regroupement des Historiens et Historiennes pour le Oui (historians in favour of a "yes" vote) published in the Bulletin d'histoire politique 4.3 (Spring 1996): 93–94, should also be mentioned. Finally, more recently, there was the "history lesson" given by Gerard Bouchard to John Ralston Saul, pointing out the latter's historical errors and oversights: "La vision siamoise de John Saul," Le Devoir, January 15–16 and 17, 2000. Saul's reply was not long in coming: John R. Saul, "Il n'y a pas de peuple conquis," Le Devoir, January 22 and 24, 2000. Others later contributed to the discussion: Jean Larose, "Pas d'histoire," Le Devoir, February 5, 2000; Jocelyn Létourneau, "Des histoires du passé," Le Devoir, February 12, 2000.

16. This is a reference to the words of René Lévesque the night of the defeat of the first referendum, on sovereignty association, on May 20, 1980. Speaking to a disheartened crowd gathered in the Paul-Sauvé Arena in Montreal, the leader of the Parti Québécois and premier of Quebec, a moderate man and an irreproachable democrat, said: "If I understand correctly, what you are saying to me is 'until the next time.' "

17. "J'ai tant besoin du 24 juin," *Le Devoir*, June 23, 1997. Author of a substantial body of literary work, Victor-Lévy Beaulieu is one of the most important popular writers of contemporary Quebec.

18. *The Fate of America*, subtitles by Robert Gray (Montreal: National Film Board of Canada, 1997), translation of *Le sort de l'Amérique* (Montreal: National Film Board of Canada, 1996). Script published in French as *Le sort de l'Amérique* (Montreal/Paris: Boreal/K-Films, 1997), 26.

19. *L'ingratitude. Conversation sur notre temps*, with Antoine Robitaille (Montreal: Québec-Amérique, 1999), 137.

20. Objectively in the sense that one is always more or less culturally determined by the particularities of one's place and one's origin, socialization, and education.

21. *L'avenir de la mémoire* (Quebec City: Nuit blanche, 1995), 58.

22. On this subject, see Hans Jonas, *The Imperative of Responsibility: In Search of an Ethics for the Technological Age* (Chicago: University of Chicago Press, 1984), translation of *Le principe responsabilité* (1979; Paris: Cerf, 1990), ch. 4, point 5.

23. These great intellectuals who in various periods formed the French-Canadian imaginary and episteme include François-Xavier Garneau, Lionel Groulx, Guy Frégault, Michel Brunet, Maurice Séguin, and Fernand Dumont; they explicitly played the role of thinkers and not only scholars. See the following works in particular: Jean Lamarre, *Le devenir de la nation québécoise selon Maurice Séguin, Guy Frégault et Michel Brunet (1944–1969)* (Sillery: Septentrion, 1993); Ronald Rudin, *Making History in Twentieth-Century Quebec* (Toronto: University of Toronto Press, 1997); Serge Gagnon, *Quebec and Its Historians, 1840 to 1920* (Montreal: Harvest House, 1982); Yvan Lamonde, *Histoire sociale des idées au Quebec, 1760–1896* (Montreal: Fides, 2000).

24. For an illustration, see J. Létourneau and Sabrina Moisan, "Young People's Assimilation of a Collective Historical Memory: A Case Study of Quebecers of French-Canadian Heritage," in *Theorizing Historical Consciousness*, ed. Peter Seixas (Toronto: University of Toronto Press, 2006), 109–20.

25. On this subject, see J. Létourneau, "La production historienne courante portant sur le Québec et ses rapports avec la construction des figures identitaires d'une communauté communicationnelle," *Recherches sociographiques* 36.1 (1995): 9–45.

26. For a recent example of this reflex, see Jean-François Lisée, *Sortir de l'impasse. Comment échapper au déclin du Québec?* (Montreal: Boreal, 2000).

27. Jean-Jacques Simard, "L'identité comme acte manqué," *Recherches Sociographiques* 36.1 (Winter 1995): 103–11, in which the author uses the expression "rebelles manqués."

28. *L'avenir de la memoire*, 55.

29. On this subject, see Emmanuel Kattan, *Penser le devoir de mémoire* (Paris: Presses Universitaires de France, 2002).

30. Disenchanted with the political situation in Quebec, which according to her was marked by apathy and indifference, stagnation, and the eternal return of the same problems and the same solutions, Hélène Jutras, then a law student at McGill University, published a resounding article in Le Devoir on August 30, 1994 ("Le Québec me tue" [Quebec is killing me]), which generated the largest volume of mail ever received by the paper. Following the publication of several letters against her position, Jutras came back with another letter with an equally provocative title, "Oui, Le Québec me tue" (Yes, Quebec is killing me), (Le Devoir, September 27, 1994). Jutras's texts were collected and published in English under the title Quebec Is Killing Me (Kemptville, Ont.: Golden Dog Press, 1995). It seems that, since her public departure in the mid-1990s, Ms. Jutras has gone through a major "(r)evolution" in her personal life and ideas (see "Le Québec ne l'a pas fait mourir" [Quebec didn't kill her], Le Devoir, August 10, 1999).

31. Serge Cantin, Ce pays comme un enfant (Montreal: L'Hexagone, 1997), 189.

32. Formulation borrowed from Serge Cantin, "Femand Dumont. La mort d'un homme de parole et d'action," Le Devoir, May 10–11, 1997.

33. The reader should bear in mind that I am using the term historian to mean a member of the community of men and women who do scholarly work—that is, systematic and rigorous work—in the study of the past, whatever their specific disciplines.

34. We know that the history we compose of the past is always the product of a complex dialectic made up of factual recollections and forgettings that share a common boundary within a single semio-narrative structure that refers somewhere to competing powers. From this point of view, forgetting is not necessarily conscious concealment of the past, but the automatic result of the fact that recollection simultaneously creates both the thinkable (remembering) and unthinkable (forgetting). This is why remembering necessarily implies that one forgets as well. In this context, what is forgotten may be defined as a memory that is not activated and that may resurface if the memory covering it disappears or the boundary between recollection and forgetting is broken down as a result of critical reflection leading to the deconstruction of a particular cultural modelling of memory.

35. Several gems are cited in Trou de mémoire, the transcription of a series of broadcasts on Radio-Canada from July 9 to August 27, 1995 (Montreal: SRC-Radio, 1995).

36. I am not claiming, because I am unable at this time to demonstrate it rigorously on the basis of a broad corpus, that these essays, which were collected as an informal classroom exercise, are representative of the historical memory of francophone Quebeckers. My intuition, however, is that they are, for two reasons: first of all, because they repeat essentially what is said in the public arena about francophone Quebeckers' past; and second, because year after year I find essentially this view of Quebec history among students interviewed. Two recent studies confirm my impression: Sabrina Moisan, "La mémoire historique de l'aventure québécoise chez les jeunes Franco-Québécois d'heritage canadien-français. Coups de sonde et analyse des résultats," master's thesis, Université Laval, 2002; Jacques Caouette, "Les représentations des élèves de quatrième secondaire de la Polyvalente Le Carrefour de Val-d'Or concernant l'histoire," master's thesis, Université du Québec en Abitibi-Témiscamingue, 2000.

37. *Act respecting the future of Québec (Bill 1)* (Quebec City: Éditeur officiel du Québec, 1995), preamble. The bill includes a declaration of sovereignty.

38. These dates correspond to the following events: 1759 (conquest of New France by the British); 1763 (formal cession of New France to Great Britain by France); 1774 (Quebec Act); 1837–38 (*patriote* rebellions crushed by British forces); 1840 (Act of Union of the two Canadas); 1867 (British North America Act); 1917 (conscription); 1942 (conscription); 1982 (patriation of the Canadian Constitution without Quebec's agreement); 1990 (failure of the Meech Lake Accord); 2001 (passage of the Clarity Act, federal law on the requirement for clarity in a referendum).

39. Louis Comellier, "Plaidoyer pour l'idéologie tabarnaco," *Le Devoir*, July 4, 1996, A7.

40. I would not dare suggest that this narrative also fuels their political imaginary, although this is taken for granted—too readily—by many observers. My feeling is that there is a growing gap between the narrative of identity and memory circulating in the public space—a narrative that people often make their own, almost always uncritically—and the political imaginary to which people aspire. This appears to be particularly true among young people, whose representations—that of the nation, for example—seem to differ substantially from those of their parents. See J. Létourneau, "La nation des jeunes," in *Les jeunes à l'ère de la mondialisation. Quête identitaire, et conscience historique*, ed. Bogumil Jewsiewicki and J. Létourneau, with Irene Herrmann (Sillery: Septentrion, 1998), 411–30.

41. Far be it from me to claim that this is not taking place. Historians are undertaking it in part, and so are members of the literary community. But the malaise of Quebec memory is deep, the struggle against demagoguery and bad faith is unequal, and the weight of politics is so crushing in any discourse on Quebec's past that the transmutation of memory is slow and difficult. For a position that has much in common with mine, see Pierre Nepveu, "Notes sur un angélisme au pluriel," and "L'impossible oubli," in *Le Devoir*, June 9, 1997, A7 and June 19, 1997, A9, respectively.

42. Discussed in Gilles Bibeau, "Tropismes québécois. Je me souviens dans l'oubli," *Anthropologie et sociétés* 19, no. 3 (1995): 151–52.

ROB SHIELDS

The True North Strong and Free

Rob Shields (b. 1961) focuses his research on the social use and meanings of social spaces such as digital and built environments, urban spaces and regions, including tourist destinations, local identities, and the impact of changing spatializations on cultural identities. This intellectual project has been extended through the peer-reviewed journal *Space and Culture* (Sage) and publications on the spatiality of the city and consumption spaces, such as the edited volume *Lifestyle Shopping* (1993) and *Places on the Margin* (Outstanding Book of the Year, 1991). Shields's recent research concerns the relevance of electronic technology, virtuality, and innovation to everyday life, built space, and engineering. After many years at Carleton University (Ottawa), Shields was appointed the Henry Marshall Tory Chair and Professor in Sociology and in Art and Design at the University of Alberta.

O Canada! Our home and native land!
True patriot love in all thy sons command.
With gloating hearts we see thee rise,
The True North strong and free!
From far and wide, O Canada,
we stand on guard for thee.
God keep our land, glorious and free
O Canada, we stand on guard for thee
O Canada, we stand on guard for thee.
—Robert Stanley Weir, translation of Adolphe-Basile Routhier's *O Canada*[1]

"The True North Strong and Free," a phrase from the English version of the Canadian national anthem, summarises many aspects of southern central Canadian myths of the North: truth or honesty to an autochthonous spirit of the land, a "strength" that defies human incursion, and freedom from conquest by those with imperial ambitions. The notions around the imaginary geography of this "True North Strong and Free" provide an example of the discursive power in spatialisation, especially when it involves nationalistic "representations of space." The concepts harnessed to the physical datum of the "North"—truth, purity, freedom, power—serve in the establishment of a particular "social spatialisation" as an order of the world and cosmos, a specification of priorities and threats, friends and foes, and help to reinforce the cultural solidarity of individuals and communities. There are, of course, competing spatial mythologies, but the "True North Strong and Free" has a striking prominence amongst English-speaking, central, southern Canadians and in the dominant political rhetoric this majority generates.

The Nationalistic "Tradition" of Images

It has been said that power, that empire came from the north. Northern
people have always stood for courage and unconquerability. They have
the muscle, the wholesomeness of life, the strength of will.[2]

Since the 1970s, a public revival of elements of Northern myths as part of a nationalistic ideology—the one, true, *Canadian* vision of the North—has become apparent. In this case spatialisation takes an unusually prominent position, appearing explicitly in ideology. One important figure in this nationalistic vision of the North has been the historian W. L. Morton. In his *The Canadian Identity* (1961)[3] he argues that the topography of the "grim Precambrian horseshoe" of the Canadian Shield (which includes the Barrens, for example) is central to "all understanding of Canada." In contrast to the United States, this cultural heartland of Canada is a forbidding wilderness. It was traversed by (male) fur traders, lumberjacks, prospectors, and miners who "wrested from it the staples by which Canada has lived," but they had always to return to their home bases (women and families) in the St. Lawrence valley, or in the prairies, for that was where their food came from. Morton claims that "this alternate penetration of the wilderness and return to civilization is the basic rhythm of Canadian life,"[4] thus enshrining (despite its entirely past nature) a gendered opposition of nature versus civilisation as the enduring rule of Canadian daily life. His work marks the transformation of the earlier climatic determinism into a geographic determinism where power becomes vested in the land rather than the weather. In this manner, Southern Canadians have integrated something of the traditional native understandings of *genius loci*—the spirit of places—into their own mythology. This vision systematises the treatment of the North as an icon and zone of purity and develops an ordering narrative of everyday life in Canada which relates habits and opinions of an idealised "typical Canadian" to the presence of this "True North." One corollary, however, is that development becomes fraught with all the problems of the violation of this purity, the sacrilege of plundering the "heart" of the Canadian nation.

Morton argues that "the ultimate and the comprehensive meaning of Canadian history is to be found where there has been no Canadian history: in the North."[5] But such a displacement of meaning and sense— of the so-called "motor of history"—to the barely inhabited North obscures some of the fundamental socio-political ingredients which have shaped the progress of Canada as a national society. There is place for neither domestic politics nor the transnational economics of the historical staples trades (first in furs, later in wheat and minerals) which have shaped Canadian settlement and class patterns, nor does it offer any historical logic for some of the great social struggles such as the Suffragettes and the workers' movements. Landscape becomes the "heart" of Canada rather than individuals. It is difficult to see how such a vision of the North, an obsessive paranoia at the back of Canadians' imagination, could be credited as the unequivocal "meaning" of Canadian history.

This environmentalism also figures in the work of other influential Canadian scholars such as the political economist Harold Innis[6] and the historian Donald Creighton whose work through the 1960s laid the historical bases for the elaboration of a nationalistic ideology. Their tendency to introduce the North as a causal factor, as opposed to the argument that it has merely "causative" status as an element of social spatialisation, is found in the work of the well-known literary critic Northrop Frye, Professor Emeritus of English at the University of Toronto, who has argued that European settlers saw nature in Canada as a hostile Leviathan.[7] "Fear of nature" is an important ingredient in this "tradition" of reporting on the Canadian character.[8] This view, based largely on an interpretation of Canadian literature, is crystallised by a so-called "garrison mentality." Historically, in many Canadian novels, the protagonists encounter a rapacious, masculine-gendered, natural environment which leads them to retreat into the safety of their frontier garrisons.[9] Thus, there is a tradition of Canadian anti-heroes: passive, poetic, and sexually ambivalent male protagonist-victims. It also often finds expression in a version of Turner's frontier thesis: whereas the American western frontier represented "the limit of knowledge or the limit of control . . . a northern frontier, in contrast, denotes the limits of endurance. . . . While the western frontier is simply a culturally defined interface, the northern frontier is an existential one."[10]

Two problems arise with this statement which characterises all these works. First, the frontier is said to "denote" rather than "connote" or "represent" a limit. That is, the "frontier" is accorded the status of a real, physical, object, rather than a feature of a historical spatialisation of Canada which exists *grace à* the imaginative capacities of people. Also, the problem of meaning is reduced to mimesis: rather than being a *metaphor* for limits, the frontier is treated as denotative signifier (as, for example, in the case of the word "tree" when used to indicate a real tree). Here is one manifestation of a particular spatialisation which takes a region as a symbol for mental and social states and then attributes causal power to the region itself (as opposed to, for example, the influence on development of distance from markets). Cook says, "It is the fashion in which . . . geography has been interpreted that provides each of these two nations [the United States and Canada] with a culture."[11] Frye comments, "The countries men live in feed their minds as much as their bodies: the bodily food they provide is absorbed in farms and cities; the mental religion and the arts. In all countries this process of material and imaginative *digestion* goes on."[12] Second, limits of existence or physical "endurance" are implied to be consonant with "existential" limits. The subtle and unexamined rhetorical gloss from "existence" to "existential" has gross implications for such analyses.

With such contradictory claims made about the North, one must be careful about accepting any one of them. They all have weaknesses and tend to stretch the available evidence to fit the purposes being advanced. One might expect at least some figures on urbanisation to be advanced (and they would be highly schematic) to support the above theory about the North as a leisure space, yet even if one could do so, comparable, historical recreation statistics would be hard to generate. Despite these difficulties, one finds Canadian intellectuals and social scientists dwelling on this question of the "Canadian Identity," and also asserting their views on radio and television—in effect campaigning to establish a hegemonic status for their views—brings this case-history to new pastures. This partly explains the wide dissemination of "Wacousta revival"[13] which originated from Toronto-area intellectuals with peerless access to the national radio and television broadcasting system, the CBC [Canadian Broadcasting Corporation], through the Toronto production studios.[14] What is doubly intriguing is the lack of alternate, perhaps more subtle, views in public discussions. Thus several questions arise about the "nationalistic" tradition of Northern space-myths and the role of central Canadian ideologues. To what extent, and why, is the exposition of this particular myth an appealing and beneficial activity for those writers involved? Why has it received such a ready and uncritical reception in the media, the public, and the government? The discourse of the "True North" is difficult to escape. When talking about the factual conditions of either the Northern spaces of Canada or about Canadian nationalism, it becomes clear that a spatialisation of the North and, indeed, of Canada as a whole, as the "True North Strong and Free" founds both the metaphors *and* is built into the commonsensical, apparently empirical, classifications through which one might describe reality. One finds this spatialisation re-stated in a hundred slightly different ways in newspapers, statistical reports, and yearbooks: "Developed or not, the North remains all important to the Canadians' self-image. It makes their country the second largest on earth. . . . Above all, its brooding physical presence over the land is a warning that Canadians have not yet conquered their universe."[15] The "True North" remains the stock-in-trade of not only government sponsored coffee-table books and tourism advertisements but also news reports and documentaries.

There is a certain sense of guilt in the face of an exploited internal colony.[16] Canadians are reluctant imperialists. It comes as little surprise that the "True North" myth also disguises the realities of the exploitation of the North for Southern profit.[17] A hypothesis for further research would be that such a spatialisation, which a Marxist would label as a *phantasmagoria*, appears to be an essential, if neurotic, part of a nation split by deep heartland-hinterland inequalities.[18] If "the region has had difficulty shedding its singular image [wherein it is seen as a single landscape of] . . . the solitary Inuit crossing an unbroken icy expanse, the light grey haze of the winter sky all but indistinguishable from the snow-covered land and sea," it is because of the *importance* of this belief to Southern Canadians. What is being discussed, after all, is the *Southern image* of the North, something that Northerners, lacking in media access, economic power, and without political control, are unable to change. As Coates continues, it seems that even with developments such as "oil exploration rigs on artificial islands . . . their perpendicular girders only reinforce the horizontal nature of the environment"[19]—in the eyes of Southerners. The "True North Strong and Free" provides an example of a great national foundation myth.

This "True North Strong and Free" is archetypally an unconquerable wilderness devoid of "places" in the sense of centres of habitation; the last reserve of a theosophical vision of Nature which must be preserved, not developed.[20] If it must be encroached upon, this should be "temporary" in the form of "men-only" style work-camps: it is as if it was a zone which was hostile to domestic order.[21] It is as if living in the North has some feared impact on the structure of society and the family: an "etching process" on human relation. The range of images available gives no hint of the existence of kitchen sinks beyond the urban and agricultural regions of Southern Canada.

To the extent that the "True North Strong and Free" is a region of the "Other," it is the "pole" in the Southern Canadian popular imagination to which everything that presents a contrast with "civilisation" and its values can be assimilated. This includes native mythologies such as the Cree Windigo myth,[22] reported sightings of creatures such as the reputed Sasquatch and fearsome animals such as Grizzlies or Wolverines. This reinforces the argument that the North is a liminal zone where "civilised" social norms are suspended on the lines of *rites de passage*. "It is mockery to speak of the Arctic as the land of the Esquimaux, for nowhere on earth is man less sovereign. . . . Nature is indeed beautiful in her northern strongholds, but her beauty shows only its terrible aspects, its dread grandure [*sic*]. The face of the mighty mother does not soften into a smile for the feebleness of her youngest-born offspring. . . ."[23] These apparently inescapable myths circulate in literary and media channels side by side with self-consciously factual accounts. Where there are attempts to present Northern conditions and life accurately, for example in National Film Board documentaries, the wildness of the region—its autochthonous "indigenous spirit"—is always contrasted with development reports which appear as figures on the common-sense ground of the mythified North. Behind the superficial oscillation of (public) homage and (private) ignorance is not merely a paranoid "fear of nature"[24] but the construction of the "North" as a zone of Otherness so alien that it cannot even be thought without beginning to criticise the fundamentals of Canadian nationalism. The "True North"—reality mediated by imagination—has come to be constituted as a space with a romantic image in the context of regional inequalities which have become more visible through news coverage of Northern development in the late 1970s (i.e., the Berger Inquiry 1977).[25] The recreational use of the North mediates repressed reality of the "Real North" and the mythology of the "True North" in the structure of ritualistic trips to summer cottages, and (still largely men's) fishing, hunting, and canoeing trips. Much could be said of the *rites de passage* of adolescent Boy Scouts and rituals of reconfirmation for greying sport-fishermen. But, the political importance of this critique is the effect this space-myth and related social spatialisation have of masking and even of promoting regional exploitation, the enforced genocidal poverty of Northern inhabitants (significantly, mostly native Indians, Inuit, and Métis), the national unity of a federal state and cultural hegemony of Canadian ideologues as opposed to the continentalistic culture of the United States. The seductiveness of this myth helps one understand why the very inegalitarian "mapping" of the Canadian nation attracts very little head-on critique from social scientists.

A systematic constellation of meanings is at once the orbit and limit of possible interpretations which can be put on the North as a myth without challenging the set of inter-related assumptions about the character of places and their suitability for specific activities. While we can disagree on the applicability of possibly idiosyncratic images we are governed by limits of an overall, naturalised (i.e., become what is understood as "natural") discourse on the North which both constitutes and organises the space, and implicitly positions us with respect to it. A personal "Canadian identity" is partially constituted through ascription into the mythology of the "True North Strong and Free." But public acceptance of this myth as part of a nationalistic ideology is often contradicted by private neglect of its premises. The "True North Strong and Free" mythology bursts out of its repressed status in jokes and clichés of Canadianness which are met with embarrassed laughter. Hence, the mismatch between public rhetoric, even if it is hotly defended, and private investment decisions. This is but one local effect of a discourse of space or better, of a "spacing," which organises reality as *geographical* coherent in three dimensions, and *rationalises* knowledge of the world. The mythological space of the "True North Strong and Free" is not a closed region but is organised in respect to and indeed, penetrates to the centre of Canadian society in much the same manner that Solzhenitsyn said that the Gulag Archipelago haunted the streets of Moscow and the minds of Russians: "And the Kolyma was the greatest and most famous island, the pole of ferocity of that amazing country of Gulag which, though scattered in an Archipelago geographically, was, in the psychological sense, fused into a continent—an almost invisible, almost imperceptible country inhabited by the 'zek' people. And this Archipelago criss-crossed and patterned that other country within which it was located, like a gigantic patchwork, cutting into its cities, hovering over its streets."[26] The nationalistic "tradition" expresses a Canadian social spatialisation which relies on the privileged territorial space of the North for differentiating and "grounding" a cultural identity opposed to the continentalism projected by the United States. In this latter spatial order,

Canada is merely an accident of historical stubbornness and refusal to accept the distinctiveness of North America from Europe. If the reality of the Canadian North, the "Real North," is one of an internal colony,[27] of a zone of systematic exploitation (of mineral wealth, of populations) and under-development, this is swept under the carpet by the force of a view of the "True North" which is comparable to an idyllic seventeenth-century vision of the pastoral countryside which neglects to notice the impoverished and demoralised peasant population.

Dorfman and Mattelart argue that each great urban civilisation creates its own pastoral myth, an extra-social Eden, chaste and pure, where: "The only relation the centre (adult-city folk-bourgeoisie) manages to establish with the periphery (child-noble savage/worker/peasant) is touristic and sensationalist. . . . The innocence of this marginal sector is what guarantees the Duckburger his touristic salvation . . . his childish rejuvenation. The primitive infrastructure offered by the Third World Countries [or 'The Countryside'] becomes the nostalgic echo of a lost primitivism, a world of purity . . . reduced to a picture postcard to be enjoyed by a service-oriented world."[28] This circulation of notions, the mythology of the "True North Strong and Free," as part of the social spatialisation of the Canadian nation serves to gloss over more than North-South disparities. It also provides a unifying sense that all those who, whether living in the East or West, are Canadians by virtue of the patrimony the North. "Now the North, which is common to both East and West is a natural bridge to unite the two divisions. I look to the North as one of the great unifying factors in the future of the Dominion."[29] It opposes the different regional interests with a strong emotional argument. Central to this counterpoint of interests is the Federal Government policy of "developing the north for the benefit of all Canadians" (i.e., as a resource-rich colony). The Northern Territories are prevented from attaining provincial status despite popular demand. This would mean relinquishing Southern control over development and resources and involve sacrificing the "for the benefit of all" policy. Nor is this only a question of power and economics. The literal re-territorialisation of the North, the re-drawing of maps, would make the North suddenly some-one's, a place where people dwelt and appropriated the land as their own. It would no longer be an "empty space" but a territorialised place, a place of communities, a landscape made meaningful by personal biographies, and acknowledged as such. This is nearly unimaginable in the terms of the current notions of purity and inviolability. The discursive economy of the "True North" coincides neatly with a set of non-discursive practices, namely, the institutions of Canadian federalism and the recreational practices of summer tourists who indulge in a type of *rite de passage* which re-confirms their self-image as "Canadian." The "True North" is a common reference "point" marking an invisible national community of the initiated.[30] It is the common appeal to self-inscription—the "writing-in"—of the North into a territorial heritage that constitutes the Vancouverite and the Newfoundlander as Canadian. This is further to say, that the "True North Strong and Free" is an essential and determining component of the view which imaginatively repositions Canada as a "Northern nation" with more in common with Norway, for example, than with the United States. It is on this basis that Canadians often set out their differences from the United States.[31]

The various images circulating around the "True North Strong and Free" constitute a system of signification, a discursive representation which requires analysis *in toto*. Yet this mythological discourse is only a part and hint of an overall spatialisation: a modern *geomancy*. In this system, places or regions mean something only in relation to other places as a constellation of meanings, that is, the North makes sense only with reference to other regions: the "urban jungle," the southern agricultural fringe, or the commodified consumer landscape of Toronto's suburban strip developments. The images are oriented towards each other in a mutually supporting dialogical exchange.[32]

The importance of the "True North Strong and Free" mythology is in its paradoxical reinforcement of a sense of Canadian identity while disguising the simultaneous exploitation and under-development of the North. This takes place through its presence as a community "yarn," a national mythology as well as its role in underpinning the institutional arrangement of the Canadian state. This is, however, at some cost to those inhabitants of the region. The manner in which the North is used metaphorically in narratives and texts to convey abstract ideas or metonymically appropriated for its nationalistic connotations quite apart from direct presentations of "The North" *per se* reveals the importance of spatialisation as a cognitive tool. A "True North" rises out of the datum of the "Real North." The North becomes "the North in men": a sort of essentialistic human nature revealed by ritualistic journeys, *rites de passage*, and re-confirmation in a landscape empty of human traces.

But, the "True North" is more than just a myth or a story. It motivates, and is articulated with a set of active practices which are both institutional and personal. It is, in view of people's personal neglect of it (despite the jokes and embarrassed clichés), a mythology which is first of all practised, and only second consciously contemplated. As a result, the "True North Strong and Free" has empirical effects on patterns of development, economic impacts on its inhabitants, political implications for the nation-state and cultural impacts on Canadian citizens.

Notes

Originally published as "The True North Strong and Free," in *Places on the Margin: Alternative Geographies of Modernity*, by Rob Shields. Copyright © Rob Shields. Reprinted with permission of the author.

1. Canadian National Anthem, official English version. Tune by Calixa Lavallee, lyrics by Adolphe-Basile Routhier as the Québécois "Chant Nationale." English translation by Robert Stanley Weir, a Toronto school teacher, approved 1967. *O Canada* was first commissioned by Theodore Robitaille, lieutenant governor of Quebec, for a banquet in Quebec City on June 24, 1880. The French lyrics were written by Sir Adolphe-Basile Routhier, a prominent Quebec City lawyer and writer, in the form of a poem, which was set to music by Calixa Lavallee. Parliament refused to accept the English words of *O Canada*; only the melody was accepted, in 1967. The principal objection was the lack of any mention of God. In 1972, a revised version of the lyrics was considered, finally being accepted in the National Anthem Act, June 27, 1980. The phrases "True North" and "White North" also appear in Tennyson's *Idylls of the King* (1873) in direct reference to Canada, and in the epigraph Tennyson wrote for Franklin's monument in Westminster Abbey (1847), respectively.

2. Lord Strathcona in a letter to William Carson cited in B. Willson, *Life of Lord Strathcona and Mount Royal* (London: Cassell, 1915), 601.

3. W. L. Morton, *The Canadian Identity* (Madison: University of Wisconsin Press, 1961).

4. Ibid., 5.

5. Morton, "The 'North' in Canadian Historiography," in *Transactions of the Royal Society of Canada*, ser. 4, no. 8 (1970): 40.

6. Harold Innis (1894–1952), Professor of Political Economy at the University of Toronto, was an influential figure in pressing for the establishment of the first geography department in Canada at Toronto. For Innis, geography was an important element in his career strategy (M. Sanderson, "Griffith Taylor: A Geographer to Remember," *Canadian Geographer* 26 [1982]: 293–99; G. S. Dunbar, "Innis and Canadian Geography," *Canadian Geographer* 29, no. 2 [1985]: 159–64). His interest in the staples trade and export patterns led him to propound what has been called the Laurentian hypothesis along with Creighton. That is, that much of Canadian history is explained by the nature and location of the St. Lawrence River which represented a "highway" to the heart of the continent. This contrasts with the barrier to westward expansion posed by the Appalachian Mountains in the case of the young United States. It might also be contrasted to the Québécois perception of the St. Lawrence which included the added dimension of the river as "mainstreet": the main communications route between the various seigneuries along the shore (for this insight I am

indebted to the participants in the seminar on the "Laurentian Hypothesis Revisited" held at the Canadian Association of Geographers meetings, Hamilton, Ont., June 1987). This hypothesis was also suggested by the British geographer Marion Newbigin in her book on Canada (*The Great River, the Lands and the Men* [New York: Harcourt, Brace, Jovanovich, 1927]) which emphasized the importance of the St. Lawrence and the lands of its drainage basin. See also R. W. Winks, ed., *The Historiography of the British Empire-Commonwealth* (Durham: Duke University Press, 1966), 80.

7. N. Frye, "Haunted by Lack of Ghosts: Some Patterns in the Imagery of Canadian Poetry," in *The Canadian Imagination: Dimensions of a Literary Culture*, ed. D. Staines (Cambridge, Mass.: Harvard University Press, 1977), 24–25.

8. See also M. Atwood, *Survival* (Toronto: Anansi, 1979); and J. G. Moss, "Canadian Frontiers: Sexuality and Violence from Richardson to Kroetsch," *Journal of Canadian Fiction* 3 (Summer 1973): 36–41.

9. On gendered spaces see also Carolyn Andrews and Beth Moore Milroy, eds., *Life Spaces: Gender, Household, Employment* (Vancouver: University of British Columbia Press, 1988); and Sophie Watson, "Gilding the Smokestacks: The Symbolic Representations of Deindustrialised Regions" (copies available from University of Bristol, Dept. of Social Policy, 1989).

10. G. McGregor, *The Wacousta Syndrome* (Toronto: University of Toronto Press, 1985), 59.

11. R. Cook, "Imagining a North American Garden," *Canadian Literature* 103 (winter 1984), 11.

12. N. Frye, *Stubborn Structure: Essays on Criticism and Society* (London: Methuen, 1971), 199.

13. John Richardson's *Wacousta* (1832) is considered to be the first novel written by a native-born Canadian. The reference here is to the return of theories of Canadian culture and identity that positions the relationship to the physical environment at the core of national narratives. These include the widely praised—and widely criticized— *The Wacousta Syndrome* (1985) by Gaile McGregor, which positions the retreat from nature as being at center of the Canadian national psyche.—Eds.

14. By virtue of their presence in and around Toronto and central southern Ontario, this group of writers, including Pierre Berton, Gaile McGregor, Northrop Frye, W. L. Morton, Carl Berger, and so on have peerless access to the nationally aired morning "chat shows" which have provided a vehicle for the wide dissemination of their ideas. Nor do they function as cautious academics, but speak as intellectuals about their work which they "boost" without reservation. These radio and television interviews are partly arranged by publishers to launch books to the Canadian public. One of the best examples is Gaile McGregor's appearance on "Peter Gzowski's *Morningside*" (the CBC's three-hour flagship Monday-Friday morning programme which has a broad "up market" national audience), January 16, 1985.

15. Government of Canada, *Canada Pent-annual Report* (Ottawa: Supply and Services Canada, 1963), ii and (1968), i.

16. M. Hechter, *Internal Colonialism: The Celtic Fringe in British National Development, 1536– 1936* (London: Routledge and Kegan Paul, 1975).

17. Coates, *Canada's Colonies*.

18. In democratic control, provision of social services, average income and so on, see T. Berger, *Northern Frontier, Northern Homeland: The Report of the Mackenzie Valley Pipeline Inquiry* (Ottawa: Supply and Services Canada, 1977); and Coates, *Canada's Colonies*, 1986.

19. Coates, *Canada's Colonies*, 15–16.

20. See for example J. Wadland, "Wilderness and Culture," in *Nastawagan: The Canadian North by Canoe and Snowshoe*, ed. B. W. Hodgins and M. Hobbs (Toronto: Betelgeuse, 1985); W. Drew, *The Wabeno Feast* (Toronto: University of Toronto Press, 1973).

21. This has also had other specific impacts which demand a full-scale study in their own right. While the pace of Northern development follows a thoroughly capitalist logic, the "style" of development and change in the North has, by the logic of purity encapsulated by the mythology of the "True North," helped to maintain the separation of the North from the inhabited lands of Canada. Partly on the basis of the antithesis of civilisation versus nature that is set up, work-camps provisioned from Edmonton, Winnipeg, or Montreal have been favoured rather than more economic, permanent towns which might act as "growth poles," such as Churchill, Manitoba. This returns to my argument that the North is treated as if it is an improper place for families, for civilisation.

22. The Windigo Myth appears in several variants amongst the Cree tribes in the Northern areas of the provinces. According to the Mistassini Cree, "Windigo" is a bush spirit which may "possess" an individual making him uncommunicative, withdrawn, and morose. According to legend (and practice) in the context of extended-family hunting groups, possessed individuals must be ritually killed otherwise they will become violent and murder-off the entire group.

23. "A Vanishing Race," *Catholic World* 1.5 (August 1865): 708.

24. J. G. McGregor, *North West of Sixteen* (Tokyo: C. E. Tuttle and M. G. Hurtig, 1984).

25. Justice Thomas Berger was the commissioner of the Mackenzie Valley Pipeline Inquiry, which was charged with investigating the environmental, social, and economic impact of a planned pipeline through the Northwest Territories. Berger broke new ground by consulting extensively with the aboriginal communities that were to be impacted by the development. Released in 1977, the inquiry recommended a moratorium on the pipeline due to the negative effect it would have on aboriginal communities and the environment. The report played an important role in heightening public awareness of environmental and aboriginal issues in Canada.—Eds.

26. A. Solzhenitsyn, *The Gulag Archipelago* (New York: Harper and Row, 1977), 1.

27. Hechter, *Internal Colonialism*.

28. A. Dorfman and A. Mattelart, *How to Read Donald Duck* (New York: International General, 1975), 96.

29. Lord Tweedsmuir, *Notes for Mackenzie King's Speeches in Britain* (Summer 1937), cited in R. M. Hamilton and D. Shields, *The Dictionary of Canadian Quotations and Phrases* (Toronto: McClelland and Stewart), 69.

30. B. Anderson, *Imagined Communities* (London: Verso, 1983).

31. This has begun to change since the 1981 constitution came into effect and made some of the social values explicit. These contrast with those given primacy in Ameri-

can constitutional and legal practice and might include an emphasis on community solidarity over individual freedom (good government over individual rights), equity over equality, and the provision of a "welfare net" as opposed to the neo-liberal social values of individual independence in the United States.

32. M. M. Bakhtin, *Rabelais and His World*, trans. H. Iswolsky (Bloomington: Indiana University Press, 1984), 10–12.

KEVIN PASK

Late Nationalism: The Case of Quebec

Kevin Pask (b. 1961) is an associate professor of English at Concordia University. He received his Ph.D. at Johns Hopkins University and is the author of *The Emergence of the English Author: Scripting the Life of the Poet in Early Modern England* (1996), as well as other essays about early modern English literature.

The experience of nationalism in Quebec remains an oddly belated affair —especially considering its proximity to the United States, with its precocious example of nation-statehood. Despite its apparent blandness, at least in the lexicon of American comedy, Canada remains a perpetually irritated anomaly in the Americas: a state comprising two nations (if not more, considering the significance of the aboriginal "First Nations"). Lord Durham's Report, the imperial response to the Rebellion of 1837, infamously observed that Lower Canada (now Quebec) consisted in fact of "two nations warring in the bosom of a single state," and the observation has been easily extended to the constitutional problems of modern Canada.[1] More than 150 years later, Lord Durham remains both a threat to Québécois nationalism—recommending the assimilation of the francophone population—and an oracle: the decisive appearance of the language of "nationhood" in British North America. Thus, in the nationalist imaginary, the only means of avoiding assimilation into the rest of anglophone North America is to realize Durham's two nations with the creation of a sovereign state, definitively marking the appearance of a mature French-speaking people in North America.

By any reasonable measure, Quebec has indeed emerged as a vibrant and progressive society in the past forty years—roughly the period since the election of Jean Lesage in 1960 ushered in the "Quiet Revolution" which transformed Quebec's former economic dependence on English-Canadian and American capital and dissolved the cultural monopoly of the Catholic Church. The Quiet Revolution also saw the explosion of a modern nationalism in Quebec and the creation of the Parti Québécois (PQ), initially led by the charismatic René Lévesque, as a social-democratic and nationalist political force. Although the PQ has governed Quebec more often than not since its first election in 1976, it has not been able to achieve in two referenda (1980 and 1995) what it sees as the culmination of the Quiet Revolution—independence from Canada. Nationalist fervour, in fact, seems to be in retreat from the high-water mark it achieved in the 1995 referendum on independence (significantly couched in the more reassuring terms of "sovereignty" and "partnership" with Canada), which failed only by the smallest of margins. Although the current PQ government remains officially committed to holding another referendum at some moment in the future, the population appears to have lost its avidity for another episode in the constitutional debate. Lucien Bouchard, the politician whose oratorical force and eloquence brought the sovereignist option close to success in 1995, resigned in January 2001 as Premier of the province, citing frustration at his inability to whip up nationalist fervour following the referendum. In the nationalist imaginary, still powerful in Quebec, this can only be taken as a collective lack of maturity and failure of nerve.

Is Quebec, almost alone in the Western Hemisphere, doomed to the status of neo-colonial atavism? No, runs the nationalist argument, Quebec's collective maturation can be postponed, but it cannot finally be deterred. As Benedict Anderson has argued in his important work on nationalism, a logic of seriality is in place here: the universalization of "nation" as the name of political and cultural identity in a world defined as one of United Nations.[2] Jacques Parizeau, the PQ Premier who organized the 1995 referendum, repeatedly invoked the moment of Quebec taking its seat at the United Nations and responsibly assuming all of the normal international duties. This was a projection without specific political content in the ordinary sense; there was no pretense of affecting world affairs or even the lives of most Québécois. A collective "self," as Anderson's argument suggests, looks for its reflection in the universality of "United Nations." The compelling power of nationalism rests upon this psychologization of the nation. It measures both the "naturalness" of the nation-state as a political form and the attractiveness of individual self-identification with a national "spirit." The defeat of the referendum, then, could be treated as a kind of existential failure. Quebec once again failed to say "Yes" to itself; indeed, failed to take up its adult responsibilities in the world at large.

This strongly felt rhetoric of existential crisis is not simply a reaction to the loss of two referenda. It suffused the culture of Quebec throughout the explosion of national feeling in the period of the Quiet Revolution. The virtual poet laureate of the time, Gaston Miron (1928–1996), could write a poem called "*Pour mon repatriement*" (For my repatriation) which declared, "*un jour j'aurai dit oui à ma naissance*" (one day I will have said yes to my birth).[3] Indeed, from at least the 1950s and throughout the period of the Quiet Revolution, Québécois nationalists have relied on a psychologized "subject-nation" whose destiny, like that of a child's, is necessarily independence from the parents. The psychoanalyst Camille Laurin, who later became a leading figure of the first PQ government (author of Bill 101, still widely celebrated as the bulwark of the French language in the province), lent his professional credentials to this collective psychology.[4] In the period of nationalist mourning after the most recent referendum, the trope could return as the spectre of perpetual childhood: a book entitled *Ce pays comme un enfant*.[5] The continuing use of the language of collective birth and maturation represents perhaps the most rhetorically powerful gesture in the nationalist repertoire—in Quebec or elsewhere.[6]

Although an advanced society, Quebec is, in the powerful optic of nationalism, retarded. It presents us, then, with an interesting example of the political and cultural vicissitudes of nationalism as a serialized, global project. Its example is especially pertinent to "new–old" nationalisms in European countries (Scotland, Catalonia) even as it is also linked to postcolonial instances by its American and colonial provenance. Its case also allows us to take the measure of the nationalist intellectual in the new cultural landscape of postmodernism. "At the base of the modern social order," writes Ernest Gellner, "stands not the executioner but the professor."[7] This aspect of "modernity" remains sharply defined in Quebec, where a clerical near-monopoly on francophone intellectual and cultural life is a living memory. (The number of Catholic priests in Quebec dropped from 8,400 around 1960 to 4,285 in 1981.) In this setting the nationalist character of secular intellectuals has been largely taken as a given: they are the organic intellectuals of the nation-state, defining themselves against the universalism of the Catholic clergy. "Intellectuals are in some degree predestined to propagate the 'national' idea," Max Weber remarked almost a century ago, and the dictum has held up remarkably well.[8] In Quebec, as Jocelyn Létourneau has persuasively argued, this destiny took the shape of a "father's" protective concern for the "*petite nation*" and its people.[9]

This destiny, however, can no longer be taken for granted in Quebec, where the national narrative and the privileged position of the intellectual within it show signs of structural fatigue. If the explanation of this exhaustion is too often a facile account of "postmodernity," it remains remarkable that the signal theorization of postmodernism was produced for Quebec. Jean-François Lyotard's account of the postmodern condition was in fact originally produced for Quebec's Conseil des Universités in the late 1970s, part of the Quiet Revolution's ongoing reconceptualization of education in the province.[10] This report, however, was likely to have appeared as entirely antipathetic to the first PQ government, as it prepared itself for the 1980 referendum on "sovereignty-association." Lyotard's contention that the new "multiversity" was no longer equipped "to train an elite capable of guiding the nation towards its emancipation" was, as far as I can tell, promptly ignored by the institutional matrix which originally commissioned the report.[11]

This does not mean, however, that the discourse of Québécois nationalism has been able successfully to evade the dilemma Lyotard presented. The 1995 referendum, in fact, saw the confluence of two forms of nationalism: both the popular appeal of a rhetoric of national "humiliation" and eventual "affirmation" powerfully mobilized by Lucien Bouchard in the referendum campaign; and, in a considerably lower and more ironic register, a late nationalism. If modernity produced the nationalist intellectual, this is now a figure subjected to "postmodern" stress. Nationalism is an increasingly suspect force, but the nation-state itself has lost none of its legitimacy. Thus, the United States can embody the "ancient" legitimacy of the nation-state while resolutely setting its sights on various forms of "bad" nationalism.[12] If this conjuncture also highlights the attractiveness of nationalism for the left, it has at the same time produced a late nationalism that divests itself of any large claims to emancipation. This is perhaps particularly true of small nations, Scotland and Catalonia as well as Quebec, that have aligned their national aspirations with supranational economic and political arrangements (the EU in Europe, NAFTA in North America).[13]

Daniel Latouche, ironist of Québécois nationalism, marks this new formation. Born in 1945, he is of a generation which grew up with the Quiet Revolution of the 1960s and the independence movement, and he is an intellectual (based at Quebec's Institut National de la Recherche Scientifique–Urbanisation) who has been closely associated at various times with the public venues of nationalism in Quebec: the PQ and the newspaper *Le Devoir*. Latouche is a supple thinker, close in some respects to a figure like Tom Nairn: constantly measuring the fate of nationalism against the larger currents of global developments, and well prepared to challenge easy assumptions about the purported irrelevance of the nation-state.

In the period leading up to the 1995 referendum, Latouche stepped into the role of ideological ambassador of Québécois nationalism to English Canada and the US, appearing on the McNeil–Lehrer Report in the US, writing for Toronto's *Globe & Mail*, and responding to Philip Resnick's *Letters to a Québécois Friend*.[14] In the early 1990s, when the failure of Brian Mulroney's Meech Lake Accord, granting Quebec the status of a "distinct society," set the stage for a new referendum on independence, Latouche essayed a kind of disillusioned nationalism in the heart of "enemy territory," the English-language *Gazette* of Montreal. "Nationalism is like a toothache. It never gets any better on its own. Its excesses come from the length of time it takes for it to run its natural course towards its equally natural goal: sovereignty."[15] The simile is striking, not least because it was later borrowed by Jacques Parizeau, himself speaking before a hostile audience of Toronto business people during the 1995 referendum campaign. Nationalism is both something entirely "natural"—a word used twice in the three sentences just quoted—but also negatively "natural," like a toothache, something to be "cured."[16] The rhetoric is of course informed by its occasion: the attempt to neutralize a hostile audience by convincing them of the inevitability of the nationalism they oppose. Still, the capacity of Latouche and Parizeau to ironize the naturalness of the nation-state is remarkable in a context where the serialization of nation-states, rather than any particular political conflict between Ottawa and Quebec City, was the true subject of the referendum debate.[17]

Latouche witnesses the antinomy of late nationalism: on the one hand the continuing power of the concept of the nation-state as the virtually universal principle of political and cultural legitimacy; on the other, the growing sense of ideological fatigue around the issue and a wistful desire for "nations without nationalism." Benedict Anderson has recently coined the term "late official nationalism" to describe the attempted—and sometimes failed—production of nationalist affects by bureaucratic elites; the term itself, moreover, suggests the possibility of periodizing nationalism in a fashion inimical to the classical nationalist imaginary, which has always insisted on the profound historical depths of national sentiment.[18] "The sovereignty of a people is an old, old, old idea," insisted Bernard Landry in his recent successful campaign to succeed Bouchard as leader of the PQ and Premier of the province. "Sovereignty is something that is unchanging, universal."[19]

It does not necessarily follow, however, that the possibility of periodizing nationalism automatically dissipates the power of its claims. The importance of a high (that is, literate) culture is a symptom of the nature of modernity itself, which produces the need for the specialization and interchangeability of functions (what Gellner terms the need to produce "context-free messages") as well as a social environment characterized by daily contact with extensive and interconnected bureaucracies. The modern nationalist, then, demands the congruence of political borders with cultural ones because, as Gellner argues, "non-congruence is not merely an inconvenience or a disadvantage: it means perpetual humiliation. Only if such a congruence does obtain can one feel 'at ease in one's skin.' "[20] To my knowledge, this fundamental condition of nationalism has not been repealed, even by the appearance of a postmodernism which dispenses with the master narratives of modernity. If, however, the experience of contemporary nationalism in highly developed societies tends to ironize the naturalness of its own deepest claims to legitimacy, it becomes perhaps useful to offer Quebec as an exemplary periodization of this experience.

Priestly Progenitors

French-Canadian nationalism developed only very slowly after the British Conquest, and throughout the nineteenth century. This was largely a result of the domination of the Catholic clergy over a mainly rural population which had little direct contact with imperial and Canadian bureaucracies. The clergy was strongly ultramontane in character, hostile both to republican France and the Protestant United States. The cities, Quebec City, but especially Montreal, meanwhile, became important centres of English-Canadian capital (its entrepreneurs often in fact Scots in origin), running empires of continental scope, the fur trade and later the Canadian Pacific Railroad, as well as resource extraction and manufacturing within Quebec itself. Urban workers were often French-Canadian habitants drawn to the cities, but also Irish, English, and Scots. Middle-class French Canadians gravitated toward the professions and the clergy rather than business, where, in any case, they were often unwelcome.

A French-Canadian nationalism found it difficult to thrive in such circumstances, and the failure of the Rebellion of 1837 decisively eliminated a liberal and republican nationalism in French Canada for several generations. It is symptomatic of the difficult genesis of nationalism in Quebec that, even in the early twentieth century, much of the nationalist movement was given over to a retrograde attempt to act as defenders of the faith, in the context of large-scale urbanization (as well as massive emigration to New England, where "Little Canadas" became the norm in industrial towns). The Catholic faith of French Canada remained the key term of this unstable conjuncture of Catholic internationalism and national, linguistically and ethnically derived particularism. Abbé Lionel Groulx, whose history of New France (*La naissance d'une race*, 1919) was central to this nationalism, epitomized the period's mobilization of the concept of an essentially modern nation-race (affiliated in Groulx's case with Action Nationale and Jeune-Canada, the French-Canadian offshoots of the fascist Action Française), while also appealing to the supposed ancien-régime purity of the Catholic peasantry before the Conquest. (The Janus of modern nationalism in Quebec, Groulx virtually invented the academic study of French-Canadian history at the Université de Montréal.) The legacy of Groulx is now an extremely difficult one for Québécois nationalism. He was a very important figure for those now in their 60s and 70s, but younger generations care little for him, especially with recent controversies about the extent of his anti-Semitism.[21] Jacques Parizeau's infamous comment on the night of the 1995 referendum—that "money and the ethnic vote" (an equation perhaps implicitly anti-Semitic) doomed the result—was widely and heatedly repudiated in the province, and Parizeau resigned as Premier the next day; but the lingering remnants of an earlier xenophobia continue to haunt Québécois nationalism.[22]

Provincial Development and Quiet Revolution

The Quiet Revolution of the 1960s and 1970s, although not itself a strictly separatist movement, transformed the landscape of nationalism in the province. It made possible a repudiation of the nationalism of Groulx's period (and associated in political terms with the reign of Maurice Duplessis, "la Grande Noirceur," which dominated the 1940s and 1950s). The province's birth rate dropped dramatically from one of the highest in the developed world to one of the lowest. The Quiet Revolution also enacted a French-style *dirigiste* economic policy, creating for example the massive Hydro-Québec, and establishing a strong presence in the provincial economy through the creation of an activist pension fund and other levers of industrial policy. The name for this convergence of public and private remains "Quebec Incorporated."

Pierre Trudeau initially claimed the Quiet Revolution as a victory over nationalism, which he associated with the era of Groulx and Duplessis. His own legacy as Prime Minister was the attempt to install French equality in Ottawa and a differential, but still pan-Canadian, identity in the place of either imperial subjects or American-style "melting pot": federal bilingualism and official multiculturalism. This turned out to be more popular in English Canada, where it bolstered a sense of distinction from the US, and in French Canada outside Quebec, in need of federal linguistic support, than in Quebec—perhaps the only place in Canada where language could spark rather than mitigate nationalism.

Left Québécois intellectuals of the period asserted their participation in the worldwide struggle of decolonization, perhaps most famously in Pierre Vallières's 1967 polemic, *Nègres blancs d'Amérique* (White Niggers of America). The great cultural achievement of this era was the work of Michel Tremblay, whose plays initially shocked the Québécois theatrical world more by their use of *joual*, the French dialect associated with the lower classes (in Tremblay's case, Montreal's francophone working class), than by their daring representation of women and homosexuals. Joual served as the cultural emblem of decolonization from "international French," an aspect of nationalism in the period almost as important as opposition to the domination of English Canada. (English Canada itself effectively declared its cultural independence from British and American norms in the same period. The idea of a specific and autonomous Canadian literature, for example, is a remarkably recent phenomenon.)

The Quiet Revolution was of course very different from the situation of the "Third World" nationalisms. Still, in terms particularly appropriate to the situation of Quebec, Peter Worsley remarks of this period that "the nationalist mystique . . . [became] grounded in an institutional practice, that of mobilization for development."[23] "*Maîtres chez nous*" (Masters of our own house) was the slogan of Jean Lesage's government, itself without a separatist project. In this light, the massive development projects undertaken by Hydro-Québec in the 1970s can appear within the same socioeconomic landscape as Egypt's Aswan Dam. Quebec was in a position to take advantage of the "nationalist mystique" partly because its francophone professional-managerial class could plausibly conceive of itself as underdeveloped and in need of a sort of Great Leap Forward. The first leader of the PQ, René Lévesque, constantly juggled the aspirations of the radical nationalists and those of an emerging professional-managerial class, linked to a rapidly expanding state. Nation was of course the crucial term of this co-existence: "We [Québécois] will decide whether an enterprise will be private, public, or mixed. But it must be Québécois."[24] Quebec Incorporated, in other words, must be managed by francophone Québécois.

The economic shocks of the early and mid-1970s brought the period of Keynesian national development to an end, but only slowly in Quebec. This was in part because of the continuing power of the "nationalist mystique" in articulating government activism in the province. (Across the border in the United States, the equally nationalist mobilization of a military Keynesianism also extended this conjuncture, if to different effect.) The long-term success of such activism, however, created the conditions in which the francophone professional-managerial class felt itself increasingly alienated from the rhetoric of national liberation. By the early 1990s, average incomes of francophones had slightly surpassed those of anglophones. A large francophone executive class, moreover, was firmly in place and was as alarmed as their anglophone counterparts (and perhaps most importantly, the province's Wall Street creditors) about the soaring provincial deficit.

It is in this socioeconomic environment that a late nationalism has emerged in Quebec. Latouche had already addressed the predicament of narratives of national liberation even before the 1995 referendum, dispensing with the rhetoric of "national development" and explicitly harnessing a postmodern nationalism to the rhetoric of neoliberalism: "Independence for Quebec should be looked upon as just another case of political deregulation. After years of trying unsuccessfully [to] down the size of both the federal and the provincial governments, there is only one way left: get rid in one stroke of most of the legislative responsibilities of at least one of them. . . . Quebec as a whole has to be 'privatized.' "[25] This late nationalism can appear as the functional equivalent of the privatization and downsizing of the post-Fordist economy. Will this turn out to be a parodic version of the "nationalist mystique," a "National Salvation Government" to cut corporate taxes and reassure international investors? The government of Lucien Bouchard, although essentially forced by Quebec's international creditors to proceed along the path marked out by Latouche, also gambled that a balanced budget and a good credit rating would give the population a taste for independence. If his recent resignation suggests that the gamble was lost, his successor, Bernard Landry, is nevertheless more *pur et dur* with regard to both independence and a neoliberal agenda. This testifies to the continuing power of nationalist imaginings. It is, after all, extraordinary that nationalism can so dramatically change its political coefficient without alienating its constituency—largely, though by no means exclusively, social-democratic in the case of the PQ. One is thus inclined to appreciate Anderson's contention that nationalism is not so much an ideology as a universally shared assumption: "It would, I think, make things easier if one treated it as if it belonged with 'kinship' and 'religion,' rather than with 'liberalism' or 'fascism.' "[26]

Intellectuals such as Latouche himself testify to the continuing pertinence of this formulation. "The human sciences," remarks Martin Thom, "are dyed with colours registered at the proof stage of the age of nations."[27] The widespread perception of the "politicization" of the universities in North America, however, betrays the anxiety that the dye is wearing thin. This has proceeded at a slower rate in the francophone universities of Quebec, and this fact might be related to the greater role for such academics in the context of a nationalism which has not arrived at its "natural" goal of a nation-state. Still, the humanities in Quebec remain subject to the same twin pressures affecting other North American universities: increasing technical specialization from "above" the traditional humanities, and "popular" or "resistant" cultures from "below." In, for example, the study of literature, a discipline often central to the national curriculum, one can now begin to see the outlines of the historical process framing the response of humanist academics: the quasi-clerical universalism of the classics replaced by the study of the national literatures, itself to be challenged in turn by a globalized (read "Americanized') cultural studies.

Gellner usefully remarks that nationalism "suffers from pervasive false consciousness" by claiming to defend folk culture while in fact forging a high culture.[28] One of the overriding characteristics of the late nationalist moment is the evaporation of this particular form of "false consciousness," at least in societies like Quebec, where it appears as outmoded and sentimental, attached to a figure like Lionel Groulx.[29] This sea change is also reflected in the world of Montreal's newspapers, where the name of the youth-oriented alternative weekly, Voir (see), is itself a jab at the nationalist daily, Le Devoir (duty), replacing the austere Weberian intellectual (Le Devoir was founded in 1910) with immersion in a highly Americanized society of spectacle. Not coincidentally, Voir advocated a vote for sovereignty during the 1995 referendum, but only in order to "get over" what it felt to be the tiresome rhetoric of humiliation and national self-affirmation. Subsequently, it has announced its intention to ignore the national debate in its pages.

Escape from the Rural Curse

If the modern use of the word "country" (in this respect similar to the French *pays*) itself betrays the characteristic nationalist valorization of the rural at the expense of the urban, how will a new "age of cities," to borrow a phrase from Martin Thom, affect the nationalist imaginary? It should be admitted that, however much this imaginary promoted the countryside, the classical age of nationalism was also the great age of urbanization, partially the result of the experience of alienation from a primary (rural) culture. Quebec's most important sociologist, Fernand Dumont (1927–1995) theorized the distinction between a "first" and a "second" culture, and later narrated his own life as an "emigration" from small-town to urban Quebec.[30] This is a narrative very close to the experience of the Quiet Revolution. It does not, however, account for the experience of a newer generation whose itinerary is increasingly one of migration between cities. Montreal remains the "natural" limit of all such migrations in the Québécois nationalist imaginary. As long as this remains the case, a thoroughly urbanized culture can be reclaimed for the age of nations. Jane Jacobs's work, perhaps more than any other, has reversed the classical nationalist image of the city as a parasite on the countryside.[31] Jacobs (by then resident in Toronto) came out in favour of the 1980 referendum on "sovereignty-association" because, in effect, it would "downsize" the scale of government, allowing both Montreal and Toronto to flourish as centres of essentially city-state capitalisms.[32] The nationalism of Latouche is crucially informed by Jacobs, and his recent work has increasingly turned to the idea of the nation defined by a single metropole.[33] Both Jacobs and Latouche tend to assume the naturalness of the nation as the unit of metropole and periphery, the former now thoroughly dominating the latter. Each great city requires its own hinterland (already a stunning demotion of the "heartland" of classical nationalism), and the nation becomes the city-state writ large.

It has in fact largely been the case that francophone migrations in Quebec terminate at Montreal. The rates of interprovincial mobility for Quebec's anglophones and "allophones" (mother tongue other than English or French), on the other hand, are well above the Canadian average (with the force of Québécois nationalism partly filling their sails). This landscape, however, is changing. Francophone parents, for example, are increasingly demanding a stronger English-language programme in the French schools, partly with an eye to a mobile North American job market. Montreal itself, moreover, has dramatically emerged in recent years as a powerful high-tech economy, with considerable strengths in aerospace, pharmaceuticals and communications technology. The province's principal exports in 1988 were newspaper and aluminium; in 1998, aircraft and aircraft parts, along with electronic parts and components.[34]

The relationship of these new industries, and thus of Montreal itself, to the rest of the province and to the nationalist government is no longer the same as when Montreal served primarily as the headquarters of resource-extraction companies. Bernard Landry (then Finance Minister) recently elicited the scorn of these industries with proposals, entirely characteristic of Quebec Incorporated, to create huge tax subsidies in order to attract a large microchip factory to Montreal and to create an "e-commerce" commercial centre. The "nationalist mystique" no longer appears particularly relevant to Montreal's development as the engine of Quebec's economy.

Exiting the Nationalist Imaginary

The high cultural emblem of this moment is Robert Lepage, who has succeeded Michel Tremblay at the centre of Québécois theatre. Unlike Tremblay, Lepage has become one of the travelling impresarios of the international polyglot production. Lepage has adroitly positioned his own theatre at the crossroads of American and European culture—in, for instance, the juxtaposition of Miles Davis and Jean Cocteau in *Needles and Opium*; moreover, he marks this international conjuncture as the almost inevitable vocation of Québécois culture, a conjuncture also marked by the firm subordination of the verbal to the visual elements of the spectacle. International French, meanwhile, has re-emerged as the dominant language of the theatre in the province. While *joual* remains quite popular, especially on television, it has lost its specifically political content. Latouche, meanwhile, has taken on the sacred cow of Bill 101 and its codification of the linguistic dominance of French in the province (the simple graffito "101" often marks condemnation of the stray English sign in Montreal), arguing that it impedes rather than promotes the cause of Québécois nationalism. The sheer fact of a Québécois nation-state will ensure the status of French, while at the same time creating the confidence for expanded forms of linguistic *métissage*: "À nous l'impureté."[35] Marshalled in the service of nationalism, the argument simultaneously bids farewell to the cultural underpinning of nationalism: the congruence of political and cultural borders. We have exited the classical nationalist imaginary.

Indeed, nomadic figures such as Lepage seem to betoken some new "imagined community" beyond that of the nation-state. John Gerard Ruggie has re-described Owen Lattimore's work on the "sovereign importance of movement" for the Mongol tribes in the context of the political order of postmodernity.[36] In the Quebec of the early 1990s, the 19-year-old Hélène Jutras could both infuriate and galvanize the readership of Le Devoir with her declaration that "Quebec is killing me" and that she, like her anglophone and allophone peers, wanted to leave, perhaps for the US.[37] Here was the voice of "Young Quebec," Anderson's "Future Perfect" around which classical nationalism had always been constructed ("Young Germany," Jeune-Canada, etc.).[38]

Jutras was in a sense the perfect embodiment of that nationalism, using the language of national existential crisis in a later elaboration of her reasons for wanting to leave: "My happiness comes before that of a country which refuses to be one."[39] Her cri de coeur needed to discover a nationalist rationale for the fact that Montreal could no longer exist as her sole metropole. In more ways than this, she was the true daughter of Québécois nationalism. Until the 1970s children of immigrants could attend either English or French schools, and generally chose English; subsequently, they have been required to attend French schools. The law was of course designed to integrate immigrants into a new national culture—Québécois rather than French-Canadian. What was not intended was the simultaneous integration of students of French-Canadian stock (primarily in the schools of Montreal, where allophones form a large percentage of children) into a kind of "World Beat" culture in which international migration is widespread. In only a few years since Jutras published her essay, such desired movement has become the norm rather than the exception: "Aujourd'hui Québec; demain le monde," boasts a current advertising campaign for the Laval University.

It is possible that late nationalism is constructed around the "Future Perfect" of cosmopolitan movement. Anderson himself has meditated on the importance of the passport to modern identity as well as the importance of "long-distance nationalism."[40] Latouche has recently insisted, with regard to the cosmopolitanism of Montreal, "A cosmopolitan city cannot be constructed outside a national time and space. Without the nation, one cannot have access to the universal."[41] The nation-state, after all, retains the passport to the cosmopolitan experience of the global cities. Even this monopoly, however, is diluted when more and more people experience multiple citizenship. The francophone writer Dany Laferrière has expatiated in an interview on the benefits of tri-citizenship —in his case, Haitian, Canadian (a former resident of Montreal), and American. His situation is no longer unusual in Montreal, and this has a very real effect on his French-Canadian peers. This maximization of one's potential for movement is the flip side of the explosion of "long-distance nationalisms." In this form, however, movement is not necessarily understood as exile from an idealized homeland, which tends to be the case for the long-distance nationalist.

The nation-state remains a powerful model of serialization: to everyone a nation and, conversely, every nation an organic and coherent "body politic." In the classical nationalist imaginary, this was necessarily a single national identity. Dual citizenship was an aberration to be rectified through the development of new standards of naturalization and expatriation. Until very recently, both the United States and Canada were insistent on the point: naturalization in another country was long one of the statutory acts that could trigger the loss of US and Canadian citizenship. Only a 1967 ruling of the Supreme Court forced the government of the US to accept dual citizenship; Canadian law did not permit it until 1973. By 1995, however, Québécois nationalists were promising voters that they did not need to fear losing their Canadian passports; they could carry both a Canadian and a Quebec passport.[42] The power of nationalism once relied on the "natural" order of unique citizenship. This order, however, is no longer guaranteed by the serialization of nation-states; it is perhaps even undermined by that product of classical nationalism— the ongoing multiplication and elaboration of national identities—in a world where global migrations make it increasingly possible to "collect" citizenships.

Late and Soft?

The multiple passport signals the arrival of citizenship as something as much akin to consumer choice as to primal identification or affiliation. Toward the end of his life, Gellner looked forward to such a lessening of nationalist fervour in a largely Western European context: at a more advanced stage, the same industrial culture that created the initial impetus for nationalism would ultimately diminish its effects. "[L]ate industrial man, like his immediate predecessor, early industrial man, still finds his identity in a literate culture, rather than anything else, but his literate culture no longer differs quite so much from that of his ethnic neighbour."[43] The result, Gellner argued, would be greater reliance on forms of shared sovereignty—federalization and cantonalization—rather than full independence. In various ways, Scotland and Catalonia, as well as Quebec, seem to bear out this speculative observation. In Quebec this is called the "soft" nationalist option, and its popularity explains the insistence of both referenda on wording that implied continued "association" and "partnership" with Canada. Brian Mulroney's attempt to enshrine Quebec's status as a "distinct society" was a version of this which attempted to accommodate Quebec's nationalism within a federalist framework. Its success (it failed at the last moment in 1990) would, I think, have been more than merely temporizing—part of the reason it was opposed by the most militant elements of the PQ. A large part of the francophone population of Quebec, including many who voted for the PQ referenda, would in fact be relieved to accept a largely symbolic enhancement of Quebec's national status that stopped well short of a nation-state.

If Gellner's analysis is correct, then the nationalist reliance on a version of post-Fordist downsizing, along with supranational political and economic arrangements to multiply the number of nation-states, is likely to yield ambiguous results. Gellner pointed to a situation of greater standardization between industrial economies in which "mutual differences become, at least in some measure, merely phonetic rather than semantic: they do similar things and have similar concepts."[44] Gellner's "high culture" of industrial production, implicitly a standardized (national) print-language, now needs to accommodate easy translatability and English as the lingua franca of the executive suite and airport hotel. This is particularly noticeable in the case of the culture industry, arriving at an advanced state when a concept such as TV's *Survivor* can be designed as a modular product easily reassembled in various national markets. Quebec has established something of a niche in such cultural products: Lepage's international spectacles, the growing empire of Cirque de Soleil in Las Vegas and Orlando, Canadian-European co-productions of children's cartoons for the EU–North American market, and Softimage's success in developing special effects for Hollywood.

Québécois nationalists hoped that such high-profile *savoir faire* in the new context of NAFTA would help to detach Quebec from any sense of economic dependence on Canada, and it is certainly the case that Quebec's economic interdependence with the Northeastern US now rivals its trade with Ontario. This has not, to this point, produced the expected upsurge in national sentiment. Rather the opposite. In Quebec, as elsewhere, the goal of arrival at the nation-state can come to feel anticlimactic when the erosion of citizenship in the advanced parliamentary nation-states has the effect of "cantonalizing" the nation-state itself. The real news appears to lie elsewhere. We are in the midst of discovering a new landscape in which the supranational organizations themselves, rather than the parliamentary institutions of the nation-state, become subjects of debate and sites of confrontation: Seattle, Quebec City, Genoa, etc., rather than the interrelated but still nationally specific conflicts in Chicago, Mexico City, or Paris of more than thirty years ago.

Theorists of nationalism have often remarked on the unlikelihood of supranational organizations generating adherence or solidarity. They are effectively the creatures of their own cadre of administrators, and to some extent rely on the continuation of "soft" nationalisms operating beneath them as the basis of community congruent with civil society and rule of law. Gellner welcomed this possibility, and spoke in Montreal several years ago of his attraction to the idea of some behind-the-scenes Whitehall coterie stage-managing the bands and hoopla of national sentiment. If, however, supranational organizations have failed to win anything like broad popular adherence, it is strikingly the case that opposition to the supranational—especially in the form of the international trade organizations—has suddenly created internationally cohesive dissent, often with the aid of the Defense Department's technology—the internet—and the language and culture of the American imperium. In Quebec the interest in this global theatre, prominent in the youth-oriented weeklies, anglophone and francophone alike, has left the PQ scrambling to retain the interest and votes of demographic segments, the left and francophone youth, it could once take for granted. There has been recent speculation, moreover, about the formation of a left alternative to the PQ, which, while probably remaining officially sovereignist, would be willing to risk the breakdown of a common nationalist front.

These developments point toward a more general challenge to what I have been calling late nationalism. Nationalist thinkers, at least of small or potential nation-states, have often been the greatest enthusiasts of NAFTA and the EU, seeing them as potentially generating sovereignties below as well as above the level of existing states. Will this process, however, avoid Gellner's picture of co-opted nationalisms? Other forms of community and solidarity become increasingly prominent alongside the still powerful nationalist one.

Notes

Originally published as "Late Nationalism: The Case of Quebec," in *New Left Review* 11 (2001): 25–54. Copyright © New Left Review. Reprinted with permission of the publisher.

1. *Lord Durham's Report*, ed. Gerald Craig (Ottawa: Carleton University Press, 1963), 23.

2. See in particular "Nationalism, Identity, and the Logic of Seriality," in *The Spectre of Comparisons* (London: Verso, 1998), 29–45.

3. *L'homme rapaillé (Poèmes 1953–1970)* (Montreal: Presses de l' Université de Montréal, 1970), 87.

4. "Autorité et personnalité au Canada français," in *Ma traversée du Québec* (Montreal: Du Jour, 1970), 19–34.

5. Serge Cantin, *Ce pays comme un enfant. Essais sur le Québec (1988–1996)* (Montreal: L'Hexagone, 1997).

6. An alternate, and widely used, figuration is that of a marriage—one which Quebec, usually understanding itself in the position of the spurned or oppressed wife, desires to leave. Since, however, even a badly functioning marriage does not necessarily lead to divorce, I take this metaphor to be a less powerful one in the nationalist imaginary— although it perhaps better accounts for the ambivalence of the Québécois toward independence.

7. *Nations and Nationalism* (Ithaca, N.Y.: Cornell University Press, 1983), 34.

8. *Economy and Society* (Berkeley: University of California Press, 1978), 915–16. See Perry Anderson's commentary, "Max Weber and Ernest Gellner: Science, Politics, Enchantment," in *A Zone of Engagement* (London: Verso, 1992), 197.

9. *Passer à l'avenir. Histoire, mémoire, identité dans le Québec d'aujourd'hui* (Montreal: Boréal, 2000), 115–40.

10. See William Coleman on educational reform and its relationship to nationalism, *The Independence Movement in Quebec, 1945–1980* (Toronto: University of Toronto Press, 1984), 157–82.

11. *The Postmodern Condition: A Report on Knowledge* (Minneapolis: University of Minnesota Press, 1984), 48.

12. See Tom Nairn, "Demonizing Nationality," in *Faces of Nationalism* (London: Verso, 1997), 57–67; also Fredric Jameson, "Globalization and Political Strategy," *New Left Review* 4 (July–August 2000), 49–68.

13. For a useful comparison of the three instances, see Michael Keating, *Nations against the State: The New Politics of Nationalism in Quebec, Catalonia and Scotland* (London: Palgrave Macmillan, 1996).

14. *Letters to a Québécois Friend* (Montreal: McGill-Queen's University Press, 1990).

15. "Ten Reasons for Sovereignty," *Gazette*, October 31, 1991.

16. For discussion of the figurative pathos of the "body politic" in Quebec, see Kim Sawchuk, "Wounded States: Sovereignty, Separation, and the Quebec Referendum," in *When Pain Strikes*, ed. Bill Burns, Cathy Busby, and Kim Sawchuk (Minneapolis: University of Minnesota Press, 1999), 96–114.

17. Québécois nationalists assert that an "overweening centralization" of political power in Ottawa deprives Quebec of the necessary tools for its development. An outsider, however, might be forgiven for failing to discern any proposals for the management of those tools in an independent Quebec strikingly different from those already in place. The role of the provincial government in the economy is massive by North American standards.

18. *Spectre of Comparisons*, 46–57.

19. *Globe & Mail* (Toronto), January 23, 2001.

20. "Reply to Critics," NLR 1/221 (January–February 1997), 84.

21. This is detailed at excruciating length by Esther Delisle, *The Traitor and the Jew: Anti-Semitism and Extremist Right-wing Nationalism in French Canada from 1929 to 1939*, trans. Madeleine Hébert (Montreal: Robert Davies Publishing, 1993). Mordecai Richler relied on Delisle's research for his caustic remarks on the xenophobic quality of Québécois nationalism in *Oh Canada! Oh Quebec!: Requiem for a Divided Country* (Toronto: Knopf, 1992), which elicited considerable uproar. Richler's opinions are widely shared in anglophone Quebec.

22. Most dramatically in the recent "affaire Michaud" concerning a long-time PQ activist, Yves Michaud, who developed an unsavoury obsession with the opposition of Jewish voters to the PQ and its national project. The controversy contributed to the resignation of Lucien Bouchard, who had succeeded Parizeau as Premier, when it became apparent that many in the PQ resented the extraordinary steps the Premier took to condemn Michaud.

23. *The Three Worlds* (Chicago: University of Chicago Press, 1984), 292.

24. *La passion du Québec* (Montreal: Éditions Québec/Amérique, 1978), 202.

25. "Ten Reasons for Sovereignty."

26. *Imagined Communities*, rev. ed. (London: Verso, 1991), 5.

27. *Republics, Nations and Tribes* (London: Verso, 1995), 4–5.

28. *Nations and Nationalism*, 124.

29. Charles Taylor (himself of mixed anglophone and francophone heritage) now represents the more pertinent intellectual model for younger intellectuals, and is frequently to be seen on the French-language Radio-Canada.

30. *Le lieu de l'homme. La culture comme distance et mémoire* (Montreal: Hurtubise HMH, 1968); *Récit d'une émigration. Mémoires* (Montreal: Boréal, 1997).

31. *The Economy of Cities* (New York: Random House, 1969); *Cities and the Wealth of Nations* (New York: Random House, 1984).

32. "Canadian Cities and Sovereignty Association," 18th Massey Lecture Series, Toronto, 1980.

33. See his discussion of Jacobs in *Le Bazar. Des anciens Canadiens aux nouveaux Québécois* (Montreal: Boréal, 1990), 233–47; also Tom Nairn's striking condemnation of the classical nationalist imaginary in this respect, "The Curse of Rurality: Limits of Modernization Theory," in *Faces of Nationalism*, 90–112.

34. Under NAFTA, moreover, international exports, particularly to the United States, have dramatically increased. Such exports represented 21.8 per cent of GDP in 1992, 37.5 per cent in 1998: an increase of 71.9 per cent.

35. "*Pour en finir avec la loi 101,*" in *Le pays de tous les Québécois. Diversité culturelle et souveraineté,* ed. Michel Sarra-Bournet (Montreal: VLB éditeur, 1998), 100. This collection indicates something of the importance nationalists have given to reconciling nationalism and "multiculturalism" in the years since the 1995 referendum and Jacques Parizeau's remarks concerning "money and the ethnic vote."

36. "Territoriality and Beyond: Problematizing Modernity in International Relations," *International Organization* 47 (Winter 1993): 139–74.

37. "Le Québec me tue," *Le Devoir,* August 30, 1994.

38. *Spectre of Comparisons,* 360–63.

39. "Oui, le Québec me tue," *Le Devoir,* September 27, 1994.

40. *Spectre of Comparisons,* 69–74.

41. Daniel Latouche, *Mondialisation et cosmopolitisme à Montréal* (Montreal: Presses de la Sorbonne, 1997), 13.

42. This created a good deal of consternation on the part of Canadian federalists, and indeed Canadian law would have likely been altered to prevent the sudden creation of seven million Canadian citizens living in the new state of Quebec while continuing to demand various Canadian benefits. See Stanley Hartt, "Divided Loyalties: Dual Citizenship and Reconstituting the Economic Union," *C. D. Howe Institute Commentary* 67 (March 1995).

43. "Nationalism and Politics in Eastern Europe," *NLR* 1/189 (September–October 1991): 131.

44. Ibid., 131.

MAURICE CHARLAND

Technological Nationalism

Maurice Charland (b. 1953) is a professor and the chair of communication studies at Concordia University, where he has taught since 1981. He is also an honorary associate director of the Centre for Rhetoric Studies at the University of Cape Town, South Africa. He completed his Ph.D. at the University of Iowa in 1983. He is one of the founders and former director of Montreal's Joint Ph.D. Program in Communication Studies. He is the recipient of the National Communication Association's 2000 Charles H. Woolbert Research Award for his 1987 essay "Constitutive Rhetoric: The Case of the People Québécois." With Michael Dorland of Carleton University, he shared the Canadian Communication Association's 2002–3 Gertrude J. Robinson Book Prize for their coauthored *Law, Rhetoric, and Irony in the Formation of Canadian Civil Culture*. His current research focuses on the rhetoric of impiety and its relationship to theories of deliberative democracy.

There was a time in this fair land / When the railroad did not run . . .
—Gordon Lightfoot

Picture clarity and intellectual clarity are limited by electromagnetic resources.—H. A. Innis

Canada, Technology, and Technological Rhetoric

Canada is a technological state. This is just to say that Canada's existence as an economic unit is predicated upon transportation and communication technology. In addition, the *idea* of Canada depends upon a rhetoric about technology. Furthermore, we can understand the development of a Canadian nation-state in terms of the interplay between this technology and its rhetoric.

That Canada owes its existence to technologies which bind space is readily apparent. Canada is a sparsely populated territory in which rock, mountains, and sheer distance inhibit human contact between those who live in its several distinct regions. The telegraph and the railroad to a degree overcame these obstacles and permitted the movement of goods and information across what was, in the nineteenth century, an undeveloped wilderness. Indeed, as Harold Innis observes, "[t]he history of the Canadian Pacific Railroad [CPR] is primarily the history of the spread of western civilization over the northern half of the North American continent."[1] Through the CPR, Innis points out, western Canadian territories became integrated into the economic and political systems which had developed in eastern Canada.

And what is the nature of this "civilization?" It is one based in the circulation or communication of commodities and capital. The civilization the railroad extended was one of commerce as the CPR extended eastern economic interests. The railroad reproduced and extended a state apparatus and economy which concentrated power in metropolitan centres, permitting the incorporation and domination of margins. If the CPR was a "national project," it was so first and foremost as an economic venture. The railroad was built with a combination of public and private capital for the advantage of the state and merchants, and the former, like the latter, saw its interests in terms of economic development. The nineteenth-century British-style state was, after all, a state of capitalists.

The railroad did more though than enhance trade. It permitted the development of a political state and created the possibility of a nation. It did so by extending Ottawa's political power: it permitted Ottawa to exclude a powerful American presence from western Canada and thus establish its political control over the territory.[2] Specifically, the CPR fostered immigration into the western plain, effectively discouraging Minnesotans from moving northward and annexing a sparsely populated area; the CPR permitted Ottawa to establish its military presence in the west, as it did when suppressing the Métis rebellion, and, of course, eastern Canadians no longer had to travel through the United States in order to reach British Columbia. Furthermore, this physical spanning of the country permitted Canadians, including those in Quebec, to unite in patriotic sentiment, as they did when militia from Nova Scotia, Quebec, and Ontario fought side by side against Riel's supporters in Saskatchewan.[3]

In a sense, the power the CPR extended could become the object of a "national" experience; the CPR offered those in Canada the experience of a technologically mediated political unity as a common denominator.

My point here is that the CPR permitted more than the physical linking of a territory. Apart from joining the country to facilitate commercial intercourse and political administration, the CPR offered the possibility of developing a mythic rhetoric of national origin. Following McGee's arguments on the development of collectivities, I would argue that such a rhetoric is necessary to the realization of the project of Canadian nationhood.[4] That rhetoric is necessary both as a *legitimation* of a sovereign united Canada within the discursive field of parliamentary government, and as an *inducement* for those in Canada to see themselves as Canadian; for Canada to be legitimated, a myth is necessary. The CPR is well suited to such mythologization because (1) its construction in the face of political, economic, and geographic obstacles can be presented as an epic struggle; (2) the CPR was a state project and thus can be represented as the manifestation of a *Canadian* will to survive politically; and (3) the steam engine itself offers Canadians the opportunity to identify with a nationalized icon of power. In sum, the CPR is significant not only as a mode of transportation and communication, but also as the basis for a nationalist discourse. The technological nation is discursive as well as political. Furthermore, the very existence of the CPR can be understood as a moment in the nationalist rhetoric it renders possible, for it was a symbolic strategy in the face of political exigencies.

The myth of the railroad, or of the binding of space technologically to create a nation, places Canadians in a very particular relationship to technology.[5] In Kenneth Burke's language, this rhetoric privileges "agency" as the motive force for Canada's construction.[6] Canada's existence would be based in a (liberal) pragmatism in which technology is more potent and more responsible for Canada's creation than the so-called "Fathers of Confederation." In the popular mind, Canada exists more because of the technological transcendence of geographical obstacles than because of any politician's will. Thus technology itself is at the centre of the Canadian imagination, for it provides the condition of possibility for a Canadian mind.

In the rhetoric and construction of the CPR, we see the genesis of technological nationalism as a component in the project of building the national state. This project has two components: one, physical, the other, discursive: (1) The existence of a transcontinental Canada required the development of a system of transportation facilitating territorial annexation, colonization, and the implantation of a military presence. (2) The existence of this Canada also required the development of a rhetoric which ideologically constituted those in Canada as Canadians, united in the national project and under the political authority of a national government.

For the moment, let us focus on the rhetorical component of technological nationalism. The Canadian tradition of parliamentary public address, which Canada inherited from Britain, places particular demands on the rhetoric of the Canadian state. In this "Whig Liberal" tradition, political power is legitimated by a rhetoric of the "people."[7] That is to say, attempts to discursively secure legitimacy will argue that a national "people" exists which authorizes the state's power. For Ottawa to successfully exercise the power the CPR extended, it must counter arguments in favour of provincial autonomy or, conversely, annexation by the United States by persuasively representing those in Canada as forming a Canadian people. Indeed, the existence of such a pan-Canadian collectivity was asserted by Georges Etienne Cartier in defense of Confederation.[8] Without such a persuasive rhetoric of "national" identity and "national" interest, Ottawa's power would dissolve.

In Canada, the constitution of a "people" of individuals united under a liberal state requires that the barriers between regions be apparently transcended. As it permits mastery over nature, technology offers the possibility of that apparent transcendence. Consequently, in order to assert a national interest and unity, Ottawa depends upon a rhetoric of technological nationalism—a rhetoric which both asserts that a technologically mediated Canadian *nation* exists, and calls for improved communication between regions to render that nation materially present. In other words Canada is a state which must constantly seek to will a *nation* in its own image, in order to justify its very existence. The CPR can be understood as one manifestation of this necessity, but as a form of *economic* communication, it gave rise neither to a common Canadian culture, nor to a Canadian "public" of citizens capable of participating in the country's political will formation. At most, it offered those in Canada the possibility of jointly participating in the rhetoric of the national project. Primarily, the CPR enmeshed Canada within a series of networks of domination. As Innis observes and the suppression of the Métis uprising of 1885 makes manifestly clear, space-binding technologies extend power as they foster empire."[9] Because of the CPR's inability to create a people or nation, another technological instrument was necessary, an instrument which would permit the representation and actualization of some form of Canadian "public" and common Canadian culture. Both the rhetoric of national identity and the fact of a Canadian political community required a cultural rather than economic form of communication. Technological nationalism required radio, and the advent of the broadcasting era advanced the project of a technologically constituted nation.

The development of electronic communication, and in particular broadcast technology, permitted a new articulation of the rhetoric of technological nationalism. Technological nationalism became a major factor in the development of the structure of broadcasting in Canada, as radio and television were enlisted into the national project. However, this rhetoric of a technologically mediated Canada is contradictory.

Significantly, Canada's first national radio network was established by a railway. While local radio had been pioneered by private entrepreneurs, national radio was the product of a state agency, the C[anadian] N[ational] R[ailway]. The national railway saw in radio a means to foster immigration, to enhance its own image, and to support the project of nationhood.[10] Canadian National Railway radio, which initially broadcast to railroad parlour cars, developed in 1924 into a network of stations in major Canadian cities from Vancouver to Moncton. It offered symphony broadcasts, comic operas, special events, and in 1931, a dramatic presentation of Canadian history.[11] State-supported radio, following the railroad's path, presented those who live in anglophone Canada with an image of Canada.[12] CNR sought to bind Canada with information just as rail had bound Canada economically. Thus was forged the link in the official Canadian mind between railroad, radio, and national identity. As the official biographer of Sir Henry Thorton, the CNR's president and instigator of its radio services, writes: "As a direct result of Sir Henry's abilities to see the possibilities inherent in a new medium of expression, the railway did for Canada what she was too apathetic to do for herself. . . . He saw radio as a great unifying force in Canada; to him the political conception transcended the commercial, and he set out consciously to create a sense of nationhood through the medium of the Canadian National Railway Service."[13]

The rhetoric of technological nationalism had incorporated radio. It sought to enlist another space-binding technology in the project of constituting a nation in the image of the state. Furthermore, this vision of an electronically constituted Canada did not remain Thorton's, but became that of the national government. Thus, one of the first "live" national broadcasts was a celebration of Canada. Prime Minister MacKenzie King's voice was heard across the country as he spoke from Ottawa on July 1, 1927, Confederation's anniversary. Commenting on that moment a month later at the Canadian National Exhibition, the Prime Minister presented radio, a gift of science, as the means whereby Canada would develop a "people" or "public" to justify its government:

On the morning, afternoon and evening of July 1, all Canada became, for the time-being, a single assemblage, swayed by a common emotion, within the sound of a single voice. Thus has modern science for the first time realized in the great nation-state of modern days, that condition which existed in the little city-states of ancient times and which was considered by the wisdom of the ancients as indispensable to free and democratic government—that all the citizens should be able to hear for themselves the living voice. To them it was the voice of a single orator—a Demosthenes or a Cicero—speaking on public questions in the Athenian Assembly or in the Roman Forum. Hitherto to most Canadians, Ottawa had seemed far off, a mere name to hundreds of thousands of our people, but henceforth all Canadians will stand within the sound of the carillon and within hearing of the speakers on Parliament Hill. May we not predict that as a result of this carrying of the living voice throughout the length of the Dominion, there will be aroused a more general interest in public affairs, and an increased devotion of the individual citizen to the commonweal?[14]

King's statement preceded a national radio policy by five years. However, it can be understood as a charge to future policy makers. Certainly, it articulated the major themes of technological nationalism in the broadcasting era. In particular, it reveals the paradoxical promise of democracy and domination inherent to the rhetoric of technological nationalism. MacKenzie King's speech reduces Canada to a community or small city which does not suffer from the isolating effects of distance, regionalism, or cultural diversity. Here, technology would create a *polis* where the proximity of speaker to audience would promote "freedom" and give rise to a "democracy" of a public sharing a commonweal. As MacKenzie King also put it: "It is doubtful if ever before . . . those in authority were brought into such immediate and sympathetic and personal touch with those with whom their authority is derived."[15] As such, technological nationalism is a form of liberalism. It proposes the electronic *polis* and affirms no value save the communication of the people's voices as expressed in Parliament. However, this vision of a society in and through communication is undermined by technological nationalism's other goal, that of creating a *united* Canada. This second goal is also implied above. Note that the speech identifies an interest in public affairs with "devotion," and that the community called into being is but an audience, subject to a voice. Radio, if it offers community, also offers domination, as Innis observes in counterpoint to MacKenzie King: "The rise of Hitler to power was facilitated by the use of the loudspeaker and radio. . . . The radio, appealed to vast areas, overcame the division between classes in its escape from literacy, and favoured centralization and bureaucracy. A single individual could appeal at one time to vast numbers of people speaking the same language. . . ."[16]

MacKenzie King's remarks capture the spirit of the rhetoric of Canadian government policy towards broadcasting as a means of binding space from his own time until the recent flirtations with cultural continentalism. As with rail service in Canada, broadcasting was consciously regarded as a means of *creating* a Canada with sufficient commonality to justify its political union, while simultaneously, it was also considered a means of simply enabling Canadians to be aware of each other and their already constituted values and identity. Such a contradictory role for broadcasting was articulated in various government reports dealing with the problems posed by broadcasting technology including the 1929 *Report of the Royal Commission on Broadcasting*, and the 1932 *Report of the Parliamentary Committee on Broadcasting*. These and subsequent reports offered a rhetoric which asserted the existence of a distinctly Canadian (and thus unitary) consciousness which required technological mediation and also charged broadcasting with the task of realizing that consciousness and its nation.

The Development of a Broadcasting Policy of Technological Nationalism

The 1932 Broadcasting Act followed rather than anticipated broadcasting's development. Canada's first commercial radio station was licenced in 1919. A decade elapsed before the Royal Commission on Radio Broadcasting, chaired by Sir John Aird, former president of the Canadian Imperial Bank of Commerce, issued a report calling for exclusive government control of broadcasting, including the nationalization of existing privately owned outlets.[17] The Commission's stance was one of "defensive expansionism," as Margaret Prang would put it, for it pointed to the threat of Americanized airwaves and called for protective federal initiatives.[18] Of course, the Commission asserted that the airwaves must be protected from an American expansion driven by market forces. More significantly, the Aird Report also echoed MacKenzie King as it asserted that radio must become a means for developing Canadian hegemony and fostering a unified culture in the face of geography and regionalism: "At present the majority of programs heard are from sources outside of Canada. It has been emphasized that the continued reception of these had a tendency to mold the minds of young people in the home to ideals and opinions that are not Canadian. In a country of the vast geographical dimension of Canada, broadcasting will undoubtedly become a great force in imparting a national spirit and interpreting national citizenship."[19]

The official Canadian mind conceives of Canada as a nation which must come to be in spite of space. Thus, even though the Aird Commission did not seek to establish a repressive single Canadian discourse, but called for a broadcasting system in which programming would be provincially controlled, it sought to create an extended community in which common Canadian interests would be articulated and a shared national identity could emerge. The popular mind, like the land, must be occupied. Note, however that technological nationalism only defines Canadian ideals and opinion by virtue of their not being from foreign sources. This is significant because, in its reluctance or inability to articulate a positive content to the Canadian identity—an identity still to be created—technological nationalism is a form of liberalism, privileging the process of communication over the substance of what is communicated. Consequently, if radio were to bring forth a nation by providing a common national experience, that experience would be one of communication, of sheer mediation. This is the first contradiction of technological nationalism: The content of the Canadian identity would be but technological nationalism itself.

Ottawa did not, of course, permit a great deal of provincial autonomy in broadcasting. Nor did it, ultimately, establish a state monopoly. The 1929 Depression began weeks after the Aird Report's publication and the government turned to more urgent matters. Meanwhile, several provinces, led by Quebec, challenged Ottawa's jurisdiction over broadcasting in the courts. This delayed the implementation of a Canadian radio policy. Canada's Supreme court upheld Ottawa's jurisdictional claim in 1931. The British Privy Council rejected Quebec's appeal of that ruling in 1932. Only then did Ottawa act.

Prime Minister Bennett, who considered radio "a most effective instrument for nation building," established in 1932 a special committee of the House of Commons to examine broadcasting and draft appropriate legislation.[20] The 1932 report echoed both the rhetoric and the recommendations of the Aird Commission. More strongly than before, radio was presented as heir to the railroad's mission. Thus, the chairman of the 1932 Parliamentary committee, Dr. Raymond Moran, asserted: "Had the fathers of Confederation been able to add this means of communication to the ribbons of steel by which they endeavored to bind Canada in an economic whole, they would have accomplished a great deal more than they did, great even as their achievement was."[21] The committee realized that national radio service, like national rail service, would not develop without state direction and capital. The Canadian culture and unity sought after would not spring from unbridled commerce, but would have to spring from the state itself. Thus the committee, linking radio to railroad, called for the creation of a radio commission empowered to nationalize private broadcasting stations. The hoped-for result would be a united Canada. The Commons committee's report led to the 1932 Radio Broadcasting Bill. That bill was introduced to the House by Prime Minister Bennett. As he presented the legislation, he charged radio with the task of creating national unity and serving the Empire. Radio, like the Canadian Pacific Railway, would permit a technologically mediated state and *nation*: "Without such (Canadian) control radio broadcasting can never become a great agency for the communication of matters of national concern and for the diffusion of national thought and ideals, and without such control it can never be the agency by which national consciousness may be fostered and sustained and national unity still further strengthened. . . . Furthermore, radio broadcasting, controlled and operated in this way, can serve as a dependable link in a chain of empire communications by which we may be more closely united one with the other."[22] Bennett's rhetoric appropriated for Ottawa the right to create a consciousness. Certainly, his discourse is apparently liberal, for it presumes that national concerns and thoughts pre-exist radio and need only to be "communicated" and "diffused." However, Bennett's address also reveals that without the common denominators of radio and state, there would be no nation, for it is a nation dependent upon technology to be created and sustained. Radio was to be a means of socialization, diffusing the ideal of the nation to be constructed, the ideal of communication. In other words, the process of communication would legitimate the state and the (British) empire whose power it extended.

The Contradictions of Economic and Cultural Communication

Canada did not end up with the exact broadcasting system these reports envisaged, of course, for the abstract principles of policy are not easily realized. In particular, the development of both communication and transportation infrastructures are based on technologies and economic forces which exist somewhat autonomously from the state. Indeed, from the outset, radio offered little promise of creating or strengthening the Canadian state or *nation*; since American signals penetrated Canada's borders far more easily than steel rails. By 1930, Canadians were more likely to receive American than Canadian signals: nearly all Canadians were within reach of an American station, while only 60% could receive a signal originating in Canada.[23] Furthermore, American-made programs were very popular among Canadians. At least 50% of Canadian listening time was devoted to United States programming.[24] While the CNR at that time operated a national network service (albeit of limited scope), it could not compete with American programs, be they distributed in Canada by Canadian stations, or by powerful stations based in the United States. In consequence, Margaret Prang points out, as I observed above, that Canadian broadcasting policy has been characterized by "defensive expansionism." It has been sensitive to American expansion, and has called for a concerted state effort to use technology both as a form of defense and as a means of establishing Canadian hegemony over its territory. Canada had secured its western territory through space-binding technology; it had not, however, secured its cultural territory. Thus the Canadian Radio Broadcasting Commission [CRBC], and its successor, the CBC [Canadian Broadcasting Corporation], were instituted to occupy and defend Canada's ether and consciousness.

While various governments in Ottawa could rhetorically call for a technologically mediated *nation*, they were in no way assured of success, especially since radio, like rail, is an extension of an economic system dominated by American capital. In spite of Prang's "defensive expansionism," and the conscientious work of broadcasters at the CRBC and CBC, anglophone Canada found itself saddled with a model of broadcasting as entertainment largely developed outside of the country, and with a timetable for its development over which Ottawa had little control. Canada was the subject of what Boyd-Barrett terms "media [as opposed to cultural] imperialism."[25] And, of course, both of these could only be countered through major government expenditures. Technological nationalism thus encountered its constraint.

In passing the 1932 Radio Broadcasting Bill, Parliament sought to empower the discourse of technological nationalism. However, while talk may be cheap, its transmission by radio is not and Parliament was ultimately unwilling to advance the funds necessary for the new radio service, the Canadian Radio Broadcasting Commission, to nationalize existing stations or establish many new facilities.[26] The federal government, under John A. MacDonald's leadership, had been willing to subsidize the CPR, but that project ultimately would promote Canadian commerce and the Canadian accumulation of capital. State radio, on the other hand, offered no financial benefits. On the contrary, state radio would always be a drain on the public purse, particularly if it were to avoid commercialization and seek to "uplift" its audience, rather than transmit popular (and predominantly American) programs.

We see here a fundamental difference between the railroad and radio. While both were and are called upon to help create a nation, the railroad's nation is economic, while radio's is cultural and ideological. That the CPR would carry American goods, or that its Canadian cargo would be undistinguishable from American freight, was unimportant. Canadian commerce could be identical in content to its American counterpart and remain Canadian. Conversely, radio is not a common carrier and is thus quite unlike rail service. If radio were treated as a common carrier, like the railroad, its item would be irrelevant. Radio would be successful if it were profitable. However, radio is Canadian by its content, and is thus quite unlike the CPR. *Canadian* radio must create its own "freight," and find a market for it as well. However, before Canadian radio had developed into a mature form, the nature of demand in the radio market had already been constituted by the distribution of American programs. Consequently, Canadian radio, unlike Canadian rail, could be either profitable or Canadian, not both. We see here then the second contradiction of technological nationalism: it identifies a medium ultimately based upon a foreign economic and programming logic as the site for Canada's cultural construction.

The CRBC's main failure was its inability to compete successfully with commercial broadcasters and so transform the airwaves into a medium fostering nationhood. This failure was not unique to the CRBC, but is endemic to Canadian broadcasting's history. The Canadian Broadcasting Corporation, established to succeed the CRBC in 1936, faced the same dilemma. From its creation until the advent of television in Canada in 1952 the CBC did, to a degree, offset the influence of American broadcasting in Canada. Certainly, without state-sponsored radio, the airwaves in Canada would have become but another market for American networks. In particular, the CBC did offer to Canadians a common experience and its popularity increased during the Second World War, as Canadians sought information on Canada's war effort. Nevertheless,

American programming remained popular in Canada—Toronto and Montreal had US network affiliates, and the CBC's most popular programs were American productions such as "Fibber McGee and Molly" and "Edgar Bergen and Charlie McCarthy."[27]

Communication technology, heralded as the means of promoting Canadian statehood and nationhood, paradoxically offered those in Canada a common "national" experience which included cultural commodities from the United States. This phenomenon was intensified with the development of more sophisticated and expensive media. New media, as they accelerated the binding of space and the rise of empire, increasingly drew Canada into the American cultural system. Thus, when CBC television was born in 1952, there were already 146,000 receiving sets in Canada with antennae pointing south.[28] Television as a medium, with expensive genres of programming, styles of production, and a star system, was already developing in the United States. Canadian television could scarcely compete. Only the CBC's monopoly over Canadian TV network programming and the still poor penetration of cable television preserved a Canadian presence on Canadian screens. Thus, the 1957 Royal Commission on Broadcasting observed that Canadian television could not be Canadian and turn a profit, and reasserted the state's role in constructing a national identity: "The choice is between a Canadian state-controlled system with some flow of programmes east and west across Canada, with some Canadian content and the development of a Canadian sense of identity, at a substantial public cost, and a privately owned system which forces of economics will necessarily make predominantly dependent on American radio and television programmes."[29] As in previous decades, the threat of American expansion is presented as warranting state action. And, as in the past, this 1957 report articulates the imperative of technological nationalism: It likens broadcasting to the CPR as it affirms that "the building of the first Canadian railway was only the first of many devices to pull together into a nation the vast expanse of Canadian territory."[30] It then asserts that without public expenditures, a Canadian nation could not exist. Within the logic of a technologically mediated nation, the committee's observations are, of course, "true." More significantly, as an argumentative justification for a public policy of nation-building, their import is rhetorical. The need to support Canadian television is based upon a vision of technology as a means of creating and maintaining a nation at will. Significantly, this rhetoric sees a Canadian nation and identity as exegetic of the state itself. Ninety years after Canada's political constitution, a national identity is still so ephemeral that the state, and its agencies, feel compelled to create it. Technological nationalism refuses to consider that Canada is not a nation but a state, and that Canadian cultures could exist outside of their technological mediation.

Conclusion

Rail and radio differ. The latter binds space much more efficiently than the former. The railroad depends upon the physical domination of geography to join distant points. Radio, on the other hand, does not so much bind space as annihilate it. The railroad binds space one-dimensionally as it links east to west; radio renders space insignificant across two or three dimensions as all points become proximate. Thus, radio, and electronic technology in general, will tend to ensnare Canada within an American web of information. The advocates of Canada's continual technological reconstitution seem to have intuitively, but naively, grasped what Innis observed, that technologies of communication extend and strengthen empires. They sought to favour the Canadian (and British Empire) domination of a geographic and cultural territory, but they failed to realize that such technologies were not merely the tools of political will permitting control over a region. As Innis saw, space-binding technologies favour and transform existing centres of power. They are not the political, economic, and cultural equivalents of string and tape, which can patch together a territory. They are media which extend power, and for Canada in the twentieth century, power is based in the United States. Thus, as broadcasting developed in Canada, it adopted the form and content of American programs.

In the absence of the American (culture as commodity) presence, it is doubtful whether the logic of technological nationalism would be any more successful. Technological nationalism, as a form of liberalism, presumes that communication will reveal a common interest uniting Canadians in spite of their differences: The CBC would both express Canada's diversity and promote a (singular) Canadian identity; Telidon[31] would be tomorrow's soapbox and town meeting hall.[32] Technological nationalism presents technology merely as a neutral medium facilitating nationhood. However, it is hardly so benign, for it locates the state's very raison d'être in the experience of technological mediation. Indeed, as Innis observed, space-binding technologies establish dominions of power by extending markets and the commodity system. Radio and television, and other communication technologies, may appear unlike the CPR or the system of trade because they distribute information rather than goods.

However, the content of media are commodities which are produced, bought and sold, and electronic media extend the economic and cultural influence of centres of production over marginal areas. Most importantly, media promote the cultural dependency of margins. While the rhetoric of technological nationalism promises a public in which Canadians would share their commonality and participate in political will formation, it offers ultimately a state in which listeners are subject to a discourse which can only be produced by specialists.

Canada is a country whose national experience follows its state experience. Consequently, a Canadian identity and culture would be rooted in the state itself, for it is through the state that Canada's populace is constituted as a people. Technological nationalism therefore cannot but offer the empty experience of mediation. Not only do communication technologies favour centres of power and promote the suppression of marginal experience, but they transform culture into the experience of commodities and of technology itself. Thus, even if technological nationalism could offer a Canadian experience and promote a national identity across space, that identity would become a disposable one.

Notes

Originally published as "Technological Nationalism," in *Canadian Journal of Social and Political Theory* 10.1–2 (1986): 196–220. Copyright © Canadian Journal of Social and Political Theory. Reprinted with permission of the author.

1. Harold A. Innis, *A History of the Canadian Pacific Railway* (1923; reprint, Toronto: University of Toronto Press, 1971), 287.

2. I am subscribing to a "metropolitan" interpretation of Canadian history. This perspective is central to Innis's analysis and is discussed in J. M. S. Careless, "Frontierism, Metropolitanism and Canadian History," *Canadian Historical Review* 35 (March 1954): 1–21.

3. Quebec initially supported, albeit with some reservations, Ottawa's decision to put down militarily the 1885 Métis uprising. Popular support in Quebec for Riel developed subsequent to his defeat. See Robert Rumilly, *Histoire de la Province de Quebec* (Montreal: Editions Bernard Valiquette, 1942), 5:1–108.

4. Michael Calvin McGee, "In Search of the 'People': A Rhetorical Alternative," *Quarterly Journal of Speech* 66 (February 1980), 1–16.

5. Various rhetorics of technology are possible. Canada's rhetoric is rooted in its colonial origins and state-supervised development. In the United States, where local development preceded the federal state, a different rhetoric of technology arose. There, "clean" electrical technology was heralded as a means to restore the pastoral ideals of a democratic community and harmony with nature. See James W. Carey and

John J. Quirk, "The Mythos of the Electronic Revolution," *American Scholar* 39.1 (1970): 226–35.

6. Kenneth Burke, *A Grammar of Motives* (Berkeley: University of California Press, 1945), xv–xxiii, 275–317.

7. McGee, "In Search of the 'People.'"

8. Georges Etienne Cartier, address to the Assembly of Lower Canada, February 7, 1865, in *Le manuel de la parole. Manifestes Québécois* (Sillerey: Editions du boréal express, 1977), 1:53–61: "Les nations sont formées maintenant par l'agglomération de divers peuples rassemblés par les intérêts et sympathies, ceci est notre position dans le moment actuel. Une objection a été suscité au projet maintenant sous notre considération [Confederation], à cause des mots, 'nouvelle nationalité.' Lorsque nous sommes unis, si toutefois nous le devenons, nous formerons une nationalité politique indépendante de l'origine nationale, ou de la religion d'aucun individu."

9. The interests of empire in the CPR are quite evident: Great Britain took an interest in the CPR's construction, Canadian Pacific instituted steamer service from its western terminus to Australia and the Orient in order to link British territories, and the railway came to be considered part of the Empire's system of communication and received a British postal subsidy. See John Murray Gibbon, *Steel of Empire* (London: Rich and Cowen, 1935), 355.

10. Frank W. Peers, *The Politics of Canadian Broadcasting, 1920–1951* (Toronto: University of Toronto Press, 1969), 23–24.

11. Ibid.

12. CNR radio did offer some French-language programming on its network, much to displeasure of many in western Canada who objected to the French language being on the air outside of Quebec. As Innis observes of radio: "Stability within language units became more evident and instability between language units more dangerous." Harold A. Innis, *The Bias of Communication* (Toronto: University of Toronto Press, 1951), 82.

13. Darcy Marsh, *The Tragedy of Sir Henry Thorton* (Toronto: Macmillan Company of Canada, 1935), 115–16.

14. William Lyon MacKenzie King, address at the Canadian National Exhibition, July 1927, in *Signing On: The Birth of Radio in Canada* (Toronto: Doubleday Canada, 1982), 190.

15. Ibid.

16. Innis, *Bias of Communication*, 82.

17. Canada, *Royal Commission on Broadcasting*, Aird Commission (1929), 12–13.

18. Margaret Prang, "The Origins of Public Broadcasting in Canada," *Canadian Historical Review* 46.1 (1965): 11–31.

19. Aird Commission, 6.

20. Reprinted in Peers, *Politics of Canadian Broadcasting*, 78.

21. Reprinted in ibid., 97.

22. Reprinted in ibid., 101–2.

23. Prang, " Origins of Public Broadcasting," 3.

24. Ibid., 4.

25. Oliver Boyd-Barrett, "Media Imperialism: Towards an International Framework

for the Analysis of Media Systems," in *Mass Communication and Society*, ed. James Curran, Michael Gurevitch, and Janet Woollacott (London: Open University Press, 1977), 116–35.

26. The CRBC's funding problems are discussed in E. Austin Weir, *The Struggle for National Broadcasting in Canada* (Toronto: McClelland and Stewart, 1965), 173–77.

27. Ibid., 281; Peers, *Politics of Canadian Broadcasting*, 283, 285.

28. Canada, *Royal Commission on Broadcasting*, Fowler I (1957), 313.

29. Ibid., 10.

30. Ibid., 9.

31. Like France's better-known Minitel, Telidon was one of many "videotex" systems that used home televisions as a platform for two-way communications. A primitive precursor to the Internet, Canada's Telidon failed commercially within a year of its launch in 1980.—Eds.

32. Canada, Ministère des Communications, *Notes pour une allocution du Ministre des communications l'honorable Francis Fox devant l'association canadienne des communications* (Ottawa, June 1982), 17: "Il est indéniable que les technologies nouvelles ont le pouvoir de nous atomiser, de faire de nous des isolés reliés individuellement à un centre informatique multimédia. Mais elles ont aussi le pouvoir de nous rapprocher, de donner naissance au village global, ou plutôt à la ville globale dont Télidon serait la place publique, le crieur et le conteur."

B

Race, Difference, and

Multiculturalism

HIMANI BANNERJI

On the Dark Side of the Nation: Politics of Multiculturalism and the State of "Canada"

Himani Bannerji (b. 1942) is a professor of sociology at York University, Toronto. She holds a B.A. from Visva Bharati University (1962, India), an M.A. from Jadavpur University (1965, India) and both an M.A. (1971) and a Ph.D. (1988) from the University of Toronto. Bannerji's research explores colonial discourse and the intersections of gender, race, and class. Through books such as *Unsettling Relations: The University as a Site of Feminist Struggles* (1991), *Returning the Gaze: Essays on Racism, Feminism and Politics* (1993), *The Writing on the Wall: Essays on Culture and Politics* (1993), and *Thinking Through: Essays on Feminism, Marxism, and Anti-Racism* (1995), Bannerji has been a major contributor to the development of Marxist-feminist theory in Canada. She is also a writer and a poet whose work has been widely anthologized, including in the *Oxford Book of Canadian Short Stories*.

Part I: In or of the Nation? The Problem of Belonging

"Canada," with its primary inscriptions of "French" or "English," its colonialist and essentialist identity markers, cannot escape a fragmentary framework. Its imagined political geography simplifies into two primary and confrontational possessions, cultural typologies and dominant ideologies. Under the circumstances, all appeals to multiculturalism on the part of "Canada Outside Quebec" become no more than an extra weight on the "English" side. Its "difference-studded unity," its "multicultural mosaic," becomes an ideological sleight of hand pitted against Quebec's presumably greater cultural homogeneity. The two solitudes glare at each other from the barricades in an ongoing colonial war. But what do either of these solitudes and their reigning essences have to do with those whom the state has named "visible minorities" and who are meant to provide the ideological basis for the Canadian state's liberal/universal status? How does their very "difference," inscribed with inferiority and negativity—their otherwise troublesome particularity—

offer the very particularist state of "English Canada" the legitimating device of transcendence through multiculturalism? Are we not still being used in the war between the English and the French?

It may seem strange to "Canadians" that the presence of the First Nations, the "visible minorities" and the ideology of multiculturalism are being suggested as the core of the state's claim to universality or transcendence. Not only in multiplying pawns in the old Anglo-French rivalry but in other ways as well, multiculturalism may be seen less as a gift of the state of "Canada" to the "others" of this society, than as a central pillar in its own ideological state apparatus.[1] This is because the very discourse of nationhood in the context of "Canada," given its evolution as a capitalist state derived from a white settler colony with aspirations to liberal democracy,[2] needs an ideology that can mediate fissures and ruptures more deep and profound than those of the usual capitalist nation state.[3] That is why usually undesirable others, consisting of nonwhite peoples with their ethnic or traditional or underdeveloped cultures, are discursively inserted in the middle of a dialogue on hegemonic rivalry. The discourse of multiculturalism, as distinct from its administrative, practical relations and forms of ruling, serves as a culmination for the ideological construction of "Canada." This places us, on whose actual lives the ideology is evoked, in a peculiar situation. On the one hand, by our sheer presence we provide a central part of the distinct pluralist unity of Canadian nationhood; on the other hand, this centrality is dependent on our "difference," which denotes the power of definition that "Canadians" have over "others." In the ideology of multicultural nationhood, however, this difference is read in a power-neutral manner rather than as organized through class, gender and race. Thus at the same moment that difference is ideologically evoked it is also neutralized, as though the issue of difference were the same as that of diversity of cultures and identities, rather than those of racism and colonial ethnocentrism—as though our different cultures were on a par or could negotiate with the two dominant ones! The hollowness of such a pluralist stance is exposed in the shrill indignation of Anglophones when rendered a "minority" in Quebec, or the angry desperation of Francophones in Ontario. The issue of the First Nations—their land claims, languages and cultures—provides another dimension entirely, so violent and deep that the state of Canada dare not even name it in the placid language of multiculturalism.

The importance of the discourse of multiculturalism to that of nationmaking becomes clearer if we remember that "nation" needs an ideology of unification and legitimation.[4] As Benedict Anderson points out, nations need to imagine a principle of "com-unity" or community even where there is little there to postulate any.[5] A nation, ideologically, cannot posit itself on the principle of hate, according to Anderson, and must therefore speak to the sacrificing of individual, particularist interests for the sake of "the common good."[6] This task of "imagining community" becomes especially difficult in Canada—not only because of class, gender and capital, which ubiquitously provide contentious grounds in the most culturally homogeneous of societies—but because its socio-political space is saturated by elements of surplus domination due to its Eurocentric/racist/colonial context. Ours is not a situation of co-existence of cultural nationalities or tribes within a given geographical space. Speaking here of culture without addressing power relations displaces and trivializes deep contradictions. It is a reductionism that hides the social relations of domination that continually create "difference" as inferior and thus signifies continuing relations of antagonism. The legacy of a white settler colonial economy and state and the current aspirations to imperialist capitalism mark Canada's struggle to become a liberal democratic state. Here a cultural pluralist interpretive discourse hides more than it reveals. It serves as a fantastic evocation of "unity," which in any case becomes a reminder of the divisions. Thus to imagine "com-unity" means to imagine a common project of valuing difference that would hold good for both Canadians and others, while also claiming that the sources of these otherizing differences are merely cultural. As that is impossible, we consequently have a situation where no escape is possible from divisive social relations. The nation state's need for an ideology that can avert a complete rupture becomes desperate, and gives rise to a multicultural ideology which both needs and creates "others" while subverting demands for anti-racism and political equality.

Part II: On the Dark Side of the Nation: Considering "English Canada"

If one stands on the dark side of the nation in Canada everything looks different. The transcendent, universal and unifying claims of its multiculturally legitimated ideological state apparatus become susceptible to questions. The particularized and partisan nature of this nation-state becomes visible through the same ideological and working apparatus that simultaneously produces its national "Canadian" essence and the "other"—its non-white population (minus the First Nations) as "visible minorities." It is obvious that both Canada and its adjectivized correlates English or French Canada are themselves certain forms of constructions. What do these constructions represent or encode? With regard to whom or what are we otherized and categorized as visible minorities? What lies on the dark side of this state project, its national ethos?

Official multiculturalism, mainstream political thought and the news media in Canada all rely comfortably on the notion of a nation and its state both called Canada, with legitimate subjects called Canadians, in order to construct us as categorical forms of difference. There is an assumption that this Canada is a singular entity, a moral, cultural and political essence, neutral of power, both in terms of antecedents and consequences. The assumption is that we can recognize this beast, if and when we see it. So we can then speak of a "pan-Canadian nationalism," of a Canada which will not tolerate more Third World immigrants or separatism, or of what Canada needs or allows us to do. And yet, when we scrutinize this Canada, what is it that we see? The answer to this question depends on which side of the nation we inhabit. For those who see it as a homogeneous cultural/political entity, resting on a legitimately possessed territory, with an exclusive right to legislation over diverse groups of peoples, Canada is unproblematic. For others, who are on the receiving end of the power of Canada and its multiculturalism, who have been dispossessed in one sense or another, the answer is quite different. For them the issues of legitimacy of territorial possession, or the right to create regulations and the very axis of domination on which its status as a nation-state rests, are all too central to be pushed aside. To them the same Canada appears as a post-conquest capitalist state, economically dependent on an imperialist United States and politically implicated in English and US imperialist enterprises, with some designs of its own. From this perspective "pan-Canadianism" loses its transcendent inclusivity and emerges instead as a device and a legitimation for a highly particularized ideological form of domination. Canada then becomes mainly an English Canada, historicized into particularities of its actual conquerors and their social and state formations. Colonialism remains as a vital formational and definitional issue. Canada, after all, could not be English or French in the same sense in which England and France are English and French.

Seen thus, the essence of Canada is destabilized. It becomes a politico-military ideological construction and constitution, elevating aggressive acts of acquisition and instituting them into a formal stabilization. But this stability is tenuous, always threatening to fall apart. The adjective "English" stamped into "Canada" bares this reality, both past and present. It shows us who stands on the other side of the "pan-Canadian" project. Quebeckers know it well, and so their colonial rivalry continues. And we, the "visible minorities"—multiculturalism notwithstanding—know our equidistance from both of these conquering essences. The issue at stake, in the end, is felt by all sides to be much more than cultural. It is felt to be about the power to define what is Canada or Canadian culture. This power can only come through the actual possession of a geographical territory and the economy of a nation-state. It is this which confers the legal imprimatur to define what is Canadian or French Canadian, or what are "sub-" or "multi-"cultures. Bilingualism, multiculturalism, tolerance of diversity and difference and slogans of unity cannot solve this problem of unequal power and exchange—except to entrench even further the social relations of power and their ideological and legal forms, which emanate from an unproblematized Canadian state and essence. What discursive magic can vanish a continuously proliferating process of domination and thus of marginalization and oppression? What can make it a truly multicultural state when all the power relations and the signifiers of Anglo-French white supremacy are barely concealed behind a straining liberal democratic façade?[7]

The expression "white supremacist," harsh and shocking as it may sound to many, encodes the painful underpinnings of the category visible minorities. The ideological imperatives of other categories—such as immigrants, aliens, foreigners, ethnic communities or New Canadians—constellate around the same binary code. There is a direct connection between this and the ideological spin-off of Englishness or Frenchness. After all, if nations are "imagined communities," can the content of this national imagination called Canada be free of its history and current social relations of power? Does not the context inflect the content here and now?

This inscription of whiteness underwrites whatever may be called Englishness, Frenchness, and finally Europeanness. These national characteristics become moral ones and they spin off or spill over into each other. Thus whiteness extends into moral qualities of masculinity, possessive individualism and an ideology of capital and market.[8] They are treated as indicators of civilization, freedom and modernity. The inherent aggressiveness and asociality of this moral category "whiteness" derives its main communitarian aspect from an animosity towards "others," signalling the militaristic, elite and otherizing bond shared by conquerors. The notion of Englishness serves as a metaphor for whiteness, as do all other European national essences. Whiteness, as many have noted, thus works as an ideology of a nation-state. It can work most efficiently with an other/enemy in its midst, constantly inventing new signifiers of "us" and "them." In the case of Canada the others, the First Nations, have been there from the very inception, modulating the very formation of its state and official culture, constantly presenting them with doubts about their legitimacy. Subsequently, indentured workers, immigrants, refugees and other "others" have only deepened this legitimation crisis, though they also helped to forge the course of the state and the "nation."[9] "English," as an official language, has served to create a hegemonic front, but it is not a powerful enough antidote as an ideological device to undermine antagonisms that are continually created through processes of ruling; it is the ideology of "whiteness/Europeanness" that serves as the key bonding element. Even though the shame of being an Italian, that is, non-English, in Canada outweighs the glory of the Italian renaissance, "Italian" can still form a part of the community of "whiteness" as distinct from non-white "others." It is not surprising, therefore, to see that one key element of white supremacy in Canada was an "Orange" mentality connecting Englishness with whiteness and both with racial purity. Books such as *Shades of Right*, for example, speak precisely to this, as does the present day right-wing nationalism of "English"-based groups. Quebec's "French" nationalism has precisely the same agenda, with a smaller territorial outreach. In fact, racialization and ethnicization are the commonest forms of cultural or identity parlance in Canada. This is not only the case with "whites" or "the English" but also with "others" after they spend some time in the country. A language of colour, even self-appellations such as "women of colour" (remember "coloured women"?), echo right through the cultural/political world. An unofficial apartheid of culture and identity organizes the social space of "Canada," first between whites and non-whites, and then within the non-whites themselves.

Part III: A Rose by Any Other Name: Naming the "Others"

The transcendence or legitimation value of the official/state discourse of multiculturalism—which cherishes difference while erasing real antagonisms—breaks down, therefore, at different levels of competing ideologies and ruling practices. A threat of rupture or crisis is felt to be always already there, a fact expressed by the ubiquity of the integration-fragmentation paradigm in texts on Canada. Instead of a discourse of homogeneity or universality, the paradigm of multiculturalism stands more for the pressure of conflict of interests and dynamics of power relations at work. This language is useful for Canada since imagining a nation is a difficult task even when the society is more homogeneously based on historic and cultural sharing or hegemony. Issues of class, industry and capital constantly destabilize the national project even in its non-colonial context. Gramsci for example, in "Notes on Italian History," discusses the problem of unification inherent in the formation of a nation-state in the European bourgeois context.[10] Unificatory ideologies and institutions, emanating from the elite, posturing as a class-transcendent polity and implanted on top of a class society, reveal as much as they hide. These attempts at unification forge an identifiable ideological core, a national identity, around which other cultural elements may be arranged hierarchically. It transpires that the ability and the right to interpret and name the nation's others forms a major task of national intellectuals, who are organic to the nation-state project.[11]

If this difficulty dogs European bourgeois nationalism, then it is a much more complicated task for Canada to imagine a unificatory national ideology, as recognized by members of the "white" ideological bloc espousing non-liberal perspectives. Ultra-conservatives in general have foresworn any pretence to the use of "multicultural" ideology. They view multiculturalism as an added burden to a society already divided, and accord no political or cultural importance to groups other than the French. The political grammar of "national" life and culture, as far as the near and far right are concerned, is common-sensically acknowledged as "English." According importance to multiculturalism has the possibility of calling into question the "English" presence in this space, by creating an atmosphere of cultural relativism signalling some sort of usurpation. This signal, it is felt, is altogether best removed. English/Europeanness, that is, whiteness, emerges as the hegemonic Canadian identity. This white, Canadian and English equation becomes hegemonic enough to be shared even by progressive Canadians or the left.[12] This ideological Englishness/whiteness is central to the programme of multiculturalism. It provides the content of Canadian culture, the point of departure for "multiculture." This same gesture creates "others" with power-organized "differences," and the material basis of this power lies both below and along the linguistic-semiotic level. Multiculturalism as the "other" of assimilation brings out the irreducible core of what is called the real Canadian culture.

So the meaning of Canada really depends on who is doing the imagining—whether it is Margaret Atwood or Charles Taylor or Northrop Frye or the "visible minorities" who organize conferences such as "Writing thru 'Race.'" Depending on one's social location, the same snow and

Canadian landscape, like Nellie McClung and other foremothers of Canadian feminism, can seem near or far, disturbing, threatening or benign.[13] A search through the literature of the "visible minorities" reveals a terror of incarceration in the Canadian landscape.[14] In their Canada there is always winter and an equally cold and deathly cultural topography, filled with the RCMP [Royal Canadian Mounted Police], the Western Guard, the Heritage Front and the *Toronto Sun*, slain Native peoples and Sitting Bull in a circus tent, white-faced church fathers, trigger-happy impassive police, the flight and plight of illegals, and many other images of fear and active oppression. To integrate with this Canada would mean a futile attempt at integrating with a humiliation and an impossibility. Names of our otherness proliferate endlessly, weaving margins around "Canada/English/ French Canada." To speak of pan-Canadian nationalism and show a faith in "our" national institutions is only possible for those who can imagine it and already are "Canada." For "others," Canada can mean the actuality of skinhead attacks, the mediated fascism of the Reform Party, and the hard fist of Rahowa.[15]

It is time to reflect on the nomenclature extended by multiculturalism to the "others" of "Canada." Its discourse is concocted through ruling relations and the practical administration of a supposed reconciliation of "difference." The term "visible minorities" is a great example: one is instantly struck by its reductive character, in which peoples from many histories, languages, cultures and politics are reduced to a distilled abstraction. Other appellations follow suit—immigrants, ethnics, new Canadians and so on. Functional, invested with a legal social status, these terms capture the "difference" from "Canada/English/French Canada" and often signify a newness of arrival into "Canada." Unlike a rose which by any other name would smell as sweet, these names are not names in the sense of classification. They are in their inception and coding official categories. They are identifying devices, like a badge, and they identify those who hold no legitimate or possessive relationship to "Canada." Though these are often identity categories produced by the state, the role played by the state in identity politics remains unnoticed, just as the whiteness in the "self" of "Canada's" state and nationhood remains unnamed. This transparency or invisibility can only be achieved through a constellation of power relations that advances a particular group's identity as universal, as a measuring rod for others, making them "visible" and "minorities."

An expression such as "visible minorities" strikes the uninitiated as both absurd and abstract. "Minority," we know from J. S. Mill onwards, is a symptom of liberal democracy, but "visible"? We realize upon reflection that the adjective "visible" attached to "minority" makes the scope of identity and power even more restricted. We also know that it is mainly the Canadian state and politics which are instrumental in this categorizing process and confers this "visibility" upon us. I have remarked on its meaning and use elsewhere:

> Some people, it implies, are more visible than others; if this were not the case, then its triviality would make it useless as a descriptive category. There must be something "peculiar" about some people which draws attention to them. This something is the point to which the Canadian state wishes to draw our attention. Such a project of the state needed a point of departure which has to function as a norm, as the social average of appearance. The well-blended, "average," "normal" way of looking becomes the base line, or "us" (which is the vantage point of the state), to which those others marked as "different" must be referred . . . and in relation to which "peculiarity" [and, thus, visibility] is constructed. The "invisibility" . . . depends on the state's view of [some] as normal, and therefore, their institution as dominant types. They are true Canadians, and others, no matter what citizenship they hold [and how many generations have they lived here?] are to be considered as deviations. . . .[16]

Such "visibility" indicates not only "difference" and inferiority, but is also a preamble to "special treatment." The yellow Star of David, the red star, the pink triangle, have all done their fair share in creating visibility along the same lines—if we care to remember. Everything that can be used is used as fodder for visibility, pinning cultural and political symbols to bodies and reading them in particular ways. Thus for non-whites in Canada, "their own bodies are used to construct for them some sort of social zone or prison, since they can not crawl out of their skins, and this signals what life has to offer them in Canada. This special type of visibility is a social construction as well as a political statement."[17] Expressions such as "ethnics" and "immigrants" and "new Canadians" are no less problematic. They also encode the "us" and "them" with regard to political and social claims, signifying uprootedness and the pressure of assimilation or core cultural-apprenticeship. The irony compounds when one discovers that all white people, no matter when they immigrate to Canada or as carriers of which European ethnicity, become invisible and hold a dual membership in Canada, while others remain immigrants generations later.

The issue of ethnicity, again, poses a further complexity. It becomes apparent that currently it is mainly applied to the non-white population living in Canada. Once, however, it stringently marked out white "others" to the Anglo-French language and ethos; while today the great "white" construction has assimilated them. In the presence of contrasting "others," whiteness as an ideological-political category has superseded and subsumed different cultural ethos among Europeans. If the Ukrainians now seek to be ethnics it is because the price to be paid is no longer there. Now, in general, they are white vis-à-vis "others," as is denoted by the vigorous participation of East Europeans in white supremacist politics. They have been ingested by a "white-Anglo" ethos, which has left behind only the debris of self-consciously resurrected folklores as special effects in "ethnic" shows. The ethnicities of the English, the Scottish, the Irish, etc., are not visible or highlighted, but rather displaced by a general Englishness, which means less a particular culture than an official ideology and a standardized official language signifying the right to rule. "Ethnicity" is, therefore, what is classifiable as a non-dominant, sub- or marginal culture. English language and Canadian culture then cannot fall within the ministry of multiculturalism's purview, but rather within that of the Ministry of Education, while racism makes sure that the possession of this language as a mother tongue does not make a non-white person non-ethnic. Marginalizing the ethnicity of black people from the Caribbean or Britain is evident not only in the Caribana Festival but in their being forced to take English as a second language. They speak dialects, it is said—but it might be pointed out that the white Irish, the white Scots, or the white people from Yorkshire, or white Cockney speakers are not classified as ESL/ESD clients. The lack of fuss with which "Canadians" live with the current influx of Eastern European immigrants strikes a profound note of contrast to their approach to the Somalis, for example, and other "others."

The intimate relation between the Canadian state and racism also becomes apparent if one complements a discussion on multiculturalism with one on political economy. One could perhaps give a finer name than racism to the way the state organizes labour importation and segmentation of the labour market in Canada, but the basic point would remain the same. Capitalist development in Canada, its class formation and its struggles, predominantly have been organized by the Canadian state. From the days of indenture to the present, when the Ministry of "Manpower" has been transformed into that of "Human Resources," decisions about who should come into Canada to do what work, definitions of skill and accreditation, licensing and certification, have been influenced by "race" and ethnicity.[18] This type of racism cannot be grasped in its real character solely as a cultural/attitudinal problem or an issue of prejudice. It needs to be understood in systemic terms of political economy and the Gramscian concepts of hegemony and common sense that encompass all aspects of life—from the everyday and cultural ones to those of national institutions. This is apparent if one studies the state's role in the importation of domestic workers into Canada from the Philippines or the Caribbean. Makeda Silvera, in *Silenced*, her oral history of Caribbean domestic workers, shows the bonds of servitude imposed on these women by the state through the inherently racist laws pertaining to hiring of domestic workers.[19] The middle-man/procurer role played by the state on behalf of the "Canadian" bourgeoisie is glaringly evident. Joyce Fraser's *Cry of the Illegal Immigrant* is another testimonial to this.[20] The issue of refugees is another, where we can see the colonial/racist as well as anti-communist nature of the Canadian state. Refugees fleeing ex–Soviet bloc countries, for example, received a no-questions acceptance, while the Vietnamese boat people, though fleeing communism, spent many years proving their claim of persecution. The racism of the state was so profound that even cold-war politics or general anti-communism did not make Vietnamese refugees into a "favoured" community. The story of racism is further exposed by the onerous and lengthy torture-proving rituals imposed on Latin Americans and others fleeing fascist dictatorships in the Third World. In spite of Canada's self-proclaimed commitment to human rights, numerous NGOs, both local and international, for years have needed to persuade the Canadian state and intervene as advocates of Third World refugees. Thus the state of "Canada," when viewed through the lens of racism/difference, presents us with a hegemony compounded of a racialized common sense and institutional structures. The situation is one where racism in all its cultural and institutional variants has become so naturalized, so pervasive that it has become invisible or transparent to those who are not adversely impacted by them. This is why terms such as "visible minority" can generate so spontaneously within the bureaucracy, and are not considered disturbing by most people acculturated to "Canada."

Visible minorities, because they are lesser or inauthentic political subjects, can enter politics mainly on the ground of multiculturalism. They can redress any social injustice only limitedly, if at all. No significant political effectiveness on a national scale is expected from them. This is why Elijah Harper's astute use of the tools of liberal democracy during the Meech Lake Accord was both unexpected and shocking for "Canadians." Other than administering "difference" differentially, among the "minority communities" multiculturalism bares the political processes of cooptation or interpellation.[21] The "naming" of a political subject in an ideological context amounts to the creation of a political agent, interpellating or extending an ideological net around her/him, which confers agency only within a certain discursive-political framework. At once minimizing the importance and administering the problem of racism at a symptomatic level, the notion of visible minority does not allow room for political manoeuvre among those for whose supposed benefit it is instituted. This is unavoidably accompanied by the ethnicization and communalization of politics, shifting the focus from unemployment due to high profit margins, or flight of capital, to "problems" presented by the immigrant's own culture and tradition.

In fact, organizing multiculturalism among and by the non-white communities amounts to extending the state into their everyday life, and making basic social contradictions to disappear or be deflected. Considering the state's multicultural move therefore allows a look into the state's interpellative functions and how it works as an ideological apparatus. These administrative and ideological categories create objects out of the people they impact upon and produce mainstream agencies in their name. In this way a little niche is created within the state for those who are otherwise undesirable, unassimilable and deeply different. Whole communities have begun to be re-named on the basis of these conferred cultural-administrative identities that objectify and divide them. Unrelated to each other, they become clients and creatures of the multicultural state. Entire areas of problems connected to "race," class, gender and sexual orientation are brought under the state's management, definition and control, and possibilities for the construction of political struggles are displaced and erased in the name of "ethnic culture." The politics of identity among "ethnic communities," that so distresses the "whites" and is seen as an excessive permissiveness on the part of the state, is in no small measure the creation of this very culturalist managerial/legitimation drive of the state.

What, then, is to be done? Are we to join forces with the Reform Party or the small "c" conservative "Canadians" and advocate that the agenda of multiculturalism be dropped summarily? Should we be hoping for a deeper legitimation crisis through unemployment and rampant cultural racism, which may bring down the state? In theory that is an option, except that in the current political situation it also would strengthen the ultra-right. But strategically speaking, at this stage of Canadian politics, with the withdrawal and disarray of the left and an extremely vulnerable labour force, the answer cannot be so categorical. The political potential of the civil society even when (mis)named as ethnic communities and reshaped by multiculturalism is not a negligible force. This view is validated by the fact that all shades of the right are uneasy with multiculturalism even though it is a co-opted form of popular, non-white political and cultural participation. The official, limited and co-optative nature of this discourse could be re-interpreted in more materialist, historical and political terms. It could then be re-articulated to the social relations of power governing our lives, thus minimizing, or even ending, our derivative, peripheral object-agent status. The basic nature of our "difference," as constructed in the Canadian context, must be rethought and the notion of culture once more embedded into society, into everyday life. Nor need it be forgotten that what multiculturalism (as with social welfare) gives us was not "given" voluntarily but "taken" by our continual demands and struggles. We must remember that it is our own socio-cultural and economic resources which are thus minimally publicly redistributed, creating in the process a major legitimation gesture for the state. Multiculturalism as a form of bounty or state patronage is a managed version of our antiracist politics.

We must then bite the hand that feeds us, because what it feeds us is neither enough nor for our good. But we must wage a contestation on this terrain with the state and the needs of a racist/imperialist capital. At this point of the new world order, short of risking an out-and-out fascism, the twisted ideological evolution of multiculturalism has to be forced into a minimum scope of social politics. Until we have developed a wider political space, and perhaps with it keeping a balance of "difference," using the avenues of liberal democracy may be necessary. Informed with a critique, multiculturalism is a small opening for making the state minimally accountable to those on whose lives and labour it erects itself. We must also remember that liberalism, no matter who practises it, does not answer our real needs. Real social relations of power—of "race," class, gender and sexuality—provide the content for our "difference" and oppression. Our problem is not the value or the validity of the cultures in which we or our parents originated—these "home" cultures will, as living cultures do in history, undergo a sea-change when subjected to migration. Our problem is class oppression, and that of objectifying sexist-racism. Thinking in terms of culture alone, in terms of a single community, a single issue, or a single oppression will not do. If we do so our ideological servitude to the state and its patronage and funding traps will never end. Instead we need to put together a strategy of articulation that reverses the direction of our political understanding and affiliation—against the interpellating strategies of the ideological state apparatus. We need not forget that the very same social relations that disempower or minoritize us are present not only for us but in the very bones of class formation and oppression in Canada. They are not only devices for cultural discrimination and attitudinal distortion of the white population, or only a mode of co-optation for "visible minorities." They show themselves inscribed into the very formation of the nation and the state of "Canada." Thus the politics of class struggle, of struggle against poverty or heterosexism or violence against women, are politically more relevant for us than being elected into the labyrinth of the state. The "visible minorities" of Canada cannot attain political adulthood and full stature of citizenship without struggling, both conceptually and organizationally, against the icons and regulations of an overall subordination and exploitation.

In conclusion, then, to answer the questions "How are we to relate to multiculturalism?" and "Are we for it or against it?" we have to come to an Aesopian response of "ye, ye" and "nay, nay." After all, multiculturalism, as Marx said of capital, is not a "thing." It is not a cultural object, all inert, waiting on the shelf to be bought or not. It is a mode of the workings of the state, an expression of an interaction of social relations in dynamic tension with each other, losing and gaining its political form with fluidity. It is thus a site for struggle, as is "Canada" for contestation, for a kind of tug-of-war of social forces. The problem is that no matter who we are—black or white—our liberal acculturation and single-issue oriented politics, our hegemonic "subsumption" into a racist common sense, combined with capital's crisis, continually draw us into the belly of the beast. This can only be prevented by creating counter-hegemonic interpretive and organizational frame-works that reach down into the real histories and relations of our social life, rather than extending tendrils of upward mobility on the concrete walls of the state. Our politics must sidestep the paradigm of "unity" based on "fragmentation or integration" and instead engage in struggles based on the genuine contradictions of our society.

Notes

Originally published as "On the Dark Side of the Nation: Politics of Multiculturalism and the State of 'Canada,' " in *Journal of Canadian Studies* 31.3 (1996): 103–28. Reprinted with permission of the publisher.

1. On multiculturalism, its definition and history, see Angie Fleras and Jean Leonard Elliot, eds., *Multiculturalism in Canada: The Challenge of Diversity* (Scarborough: Nelson, 1992).

2. On the emergence of a liberal state from the bases of a white settler colony, see B. Singh Bolaria and Peter Li, eds., *Racial Oppression in Canada* (Toronto: Garamund Press, 1988); also see Peter Kulchyski, ed., *Unjust Relations: Aboriginal Rights in Canadian Courts* (Toronto: Oxford University Press, 1994), and Frank Tester and Peter Kulchyski, *Tammarniit (Mistakes): Relocation in the Eastern Arctic* (Vancouver: University of British Columbia Press, 1994). For a "race"/gender inscription into a semi-colonial Canadian state, see Patricia Monture-Angus, *Thunder in My Soul: A Mohawk Woman Speaks* (Halifax: Fernwood, 1995).

3. For an in-depth discussion of mediatory and unificatory ideologies needed by a liberal democratic, i.e., capitalist state, see Ralph Miliband, *The State in Capitalist Society* (London: Quartet Books, 1984), chaps. 7 and 8.

4. For a clarification of my use of this concept, see Jurgen Habermas, *Legitimation Crisis* (Boston: Beacon Press, 1975). This use of "legitimacy" is different from Charles Taylor's Weberian use of it in *Reconciling the Solitudes*.

5. See Benedict Anderson, *Imagined Communities: Reflections on the origin and spread of nationalism* (London: Verso, 1991), introduction and chap. 2. Anderson says, "I . . . propose the following definition of the nation: it is an imagined political community —and imagined as both inherently limited and sovereign. It is *imagined* because the members of even the smallest nation will never know most of their fellow members, meet them, or even hear of them, yet in the minds of each lives the image of their communion" (6).

6. Ibid., chap. 2.

7. On the development of active white supremacist groups in Canada, and their "Englishness," see Martin Robb, *Shades of Right: Nativist and Fascist Politics in Canada, 1920–1940* (Toronto: University of Toronto Press, 1992); also William Peter Ward, *White Canada Forever* (Montreal: McGill-Queen's University Press, 1978).

8. See Stoler, *Race and the Education of Desire*; but also Mrinalini Sinha, *Colonial Masculinity* (Manchester: Manchester University Press, 1995).

9. The history of immigration and refugee laws in Canada, and of the immigrants, indentured workers and refugees themselves, must be read to comprehend fully what I am attempting to say. See The Law Union of Ontario, *The Immigrant's Handbook* (Montreal: Black Rose Books, 1981); also *A Report of the Canadian Immigration and Population Study: Immigration Policy Perspective* (Ottawa: Department of Manpower and Immigration and Information Canada, 1974); and *Equality Now: Report of the Special Committee on Visible Minorities* (Ottawa: House of Commons, 1986).

10. Antonio Gramsci, "Notes on Italian History," in *Selections from the Prison Notebooks*, ed. and trans. Quentin Hoare and Geoffrey Smith (New York: International Publishers, 1971).

11. On organic intellectuals as intellectuals who are integral to any ideological and class project, see Gramsci, "The Intellectuals," in ibid.

12. This becomes evident when we follow the controversies which are generated by writers' conferences, such as "Writing thru 'Race,'" or the black communities' response and resistance to Royal Ontario Museum's exhibition on African art and culture—"Out of the Heart of Africa."

13. Nellie McClung (1873–1951), feminist and social activist who was instrumental in the women's suffrage movement in Canada. A well-known and influential figure during her lifetime, from 1921 to 1926 McClung was a member of the Alberta Legislative Assembly.—Eds.

14. See, for example, Dionne Brand, *Winter Epigrams* (Toronto: Williams-Wallace, 1983); Krisantha Sri Bhaggiyadatta, *The 52nd State of Amnesia* (Toronto: TSAR, 1993); Himani Bannerji, *Doing Time* (Toronto: Sister Vision Press, 1986); and collections such as Diane McGifford and Judith Kearns, eds., *Shako's Words* (Toronto: TSAR, 1990).

15. The acronym for Racial Holy War, a neo-Nazi rock band.

16. Himani Bannerji, "Images of South Asian Women," in *Returning the Gaze: Essays on Racism, Feminism and Politics*, ed. Bannerji (Toronto: Sister Vision Press, 1993), 148. On this theme of social construction of a racialized "minority" subject and its inherent patriarchy, see Linda Carty and Dionne Brand, "Visible Minority Women: A Creation of the Colonial State," and Roxana Ng, "Sexism, Racism, Canadian Nationalism," both in ibid.

17. Bannerji, "Images of South Asian Women," 149.

18. See Donald Avery, *Reluctant Host: Canada's Response to Immigrant Workers, 1896–1994* (Toronto: McClelland and Stewart, 1995). Much work still needs to be done in this area in which class formation is considered in terms of both "race" and gender. But a beginning is made in Dionne Brand's *No Burden to Carry: Narratives of Black Working Women in Ontario, 1920s to 1950s* (Toronto: Women's Press, 1991); and Dionne Brand and Krisantha Sri Bhaggiyadatta, eds., *Rivers Have Sources, Trees Have Roots: Speaking of Racism* (Toronto: Cross Cultural Communications Centre, 1985).

19. This is powerfully brought forth through the issue of importation of domestic workers in Toronto from the Caribbean by Makeda Silvera, *Silenced: Talks with Working-Class Caribbean Women about Their Lives and Struggles as Domestic Workers in Canada*, 2nd ed. (Toronto: Sister Vision Press, 1989).

20. J. C. Fraser, *Cry of the Illegal Immigrant* (Toronto: Williams-Wallace Productions International, 1980).

21. Aboriginal leader Elijah Harper (b. 1949) was a member of Manitoba Legislative Assembly from 1981 to 1992 and a member of Parliament from 1993 to 1997. Harper played a historic role in the negotiations over the Meech Lake Accord, which was an attempt to amend the Canadian Constitution so that the province of Quebec would finally endorse the Canada Act (the repatriation of the Canadian constitution in 1982). In order for the Accord to be accepted, it required ratification by all of the provinces of

Canada. In Manitoba, ratification required unanimous consent by all members of the legislative assembly. Because the Accord did not constitutionally guarantee rights for Canada's aboriginal peoples (First Nations, Inuit, and Métis), Harper refused to vote in favor of Meech Lake, which effectively led to the death of the proposed constitutional amendment.—Eds.

KATHARYNE MITCHELL

In Whose Interest? Transnational Capital and the Production of Multiculturalism in Canada

Katharyne Mitchell (b. 1961) is a professor of geography and the Simpson Professor of the Public Humanities at the University of Washington. She received a B.A. in art and archaeology from Princeton University before studying geography at the University of California, Berkeley, where she received her M.A. and Ph.D. In addition to numerous articles and book chapters dealing with the city, geography, and globalization, Mitchell is the author of *Crossing the Neoliberal Line: Pacific Rim Migration and the Metropolis* (2004) and coeditor of *A Companion Guide to Political Geography* (2003) and *Life's Work: Geographies of Social Reproduction* (2004).

In this paper, through a critical examination of the appropriation of the liberal rhetoric of multiculturalism by Canadian business interests, I join with those who believe abstract celebration of travel, hybridity, and multiculturalism to be premature.[1] In numerous celebratory representations of these "new" transnational cultures and hybrid subject positions, the powerfully oppressive socioeconomic forces underlying the changes are neglected, as are many of the people caught within them. As bell hooks has noted of Clifford's somewhat playful evocation of travel and "hotel lobby" culture, the actual, terrorizing experience of border crossings for many people of color is effectively elided.[2] On-the-ground experiences are relegated to a secondary position (if included at all) in the general rush to proclaim the beneficial potential of hybrid forms and state-sponsored drives toward increasing cultural diversity and mutual tolerance. In an era of global capitalism, the heralding of subject positions "at the margins" too often neglects the actual marginalization of subjects. And positive readings of the forces of deterritorialization inadequately address "the powerful forces of oppression unleashed by them."[3]

In addition, the abstract promotion of liberal tenets such as multiculturalism neglects the numerous ways in which liberal cultural projects are always at risk of appropriation. The concept of culture as a "way of life" and a manifestation of national identity has a historical legacy that Williams traces to the English social critics of the nineteenth and early twentieth centuries.[4] He argues that the idea of culture in the modern sense, as the daily practices and everyday life of a whole people, emerged during the formation of industrial liberal society. Attempts to define culture as a way of life are linked to an effort to politicize and harness all aspects of life in the context of a rapidly changing and increasingly fragmented "modern" industrial society. By controlling the meaning of culture and broadening it to include the minutiae of everyday existence, the process of hegemonic production, as outlined by Gramsci and others, can be initiated and extended into the very fabric of social life.[5]

Thinking of culture as "our common life" allows lifestyle and the habits of everyday life to be normalized and reconstructed by the state and by social institutions through the process of ideological production. In this paper I look at how the image of multiculturalism as the correct Canadian "way of life" becomes manipulated in this cultural project during the period of hypermodernity of the late 1980s.[6] In particular, I examine how this concept has been politically appropriated, normalized, and reconstructed by the Canadian state and by private institutions to facilitate international investment and capitalist development in Vancouver, British Columbia. In this manner, I hope to show how terms like multiculturalism are not *naturally* emancipatory, but must be constantly monitored and interrogated—especially with regard to their symbiotic relationships with the transnational movements of capital.

Vancouver's Integration into the Global Economy

In the 1980s, Vancouver's increasing integration into the global economy had many negative effects for urban residents and led to new types of resistance to transnational capitalist ventures. During this time, an increasing number of business ventures and agreements were occurring between Canadian businessmen, government bureaucrats, and wealthy Pacific Rim players, particularly those operating out of Hong Kong. These connections became highly visible in December 1988, when buyers in Hong Kong purchased 216 luxury condominiums on the south shore of False Creek in downtown Vancouver. The condominiums were marketed exclusively in Hong Kong and sold out within a period of three hours. The sale prompted a tremendous outcry among Vancouver residents and fueled major anti–Hong Kong sentiment in the city. Members of various political parties became involved in the fray, as did representatives from international business centers, universities, multicultural institutes, and neighborhood organizations.

Politicians who spoke scathingly of the condominium sales included Committee of Progressive Electors (COPE) councillor Harry Rankin. Rankin, a progressive leftist, said at the time, "The basic issue is to give Canadians the first and only chance to buy: that means Canadian residents or landed immigrants. No offshore people should be allowed to speculate in this market."[7] Michael Goldberg, chairman of the Vancouver International Financial Centre (a nonprofit society acting as conduit between government and business to promote Vancouver as an international business center) responded by dismissing negative reactions such as those of Rankin's as fueled by racism and fear of change. "People who experience change . . . look for a bogeyman to blame. Now it is really easy to blame foreigners, especially visible minorities for these changes. If the same units had been marketed in London, I suspect the outcry would have been much less."[8]

In the preceding remarks by Rankin and Goldberg, the age-old theme of globalism versus localism emerges. This theme has been part of an ongoing debate in Vancouver since the late 1960s and has recurred with each successive period of prosperity and renewed urban development. Most frequently the politicians who have aligned themselves on the side of localism and slow-growth development have been members of left or liberal parties such as COPE. Believing that uncontrolled international investment and rapid development often produce major, unacceptable dislocations within the city, these politicians and parties have fought (usually unsuccessfully) for more stringent local controls over land and urban form over the past quarter century.

This is an old story. But the twist introduces a new dimension to this pervasive development conflict. When Goldberg accused Rankin of inhibiting international capitalism, he accused him of being a racist at the same time. This new strategy, involving the political manipulation of the meanings of race and racism, has had profound repercussions for political and economic alliances, consciousness formation, and urbanization in Vancouver. Capitalists and politicians seeking to attract Hong Kong Chinese investment target "localists" as racist and endeavor to present themselves and the city as nonracist. Their willingness to attract foreign capital and to advertise the city as "open for business" is deliberately conflated with a willingness to engage with Chinese immigrants and businesspeople in the spirit of racial harmony.

Racism, particularly against the Chinese, has been a long-standing problem in British Columbia that has been addressed seriously only in the past decade. As racism hinders the social networks necessary for the integration of international capitalisms, it has been targeted for eradication. Multiculturalism has become linked with the attempt to smooth racial friction and reduce resistance to the recent changes in the urban environment and experiences of daily life in Vancouver. In this sense, the attempt to shape multiculturalism can be seen as an attempt to gain hegemonic control over concepts of race and nation in order to further expedite Vancouver's integration into the international networks of global capitalism.

Vancouver's urban environment has been shaped by several periods of capital investment, following the boom cycles of the economy. The most recent period of rapid transformation prior to the late 1980s occurred two decades earlier, when mammoth glass office buildings began to crowd the city skyline.[9] The most recent changes introduced by international investment are thus part of an ongoing cycle, but reflect the shock of the new in a particularly acute manner owing to the intensity and speed of the transformations. Statistics on Vancouver's rapid growth and internationalization in the past decade have been documented in a number of places,[10] as have the city's increasing links to the Pacific Rim and shift to a more service-oriented economy.[11] Increasingly high-profile trade with Asian countries has been crucial for Vancouver's growth and establishment as the primary commodity gateway for the U.S. market since the final settlement of the North American Free Trade Agreement (NAFTA) in 1993.

In the early 1980s, there was a determined effort by municipal and provincial representatives and businesspeople to attract offshore Asian capital into Vancouver. In the hopes of enticing some of the wealthy Hong Kong elite to make investments in advance of 1997, there was a campaign to "sell" Vancouver as a secure, profitable and livable city in which to do business and reside.[12] This campaign crossed political divides and led to unlikely alliances between liberals and conservatives; it was advocated by B.C. Premier Vander Zalm of the Social Credit (Socred) party throughout his term of office, and is currently a major concern of Premier Harcourt of the New Democratic Party (NDP). Harcourt visited Hong Kong as mayor of Vancouver and returned to reassure Hong Kong residents of his ongoing loyalty to the city one month after his election as premier.[13]

The major reason for the heightened interest in attracting Hong Kong capitalists to Vancouver is quite simple: there is a lot of money there. Estimates of the actual amounts of capital flowing between Hong Kong and Vancouver vary widely and figures are not documented by statistical agencies connected with either city government. At a private banking conference in Geneva in 1990, however, president-elect of the Swiss Private Banker's Association, Pierre Mirabaud, was quoted as saying that people in Hong Kong and Taiwan transfer about a billion Canadian dollars a month to Canada.[14] How much of this capital stays in Canada, how much goes to Vancouver, and how much flows to the United States, back to Hong Kong or elsewhere is impossible to even estimate. One more specific measure of capital flow between Hong Kong and Vancouver, although still highly approximate, is through the business immigration program statistics. The category of business immigration was initiated in Canada in 1984 and was targeted for the Hong Kong elite diversifying their portfolios in advance of the 1997 changeover to Chinese communist control. The category includes investors and entrepreneurs who are required to bring a certain amount of money into Canada and are then given higher processing priority for immigration. As of 1991, the total amount required for investors in British Columbia was a minimum personal networth of c$500,000 with a promise to commit c$350,000 to a Canadian business over a three-year period.

The business immigration program set up by the Canadian federal government attracted a great proportion of wealthy immigrants from Hong Kong during the late 1980s. From 1984 through 1991, Hong Kong led as the primary source country under the program, jumping from 338 landed immigrants in 1984, to 6,787 by 1990.[15] Although Vancouver is second to Toronto in the preferred destination for most of these immigrants, the amount of estimated funds brought to British Columbia in 1988 (most of the funds brought into the province wind up in Vancouver) was nearly one and a half billion Canadian dollars, three hundred million dollars more than to Ontario.[16] Figures from 1989 show an approximate capital flow of c$3.5 billion from Hong Kong to Canada, of which c$2.21 billion or 63 percent was transferred by the business migration component.[17] I consider these figures quite conservative. Most applicants under-declare their actual resources by a significant margin for income tax purposes. Bankers and immigration consultants I interviewed in Hong Kong put the overall figure as high as c$6 billion being transferred from

Hong Kong to Canada in the late 1980s and early 1990s. Of that amount, over one-third would be destined for British Columbia.[18]

Banking networks between the cities have grown tremendously in order to accommodate and encourage the financial activity. The Hong Kong and Shanghai Banking Group (Hongkong Bank), the largest non-Japanese bank in Asia, has, through rapid expansion in the past two decades, incorporated many wholly owned and subsidiary firms in Canada. For example, the Hong Kong Bank of Canada was founded in 1981 as a small branch of the international giant. In 1986 the bank acquired the assets of the Bank of British Columbia for C$63.5 million, and in 1990 it bought out Lloyds Canada. By 1991 the bank had the largest consumer presence of any foreign-owned bank in Canada and had opened 107 offices—including sixteen which specialized in Asian banking. Twenty-five percent of its retail deposits (totaling over C$5 billion) originated from Asian customers.[19]

Race and Place

Racism, like capitalism, is an old story in Vancouver. The power of definition over what constitutes race and racism is central to the forms it takes over the years. White Vancouverites' conceptions of "Chineseness" have often been bound to these definitions and also to the construction of an Anglo-Canadian identity through this process of othering. The identities that have been constructed along racial lines for Chinese Canadians and Anglo-Canadians have been historically tied to place in Vancouver, with Chinatown and Shaughnessy exemplifying two contrasting neighborhoods with formerly rigid racial boundaries and class distinctions.[20]

Until recently, wealthy Anglo neighborhoods in Vancouver's westside, like Shaughnessy, were almost completely homogeneous. The symbols of distinction in these neighborhoods were predicated on the links to a British aristocratic past, one that expressed both class and racial separateness. Recent expressions of racism against wealthy Hong Kong Chinese immigrants, which have increased in number in the past decade,[21] often become manifest in struggles over boundary protection and land control in these areas. These struggles reflect an anxiety about the loss of both economic and symbolic control over the defining and marking of place.

Some long-term white residents fear exclusion from the business practices of the Hong Kong entrepreneurs, whom they perceive as directing or channelling their capital and opportunities along racial, regional, or family lines. Much of the anger and resentment at the 1988 marketing of the Vancouver Regatta condominiums in Hong Kong stemmed from this fear of exclusion. At the same time, media articles, popular books, jokes, and anecdotes from the late 1980s also emphasized the threat of engulfment. Words relating to water, such as "tide" or "wave," were used frequently in reference to the new business activities and immigration of the Hong Kong Chinese.[22] Floods and tides of destruction had been evident in images of "Asian" takeovers in earlier years as well, with Lothrop Stoddard's postwar treatise *The Rising Tide of Color*, a popular book in Vancouver in the 1920s. In this book, Stoddart wrote of the vulnerability of "white race-unity" and the "very imminent danger that the white stocks may be swamped by Asiatic blood."[23]

Other conflicts centered on the transformation of the urban environment. In the late 1980s, demolitions, "monster" houses, and the destruction of trees and gardens were the source of greatest strife. "The monster house" is a term that is used for recently constructed houses that are especially large in the context of Vancouver neighborhoods on the west-side of the city.[24] The original, smaller houses, built on Canadian Pacific Railroad land in the 1920s, were demolished to make space for the new monster houses, which often extend to the extreme edges of the lots. Before the demolitions began in the early 1980s, one long-term resident of Kerrisdale described his west-side neighborhood as "one of the most conservative, fossilized landscapes in the province."[25]

Many of the new houses are perceived as ugly and cheap by the older, white residents, who are drawn primarily from the ranks of the upper middle class and wealthy.[26] Although the new houses are much larger than most of the buildings that were there formerly, the general neighborhood impression of these houses is that the quality of materials is poor, the architectural style is boxy and clumsy, the landscaping is unappealing, and the entire package is noncontextual. Residents spoke to me frequently about the loss of ambience, tradition, and heritage in their neighborhoods, bemoaning the new buildings' lack of "character." Implicit in many of the statements was a perceived threat to an established way of life, a way of life predicated on the symbols, values, and distinction of a white, Anglo tradition.[27] One person wrote in a letter to Vancouver City Council, April 10, 1990: "I grew up in Shaughnessy, on Balfour Street, and have watched closely the changes happening within it. I am saddened and disgusted when I walk through it today to see so many of the trees and houses gone, only to be replaced by hideous monster houses!! . . . I talked to a construction worker who was working on one of these new atrocities they call a house . . . he said, and I quote, 'the house is a piece of shit, and will probably be falling to pieces in ten years:' So, is this what Shaughnessy is to become? . . . We need assurances that the character of the neighborhood will be maintained!"

In addition to the actual physical changes in the landscape, there have been extreme economic changes as well. The most prominent real estate company in Vancouver, Royal LePage, shows average prices for an executive detached two-story in the west-side, rising from c$185,000 in 1979 to c$500,000 in 1989. The price for a detached bungalow doubled in just four years, from c$200,000 in 1985 to c$400,000 in 1989.[28] Forecasts by real estate agents for the future show prices soaring to c$700,000 in 1995 and c$800,000 by the year 2000 for the average Kerrisdale home.[29] Word-of-mouth stories and newspaper accounts depict far more acute price changes, including stories of houses that were flipped for great profit three or four times within a single year.[30]

The association of the influx of wealthy immigrants from Hong Kong with the aesthetic and economic changes in neighborhoods like Shaughnessy and Kerrisdale was made both directly and obliquely in letters to the Vancouver City Council, letters to the editor, and in interviews with me. The anxiety surrounding the loss of a way of life was often expressed as a concern about individual and national identity as well as a concern about urban change. One person wrote in a letter to the editor: "Canadians see monster housing as an arrogant visible demonstration of the destruction of Canadian culture. Yes, we have a Canadian identity and Canadians should beware of persons who say we don't while they try to rebuild Canada in a different mould for their own purpose and profit."[31]

The reference to profit is a direct jab at the Hong Kong Chinese, who are perceived as responsible for house price escalation as a result of using homes for profit through the practice of speculation, rather than as places to live. For wealthy white residents, investing in "tasteful" or "high" culture in Vancouver society, which includes the home where one lives, secures profit yet *does not have to be pursued as profit*. Living in an established and wealthy area such as Shaughnessy purportedly because the character of the neighborhood "feels right" allows the homeowners to profess ignorance and innocence of any cynical or mercenary motives such as profit, yet establishes their fundamental connection to the underlying systems that generate it.[32]

Although the letter refers to the destruction of a national identity, the concern over social identity is implicit; profit-generating development in Vancouver's east-side and outlying areas is rarely contested, nor are those areas (which are far more economically and racially mixed) defended on the grounds of preserving heritage, tradition, character, or identity of any kind. The violence of the reaction against the aesthetic and economic changes in Kerrisdale and Shaughnessy betrays the profound fear that the symbols and meanings of the established and dominant Anglo group are being eroded, and with them the chance of appropriating and naturalizing the appropriation of the rare rights and assets that are dependent upon one's position in social space as well as the distribution of those assets in geographical space.[33]

The repercussions of these economic, morphological, and social changes in west-side neighborhoods have been extreme. Many people living in areas such as Kerrisdale have expressed a twofold anxiety: first, that the quality of the neighborhood that they are living in is being eroded through the imposition of large and "ugly" buildings and the influx of people with different tastes and values and, second, that because of the fantastic price leaps in housing, their children will not be able to live in the same area where they grew up.[34] The anxiety expressed is that an elite lifestyle, represented largely through both the choice of neighborhood and the style of house and gardens within that neighborhood, can no longer be reproduced in succeeding generations.

Although the rise in house prices and the construction of the monster houses may derive from a number of causes, including intraprovincial migration and demographic shifts, there is a general feeling among many residents of these neighborhoods that the Hong Kong Chinese are largely responsible for the changes. Some residents I spoke with felt that the cultural differences, the different practices of daily life that they envisaged as the norm for people in Hong Kong, were changing the patterns of daily life in Vancouver. Here the conflation of race and culture operates in an insidious way to legitimize the exclusion of the Hong Kong Chinese from west-side neighborhoods. Residents invoked cultural difference as the reason that they felt uncomfortable with the new immigrants and were thus able to mobilize resistance to the changes on relatively neutral grounds. One woman in her fifties, a resident of Vancouver who had been born and raised in England, said of the changes in her Kerrisdale neighborhood:

A: It's a shame because we have many friends. . . . I hate to single out one race but you're particularly thinking about one race . . . but we have many friends and they're fine people. But I just think their way of life is so totally different.

K: So assimilation is difficult?

A: It's very difficult. The very thought of having an apartment lot would make my husband sick. Whereas to a Chinese, it's great. It's business. It's just so different. This is the thing that's interesting. We put our house up for sale and it's quite big and I love it; I think it's a beautiful house. This lady came in and looked around and looked around and walked out. And the real estate lady said, she probably doesn't even know what color your drapes are. She's going to knock it down.

K: Is this a Chinese woman?

A: Yes. And so, we're just so completely different.[35]

Multiculturalism and Capital Accumulation: Whose Interest?

In the following section I will examine some of the strategies that have been taken to combat racism, localism, and patriotism in the context of Vancouver's integration in the global economy. The ongoing attempt to influence and guide the production of meanings and the new articulations of race and nation are directly implicated in the production of a multiculturalist rhetoric in Canada. This rhetoric, in turn, is implicated in the strategy of spatial integration and the articulation of international capitalisms. The multiculturalist ideology has been produced and contested by many groups and individuals in Vancouver, but I will focus in particular on the role of the state and on one private institution.

Cultural pluralism has been promoted in Canada in different forms and with different meanings since the time of Sir Wilfrid Laurier's term in office.[36] At the time that he was elected in 1896, Canada was experiencing an economic boom, and Laurier saw his mission as prime minister to be one of easing "racial" tensions so that the country could expand geographically and economically without the drag of conflicting sentiments from the two charter groups. For most of the twentieth century, government policy initiatives around the concept of cultural pluralism functioned as a relief valve for growing tensions with Quebec and as a framework for a national discourse on the possible reconstitution of Canadian society and Canadian identity.[37]

The term "multiculturalism" became common after Prime Minister Trudeau's speech in October 1971, in which he introduced a new plan for the country called "multiculturalism within a bilingual framework." The specific "multicultural" programs that were funded and the types of conferences that were convened in the first decade after this speech did not deviate much from the earlier initiatives, which had focused on general questions of Canadian national identity and on the reduction of animosity with the Quebecois. Critics of multicultural policy in the early 1980s noted that the weakest policy programs were those that were aimed at reducing racial and ethnic discrimination, and that aside from a noisy rhetoric, the general effort by the government was minimal at best. The budget allocated for the implementation of multicultural programs in 1980 was a miserly c$10.8 million, and relatively little labor or energy was expended by government agencies—aside from a cursory interest in producing a few films and a couple of new radio programs.[38]

In the mid-1980s, however, the emphasis began to shift. The early concern about identity in the context of friction with Quebec became more widespread and all-encompassing. Canadian national identity was no longer just manifested in expressive instances of multicultural unity and harmony, it was explicitly linked in language and law to the multicultural ethic. At the same time, the policy initiatives of the government shifted from interest in the maintenance of cultural language and heritage (which had been primarily focused at the French Canadians) to a far more extensive and stronger commitment to the improvement of what it terms "race relations." Government funding nearly tripled between 1980 and 1991, with a far greater proportion of federal money allocated to programs dedicated to the improvement of race relations.

Alongside the increase and shift in government funding, there were concrete moves toward the entrenchment of multiculturalism in the constitutional and statutory levels of government. The 1982 Canadian Charter of Rights and Freedoms included two provisions that were related to multiculturalism; Section 27 explicitly linked the interpretation of the charter as consistent with the "preservation and enhancement of the multicultural heritage of Canadians." The Canadian Multiculturalism Act of 1988 was even more direct in its affirmation of the cultural diversity of Canada and the role of the government in "bringing about equal access for all Canadians in the economic, social, cultural and political realms."[39]

With the commitment to multiculturalism enshrined in the Constitution Act of 1982, and entrenched in the nation's statutes with the Multiculturalism Act of 1988, yet with a clear emphasis on maintaining the privileging of the English and French languages, the first steps in the nation-building of a new Canadian order were taken. The language used in reference to the new act is explicit in the linking of multiculturalism with identity, nationhood, and progress. The connection of a new Canada with a new world order involving international cooperation and increased economic prospects is similarly categorical. David Crombie, the secretary of state of Canada and the minister responsible for multiculturalism, wrote in 1987:

> Dear fellow Canadians,
> I am pleased to introduce a Bill which, upon passage, will become the world's first national Multicultural Act. It contains the government's new policy respecting multiculturalism, an essential component of our Canadian identity. . . . Its intention is to strengthen our unity, reinforce our identity, improve our economic prospects, and give recognition to historical and contemporary realities. . . . Multiculturalism has long been fundamental to the Canadian approach to nation-building. . . . Canadians are coming to realize that substantial social, economic and cultural benefits will flow from a strengthened commitment to multiculturalism.[40]

Crombie's words echoed the sentiments of Prime Minister Brian Mulroney, who had emphasized the potential economic benefits of multiculturalism in 1986, at a conference called, appropriately enough, "Multiculturalism Means Business." In his speech, Mulroney is unequivocal about the pragmatic reasons for promoting a new multiculturalism. He makes the link between Canada's need for export markets and increased trading opportunities with a more nurturing, progressive stance of government vis-à-vis the nation's ethnic members who might perhaps have links to "other" parts of the globe. The changing patterns of immigration into Canada make it more than likely that the "other" parts of the globe to which Mulroney refers will be located in Asia. The gamble for increased business opportunities with the booming Pacific Rim countries through the particularist ties of well-coddled Asian-Canadians is unambiguous and unapologetic, couched as it is in the lingo of humanitarianism and the entrepreneur spirit: "We, as a nation, need to grasp the opportunity afforded to us by our multicultural identity, to cement our prosperity with trade and investment links the world over and with a renewed entrepreneurial spirit at home. . . . In a competitive world, we all know that technology, productivity, quality, marketing, and price determine export success. But our multicultural nature gives us an edge in selling to that world. . . . Canadians who have cultural links to other parts of the globe, who have business contacts elsewhere are of the utmost importance to our trade and investment strategy."[41]

The connection between the government's promotion of better race relations and human rights and the increasing immigration of wealthy Asian investors is made in several government publications, albeit indirectly. In a statement by the Economic Council of Canada in 1991, called "New Faces in the Crowd," the authors juxtapose statistics showing the decline of British immigration and growth of Asian immigration, discussions of the economic impact of the immigrant investor category, and government expenditures showing increases in funding for multiculturalist programs engaged with group acceptance and tolerance and improved race relations.[42] The interconnections are implicit but fairly clear: the government has embarked on a new ideological strategy involving the mitigation of racial tensions surfacing around the increase of wealthy Asian immigrants into the society. Two new bills and a national campaign in 1989 and 1990 were directly engaged with defusing racial animosity and educating people about racial discrimination.[43] It cannot be entirely coincidental that the national public education campaign to mark the International Day for the Elimination of Racial Discrimination was organized less than a month after the following two articles appeared in Canada's major daily newspaper, the *Globe and Mail:*

> What, for Vancouver, is tomorrow?
> The answer: to call what is taking shape here startling is an understatement. Vancouver, barely past its birthday, is going to become an Asian city.[44]
> The Hong Kong immigrants are of a different breed from the usual new arrivals: they're rich. . . . Choice blocks of condominiums are being built that are sold only to Hong Kong buyers. Old houses are being bulldozed and replaced by unattractive megahouses for Hong Kong buyers. Hong Kong investment—about $800 million a year in the province, most of it in Vancouver—is gobbling real estate.[45]

The set of beliefs around what multiculturalism is and should be reflects private concerns as well as those of government agents. In addition to a flourishing of government organizations in Vancouver in 1989 and 1990 such as the Hastings Institute and the Affiliation of Multicultural Societies and Services Agencies of B.C. (AMSSA), there have been some key private institutions involved in promoting multicultural understanding, particularly between Vancouver and Hong Kong. The Laurier Institute, headquartered in Vancouver, is the most prominent and well-financed of these organizations.

The Laurier Institute came into existence legally in the middle of 1989 but, according to the executive director, was operational for a year prior to that time. The goals of the institute are quoted in a number of brochures and publications. In short, they are "to contribute to the effective integration of the many diverse cultural groups within Canadian society into our political, social and economic life by educating Canadians of the positive features of diversity."[46] Orest Kruhlak, the executive director of the institute, specifically mentioned the attempt to defuse potential racial friction as an important principle of the organization. He cited the organization's worry about future problems arising as a result of the increase in immigration and the growing racial diversity of Vancouver. "Nobody seemed to be looking at the long-term implications of increased diversity. What we wanted to do was say how can we start working with some of the issues that might come forward in the future with the idea of trying to get ahead on the issue and do research and educational programming to try and prevent the problems that we have come to understand were going to be major problems in the future."[47]

One of the first projects that was commissioned by the institute was a study on real estate price increases in Vancouver. According to Kruhlak, this study had not been planned but was in response to "a growing and emerging problem." In the report, entitled "Population and Housing in Metropolitan Vancouver: Changing Patterns of Demographics and Demand," the author's results seemed to indicate that the rising house prices were a product of demand from the aging postwar baby boomers. The author of the report, David Baxter, wrote in the executive summary: "Regardless of the level of migration assumed (none, normal, or high) and regardless of the level of household headship rates assumed (constant or increasing), it is the demographic process of the aging of the postwar baby boom into the 35 to 44 age group (1986 to 1996) and then into the 45 to 54 age group (1991 to 2006) that will determine the characteristics of changes in housing demand in metropolitan Vancouver in the future."[48]

Although this paragraph is fairly general, seeming to indicate that demographic change is at least partially responsible for changes in housing demand in Vancouver (with the implication of increasing house prices), the following paragraph in the summary demonstrates the persuasive rhetorical strategy that is at the heart of the study. In this section, Baxter makes it clear that the report is not so much concerned with showing the possible reasons for price increases as showing what are not possible reasons. What is not possible and not acceptable in the dictates of multiculturalism and the Canadian way would be to label and identify and otherwise pinpoint a particular group. In an avuncular, warning tone, he writes: "If we seek someone to blame for this increase in demand, we will find only that the responsible group is everyone, not some unusual or exotic group of residents or migrants. In fact, there is no one to blame: the future growth in housing demand is a logical and normal extension of trends in the nation's population."

The findings of Baxter's report, part of a series of joint research projects sponsored by the Canadian Real Estate Research Bureau and Bureau of Applied Research (at the Faculty of Commerce and Business Administration at the University of British Columbia) as well as the Laurier Institute, were picked up and commented on by nearly all of the major newspapers in Canada. The effect of Baxter's warning statement on the media was immediate, and immediately conveyed to the public. The *Vancouver Sun* and the *Globe and Mail*, still recovering from the accusations of racism in articles written on Hong Kong and Vancouver in 1988 and early 1989, made the connection between Baxter's statement on "unusual or exotic groups" with wealthy immigrants from Hong Kong. This connection, although implied, was not explicitly mentioned anywhere in the text. The media, in an ecstasy of self-flagellation and expiation for former sins, printed the story with explicit reference to Hong Kong. The *Globe and Mail* wrote in November 1989, "Aging baby boomers, not foreign immigrants, are the main reason Vancouver housing prices are rising, a study says. . . . [The study] was prompted by public complaints that home-buying by affluent Hong Kong immigrants had been forcing up Vancouver home prices."[49]

The other Laurier project reports, all focused in some way on housing and real estate in Vancouver, were also broadcast nationally in several forums. Professor Hamilton's study, entitled "Residential Market Behavior: Turnover Rates and Holding Periods," claimed the immigration levels did not contribute to speculation (flipping) in the housing market. The *Vancouver Sun* declared soon after in headlines, "Foreign buyers absolved."[50] And the local Vancouver paper, the *Courier*, wrote in April 1990, "Home speculation not immigrants' fault."[51] A study by Dr. Enid Slack on the impact of development cost fees charged by municipalities (the fourth in the series) showed that the levies on developers (for financing water supply systems, sewage treatment plants, etc.) are often passed on to new home buyers in increased house prices. The *Real Estate Weekly* in Vancouver wrote of these findings, "Slack's report is part of a major study commissioned by the Laurier Institute to determine whether any basis exists for suggestions that Chinese immigrant buyers are driving up Vancouver real estate prices. So far, the Institute has found, 'in fact there is no one to blame. . . . [T]he responsible group is everyone.' "[52]

The continual reiteration of Baxter's statement that no one is to blame appears to operate like a mantra for warding off the evil spirit of racism. But in fact, the statement operates on a number of levels. In denying that blame for the specific results of higher real estate prices can be pinned on anyone in particular, the proponents of this belief achieve two results: first, those who disagree with this belief are not joining in the valiant effort to defeat racism, and thus can be seen as somewhat suspect in this area; and second, since everyone is responsible and no one to blame, there is no obligation and no need to uncover and demask the agents or systems involved in the process that has, in fact, led to higher prices. The workings of capitalism thus remain opaque, the agents involved in capital transfer remain faceless, and the spatial barriers and frictions that may disrupt the free flow of capital over and through municipal and international borders are eradicated.

The implications of Dr. Slack's report go one step further. Not only is no one to blame for the unfortunate (for house buyers) rise in house prices, but if anyone should be held accountable, it is city government. Although house prices have doubled and tripled in a single year, adding hundreds of thousands of dollars to house prices in certain neighborhoods, Slack's findings focus on the development costs imposed by *municipalities* on new housing projects. These costs (which only affect new houses, not those that are the main source of the controversies discussed earlier) range from about C$1,500 for new homes in Burnaby to about C$12,000 for a new home in Richmond. Furthermore, the costs are not imposed in many communities in Vancouver or North Vancouver. Nevertheless, Slack's report was commented on in the *Vancouver Sun* with the headline: "Study finds extra charges placing heavy burden on new home buyers."[53] Here, it is the extra charges that are to blame; the charges, levied by the municipalities, are forcing people to pay more. Too much government obviously throws the whole supply and demand system off, and developers are naturally forced to pass off these onerous tax burdens onto the buyer. If anyone is to blame it is an overly controlling and paternalistic city government.

Why would the Laurier Institute, an organization whose express mission and role is to "promote cultural harmony in Canada" and "encourage understanding among and between people of various cultures" commission these particular reports? Although my sources indicate that the

Laurier Institute was founded by "a group of businessmen," the organization's brochures do not identify the founders by name. The list of the board of directors of the institute in 1990 included thirteen people and their positions. Of this group there are four lawyers in major law firms, three executives in large corporations, two investment and management counselors, and one real estate executive. Of the corporations or firms represented, nine are directly or indirectly involved with Hong Kong business or investment. Of the seven founding donors (donating C$25,000 or more), there is a similar overlap with Hong Kong business concerns.[54]

The role of the Laurier Institute to provide guidance through the education of the benefits of multiculturalism has been expressed in a number of areas, including a video and curriculum guide for use in the schools called "Growing Up Asian and Native Canadian."[55] The dissemination of general information from studies that educate and persuade readers about "what is really happening" is made public and broadcast via the media. In addition, the information generated from commissioned research is offered to companies who become corporate members of the institute. In seeking to attract corporate members, one brochure enumerates the advantages of having insider information on changes regarding cultural diversity in Canada that may be economically fruitful. Like Mulroney's speech quoted earlier, the emphasis on the economic potential of contributing to the multicultural ideology is clear: "The cultural diversity of Canada's population has brought, and continues to bring, significant change to the Canadian workforce and the Canadian marketplace. Companies which recognize the potential of this diversity and act accordingly will have enormous advantage over those who do not. Membership in The Laurier Institute offers assistance in terms of both recognizing the potential and implementing programs which will deliver that advantage."[56]

Other corporate members and major supporters of the Laurier Institute include the Bank of Nova Scotia, the Canadian Maple Leaf Fund Ltd., Concord Pacific Developments, Grand Adex, Hong Kong Bank of Canada, Pacific Canadian Investment and the Royal Bank of Canada. All of these corporations have major stakes in Hong Kong and in the continued flow of people and capital from Hong Kong into Canada. Those who helped to fund the real estate reports mentioned earlier, plus sponsoring a number of Laurier Institute events and conferences, include the major real estate companies and foundations in Vancouver, most of whom have profited enormously as a result of the increased connections with Hong Kong over the past decade.

Reclaiming Multiculturalism

Is it possible then to reclaim multiculturalism as a possible counter-public sphere?[57]

In *Political Power and Social Classes*, [Nicos] Poulantzas describes how the dominant discourse of bourgeois ideology presents itself as innocent of power, often through the concealment of political interests behind the objective facade of science.[58] In the production and promotion of multiculturalism in Canada, the particular configurations of power remain similarly concealed, but in this case, behind the façade of national identity and racial harmony. The struggle over ideological formation, such as the language and meaning of race and nation, resonates as an effort to shape a dominant discourse for specific *material* ends. Culture-workers who ignore the socioeconomic elements involved in this struggle run the risk of celebrating new voices and cultural opportunities, just as those voices risk being appropriated and/or extinguished.

In Vancouver, for example, increasing global connections and rapid urban development have been accompanied by an influx of wealthy "Asian" immigrants and by several high-profile development projects by Hong Kong investors. Tensions around city transformation have reflected anger toward the unacceptable dislocations occasioned by rapid capitalist development, as well as increased antagonism toward Chinese investors from Hong Kong, who are often represented as invaders flooding the city on a tidal wave of capital. As tensions have grown, resistance to change has become more vociferous, culminating in several local attempts to halt "flows" of any kind. In this context, the reworking of multiculturalism as an ideology of racial harmony and bridge-building in the city operates as both a localized effort at damage control in a specific situation and part of a much broader strategy of hegemonic production in the interests of multinational capitalism.

By identifying the production of multiculturalism on the ground rather than heralding it in the abstract, it is possible to recognize sites of resistance as well as sites of control. When examining *who is* saying *what* and *why* about multiculturalism, one can identify the ways in which representations are made and appropriations are occurring. Unmasking the individuals and institutions responsible for these appropriations is the first step in contesting and reclaiming meaning. Despite the difficulties of disentangling agendas and interrogating material gain, it is only through this process that more positive interpretations of liberal concepts like multiculturalism can be won.

Notes

Originally published as "In Whose Interest? Transnational Capital and the Production of Multiculturalism in Canada," in *Global/Local: Cultural Production and the Transnational Imaginary*, ed. Rob Wilson and Wimal Dissanayake, 219–54. Copyright © Duke University Press 1996. Reprinted with permission of the publisher.

1. See Anne McClintock, "The Angel of Progress: Pitfalls of the Term 'Post-Colonialism,'" *Social Text* 10. 2–3 (1993): 84–98; Gayatri Chakravorty Spivak, "Neocolonialism and the Secret Agent of Knowledge: An Interview," *Oxford Literary Review* 13.1–2 (1991): 220–51; Ella Shohat, "Notes on the 'Post-Colonial,'" *Social Text* 10.2–3 (1992): 99–113; Sneja Gunew, "Denaturalizing Cultural Nationalisms: Multicultural Readings of 'Australia,'" in *Nation and Narration*, ed. H. Bhabha (New York: Routledge, 1990); and Talal Asad, "Multiculturalism and British Identity in the Wake of the Rushdie Affair," *Politics and Society* 18.4 (1990): 445–80.

2. bell hooks, "Representing Whiteness in the Black Imagination," in *Cultural Studies*, ed. L. Grossberg, C. Nelson, and P. Treichler (New York: Routledge, 1992); James Clifford, "Traveling Cultures," in ibid., 101.

3. Kamala Visweswaran, *Fictions of Feminist Ethnography* (Minneapolis: University of Minnesota Press, 1994), 109.

4. Raymond Williams, *Culture and Society, 1780–1950* (Harmondsworth: Penguin Books, 1961), 285.

5. Antonio Gramsci, *Selections from the Prison Notebooks* (London: International Publishers, 1971).

6. The term "hypermodernity" is used by Allan Pred and others to emphasize both the chronic and ongoing symptoms of modernity and capitalist development as well as their acute acceleration in the past two decades. See Allan Pred and Michael Watt, *Reworking Modernity: Capitalisms and Symbolic Discontent* (New Brunswick: Rutgers University Press, 1992).

7. "Reaction to Sale of Condominiums Felt Fuelled by Fear of Change Racism," *Vancouver Sun*, December 19, 1988.

8. Ibid.

9. For a discussion of this earlier period of development, see Donald Gutstein, *Vancouver Ltd.* (Toronto: James Lorimer, 1975). I am indebted to David Ley for pointing out the historical nature of these real estate booms.

10. See, for example, City of Vancouver, *Vancouver Trends* (May 1990); Province of British Columbia Ministry of Regional Development, *Vancouver Perspectives* (1991).

11. See, for example, Thomas Hutton and H. Craig Davis, *Vancouver as an Emerging Centre of the Pacific Rim Urban System*, U.B.C. Planning Papers, Comparative Urban and Regional Studies, no. 19 (August 1989); David Edgington and Michael Goldberg, "Vancouver and the Emerging Network of Pacific Rim Global Cities," paper presented at the North American meeting of the Regional Science Association, Santa Barbara, Calif., November 10–12, 1989, revised August 1990; David Ley, "Liberal Ideology and the Postindustrial City," *Annals of the Association of American Geographers* 70.2 (June 1980): 238–58.

12. Pamphlets in B.C. [British Columbia] Government offices in Hong Kong are full of details on how to invest in Canada; Canadian and Hong Kong banks also provide information on the transfer of funds, tax holidays through the offshoring of funds, and general services for individuals moving from Hong Kong to Canada. See, for example: *Invest Canada: The Magazine of Canadian Opportunity*, *Prospectus Canada* (in Chinese), *Your Future Is British Columbia: A Guide to Business Immigration*, *Gateway to Canada: Canadian Imperial Bank of Commerce* (in Chinese).

13. Harcourt said in a speech at a British Columbia reception for the Hong Kong trade and investment community on November 21, 1991: "As British Columbia's new premier, I am committed to strengthening and expanding BC's ties with Hong Kong." *Canada and Hong Kong Update* (Winter 1992): 10. See also "Asia's Big Money Players Get Some Political Reassurance," *Vancouver Sun*, November 23, 1991. [Harcourt's term as premier ended in 1996. Since 2001, the premier of British Columbia has been the Liberal Gordon Campbell.—Eds.]

14. Jack Moore, "Swiss Banker Estimates Billions Pouring into Canada from Hong Kong, Taiwan," *Courier*, June 17, 1990.

15. Diana Lary, "Trends in Immigration from Hong Kong," *Canada and Hong Kong Update* (Fall 1991): 6.

16. Employment and Immigration Canada, *Immigration to Canada: A Statistical Overview* (November 1989).

17. Alan Nash, "The Emigration of Business People and Professionals from Hong Kong," *Canada and Hong Kong Update* (Winter 1992): 3.

18. My estimate, based on interviews with nine immigration consultants and five high-level bankers in Hong Kong, is far lower than one given by Hong Kong economist and businessman Simon Murray, who believed that Hong Kong lost HK$2.25 billion per month to Vancouver in 1989. In Canadian dollars, this comes to nearly C$4 billion per year being transferred from Hong Kong to Vancouver. See F. Wong, "Confidence Crisis Costing Billions," *Hong Kong Standard*, September 21, 1989.

19. *Globe and Mail*, August 5, 1991.

20. See Kay Anderson, *Vancouver's Chinatown: Racial Discourse in Canada, 1875–1980* (Montreal: McGill-Queen's University Press, 1991) for an insightful look at these processes as they apply to the construction of Vancouver's Chinatown.

21. According to Lydia Chan, a coordinator at SUCCESS (United Chinese Community Enrichment Services Society), incidents of racism against Chinese Canadians have risen markedly in the late 1980s, but rarely involve physical violence. She said in an interview, "The reception here has changed. I guess now some people feel that there are too many Chinese people, too many Asian immigrants . . . and that's why we feel that the racial tension is there." Interview, October 1990. See also, "Racism Is an Ugly Word," *Equity* (June 1989).

22. A few examples include: *China Tide* (Toronto: Harper and Collins, 1989), a popular book by Margaret Cannon chronicling Hong Kong investment in Vancouver; "Asian Capital: The Next Wave," from *B.C. Business*, July 1990; "Tidal Wave from Hong Kong," *B.C. Business*, February 1989; "Flippers Awash in Profits," *Vancouver Sun*, February 8, 1989; and "Hong Kong Capital Flows Here Ever Faster," *Vancouver Sun*, March 21, 1989.

The metaphor of destruction and engulfment by water has been shown by authors like Theweleit, in his study of the German Freicorps, to have been a symptom in writing and fantasy that related to deep fears about dissolution and the transgression of boundaries. These anxieties were largely related to concerns about the wholeness and stability of identity and masculine sexuality. See Klaus Theweleit, *Male Fantasies*, vol. 1, *Women, Floods, Bodies, History*, trans. Stephen Conway (Minneapolis: University of Minnesota Press, 1987).

23. Lothrop Stoddard, *The Rising Tide of Color* (New York: Charles Scribner's Sons, 1920), 301. Quoted in Anderson, *Vancouver's Chinatown*, 109–10.

24. Extra-large houses have also been built in east-side neighborhoods, but these have been called "Vancouver Specials" by the local populace.

25. Interview, February 1992.

26. In 1986 average family income for residents of the Kerrisdale area was C$76,451 per year (with a standard error of C$2,522) and approximately C$96,034 for residents of Shaughnessy—with over 67 percent earning over C$50,000 per year, according to census statistics. (The Economic Council of Canada defined "middle-income families" as those with an income between C$33,800 and C$56,400 in 1990.) See City of Vancouver Planning Department, *Vancouver Local Areas, 1986* (June 1989).

27. Duncan and Duncan discuss the instrumental use of pastoral symbols to evoke an image of a romanticized (aristocratic) English past in the west-side suburb of Shaughnessy. See James Duncan and Nancy Duncan, "A Cultural Analysis of Urban Residential Landscapes in North America: The Case of the Anglophile Elite," in *The City in Cultural Context*, ed. J. Agnew, J. Mercer, and D. Sopher (Boston: Allen and Unwin, 1984). Prior to the 1980s, most west-side neighborhoods were composed almost exclusively of white residents, most of British heritage. In 1914, 80 percent of the social register of Vancouver was composed of members who resided in Shaughnessy Heights.

28. From the 1991 Royal LePage Survey of Canadian House Prices.

29. C. Smith, "Prime Time," *Equity* (March 1990).

30. See, for example, "City Housing Market Flipping Along," *Business*, September 1, 1989; "Flipping Is Hong Kong Game," *Vancouver Sun*, March 20, 1989; "Flippers Awash in Profits," *Vancouver Sun*, February 8, 1989.

31. *Western News*, July 26, 1989.

32. Bourdieu writes that legitimating culture as a second nature allows those with it to see themselves as disinterested and unblemished by any mercenary uses of culture. See Pierre Bourdieu, *Distinction: A Social Critique of the Judgement of Taste* (Cambridge, Mass.: Harvard University Press, 1984), 86.

33. Ibid., 124.

34. A housing survey in 1991 showed that 96 percent of Vancouver residents said that their children will not be able to afford to live where they were raised. *Vancouver Sun*, November 9, 1991. In the expressed anxiety about the "ugly" buildings and erosion of the neighborhood, what is often left unstated is the anxiety felt about the difference in race of the people moving into the neighborhoods. In this case, the emphasis on cultural values and taste can be seen to operate as an alibi or "screen-allegory" for a

foreclosing of the broader narrative of racism. See Gayatri Chakravorty Spivak, "Can the Subaltern Speak?" in *Marxism and the Interpretation of Culture*, ed. C. Nelson and L. Grossberg (Chicago: University of Illinois Press, 1988), 291.

35. Interview, October 11, 1990.

36. Laurier was Canada's seventh prime minister and first French-Canadian prime minister.

37. Jean Elliot and Augie Fleras, "Immigration and the Canadian Ethnic Mosaic," in *Race and Ethnic Relations in Canada*, ed. Peter Li (Toronto: Oxford University Press, 1990).

38. Ronald Wardhaugh, *Language and Nationhood: The Canadian Experience* (Vancouver: New Star Books, 1983), 201; Evelyn Kallen, "Multiculturalism: Ideology, Polity, and Reality," *Journal of Canadian Studies* 17.1 (1982): 55.

39. Canada, *The Canadian Multiculturalism Act: A Guide for Canadians* (Ottawa: Ministry of Supply and Services, 1990).

40. Canada, *Multiculturalism . . . Being Canadian* (Ottawa: Ministry of Supply and Services, 1987), 1–2.

41. Quoted in Elliot and Fleras, "Immigration," 67.

42. Canada, *New Faces in the Crowd: Economic and Social Aspects of Immigration* (Ottawa: Ministry of Supply and Services, 1991).

43. Canada, *Working Together towards Equality: An Overview of Race Relations Initiatives* (Ottawa: Ministry of Supply and Services, 1990).

44. "Face of Vancouver to be Radically Altered," *Globe and Mail*, February 20, 1989.

45. "Is Vancouver Trading Furs for Beads?" *Globe and Mail*, March 1, 1989.

46. Laurier Institute, newsletter/announcement.

47. Interview, January 3, 1991.

48. David Baxter, "Population and Housing in Metropolitan Vancouver: Changing Patterns of Demographics and Demand," unpublished manuscript, 1989.

49. "Study Says Baby Boomers behind Home Price Surge," *Globe and Mail*, November 16, 1989.

50. B. Constantineau, "Foreign Buyers Absolved," *Vancouver Sun*, March 28, 1990.

51. B. Truscott, "Home Speculation Not Immigrants' Fault," *Courier*, April 22, 1990.

52. "Burb Buyers Hit with Levies," *Real Estate Weekly*, April 6, 1990.

53. Constantineau, "Foreign Buyers Absolved."

54. The founding donors are Lieutenant-Governor Dr. and Mrs. David C. Lam, Asa Johal, Dr. Peter Lee, Milton K. Wong, the Chan Foundation, the Bank of Montreal, and the Pacific Canadian Investment Group.

55. Laurier Institute, letter to potential members, November 2, 1991.

56. Laurier Institute, *Corporate Member Benefits, Cultural Harmony through Research, Communication, and Education*.

57. Sneja Gunew, "Denaturalizing Cultural Nationalisms," 114.

58. Nicos Poulantzas, *Political Power and Social Classes*, trans. Timothy O'Hagan (London: NLB and Sheed and Ward, 1973), 217.

EVA MACKEY

Postmodernism and Cultural Politics in a Multicultural Nation: Contests over Truth in the Into the Heart of Africa Controversy

Eva Mackey (b. 1956) is an associate professor at the School of Canadian Studies, Carleton University. Her doctorate, from the University of Sussex, was completed in 1996. Publications include The House of Difference: Cultural Politics and National Identity in Canada (1999, 2002) and numerous book chapters and journal articles. She is currently writing a book provisionally entitled Contested (Home)lands: Property, Rights, and Citizenship.

This essay examines some of the new forms of control and resistance to challenge that elite producers of culture and representations are mobilizing in the local, yet radically transformed, representational arena. The focus of this article is an analysis of the cultural politics of a controversy concerning race, representation and history that occurred in Toronto, Canada. The controversy centered on a self-consciously postmodern museum exhibit entitled Into the Heart of Africa. Although the exhibit attempted to present colonialism and museum collections in a reflexive and critical way—focusing on the worldview of the colonialist collectors of the objects—it aroused outrage and accusations of racism from black individuals and organizations in Toronto. Through analyzing the controversy I explore some of the limits of the increasingly sophisticated ways issues of difference and representation are articulated by elites, in this case through postmodern representational tactics and the Canadian version of multiculturalism.

Every week during the spring and summer of 1990 the Coalition for the Truth about Africa demonstrated outside the Royal Ontario Museum in Toronto. The group, made up mostly of Toronto African-Canadians, charged that the Into the Heart of Africa exhibit, which was curated by a white Canadian anthropologist, was "racist," and "promoted a white supremacist view of Africa." In the beginning the Coalition simply wanted its views heard, specifically its views about the important contributions Africa had made to the history of "civilization." Later, although the exhibit addressed the past, specifically Canadian colonialism in Africa between 1875 and 1925, the Coalition used the exhibit as a focus for discussing and mobilizing against racism in contemporary multicultural Canada. It renamed the Royal Ontario Museum (ROM) the Racist Ontario Museum. Eventually, claiming to speak in the authentic voice of diasporic Africans, the Coalition demanded that the show be closed and remounted with the input of African-Canadians. In this struggle over representations of history, violence erupted between the police and the demonstrators on two occasions, eleven members of the Coalition were arrested, and the exhibit's tour was canceled. Finally, the curator left her teaching job when the conflict moved into the university. The controversy catapulted into months of heated debate in the press, on the street, and in anthropology departments and museums in Canada. These debates centered on contested views of racism, history, cultural appropriation, academic freedom, and the nature of multiculturalism in Canada. The exhibit received more press attention than any other museum exhibit shown in Canada, with the possible exception of [Calgary's] Glenbow Museum's *The Spirit Sings*.[1]

One of the most ironic and difficult aspects of the controversy was that the curator's stated aims and intentions in the exhibit were to critique the "ethnocentrism and cultural arrogance" of the Canadian colonialists in Africa. She and the Royal Ontario Museum intended the exhibit to be on the cutting edge of new approaches to museology, art history and anthropology.[2] The exhibit was meant to deconstruct, albeit very subtly and ambiguously, the worldview of Canadians during the colonial period and the truths and knowledges institutionalized by museums. In the exhibition catalogue the curator suggested that "by studying the museum as an artifact, reading collections as cultural texts, and discovering the life histories of objects, it has become possible to understand something of the complexities of cross cultural encounters."[3] In short, her exhibit sought to integrate many postmodern assumptions and analytical practices concerning the construction of meaning, culture, history and identity-assumptions which have now become very influential if not dominant in the humanities and social sciences. What happened? The people calling this work racist were the very people whose ancestors were the subjects of the racist colonial discourses and practices the exhibit was intended to critique. Why were they calling it racist when it seemed the curator saw the exhibit as a form of cultural retribution for the past? What can examining this controversy contribute to our understanding of the cultural politics of public culture?

Truth, Power and Subjectivity

A central feature of the controversy surrounding *Into the Heart of Africa* was the way in which it brought into focus contrasting discourses about truth and divergent claims to truth. The deconstruction of truth claims was an integral part of the curator's approach to the exhibit, and is a principal preoccupation of postmodern theory and strategy. Jane Flax, for example, describes postmodern discourses as "all deconstructive"; they seek to distance us from Enlightenment beliefs concerning truth, knowledge, power and the self, beliefs that are taken for granted within, and serve as a legitimation for, contemporary Western culture.[4] The Coalition for the Truth about Africa, as is clear by its name, was unequivocal about its possession of the truth and its moral right to promote it. The Coalition was widely ridiculed and pilloried by academics and by the press for what was seen as their unsophisticated and "politically correct" approach to history and identity.

In order to analyze these battles around truth and representation it is first necessary to consider not only the qualitative differences between the discourses deployed by defenders of the exhibit and those used by the Coalition but also the range of social locations of the speakers. Immense social, economic, and cultural power buttresses the postmodern discourse of the exhibit and its defenders, whereas the Coalition speaks from a marginalized and oppositional position. Understanding the cultural politics of the controversy requires much more than examining the internal inconsistencies of the respective discourses and comparing them as if they were equal.

Much of the scholarly writing about the exhibit focuses on "what went wrong," or, implicitly, on how to avoid such controversies in the future[5] or on how the curator's intentions were misinterpreted.[6] I look more broadly at the events, discourses and context of the controversy in order to examine the contests for interpretive authority which were enacted between its socially located agents. What does this reveal about the political and cultural effects of postmodern theories and practices when they are released into specific contexts? Such contexts entail a cultural politics which is not confined to interpreting texts, but rather can include violent confrontations between blacks and police on the street while anthropologists and experts wait inside. Finally, what is the significance of this controversy in the context of an official policy of multiculturalism?

Imagining Multiculturalism

Canada has had an official policy of multiculturalism since 1971. The aims of that policy were to "help minority groups preserve and share their language and culture, and to remove the cultural barriers they face."[7] Although an extensive discussion is not possible here, the original policy has been critiqued for many reasons. It has been described as a ploy by the federal government to "divert attention from Quebec separatist energies."[8] It has also been critiqued for maintaining the idea that being British Canadian is the norm, while other Canadians are viewed as "multicultural" in relation to them. Also, Aboriginal people and the Québécois have argued that multiculturalism is not relevant to them. They maintain that their position within the nation-state of Canada is different from that of more recent immigrants because they have special status as either First-Nations peoples, or in the case of French-Canadians, as one of the two "Founding Nations."[9] Furthermore, it has been argued that multiculturalism promotes fragments of cultures, constructed from folkloric and culinary remnants.[10] In this multicultural model of culture the cultural fragments become conceptually divorced from politics and economics, and become commodified cultural possessions; multiculturalism enacts a process akin to what [Richard] Handler calls "cultural objectification."[11] Kogila Moodley argues that Canadian multiculturalism promotes the "three Ss" model of culture: "saris, samosas and steel bands"—in order to diffuse the "three Rs": "resistance, rebellion and rejection."[12]

The institutionalized ideology and policy of multiculturalism in Canada differs in fundamental ways from versions of multiculturalism and cultural pluralism in the United States and Britain. Recently in the United States multiculturalism is often twinned with the term "politically correct," and refers to debates about decanonisation on university campuses. In Britain multiculturalism is also mainly an educational policy, although it does have further implications at local levels of government. Multiculturalism in Canada is much more widespread as an institutionalized strategy for political legitimation. It is a federal policy and attempts to define Canada as a nation.

Since 1971 Canada's official ideology of multiculturalism has changed. It has, at least rhetorically, become much more rights-oriented, and, according to government documents, focused on transforming the dominant society. The discourse of helping remove "cultural barriers" has been transformed into one of "race relations." In 1982 the Canadian Charter of Rights and Freedoms guaranteed "equal rights that respect the multicultural heritage of Canadians." In 1988 the policy was enshrined in Bill C-93, "An act for the preservation and enhancement of multiculturalism in Canada." The act, among other things, "recognizes and promotes" the understanding that multiculturalism is "a fundamental characteristic of the Canadian heritage and identity" and "promote[s] the full and equitable participation of individuals and communities of all origins in the continuing evolution and shaping of all aspects of Canadian society and assist[s] them in the elimination of any barrier to such participation."[13] There is a federal Department of Multiculturalism and Citizenship which makes funding available for individuals, groups and institutions under programs such as Race Relations and Cross-Cultural Understanding, Community Support and Participation and Heritage Cultures and Languages. According to the Department of Multiculturalism and Citizenship, the new Multiculturalism Act, "addressed to all Canadians . . . is based on the idea that everyone, including the government, is responsible for changes in our society. This includes the elimination of racism and discrimination."[14]

The focus of this discussion of the Act is not so much the policy of multiculturalism but its imaginary. How does the notion of Canada, imagined as a multicultural nation, intersect with the discourses in the controversy? Although the imagined community is inclusive and pluralistic, and the federal government spends millions of dollars representing multicultural Canada to Canadians, what actually happens at an institutional level?[15]

Blacks as Conceptual Exiles from Nationhood

The Royal Ontario Museum—in its seventy-seven-year history—had never targeted blacks in Toronto. This oversight is a glaring exclusion, considering the long history of the black presence in Canada.[16] It is all the more surprising when one considers Toronto's large and vibrant black population and Canada's official policy of multiculturalism. The interactions between the Museum and Toronto blacks before the exhibition exemplify the practice of multiculturalism as distinct from its ideology. The Royal Ontario Museum—a powerful and influential cultural institution dominated by, and directed to, the white majority in Canada—

organized an exhibit based on artifacts that white colonists had brought back (some say had stolen) from Africa. The Museum hired a white Canadian anthropologist to curate it, despite Toronto's large African-Canadian population. However, and more importantly, the Museum invited the black community to approve the exhibit after it was already completed. The Museum, a powerful agent in defining public culture, invited blacks to share in their culture (by approving the exhibit), but did not share any of the power to control and define the content of that culture. In other words, it refused to share any of its institutional power. Furthermore, the Museum and the exhibition excluded African-Canadians from the imagined community of Canada.

Museums have played a complex role since the sixteenth century in representing the story of Western expansion. One function of the museum in our culture is to represent nations, and nations' relationships with others, both inside and outside their borders. Appadurai and Breckenridge write, "Museums, which frequently represent national identities at home and abroad, are also nodes of transnational representation and repositories for subnational flows of objects and images."[17] As is the case with the Into the Heart of Africa controversy, this act of representing the nation (and the transnation) is extremely problematic because, as Ivan Karp points out, museum displays "are all involved in defining the identities of communities—or in denying them identity."[18] Bourdieu points out that the true function of museums is to "increase the feeling of belonging for some, and of exclusion for others."[19] Who does the imagined community of multicultural Canada include and exclude in the terms of this exhibit?

The stated focus of the Into the Heart of Africa exhibit was the white Canadians who took part in the colonial venture. It analyzed their worldview, not the worldview of Africans or African-Canadians. As a means of defense the Museum, the curator and the press argued that this was an exhibit about Canadian history, and that the Coalition just did not understand the exhibit was not about Africa. Indeed the opening text panel of the exhibit warned that the Canadian "experience of Africa, as seen in this exhibition, was very different from the way that Africans perceived themselves, their own cultures, and these events." The panel also informed viewers that the objects "remind us of a little remembered era of Canada's past." The first person plural pronoun here has "implicit exclusions."[20] The "us" in this sentence is subtly addressed to white Canadians—probably with all good intentions—as a critical strategy intended to inspire a reflexive critique of Canada's role in colonialism. However, by conceptually distinguishing Canadians from Africans, and then giving no space in the exhibit for the way that "Africans perceived themselves, their cultures, and these events," the exhibit not only excluded historical African voices, but also present day African-Canadian viewers, who locate and identify themselves as both Canadian and African or diasporic African. Further, in a news release about the exhibit potential viewers were told that in the Military Room they "will be able to understand Zulu warfare from the other side of the battlefield."[21] This *other* side is implied to be the Zulu side. By assuming that this side is that of white Canadians, the ideal viewer is presumed to be a white Canadian. In the process of hailing and interpolating white Canadians, the exhibit "othered" the Africans of the colonial time, as well as African-Canadians in Toronto in 1990. As Marlene Nourbese Philip writes:

> The ROM argued that this was a part of Canadian life that Canadians did not know about. This immediately begs the questions: Which Canadians did the ROM have in mind? European or African Canadians? Or was the ROM perhaps defining "Canadian" as someone from European heritage?
>
> This exhibit, was, however, also about African history and African Canadians, some of whom have been here for a few centuries. African Canadians know the history of colonialism in a painfully intimate way and often live its implications and repercussions every day of their lives in this country. It is, of course, a not-so-astonishing and racist oversight that the ROM would assume that the only meaningful audience of this exhibit would be white Canadians.[22]

African-Canadians, a group with a profound and legitimate interest in the history of the relationship between Africa and Canada, were excluded both from the planning of the exhibit and implicitly from the position of the ideal viewer. The exhibit's mode of address, in its construction of a white community of viewers, marginalized African-Canadians and transformed them into conceptual exiles from Canadian citizenship, or perhaps, more specifically, Canadian identity.

However, this was not a direct and uncomplicated process of exclusion. As my description of the pre-opening interactions between the Museum and the black community shows, the Museum attempted to bring in the black community—if not as active participants in the planning process, well then certainly as viewers. For instance, the most common newspaper ads for the exhibit proclaimed: "*Into the Heart of Africa*: An historical journey through the world of Sub-Saharan Africa from 1875 to 1925. Celebrate the rich cultural heritage of African life." This advertisement seriously misrepresents the exhibit. It did not celebrate the rich cultural heritage of African life, yet many African-Canadians came expecting this. One woman said, "All my life I have been looking for my roots. I came here looking for them and you gave me nothing."[23]

The new brochure, which was written in collaboration with the black community, now referred to "Africa. Birthplace of humanity. A continent of Ancient civilizations and complex cultures." In attempting to manage potential conflict, the Museum integrated into the revised brochure some of the discourses of the African-Canadians who had critiqued the original version. But the new brochure did not reflect the analytic thrust of the exhibit. In one paragraph it states, "The rich cultural heritage of African religious, social and economic life is celebrated through objects brought back by Canadian missionaries and military men over 100 years ago." The confusion and conflation of two foci, a celebration of Africa on the one hand and an examination of colonialism on the other, is evident in this sentence. There is no overt reference to the fact that the exhibit is supposed to be critical of the ethnocentrism of the colonialists. It seems that in trying to manage potential conflict and to please all sectors of the potential audience—African-Canadians, art historians, and white people who might remember or have relatives who partook in Canada's colonial or missionary past—the exhibit presented a perverse and confused melange of discourses that many African-Canadians found inflammatory and degrading. The Coalition argued at one point that the show was like an exhibit about the Holocaust from the Nazi perspective. Is the Museum's advertising strategy not akin to advertising an exhibit celebrating Jewish civilization for a show based on "artifacts" taken from Jews in the concentration camps? Would it be possible to advertise an exhibit such as that (if anyone would do such a thing) without reference to the absolute horror of fascism? In any case, the Museum's attempt to manage, commodify and domesticate race in a volatile and rapidly changing context reflects some of the tactics, as well as limitations of a liberal multiculturalist framework. Although the exhibit was intended to be critical of what Canadians thought about Africans in the past, it excluded African-Canadians in the present from being potential viewers of the exhibit and active definers of culture in Canada. Instead, it constructed them as conceptual exiles from the Canadian community.

From the early critical coverage of the exhibit it soon became apparent that the curator's reflexive strategy of focusing on the worldview of colonialist collectors of the objects, in order to critique colonialism, was backfiring. She intended for visitors to question the supposedly objective truths museums tell, by suggesting that the meanings connected to objects arise from various social locations. The exhibit utilized a postmodern notion of truth as contingent, multiple and eliding. However, many of the visitors experienced the exhibit as promoting a particular and a singular truth about Africa. For some visitors this perceived singular truth conflicted with their own. The irony and ambiguity of the exhibit was simply lost on many viewers; one could say that it critiqued the "cultural arrogance of the colonialists" (the curator's phrase) in an elitist, culturally arrogant manner, which was difficult for the public to read.[24] In fact, many critiques of the exhibit focus on its elitism, for instance, its use of irony.

The defenders of the exhibit continually argued that *Into the Heart of Africa* was meant to be understood as ironic—and cited the quotation marks around the words "savage" and "barbarous" as an example. However, Harry Lalla, an adviser for race relations and multiculturalism for the Toronto Board of Education, argued that "in dealing with issues as sensitive as cultural imperialism and racism, the use of irony is a highly inappropriate luxury."[25] Brenda Austin-Smith wrote that the irony placed another burden on blacks who felt offended by the exhibit: "Either black viewers submit to a white culture's model of ironic art, or they listen to art critics [or curators] tell them that they just aren't culturally literate enough to know irony when they see it."[26] One of the guards who had been on duty at the exhibition at least three times a week over its ten-month run said that although it had taken him a long time to figure it out he came to realize that it was a specialist show, comprehensible only to a select few, and open to misinterpretation by all others.[27]

For example, a teacher who brought his students to see the exhibit said that one of the museum guides had told his class that "the missionaries civilized the pagans of Africa," and that the Zulus were "an extremely vicious tribe and that's why we would be looking at so many of their weapons."[28] Leaving aside the obvious question concerning the training of guides, clearly, if the guides were reading the colonial images literally rather than ironically and deconstructively as intended, the general public could not be faulted for doing so too. The professional postmodern discourse of irony ignores the way museums are perceived by large sectors of the general public. The public's misinterpretation of the intentions of the exhibitors has a lot to do with the way in which many people experience the museum as an institution where one gains an understanding of "objective history" through the veneration of historical objects.[29]

In this context it is conceivable that many visitors to the exhibit felt they were being asked to venerate not only African art but simultaneously the ideology of its collectors. The curator's strategy of ambiguity was transformed in the eyes of the public into a problematic claim to truth. The institutional power of the Royal Ontario Museum authorizes the truth claims of its exhibits. Museums constitute, in Shelton's words, "the essential mechanisms of a ministry of truth."[30] The exhibitors had attempted to critique—from within—the museum's status as cultural institution. Yet the public's perception of the museum as purveyor of truth overpowered this critique, and the show's use of irony: in other words, much of the public saw the show as a presentation of facts, rather than as a comment upon the truth value of those facts. Although the curator had attempted to utilise a postmodern notion of truth as constructed and multiple, many viewers, in particular the Coalition, saw the exhibit as promoting, within its institutional context, a singular and fixed truth.

The Truth about Blacks

Paul Gilroy writes that one of the main ways that black people are represented in racist discourse is as either problem or victim.[31] The majority discourses of the controversy positioned blacks in these roles. In both the curator's ambiguous discourses and the Museum's defense claiming historical accuracy, black people were presented as victims, either of colonialism or of their own savagery. In the exhibit's representation of the past whites were the focus and the agents. This was reversed, with negative results, in the press coverage of the protests. In the press the blacks involved in the controversy were largely portrayed as causing problems by "deliberately," as one Toronto Star writer suggested, "distorting the truth to suit their own ends."[32] They were presented as extremists who were oppressing rational mainstream society. The shift in the press's attitude towards the protesters, which became less and less sympathetic to the Coalition's struggle, can be seen in the marked difference between two quotes, one from the beginning of the controversy, the other from more than a year later, by reporter Bronwyn Drainie in the

Globe and Mail. At first she writes: "Unfortunately what thoughtful white Canadians see as an ironic examination of our great-grandparents' dubious and racist role in bringing Christianity, Commerce, and Civilization to "the dark continent," black Canadians see as a celebration of colonialism and an unambiguous demonstration of white superiority over native Africans and their cultures."[33] One year later Drainie wrote: "But what many visitors saw as an ironic and self-searching examination of white Canadians' historical intolerance toward Africa was viewed by a small number of radical blacks in Toronto as a perpetuation of those old racist attitudes. The dubiously named Coalition for the Truth about Africa . . . picketed outside the ROM's doors for months. . . . More moderate blacks, while not deeming the show racist in intent. . . ."[34] The first quotation implies that there is some legitimacy to the black Canadians' claims, and recognizes the validity of both opposing interpretations. Furthermore, when Drainie states that "thoughtful" Canadians see the exhibit as critical, she is suggesting that there are many people who will not perceive it in this way. In the later quote she constructs the Coalition as isolated extremists, comparing the view of "many visitors" to that of "a small number of blacks" who are in opposition to the more moderate black majority.

Gill Seidel examines a similar process in her discussion of the British New Right's cultural racism. Cultural racism redefines key concepts such as racism as a "vulgar and banal catch phrase," thereby trivializing the analytic concept of race.[35] This process involves what she calls the "criminalisation of anti-racists" through "semantic mythical reversals."[36] Anti-racists are described by the British New Right as "multiracial zealots" whose behavior constitutes "anti-British prejudice."[37] The more powerful group thereby constructs the minority group as the oppressor. Those in power come to be seen as victims. These processes ultimately deny the legitimacy and autonomy of "other (black) subjectivities and struggles."[38] Indeed, in much of the later press coverage of the controversy protesters were constructed as dangerous to all the things "our" society holds dear—academic freedom, the integrity of history, and even cultural pluralism. The Coalition came to be seen as an aggressor besieging the apparently innocent Museum, and society as a whole. On August 10, 1990 the *Toronto Star* reported that the protesters "seem to have willingly misread" the exhibit, "and this is where the whole matter turns serious. For their attack on the exhibition challenges both academic freedom and the integrity of history."[39] An article two and a half months later in the *Toronto Star* stated: "People who are troubled by the exhibit have every right to picket the ROM and to bring to public attention the reason why they object to the exhibit's particular approach. These are reasonable responses in a democratic society. However, by calling [the curator] a racist rather than simply viewing her as someone who has failed to emphasize things which they would have preferred to see emphasized, these people not only deny the complexity of life itself, but do grievous harm to an ideal which they claim to serve—pluralism."[40] The press and many others critiqued the Coalition for asserting that it held the "truth about Africa," especially in relation to the curator whom the press did not perceive as making any truth claims. For example, David Cayley in the *Toronto Star* declared: "By calling themselves 'the Truth about Africa' the protesters contended that one monolithic truth about Africa exists. [The curator] was more modest and intellectually honest—she clearly does not believe that there can be knowledge about Africa, or anything else, that exists apart from the particular context in which the knowledge is constructed and reconstructed."[41]

Regarding the Coalition's claims to truth Donna Laframboise of the *Toronto Star* contended: "The umbrella group which organized the protests against the exhibit calls itself the Coalition for the Truth About Africa. However unconscious they may be of the fact, such a name implies that there is *the truth* (their version) and nothing else. . . . While there is nothing wrong with insisting that other stories deserve to be told, there is something truly appalling about believing that only you have the right story—and that anyone who tells a different one is, by definition, evil."[42] These statements are typical of majority discourse about minorities. They discount, and essentially render invisible systemic structural inequalities, and belittle the experiences of marginalized people. They also construct an authoritative truth about the Coalition, labeling the group as a problem within an otherwise unified multicultural Canada.

Yet the significance of the two press quotations cited above goes beyond the fact that they attempt to discount and delegitimate the Coalition. The line of discourse in these quotes mobilizes a belief in the multiplicity of truths, and in the notion that knowledge is constructed and reconstructed in this process. These notions sound terribly familiar, in that they have become central to much recent anthropological thought. Here they are used in ways which, in this particular context of competing truths and socially constructed knowledges, support those in positions of privilege and power. The radical oppositional potential in the notions has been shifted; they have become weapons for silencing opposition.

The idea of multiculturalism was mobilized in a similar way. In a major group of pieces on the Opinions page of the *Toronto Star* (June 5, 1990) both the curator and Charles Roach, a leading member of Toronto's black community, end their articles on the controversy by referring to multiculturalism. However, the two authors attach very different meanings to this term. Roach argues, "In our multicultural society let us engage or invite representatives of the various communities to be the exponents of their own cultural heritage."[43] Central to his definition of multiculturalism is the word "engage," which implies active power by minority groups in defining their history. The curator writes, "Thinking critically about our collective past, and about one of our most important public institutions, the museum, as this exhibit does, is vital to the health and future of a multicultural democracy." Here the key verb is "thinking." Multiculturalism becomes an intellectual activity, which helps us to understand past events and the way museums represent these events. The curator's attitude here enacts a selective erasure of the Coalition's demand for recognition and actions in the present. She proposes an intellectual model of pluralism which negates the political accountability being demanded of the exhibit and the Museum. She constructs herself as an active proponent of multicultural thinking in the imagined community of Canada, from which the Coalition is implicitly excluded. By attacking her, the Coalition is constructed as dangerous and opposed to the "health and future of a multicultural democracy." By mobilizing the concept of multiculturalism in this way, it becomes, as does postmodernism, an intellectual weapon used to bolster authoritative majority discourse. Multiculturalism and postmodernism are thus deployed offensively and defensively by powerful groups when their authority is being challenged by less socially or politically powerful groups.

Conclusion

At the outset the Royal Ontario Museum controversy seemed to involve a fairly clear set of oppositions. On one side were the proponents of a sophisticated and ironic postmodern reflexive discourse which proclaimed a distrust of metanarratives and questioned the fixed nature of meaning. In the opposing position was the Coalition for the Truth about Africa, whose discourse made unequivocal truth claims and constructed the history of Africa as an emancipatory metanarrative. Closer analysis reveals that all of the agents in the controversy made truth claims. Although the curator claimed to be actively challenging the idea of fixed truths in her postmodern exhibit, as the controversy intensified, she eventually did solidify her position and proclaim an authoritative truth. So did the Museum, and its truth claims were backed up by its institutional power. The Museum did not limit itself to discursive strategies; it also relied on legal tactics. The Museum won a bid for an injunction to keep protesters away from the Museum, and as a result the police arrested eleven protesters. Later, the Museum attempted to sue the Coalition for $160,000 in damages.[44] Although the suit was eventually dropped, the mainstream press implicitly supported the curator's and the museum's claims to authority, and created their own authoritative truths about blacks as problems in multicultural Canada.

Amidst this cacophony of competing truth claims about the past and present, we can begin to contextualize the discourses of the Coalition. Although they were presented as the only ones in the controversy making truth claims, they were in fact surrounded by, even drowned out by, other less obvious claims to truth in the majority discourses about minorities.[45] Many defenders of the exhibit presented these as common-sense truths. The majority discourses about the Coalition were backed up by hefty resources of material and symbolic power. By contextualizing and examining the discursive battles in the controversy, I have mapped out the cultural conditions of the Coalition's discourse, which was oppositional minority discourse. Gilroy, in his analysis of similar oppositional groups in Britain, sees them as "urban social movements" and emphasizes that they are, at heart, defensive organizations.[46] In placing oppression at the center of their discourse, the Coalition sought to publicize and challenge the ubiquitous and subtle domination blacks experience in contemporary Canada. The Museum controversy illustrates how the discourses of postmodernism and multiculturalism can be used both to mask and defend this domination.

Notes

Originally published as "Postmodernism and Cultural Politics in a Multicultural Nation: Contests over Truth in the Into the Heart of Africa Controversy," in Public Culture 7.2 (1995): 403–31. Copyright © The University of Chicago. Reprinted with permission of the publisher.

1. Enid Schildkrout, "Ambiguous Messages and Ironic Twists: Into the Heart of Africa and The Other Museum," Museum Anthropology 15.2 (1991): 16–23.

2. Jeanne Cannizzo, "Into the Heart of a Controversy," Toronto Star, June 5, 1990.

3. Jeanne Cannizzo, Into the Heart of Africa (Toronto: Royal Ontario Museum, 1989).

4. Jane Flax, "Postmodernism and Gender Relations in Feminist Theory," *Signs* 12.4 (1987): 624.

5. Schildkrout, "Ambiguous Messages"; Michael Ames, "Biculturalism in Exhibits," *Museum Anthropology* 15.2 (1991): 7–15.

6. Jeanne Cannizzo, "Exhibiting Cultures: 'Into the Heart of Africa,' " *Visual Anthropology Review* 7.1 (1991): 150–60.

7. Multiculturalism and Citizenship Canada, *Multiculturalism: What Is It Really About?* (Ottawa: Ministry of Supply and Services, 1991).

8. Linda Hutcheon, "Beginning to Theorize Postmodernism," in *A Postmodern Reader*, ed. Joseph Natoli and Linda Hutcheon (Albany: State University of New York Press, 1993): 31.

9. Eva Mackey, "Multiculturalism in Canada as Ideology and Practice: Peeling off the 'Great National Bandage,' " unpublished manuscript (University of Sussex, 1991).

10. J. J. Smolicz, "Multiculturalism in Australia: Rhetoric or Reality," *New Community* 12.3 (1985): 455.

11. Richard Handler, *Nationalism and the Politics of Culture in Quebec* (Madison: University of Wisconsin Press, 1988).

12. Kogila Moodley, "Canadian Multiculturalism as Ideology," *Ethnic and Racial Studies* 6.3 (1983): 320.

13. Canadian Multiculturalism Act of 1988. R.S.C. 1985, Ch. 24 (4th Supp.).

14. *Together: A Newsletter about Multiculturalism Today* (Ottawa: Multiculturalism and Citizenship Canada, 1990), 6.

15. My current dissertation research focuses on the cultural construction of national identity and the "multicultural imaginary" in Canada. Recent fieldwork examined the relationship between government-produced multicultural representations and other more localized sites of the construction of national identity.

16. Blacks have been in Canada for almost two hundred years. The first recorded arrival was in 1796, when a group of runaway slaves were shipped from Jamaica to Nova Scotia by the British. S. Ramcharan, *Racism: Nonwhites in Canada* (Toronto: Butterworths, 1982), 19. [The 1796 reference is to the resettlement of the Jamaican Maroons in Nova Scotia. However, peoples of African descent had a presence in Canada long before this date. The translator Mathieu Da Costa arrived in Canada between 1604 and 1608; African slaves came to Canada with French settlers in the seventeenth and eighteenth centuries; Loyalists in the American Revolution brought their slaves with them to Canada. There are records of the African slave Olivier Le Jeune being sold in New France in 1628.—Eds.]

17. Arjun Appadurai and Carol A. Breckenridge, "Museums Are Good to Think: Heritage on View in India," in *Museums and Communities: The Politics of Public Culture*, ed. Ivan Karp, Christine Mullen Kreamer, and Steven D. Lavine (Washington, D.C.: Smithsonian Institution Press, 1992), 44.

18. Ivan Karp, "On Civil Society and Social Identity," in ibid., 19. The problem of comparison across geopolitical sites, and the importance of taking into account specific national and local contexts, is illustrated by the following example. An ex-

hibit, of a very similar style and critical focus, was the centre of a fierce political battle in the United States in 1991. *The West as America: Reinterpreting Images of the Frontier*, at the National Museum of Art—an exhibit of American art that portrayed the nation's expansion to the Pacific—also took a critical, deconstructionist approach. It argued, in text on plaques, that the images were "carefully staged fiction" meant to justify the "hardship and conflict of nation building." Martin Walker, "How the West Was Won, or Was It?" *London Review Guardian*, June 13, 1991. Like *Into the Heart of Africa* the show's curators attempted to take what was previously seen as truth and reveal it as fiction. As in the case of the Royal Ontario Museum the exhibit elicited angry editorials in the press and its tour was canceled. Although *The West as America* was undoubtedly less ambiguous and more directly critical, Native Americans, the group represented in the images, did not to my knowledge vehemently oppose the exhibition. Instead, senators from Western states objected to it and threatened budgetary retaliation against its sponsor, the Smithsonian Institution. They charged that the exhibit "effectively trashes . . . most of our national history . . . reducing the saga of America's Western pioneers to little more than victimization, disillusionment, and environmental rape" (cited in Walker, ibid.). It was seen as unpatriotic. Why did the deconstruction of the history of the imagined nation of the United States outrage the Right, whereas a similar, if less direct deconstruction of Canadian imagined innocence in colonialism, outraged not the Right but African-Canadians?

19. Quoted in Nick Merriman, "Museum Visiting as a Cultural Phenomenon," in *The New Museology*, ed. Peter Vergo (London: Reaktion, 1989), 163.

20. Linda Hutcheon, "The Post Always Rings Twice: The Postmodern and the Postcolonial," *Textual Practice* 8.2 (1994): 212.

21. Hutcheon, "Beginning to Theorize Postmodernism," 11–12.

22. Marlene Nourbese Philip, *Frontiers: Essays and Writings on Racism and Culture* (Stratford: Mercury Press, 1992), 105.

23. Howard Goldenthal, "Activists Dissatisfied with ROM's Apology Letter," *Now Magazine* (April 1991): 4–10.

24. I thank Sue Reinhold for pointing this phrase out to me.

25. "Analyzing Racism at ROM," *Varsity* (June 1990).

26. Cited in Robert Fulford, "Into the Heart of the Matter," *Rotunda* (Summer 1991): 24.

27. Ibid., 25. For example, I could be seen as an ideal viewer: white, educated in postmodernism, anthropology, feminism and colonial history. I could therefore read the subtlety and ambiguity of the exhibit, and appreciate the irony. I am not, however, in any way representative of the general public of Toronto or Ontario. This raises the question of the contradictions between museum curators' intellectual and aesthetic ambitions and their audiences and political environments (see Merriman, "Museum Visiting as a Cultural Phenomenon," 54).

28. J. McClelland, "Exhibit Diminishes African Cultures," *Contrast*, April 12, 1990.

29. Anthony Shelton, "In the Lair of the Monkey: Notes Towards a Postmodernist Museography," in *Objects of Knowledge*, ed. Susan M. Pearce (London: Athlone Press, 1990), 97.

30. Ibid., 96.

31. Paul Gilroy, *There Ain't No Black in the Union Jack: The Cultural Politics of Race and Nation* (London: Hutchinson, 1987).

32. Christopher Hume, "ROM Critics Confusing Content with Context," *Toronto Star*, May 19, 1990.

33. Bronwyn Drainie, "Black Groups Protest African Show at 'Racist Ontario Museum'," *Toronto Globe and Mail*, 17 March, 1990: C3.

34. Bronwyn Drainie, "ROM Adds Insult to Injury in Debacle over African Show," *Toronto Globe and Mail*, 4 April, 1991.

35. Gill Seidel, "The White Discursive Order: The British New Right's Discourse on Cultural Racism with Particular Reference to the Salisbury Review," in *Approaches to Discourse, Poetics and Psychiatry*, ed. Iris M. Zavala et al. (Amersterdam: John Benjamins, 1988), 131.

36. Ibid., 136.

37. Ibid., 41–42.

38. Ibid., 134–38.

39. David Cayley, "Trouble out of Africa," *Toronto Star*, August 10, 1990.

40. Donna Laframboise, "ROM Protesters Miss Own Point," *Toronto Star*, 22 October, 1990.

41. Cayley, "Trouble out of Africa."

42. Laframboise, "ROM Protesters."

43. Charles Roach, "Into the Heart of a Controversy," *Toronto Star*, June 5, 1990.

44. "ROM Sues Protest Group," *Toronto Globe and Mail*, August 16, 1990.

45. Seidel, "Right-wing Discourse and Power: Exclusions and Resistance," in *The Nature of the Right*, ed. G. Seidel (Amsterdam: John Benjamins, 1988), 8–9.

46. Gilroy, 231.

LEE MARACLE

Another Side of Me

Lee Maracle was born in 1950 and raised in Vancouver, British Columbia. She belongs to the Sto:loh Nation and is of Salish and Cree heritage. She studied at Simon Fraser University. Her recent books (fiction and nonfiction) include *Ravensong* (1995), *I Am Woman: A Native Perspective on Sociology and Feminism* (1996), a book of poems entitled *Bent Box* (2000), *Daughters are Forever* (2002), and *Will's Garden* (2002). Maracle was the Stanley Knowles Visiting Professor in Canadian Studies at the University of Waterloo (2001) and Distinguished Professor of Canadian Culture at Western Washington University (2003); at present she is the traditional cultural director of the Centre for Indigenous Theatre in Toronto, Ontario.

The aspect of the movement which is under constant attack, even by people who know little or nothing about it, is the communist element. I am most sensitive about this aspect for within it lies the kernel of truth of my own political vision.

Native students of leftist politics that grew out of the 1960s deserved some of the criticism that people raised. Our communism had both feet rooted in European labour history. In this country, that history is an inglorious one. The foundation of unions here was rooted in racism.

Marx himself was full of arrogance and racial supremacist attitudes; that does not negate his sense of history nor his science of revolution. Revolution! Even the most patriotic militants balk at the word. That the European labour movement was built on our backs, that the workers of this land have always had us as a cushion to soften the blow of recession is undeniable. That white Marxists, communists and would-be leftists are tainted with racism is equally undeniable. But to renounce the principles of communism because its adherents are flawed is absurd.

Marxism is founded on the expropriated knowledge and principles of our old societies, which were handed to Marx in distorted fashion. Coloured by the bias of the church, Marx's research was hindered by the brothel-tinted sunglasses of the clergy. The settlers of this country began life with a lie. They cannot carry the truth of communist theory to fruition. Marx was sensitive to the limitations of his theory. He was sensitive to the colonial reality of capitalism's beginning. He was also very sensitive about the basic reactionary character of those sectors of the labour movement that were racist. He must spin over in his grave once a day at the behaviour of his flagbearers.

Our most brilliant movement leaders have been Native Marxists. Against all odds, they have courageously fought to analyze our history so that we could alter it. Marx died, hungry and ill, struggling to synthesize the lessons of world history, that the history of the world might change. He took his knowledge of the people of the world and found the thread with which we might weave a whole new social fabric. All we needed was the courage to turn around: to make revolution.

That white people are unable to make revolution without our assistance—to turn around the society they created—does not negate the necessity and inevitability of turning it around. It has been my experience that those who are rabidly anti-communist are themselves parasites. They live off the movement. They live off the toil of others.

Revolution means to turn around. Square boxes do not turn around. Circles do. This society is made up of a hierarchical system of classes: rectangles that pile up on one another, with the smallest rectangle and the fewest members at the top of the pyramid. The majority fit into the rectangle at the base. The thinking of the people in this country is married to that reality. It is stratified, linear and racist.

Every time Native people form a circle they turn around. They move forward, not backward into history. We don't have to "go back to the land." We never left it. We are not reptiles or amphibians that lived in the sea and now wish to go back to the land. Critics of communism cling to the delusion that the cities we now inhabit do not exist on land. Innocently, some of the people that left their original communities feel this way too. Such thinking is promoted by those who wish to throw the movement into reverse.

Along with the mistaken notion of land, comes the distortion of traditionalism. We are and always have been culturally Cree, Salish, Nis'ga'a and so forth. One does not lose culture. It is not an object. Culture changes, sometimes for the better, sometimes for the worse, but it is constantly changing and will do so as long as people busy themselves with living. Culture is a living thing. It grows and stagnates by turns. The philosophical premise of a people rarely alters itself fundamentally, however. The cultural expression of philosophy may change, but to alter the foundations takes a great deal more effort than simple legal prohibition.

Certainly the prohibitive laws surrounding language and cultural expression were both painful and damaging for our cultural initiative. This is unarguable. We now are paralyzed with fear at cultural innovation. The basis for this fear is the inequitable relations inherent in colonialism. Let's just think about how the Salish came by quillwork: by trading with other Native people. We did not fear this new cultural innovation. Why? Because we were equals. The trade is indeed a trade; moccasins for dried fish, so to speak. However, when we adopt the guitar and country-style music, then we get a little nervous. Likewise with European philosophy.

Cultural imperialism means altering a colonized people's cultural expression without consideration for the aspirations of the people. Fortunately, this does not occur with the degree of thoroughness desired by the imperialists. Even while we use the medium of European-style music, we infuse our own language, our own words and our own meaning. Floyd Westerman is a country singer, but "Custer Died for Your Sins" will not likely be sung by white country singers for some time to come. It is a song that is culturally ours.

If a culture does not express the conditions, the aspirations and the dreams of a people at any period in their history, then it is a dead culture. Culture is a mirror of a people's way of life. We now live not in longhouses or tipis, but in townhouses and apartment blocks. We purchase our food from a grocery store (though given the condition of the food that is sold at these grocery stores, I am not sure this is a good innovation).

No people ever totally deserts its ancestry. The actual ceremonies of the past, the manner in which they were conducted is a matter of speculation by white anthropological experts. There are few elders alive who were not raised in the tradition of the Catholic church, who were not influenced in some fashion by early colonialism. The ceremonies of those spiritual leaders are, likewise, a matter of personal conjecture.

There is no problem with that. Anything that brings people closer to themselves is a ceremony. The search for the truth of one's spirit is a private one, rich in ceremony. The manner in which a person seeks the self is always based on the sacred right of choice.

The question of the existence of a "Great Spirit" is one that is personal and not the basis of our philosophy. Religion and the manner in which a person resolves their own morality, code of conduct, principles, etc., is based on the laws governing choice. As we all know, communists are self-avowed atheists. They are purported to persecute religious people the world over. Native communists have been patient beyond reason with the religious beliefs of others while being persecuted by those who accuse them of persecution.

The extent to which we cannot tolerate communists, Christians and Buddhists in our midst is the exact measure of our integration into the negative aspects of European culture. The principles of communism regarding religion are simple: everyone has the right to worship and conversely, all have the right to oppose worship—peacefully. No one has the right to use religion to exploit others. Communists do not budge on the question of persecution for the purpose of exploitation. This is most annoying for parasites. The American Indian Movement hates communists.

I firmly believe that the philosophy of my ancestors lines up quite tidily with the philosophy of communism. I make no apology for my principles. What I hold myself to account for is not having fought hard and long for the principles that I hold dear to my heart. I should have thrashed the opponents of anticommunist treachery long ago and didn't. Not because I was afraid of the consequences, but rather because I loved some of the people influenced by anti-communist bogeymen. These are some of the "terrible" principles of communism to which I ascribe:

- End the unequal and oppressive relations between European and Third World Nations.
- End the violent competition between nations of exploiters. Work for peace.
- End the rape and plunder of the earth and its treasures in the interest of profit.

Are these principles frighteningly close to the words of our leaders? Are they terrifyingly close to the laws of our ancients? On the flip side of the coin, I can well understand why Native people scorn leftist ideology in North America. They point to the white left, the myriad communist parties, their history of treachery against us, and ask me if I am out of my mind. (I wouldn't be surprised if the answer was a categorical yes, but I am no shrink so I am not going to answer that one directly.) All I can say is: I know how it feels to be truly alone. I do not accede to their lusting after our homelands. I know how they are. The white left in this country seeks to remake us, to wrest control of the country from their own enemy and divide the spoils among themselves. Obviously, no Native person could agree with that.

The subject of the development of the left, its history of betrayal of

Native people, is not for this work. I intend to treat this subject very seriously elsewhere in another work. Herein, I wish to paint my own life in all its complexity. The side of Native people most impossible for the left to deal with centres on our concept of "spirituality." Not surprisingly, we ourselves find it difficult to grasp. It must be borne in mind that the left in CanAmerica is predominantly white and male. These leftists have traditionally pooh-poohed that which is, for them, inexplicable. Along with sexism/racism, there is dogmatism. Being a white leftist in Can-America is tantamount to joining the holy church of Karl Marx, the atheist. If that is contradictory and confusing, never mind; you have just experienced the illogic of the middle class—confusion is their general state of mind. Being an atheist does not mean that we ignore the very phenomenon which defines all things—spirit, essence. To possess a spirit is to be alive. It does mean that we strip spirit of its mystical cloak and look at it in the cold light of reality.

To acknowledge the existence of spirit, to say that it is spirit that defines a living thing, to say that spirit is the motive force governing every living thing is not equal to a belief in a Great Spirit, Supreme Being or God. To define Indian-ness, Native culture, through belief in mono-theism or a Great Spirit deity, is to blind yourself and confine all others to the narrow parameters of your own vision.

The body of a person in its death-state shrinks. From life to death, a person loses six or eight unaccounted-for pounds. I am no scientist, but logic tells me that the spirit has mass and weight. Science has not yet unravelled the mystery of the spirit; thus, no dollars are allocated to such research. This does not negate spirit's existence, it only shrouds it in mystery.

"I hear my grandmothers speak" is one remark which brings either howls of laughter or nervous looks of skepticism from the faces of most atheists and even Christians.

What is often attributed to creativity, I believe is more properly con-nected to spirit. Most poets agree. They will go to great lengths to achieve the inspiration necessary to write. Spiritualism is not a learned or bequeathed gift. It is natural to us all. It can, however, be obstructed and even crushed. It can also be harnessed. A person can be taught to reject its vitality. She or he can be prevented from making use of its potential. But spirit cannot be handed out. Only death causes spirit to depart from the body. "Indian doctoring" is the harnessing of spiritual energy. Our healing process is based on the assumption that illness, dis-ease, is inside the body. The whole of the body is ill. Healing will be done primarily through the spirit. Spirit and body join together against the illness. What Native medicine does is harness the reserve of spiritual strength to assist the body in purifying itself of the disease. All the methods of healing that Native doctors use are directed at purification. This makes sense if one considers that the major cause of disease is the presence of toxins and foreign bodies in the body.

I find it hard to believe that our people prayed before the days of conquest. To pray means "to beg, plead, beseech." It is my understanding that begging was against our ancient laws. Prayer is not synonymous with ceremony. Spiritual healing is referred to by many Native doctors as "putting our minds together to heal." That is not the equivalent of prayer. However, there is no word for this process in the English language. We then must make one up or integrate our own word into the language.

English does not express the process of ceremony. Yet, we are forced to communicate within its limits. We must differentiate and define our sense of spirituality in English.

I am going to defy orthodox science in the European sense, Marxism in every sense, and some of our own people whose spiritualism is limited to monotheistic prayer. I have no interest in being the scholar who researches the phenomenon of spiritual healing. I am not going to test its validity or even justify my experience with it. I will merely state that when I speak with my grandmothers before me, they answer. I do not believe in a Great Creator.

I believe that creation is and will remain a mystery until I die. To have some guy come along and tell me that the whole of creation rests on a mythical male creator, or a male monkey, is just too narrow a range of options for me. I am not an impatient person. I can wait until I depart the earth before presuming that I know the answer. Until then, I content myself with repeating something one of our ancestors understood about Europeans: "White men are arrogant; they think that while still living they can solve the great mystery."

I think that white people who indulgently refer to us as a spiritual people are unable to escape the chains of a parasitic culture. Parasites need a host to sustain them. They cannot sustain themselves. White people do not produce the stuff of life for white folk. Even in their own land, the majority of farm labourers are non-whites or children. Since white adults rarely work at productive labour that is physical, they cannot conceive of laboriously unravelling their bodily person and discovering their spirit within. They gape at us in the hope that through the process of osmosis they will acquire some sense of spirituality.

We bare our spirit naked for them that they might ingest some of it. After having robbed us of land, wealth and livelihood, they now want our spirit. And we strive to give it to them. Well, I don't remember my grandmother ever telling me that there was any virtue in surrendering my spirit, so I don't. For those white people who seek to discover their spiritual being I say: fast, walk in the mountains or on the bald prairie, bathe in the rivers, eat only what nature provides, sweat and rediscover your spirit. There is no easy route to spiritual re-birth.

Note

Originally published as "Another Side of Me," in I Am Woman: A Native Perspective on Sociology and Feminism, by Lee Maracle. Copyright © Press Gang Publishers 1996. Reprinted with permission of the publisher.

KRISTINA FAGAN

Tewatatha:wi: Aboriginal Nationalism in Taiaiake Alfred's *Peace, Power, Righteousness:* An Indigenous Manifesto

Kristina Fagan (b. 1973) is an assistant professor of English at the University of Saskatchewan. Her research focuses on aboriginal writing and storytelling. She has a long-term interest in exploring how new cultural and literary critical methodologies may be derived from oral traditions. Her current research examines autobiography and storytelling among her own community of the Labrador Métis.

In recent years the idea of Aboriginal nationalism has been creeping into public language in Canada through the widespread use of the term "First Nation." The idea that Aboriginal peoples are "Nations," not just "cultures," has also begun to influence the Canadian government, the courts, and the study of law and political science. The principle that Aboriginal peoples have the right and responsibility to determine their own paths is an ancient one, however. The Great Law of Peace of the Rotinohshonni, which is itself at least five hundred years old, claims the long history of this principle: "By birthright, the Onkwehonweh (Original Beings) are the owners of the soil which they own and occupy and none other shall hold it. The same law has been held from the oldest times."[1] The idea of Aboriginal nationalism has not significantly impacted the study of Aboriginal literatures, however, particularly in the territory known as Canada.[2] Canadian critics of Aboriginal literature have tended to look through the lenses of culture and colonialism. This article examines some of the shortcomings of these widespread approaches and explores the idea of thinking about Aboriginal literature in terms of Aboriginal nationalism. As a test case, I will read Taiaiake Alfred's *Peace, Power, Righteousness: An Indigenous Manifesto* in terms of its place within the Kanien'kehaka (more widely known as Mohawk) Nation and the Rotinohshonni (or Iroquois Confederacy).[3]

Criticism of Aboriginal literature in Canada has tended to divide the literature from concrete political issues of law, land ownership, and governance. I would like to begin with a story that demonstrates this division. Recently, during a Canadian literature course in which we repeatedly dealt with the idea of Canadian nationalism, I decided to include a segment on Aboriginal nationalism. I began the segment with two examples of traditional oral narratives, one by Ghandi, of the Haida Nation, and one by Angela Sidney, of the Tagish and Tlingit Nations.[4] Both of these texts depict the importance of an Aboriginal homeland and the difficulties of displacement from that homeland. Nearly all of the students in the class were non-Aboriginal, and these narratives were unfamiliar to them, both in terms of content and form. Nevertheless, they responded to the stories with enthusiasm and interest. We then moved to an editorial column by Taiaiake Alfred entitled "Who Are You Calling Canadian?"[5] In it Alfred argues that the people of the First Nations should not be considered citizens of Canada. The path of Canadian citizenship and equal opportunity, he says, has only led to the dilution of Aboriginal land claims, languages, and traditions. I was unprepared for the students' extreme negative reaction to this piece. Many students were angry, insisting that Aboriginal people were defeated and must accept the dominant nation's rules, while others argued for the Canadian cultural mosaic model into which Alfred, they said, should learn to fit.

While I saw all three texts as belonging to Aboriginal national traditions and as deeply political, the students clearly put the traditional stories and Alfred's editorial into different categories. They viewed the stories, I suspect, as interesting cultural artifacts that belong to Canada's past (though Sidney's story was recorded in the 1970s). Alfred's overtly political writing, on the other hand, was clearly contemporary and challenged many of the students' ideas about Canadian identity. In dividing Aboriginal culture from Aboriginal politics, the students were part of a widespread tendency in Canadian society. Investigating this tendency, Renee Hulan has surveyed Canadian media representations of Native people as well as reviews of Canadian Native literature and concludes that both tend to divide "Native culture" and "Native politics" into separate spheres.[6] Indeed, while critics of Aboriginal literature would of course be more sophisticated in their responses than my Canadian literature students, I would argue that the same kind of preferences and divisions can be seen in much of their work.

The "cultural" approach (sometimes called "culturalism") has been the most popular way of thinking about Aboriginal literature and identifying particular aspects of Aboriginal cultures (such as tricksters or medicine wheels) in a text.[7] Compared to "nation," however, "culture" can be a politically soft and shifty term. Our ideas about culture walk close to "folklore," associated with identifiable external symbols: distinctive clothing, food, housing, language, and so on. Canada has a long history of fascination with such symbols; they represent a non-challenging form of difference where Aboriginal peoples become yet another culture in the mosaic.

A potential problem with "culturalism" as an approach to Aboriginal literature is that it is often cut off from politics. As Cathryn McConaghy argues, categories of cultural difference are too often separated from "social, educational, and political contexts" as well as "disassociated from issues of class, gender, racialization and other forms of social analysis."[8] Métis writer Howard Adams sees this critical division of culture from politics as part of an effort by the dominant culture to depoliticize Aboriginal people by "stressing legends and myths . . . to direct Natives' attention away from revolutionary nationalism."[9] In the context of Aboriginal nationalism, indeed, focusing on markers of "culture" can allow people to avoid dealing with the underlying principle of nationhood and its concrete consequences. For instance, non-Aboriginal judges working in Aboriginal communities have been instructed in greater cultural sensitivity; however, such cultural issues do not address the fact that a foreign justice system has been imposed on Aboriginal nations. Similarly, criticism of Aboriginal literature, in persistently avoiding the topic of Aboriginal nationalism, is choosing to avoid a demanding political issue. As Craig Womack writes, "America loves Indian culture. America is much less enthusiastic about Indian land title."[10] I am not arguing that the maintenance of Aboriginal cultures is unimportant but rather that persistently focusing on culture over politics can be a way of disengaging from important parts of Aboriginal peoples and their literatures.

It may surprise some to hear the claim that the study of Native literature avoids politics when so much criticism in the area deals with questions of power and colonization. Literary scholars, however, have tended to stay away from specific political (with a big P) topics within Native literature, such as land ownership, law, and governance. They tend instead to focus on small-p politics, that is, on power relations and on large-scale issues such as colonization, sexism, and so forth. Of course, colonization and power are essential critical concepts, but they easily can also become vague terms that sidestep the complicated and distinct situations and demands of specific Native groups. While it is easy to understand general concepts of colonialism, it is much more difficult and time-consuming to learn about the specific traditions, languages, histories, and political priorities of particular First Nations. Moreover, while it is easy for non-Natives to decry generalized Native dispossession, it may be less easy to support Native people's specific claims to self-determination, claims that have material consequences.

The critical resistance to politically "strident" or activist works probably arises out of the current critical climate, one that is widely suspicious of truth claims. In this climate, it is not surprising that the idea of nation, which is based on claims to truth, identity, and unity, has largely come to be seen as naive. It is now a critical truism that, as Benedict Anderson famously argued, a nation has no natural basis, but is a figment of our collective imaginations, a way of giving a diverse, scattered, and fairly random group of people a sense of togetherness. But more than that, the idea of nationalism has come to be ethically suspect, widely seen as a way of masking injustice. Claudia Bell, writing about New Zealand nationalism, bluntly defines nationalism as "the politics that enables one culture to obliterate or assimilate another, through such processes as colonisation, genocide, and immigration policies."[11] Partly because of Aboriginal, Québecois, and various regional and ethnic claims, Canadian nationalism now seems highly problematic. Thus, Canada is widely referred to as a postmodern, or postnational, nation and Jonathan Kertzer is typical in beginning his recent study of Canadian literature with the assumption that "the very idea of the nation has been set in doubt."[12] Considering that this is a working assumption, it is not surprising that critics have been hesitant to approach the question of nationalism in Native literature. Confusion over what Aboriginal nationalism might mean may be another element in literary scholars' hesitance to use the concept. Canadian nationalism is based on a shared governmental structure and a presumably shared sense of national community, despite citizens' different national origins, races, ethnicities, regional identities, religions, and innumerable other forms of diversity. Aboriginal nationalism appears to be quite the opposite. The First Nations often do not have a government in place that reflects their status as nations. Each Aboriginal nation, however, does share a genetic connection, as well as a certain sense of a shared history and culture.[13]

I am not arguing that scholars should reject a postmodern critical framework for examining Aboriginal literature. I would suggest, however, that Aboriginal nationalism offers an approach that is more grounded in Aboriginal people's perspectives and values. Furthermore, given the limitations of culture and colonialism as ways to categorize and approach Native literature, I would argue that nationalism offers another meaningful option, one with a number of advantages.

For one, critically looking at the work of a particular Aboriginal nation immediately moves the critic into a realm of tribal, political, and very concrete and specific concerns. Very little criticism of Aboriginal literature in Canada has examined texts in terms of their specific national identity and culture. Once we begin to focus on a particular nation, however, we can begin to investigate its particular language, history, narrative structures, symbols, heroes, influential songs and stories, and so on.

For example, within the Rotinohshonni, the apparently simple words "house," "fire," and "tree" all have specific symbolic meanings and complex connotations, meanings that are not necessarily shared by other First Nations. This kind of specific knowledge, much of which is not crosstribal, can greatly enrich our understanding of works by Aboriginal authors.

Beyond being an eye-opening analytical tool, working with the concept of Aboriginal nationalism also moves critics into a politically charged space. Cree poet Louise Halfe once asked a group of Aboriginal literature critics why they were not out marching on the streets with Aboriginal activists.[14] The likely answer is that most work on Aboriginal literature, as I have argued, does not engage in concrete political issues. In contrast, Aboriginal nationalism involves specific political demands with which the critic must try to come to terms. If we choose to work with the concept of Aboriginal nationalism, we must consider to what extent we support Aboriginal nationalist claims. And if we do support those claims, what does that mean in terms of literary value? From an Aboriginal nationalist perspective, art should come out of a tribal and communal base. And it should work toward the defense of Aboriginal lands, resources, languages, and future, helping to build self-determining Aboriginal nations.

These concerns, in turn, will inevitably lead us to examine texts that have thus far received little literary attention. Within Aboriginal literature in Canada there is a strong tradition of tribal nationalism, particularly in tribal histories, oral traditions, nonfiction, and activist writings. This tradition, however, has been persistently ignored by critics in favor of more conventionally literary (read European literary) and more individualistic genres, such as novels, poetry, drama, and autobiography. This nearly exclusive attention to the "literary" genres, in turn, leads to analysis of individualistic and cultural, rather than collective and political, issues. Nonfictional, political, and "activist" works have been a significant part of Native literature and have been subject to as much creativity and formal innovation as other genres."[15] Yet scholars of Aboriginal literature have very rarely examined the argumentative nonfiction of Aboriginal writers. Robert Warrior, who is a notable exception to this generalization, agrees that Native people have been acknowledged as producers of literature and culture but rarely as critics.[16]

As a test case for how one might use the concept of Aboriginal nationalism within literary criticism, let us turn to Taiaiake Alfred's *Peace, Power, Righteousness: An Indigenous Manifesto*. Alfred is a Kanien'kehaka traditionalist and a supporter of the Rotinohshonni. I want to argue that we can place *Peace, Power, Righteousness* within the traditions of the Rotinohshonni and the Kanien'kehaka Nations.

Alfred's book is indeed a manifesto, and his argument has been the subject of much contention. In short, Alfred claims that most Aboriginal leaders have sold out. These leaders, he says, may put on some of the trappings of tradition, but they have achieved personal power by working within the colonial system. Under such leadership Aboriginal nations may achieve a degree of power through Canadian-controlled Aboriginal rights, treaties, self-government agreements, and economic development. According to Alfred, however, this path entails nations giving up their true source of power in the Indigenous sense, power that is achieved only through adherence to Indigenous traditions. Thus, he calls for a new kind of leader, one that takes a contentious attitude to colonial structures and is committed to traditions of Aboriginal autonomy.

Alfred's sense of what "Aboriginal autonomy" means is grounded in his Kanien'kehaka upbringing. The Kanien'kehaka conception of nationhood has been formed by their place within the Rotinohshonni, a confederation of six Aboriginal nations. A Wendat (Huron) man, known in English as "the Peacemaker," founded the confederacy long before European contact and established "The Great Law of Peace," a massive oral text. Under the guidance of the Great Law, the Rotinohshonni developed a powerful and elaborate system of governance, with fifty chiefs, fifty clan mothers, and a consensus based political process. While in the eyes of the Canadian government band councils now run the various Iroquois communities, the Rotinohshonni government is still very much in business and supported by a large portion of the communities.

With its large population, agricultural settlements, and elaborate formal laws, the Rotinohshonni is extremely different from, for instance, the northern Cree nations who were traditionally hunter-gatherers and lived in much smaller family-based groups. Because of such differences, problems arise when we try to find a definition of nationhood that is appropriate to all Aboriginal nations. Often the words used to express nationhood in English have no equivalent in Native languages, and, furthermore, the word means different things to different peoples. Audra Simpson, a Kanien'kehaka anthropologist, describes the debate over what the word means as a "tired point," saying, "we are all different people, different nations, and would have different ideas about what nationhood is and what it means to us. The Sechelt conception or Northern Cree conception will certainly depart from Mohawk ideas about who we are. Each people will have a term in their own language that will mean 'us.' I think that is what our concept of nationhood is."[17]

The Kanien'kehaka have no word for nationalism per se. According to both Alfred and another Kanien'kehaka writer, Patricia Monture-Angus, the closest equivalent is the word "tewatatha:wi," meaning "we carry ourselves," or according to another translation, "We take care of ourselves." "Tewatatha:wi" tells us more about literary forms of nationalism than can be learned from static nouns such as "nation" and will guide how I will approach the analysis of nationalism in Alfred's text. The idea that "we" must do the carrying emphasizes the idea of community and collectivity; a nationalist writer never writes fully for him or herself. The verb "to carry" points to responsibility; what must be carried is one's people, their history, their stories, their traditions. And the fact that this is a verb-based phrase reminds us that Aboriginal nationalism is not just an idea but an action. In examining the values of community, responsibility, and action, I attempt to move away from a superficial look at symbols of traditionalism to explore traditional principles and values.

"We Carry Ourselves": Community

The English literary tradition is often focused on the individual: his or her struggles, triumphs, and reflections. So how does one write in order to place the focus on the community instead—as Aboriginal nationalist writers wish to do? The Kanien'kehaka language actually offers a model for how to reflect the importance of community. As Kanien'kehaka writer Brian Maracle describes the language, "Only when the individual is placed in context does the individual appear."[18] Maracle goes on to use the analogy of a movie shot where we see a stretch of forest with a river running through it, then the camera focuses more closely on the river, then on a canoe in the river, and finally on the man in the canoe.[19] In the same way, he explains, the Kanien'kehaka language begins with the context before moving to the subject. The structure of Alfred's text is similar to this linguistic structure; he situates himself within the context of a community of voices before moving to himself or his particular concerns. He begins with a passage from the Great Law of Peace—the original text of the Rotinohshonni. He then moves to a passage from the "Thanksgiving Address," which is spoken at the beginning of all Rotinohshonni ceremonies and explicitly brings all people together as "one mind."[20] This section places Alfred in thankful relation to all elements of creation. He then zooms in further to thank the many people who helped him with his book. Even as he finally moves to speak of himself, Alfred positions himself within the community: "It will become abundantly clear that I am Onkwehone, shaped by my upbringing in Kahnawake and my political life among the Rotinohshonni."[21]

Throughout his text Alfred continues to mingle his voice with those of others. In fact, we could think of this writing technique as one of conversation with the Aboriginal community. Alfred writes, he says, with "a self-imposed demand for accessibility, particularly among Native people."[22] His first book, *Heeding the Voices of Our Ancestors*, was a conventional academic study, but with *Peace, Power, Righteousness* we can see him moving toward a more accessible and explicitly political form. He is also in conversation with Aboriginal people within his work, including long quotations from various elders, from the Condolence Ritual, and from the Great Law, as well as four lengthy conversations with other Aboriginal thinkers.

Alfred's use of conversation is specifically linked to his nation's political traditions. Leaders of the Rotinohshonni must converse together until they reach consensus. The belief is that, through rational thought and discussion, the chiefs will eventually arrive at the best shared truth for the community. Clearly then, communication, argument, persuasion, and debate are central to the functioning of the confederacy. So within the Rotinohshonni political power lies not in force but in persuading others of your point of view: "For a people convinced that their vision of peace [through rational debate and consensus-building] can save the world from strife and conflict by restoring harmony and balance, the development of powerful oratorical abilities is imperative."[23] In fact, Alfred's first conversation in the text seems to be primarily a demonstration of his own oratorical abilities: a transcription of him orally explaining to an unnamed friend the way in which the Condolence Ritual parallels the themes of his book.[24] With this section, which is a monologue rather than a dialogue, we can see Alfred taking on the role of leader by carefully and deliberately speaking his truth.

Alfred also records extensive conversations with a Kwa'kwala'wakw woman activist, with a young female Kanien'kehaka graduate student, with Sioux philosopher Vine Deloria, and with a traditional Kanien'kehaka leader named Atsenhaienton, thus consulting with both young and old, male and female, as is necessary to achieve community consensus. Alfred describes this responsibility for wide consultation as a "requirement for universal inclusion and the maintenance of strong links between those charged with the responsibility of decision-making and those who will have to live with the consequences of their decisions."[25] All of these conversations are notably agreeable, with the participants sharing basic assumptions about nationhood. Alfred expresses his own views at some length, and the speakers are clearly responding to each others' ideas. For instance, in conversation with a Kwa'kwala'wakw woman on the loss of traditional Indigenous principles, after a long discussion of their own communities' distinct issues, they come to a moment of consensus, echoing one another's thoughts. The woman speaks of the danger of being pacified by the Canadian government's $58 million Royal Commission Report on Aboriginal People, and it reminds her of an element of the Rotinohshonni Condolence Ritual that Alfred has described:

> Watch out for what is it again?
> "Beware the magic."
> The magic, and the lurking dangers.[26]

The transcription of the conversation ends here, thus emphasizing the two thinkers' arrival at a shared conclusion. In this sense Alfred is recreating on paper the way in which consensus building would have traditionally worked among the Rotinohshonni where all community members would have had their own ideas, but where they would also have shared basic assumptions about the organization and governance of their society. This shared base is why consensus building worked for the Rotinohshonni in precontact times and also why it is so difficult today, now that those shared assumptions have been undermined.

In writing an expository and argumentative text, Alfred is upholding Rotinohshonni traditional beliefs. As explained earlier, the Rotinohshonni is founded on the belief that all human beings possess the power of rational thought and, if used, that power will inevitably move people toward peace. Furthermore, since decisions must be made through group consensus, the only way a person can have influence within that system is to convince others. Hence, the ability to argue rationally and convincingly is at the centre of the Rotinohshonni system of value. Alfred writes in the argumentative tradition of great Kanien'kehaka orators such as Thayendanegea (Joseph Brant), Oronhyatekha (Peter Martain), and E. Pauline Johnson. While some may see his tone as angry or adversarial, his people see argument as the path to peace: "Active and fractious disagreement is a sign of health in a traditional system."[27] This may help us understand why Alfred is so harshly critical of current Aboriginal leaders—intense criticism is how leaders of his people were traditionally held accountable.

In addition to selecting a traditional genre, Alfred also structures *Peace, Power, Righteousness* around a practice of his people—the Condolence Ritual. This ritual is held when a chief of the Rotinohshonni dies, and it is intended to serve two functions. The first is to encourage the spirit of the dead to go to the Creator and not be tempted to linger on earth among his friends and family, causing further sickness and death. The second purpose is to reconcile the living to the death, to free them from excessive grief so that they can live in peace. This ritual is particularly appropriate to Alfred's argument about Aboriginal leadership. He feels that Aboriginal communities have lost most of their strong, traditional leaders; current leaders, he argues, have largely bought into the Canadian-imposed system of band councils, leaving behind Aboriginal political principles and processes. This loss, he says, has caused grief and confusion in Aboriginal communities, and there is a danger that people will continue to be haunted by it. The Condolence Ritual thus offers a way for Alfred to try to help Aboriginal communities put aside their grief and make way for a new generation of traditional leaders. He moves through the ritual stage by stage and interprets each as having symbolic significance in the current political situation. For example, the ritual involves the wiping of the eyes, clearing of the throat, and unblocking of the ears.[28] In the same way, he writes, we must open our eyes to the problems in Aboriginal communities. By re-enacting the Condolence Ritual, Alfred is doing more than wishing for his community to heal; he is, within the traditions of his community, making it so.

"We Carry Ourselves": Action

Arguing that a text can function as a ritual reminds us that a written work is not only an object but also an interaction between a writer and a reader, an event with real-life consequences. This view is in keeping with the oral tradition, where a song, prayer, or chant can, for example, cure or cause an illness. In this tradition, we can think of *Peace, Power, Righteousness* as an act of nation building. And, as Oren Lyons of the Six Nations states emphatically, nationalism is a series of such actions, not a thing: "Sovereignty is the act. Sovereignty is the do. You act."[29] The idea that writing can be an action with political effect is clearly important to Alfred. He writes extensively for Aboriginal newspapers, trying to stir up change within his own community. And he was, at one time, a speech-writer for Matthew Coon Come, then Chief of the Assembly of First Nations. The influence of speech writing, in fact, seems audible in the last words of the book, which are a call to action: "These words are a manifesto, a challenge, and a call to action. Don't preserve tradition, live it! Let us develop a good mind and do what is necessary to heal the damage done to us and bring back to life the culture of peace power righteousness that is the indigenous way."[30] With this commanding tone, Alfred is also echoing the imperatives that make up the Great Law of Peace.

Despite the fact that Alfred is clearly action-oriented, however one of the criticisms that has been brought against him is that his argument, because it is focused on leaders, is not grounded in the lives of the majority of Aboriginal people. For instance, while he argues that Aboriginal people must "live" their traditions, he gives very few examples of what this would mean in practice. He also gives virtually no examples from his own experiences in trying to live the principles that he pronounces. This emphasis on philosophy over practice becomes especially striking when we compare his book to those of two other Kanien'kehaka nationalist writers, Brian Maracle and Patricia Monture-Angus—both of whose writing embraces the idea that the personal is political. While both Maracle and Monture-Angus believe, like Alfred, that their people should be self governed by the Rotinohshonni, their personal experiences in trying to implement and live such a governance keep their views complicated and continually qualified. Maracle, for instance, admits that he idealized the Rotinohshonni before he actually lived on the Six Nations Reserve. Now, while still a believer, he is nevertheless critical of the slow pace of the confederacy and their lack of impact on everyday reserve life.[31] Monture-Angus similarly contemplates the difficulty in fitting her political principles with life on her husband's reserve. For example, she describes her idea that people on the reserve should, as an act of sovereignty, try to deal with crime within their own community whenever possible rather than turning to the RCMP (the Canadian police force). Yet when her own son was assaulted by someone in power within the band government, she felt she had no choice but to go to the police.[32] These are the kinds of tensions that emerge from the complexity of real life—tensions with which Alfred chooses not to deal. As a result, his argument often seems overly simplistic; Aboriginal people are presented as either traditional nationalists, or assimilated sellouts. For most Aboriginal people, I would suggest, the issue is not so black and white. As Joyce Green writes, Alfred's nationalist model does not address "the syncretic nature of cultures . . . and of the many contingent choices individuals make in their cultural selections," and she worries that such an argument has the potential to become "oppressive fundamentalist formulations."[33]

Alfred himself admits that his views are quite different from those of 95 percent of Aboriginal people in Canada.[34] The Rotinohshonni style of nationalism is unique. This is in part because Iroquois communities still have a functioning traditional government that many people see as more valid than the band councils (in fact, on the Six Nations Reserve, less than 10 percent voted in the 1993 band council election).[35] Furthermore, Atsenhaienton claims that a nationalist stance is deeply embedded in his people: "it's culturally within the makeup of our people because of our constitution, our state of mind, our worldview that we look at ourselves as an independent people."[36] And the Kanien'kehaka in particular were deeply impacted by a prolonged and violent standoff in Oka, Quebec, in 1990, leading to great anger toward the federal government and a strong stirring of Kanien'kehaka nationalism. It would be a mistake to look for Alfred's style of nationalism in Aboriginal writers from across Canada.

This is not to say, however, that Alfred cannot be seen as part of a literary tradition; we can see him as writing within a Kanien'kehaka tradition that includes writers such as Brian Maracle, Patricia Monture-Angus, Beth Brant, Maurice Kenny, and Michael Doxtater, as well as visual artists such as filmmaker Shelley Niro and painter Bill Powless. All of these artists draw on Kanien'kehaka cultural symbols; they are creating the art of their nation. As Brant writes: "We do not write as individuals communing with a muse. We write as members of an ancient cultural consciousness. Our 'muse' is us. Our muse is our ancestors."[37] The most famous Kanien'kehaka writer is certainly E. Pauline Johnson who, before her death in 1913, was one of the most famous and successful poets in Canada. Much critical attention has been paid to how Johnson carefully constructed her public image as an Aboriginal woman, but very little has been written on her as a Kanien'kehaka writer, despite the fact that, according to Brant, "Johnson belonged to only one Nation, the Mohawk Nation."[38] Johnson herself complained that Canadian writers were not competent to recognize tribal characteristics:[39]

> The term "Indian" signifies about as much as the term "European," but I cannot recall ever having read a story where the heroine was described as "European." The Indian girl we meet in cold type, however, is rarely distressed by having to belong to any tribe, or to reflect any tribal characteristics. She is merely a wholesome sort of mixture of any band existing between the Mic Macs of Gaspe and the Kwaw-Kewiths of British Columbia, yet strange to say, that notwithstanding the numerous tribes, with their aggregate numbers reaching more that 122,000 souls in Canada alone, our Canadian authors can cull from this huge revenue of character, but one Indian girl.[40]

Over a century has passed since Johnson wrote these words, but among Canadian literary critics little has changed. There is still a lack of awareness of and lack of willingness to investigate the specificity of Native people. There is a need for more research that views Aboriginal literature in terms of specific First Nations traditions.

As I have shown, viewing Taiaiake Alfred's work in terms of his place within his nation offers us a way to understand his writing, not just his ideas, and to see him as creatively engaged in a tradition, though not one that is conventionally literary. Furthermore, we can see him not only as "culturally" Kanien'kehaka but as an active member of his nation, acting on its principles and invoking change. As he comments, "It's all just folklore unless you act on it."[41]

Notes

Originally published as "Tewatatha:wi: Aboriginal Nationalism in Taiaiake Alfred's *Peace, Power, Righteousness: An Indigenous Manifesto*," in *American Indian Quarterly* 28.1–2 (2004): 12–29. Copyright © 2004 The University of Nebraska Press. All rights reserved.

1. "The Iroquois Constitution," A Chronology of U.S. Historical Documents, University of Oklahoma Law Center, http://www.law.ou.edu/hist/iroquois.html (accessed January 2003).
2. I use the word "Canada" in this article, but, in doing so, I do not wish to efface the claim of other nations to the land commonly known as Canada.
3. Taiaiake Alfred, *Peace, Power, Righteousness: An Indigenous Manifesto* (Don Mills, Ont.: Oxford University Press, 1999).
4. Ghandi, "There Was a Child of Good Family," in *A Story as Sharp as a Knife*, ed. and

trans. Robert Bringhurst (Vancouver: Douglas and McIntyre, 1999), 33–44; Angela Sidney, "Kaax'achgóok," in *The Social Life of Stories: Narrative and Knowledge in the Yukon Territory*, ed. Julie Cruikshank (Vancouver: University of British Columbia Press, 1998), 28–35.

5. Taiaiake Alfred, "Who Are You Calling Canadian?" *Eastern Door Newspaper*, September 1, 2000, 4.

6. Renee Hulan, "Cultural Contexts for the Reception of Marilyn Dumont's *A Really Good Brown Girl*," *Journal of Canadian Studies* 35.3 (2000): 73.

7. See Cathryn McConaghy, *Rethinking Indigenous Education: Culturalism, Colonialism, and the Politics of Knowing* (Flaxton, Australia: Post Pressed, 2000), for discussion of "culturalism."

8. Ibid., 43–44.

9. Howard Adams, *A Tortured People: The Politics of Colonization* (Penticton, B.C.: Theytus, 1995), 103.

10. Craig Womack, *Red on Red: Native American Literary Separatism* (Minneapolis: University of Minnesota Press, 1999), 11.

11. Benedict Anderson, *Imagined Communities: Reflections on the Origin and Spread of Nationalism* (London: Verso, 1983).

12. Jonathan Kertzer, *Worrying the Nation: Imagining a National Literature in English Canada* (Toronto: University of Toronto Press, 1998), 5. On Canada as a postnational nation, see Daniel Francis, *National Dreams: Myth, Memory, and Canadian History* (Vancouver: Arsenal Pulp, 1997), 108–10.

13. For more on different ways of conceptualizing nationalism, including nationalism that is not state based, see Alfred's *Heeding the Voices of Our Ancestors: Kahnawake Mohawk Politics and the Rise of Native Nationalism* (Toronto: Oxford University Press, 1995), 8–12.

14. Louise Halfe, Roundtable discussion on Aboriginal literature, Congress of Social Sciences and Humanities, Edmonton, Alberta, May 1999.

15. For example, in Canada Aboriginal writers who write nonfiction (not including traditional stories and autobiographies) and activist writing include Howard Adams, Marie Battiste, Harold Cardinal, Roland ChrisJohn, Olive Patricia Dickason, Sakej Henderson, Brian Maracle, Patricia Monture-Angus, George Sioui, and Drew Hayden Taylor, to name a few of many.

16. Robert Allen Warrior, *Tribal Secrets: Recovering American Indian Intellectual Traditions* (Minneapolis: University of Minnesota Press, 1995), xvi.

17. Alfred, *Peace, Power, Righteousness*, 65.

18. Brian Maracle, *Back on the Rez: Finding the Way Home* (Toronto: Viking, 1996), 264.

19. Ibid., 263.

20. Ibid., 295.

21. Alfred, *Peace, Power, Righteousness*, xix.

22. Ibid., xxiv.

23. Ibid., xix.

24. Ibid., xx–xxiii.

25. Ibid., 91.

26. Ibid., 34.

27. Ibid., 92.

28. Ibid., xx.

29. Patricia Monture-Angus, *Journeying Forward: Dreaming First Nations Independence* (Halifax: Fernwood, 1999), 38.

30. Alfred, *Peace, Power, Righteousness*, 145.

31. Maracle, *Back on the Rez*, 206–10.

32. Monture-Angus, *Journeying Forward*, 162.

33. Joyce Green, *Cultural and Ethnic Fundamentalism: The Mixed Potential for Identity, Liberation, and Oppression*. The Scholar Series, Saskatchewan Institute of Public Policy (Regina, Sas.: University of Regina, 2003), 16–17.

34. Alfred, *Peace, Power, Righteousness*, 113.

35. Maracle, *Back on the Rez*, 25.

36. Alfred, *Peace, Power, Righteousness*, 113.

37. Beth Brant, *Writing as Witness: Essays and Talk* (Toronto: Women's Press, 1994), 10.

38. Ibid., 7.

39. E. Pauline Johnson, "A Strong Race Opinion on the Indian Girl in Modern Fiction" (1892), in *Postcolonialism: Critical Concepts in Literary and Cultural Studies*, ed. Diana Brydon (London: Routledge, 2000), 997.

40. Ibid., 992.

41. Alfred, *Peace, Power, Righteousness*, 11.

LEN FINDLAY

Always Indigenize! The Radical Humanities in the Postcolonial Canadian University

Len Findlay is a professor of English and the director of the Humanities Research Unit at the University of Saskatchewan. Educated at Aberdeen and Oxford, he came to Canada in 1974. Widely published in nineteenth-century European topics and increasingly in Canadian studies, his recent work includes a new edition of *The Communist Manifesto* (2004), "Spectres of Canada: Image, Text, Aura, Nation" (*University of Toronto Quarterly*, 2006), and collaborative projects for the *Australian Journal of Aboriginal Education* and for the Office of the Treaty Commission of Saskatchewan. He is currently writing an intellectual biography of Alexander Morris.

The word itself, research, is probably one of the dirtiest words in the
indigenous world's vocabulary.
—Linda Smith, *Decolonizing Methodologies*

I'm not human. I'm an Indian.
—Alphonsine, three-year-old daughter of Judge Mary Ellen Turpel-Lafond,
as told by her mother

This essay is in four parts. The first part deals with the form and force of
the exhortation, *Always Indigenize!* The second part offers no single solution to the struggle for justice inside and outside universities but instead
suggests the doublet *vision and conspiracy*, as a way of taking advantage of
millennial dependencies in governments and elite institutions while recognizing that such dependencies exist within neo-paternalistic structures designed to be perceived as ethical and inclusive while practicing
an oppressive and contradictory politics of difference. The third part
argues for the radical humanities as a crucial piece of the decolonizing
puzzle and offers an example of the kind of critique that non-Indigenous

scholars should undertake as one element in their contribution to the Indigenization process. And finally, I turn more particularly to the discipline of English within the grand narrative of English as a world language, a narrative constantly and uncontrollably interrupted and abducted by both native and non-native speakers in familiar as well as exotic settings. Here I argue for a more concertedly activist disciplinarity which will have at its centre new alliances between English literary studies and Indigenous studies. This argument, like the exhortation always to Indigenize, gestures towards rather than guarantees a particular future. In transforming each other through new rapprochements and *articulations* that both express and connect in strategically contingent ways,[1] academic English and Indigenous studies can help transform the institutions that house them and the publics which fund them, but only if "we" work together to make that happen.

Always Indigenize!

In the (human) beginning was the Indigene. This hypothesis is a necessary but inscrutable pretext for the historical and current distribution of our species in diverse groupings across the globe. With oral and written histories of a recoverable past have come difference and conflict, competing versions of residency, conquest, settlement, entitlement, and the limited circulation and decidedly mixed benefits of Indigenous status. It seems fair to say that all communities live as, or in relation to, Indigenes. And so there seems a general warrant for supplementing Fredric Jameson's famous exhortation, "Always historicize,"[2] with *always Indigenize.* In so Indigenizing, however, we should bear in mind James Chandler's recent demonstration of how unclear and general Jameson's urging to historicize is and how divergently it has been interpreted by literary scholars.[3] And we should also clarify at the outset who the "we" in question are and how they stand in relation to Indigenousness and its increasingly explicit protocols of self-determination and self-representation.

The employment of the English language to express a sentiment like "Always Indigenize!" that may have important consequences for Indigenous peoples, in Canada and elsewhere, is neither innocent nor "merely" practical. But the dangers of Anglocentric presumption are perhaps offset somewhat by the form this exhortation takes, specifying no particular addressee, definition, or outcome, but instead promoting participation in an activity whose nature and consequences will depend on who is listening and how they understand and act upon what they hear or read. It can be understood as an allusive command to include Indigeneous issues within the broader and more "developed" project of Western Marxism. It can be understood as academic vanguardism playing variations on its own dearest illusions about what it can make happen. Or it can be heard, as I intend it to be heard, as a strategically indeterminate provocation to thought and action on the grounds that there is no *hors-Indigene*, no geo-political or psychic setting, no real or imagined *terra nullius* free from the satisfactions and unsettlements of Indigenous (pre)occupation. The necessity and difficulty of Indigenizing is therefore no global shell game involving entities and essences that come and go according to sleight of hand or mind or cartographic ruse but an overdetermined play of forces and processes that produce particular determinate moments subjected in their turn to contestation and change. Indigenizing today is undertaken in face of the realities and dangers of "aggravated inequality,"[4] the fact that development's twin continues to be underdevelopment, and the reality that the emergence of a so-called new economy has so far altered little the only too predictable global distribution of poison and prosperity.

Having drawn in a general way on deconstruction for some of my comments so far on Indigenizing, let me now turn to an Indigenous authority to frame what follows more firmly and prescriptively. The Maori educational theorist Linda Tuhiwai Smith has just published a powerful book, *Decolonizing Methodologies: Research and Indigenous Peoples*, which provides what Terry Goldie, for example, lacked (and mourned) in his analysis of the reified and commodified Indigene within white-settler semiotic economies.[5] Smith's work deserves to inspire other Indigenous scholars and to direct the efforts of non-Indigenous colleagues. She defines Indigenization variously as demystification, recentering, "researching back," "rewriting and rerighting," as multi-level and counter-hegemonic, and as "inevitably political" and connected to "broader politics and strategic goals." Smith identifies Indigenizing with the processes of "decolonization, healing, transformation, and mobilization" and with "Twenty-Five Indigenous Projects."[6] There is clearly much work to be done, and to be done according to an Indigenous division of labour which simultaneously employs and critiques the division of labour's Euro-imperial and now transnational corporate agenda. This double strategy of working with and against, defining by connection and by difference, suggests that, despite Linda Smith's approving citation of Audre Lorde, some of the master's most important tools—like the domestic and international division of labour—*can* be used "to dismantle the master's house," though not if they are the only tools used and if they remain within dominant patterns of ownership of the means of production.[7]

Vision and Conspiracy

Canadian universities have made *some* progress in the last two decades in moderating their traditional Eurocentrism. That Eurocentrism has for more than a century been underpinned by two related fictions which, in their most extreme forms, are captured in the doctrines of *terra nullius* (empty land) and *scientific objectivity*.[8] The legal, religious, political, and cultural armatures of colonization constantly circulated the notion that Canada was an *empty land*: empty, that is to say, in the sense of being largely uninhabited, or empty of any social organization capable of meeting European standards for the fully "human."[9] At the same time, European colonization came to depend on an ever more ascendant science and technology to ensure the profitability of its civilizing mission. Commercial society extended its domains and enhanced its profit margins in part by using science and technology to reinforce stereotypes of Canada's First Nations as hostile to or incapable of participating in modernity and hence ripe for assimilation or elimination. This stark picture of greed and genocide needs to be modified in light of the treaties signed between (often competing) colonizing powers and the First Nations, but much of the modification to date has attempted to reconceal, minimize, sanitize, or even justify colonial practices radically at variance with Canada's professed sense of itself, domestically and internationally.

The consequence of academic complicity with colonialism has been a massive and persistent deficit in the national understanding of the rights of Indigenous peoples and the value and potential relevance of Indigenous knowledge to economic prosperity and social justice in Canada. The Canadian academy continues to face a formidable challenge in self-education and public education in this area. The academy must therefore begin anew to decolonize its traditional presumptions, curricula, faculty complement and student body, and research and teaching practices, and do so more radically and more rapidly than hitherto.

But where do we begin (again)? How do we proceed? Who are the "we" in question, and why? And how can scholars best record and most effectively share the most successful decolonizing practices across disciplines, institutions, regions? One might decide to start where one might presume progress most likely, "enlightenment" most assured—namely, in the humanities. And such a presumption could find support in the massive outpouring across the world recently of creative and scholarly work dealing with or claiming to exemplify one or another version of the postcolonial.[10] Yet Canadian universities, despite (or because of) their crucial role in producing and responding to social change, have not themselves featured very prominently as an object of anti-colonial or actively decolonizing inquiry (compared, for instance, with the case of India in, say, Symonds, Viswanathan, and Majeed).[11] Alas, more often than not Canadian universities have been seen (and seen themselves to be) sites of feuding about so-called political correctness,[12] feuding which coexists as a distraction or embarrassment beside a wide range of traditional disciplinary activities which are assumed or asserted to be "objective." Canadian universities remain complicitous with residually colonial and defiantly neo-colonial policies and practices that continue to produce Indigenous academic "homelessness" and that define what counts as knowledge and who will benefit from its acquisition and exercise, while the beneficiaries and casualties of colonialism stay much the same as they have always been.[13]

Of course, colonialism has a particular history within and across all disciplines, old and new, and it is not only theology and law and genetics that need to hang their heads when invited to return the increasingly emboldened gaze of Canada's First Nations, and Inuit and Métis peoples who are currently "looking white people in the eye."[14] Professedly objective methods have brought many benefits to Canada, but only at a price—a price that has been paid disproportionately by so-called surplus populations standing inconveniently in the way of "progress" and "development." The claim to objectivity, whether made in published form or from a podium, habitually depends on formulations and explorations of research questions that play down or attempt to suspend socio-political determinants without ever fully or permanently erasing evidence of their agency. Elite institutions are still much too implicated in inappropriate presumptions and practices which in effect replay colonial encounters in the names of excellence, integration, modernity, and so on (as part of a more general threat to difference posed by the "University of Excellence").[15] The persistence of this reality, despite abundant good will and public commitments by universities to Indigenous issues, recalls a similar discrepancy between the institutions' professed enthusiasm for interdisciplinarity and the zealous and narrow disciplinary nature of most of their teaching and research. These related discrepancies suggest an analogous solution in Indigenously-led, strategic interdisciplinarity which draws on the fluid, permeable, holistic features of Indigenous knowledge to suspend or renegotiate academic territoriality (and the property regimes that underpin it).[16] We may still in general be far short of a *postpaternalistic* research and teaching agenda centred in and productively addressing the concerns of Indigenous peoples and the conceptual and practical deficits and disfigurements in the residually colonial or aggressively biotechnologizing, neo-colonial Canadian academy. However, Linda Smith offers very constructive as well as sobering advice for the development of new academic and more broadly social formations involving "non-indigenous activists and intellectuals" while "centr[ing] a politics of indigenous identity and indigenous cultural action."[17]

Following Smith's advice, we may be able to produce and reproduce the conditions of possibility of innovative, non-appropriative, ethical cross-cultural research, postcolonial institutional ethnographies, and a juster understanding and achievement of the strategic as such. But what counts as strategy here, as strategic research and teaching in particular, and how does it connect to postcolonial notions like "strategic essentialism" as understood and practiced by Gayatri Spivak, Sherene Razack, and others? What might strategic interdisciplinarity look like in future? Such questions seem to me straightforward in the context of Indigenization, because essentialism is "the galvanizing idiom of insurgency but the lethal accomplice of hegemony,"[18] and not fully allowable when the Indigenizing is being undertaken by the non-Indigenous academic collaborator rather than the insurgent Indigene. Outsider essentializing of Indigenous history and cultural practices must be respectfully strategic rather than presumptuously exotic, and driven by the need to benefit Indigenous people according to their lights, needs, and aspirations. Non-Indigenous learning which crosses disciplines and cultures but remains unidirectional cannot avoid reinscribing diffusionist colonialism and the only too predictable classification of polymaths and primitives, masters and servants.

There is no single remedy for the problems of colonialism, neo-colonialism, and the prematurely postcolonial. The (re)doubling remedies I propose deliberately eschew singularity by attempting to be always constructive as well as deconstructive, addressing both a deficiency and an oppressive reality. By invoking *vision* as the first term in my doublet here, I point to the fact that millennial federalism in Canada is conceptually challenged, woefully lacking in vision (as well as literal and metaphorical millennial fireworks!), the proliferation of institutional and official "vision statements" notwithstanding. Indigenizing vision can be of enormous benefit to all people, as will be more evident once Marie Battiste's new collection of essays is published. Whether one is thinking of new pedagogies or sustainability, or institutional internationalization, or other topical issues, Indigenous knowledge can be an invaluable resource, if only in the first instance on its own terms. As we seek new national imaginaries in the new millennium, while federal budgetary surpluses melt away in the reactive restitution of things as they (arguably) were, publicly funded institutions will be looked to for inspiration, guidance—in sum for *content* for new information networks and a freshly skeletal cyber-state. Universities, meanwhile, will be doomed to recycle the neo-imperialist platitudes of *Star Trek* as *their* vision, unless they act on their obscured dependency on Indigenous vision and knowledge. Such vision honours the Other of Eurocentric, instrumental reason while exposing the latter's arbitrariness and connections to injustice. Such vision is available in the traditional teachings of Indigenous peoples, though no longer as part of the larcenous practice of "trading the Other";[19] it is available also in colonial forms of hybridization and resistance such as the ledger drawings readable by non-Indigenous scholars;[20] and it is perhaps most compellingly available as mobilization and critique in such strategic Indigenizing of Canadian identity as Sharilyn Calliou's "Peacekeeping Actions at Home: A Medicine Wheel Model for a Peacekeeping Pedagogy," or the strategic traditionalism of J. Y. Henderson's "Postcolonial Ghost Dancing."[21]

In contrast to vision, *conspiracy* may seem to pose problems associated with aversion rather than narrowly instrumental understanding. Conspiracy may seem like the wrong term for facilitating new solidarities and coalitions across the Indigenous/non-Indigenous line. Indeed, it may seem to concede too much in a self-incriminating way. However, I prefer it to a more positive term like *concert* from which Victor Ramraj elicits such power in his recent collection of *World Literature Writing in English*. Ramraj convenes and skillfully plays up commonality while respecting difference and promoting imagination as one of politics' invaluable Others. In contrast to Ramraj's emphases in what is an even-handed but not at all a wishy-washy introductory anthology, I am more concertedly political in aiming to mobilize difference as dissonance and dissent against the dominant ideology which so often presents itself as social and other forms of harmony—whether in readings of Ulysses' great speech on social degree in *Troilus and Cressida*[22] or Sir William Jones's export to Bengal of the idea of "the great *orchestra* of the nation."[23]

Another reason for preferring conspiracy to concert may lie in the latter's source in Ramraj's epigraph from Geoffrey Hartman, whom I will take to task in the next section of this essay. More importantly, however, I wish to rehabilitate conspiracy as a valuable term for articulating resistance by aligning its Indigenization with the so-called "Pontiac Conspiracy" of which Francis Parkman wrote so revealingly and influentially in 1851, a conspiracy explicitly and prominently linked to the deeply problematic notion of "the Conquest of Canada." In the Preface to the sixth (1870) edition of this his first historical work, Parkman reaffirms its value as a portrait of "forest life and the Indian character" within which the use of smallpox and rum as official means of pacifying Indigenous peoples is thought "sufficiently startling."[24] From the outset, however, Parkman worked from the conviction that he was writing of "the American forest and the American Indian at the period when both received their *final* doom."[25] And he was writing in a tradition that had already firmly racialized conspiracy in the so-called New York Conspiracy or Negro Plot of 1741–1742,[26] a tradition that has received a "fresh lease on life" in the United States today in the prejudging and demonizing of marginal groups thought to threaten dominant American interests at home and abroad.[27]

In endeavouring to rehabilitate conspiracy as a necessary strategic step on the way from the Indigenous margin toward the academic centre, I wish to invoke especially the history of Pontiac even while running the risk of new, conspiratorial knowledge-coalitions being mistaken for the work of the Michigan Militia and their ilk. What I am proposing is not conspiracy marked by silence, secrecy, violence, and hate, but linked instead to vigorous self-representation and to a very public process of envisioning, and then achieving, a thoroughly Indigenized future for all citizens. Indigenous insurgency may be driven to, but not necessarily driven by, conspiracy. Official academic channels remain inadequate and zealously self-sustaining in the name of tradition, academic freedom, and institutional autonomy.[28] How otherwise can one account for the meagre and overwhelmingly cultural rather than scientific presence of Indigenous scholars and Indigenous knowledge in Canadian universities, still, today?[29] But a self-identified conspiracy might remind Indigenizers and others of a rhetoric and politics of dismissal which both deplored and denied the possibility of Indigenous leadership and solidarity in Parkman's version of Pontiac's case—there was little to be expected yet much to be feared from the "radical peculiarity of Indigenous language[s]" and the paradoxically fierce individualism of "an all-believing race."[30] Parkman's contradictions proliferate as Pontiac's power is attributed to the "hero-worship" recently popularized by Thomas Carlyle but also to the essentially uncontrollable members of "one of these savage democracies."[31] The latter description of Indigenous polities was intended as a self-destructive oxymoron giving way to spasmodic forms of social cohesion: positively cast as "alliances" when connected to the colonial French or English, but negatively cast as plot and political seizure among "the great mass of Indians"[32] when a modestly legitimating European connection was absent. Parkman aggravates the ambivalence of the Harvard scholar towards his less educated fellow Euro-Americans while projecting it into political analysis of "savage democracies." There, instead of revolution by virtue of the general will, he could find only conspiracy in the course of which "the Indians concealed their designs within the dissimulations of their race."[33]

Such "dissimulation" is part of a larger problematic of representation which elicits from Parkman an imperious intervention concentrating in one place many of the terms and tactics still used in some quarters of the academy and society today:

> Of the Indian character, much has been written foolishly, and credulously believed. By the rhapsodies of poets, the cant of sentimentalists, and the extravagance of some who should have known better, a counterfeit image has been tricked out, which might seek in vain for its likeness through every corner of the habitable earth; an image bearing no more resemblance to its original, than the monarch of the tragedy and the hero of the epic poem bear to their living prototypes in the palace and the camp. The shadows of his wilderness home, and the darker mantle of his own inscrutable reserve, have made the Indian warrior a wonder and a mystery. Yet to the eye of rational observation there is nothing unintelligible in him. He is full, it is true, of contradiction. He deems himself the centre of greatness and renown; his pride is proof against the fiercest torments of fire and steel; and yet the same man would beg for a dram of whiskey, or pick up a crust of bread thrown to him like a dog, from the tent door of the traveller. At one moment, he is wary and cautious to the verge of cowardice; at the next, he abandons himself to a very insanity of recklessness; and the habitual self-restraint which throws an impenetrable veil over emotion is joined to the unbridled passions of a madman or a beast.[34]

AMERICAN HISTORY is self-consciously speaking here. The *Conspiracy* was dedicated to Parkman's teacher and the first Harvard professor of modern history, "Jared Sparks, LL.D, President of Harvard University[,] . . . as a testimonial of high personal regard, and a tribute of respect for his distinguished services to American history." The modern and the American converge to execute narrative interruption of chilling confidence and evil omen. The passage moves from the "counterfeit" as emotional, imaginative, and irresponsible to "rational observation" and complete intelligibility. Parkman proceeds according to a visual schema that panoptically commands "every corner of the habitable earth" *and* arterioscopically invades the innermost recesses of the living Indigene. Tragic and epic mimesis are no longer up to the task, especially in a new republic where any actual monarch will always turn out by definition to be worse than his or her dramatic image, and where only the historical fiction of Fenimore Cooper comes close to sharing history's epic vocation to define the heroic anew. Human inconsistency is read harshly so as to distract the reader from the displacement onto the Indigene of precisely those contradictions on which colonialism depends in order to function. Educated reason offers the Indigene a "home" in insanity, animality, or inferiority, while the attribution to him of "inscrutable reserve" ironically anticipates the only too scrutable reserves to which Native Americans would soon be confined and also the impending treatment of the inscrutable oriental immigrant. It is in the face of just such selective reading and mono-disciplinary imperiousness as Parkman exemplifies that we urgently need a transdisciplinary, oppositional politics of reading which embraces conspiracy in order to redefine it, while looking to Indigenous vision to help meet Canada's substantial discursive, ethical, and social deficits.

The Radical Humanities

In conjunction with an emergent, counter-hegemonic Indigenous humanities which alone will be able fully to expose injustice while remaining partially, deliberately unreadable to the dominant Other,[35] there needs to be a radicalizing of the Eurocentric humanities from within. What this requires is not an abandonment of traditional humanist competencies (and Parkmanian deficiencies), but their Indigenizing employment otherwise to redefine the human, as may become clearer from the following, only too recent example.[36]

In 1998–1999 Emory University inaugurated a lecture series with a talk by the distinguished comparativist and deconstructionist Geoffrey Hartman of Yale University. Hartman's theme was *AESTHETICIDE: or,*

Has Literary Study Grown Old? Multiple copies of the published version of this talk have been widely disseminated at no charge to Humanities Centres and Institutes across North America and across the world. Emory clearly thinks its new series has got off to a good start, and there is institutional pride as well as generosity behind the free dissemination of Hartman's lecture and in the covering letter. One of the many remarkable features of this lecture is how it combines radical textualism and cultural conservatism. This combination is used to convey concerns about a decline in academic standards in the shift from Comparative Literature to Cultural Studies and about the "politicization" that the latter apparently brings with it. According to Hartman these developments are two of the "many reasons for the recession of literary criticism and a diminishment in its standards and quality."[37] He attempts to discredit this recession further by connecting it to the early-modern relocation of liberty in western Europe, and its subsequent "translation" to the "universities of the New (now not so new) World [which now may be] weakening in their will to teach and transmit the Western heritage."[38]

Hartman deals with diversity as academically unmanageable excess and "demographic upheaval" in three main moves: reaffirming deep rather than superficial learning, returning to sacred hermeneutics and the canons it authorizes, and rediscovering the Western tradition as sufficiently rich and complex to warrant continued educational concentration in a world where no one can or should seek to know all that qualifies as art and culture. Hartman's argument turns on a reading of the following passage from Tacitus's *Agricola*, which he cites selectively, and paraphrases tendentiously:

> The winter which followed was spent in the prosecution of sound measures. In order that a population scattered and uncivilized [*dispersi ac rudes*], and proportionately ready for war, might be habituated by comfort [*voluptates*] to peace and quiet, [Agricola] would exhort individuals, assist communities, to erect temples, market-places, houses: he praised the energetic, rebuked the indolent, and the rivalry for his compliments took the place of coercion. Moreover, he began to train the sons of the chieftains in a liberal education [*liberalibus artibus erudire*], and to give a preference to the native talents [*ingenia*] of the Briton as against the trained abilities [*studii*] of the Gaul. As a result, the nation which used to reject the Latin language began to aspire to rhetoric [*eloquentia concupiscerent*]: further, the wearing of our dress became a distinction, and the toga came into fashion, and little by

little [*paulatimque*] the Britons went astray into alluring vices [*delenimenta vitiorum*]: to the promenade, the bath, the well-appointed dinner table. The simple natives [*apud imperitos*] gave the name of "culture" [*humanitas*] to this factor of their slavery [*servitutis*].[39]

Hartman sees this passage as "anticipat[ing Cultural Studies] scepticism" about "the link between liberty and the art of the past" and "remind[ing] us of what postcolonial literary and political critics have been saying: the colonizers use culture to weaken the resolve of the colonized, to prevent them finding their own genius and resources."[40] This is in every sense a powerfully *partial* reading, a telling example of patronizingly weak Indigenizing and depoliticizing deconstruction.

Hartman uses humanist learning to imply that the Western canon already knows what its critics (in this case he cites Fanon) are eager to tell it. But that prior knowledge exists within a commitment originating in the ancient world to the "idea of a sacred succession, or of a canonical order of works, guiding both scholarly and artistic tradition."[41] While sloppily renaming Agricola Agrippa in his discussion of Tacitus's account of his father in law, Hartman seizes on the Loeb translation of *humanitas* as "culture" to underscore the prescience of an ancient text and to confirm his personal awareness that particular translations of "humanity" have been exposed at the racist heart of modern colonialism and boldly brandished by postcolonial culturalism. But it is not enough simply to register the fact of "humanity's" portentousness; it has to be read as rigorously as Hartman reads Wordsworth or Nietzsche. And such a reading might be introduced as a reflection on the lesson that Agricola learned from his predecessors, namely, that "little was accomplished by force if injustice followed."[42] The problematic of pacification[43] and the unhealthy undertow of "sound measures" (*saluberrimus consiliis*) begin to disclose desire, stress, contradictions, circularities. The presence or absence of "civilization" turns unhelpfully on the same root in *rudes/erudire*, but is clarified by connection to urbanization, education, language acquisition. Agricola's civilizing mission depends (as does my counter-civilizing mission) on an exhortation (*hortari privatim*) and is confirmed by an act of naming (*vocabatur*), that is to say, by rhetorical details which ought to have been grist to Hartman's deconstructionist mill. However, he passes them over in favour of the lexical reduction of *humanitas* to "culture," and his later preference of *studium* to *ingenia*.[44]

Hartman recognizes the loaded nature of a liberal arts education in the context of colonization, but he fails to comment on the irony of translating *erudire* as "training," when later in the same sentence training is associated with the Gauls rather than the Britons. This irony points to the substantial biases of the English translation, biases evident also in the interpolated description of the Britons as a "nation." The contribution of cultural presumption and projection to hegemony are scarcely acknowledged, never mind adequately translated. The process here is composite, involving contamination as well as education, going "astray" as well as going straight, while Indigenous deficiency and error keep pace with civilizing activities and policies. Eloquence seems possible only in Latin, and only as an object of desire for Britons who are learning Latin as a second language. The Roman vices that some subject Britons *do* readily master lead them to a humiliating socio-linguistic catchresis—taking as emblems of *humanitas* sartorial self-display, sensual hygiene, and gluttony in a proto-decadent care of the self. Tacitus keeps them in their inferior place, yet the enslaved Britons are both right and wrong in naming a set of overdetermined practices *humanitas*. These signifiers of "distinction" (*honor*) draw on political and material surpluses unjustifiable and unsustainable over time. They represent Roman superiority and also the empire's "final doom." What Tacitus both welcomes and worries about as acculturation will both perpetuate the empire and create the conditions for its dissolution from within. Motivated and partial appropriation of the past in the present, as is done by Tacitus the historian, his Loeb translators, by Hartman, and by me, is ideological as well as intellectual work, and it is unnecessary and dangerously "humane" to pretend otherwise in the name of scholarly standards that too often appeal to the best and the brightest in order to privilege the best-off and the whitest.

Such humanistic resistance to Hartman's reinscription of Eurocentric privileges—and problematic outcomes like an apolitical academy, reluctantly inclusive canon and curriculum, and self-renewing but exclusive civil society—needs to be effective and influential. Otherwise, Tacitus and his heirs (like Parkman who admiringly cites the *Germania*)[45] will never be made to yield an adequate measure of anti-colonial truth, nor will scholarship fully demonstrate "the power to transform history into justice."[46] So, the capacity for careful reading and the knowledge of dead languages must coexist alongside anticolonial resolve, if "real" rigour and scholarly distinction are not to confine themselves even more obsessively to "the" Western tradition. The new, radical (and hence Indigenizing) humanities need to retain as well as supplement and redeploy the benefits of a "classical" education.

Englishes and Others

I want to conclude by arguing against "English" as imperious singularity and academic accomplice of the current hegemony, and by urging a new beginning for Englishes as the redrawing of the academic map and redistribution of cultural legitimacy and territoriality under Indigenous educational leadership. This I take to be an explicitly interested and interesting endeavour, an energizing departure from the colonial practice of Kantian and Arnoldian disinterestedness. Englishes ought to be a source of good instrumentality, by which I mean in part traditional disciplinarity but also a set of interdisciplinary and multidisciplinary connections that define more by (politicized) commonality than by difference, and that defetishize expertise and writing at least so far as to re-empower generalists and the work of going public and "going native" alongside publishing in academic journals and with academic presses. I mean also a set of activities self-defined and widely recognized as forms of useful knowledge—useful today and tomorrow as enhanced communicative and interpretative skills, and invaluable over a lifetime of engaged and critical citizenship and development of new solidarities.

Engaged and critical citizenship should start inside universities but not stop there or prove separable from the rest of life. The critical citizenry that looks to the political and cultural history of English as a world language and "family" of literatures must see or be taught to see in this living archive, and in its old and new technological modalities and mediations, the endlessly artful masking of "the violence of production,"[47] the endlessly adroit yet oppressive management of the meanings of class, race, and gender, the endless silencing and mockery imposed or undertaken in the name of humane ideals and moral universals. The meaning of literary knowledge resides primarily not in the elitist interactions of guardians with their own underclass and with student consumers under the aegis of excellence and standards; it resides in the social relations of production and reproduction of the linguistic and the literary. Focus on the latter version of productivity can lead, and quickly, to the transformation of pedagogy, curriculum, merit, status, that bourgeois individualism that claims originality for itself, and that capitalist value form at the heart of everything we currently do, or fail to do, or are prevented or prohibited from doing. It can and should also involve the radical, Indigenizing redefinition of what is meant by "culture" from all quarters of the Canadian academy, and perhaps especially from the radical humanities.

The nature and value of academic disciplines are determined by economic and social forces. The precise effects of such determination of the academic agenda can and should be demonstrated, and the task of doing so is important scholarly as well as administrative work, but such demonstration can never be complete or unequivocal. Disciplinarity remains a site for the staging of invidious, oppressive, or productive difference, but also, alas, disciplinarity remains a set of determinations and symptoms of unexamined privilege or indifference or fear. The humanities are in particular danger, perhaps most of all in English-speaking countries. Certainly they are in danger all across Canada. The current beleaguerment of the humanities is in part the consequence of "external" misunderstanding and hostility elsewhere in the university and in society at large. Much of this misunderstanding and hostility can be captured by the expression *bad instrumentality*. However, the current beleaguerment is also the result of what happens—or fails to happen "inside" the humanities. Many of the problems internal to the humanities can be captured in the notion of *anti-instrumentality* or *knowledge-for-its-own-sake*.

The past, present, and future of English Literary Studies in particular is intimately connected to the legacy of nineteenth-century philology as a Euro-imperial tool,[48] and to the related fate of "the" English language: English as a world language but not necessarily as a compliantly technocratic, multi-national corporate instrument and/or conduit for cultural dumping or defoliation. Any quasi-imperial formation, including cultural formations like a *lingua franca* and the canon it sustains and is sustained by, acquires "impurity" while extending its authority or penetration across differences of class, race, gender, nationality. Such "impurity" will be the locus of intensified oppression, but also the focus of resistance and critique such as that offered by the Terra Lingua group of scholar activists who work for the preservation and promotion of Indigenous languages across the world. The end of English-in-the-singular—understood as a project for the extension of hegemony combined with the ever more zealous policing of purity and maintaining of "proper standards"—is long overdue and too long delayed by the passing of the Anglo-imperial torch from Britain to the United States. A new goal for Englishes is an enhanced capacity for analytical and imaginative critique of the current (Amerocentric, neo-colonial, capitalist) hegemony. In making this end explicit and effective, English(es) will not be politicizing the university but simply endeavouring to change its tacit but well established politics. And in taking their lead from a new generation of Indigenous theorists and activists, Englishes and their critical promoters can contribute in highly practical ways to economic and social justice for all—for as long as the sun shines, the curriculum flows, and the text of treaties between the Crown and Canada's First Nations is not reduced to the rhetoric of entreaty.

Notes

Originally published as "Always Indigenize! The Radical Humanities in the Postcolonial Canadian University," in *Ariel: A Review of International English Literature* 31.1–2 (2000): 307–26. Copyright © Len Findlay. Reprinted with permission of the author.

1. Stuart Hall, "On Postmodernism and Articulation: An Interview with Stuart Hall," in *Stuart Hall: Critical Dialogues in Cultural Studies*, ed. David Morley and Kuan-Hsing Chen (London: Routledge, 1996), 131–50.

2. Fredric Jameson, *The Political Unconscious: Narrative as a Socially Symbolic Act* (Ithaca: Cornell University Press, 1981), 9.

3. James Chandler, *England in 1819: The Politics of Literary Culture and the Case of Romantic Historicism* (Chicago: University of Chicago Press, 1998), 51ff.

4. Paul Martin, "Education and the Public Good." Unpublished address, Breakfast on the Campus program, University of Ottawa, 1998.

5. Terry Goldie, *Fear and Temptation: The Image of the Indigene in Canadian, Australian, and New Zealand Literatures* (Kingston: McGill-Queen's University Press, 1989), 4, 13, 19, etc.

6. Linda Smith, *Decolonizing Methodologies: Research and Indigenous Peoples* (London: Zed Books, 1999); see 16, 10, 39, 7, 149, 20, 189, 178, 189, 116, and 142ff respectively.

7. Ibid., 19.

8. Ibid., 53.

9. J. Y. Henderson, Marjorie Benson, and Isobel M. Findlay, *Aboriginal Tenure and the Constitution of Canada* (Toronto: Carswell, 2000). See also Smith, *Decolonizing Methodologies*, 26.

10. See, for example, Gayatri Chakravorty Spivak, *A Critique of Postcolonial Reason: Toward a History of the Vanishing Present* (Cambridge, Mass.: Harvard University Press, 1999); Gyan Prakash, ed., *After Colonialism: Imperial Histories and Postcolonial Displacements* (Princeton: Princeton University Press, 1995); Aijaz Ahmad, *In Theory: Classes, Nations, Literatures* (London: Verso, 1992); Patrick William and Laura Chrisman, eds., *Colonial Discourse and Post-Colonial Theory* (New York: Columbia University Press, 1994); Majid Rahnema and Victoria Bawtree, eds., *The Post-Development Reader* (London: Zed Books, 1997); John Willinsky, *Learning to Divide the World: Education at Empire's End* (Minneapolis: University of Minnesota Press, 1999).

11. Compared, for instance, with the case of India in, say, Richard Symonds, *Oxford and Empire: The Last Lost Cause?* (Oxford: Clarendon Press, 1986); Gauri Viswanathan, *Masks of Conquest: Literary Study and British Rule in India* (New York: Columbia University Press, 1989); and Javed Majeed, *Ungoverned Imaginings: James Mill's The History of British India and Orientalism* (Toronto: Oxford University Press, 1992).

12. Michael Keefer, *Lunar Perspectives: Field Notes from the Culture Wars* (Concord, Ont.: Anansi, 1996).

13. Patricia Monture-Angus, "On Being Homeless: One Aboriginal Woman's 'Conquest' of Canadian Universities," in *Crossroads, Directions, and a New Critical Race Theory*, ed. Frank Valdez, Jerome Culp, and Angela Harris (Philadelphia: Temple University Press, 2002).

14. Sherene Razack, *Looking White People in the Eye: Gender, Race, and Culture in the Courtrooms and Classrooms* (Toronto: University of Toronto Press, 1998).

15. Bill Readings, *The University in Ruins* (Cambridge, Mass.: Harvard University Press, 1996), 21ff.; Len Findlay, "Runes of Marx and *The University in Ruins*," *University of Toronto Quarterly* 66 (1997): 677–90.

16. Marie Battiste and J. Y. Henderson, *Protecting Indigenous Knowledge* (Saskatoon: Purich Press, 2000).

17. Smith, *Decolonizing Methodologies*, 39.

18. Len Findlay, "Retailing Petits Recits or Retooling for Revolution? Cultural Studies and the Knowledge Industries in Canada," *University of Toronto Quarterly* 64 (1995): 503.

19. Smith, *Decolonizing Methodologies*, 89.

20. Len Findlay, "Interdiscipling Canada: 'Cause Breaking Up is Hard to Do," *Essays in Canadian Writing* 65 (1998): 1–15.

21. Sharilyn Calliou's "Peacekeeping Actions at Home: A Medicine Wheel Model for a Peacekeeping Pedagogy," in *First Nations Education in Canada: The Circle Unfolds* (Vancouver: University of British Columbia Press, 1995); or the strategic traditionalism of J. Y. Henderson's "Postcolonial Ghost Dancing" in *Reclaiming Indigenous Voice and Vision*, ed. M. Battiste (Vancouver: University of British Columbia Press, 2000), 57–76.

22. Len Findlay, "Valuing Culture, Interdiscipling the Economic," *Aldritch Interdisciplinary Lecture and Conference for Graduate Students* (St. John's: Memorial University of Newfoundland, 1998), 7ff.

23. Cited in Len Findlay, " '[T]hat liberty of writing': Incontinent Ordinance in 'Oriental' Jones," *Romantic Circles Praxis Series* (November 2000): 10.

24. Francis Parkman, *The Oregon Trail [and] the Conspiracy of Pontiac*, ed. William R. Taylor, Library of America 53 (New York: Viking Press, Library of America, 1991), 345.

25. Parkman, *The Oregon Trail*, 347; emphasis added.

26. Daniel Horsmanden, *The New York Conspiracy, or a History of the Negro Plot, with the Journal of the Proceedings against the Conspirators at New-York in the Years 1741–2* (New York: Negro University Press, 1969).

27. See Fredric Jameson, *The Geopolitical Aesthetic: Cinema and Space in the World System* (Bloomington: Indiana University Press, 1992), xvii, 9ff.

28. See essays by Marie Battiste and Len Findlay in *Pursuing Academic Freedom: The History and Future of Defining Idea*, ed. Paul Bidwell and L. M. Findlay (Saskatoon: Purich, 2000).

29. Madeleine MacIvor, "Redefining Science Education for Aboriginal Students," in *Reclaiming Indigenous Voice and Vision*, ed. Marie Battiste (Vancouver: University of British Columbia Press, 2000), 73–98.

30. Parkman, *The Oregon Trail*, 359, 371.

31. Ibid., 360–61.

32. Ibid., 489.

33. Ibid., 487.

34. Ibid., 386.

35. Cited in Spivak, *Critique of Postcolonial Reason*, 245.

36. See Smith, *Decolonizing Methodologies*, 26; Findlay, "Valuing Culture, Interdisciplining the Economic."

37. Geoffrey H. Hartman, *Aestheticide: or, Has Literary Study Grown Old?* (Atlanta: Emory Humanities Lectures 1, 1998), 2.

38. Ibid., 3.

39. Tacitus, *Agricola*, trans. M. Hutton, rev. R. M. Ogilvie (Cambridge, Mass.: Harvard University Press, 1970), 21.

40. Hartman, *Aestheticide*, 2–3.

41. Ibid., 3.

42. Tacitus, *Agricola*, 19.

43. See also Findlay, "Liberty," 15.

44. Hartman, *Aestheticide*, 5.

45. Parkman, *The Oregon Trail*, 495.

46. Smith, *Decolonizing Methodologies*, 34.

47. Howard Caygill, *Art of Judgement* (Oxford: Blackwell, 1989), 389.

48. Maurice Olender, *The Languages of Paradise: Race, Religion, and Philology in the Nineteenth Century*, trans. Arthur Goldhammer (Cambridge, Mass.: Harvard University Press, 1992).

C

Modernity and

Contemporary

Culture

STEPHEN CROCKER

Hauled Kicking and Screaming into Modernity: Non-Synchronicity and Globalization in Post-War Newfoundland

Stephen Crocker is an associate professor in the Department of Sociology at Memorial University, St. John's, Newfoundland. He received his Ph.D. from the interdisciplinary program in social and political thought at York University in 1995. He conducts research and teaches in the areas of sociological theory, philosophy and sociology of time, and globalization.

Introduction: Non-Synchronicity and the Colonial World

"Not all people live in the same now," Ernst Bloch writes.[1] Futuristic and archaic moments of economy, technology, and social life can sometimes coexist alongside one another. In conditions of uneven development, our experience is made of a strange simultaneity of two non-synchronous worlds. Bloch developed the idea of "non-synchronicity" to describe the uneven development of Germany. But I want to make a case here for its usefulness in describing a form of time-consciousness peculiar to colonialism.

The basis of colonialism has always been that the objects and contents of everyday life are experienced at a distance from the social and economic conditions that organize and regulate them. The entire object world of the colony—manufactured commodities, machines, textbooks, institutions, technical expertise, literature, science—all originate somewhere else, outside the immediate life-world where they are consumed or practised. And, curiously, instead of producing a standardized and homogenous experience, as is commonly thought to be the result of global integration, the separation of system and life-world has often served to accentuate and provoke local differences in culture, language, and politico-economic organization from the cosmopolitan experience that the colony in fact makes possible. So, paradoxically, the greater a colony's fusion with global flows of information and capital, the greater may be its sense of differentiation and divergence from the cosmopolitan modernity in which it plays a constitutive role.

This difference can mean several things. Local culture may, for example, be experienced as independent of the world system and shrouded in the mysteries of a (sometimes narcissistic) autonomous folk culture. We might say that, in such cases, globalization and colonialism (leaving aside the larger question of whether these describe different phenomena) are experienced in a fundamentally "spatial" way, that is, as the juxtaposition of independent entities. Frantz Fanon's descriptions of the colonial world often give this sense of an opposition of two wholly separate and reciprocally exclusive spaces when he describes the colonial world as "a motionless, Manicheistic world, a world of statutes," but so too does much of our current discussion of globalization as a social and technical interconnection of the globe.[2] It is common to imagine globalization as a progressive unification of independent and discrete entities which, somewhat like patches of grass, slowly merge together to form a single field. That image possesses a certain truth, but it remains a fundamentally spatial image. What I want to explore here, through the instance of post-war Newfoundland, is the temporal nature of global integration. Bloch's notion of non-synchronicity is valuable in this respect because it describes a situation in which my local action (my "now") consists of one serial continuum of events participating in a larger (global) sequence, and it is only in the synchronization of these two temporal series that my own phenomenal experience can be made intelligible. The emphasis here is not only on the physical connections between locations but on the interval that differentiates my space of experience from a horizon of expectation. It matters how we think about that interval, whether we see it, for example, as an obstacle between the present and an already determined future, or as the site of active creation of very different possible futures.

To best appreciate the way that the interval between experience and expectation is organized in the project of post-war colonial modernization, it may help to set it in contrast to the earlier European experience of modernity, as described by Rheinhart Kosseleck. Kosseleck has shown that, in early Europe, modernity was experienced as "Neuzeit," or new time, the sense of living through a completely novel, unprecedented course of events. To be modern is to experience a new dynamism, or a "temporalization" in social events, which Kosseleck describes as a tension that emerges between the space of experience and the horizon of expectation. The horizon of expectation is defined by a line "behind which a new space of experience will open, but which cannot yet be seen."[3]

In the case of colonial modernization, on the other hand, the horizon of expectation is defined by a repetition of what is already real and being lived elsewhere. The political institutions, industries, and social and technical developments that reshaped colonial society after World War II were already recognizable features of the metropolis. The task of modernization was to transplant these developments to colonial soil. The future was not an unknown space of experience; it was visible elsewhere. And so the themes of newness, progress, and innovation associated with the modernity of the metropolis were replaced, in the post-war colonies, by a pervasive sense of repetition and imitation. Colonial modernization thus produced what I will call a "proleptic" structure of experience.[4] Prolepsis is a narrative device in which a future, expected event is regarded as though it were an already accomplished fact. Actions taking place in the present proceed on the understanding that a second, future action is already secured. As a result, whatever events emerge in the interval between now and then will not affect its accomplishment. The colonial present, with all its distinctive markers of non-synchronicity, was redefined, in the post-war years, as the past of a future which the colony did not create but nonetheless had to bring into being. This structure of experience had, furthermore, a deep underlying parodic nature. We may speak of a parodic character of modernization, not because social life is theatre (though that may be true) but rather because, as Linda Hutcheon has shown,[5] parody rests on a specific logic of repetition and difference which we shall explore in more detail later. And, as we shall see, parody has the added conceptual benefit of allowing us to distinguish between critical and conservative forms of repetition and thus to determine not only the new post-war forms of global inequality but also the new kinds of agency and resistance made possible by the peculiar non-synchronous heritage of colonialism, which I shall study here through instances of critical parody in the theatre and film of Newfoundland.

Colonialism and the Non-Synchronous Heritage

The post-war history of Newfoundland, and perhaps of other former colonies as well, may be viewed as a series of different experiences of non-synchronicity. Driving their leather-lined British Austin around the

Avalon Peninsula of Newfoundland in the 1930s, Lady and Sir John Hope Simpson found "a microcosm very little affected by the tide of European progress. In many ways we are here in the 18th century."[6] It is the fact that one could motor through eighteenth-century social conditions that defined the colonial experience of globalization. Or, to take an example more in keeping with our current tele-technological image of globalization, the transatlantic cable, the mid-nineteenth-century invention that made possible global financial synchronization, emerged from its long sea voyage into Heart's Content, Newfoundland, which remained for almost an entire century more a "truck," cashless economy. Is there a more powerful or concrete metaphor of non-synchronicity than the super-modern electrical sign of money passing through the archaic, near-feudal economic structure of rural Newfoundland?

In the early 1970s, I travelled around the island with my father, who was a technologist employed in various modernization projects. At the time, it was common to see new post offices in the style of futuristic Frank Lloyd Wright buildings among the traditional outport architecture. Hippies escaping from the fast food and electricity of urban America could be found living among the newly modernized population of Placentia Bay, who were enjoying the same things for the first time. The strange coexistence of these communities, united by their problematic relation to modernity, prompted Ray Guy to suggest once that "Newfoundlanders have always been hippies waiting for the rest of North America to catch up."

Now, in the late 1990s, after the failure of that earlier, post-war moment of modernization and the destruction of the cod fishery, Newfoundland has entered a new phase of non-synchronicity. The rural population is fed into increasingly global flows of labour. Men and women abandon the fishing berths of rural Newfoundland for the language schools of South-East Asia and the chicken factories of Alberta. The villages they leave behind are turned into museums. Houses, root cellars, and furniture have lost their functional value. Family homes are being liberated from the Formica and mac-tac with which they had been renovated in an earlier moment of modernization and are now transforming into consumable anachronisms for the tourist trade. The recently renovated traditional salt-box houses look newer than the now-weathered suburban homes which replaced them in the 1960s and 1970s. We now see the strange juxtaposition of trap skiffs rotting on the beach and pleasure crafts tied up at the government wharf. This is the moment of non-synchronicity that provides the peculiar setting for *The Shipping*

News, E. Annie Proulx's Pulitzer Prize–winning novel set in Newfoundland. Quoyle, a broken and disenchanted American, comes to rural Newfoundland seeking shelter from the sped-up, stressed-out grind of urban America. He renovates the old, abandoned family home while behind it, off in the woods, a now-defunct factory is reclaimed by nature. Thus the strange temporal experience of Newfoundland today is illustrated: the old and anachronistic once again come to life and thrive on the remains of the formerly new and the formerly super-modern.

The New Future of Colonial Modernization

From the start, the colonial world had been defined by the co-presence of two dissimilar worlds. Frantz Fanon, writing in the context of Africa, said that these worlds "remain obedient to the rules of Aristotelian logic (and) follow the principle of reciprocal exclusivity."[7] Joey Smallwood, who helped to engineer and document the post-war transformation of Newfoundland (in various biographical and encyclopedic works on Newfoundland), described a remarkably similar experience when he said that "we have often felt in the past, when we learned something of the higher standards of the mainland, that such things belonged to another world, that they were not for us."[8] To move from this world to that other, modern one involved not only a physical change, but a sort of existential metamorphosis because when we go there, to what Smallwood once called "the flesh pots of North America,"[9] our horizon of expectation changes: "a metamorphosis steals over us the moment we cross the border that separates us from other lands. . . . Our minds undergo a transformation."[10] What we accept, and what we expect of life, also changes: "we expect and take for granted what would have been ridiculous or avaricious to expect at home."[11]

And because of this irreconcilably dichotomous character of the two worlds, to return to Newfoundland, after having been thus modernized, required an equally radical change, which Smallwood called a "reverse transformation": "when we return to Newfoundland our minds undergo a reverse transformation: [and] we readjust ourselves unconsciously to the meaner standards under which we grew up."[12]

These remarks were part of a speech Smallwood delivered in 1946 to the National Convention, which debated Newfoundland's then impending postcolonial future. Richard Gwyn said that the speech "precised all that is essential in the sociology of Newfoundland."[13] He was right, I think, not because Smallwood identified any specific custom or tradition, but because he identified something more fundamental and abstract—a change in the relation of experience and expectation, and, ultimately, in our relation to metropolitan modernity. In his speech, Smallwood first describes the past as an opposition of two separate worlds—much like Fanon's Manicheistic worlds. He then identifies the post-war present as a new historical turning point that opens the space of experience to something unprecedented: "Our people's struggle to live here began 400 years ago and continues to this day. The struggle is more uneven now than it was then, and the people view the future now with more dread than they felt a century ago. The newer conceptions of what life can be, of what life should be, have widened our horizons, and deepened our knowledge of the great gulf that separates what we have and are from what we feel we should have and be."[14]

What the people now dread is not the future *per se* but the possible persistence into the future of the Manichean separation of two worlds that had defined, up to this point, the experience of global integration. If the future of the colonial present is suddenly more dreadful, it is because "higher, more modern conceptions of what life can be" now appear to exist in a state of tension with our own experience. The signs of modernity and progress brought to us by radio, film, newspapers, and visitors (by a new phase of time-space compression) do not simply belong to another distinct world. They now appear to reveal what ought to be but is not yet real for us. Perhaps we could say that what had been largely experienced as a spatial juxtaposition of two incongruous worlds became a temporal relation between present and future. The metropolitan space of experience appeared as our horizon of expectation; our future historical destiny was already real and extant elsewhere. Consequently, what defined the incipient modernity of Newfoundland was not newness *per se* but the anticipated integration into what was already someone else's space of experience.

This sense of change from a coexistence to a succession of non-synchronous worlds was not peculiar to Newfoundland. Arjun Appadurai describes a similar change in the Indian project of modernization which also gave rise to a new colonial sense of progress as repetition.[15] Railroads, cinema, sanitation, even the model of nationhood were all derived from someone else's history. Similarly, in Cuba, shortly after the revolution, signs appeared on office buildings. Some read "Viva, the People's Pepsi," but others said "Hurry up, we are fifty years behind!"[16] What unites these examples is an image of historical time as a repetition of a process that has already taken place elsewhere. Backward peoples skip stages and jump historical intervals in order, as Trotsky once said, "to adopt whatever is ready in advance of the specified date."[17]

To better describe the new structure of historical time that emerged in the post-war period, and in particular the new relation to the future that it supposed, we may borrow a concept from narrative theory. As I stated earlier, colonial modernization resulted in what I refer to as a "proleptic" structure of experience. The concept of prolepsis directs our attention to a fundamental feature of experience in conditions of underdevelopment. The future—and not only the future of large-scale economic and social events but that of matters of everyday life too, such as the appearance of new books, films, and ideas—appears to be created elsewhere, so that we have to wait for its late arrival. We regard the future less as something that we are actively creating and more as a ready-made space into which we are leaping. As a result, the speed at which we can erase the colonial present and replicate the other future space of experience becomes the central motivating force in historical movement.

We are fortunate to have a documentary record of the new "proleptic" image of the future and the preoccupation with speed and repetition that defined the post-war modernization of Newfoundland. In the early 1950s, the Newfoundland government produced a series of films which bear such ambitious titles as *Newfoundland Progress Report* and *Newfoundland Builds*. These newsreel-style films, which both document and promote Newfoundland's modernization, consist of voice-overs on collaged images depicting the contents of that new space of experience which Newfoundlanders were rushing toward: the industries, office buildings, welfare services, commerce and consumer goods, the university, technical schools, and road construction that were all transplanted to Newfoundland. A Chubby Chicken outlet, a billowing smokestack, a classical symphony, earth-moving equipment, supermarkets, pavement, and water and sewer pipes become a montage of the elements of a moveable, modular experience of the modern.

These images are accompanied by a kind of "fetishism of the machine," which is conveyed through close-ups of workers' hands on giant gears, screws, wheels, and pulleys. The camera pans across commercial and industrial spaces, coming to rest on determined, sweaty faces, while the voice-over announces boldly: "Yes, to the staccato rhythm of the industrial era, Newfoundland workers find their place in the new scheme of things." The narrator's voice is, significantly, of no particular time and place. Like the places it describes, it has been cleansed of any recognizable markers of non-synchronicity. What we hear and see is just one more instance of a standardized world. All the markers that might display economic, social, and cultural divergence are absent. The narrator says that

> The typical old-fashioned stores have been replaced in the larger communities by bright efficient supermarkets and specialty shops of all types. The best of the materials of world wide trade find their way to these modern markets.
>
> Now in Newfoundland the traveler finds the clean and comfortable motels that make today's travel both easy and pleasant. And the visitor from far away finds the same catering to world wide taste he'll find in the major capitals of the world.
>
> Cities and towns seem to have changed overnight from listless groupings of drab dwellings into fresh bright modern communities.[18]

But, apart from the substance or contents of that new space of experience, the films describe a new form of experience, a novel accelerated sense of time. Life is speeding up, and this itself is as clear a marker of modernity as the consumer items and industrial spaces that we see. *Newfoundland Progress Report* begins with a segue device of spinning newspaper headlines, which formally conveys the sense of a rapid passage of time. The film then documents the new time-consciousness of acceleration, speed, and proleptic time. Here are some examples:

> Overnight the men, the machines, and the money went to work, building roads, building airstrips in the wilderness, building schools and hospitals, and factories and harnessing the wasted power of the magnificent rushing waters.
>
> The erection of the mill was rapid. The buildings took shape so fast that motorists driving along the nearby highway could scarcely believe their eyes.
>
> This new industry was ready to start production in a remarkably short time.
>
> With speed once again the key note, the massive structure of concrete and steel was rushed ahead despite snow storms and many other difficulties.
>
> Huge pieces of equipment were hauled to the site over rough roads and under the worst possible conditions, for speed was vital.[19]

Many of the industries shown in the films, and described there as the most modern and the most swiftly constructed, were born in a rapid explosion of industrial growth aimed at the production of consumer commodities—chocolate bars, optics, glue, leather goods, maps, car batteries. However, few of these lasted more than a couple of years because the equipment was already out of date when it was purchased and could not compete with newer machines that could get the same products to market faster and cheaper. Some of the equipment, in fact, had been donated to Europe by the Americans under the Marshall Plan. At least one factory, when erected, still bore a plate which read "Gift of the People of the United States for the Rehabilitation of Europe."[20] What we Newfoundlanders received as modern was someone else's recently outmoded anachronism.

Modernization as Parody

The proleptic structure of colonial modernization displays an imitative and parodic impulse which I would now like to explore in more detail. In order to become what we can be, or even ought to be, we imitate what someone else already is. In suggesting that we think of modernization as parody, I do not mean that social life is simply theatre or that we are only acting instead of doing something more real. I mean that the structure of historical time that emerged in the post-war years was defined by a certain relation of repetition and difference best described in the theory of parody.

Linda Hutcheon has suggested that parody can be distinguished from borrowing, quotation, and adaptation because it does not simply copy an original. Parody is a kind of repetition which acknowledges, and even emphasizes, the divergence of the repetition from the original. Parody gives us an exaggerated version of both the original and the site of its repetition. Exaggeration has the singular ability to identify in an original element that which we might otherwise not see, much as when we enlarge a photograph or play a film in slow motion, we notice details that we might otherwise have skipped. Parody calls on this property of exaggeration in order to set into relief the difference between what is being repeated and the place in which it is repeated. But parody can be either conservative or critical. Conservative parody holds up the original as an ideal against which the divergent repetition pales. It disavows the specific situation of its enunciation in order to better emphasize the qualities of the original.

As a result of this disavowal, the present through which we are actually living loses any imminent value of its own. In relation to the new space of experience into which the present is now to be integrated, the colonial life-world is an anachronism. It is not itself the source of any historical potency or temporalization. In fact, it is an obstacle in the way of its own realization. To learn from history now is to repeat it and to be condemned, as in V. S. Naipaul's The Mimic Men, to use and to never create the intellect and machinery with which we cultivate modernity.[21] Twenty years after Confederation with Canada, Joey Smallwood could write, "We have not, in the last twenty years produced any new or original education theory, philosophy or practice. But we have put indoor toilets in 744 schools that didn't have them. That's progress."[22] That Smallwood could say, as he famously did on several occasions, that he would haul Newfoundland "kicking and screaming into the twentieth century" already implied that he regarded the future into which we Newfoundlanders were being dragged as nothing that our own present actions were helping to create. That the colonial present was defined as an inert anachronism is clear when one considers the various programs of social and cultural modernization that were initiated during those years. The most notorious of these was the (still) deeply resented program of resettlement, which involved the forced movement of communities from isolated outports to the "growth centres," where modern infrastructure and factory based wage-labour employment were to be made available.[23]

Urban centres, on the other hand, participated in what might be called a new "civilizing project," which included the introduction of elocution lessons in the university, with the aim of purging from rural students the lexicons and accents that identified their non-synchronous heritage. In Newfoundland today, one still often meets people who speak in a practised British accent, even though they have never lived in, or even visited, Britain. Perhaps this is because, as Stuart Hall has argued,[24] in the colonies, British ethnicity functioned not as one among other ethnicities but as a standard in relation to which local cultures were viewed as a deviation. The self-styled British accent displays not so much an identification with British ethnicity as a more general attempt to cover up any divergence from what is perceived to be a general cosmopolitan modernity.

The same civilizing project motivated the development of arts and culture centres which were designed initially to import American and British plays. Chris Brookes rightly compared this new cultural program to a cargo cult—if you build metropolitan-styled cultural centres, you will get metropolitan culture.[25] These developments in cultural and social policy display the same structure of historical time that one finds in more economic and social concerns. They are legitimated by an underlying premise that the cultural horizon of Newfoundland is already given in metropolitan space. The moment of decision regarding what is to be done and how it is to be done has already taken place. My own present (the period of kicking and screaming) is therefore an obstacle in the way of the realization of a sequence of events that has already been set into motion.

There is a whole phenomenology of backwardness that we might explore here. We wait for modernity, and to wait, as Thomas Mann says, is to "consume whole spaces of time without our living them, or making any use of them as such."[26] To wait is to regard the present as obstructive, inert, and void because we have already (conceptually at least) overleaped it. Mann further says that we may compare someone who waits to a greedy man "whose digestive apparatus works through quantities of food without converting it into anything of value or nourishment to his system."[27] Waiting, when it takes this form, rests on the illusion that there already exists a temporal whole, of which our contemporary actions form a part. In this light, the present appears valueless. So, ironically, the task of historical change is to neutralize and eliminate the present. In post-war Newfoundland, local forms of dialect, architecture, work organization, and cultural enjoyment were redefined as the past of a future which we did not create but nonetheless had to bring into being. The novelist Paul West, who taught at Memorial University of Newfoundland during those years, complained that his students had "never heard of Hemingway or T. S. Eliot . . . they have to assimilate so much so fast."[28]

Critical Parody: The Colonial Comic

The project of post-war modernization had the structure of a conservative parody; it disavowed the particulars of the new situation—the colonial present—in order to emphasize the qualities of the original, that is, the metropolitan space of experience that was to be replicated. But conservative parody is only one of many "strategies for getting in and out of modernity" pursued in the postcolonial world.

Critical parody is a much different creative project which undermines the authority of the original by demonstrating the extent to which the original is changed by the specific context of its repetition. The point here is to show that the original "is" only to the extent that it is instantiated in a place, the particular qualities of which determine its reception and interpretation. Critical parody therefore reveals a reciprocal influence between the original and the place of repetition.

I now want to discuss some of the critical impulses that emerged in reaction to the conservative project of modernization. One popular oppositional strategy was (and still is) to try to separate out the contents of what had previously been experienced as the spatially opposed worlds of the local and the cosmopolitan and to valorize the former over the latter. This desire to return to an earlier moment of globalization was the spirit of salvage anthropology, of realism and nostalgia in the arts, and, more generally, the spirit of what Gerald Pocius has rightly called "nativism"— the attempt to isolate a pure Newfoundland culture. These efforts of romantic purification—similar instances of which have been well documented in the Mexican case by Nestor Garcia Canclini[29]—operated on a kind of "bad faith." To enjoy the authenticity of Newfoundland culture, one had first to disavow the deep entwinement of Newfoundland culture in the global system and to overlook the fact that the peculiar forms of divergence that characterized "Newfoundland culture" were themselves products of global integration. This often amounted to a top-down cultural initiative carried out by a newly emergent cultural elite. A well-known and humorous story displays the limited appeal of this attempt. In the late 1970s, a popular traditional band was playing folk music in a bar in St. John's. When the audience grew uninterested and noisy, the singer turned on them. "Shut up," he said, " . . . we're preserving your fucking culture!"

In the theatre, film, and television that emerged in Newfoundland, something more interesting and more like critical parody took place. Laughter is (still) often provoked through a certain parodic imitation of metropolitan characters and events. The most mundane situations become humorous if they can be shown to involve a modern, cosmopolitan character carrying out some activity that we associate with Newfoundlanders (fishing, speaking in a thick accent, traditional singing, dancing, or other forms of enjoyment). Or, conversely, we can show that what we had regarded as a modern and metropolitan character is in fact a Newfoundlander in disguise. Things take place as if recognizably Newfoundland characters were modern, or as if patently cosmopolitan characters— artists, TV broadcasters, experts, entrepreneurs, and so on—were actually Newfoundlanders.

In Newfoundland theatre, the classic example is the CODCO character Ricardo Heurta. Ricardo presents himself as an eminently cosmopolitan dancer, singer, film-maker, and writer. He is a modern artist who is as at home in the cafés of Paris as in the theatres of Milan. The artist maintains this disguise until a TV talk show host recognizes him as Ricky

Reardon, a former street urchin from downtown St. John's. In other versions of the same plot, it is Bob Dylan or Harry Houdini who is revealed to be a Newfoundlander in disguise. Yet another variation parodies the elocution lessons given to rural students at the university. Here, Sir Laurence Olivier is taught to speak in a Newfoundland accent, "I am a Newfownd laaaander, laaahhhh." In his recent one-man comedy show, *The King of Fun*, Andy Jones presents the most sublime version of this device when he proposes a television series called simply *If* in which all famous historical figures—starting with Plato and Socrates—are portrayed as though they were Newfoundlanders.

We find this device of unmasking throughout the contemporary period, but we can trace it back at least to the vaudeville of the 1920s. Johnny Burke's *The Topsail Geisha* was a parody of the elite operetta in which members of a Japanese chorus with their ornamental fans are replaced by a team of fishermen from the community of Topsail, cooling themselves with triangles of dried salt cod. Time and again, this device provokes laughter. But we search in vain to find the humour in either the colonial space of experience or the metropolitan one that gets imitated. Neither of these is funny in and of itself. What is funny is the relation—specifically the temporal relation—that exists between them. I believe that relation can be best described in light of Henri Bergson's thesis on laughter.

In this essay, Bergson said that comic figures and situations reveal a basic illusion about the temporal nature of experience.[30] The comic figure is one who is so caught up in plans and projected schemes of action that he is surprised and defeated by the contingencies that emerge in the interval between a present and projected future moment. Running ahead toward some future event, he stumbles over the reality of his present. His schemes break down in such a way as to reveal the temporal organization that underlies them, and this is what provokes laughter. We laugh at the absent-minded professor who trips over her laces because her thoughts are so fixated on her abstract formulae that she forgets the more mundane but inescapable particulars of her situation. Don Quixote is the paradigm comic figure because all that he recognizes around him are the chivalric fantasies he has created.[31] These fantasies clash with the very real demands in which the knight finds himself: he falls into a well because, in it, he sees not a light shining on water but a star. He battles a windmill because his head has been filled with the image of giants prowling about the countryside. Time and again he is suspended between the projected, future schema on which he is fixated and the incorrigible present which he cannot yet escape. In the comic, simultaneous acts of projecting toward the future and disavowing the present are made visible. All humour originates in an unexpected interruption of our movement toward a horizon of expectation.

If this is true, and the comic exposes this absurd relation of time and action that underlies our habitual encounters with the world, then the colonial comic shows us how this absurdity informs the images of stagism[32] and prolepses that underlie programs of modernization and the phenomenology of backwardness on which these programs rest. The characters in Newfoundland theatre are interrupted on the way to modernity. They are no longer in one world and not yet in another. They belong neither to a traditional place, nor to a more modern state of existence. They are caught in between. They are creatures of the interval. They pretend to be modern because they perceive that, in relation to the advanced state of the cosmopolitan world, they are late and should be further along the road to modernity than they are. But because the colonial world still places a claim on them, and the markers of non-synchronicity still betray them, they have no rightful place in the future which they have prematurely assumed. They have at best a dubious claim on modernity. They have arrived too soon, thus oscillating between being too early and being too late for modernity because they cannot sustain the "proleptic" fiction that their future is already formed and real.

Conclusion: Non-Synchronicity Today

By way of conclusion, I now want to say something about the contemporary relevance of these remarks for current concerns about the control of time and the orientation of our actions around projected future events. The proleptic time-consciousness that marked an earlier moment of colonial modernity is visible today in a whole new phase of globalization and time-space compression that is characterized not only by the wonders of telecommunication but by the "new modernization" of finance with its more advanced devices for eliminating time and placing claims on ever more distant future events. I am thinking of post-war developments such as the manipulation of genetic systems and the development of pesticides and growth hormones, as well as the rise of flexible labour, rapid reskilling, and international trade agreements such as NAFTA [North American Free Trade Agreement], FTAA [Free Trade Area of the Americas], and MAI [Multilateral Agreement on Investment]. These scientific, social, and political developments have been accompanied by more precise means for controlling the interval between present and future, or experience and expectation. Each of these advances requires of us an ever greater trust in their ability to neutralize time and to subordinate more of the living, social present to some projected, future moment of planning. If we still have something to learn from colonial modernity, it is that, in instances of non-synchronicity, the leap of faith necessary to join experience and expectation is most visible and sometimes, but only sometimes, vulnerable. The parody of colonial modernity betrayed, in a form often achieving comic proportion, is in the illusion that there already exists a temporal whole of which our present actions form a part. This illusion still remains the horizon of any critique of globalization today.[33]

Notes

Originally published as "Hauled Kicking and Screaming into Modernity," in Topia 3 (2003): 81–94. Copyright © University of Toronto Press. Reprinted with permission of the publisher.

1. Ernst Bloch, "Non-synchronism and the Obligation to Its Dialectics," New German Critique 2 (1977): 22.

2. Frantz Fanon, The Wretched of the Earth (New York: Grove Press, 1968), 38.

3. Reinhart Koselleck, Futures Past: On the Semantics of Historical Time (Cambridge, Mass.: MIT Press, 1985), 273.

4. See Stephen Crocker, "Prolepsis: On Speed and Time's Interval," Cultural Values 2.4 (1998): 485–98.

5. Linda Hutcheon, A Theory of Parody: The Teachings of Twentieth-Century Art Forms (New York: Methuen, 1985).

6. John Hope Simpson, White Tie and Decorations: Sir John and Lady Hope Simpson in Newfoundland, 1934–36, ed. Peter Neary (Toronto: Toronto University Press, 1986), 135. John Hope Simpson was one of the British-appointed Commissioners of Government sent to Newfoundland not only to govern but to instruct the population in the manners of fostering and regulating civil society. The commission and the suspension of democracy lasted from 1934 to 1949, at which point Newfoundland, with a good deal of encouragement from a Britain eager to unload its responsibilities, became a province of Canada.

7. Fanon, Wretched of the Earth, 38–39.

8. Joseph Smallwood, "Let Us Draw Close to Canada," in The Book of Newfoundland, ed. Joseph Smallwood (St. John's: Newfoundland Book Publishers, 1967), 3:36. From a speech Smallwood delivered to the National Convention in 1946, later reproduced as "Let Us Draw Close to Canada."

9. Challenge for Change (St. John's: National Film Board, 1967).

10. Smallwood, "Let Us Draw Close to Canada," 36.

11. Ibid., 36.

12. Ibid., 36.

13. Richard Gwyn, *Smallwood: The Unlikely Revolutionary* (Toronto: McClelland and Stewart, 1975), 81.

14. Smallwood, "Let Us Draw Close to Canada," 36.

15. Arjun Appadurai, "Repetition," talk given at International Conference on Time and Value, Lancaster University, Bailrigg, Lancaster, U.K., April 12, 1997.

16. See Lisandro Otero, "Utopia Revisited," trans. Nancy Westrate, *South Atlantic Quarterly* 96.1 (winter 1997), 17–31.

17. Leon Trotsky, "The Law of Combined and Uneven Development," in *The Age of Permanent Revolution: A Trotsky Anthology*, ed. Issac Deutscher (New York: Dell, 1973), 85.

18. *Newfoundland Builds* (St. John's: Atlantic Films, 1952).

19. *Newfoundland Progress Report*, 1951, 4 vols. (St. John's: Atlantic Press, 1951–54). There are four Progress Reports, one for each of the years 1951–54.

20. Harold Horwood, *Joey: The Life and Political Times of Joey Smallwood* (Toronto: Stoddart, 1989), 178.

21. V. S. Naipaul, *The Mimic Men* (Harmondsworth, U.K.: Penguin, 1967).

22. Smallwood, "Let Us Draw Close to Canada," 37.

23. Growth centres already had a precedent in a series of agricultural communities set up at the height of the Depression in the mid-1930s which not only aimed to reduce the number of people dependent on the fishery, but also fostered lessons in civility. Lady Simpson called these communities "the salvation of slum dwellers. . . . The children taught to wash ears and necks—the women have instruction in management of children and of the house, in cooking, dress making and the other female arts" (qtd. in Simpson, *White Tie and Decorations*, 134).

24. Stuart Hall, "The Local and the Global: Globalization and Ethnicity," in *Culture, Globalization and the World System*, ed. Anthony D. King (London: Macmillan, 1991).

25. Chris Brookes, *A Public Nuisance: A History of the Mummer's Troupe in Newfoundland* (St. John's: Institute for Social and Economic Research, 1988), 38.

26. Thomas Mann, *The Magic Mountain* (New York: Vintage, 1967), 239.

27. Ibid., 239.

28. Paul West, "Newfoundland's University," *Atlantic Advocate* 48.9 (1958): 19.

29. Nestor Garcia Canclini, *Hybrid Cultures: Strategies for Entering and Leaving Modernity* (Minneapolis: University of Minnesota Press, 1995).

30. Henri Bergson, "Laughter," in *Comedy*, ed. Wylie Sypher (New York: Doubleday, 1956).

31. Miguel de Cervantes, *The Ingenious Gentleman, Don Quixote de la Mancha*, trans. Samuel Putnam (New York: Viking Press, 1967).

32. The belief that history consists of a series of distinct changes through which different societies must pass.

33. For more on the neutralization of time in capitalism, see Theresa Brennan, "Why the Time Is Out of Joint: Marx's Political Economy without the Subject," *South Atlantic Quarterly* 97.2 (1998): 263–80.

IOAN DAVIES

Theorizing Toronto

Ioan Davies (1936–2000) was born in the Belgian Congo to missionary parents. He pursued his postsecondary education at the University of London (B.Sc. in economics and sociology, 1961) and the University of Essex (Ph.D. in social history and comparative politics, 1970). During this time, Davies completed his national service in Britain and also worked as a journalist. He was also involved with the Campaign for Nuclear Disarmament and, for a time, was the chair of the London New Left Club. Davies immigrated to Canada in 1970, and, in 1972, he joined the Sociology Department at York University, where he taught until his death in 2000. Davies was among the earliest translators of British cultural studies to the Canadian scene. He was one of the founders of Border/Lines (in 1984), Canada's first cultural studies magazine. His influential book Cultural Studies and Beyond: Fragments of Empire (1995), based on his lectures at York University, remains a key text in understanding the history of cultural studies in Canada. His other books are Writers in Prison (1990), Social Mobility and Political Change (1970), and African Trade Unions (1966).

I. Introduction. Toronto: Spectres and Spectacle

The spectres drift across the square in rows.
How empire permeates! And we sit down
in Nathan Phillips square, among the sun,
as if our lives were real.
Lacunae. Parking lots. Regenerations.
Newsstand euphorics and Revell's[1] sign, that not
one countryman has learned, that
men and women live that
they make that life worth dying. Living. Hey,
the dead ones! Gentlemen, generations of
acquiescent spectres gawk at the chrome
on American cars on Queen St., gawk and slump and retreat.

And over the square where I sit, congregating above the Archer
they crowd in a dense baffled throng and the sun does not shine through.
—Dennis Lee, *Civil Elegies*

Thus wrote the Toronto poet Lee in the early 1970s, contemplating the new Toronto City Hall and the installation of Henry Moore's statue, the Archer, which had caused a major civic upheaval when it was unveiled. It marked the moment when the city began to think seriously about its space, as the introduction of new forms of architecture took over from the old: the City Hall itself (commanding a space beside the red sandstone, gothic, old City Hall), Mies van der Rohe's 1967 construction of the Toronto Dominion Bank on Wellington Street (a massive black glass block replacing older, interwar stone and brick offices), and the freeing of the old Harbour and the Railway lands beside Lake Ontario for commercial and public development. Throughout the 1960s and 1970s, the debates over the physical form of the future city centred on which parts of the old should be preserved, and to what use; where and for whom the new developments should take place; and what the pattern of transportation would be (expressways? public transport?). One of the great ravines (the Don Valley) had already been savaged by the running of an expressway down it, and another expressway blocked the lake off from the city: would more follow? A rapid growth of population (fuelled mainly by immigration) and commerce was pushing the city further north as well as east- and westward: issues of governance, social class, ethnicity, gender, land use, architecture, technology, and civility were major features of all discussions about the emerging character of the growing city.

Central features of these debates involved exploring the notions of culture, communication, and the "character" of the city, issues which have become common to all cities in the process of transformation, but perhaps in the case of Toronto strikingly pertinent because of the national discussions within Canada of bilingualism and multiculturalism, of federalism and provincincialism, which took on a major dimension precisely during the same period. During the 1960s and 1970s, Montréal played host both to Expo and to the Olympic Games, and saw the "apprehended revolution" of the Front de Liberation du Québec in 1970 as well as the first separatist government of René Lévesque in the late 1970s. For most of this period, federal politics was dominated by the Liberal governments of Lester Pearson and Pierre Elliott Trudeau, while Ontario provincial politics was dominated by the centre-left Progressive Conservatives. That Montréal might appear to be the focus for the image of

Canada in the world was surely not lost on the politicians, businessmen, and urban planners who debated the future shape of Toronto, the largest non-French-speaking city in Canada.[2]

None of this took place in a vacuum. Like most cities, Toronto was a set of palimpsests of cultures settled on top of each other, from the earliest Indian settlements and the first French colonizers through to the Scots and the English who established the contours of the present city in the late nineteenth century. In parts of the old city, the visual traces of earlier inhabitants remained, as Rosemary Donegan and Rick Salutin[3] showed in their book on Spadina Avenue, that road by which immigrants entered the city from ships or trains and established shops, factories, churches, synagogues, restaurants, theatres. What was noticeably the Jewish section of the interwar years, with the garment trade, a street market, and various synagogues and temples, is now Chinatown, though the Chinese community centre still has Hebrew inscriptions on its walls honouring the Jewish dead, and Grossman's Tavern, the centre of jazz and poetry readings decades ago, holds its own between Vietnamese and Cantonese restaurants.

But, of course, where much of the contemporary city now stands, there were no such buildings but open fields, small hamlets, and wild ravines. The sense of what to build, what to recover or preserve, and what to destroy is thus built upon a set of conflicting notions of what is significant and alive. I would like to argue that, to understand the evolving pattern of the city, it is important to trace the ideas of culture and communication that have been generated both by an intellectual debate around it and by the practices of the various people who inhabit it. To do that, I want to preserve the notions of space (physically, kinetically, culturally) and of communication as an important part of our sense of community, and thus to talk about the habitable city—both in the imagination and in the everyday. This means, for me, taking the imagined city as being equally significant to our understanding as the "real" city and exploring the connection between them. Thus, the Spectres of Lee's poem must necessarily contend with the physical Spectacle—commodified or otherwise.

The notion of theorizing that I wish to employ in understanding Toronto—and indeed any city—does not involve providing a total vision of the city as a definable unit, nor indeed as a set of hypotheses to be tested against "facts," but rather as a series of probing interpretations of aspects of city life and culture which provide clues to making sense of the connections which (possibly) add up to an understanding of the city's biography. In this I think that I am one with Italo Calvino, who, in *Invisible Cities*,[4] provides a "reading" of Venice that is based on partial views of the city but ultimately provides clues for reading more than Venice, even extending to Osaka-Kyoto and Greater Los Angeles. And yet, by disconnecting his various versions of Venice from each other, Calvino leaves us asking, "So what is your Venice? Why is it important?" With my conclusion, I hope to lay the grounds for doing that in Toronto. This, it will be noted, is rather different from Walter Benjamin's initial approach in his "Paris, Capital of the Nineteenth Century," which was written precisely to show why Paris was the modern city par excellence. I make no such claims for Toronto, and it would be futile to try to do so. A more modest aim, I hope, is to argue that thinking about the various theorists helps us to understand Toronto, and, in understanding that process, we learn more about ourselves. But, like Benjamin, I felt it was important to begin with those who had written in and around Toronto— those whose worlds were galvanized by the city, even if they had wider concerns and influences—and weave their thinking into the great phenomenology, epistemology, and semiology of being in the city.

The theoretical discussions generated in Toronto are part of those common to all societies which confront the issues of survival, freedom, and spiritual awareness: the philosopher George Grant, the literary critics Northrop Frye and Marshall McLuhan, the political theorist C. B. Macpherson, various creative writers and artists, musicians, architects, and academics (including the feminist sociologist Dorothy Smith, the urban utopian Jane Jacobs, the agronomist Alex Wilson, the poet bp nichol, and the critic/instrumentalist Glenn Gould) have all provided important accounts of reading the contemporary culture of the city. And yet their work was written in/against this city, in part framed by its institutions and activities, and in no small measure fed back into the living culture. No book that has set about theorizing the city quite pulls off a theoretical engagement with city culture. With Marshall Berman,[5] a Marxian aphorism becomes a wrap-around for a series of discrete narratives; on the other hand, with Mike Davis,[6] economy and power provide the mechanisms for understanding the architecture and texture of Los Angeles. This paper attempts, rather, to consider Toronto as a place where theory is produced and to suggest ways that theorizing provides a means for coming to terms with the city.

In the first seven sections of this paper[7] I suggest what seem to me to be the various key ways in which writers connected with the city have conceptualized the problems of it existing as a cultural unit. In the concluding two sections I try to reformulate these concerns by turning back to the city as its own spectacle and viewing it from inside.

[. . .]

III. C. B. Macpherson, Jane Jacobs, and the Idea of a Bourgeois Civic Culture

The justification of liberal democracy still rests, and must rest, on the ultimate value of the free self-developing individual. But in so far as freedom is still seen as possession, as freedom from any but market relations with others, it can scarcely serve as the ultimate value of modern democracy.[8]

The political theorist C. B. Macpherson spent most of his life writing and thinking about the bourgeoisie and the relationship of democratic theory and practice to the power of capitalism. His books, *Real World of Democracy*[9] and *Democratic Theory*, explore in sophisticated detail the relationships between the market, property, and democracy, while through his teaching he educated a generation of political theorists and activists. John Porter, whose *Vertical Mosaic*[10] became something of a paradigm for understanding Canadian elites through the Weberian matrix of class, status, and power, concluded, at the end of his survey, that the people who ruled Ontario were important property-owners in Toronto and its environs who also had the opportunity to send their children to the elite private schools and universities. At the time that Porter wrote his book, the people who ruled Canada came either from Upper Canada College in Toronto or from the classical colleges in Montréal.

It is useful to contrast the works of Macpherson and Porter with that of Jane Jacobs, whose *Death and Life of Great American Cities*[11] provided a critique of certain kinds of urban development, and who established a manifesto for an urban culture that was not beholden purely to market forces but rather to the self-preservation of the bourgeoisie. This analysis called into being a bourgeois class that was profoundly conscious of civil culture, the preservation of aspects of tradition, and the market advantages of being regarded as global in its cultural ambitions. It was an urban culture that saw Culture as being the work of cultured people. But it was also the culture of a propertied class which tried to preserve its own enclaves and decentre government to the community level, a bourgeois culture which resisted the government's teaming up with the construction industry to create expressways by tearing through middle-class areas like Forest Hill. Battles lost in New York might be won in Toronto.

It is especially important to contrast this view with Macpherson's. For Jacobs, the campaign to renew the city was The View from Greenwich Village, not the Bronx (the area most affected by the modernization of Robert Moses). It was a property-owners' democracy. If Macpherson agreed about property being the basis for democracy, his definition of property was different: "Political writers in the seventeenth century spoke of a man's property as including not only his rights in material things and revenues, but also his life, his person, his faculties, his liberty, his conjugal affection, his honour, etc, and material property might be ranked lower than some of the others, as it was specifically by Hobbes. The fact that property once had such a wider meaning opens up the possibility, which our narrower concept has not allowed, that property may once again be seen as more than rights in material things and revenues."[12] The shape that current cultural institutions, architecture, and perambulating spaces have taken owes much to these competing visions. But we should be conscious of the interests involved in such competitiveness. Jacobs herself operates as something of a weathervane. Against this, there always was, and is now more stridently, a bourgeoisie of the *nouveau riche*, whose models of the civic are precisely those attacked by Jacobs, whose figureheads are the property-developers, and whose concerns for civic culture are marked totally by market rhetoric. If we wish to think about the culture of the bourgeoisie in Toronto, we have, of course, to think about the bourgeoisie in its different guises.

Robertson Davies's bourgeoisie are the British in disguise, those ghostly echoes on paper who pull Toronto back to the BBC, PBS, and Conan Doyle (draped in the pseudo-psychology of Jung). Both Atwood and Lee represent the bourgeoisie in retrieval, mourning, and ultimate (in Atwood's case) feminist transcendence. Ondaatje represents the underbelly of the British influence, the chiaroscuro of imperialism as it presents the immigrant road-builders, the *médecins sans frontières*, the swashbuckling Italian truckers. In a city built by the British, where over seventy percent of the population now has non-British roots, Ondaatje's writing adds a new twist to the sense of bourgeois culture by bringing in the immigrants of recent years who move from being construction workers to being owners of construction sites. In this way the bourgeoisie, who made the culture of the city—the city of Toronto the Good (meaning Toronto the British as it would like to be seen)—are replaced by a cosmopolitan bourgeoisie, but also a bourgeoisie which sees culture as a product to be bought and sold: thus the culture of reflection and civility is replaced by the culture of commodification.

The 1990s have seen the ultimate stand-off between the various levels of the bourgeoisie. The proposal to amalgamate the five Toronto "cities" into one "mega"-city tested the various definitions of civility. The provincial government of "Mike" Harris clearly saw that its support came from the petty-bourgeoisie of the Toronto hinterlands, the nascent bourgeoisie of the new immigrant communities who live in the various suburban regions around Toronto, and the hidden agents of a global financial agenda. If this was a relationship created on the golf courses, it was one that bore little relationship to democracy, civility, or a common culture (the Asian economic crisis of late 1997 was, as *The Economist* put it, summed up in one four-letter word: g-o-l-f). The provincial election had voted in a group of those who saw the idea of the civic as being bound up with private territoriality, a suburban garrison state mentality, a rejection of the idea of a common good, and the belief in the market as necessarily being right. Thus, anything sponsored by the "state" was necessarily evil; any organization—schools, universities, publishing houses, films, TV organizations, even welfare systems, and, presumably, all levels of government—which had not been proven to be effective in terms of the market was shown to be defective in practice and intent. Any discussions about rights, constitutions, civilities, even culture (whether regional, national, or creative) were ultimately inconsequential. In opposition, the "old" bourgeoisie of Toronto, with the cultured lumpenproletariat, the intelligentsia, the media, the creative body of the downtown, rallied itself to redefine civility as something that was coherently sociable. In spite of a marvellous e-mail campaign and a coherently catholic website, the downtown lost (only 5 percent of Toronto's population in 1997 had access to the Web). The "mega"-city came into existence, and its first mayor was Mel Lastman, formerly mayor of Glenn Gould's anonymous suburban city. (The appearance of Barbara Hall, former mayor of the City of Toronto and the main contender against Lastman, on the front page of *The Toronto Star* accompanied by the CBC's Adrienne Clarkson and her partner, author John Ralston Saul, cannot have helped things much. The CBC—as opposed to The Sports Network—and Governor General's Award-winners do little for mayoral candidates when the electorate is composed largely of anti-intellectual *nouveaux riches*.)

Coming from a quite different set of concerns, the sociologist Dorothy Smith (who has taught for the past twenty years at the Ontario Institute for Studies in Education), drawing on phenomenological and

Marxist points of departure, has called for the making of everyday life as a problem of knowing as it affects the ongoing relations of power. Because her books—*The Everyday World as Problematic* and *The Conceptual Practices of Power*[13]—are primarily written from a feminist perspective, their implications affect all aspects of social control and the practice of being. The groups that she addresses may, or may not, be part of the cultured bourgeoisie and may therefore have quite different senses of the civic. But the problematic exhibited in Smith's approach confronts another tension in the city—between the sense of civic well-being displayed in the various modalities of the bourgeoisie and the tentative modalities of experiential negotiation. In this, it is important to consider the housewife negotiating her way to the rape shelter, the immigrant with the police, the bag lady with the shopping mall security guards, and the indigent artist with would-be sponsors. Toronto is a city, like most others, where people who inhabit its spaces have to negotiate their well-being against the perils of the state, corporate capitalism, and each other.

[. . .]

VI. Objects without Theorists: The Group-of-Seven-or-Twenty-Five-or-So

Toronto, at that time, was not exactly a hospitable place for contemporary art of any sort, and the decision to situate a large sculpture by Henry Moore in front of the New City Hall was the straw that broke the political camel's back. In fact, it was largely responsible for the electoral defeat of the mayor, who supported its purchase. His chief opponent proclaimed that "Torontonians do not want abstract art shoved down their throats," and, of course, won the subsequent election handily. Perhaps one indication of the remarkable change in Toronto's outlook during the last decade is that we now possess the largest collection of sculptures by Henry Moore in the Western Hemisphere; oddly enough, in view of the earlier fuss, the collection was initiated by a gift from the sculptor himself.[14]

One of the most curious features of English Canadian intellectual life up to the 1980s is the almost total lack of art criticism, whether about Canadian or any other art. When any of the major theorists discuss fine art, it is by means of illustration. With Northrop Frye, paintings are images to illustrate some other point he is making. Thus there is no ongoing discourse into which Canadian art might be inserted. Instead such discourse as there might have been is pre-empted by images which have been promoted to iconographic status. If Glenn Gould's music is a music without bodies, the Group of Seven is art of the wilderness without people, an art fit for bed and breakfast places, the Bay catalogues, or to be collected by Kenneth Thompson so that segments can be displayed by the *Globe and Mail* as Christmas cards. With Joan Murray and Robert Fulford, the Seven and their various hangers-on were transformed into a heritage industry long before anyone decided whether they were any good. The two satellite galleries of Toronto, the Robert McLaughlin Gallery in Oshawa and the McMichael Canadian Art Collection in Kleinburg, are monuments to Canadian Kitsch, to the nostalgic longing for roughing it in the bush. That virtually the same pseudo-Impressionist art might be found anywhere in the subarctic (Sweden, Norway, Finland, Latvia, Russia: the Tretyakov Gallery in Moscow is plastered with the stuff) has hardly occurred to the promoters of Group-of-Seven folklore (and a comparative study would be helpful and instructive). Prior to the 1980s, instead of art criticism and theory, we have hagiography and insane public disputes about preserving the "heritage" intact.

The reasons may be speculated, but the dramatic feature of the city from the end of the 1970s to the present has been the growth of alternative (parallel) galleries and a series of magazines which concern themselves with visual art as a dynamic part of our entire environment and culture. The interrelationship of performing and visual art is part of the reason (but that was true of religious art in the past and surely always of the art of the Salons). But, as Berland, Straw, and Tomas's *Theory Rules*[15] indicates, the liveliness of art is bound up with the liveliness of theory. The banality of much Canadian art is surely related to both the absence of theory and the absence of a creative pedagogical centre. The experience of literature is surely—after Frye—an indication of this. Unfortunately, Toronto, as far as visual art goes, is likely to see more of the same. Corporations, who are by far the largest consumers of paintings and sculptures, seem to prefer Group of Seven-ish or Norval Morriseau-ish stuff. Contemporary urban artists are hardly likely to find their way into the halls of commerce.[16]

Together with the experience of the visual arts is the curious experience of architecture. The growth of the new suburbs in Vaughan and Markham displays something of the same antisocial tendency as the Dome does. The houses are built so that their bums fart on the main street, with high walls preventing anyone seeing the backyards themselves. The streets are very wide, the shops locked into shopping malls.

Going for a walk would be unthinkable—too far to walk and nothing to see. High security and the dominance of the automobile have conspired to turn this area into a hostile, predatorial land. Who chose these designs? How did the walkable downtown invent Glenn Gould's anonymous city?

VII. Poetic Playfulness

how could you? saint reat's been
such a sad guy. maybe you'll bring joy into his life.
maybe the maybes can come to be!
suddenly it makes sense. is it the poem makes us dense?
or simply writing, the act of ordering
the other mind
blinding us
to the greater vision
what's a
poem like you doing in a
poem like this?
—bp nichol, *Martyrology*

This sad city (even the gays are sad) is a city of comedy, of art, of playfulness, the dance of the other in a dance for the other. It needs its martyrs. It finds its martyrs,

but
dedicate this poem to a whim
and
as there are words i haven't written
things i haven't seen
so this poem continues
a kind of despair takes over
the poem is written in spite of
all the words i once believed were saints[17]

The poet bp nichol not only encourages the playfulness of language but surely also helps us to find a St. Ance, where the performance is both tragic and comedic.[18]

bp nichol introduces us to a Toronto which spins the theorists on their heads. For nichol, this is a city where the words walk and where the spaces resound with music. This is the jazzed-up city, which takes the metaphors of the global village, the trips to the cottages, the nutritionist, and the psychiatrist, the vertiginous pressure of city life and puts them together into an ongoing myth of city life, the myth of living in death, the confrontation of self as work, as the making of a poem. nichol provides a sense of the (bittersweet) excitement of creation:

> simply writing, the act of ordering
> the other mind
> blinding us
> to the greater vision[19]

With nichol, we stand back from McLuhan, Innis, Gould, and the others because we have absorbed them as the "greater vision." We are confronted instead with the mundane reality of getting by with whatever equipment we have. Behind the façade of the theorists, we make poetry, music, and art. Not because we despise them but because, in their words and architectures and images, we have ingested them too powerfully. That is part of the space we inhabit.

VIII. Imaginary Cities

In his studies of Paris, Walter Benjamin noted the connection between the new bourgeois living spaces in the late nineteenth century and the rise of the detective novel (even truer, perhaps, in London than in Paris). In Toronto, the city is written on and about in many different forms than the novel. The living spaces of this city now include high-rise apartments, lofts, recycled industrial warehouses, and condominiums, as well as the imagined living spaces of film, television, theatre, music, the Internet (including chat rooms and electronic mail), magazines, journals, newspapers, and radio. Much of this is ephemeral. And yet, as Peter Fritzsche[20] notes in his marvellous study of literate Berlin, it is this sense of the writing of the city that is essential to understanding the way in which the city is read, written, lived. Toronto is a city that is much written around, yet the ontological vision of the city into which we who live here write ourselves is rarely encountered: it is invariably read against the epistemological, where the shifts in knowledge and the codes that frame reality become more real than reality itself. If we are to rethink writing as imagination, surely it is important to put the two together. This is perhaps why the novel is taken as the basis for coming to terms with the city as the intersection between the imaginary and the epistemological: it allows us to conflate ourselves as sensitive beings and the great chain of knowledge as processes which we can imagine to be at the core of the flow of experience. But it is, of course, a particular and privileged core. Everyone else lives in fragments. But do the fragments add up? To understand this, it is, perhaps, important to return to the themes of my earlier sections.

The major theorists introduced here proposed a series of understandings of Canada, Toronto, and ourselves as integral to the world's vision of itself that spun not only around the notion of different realities—different cultures—but where those notions intersected. Of course, these visions may not intersect except in particular circumstances. They are imaginations of places where we might be. Calvino tried to imagine the same place as having different realities. The various theorists and creative writers who have engaged Toronto have likewise imagined different spaces: the space of perfect democracy, of a "global village," of a feminist utopia, of a bourgeois urban paradise, of the city with perfect acoustics. While Toronto is none of these, their contrary images contend in the making of the city and the structure of the city's many forms of architecture, as well as the multiple forms of life that inhabit these structures, provide marks of these contestations, indications of competing imaginaries.

In his collection of articles on Toronto places, *Globe and Mail* columnist John Bentley Mays[21] provides an indication of the variety of building structures and the various ways that styles have emerged over the past century. At one level this might be read as an account of the evolution of architectural styles—and the organization of Mays's sections partly encourages us to look for these, with titles like "Modern," "Moderne Variations," "High Styles"—but the book is rather a collection of pieces on places which are very conscious of the theoretical concerns indicated above. Mays is concerned with how nature is incorporated into the buildings (rivers, ravines, gardens, cemeteries, the edges of the city, the waterfront); on where we shop, pray, read, live, work, and play; and of the whole notion of the streetscape and the idea of cyber and acoustic spaces. Throughout it all, the idea that architecture is somehow independent of what we do with it is avoided. Of course, there are some important indications of pieces of architecture which altered the shape of the city— the Canadian National Exhibition grounds (opened in 1892), the Toronto Dominion Bank (1967), the Sky Dome (1989)—but these are not given pride of place; rather, we are invited to explore their meaning along with the many other sites that the population inhabits.

Architecture is not put on any kind of pedestal but is an artefact like any other that is part of the process of civic and commercial decision-making.[22] Mays invites us to explore both the drama of a well-executed intervention into the cityscape and also its use, abuse, and disuse. And thus, because architecture is part of the process of being, he takes us to the expressways under whose ramps the destitute live, to the railway station which was built to take people out of the city—not into it—to Parkdale, which was once the open gate to the city but is now a cul-de-sac populated by the poor, and back to the Toronto Dominion Centre, whose original concept is now flawed by an ill conceived architectural attachment. Thus, if many outsiders see Toronto as a "modern" city, it is a flawed modernity, reorganized by the happenstance of being lived in.

Another route to viewing cities as a collection of places with attendant spectacles is to think about what people actually do there. Of course, like a map-reader, Mays provides a guide to what spaces we might inhabit. It is a reading which, in spite of himself, is predicated on place as itself. But spaces move into each other because we move. bp nichol's world is a world of moving words, Glenn Gould's is a world of remaking old sounds, Marshall McLuhan's is a world of moving kinetic sensibilities, C. B. Macpherson's and Dorothy Smith's worlds compel us to confront the alternative spaces of sociability and civic presence. In their different ways, Frye, Grant, Wilson, or even the Group of Seven compel us to confront ourselves in the great spaces of nature and ultimate meaning. What I am suggesting is that, in this city, Toronto, as we sit on the subway, or stand on the corner of Broadview and Danforth, or go to Toronto Island to celebrate Caribana (that superb midsummer evocation of Trinidad and Jamaica), the different spaces suggested by these writers and artists shift into each other. The imagined cities that are named "Toronto" are not one city but many cities. They meet in a fleeting moment, the glance of an eye, the brush of a skirt, the recognition of a piece of music.

In one way, there is no *one* Toronto for those who live in it. Lynn Crosbie has tried to reclaim the moments of these intersections in a powerful series of prose poems which use the letters of the alphabet (as good an excuse as any) to sing the modalities of the city. She writes: "I am a punk with two inches of spiked hair, a fish out of water. Trying to breathe. Sending long letters home and cultivating a depression that borders on nerve."[23]

Toronto is a city, like many more, to which people come because it encapsulates a version of a world beyond their own but which, for most, cannot deliver everything it seems to promise. Looking at those intersections in the city reveals more than Mays's spaces; it reveals the movements of real people as they slip between different places. Not that there are no flâneurs in Toronto, but this is a flânerie that sometimes reveals itself as the desperate statement of the impoverished. Toronto, in spite of its reputation, is not a kind city. The current mayor is attempting to send the "squeegee kids" (unemployed young people who clean car windscreens at major intersections) to "boot camps" so that they can learn to do something productive. In contrast to John Bentley Mays's aestheticization of the city, Lynn Crosbie tries to position Toronto as a city with worry about life, jobs, and identity at its core.

IX. Concluding

In the beginning, I introduced Toronto through the pen of Dennis Lee, who was concerned that a proud city with its own Presbyterian and Anglican heritage was being dragged into the maelstrom of the "modern," with buildings and art that would change it beyond recognition. Lee's spectres were those of the founders of the city. His spectacles were the buildings, art, and sculptures but also the founding fathers of the city. In thirty years the city has gone through a series of transformations: the population has increased to four million, the city has taken over a large portion of the hinterland; today there are more (Italian, Chinese, Korean, West Indian, African, French) Catholics than Presbyterians or Anglicans; the buildings have moved from Gothic to Panopticon. The government has changed to such an extent that the comforting inner-city sense of community has given way to the driving sense of the "global." If in the 1960s and 1970s Montréal was a real issue of civic competition, by 1998 Toronto is assured of its global space. It has overtaken Montréal in population: the banks have all relocated there, as have many businesses.

There is, of course, a conflict between this sense of *élan*, represented by the current Ontario provincial government and the new City of Toronto, and the reality of a city. In a recent article on architecture, Fredric Jameson (1998) tried to show how the idea of architecture as a space for city growth is bound up with the notion of land speculation and that speculation is bound up with the idea that the space of the city is always up for land-grabs.[24] This is not a new story, but the idea that the city's public art is totally beholden to capitalism presumably puts it in the same league as feudal Catholicism or Ottoman Islam as occasions for censorship of what is, or what is not, allowed to be built. But Jameson, in discussing the Rockefeller Center in New York, invokes Hegel's "ruse" of history, where unintended consequences of a capitalist project are realized as something else. Now Fredric Jameson is not new to Toronto, and New York, though it might be a figment of Toronto's wannabe imagination, is not Toronto, but in many ways the two cities collide in the image-spaces we inhabit.

If we go to the Manulife Centre in Toronto, a building established to sell insurance and banking, where the Toronto Film Festival moves and has its being, I meet Fred, and we go to watch Iranian films and think about Jean-Luc Godard and meet graduate students. Or not. We escape to the "ruse" of history. We *are* the ruse of history.

Toronto is that kind of place. A slippage between then, now, and becoming.

Notes

Originally published as "Theorizing Toronto," in *Topia* 3 (2003): 14–36. Copyright © University of Toronto Press. Reprinted with permission of the publisher.

1. Finnish architect Viljo Revell designed the new City Hall. It was built in the early 1960s, and Revell died almost as soon as the building was completed.

2. "Non-French" because, by the early 1970s, the influx of immigrants—from Italy, Central and Eastern Europe, India, and China—had created a new city of people whose first language was generally not English.

3. Rosemary Donegan and Rick Salutin, *Spadina* (Toronto: Douglas and McIntyre, 1985).

4. Italo Calvino, *Invisible Cities* (New York: Harcourt Brace, 1974).

5. Marshall Berman, *All That Is Solid Melts into Air: The Experience of Modernity* (New York: Simon and Schuster, 1981).

6. Mike Davis, *City of Quartz: Excavating the Future of Los Angeles* (London: Verso, 1991).

7. For reasons of length, several sections of this paper have been removed. In section II, Davies considered Frye, Grant, and the nature-culture divide in Toronto; section IV explores Innis, McLuhan, and the "Wired City"; and section V discusses Glenn Gould as an exemplum of the tensions in Toronto between technology and the social.—Eds.

8. C. B. Macpherson, *Democratic Theory: Essays in Retrieval* (Oxford: Oxford University Press, 1973), 194.

9. C. B. Macpherson, *The Real World of Democracy* (Toronto: Canadian Broadcasting Corporation, 1969).

10. John A. Porter, *The Vertical Mosaic: An Analysis of Social Class and Power in Canada* (Toronto: Toronto University Press, 1965).

11. Jane Jacobs, *The Death and Life of Great American Cities* (New York: Vintage Books, 1961).

12. Macpherson, *Democratic Theory*, 139.

13. Dorothy Smith, *The Everyday World as Problematic: A Feminist Sociology* (Toronto: Toronto University Press, 1987); *The Conceptual Practices of Power: A Feminist Sociology of Knowledge* (Toronto: Toronto University Press, 1990).

14. Glenn Gould, "Toronto," in *The Glenn Gould Reader* (New York: Knopf, 1984), 410–11.

15. Jody Berland, Will Straw, and David Tomas, eds., *Theory Rules: Art as Theory, Theory and Art* (Toronto: YYZ Books/University of Toronto Press, 1996).

16. Ioan Davies, "Theory and Creativity in English Canada: Magazines, the State and Cultural Movement," *Journal of Canadian Studies* 30 no. 1 (1995): 5–10.

17. bp nichol, *Martyrology*, bk. 1, *Scenes from the Lives of Saints* (Toronto: Coach House Press, 1972), 12.

18. With bp nichol we walk the St. Reets looking for the gods and saints who will save us from the world that is around us. Instead we find St. Erling, St. Ranger, St. Ratified, flying the flag of St. Ars and St. Ripes, comforted by St. Ripteaser and St. Rumpet. We put on our St. Ereo and wonder whether we can St. And it much longer. (Apologies to David St. Alwart's "Afterword" to *The Martyrology*.)

19. nichol, *Martyrology*, bk. 2, *Friends as Footnotes*, 16.

20. Peter Fritzsche, *Reading Berlin 1900* (Cambridge: Harvard University Press, 1996).

21. John Bentley Mays, *Emerald City: Toronto Visited* (Toronto: Viking, 1994).

22. One of the ongoing problems of thinking about cities and any aspect of post-Enlightenment culture is to take architecture as a metaphor for all that we think the creative potential to be about. Much of the rhetoric surrounding postmodernism has been borrowed from architectural accounts. In a succinct but dense little book, the Japanese critical philosopher Kojin Karatani has argued that the architectural metaphor has been developed since Descartes to overrule the more substantial socioeconomic features which are at the core of understanding the processes of capital development. In relation to understanding the growth of the contemporary city, Karatani's writing should surely be conjoined with that of Benjamin, Foucault, Simmel, and de Certeau in order to relocate architecture as materiality, rather than a metaphorical closure. See Kojin Karatani, *Architecture as Metaphor: Language, Number, Money*, trans. Sabu Kohso, ed. Michael Sparks (Cambridge, Mass.: MIT Press, 1995).

23. Lynn Crosbie, "Alphabet City," in *Queen Rat: New and Selected Poems* (Toronto: Anansi, 1998), 53.

24. Fredric Jameson, "The Brick and the Balloon: Architecture, Idealism and Land Speculation," *New Left Review* 228 (1998): 25–46.—Eds.

WILL STRAW

Shifting Boundaries, Lines of Descent: Cultural Studies and Institutional Realignments

Will Straw (b. 1954) teaches in the Department of Art History and Communications Studies at McGill University. Before joining McGill in 1993, he held an appointment in film studies in the School for Studies in Art and Culture at Carleton University. Straw received his M.A. in communications from McGill University in 1980 and a Ph.D. from the same institution in 1990. He is a former president of the Canadian Communications Association and the author of over seventy articles on film, music, and culture. *Popular Music: Scenes and Sensibilities* (2007) is a recent collection of his writings on music. In addition to his pioneering work on contemporary music, Straw has long been an important figure who has linked cultural studies communities in and outside of Canada.

My concern, in this paper, is with mapping out certain tensions and anxieties as they have shaped the ongoing development of a cultural studies project in English Canada. The value and legitimacy which I ascribe to this project itself is largely unstated here, and I would hope that the analysis which follows is not seen simply as a cynical recounting of localized struggles for prestige and influence. Nevertheless, if one accepts that the terrain of cultural studies is one which will forever be marked by disputes and jurisdictional battles, and that the final dissolution of these is neither imminent nor possible, then an analysis which seeks to specify their effects within a context such as that of English Canada serves to clarify the conditions under which cultural studies communities take shape.

Geographical Realignments

By the mid-to-late 1980s, one could reasonably claim that cultural studies (from which the qualifying "British" had now detached itself) was flourishing most visibly within the academic culture of the United States. In part, this repeated the predictable itinerary of recent projects of theoretical revision; like psychoanalytic film theory or literary deconstruction, cultural studies had crossed the Atlantic and settled into the elephantine infrastructure of the U.S. academy. More accurately, perhaps, cultural studies in the United States represented the turn within a number of disciplines in the humanities to concerns and methods which one might risk calling sociological towards, for example, the ethnography of audiences in media studies, the study of intellectual formations and institutional power in literary history, or accounts of the construction of social space in a variety of cultural forms. In many cases, as well, disciplines such as film or English studies which had lived through their poststructuralist moments found themselves newly authorized by a politics of social identity to investigate the representational status of cultural artefacts. Media or cultural texts were increasingly examined in terms of their role as sites for the figuring of social identities, from perspectives which remained cognizant of the specificities of particular textual forms but no longer obsessively insistent upon them.

More so than has been the case elsewhere, I would argue, cultural studies within the United States has been marked by the minor role played within it by the established social sciences. The sociological turn described above has been produced within the humanities, as part of a larger transformation by which a politics of cultural identity (of race, gender and sexuality) has come to dominate the wider space of oppositional politics generally, within and outside the academy. The symptomatic development here is not merely the cohering of most oppositional politics under the sign of the cultural, but the extent to which the humanities (and the discipline of anthropology, which has moved to embrace them) have come to authorize within their boundaries the discussion of virtually any question of sociocultural interest. (Communications studies, situated conceptually and institutionally at the boundary between the humanities and social sciences, may be seen to function as a bulwark between the two, as far as the migration of cultural studies is concerned.) In this respect, the situation is an inversion of that observable in the 1960s, when sociology and neighbouring disciplines within the social sciences opened their doors to embrace most of the resonant questions of the period.

At the beginning of the 1990s, I shared with many the sense that, while cultural studies had begun within Great Britain and undergone remarkable expansion within the United States, it promised to become increasingly Canadian and Australian. Discounting those biases rooted in my own geographical location, one can see in the evolving agenda of cultural studies the emergent centrality of questions with a particular relevance to these two countries. The current interrogation of notions of nationhood and cultural identity, and the debate over the relationship of cultural theory to questions of public policy and economic development, have at the very least encouraged the migration of theoretical and intellectual work between Canada and Australia. For those working in these countries, I suspect, this development has partially resolved a longtime tension between the appeal of cultural studies as an ongoing, multinational project of theoretical revision and our commitment to working simultaneously in areas, like those of media policy studies or political economy, which seemed more concretely interventionist. Within media analysis in Canada, the turn towards "thick policy" studies, to work which is not simply a chronicling of victimization or dependency but a rethinking of the terms of cultural identity, has been nourished in part by the larger shift in cultural studies within the Anglo-American world.

Institutional Reorderings

Tony Bennett's call for an analysis of the "institutional conditions of cultural studies"[1] invites attention to the ways in which cultural studies has produced new relationships between individual intellectual activity and a variety of communities of interest whose scale, geographical location and institutional position vary widely. In this respect, Ellen Rooney's appealing definition of cultural studies as "an antidisciplinary practice defined by the repeated, indeed, endless rejection of the logic of the disciplines"[2] demands a measure of qualification. As a collective conversation, cultural studies has not threatened the boundaries between disciplines so much as it has altered the terms under which change within them occurs. By continuously redefining the priorities and procedures of cultural analysis, cultural studies has produced and perpetuated the sense of there being a "centre" within cultural research. It has, however, simultaneously ensured that the location of this centre, relative to the place of different disciplines and currents of intellectual work, will shift over time.[3]

In my own institution, for example, the emergent appeal of a social geography has, in minor but observable ways, diminished the prominence of film theory, whose centring of questions of gender and ideology around issues of spectatorship once proved more resonant across a number of disciplines and constituencies. The relationship of individual or disciplinary intellectual projects to cultural studies is partly a function of the extent to which currents within these projects are tied to the latter's trajectories of change. It is an effect, as well, of the degree to which shifts in the relative prominence of different disciplines within cultural studies will alter the range of questions about which such disciplines feel authorized and compelled to speak.

Decisions by disciplines to embrace many of the concerns of cultural studies are often made in response to a perceived diminishing of their status and influence within intellectual culture, and are not inevitably or exclusively the result of projects of radical transformation. Crises of purpose within literature, music or anthropology departments, for example, which one might read as evidence of their historical decline, often result in processes of disciplinary rejuvenation which maintain these disciplines' intellectual and institutional hegemony. The most common response to these crises is the observation that these disciplines are becoming interesting again, as their own processes of internal critique come to be monitored by those working in a variety of adjacent disciplines. To take the most prominent recent example, the demonstration that forms of ethnographic or anthropological writing are ultimately "literary" constructions, whose inseparability from regimes of geopolitical power is now evident,[4] has served to invigorate and recentre the discipline of anthropology as much as it has produced calls for its disappearance. In important ways, obviously, these internal changes are welcome, and their effects on pedagogical substance and faculty composition are not negligible. At the same time, however, by invoking their past importance and power to justify the urgency and prioritizing of their own projects of internal transformation, these disciplines are often able to maintain their institutional privilege.

The risk of an engagement with cultural studies is that of participation in an intellectual field in which, as a feminist film theorist described it recently, race has displaced gender, or in which a rethinking of nationhood has taken over from a preoccupation with questions of subjectivity. In one sense, cultural studies exists only to the extent that we can identify certain collective shifts of interest or movements of theoretical development across a broad intellectual terrain. Arguably, then, cultural studies may not be defined in substantive terms, but functions as the name given to a relatively unitary enterprise of theoretical revision, in which ideas are scrutinized and debated while their usefulness to ongoing and long-term disciplinary and political projects is determined. The advantage of ongoing theoretical revision over time is that, like most enterprises which produce temporary orthodoxies, it can forge a sense of collective purpose among those participant in it. The well-intentioned claim that work within cultural studies responds directly to contextual political imperatives, and that fashions and orthodoxies constitute distractions from these, misses the extent to which the emergence and gravitational pull of points of reference serve to perpetuate exchange between otherwise disparate projects. The danger, of course, is that the regular displacement of one set of theoretical questions by another may be taken as evidence, that political and quotidian realities are themselves necessarily changing.

In English Canada (as in Great Britain) the emergence of a cultural studies has been marked by a more persistent enterprise of dialogue between the humanities and social sciences. "Culture" has continued to be a question of sociological importance within Canada, at the centre of ongoing political tensions and disputes over regional and linguistic diversity, so that attempts to demarcate those academic boundaries within which it will be studied have not usually succeeded. While historical borders between domains of intellectual practice in Canada have thus been less rigid than in many other contexts, it would be misleading to claim that they have been dissolved or transcended. One effect of the circulation of "cultural studies" (as, simultaneously, a term, a project and a set of theoretical legacies) has been the institution of an almost permanent unease with prevailing institutional definitions of intellectual work. At one level, this unease contains an implicit teleology positing that moment when these definitions will disappear. At the same time, however, one of its concrete effects has been a preoccupation with the relative influence of particular centres and currents of intellectual activity. Cultural studies is characterized (and its development driven) by the contradiction between its self-conception as the institutor of permanent dialogue and its status as a field marked by shifting agendas. This contradiction has given rise to a significant paradox within the politics of intellectual communities. While, on the one hand, cultural studies has created a space for transdisciplinary dialogue; a dialogue institutionalized within interdisciplinary programs, cross-disciplinary research groups and academic conferences. This space has also become the vantage point from which the relative value of different traditions and sites of cultural analysis may be newly observed and measured. In particular, it has magnified long-standing tensions between those who call regularly for work which is "grounded" in political or economic realities and others for whom the style appropriate to cultural analysis is to be an interpretive or broadly speculative one.

In this respect, debates over the theoretical and political substance of cultural studies often elide the function of the term itself within academic and intellectual culture. "Cultural studies," in the English Canadian context, has come to designate a space to be occupied and claimed as much as it has named a substantive theoretical heritage to be perpetuated and adapted. The simple existence of the term, it might be argued, has called forth this space as the stake and pretext underlying new forms of interaction between intellectual domains. Increasingly, the only agreement concerning cultural studies in English Canada resides in the implicit assumption that it will serve to circumscribe a certain unifying impulse in cultural research, but the nature and purpose of this unification elicit ongoing disagreement, as does the question of who will dominate it. Thus, for certain currents within English Canadian academic culture, "cultural studies" designates the pulling together and scrutinizing of a variety of dispersed writings on Canadian culture, many of which predate or have been untouched by the legacy of British cultural studies. In this sense, the term has encouraged and been affixed to the retrospective construction of a tradition which might sustain and renew longstanding debates over the character of English Canadian culture. For others, cultural studies represents participation in the ongoing, multinational project of theoretical revision and debate discussed above, in which political priorities and theoretical agendas constantly succeed and displace each other. The unity of cultural studies, defined in this way, has less to do with the persistence of shared concerns than with collective commitment to an unfolding dialogue whose points of reference, orthodoxies and pertinence to the Canadian situation are constantly changing.

Tensions over these very different conceptions of "cultural studies" manifest themselves regularly in familiar, even gossipy disagreements over the long-term value or momentary trendiness of particular positions. In this respect, analogies between cultural studies and punk music (which arrived in Canada at approximately the same time) are not entirely frivolous and occasionally invoked. The communities which took shape around each in Canada have been marked by contradictions between an avowed, even platitudinous, commitment to the local and a cosmopolitan investment in criteria of authentication and expertise elaborated elsewhere. Extending this analogy, one might note the prevalence in both communities of recurrent anxieties over fashionability, institutionalization and celebrity. These concerns are obviously common within subcultures self-defined as those of opposition or resistance. They are magnified, nevertheless, in the Canadian case, by the long-standing suspicion that status or currency are ultimately validated within centres of power and legitimation located somewhere else.

This is a well-known quality of Canadian intellectual life, concisely expressed in Michael Dorland's account of the prominence of *ressentiment* as a political impulse.[5] In the debate over intellectual cosmopolitanism, however, lines of political demarcation are not easily drawn between those whose context of intervention is locally circumscribed and others whose work circulates elsewhere. Progressive work within Canadian cultural studies has long held as one of its imperatives the deployment elsewhere of the Canadian example as one with wider applicability, particularly within debates such as those over cultural globalization or postmodernity. The project of a "Canadianized" cultural studies, therefore, has not confined itself to the adaptation and domestication of theoretical agendas emergent elsewhere. It has often promised, as well, the insinuation of Canadian preoccupations and theoretical insights into the larger agenda of cultural studies internationally.

What follows is one personal account of the institutional situation and development of cultural studies within English Canada. This account draws on my own intellectual and professional trajectory, and is inevitably distorted by the institutional contexts and generational solidarities which have shaped my experience and understanding of cultural studies. It privileges, as well, the place of communications studies as a discipline within this development, and there are no doubt alternative points of departure from which this history could be written. I would argue, nevertheless, that the elusive character of cultural studies within English Canadian intellectual culture is best grasped, at least initially, in the unfolding and intersection of such individual trajectories.

The Communications Context

In the fall of 1978, I arrived in Montreal to begin a Master's degree in McGill University's Graduate Program in Communications. My Bachelor's degree had been in film studies, but the absence of postgraduate film studies programs in Canada meant I could not continue within that discipline without going to the U.S. or Great Britain. I chose, for financial and personal reasons, to remain in Canada, reassured by those familiar with McGill's program that I could "do film" and virtually anything else I wished within its boundaries. (I stayed on, in 1980, to do a Ph.D.) The Graduate Program in Communications had grown out of McGill's English department; personal ties and intellectual sympathies linked it, in its early years, to the figure of Marshall McLuhan. The project of a McLuhanist communications studies encouraged approaches to the study of media which were speculative, humanistic and explicitly rooted within English Canadian intellectual traditions. Prominent among these were an interest in the historical role of communications technologies in processes of nation-building (which drew on the work of the historian Harold Innis) and a concern (part of the legacy of John Grierson and the National Film Board) with the role of documentary media forms in the construction of a national imaginary. However marginal these influences might become in subsequent years, they could be invoked thereafter to support claims that communications studies in Canada need not be tied inevitably to models enshrined elsewhere.

These interests would persist within communications studies in Canada, but the symptomatic development over the next five years, in my view, was the consolidation of two very different poles of attraction to graduate students within the discipline. One of these poles was that of media policy studies, the chronicling of economic dependence and governmental complicity in the development of the Canadian broadcasting and cultural industries. By this historical point, the Canadian Broadcasting Act of 1968 (with its institution of Canadian content quotas for radio and television) and governmental support of the film industry had been in place for a decade or so. Their effects, and the historical conditions which had led up to them, were scrutinized in a number of theses and publications. In a very different trajectory, other graduate students (myself among them) were drawn further into the project of monitoring and becoming conversant with critical and cultural theory, refining our own positions (and policing those of others) in the debates over western Marxism and theories of subjectivity. In the context of McGill, both directions led away from the English department, and from the combination of humanistic and nationalist impulses which had been present at the program's founding.

Communications programs in Canada, as elsewhere, are commonly marked by divisions between those students or faculty with interests rooted in the humanities and others educated within the social sciences. While the background and student recruitment practices of the McGill program in the early 1980s appeared to favour the humanities, the national growth of the discipline as a whole coincided with the rise to prominence of media-related questions within public policy, and with a widespread concern with the effects upon Canada of emergent new communications technologies. I remember this period in part for the abundance of contract research projects employing students, and for the sincerity with which many of us believed that unfolding theoretical developments (such as the refinement of the encoding/decoding model for audience research) might prove useful within these projects.

It was often within these collective enterprises that divisions rooted in the disparity of academic backgrounds were most obvious. The significant differences here were not simply those, long-standing within the discipline, between qualitative and quantitative methodologies, or textual and sociological forms of analysis. They manifest themselves more fundamentally in what might be regarded as differences of intellectual taste or disposition. In the contexts in which I worked, the most typical of these emerged between those whose approaches were marked by a privileging of specificity or complexity (of textual structures or practices of reading) and others whose work required the finality of political or sociological characterization, These differences were often homologous to those between the anglophone and francophone scholarly communities, in the context of a city with two prominent communications programs in each language. While the graduate student culture of anglophone departments was often marked by personal, geographical displacement and an implicitly bohemian conception of intellectual work, that of the francophone institutions offered a more readily available connection to state and media institutions and to collaborative projects which sought to study or transform them. In this respect, the peculiar role of "French Theory" within Canadian intellectual life (and in highlighting the divisions just mentioned) deserves comment. With then stronger ties to the humanities, anglophone communications programs within Quebec and English Canada included large numbers of people participant in the long winding down of French marxist, psychoanalytic and semiological perspectives which dominated Anglo-American critical theory through the 1970s and 1980s. For many francophones involved in communications studies, this seemed little more than an anachronistic attachment to paradigms, works and conceptions of intellectual politics which they had studied and left behind in their undergraduate years. It stood, as well, as evidence of an unfamiliarity with more recent developments within French theory (such as the emergent sociologies of cultural production or postmodern culture), whose gravitational centre was closer to the social sciences, and whose presence within Anglo-American cultural studies had not yet been felt.

The role of communications as a discipline in nurturing the growth of cultural studies in the United States has been noted elsewhere.[6] At the beginning of the 1980s the field seemed, to many of us at McGill and elsewhere, the most appropriate context for an articulation of British cultural studies with the legacies of the Chicago School of Sociology and the McLuhan-Innis tradition of Canadian research. Informal links between Canadian departments and others within the United States (most notably, that at the University of Illinois, Urbana-Champaign) took shape around such an enterprise, and the contemporary work of James Carey was an important and shared point of reference. If this project stalled or was postponed, it was in large measure because ongoing developments within critical and cultural theory pulled many individuals in other directions. Lines of fracture appeared between those for whom the theoretical unity of communications studies was to grow from an ongoing refinement of the marxist or culture-and-nation traditions (in particular, those of Williams and Innis), and others for whom that same unity required participation in a larger, international enterprise of theoretical movement which threatened (rightly or wrongly) to leave those traditions behind. Feminist theory, in particular, circulated within and between intellectual communities whose solidarities and frameworks of reference exceeded the national and the disciplinary. The increased velocity of change within Anglo-American cultural theory itself rooted in the expansion of an infrastructure of conferences, academic units, books and journals produced cleavages within departments and interpersonal networks based in part on differences in levels of investment and involvement in this change. My own reading of developments in the early-to-mid 1980s suggests that "cultural studies," during this period, came to function less and less as a project for the redefinition of communications studies as a discipline. Increasingly, it designated a subculture which was highly visible within the discipline but involved in a variety of ways with communities outside it.

In Canada, where cultural studies established its initial presence largely within communications studies, it did so in a disciplinary space which had no "logic" to speak of. While the McLuhanist legacy implicitly authorized a nonpositivist approach to communications-related research within Canada, the close links between regulatory or media institutions and the academy have encouraged (and often underwritten) an ongoing tradition of what Todd Gitlin has designated as "administrative" research.[7] Inasmuch as each of these conceptions of the discipline has been able to claim for itself a nationalist and progressive purpose, lines of political demarcation between them are not easily drawn. (The distinction between "administrative" and "critical" work, elaborated within the United States, has proved much less appropriate in characterizing Canadian research.) The failure of either tradition to establish absolute hegemony within processes of disciplinary formation and consolidation allowed cultural studies to enter the mix with relative ease. The subsequent development of cultural studies within Canada, nevertheless, was shaped by the growing importance of an intellectual space whose disciplinary and institutional boundaries were less concretely defined.

Evolving Spaces

Over the course of the 1980s, the outlines of a broader Canadian cultural studies "scene" which included currents within communications studies but encompassed a variety of other intellectual communities would become apparent. To a degree determined in no small way by the academic hiring crisis of the late 1970s and early 1980s, conferences had assumed a central role in the dissemination of new intellectual work, and in the forging of interpersonal networks between graduate students.[8] Most Canadian academic associations meet concurrently, in a nod to economies of scale, at an annual event known as the Learned Societies Conference. (Its title usually offers an irresistible target to editorial cartoonists in the host cities.) By 1983, panels on "cultural studies," sometimes offered jointly by the communications and sociology/anthropology associations, were regular events at these conferences. These panels attracted a wide range of constituencies: faculty from the only cultural studies program in Canada (the undergraduate unit at Trent University in Peterborough, Ontario), sociologists associated with the traditions of continental critical theory, and, influentially, those working within feminist theory and women's studies. Links between graduate students, which would later be formalized within publishing projects or collegial collaborations, were initiated at these events, and transdisciplinary communities of interest (such as that around popular music) often took shape.

With the rise to prominence of postmodernist currents within cultural studies, around the middle of the decade, these cross-disciplinary events were themselves displaced by one-day mini conferences on cultural theory, sponsored by the *Canadian Journal of Social and Political Theory* and organized by Arthur and Marilouise Kroker. These occasions, and the discourses which circulated within them, would intensify ongoing debate over the appropriate stakes and styles of cultural analysis within Canada. At one level, differences in the response to postmodernist theory within Canada perpetuated tensions which had surrounded cultural theory generally, though these were frequently magnified within the observable giddiness and perceived urgency of the moment. For a number of constituencies, the rhetorical forms of postmodernist writing exemplified and confirmed the cosmopolitanism and detachment from a locally or nationally constituted politics with which the cultural studies project had long been tainted. Briefly, these tensions organized themselves around a Montreal-Toronto rivalry, wherein those affiliated with the Toronto-based Ontario Institute for Studies in Education claimed for their work a more highly interventionist purpose seen to be lacking within that of the *Canadian Journal of Political and Social Theory* and those within its orbit. Within communications studies, as well, one could perceive moves towards disciplinary retrenchment, as many for whom cultural studies had meant a revitalized sociology of popular culture or developmental phase within marxist media theory balked at its new association with questions derived from the visual arts or philosophy. In an important sense, however, this moment was marked as well by the intermittent sense that the substance and style of postmodern theories broadly speculative and diagnostic as they often were might authorize a new realignment of Canadian cultural studies with an indigenous tradition (that of McLuhan, Innis and the philosopher George Grant) which had earlier articulated similar concerns. From quite distinct points of departure, those works constituting this tradition had investigated the relationships between technological change and culturally specific forms of subjectivity, and in the work of Kroker, for example, the attempt to give these works a distinctly postmodernist turn is evident.[9] As a result, the lines of demarcation which emerged in response to postmodernist theory in Canada were not entirely coterminous with those produced earlier by post-structuralism and related developments in theory. Currents within the study of Canadian literature or the visual arts, and others involved within the institutional space of Canadian studies, frequently found within the terms of postmodernist writing the bases for a new or reformulated account of Canadian distinctiveness.[10]

More so than in the United States, many Canadian universities accommodating interdisciplinary work in the humanities are located in large centres of political and economic power, such as Montreal, Toronto, Vancouver and Edmonton. One effect of this, generally unacknowledged, has been the geographical proximity of academic programs offering an interdisciplinary grounding in cultural theory to the informally organized artistic scenes which are a feature of these cities.[11] This proximity has shaped the political economy and theoretical preoccupations of cultural studies in important ways, which I can enumerate only briefly here.

The growing centrality of cultural theory within artistic and intellectual communities has made passage through an academic program in which that theory is disseminated common within the personal trajectories of those involved in such communities. Large numbers of students typically emerge from undergraduate programs in literature, art history or film studies or from local artistic scenes with a keen interest in broadening and pursuing newly acquired theoretical interests. Inasmuch as graduate departments within the relevant specialized disciplines in Canada are often nonexistent or unsympathetic to theoretical work, programs in communications studies—and, in particular, those at McGill and Concordia Universities in Montreal—have emerged as major poles of attraction. Pressures upon such programs to admit students from a diversity of disciplinary backgrounds, and to meet their demands for a curriculum which completes or extends their grounding in the broad range of contemporary cultural theories, are increasingly felt. In many cases, these pressures conflict with the ongoing research agendas or pedagogical imperatives of the faculty members most likely to encounter them.

The advantage, of course, is that pressures from these constituencies work against impulses towards disciplinary retrenchment. In this respect, the significant current shifts within cultural studies in Canada are not exclusively those towards an accommodation with the traditions and preoccupations of cultural policy analysis. The growing weight and allure of cultural theory within artistic practices, and in the scenes which surround them, has produced another gravitational pole which has proved equally compelling. As publishing, and the organizing of public talks or symposia have become central activities within these scenes, the forms of entrepreneurship and collaboration which they involve have altered the ways in which cultural studies work in Canada is supported. The new prominence of cultural theory within artistic scenes has produced a host of problems for these scenes which cannot be discussed here,[12] but from the perspective of an academic, it has noticeably and positively expanded the ways in which intellectual work is supported. It has, as well, worked to slow the institutional ossification of cultural studies within the Canadian university. In claiming this, I am hopefully not evoking those fantasies of extra-institutional intervention of which I am normally highly suspicious. Nevertheless, it has become increasingly clear in recent years that cultural studies in Canada is sustained as much in the spaces between institutions as it is within those institutions themselves. This is not merely (if at all) the result of a willful marginality, and the role of universities in the unifying and indirect subsidization of these spaces should not be underestimated. To a considerable extent, nevertheless, the recent liveliness of intellectual life in Canada has been nourished by traditions of public support for an infrastructure of publishing and exhibition ventures or curatorial and critical activities wherein the influence of cultural studies has been evident (traditions increasingly threatened within the current financial and political climate).

The influential magazines within English Canadian cultural studies— *Public, Parallelogram, CinéAction, Borderlines* and many others—have grown within the overlapping spaces of graduate student cultures, editorial collectives and the parallel gallery system, and have not, for the most part, been attached to university or commercial publishers. While the initial concerns of most of these publications took shape around specific artistic media or relatively coherent political projects, most have moved, in the course of their histories, to participation in a broader and more diverse intellectual dialogue. In this respect, and to return to a link evoked near the beginning of this essay, the Canadian scene has come more and more to resemble another which proved highly attractive to many of us during the 1980s: that of Australia. Distance and a high level of publishing activity may very often disguise fragile and marginalized conditions for intellectual work, as many who made the pilgrimage to Birmingham in the 1980s would discover. Nevertheless, the range of publications, sense of sustained dialogue and presence of shared concerns which seemed to many Canadians to characterize cultural studies in Australia has offered a more appealing and viable model than those of either Great Britain or the United States.

Notes

Originally published as "Shifting Boundaries, Lines of Descent: Cultural Studies and Institutional Realignments," in *Relocating Cultural Studies: Developments in Theory and Research*, ed. Valda Blundell, John Shepherd, and Ian Taylor, 86–102. Copyright © Routledge 1993. Reprinted with permission of the publisher.

1. Tony Bennett, "Putting Policy into Cultural Studies," in *Cultural Studies*, ed. Lawrence Grossberg, Cary Nelson, and Paula Treichler (London: Routledge, 1992), 23.

2. Ellen Rooney, "Discipline and Vanish: Feminism, the Resistance to Theory, and the Politics of Cultural Studies," *Differences* 2.3 (1990), 21.

3. This aspect of cultural studies is taken up in greater detail, and with somewhat different conclusions, in Cary Nelson, Paula Treichler, and Lawrence Grossberg, "Cultural Studies: An Introduction," in Grossberg, Nelson, and Treichler, *Cultural Studies*, 1–16, which I read only after this section of my essay was written.

4. See, for example, James Clifford and George Marcus, *Writing Culture: The Poetics and Politics of Ethnography* (Berkeley: University of California Press, 1986).

5. Michael Dorland, "A Thoroughly Hidden Country: Ressentiment, Canadian Nationalism, Canadian Culture," *Canadian Journal of Political and Social Theory* 12.1–2 (1988): 13–64.

6. Nelson, Treichler and Grossberg, "Cultural Studies," 16.

7. Todd Gitlin, "Media Sociology: The Dominant Paradigm," *Theory and Society* 6 (1978): 20–53.

8. I owe this reading of the role of conferences to David Galbraith.

9. Arthur Kroker, *Technology and the Canadian Mind: Innis, McLuhan, Grant* (Montreal: New World Perspectives, 1986).

10. For example, Linda Hutcheon, *The Canadian Postmodern: A Study of Contemporary English-Canadian Fiction* (Toronto: Oxford University Press, 1988).

11. Communications studies programs, to a considerable extent, sustain this interdisciplinary work in Montreal and Vancouver. In Toronto, the Social and Political Thought program at York University and Ontario Institute for Studies in Education have been important centres of activity within cultural studies.

12. These problems were the focus of the conference "Art and Theory / Theory as Art," organized by Jody Berland, David Tomas and myself, and held at the University of Ottawa from November 29 to December 1, 1991.

JODY BERLAND

Writing on the Border

Jody Berland is an associate professor of humanities at Atkinson College and a member of the Joint Graduate Programme in Communication and Culture, the Department of Music, and the Graduate Programme in Social and Political Thought at York University. She is the founding editor of *Topia: Canadian Journal of Cultural Studies* and has published widely on cultural studies, Canadian communication theory, music, radio and video, feminist bodies, cultural environmental studies, and social space.

Culture is always an idea of the Other (even when I reassume it for myself).
—Fredric Jameson, "On 'Cultural Studies' "

Crossing the Border

I was twelve when I first crossed the border from the United States into Canada. My American classmates viewed my departure to that country with a combination of envy and alarm. Like them I would not have been surprised to find igloos in the towns with the streets full of dog sleds. My ignorance about my new country was astounding.

But it was commonplace. I was reminded of this recently by a storyline featured for some time in the Canadian Broadcasting Corporation's (CBC) weekly television satire, *This Hour Has 22 Minutes*. Rick Mercer, author and performer of the "Talking to Americans" stories, is a caustic political commentator and Canada's most popular comedian—he hosted the 2000 and 2001 Geminis, Canada's film industry awards ceremony, and the Junos, our music awards ceremony, and has won Canada's top television comedy award with his *22 Minutes* colleagues five times. Each week, and in early 2001 in one glorious, widely viewed hour-long "best-of" special, Mercer travelled to the United States and interviewed Americans about Canada. In 2002 Mercer was awarded a Gemini (subsequently renounced, in honour of the victims of the September 11 massacre) for the

Special, "Talking to Americans." Whether interviewing ordinary people on the street, venerable ivy league academics, political staffers or a presidential candidate, he turned their ignorance about their northern neighbour into ludicrous jokes. Over several years, viewers of Canada's top-rated comedy show witnessed friendly Americans congratulating Canada on the arrival of FM radio, personal fax machines, a second area code, and power steering. Americans don't know that Canada houses some of the continent's largest automobile factories, generates significant innovations in communication technology, and remains their country's major trading partner. But of course we do.[1] They sent cheery messages to Canadian Prime Minister Tim Horton, congratulating him on his "double double," as though Canada might be the sort of country where that sounded like a prime ministerial accomplishment. (Tim Horton's, a popular doughnut shop chain named after a hockey star wherein a "double double" translates as coffee with double sugar double cream, ran a television ad campaign in which customs officials distinguished returning Canadians from imposters by their knowledge of the Tim Hortons' coffee cup contest.) They begged the government not to close down Canada's last remaining university, Eaton's U. (Eaton's, a prominent family-owned department store chain and home catalogue publisher, was recently bankrupt. Our universities are still open for business.) Although a larger percentage of Canadians own VCRs and telephones than their American counterpoints (Sauve 1994, 119),[2] they urged Canada to legalize VCRs, allow the introduction of a daily newspaper (though Toronto, where I live, produces five dailies in English and several in other languages), and change their clocks, which they were easily persuaded now run on a 20-hour cycle, to a 24-hour day to avoid disruption with American schedules. A parade of camera-ready Americans urged the mayor of Toronto not to restore the Toronto Polar Bear Hunt, which, they feelingly insisted, would be a "naive and uneducated" act. (Do I need to remind readers that there are no polar bears here outside the zoo?) And, amicably ignorant of the social policies that Canadians so value about themselves, they signed a petition, on camera, urging Canadians to cease the practice of putting their elderly out to die on icebergs.

On the much-publicized February 28, 2000 episode, one of the most watched in Canadian television history (and prominently featured in Mercer's ratings giant one-hour special), Mercer interviewed U.S. presidential candidate George W. Bush and the Governor of Michigan (a border state), a key supporter of Bush's presidential campaign. Pausing in the midst of a crowd of cameras and microphones, both men gracefully acknowledged the endorsement of Prime Minister Jean Poutine ("poutine" is the name of a popular Quebec dish of fries, gravy and melted cheese curds) despite the fact that Prime Minister Jean Chrétien shares his surname with Canada's then ambassador to the United States, Raymond Chrétien, his nephew.[3]

Of course this all says something about Canada, as well. After all it is Canadians who are watching, Canadians who are laughing, Canadians who are piling the cameras on the planes to fly home to Halifax, Nova Scotia, where 22 Minutes is produced. You don't have to be Canadian to get the joke, but you do need to be Canadian to understand it in all its ironic complexity. For some analysts, "getting it" in the more complete sense is what makes Canadians Canadian.[4] What made these interviews work so well for so many Canadian television viewers was the implicit understanding that "getting it" has nothing to do with countering the invisibility mocked by them, except ironically, of course, amongst ourselves.

But we need to approach this much-publicized romp on a more obvious level. To write, represent or reflect in Canada is to write to, about, against and sometimes across the border. Canadian studies scholars concur that "Canada is unthinkable without its border with the USA"[5] and the most cursory review of Canadian scholarship confirms that the 49th Parallel has a huge symbolic status in the culture that has no parallel in American consciousness. This is the truism north of the 49th: Canadians live and write as though the border is everywhere, shadowing everything we contemplate and fear; Americans as though there is no border at all. To them the Other is either identical or invisible, or, in the Canadian case, an oscillating combination of the two. This difference in the social construction of the border and what is on the other side of it pinpoints a fundamental difference between these closely intertwined countries that has important consequences in terms of the collective construction of narrative, knowledge, and power. It suggests a radically different relationship to what borders themselves define: the social inhabiting of space, and the self-delineation of collective selves in relation to others. In short, "the longest undefended border in the world," as it is somewhat inaccurately called, produces radically different meanings to the territories it divides.

This narrative of the border involves two protagonists, an attentive one and an inattentive one, which is not unusual in a close partnership between two unequal powers. "The beauty of being a ruler," Terry Eagleton comments, "is that one does not need to worry about who one is, since one deludedly believes that one already knows. It is other cultures which are different, while one's own form of life is the norm, and so scarcely a 'culture' at all."[6] This accurately describes the taken-for-grantedness of a parochial imperial culture. Eagleton seems to conclude from this that it is the powerful who are driven to observe "difference" in the less powerful. But if globalization means anything, it is the reversal of this anthropological conceit. It is the "other cultures" that are forced to pay attention, and America that knows least of all. Less powerful nations are either dangerous enemies or reiterations of the impoverished groups in their own country: simply less successful, wannabe versions of themselves. Staunch exemplars of what Lukacs called, in another context, "power-protected inwardness," they might look; they might develop innovative observational technologies to study and observe; but they do not see.

The idea that relationships of unequal power involve a kind of one-way mirror surrounding the imperial centre is precisely the point of Mercer's performance. The Mercer interviews clearly interpellate Canadians as a more attentive and knowledgeable audience. They remind their viewers that that we know more than we might want to know about American politics, entertainment, social problems, and gossip, and that this knowledge gives us a special edge as we traverse invisibly through their midst. As historian Kenneth McNaught wrote in a 1976 Dominion Day commentary, "It is sometimes said that Americans are benevolently uninformed about Canada while Canadians are malevolently well-informed about the U.S."[7] His point was confirmed a quarter of a century later, when a survey found that 25% of Canadians object to the "superior attitude" of Americans, while Americans find nothing objectionable in their Canadian neighbours (the latter having politely kept to themselves their knowledge of the stunning collective ignorance across the border).[8] Mercer's running joke is not just about Canada's superior knowledge, then, but concerns the inescapable imbrication of this knowledge with Canada's collective invisibility, a concise term for describing a situation in which Americans might see igloos, Mounties, or wilderness parks, but certainly not Canadians, most of whom live in cities, and well over 90% of whom (at this point you have to laugh, it is ridiculous to feel defensive about it) have easy access to FM radio.

The knowing, laughing observers evoked by Mercer are urban, English- (or other hyphenates) Canadian, and ready to be consternated and amused at their own invisibility. In participating in this narrative we become complicit in it, and arrive together with the performers at that delicious moment when such invisibility becomes strategic, invoking the one-way mirror-wall to reflect two sides of the border, one gullible and the other wily and even deceptive. This too has a history of satiric performance. In the memorable SCTV [Second City Television] mock-documentary *The Canadian Conspiracy*, a terrified journalist (Eugene Levy), hiding in a motel room with the shades drawn, exposes a conspiracy of Canadians trained by state-owned institutions like the CBC [Canadian Broadcasting Corporation] and the National Film Board (NFB) to infiltrate and take over the American entertainment industry undetected.[9] Anne Murray, Lorne Greene, Margot Kidder, Martin Short, Dave Thomas, William Shatner and other popular performers are revealed as secret saboteurs of the American way of life. Confronted by cameras, each suspect ostentatiously denies acquaintance with the other. Because their racially and ethnically unmarked bodies have permitted them to "pass" as Americans, their difference is invisible, but not at all (in this satire) insignificant. However amenable Canadians might be to friendly clichés and stereotypes, their presence as undetected aliens is hazardous to the health of the entertainment industry and a danger to the country as a whole.

The mockumentary "exposés" Canadians as undetected saboteurs the way Americans once sought to expose communists. The connection is not an accidental one. The black and white aesthetic, the raised hands and closed window blinds, the denial of friendships, the portentous narrator. . . . In this atmospheric generic framing, witch-hunts can search out any enemies, even Canadians. As its writers imply, Americans have let their anxiety about hidden enemies run amok. This anxiety is not just an internal matter. Every Canadian has heard a visiting American saying that Canada is "just like home," congratulating his or her listeners for their apparent sameness on the basis of a half-day of profound ethnographic experience involving cars, billboards, hotel menus, and conference programs. This gesture allows the visitor to seize control of his [sic] ignorance and to offer it as a friendly, patronizing gift to his listeners.

But there is an uneasy sense of difference behind the familiar. In particular, Americans have long been suspicious of Canada's "socialist" leanings. The history of communication battles between the two countries is marked by continuous efforts by U.S. officials to label Canadian films as "government propaganda," cultural policy as "government subsidy," protectionist measures as "unfair trading practices." U.S. government officials have accused "Canuckistan" (a term affectionately appropriated from one such attack) of being soft on communism since the beginning of the Cold War, and drove one high-ranking diplomat to suicide with their denunciations. Former Prime Minister Pierre Elliot Trudeau, a Keynesian liberal who travelled to the Soviet Union before assuming leadership of the government, and to Cuba afterwards; our Medicare system, which provides free medical care to everyone equally and universally; foreign policy; gun legislation; public broadcasting; all smell like socialism to some American observers who deploy their own rhetorics of differentiation against the invisible enemy. SCTV's conspiracy-exposé provides a perfect frame for this countering enactment of strategic invisibility. Aside from parodying stereotypical American film and television conventions, like cold-war propaganda films and tabloid-style "real crime" exposés, *The Canadian Conspiracy* conveys the creators' amusement at the shocking suggestion that entertainment might be subtly managed for diverse political ends, a very un-American idea that otherwise eludes the grasp of so many Americans.

The knowing play with the theme of invisibility was taken up again in the summer of 2000 in an unprecedentedly popular television commercial for the beer brand named "Molson Canadian." In this commercial, widely known as *The Rant*, "Joe," standing in front of a large screen projecting various stereotypical/multicultural images, emotionally proclaims the unrecognized virtues of being Canadian. I don't know Susy or Nancy, he proclaims (addressing the strange but commonplace idea that Canadians must all know one another), though they are probably very nice people (no comment required there). We don't own igloos or dog sleds; we believe in gun control and military peacekeeping, not global war-mongering; in diversity, not assimilation; we say zed not zee; our national animal is not the eagle but the beaver, a noble animal; and, in sum, Joe refuses to be or speak "American." His crescendoing Rant, backed by the exultant swell of Elgar's "Pomp and Circumstance," concludes with the heroic proclamation, "I Am Canadian!" followed by an apologetically mumbled, endearingly anti-heroic "thank you."

"Joe" has simultaneously performed a patriotic tirade, and mocked the rhetoric of patriotic declamation. Everything the Canadian is, is a "not." Patriotism itself, like the collective ignorance implicitly attacked by the commercial, is through ironic distancing associated implicitly with the "Other" against whom Canada must struggle to define itself. The music reminds Canadians of its colonial ties to England while working simultaneously for and against the charismatic presence of the speaker. This is the hyper-conscious rhetoric of a middle power who as Trudeau once famously described it, is forced to sleep with an elephant.

Not surprisingly, the writer of Joe's script had just returned to Canada after living and working for three years in New York, and was ready to unburden himself of his experiences. And, again not surprisingly, he did so by saying at least two things at once: we must defend ourselves with patriotic tirades, patriotism is a characteristic of the Other against whom we must defend ourselves; I wish to make a heroic statement, modesty is better than heroism; I speak on behalf of all of us, all of us are already laughing.

Like many other recent television commercials, The Rant interpellates viewers as sophisticated viewers who know exactly what they are watching. By claiming to be more than a television commercial, its script reharmonizes the glitches of previous corporate-sponsored nationalist events, in the course of which popular bands like Tragically Hip and Bare Naked Ladies have simultaneously acknowledged and mocked the "patriotism" of their beer company sponsors.[10] Beer, coffee, athletic gear—it is commodity advertising that now most eloquently articulates the nostalgia for the national that followed the political devastations wrought by free trade. But this commercial did not produce the cynical acquiescence evoked by other cleverly self-referential commercials. Judging from its emphatic popular reception, the performance reveals the mental habitus of the ordinary English Canadian: a chronic inhabiting of a space between, the moderate stance of a middle power but also something more fraught, a life in the midst of a "split screen," a space that is, or can be, more reflective. People almost forgot it was a beer commercial, judging from the crop of colloquialisms that rose in its wake, but a legal battle over the rights to a web address reminded us that it was indeed a private company that sponsored the ad (they lost the battle to own "Canadian.biz").

The commercial's effects reverberated for months. The actor's live performance of The Rant at major league hockey games where sponsorship conflicts prohibited the screening of the commercial produced an exorbitantly enthusiastic response. Newspaper columnists could not get enough of cavorting with this commercial, suggesting, for example, that the actor, a young Maritimer, should serve as Canada's next Prime Minister. An inappropriate muddling of public and private spheres? Sheila Copps, then federal Minister of Heritage, screened the ad at a meeting of culture administrators in Boston to explain Canadian attitudes on culture. The Rant was adapted and widely circulated in newspaper cartoons and Internet jokes, where it appeared as the self-differentiating proclamations of Italians, Pakistanis, Ukrainian-Canadians, and patriotic cats, among others, and it reappeared in parodic form several times in *This Hour Has 22 Minutes.*[11] An informal poll, circulated by email, suggested that 95% of Canadians identify with the ad, while 5% are disturbed by its anti-Americanism. Two years later, I still see supermarket cashiers sporting t-shirts with citations from *The Rant.* The sense of an aggrieved collective invisibility, anxiety about losing Canada's more equitable social policies, and the articulation of these with a clear if still ironic rhetoric of anti-Americanism, is obviously not restricted to writers and intellectuals. Indeed the popularity of such sentiments is the precondition, as well as the implied meaning, for the now prominent mobilization of symbols of national identity in the corporate sponsorship of hockey and music events.

A sequel has the "noble animal" the beaver emerge from under someone's coat and attack the throat of an American belittling Canadians at a bar. The "I am Canadian" figure looks distantly bemused and does not watch or intervene. Of course, beavers don't really do that. We know that. They build dams.

Notwithstanding the sentimental and ironic tone, Joe's refusal (and his audience's) to merge with "America" is identified here with a number of political claims: the need to defend Canada's social policies (peace-keeping, cultural diversity, nonviolence), the demand for respect of Canada's more inclusive social values, and the rights of marginal peoples to fair and respectful representation. *The Rant* thus provides an uncharacteristically dramatic expression of what Charles Taylor terms the "politics of recognition" for English Canada. Taylor posits a dialogical relationship between how we see ourselves and how others see us; a sense of individual or collective worth develops in interaction with others, since agency and identity are dialogical, and "the projection of an inferior or demeaning image on another can actually distort and oppress."[12] *The Rant* articulates for English Canadians an ordinarily mute frustration at the failure of a globalizing U.S. culture to challenge itself with otherness.

For some, this idea of living in the shadow of a myopic giant—by now a convention of English Canadian writing—makes the ambiguity of the collective subject a strategic choice. "We live with the exquisite fear that we are invisible people," notes writer Robert Kroetsch. "And yet we are reluctant to venture out of the silence and into the noise; out of the snow; into the technocracy. For in our very invisibility lies our chance for survival."[13] Philip Resnick calls English Canadians "a nation that dares not speak its name."[14] To name or speak for this grouping as an identity is, according to some critics, an act of exclusion against everyone who originates elsewhere, and denies the "multicultural" nature of the country. This critique is renounced by writers who argue that "English Canada" is properly a linguistic, not an ethnic category, and that this distinction is precisely what distinguishes it from other nationalisms, for it excludes no one who wishes to belong. Both advocates and opponents of this view can be found among the large immigrant and ethnically diverse populations. In the annual ritual spectacles of national television, when "Canada" is evoked with unproblematic passion, it is an assiduously bilingual, trinational, multicultural subject represented; English Canada is the sum of all that it itself invokes.

Like the opposition between ignorance and knowledge I have described, the trope of invisibility is a constant presence in English Canada's discourse on the border, and connects the disparate voices of its philosophers, critics, artists, and comics. The theme of the invisible subject touched upon by Joe, archetypical beer drinker, and Kroetsch, novelist and literary critic, recurs also in Canadian political philosophy, which maintains, as Ian Angus puts it, that " 'English Canada' is nearly impossible to grasp. It tends to disappear downwards into the elements that make it up or upwards into the nation-state. We do not seem to have the necessary concept to grasp it for itself."[15] Something is being sought or evoked, but no matter how commanding the discourse that seeks to claim its object, it can't be found. Is this absence, this lack, a failure of collective mobilization, or a moral triumph? For Angus it is the manifestation of a kind of positive abjection, not just a failure of one culture to establish a stable hegemony over others but a morally emancipating willingness to recognize the boundaries of self and the claims of others. For many Canadians, including the bracketed ones (Chinese-Canadian, Pakistani-Canadian etc.), it is the social expression of an ideal of difference, more particularly of equality in difference, whose lasting power, some critics suggest, lies precisely in its unattainability.[16] Of course global supremacy, racial purity, planetary policing, and religious absolutes are also unattainable ideals that effectively mobilize national communities to act as well as to dream. If I am going to inhabit a shared dream space I personally prefer equality in difference to supremacy in action. The question whether any one of us stands outside of the realm of shared affect is beyond the purview of this discussion. But what if the ideal itself is subject-less? Northrop Frye, in *The Modern Century*, argues that it is: he says that "Perhaps the real Canada is an ideal with nobody in it. The Canada to which we really do owe loyalty is the Canada that we have failed to create."[17] An undifferentiated other, superimposed on an ideal with nobody in it; these ideas evoke the theme of ghosts, which recurs in Frye's writing and is taken up subsequently by Kroetsch and other thinkers. "In his analysis, such politics arise from a realization of the close connection between identity and recognition. We have been told by various people that Canada lacks ghosts," Kroetsch says. "Ha. We are our own ghosts."[18]

These are now privileged texts in the canonical study of Canadian culture; they provide a common language for scholars wishing to reflect on the existential status of the national (non)subject. At the same time the expression of ambivalence bordering on self-erasure is elaborated more diffusely across the country's culture, which is replete with ironic gestures, not only toward national culture, or the lack thereof, but more broadly toward Canada's performance in the international political domain, where Canada asserts itself bravely on behalf of internationalist values—peacekeeping, forgiving the debt of poor countries, active sponsorship of refugees, nuclear disarmament, etc.—but seems quite unable to do so on behalf of itself as a political-economic community. This paradox, while holding out definite political implications, is also suggestive for understanding the relative absence of popular culture analysis in cultural studies in English Canada, if we compare its traditions to those of the U.S. and Britain. What constitutes an active or emancipatory cultural practice when the actors are in such a complicated mood?

In both everyday social exchange and symbolic culture, the ambivalence described by these theorists commonly takes the form of irony, as Mercer ably demonstrated on a weekly basis. As we have seen with The Rant, this attitude requires the capability of saying at least two opposing and even incompatible things at once—for instance, that we are proud to be Canadians and that patriotic pride is not a Canadian attribute—without seeking a means to resolve the tension between them. Canadian comics are adept at such unresolved dualism, which helps to explain the magnitude of their huge (and apparently conspiratorial) success in the U.S. as well as here; their performances enact a highly reflexive ambiguity that casts an ironic light on American heroic stereotypes and conventions. Crucially, the irony works to maintain the marginal stance of its performers, who stand poised with one foot inside and the other outside the subjectivity they portray, rather than fighting for a simple identificatory recognition—see me! I am Canadian!—from a hierarchical other.

The elusiveness of the Canadian subject involves the complicity of its actors, then; whatever its genealogy, it has become a purposeful, tactical invisibility, closely linked to the idea of being hard to locate or pin down, whether this is realized as fiction, multiculturalism, gender-bending, unpeopled landscape art, or humour. "The fact that the country grew up from two peoples speaking different languages," notes Frye in his essay on ghosts—note the haunting absence of the people of the first nations, who were presumably all grown up when these two peoples got here— "meant that nobody could ever know what a 'hundred percent Canadian' was, and hence the population became less homogeneous."[19] A Canadian can be anything, and—according to these modernist thinkers at least—is therefore nothing. The contrast with the all-American athlete, commodity or ideal is obvious.

"That's why I like it," counters Stephen Schecter. "If nothing else, it's a reminder about the incomprehensible knot at the centre of things. . . . By flattening itself into a country that refuses to be one, it has also posed the paradox of our need for a country even as we would do without one."[20]

For Schecter, and he is not alone in this, the lack of an (acknowledged) ethnic or cultural centre is not Canada's failure but an indication of the promise (if not full achievement) of tolerance and multiplicity for nations still caught up in the political and ethnic battles of modern nationalism. In a similar vein, writer John Raulston Saul admires the lack of the standard monolithic mythology of the other nation-states: "This is described by most federalists and anti-federalists alike as the failure of Canada. The failure to become like the others. To regularize a monolithic mythology. Some weep before the ever-retreating mirage of the un-hyphenated Canadian. Others say its continued existence proves the country is not real and cannot exist. For me, this failure to conform is in fact our greatest success. A proof of originality which we refuse to grasp as positive."[21] "Diversity, not assimilation," Joe proclaims in his "I am Canadian" rant. The fact that there is no such a thing as a "Canadian" according to the classical conception of national identity is not just a conceit by Canadian literary critics. It was reiterated in the last census, when 3% of respondents chose to write in "Canadian" under ethnic origin because this option did not appear on the list of identities. In this context, the self-identification as "Canadian" functions as a protest against government's ethnicity-based statistical strategies. By writing "Canadian" their ethnicity is erased—which, of course, holds different meanings for different social subjects. In this census, the nominal "Canadian" functions not as a singular, internally differentiating term (as do "white" or "Chinese") but as one that encompasses all potential answers on the list, simultaneously heterogeneous and auto-generated, signifying both too little and too much for the demographic matrix of the census.

These symbolic acts and statistical self-assertions share with literary culture a conscious ambivalence on the reflexive side of a border across which narratives, identities, and agendas seem all too certain. These continuing identity crises serve then as a kind of prophylactic against the American virus of collective unselfconsciousness. That externalized unselfconsciousness, like the fragmentary self-consciousness which rhetorically opposes it, is clearly revealed in how each of these protagonists understand the status and meaning of their borders.

Whose Border?

It is a nice coincidence that the eruption of nationalist emotion constellated in The Rant was so closely followed by the Canadian edition of Time Magazine, July 20, 2000, with the cover story, "What Border?" Needless to say, this carefree capitalist caprice appeared before the 9/11 events that so changed the constitution of many borders, especially this one. The story describes the rise of cross-border regional economies and new levels of political cooperation between governments in these regions, and argues that the increasing consolidation of business interests in the Maritimes, southern Ontario, and the west proves the efficacy of commerce and technology to "leave behind" the political fiction of the border. Time writes that "Ottawa and Washington, which still dictate the formalities between two sovereign nations, have less and less to do with the way that Canadians and Americans actually relate to each other on issues that matter the most."[22]

The feature article highlights a dispute in which New Brunswick was persuaded to promise health insurance to workers who live in Maine, and thus to distribute benefits that are part of the political enfranchisement of Canadians, regardless of their employees' place of residence. This means that Maine residents employed by specific New Brunswick companies could pay U.S. taxes but receive Canadian health benefits. It is unclear who is supposed to pay for this windfall, but the authors for Time seem certain that it will not be the packing plant or the government of Maine. It is important to note (though this enthusiastic report does not make the connection) that nearly 45% of what the U.S. buys from Canada involves trade between branches of the same company. In this instance, lobbyists for the transnational corporate consolidation of meat-packing have persuaded New Brunswick business managers to subsidize their personnel costs with Canadian public money in order to keep Canada's residents employed. The University of Maryland business professor who produced this statistic on cross-border trade warns against any move "that would undermine the advantages of free trade," arguing that "A larger, more efficient integrated market enhances the worldwide compettitveness of U.S. companies."[23]

Of course, *Time* does not consider its perspective to be controversial.[24] Because the post-industrial evolution of financial and technological realities demands the co-operation of previously distinct entities who wish to survive the economic jungle (according to this logic), it is incumbent upon the government of New Brunswick, and consequently its citizens, to subsidize the transnational corporate entity in control of eastern meatpacking. Readers with longer memories may recall similar statements from the past, like that of the former under secretary of state (U.S.) who, in 1968, before the rise of the "Information Society," opined that: "Sooner or later, commercial imperatives will bring about the free movement of all goods back and forth across our long border. When that occurs, or even before it does, it will become unmistakeably clear that countries with economies inextricably intertwined must also have free movement of the other vital factors of production—-capital, services, labour. The result will inevitably be substantial economic integration, which will require for its full realization a progressively expanding area of common political decision."[25] This statement acknowledges the levelling of social policy— what American lobbyists referred to as an impending "scorched earth," should Canada attempt to maintain its own, during free trade negotiations with Canada—that is sought by the larger power. It is not only movements between countries that are subject to greater surveillance, then, but also disparate policies within them.

Democratic public policies like universal health care, public broadcasting, affordable public post-secondary education, regional equalization grants or the admission of political refugees can be dismissed as the traces of a former era, a theme we hear frequently from neoconservative governments within Canada.

How interesting, then, that attesting to national difference has become so prominent in Canadian popular culture. Is this merely a sentimental, corporately managed reiteration of values that no longer matter in the "real" domain, what [John] Tomlinson calls a "simulacrum of anthropological place?"[26] This idea has some explanatory power, since Canada's ad agencies have come to excel at presenting Canadian situations permeated with tacit irony, and acted out in the most iconic scenarios: street hockey, snowball fights, skating rinks, blizzards, sports bars, cross-border cultural misunderstandings with ignorant Americans, all form part of the local horizon in advertising for local beer and petroleum. Is nationalism now simply a preferred motif for slick Toronto advertising executives and corporate brand promotions? Is national culture an optional product in a marketplace of identities?

This depends at least in part on where you ask the question. There is a spatial as well as a temporal context in which to seek an answer. Borders, according to contemporary theory, connect as much as they separate. But we cannot conclude from this that what they connect is shared meanings. On this side of the border, reference to the 49th Parallel evokes more than scenery, and more than culture. It evokes a rejection of market ideology, an acceptance of cultural complexity, and an antipathy to bigness and imperial expansionism. Whether the projection of regressive neoliberal values onto our southern neighbour is an accurate portrayal of social difference across the 49th Parallel or a denial of powerful forces at work within our own polity, it has important implications and effects that both incorporate and exceed the symbolic. Political satire heavily populated by willingly trapped politicians; weekly two-way cross-dressing on prime time television; hockey players making mythic disruptive inroads into the streets of the finance district; miscellaneous self-discoverers stumbling over patriotic tirades, comical bits mocking Canada's "heritage moments," and talking to Americans: each of these messages places the stereotypical roles of cultural difference in quote marks, yet reiterates a performative action with powerful political resonance that cannot be separated from the wider discourse on the border. The resilience of each of these debates accentuates the degree to which popular defence of the border is not (or not only) an icon for select brands; it is also a political choice, consciously and pleasurably (if not always effectively) defiant of classical approaches to global economics, traditional nationalism, geopolitics, and culture itself.

Notes

An earlier version of this essay was published as "Writing on the Border," in *The New Centennial Review* 1.2 (2001): 139–69.

1. To be precise, approximately 12% of Americans are aware that Canada is its largest trading partner, while 83% of Canadians know this fact; Roger Sauve, *Borderlines: What Canadians and Americans Should—But Don't—Know about Each Other . . . a Witty, Punchy and Personal Look* (Toronto: McGraw-Hill Ryerson, 1994), 27.

2. Sauve, *Borderlines*, 119.

3. In an interview about this series, Mercer refers to this interview to illustrate the fact

that he has not had to work hard to find appropriate responses to his questions: "I interviewed hundreds of presidential candidates, all named George W. Bush."

4. See John Robert Colombo's poem, "A Canadian Is Somebody Who":

> Thinks he knows how to make love in a canoe
> Bets on the Toronto Maple Leafs . . .
> Possesses "a sound sense of the possible"
> Is sesquilingual (speaks one and a half languages)
> Has become North American without becoming
> Either American or Mexican.
> Knows what the references in this poem are all about"
> (quoted in Linda Hutcheon, *Splitting Images: Contemporary Canadian Ironies* [Toronto: Oxford University Press, 1991], 13).

5. W. H. New, *Borderlands: How we talk about Canada* (Victoria: University of British Columbia Press, 1989), 6.

6. Terry Eagleton, *The Idea of Culture* (London: Routledge, 2000), 46.

7. "Canadian Independence, Too, Was Won in 1770s," *Toronto Star*, July 1, 1976, cited in Marshall McLuhan, "Canada: The Borderline Case," in *The Canadian Imagination: Dimensions of a Literary Culture*, ed. David Staines (Cambridge, Mass.: Harvard University Press, 1977).

8. Sauve, *Borderlines*, 27: "Americans Know Very Little about Canada," according to a 1992 Gallup survey.

9. "The foundations for the Canadian conquest of the American entertainment industry were laid in 1909 when 'America's sweetheart' and Toronto, Ontario native Mary Pickford arrived in Hollywood on orders from Canadian Prime Minister Sir Wilfred Laurier. Her plan was to endear herself to the American populace through cinema and then use her clout to take over the industry." Thus begins the chronicle, now immortalized on www.xone.net/conspiracy/. Key conspirators include Lorne Greene, Lorne Michaels (two Lornes!), Anne Murray, Wayne and Shuster, Michael J. Fox, Pamela Anderson, Jim Carrey, David Cronenberg, William Shatner, and, of course, SCTV comedians John Candy, Catherine O'Hara, Rick Moranis, Dave Thomas, Martin Short, and Eugene Levy. An update names Jim Carrey Lead Agent, Humor Control Initiative, and Alannis Morisette Lead Agent, Musical Control Initiative.

10. See Mark Duffett, "Going Down Like a Song: National Identity, Global Commerce and the Great Canadian Party," *Popular Music* 19.1 (2000): 1–11.

11. "There is nothing wrong with driving 10 m/hr in Bloor West Village on a Saturday, eating Kobasa and fried eggs for breakfast, and having a shot before church! My name is Dmytro and I am Ukrainian! Dyakuyu." Thus ends the Ukrainian Rant, set in the Ukrainian neighbourhood of Toronto, and circulated on the Internet. Thanks to Marcia Ostashewska for passing it on.

12. Charles Taylor, "The Politics of Recognition," in *Multiculturalism: Examining the Politics of Recognition* (Princeton, N.J.: Princeton University Press, 1994), 36.

13. Robert Kroetsch, *The Lovely Treachery of Words* (Toronto: Oxford University Press, 1989), 57.

14. Philip Resnick, *Thinking English Canada* (Toronto: Stoddart Publishing, 1994), 112.

15. Ian Angus, *The Border Within: National Identity, Cultural Plurality, and Wilderness* (Kingston: McGill-Queen's University Press, 1997), 26.

16. See Richard Day, "Constructing the Official Canadian: A Genealogy of the Mosaic Metaphor in State Policy Discourse," *Topia: Canadian Journal of Cultural Studies* 2 (1998): 42–66.

17. Northrop Frye, "Haunted by Lack of Ghosts: Some Patterns in the Imagery of Canadian Poetry," in *The Canadian Imagination: Dimensions of a Literary Culture*, ed. David Staines (Cambridge, Mass.: Harvard University Press, 1977), 122–23.

18. Kroetsch, *Lovely Treachery of Words*, 57.

19. Frye, "Haunted by Lack of Ghosts," 23.

20. Stephen Schecter, *Zen and the Art of Postmodern Canada* (Montreal: Robert Davies Publishing, 1993), 106, 108.

21. John Ralston Saul, *Reflections of a Siamese Twin: Canada at the End of the Twentieth Century* (Toronto: Penguin, 1997), 8.

22. *Time*, June 20, 2000, 23.

23. Ibid., 25.

24. *Time* itself was the subject of considerable hostility between the two countries through the 1970s, when Canada sought protection for Canadian advertisers in the Canadian edition. See Frank Swanson, "Canadian Cultural Nationalism and the U.S. Public Interest," in *Canadian Cultural Nationalism*, ed. Janice L. Murray (New York: New York University Press/Canadian Institute of International Affairs, 1977), 33. Swanson notes "the temptation for U.S. officials to misread the overall phenomenon of Canadian cultural retrofitting by interpreting it as a simple case of economic protectionism" (61). In 1976 a group of Republican congressmen noted that "the Canadian government has charted a course in communications policy which is discriminatory to trading interests in the United States. How far Canada follows that course will ultimately determine the need for and the character of our response" (cited in ibid., 72).

25. George Ball, *The Discipline of Power* (1968), cited in Ramsey Cook, "Cultural Nationalism in Canada: A Historical Perspective," in *Canadian Cultural Nationalism*, ed. Janice L. Murray (New York: New York University Press/Canadian Institute of International Affairs, 1977), 20. This is the context in which Trudeau began his administration.

26. John Tomlinson, *Globalization and Culture* (Chicago: University of Chicago Press, 1999), 110.

RICK GRUNEAU AND DAVID WHITSON

Communities, Civic Boosterism, and Fans

Richard Gruneau (b. 1948) attended the universities of Guelph and Calgary before going on to complete his doctorate in sociology at the University of Massachusetts. He taught at Queen's University (Kingston, Ontario) from 1974 to 1983, and at the University of British Columbia from 1983 to 1987. Since 1987 he has been a professor of communication at Simon Fraser University. In 1978 Gruneau cofounded (with Hart Cantelon) the Queen's Centre for Sport and Leisure Studies, one of the first research groups in Canada to advance the cause of cultural studies through a coordinated program of workshops, conferences, and publications. His books include *Class, Sports and Social Development* (1983, 1999); *Hockey Night in Canada: Sport, Identities, and Cultural Politics* (coauthored with David Whitson, 1993); and *The Missing News: Filters and Blind Spots in Canada's Press* (coauthored with Robert Hacket and NewsWatch Canada, 2000). His edited works include *Sport, Culture and the Modern State* (with Hart Cantelon, 1982); *Popular Cultures and Political Practices* (1989); and *Artificial Ice: Hockey, Culture and Commerce* (with Dave Whitson, 2005).

David Whitson (b. 1945) is a professor of political science at the University of Alberta. He received his Ph.D. at the University of Queensland, after receiving an M.Ed. from the Ontario Institute for Studies in Education. In addition to the works that he has cowritten with Rick Gruneau, he has authored numerous essays in areas such as the political economy of leisure, sports studies, and globalization and Canadian popular culture.

Historically hockey has had a special relationship to the experience of life in Canadian communities and, indeed, to the very idea of community in Canada. Canadians have experienced the game both as a community practice and as a commercial product—variously connected to the local community, to broader "communities" of loyal fans who follow professional teams, and, finally, to an imagined national community. The local game has been the stuff of community volunteer work, sociability, pride, and entertainment. The professional game has provided a common source of entertainment and national conversation, an opportunity to share a common passion as well as to rehearse old rivalries. When Calgarians anticipate a visit from the rival [Edmonton] Oilers, when Toronto fans desperately hope that the Leafs will beat the Canadiens, when the Nordiques carry the pride of Quebec City into Montreal, Canadians become involved with one another in a particularly dramatic way. Furthermore, come playoff time, when East plays West, or when Canadian teams play U.S. teams, most of the country watches. And even though sides are taken and historic rivalries relived, the games provide country-wide points of interest and a tableau of common memories.

Yet even though hockey continues to provide occasions when shared interests and identities appear to transcend, temporarily, the economic, political, and cultural struggles that divide the country—something that helps create a sense of being *Canadian*—we have to ask whether the game continues to have the same relationship to Canadian communities and identities that it once had.

Hockey and Community in Small-Town Canada

In the days before satellite dishes and paved highways were common in rural areas, hockey emerged as a centrally important communal activity in Canada. Churches and women's institutes were important focal points of community life too, but sports often cut across occupational, religious, and ethnic divisions and offered fun and entertainment for most of the community. For well over a century, baseball tournaments were regular features of rural fairs and generated great interest as teams of local men (and women) competed against neighbouring areas or touring teams. Nonetheless, the place of baseball in rural community life was always limited by the short summer and, in farming communities, by the rhythms of agricultural work. Hockey was different in several important respects. On the Prairies the long winter was the slack period for farm work and thus a season when people had more time for socializing and leisure activities. Euchre, crib, and bingo were popular in pre-television days, but men and boys played hours and hours of hockey on ponds, rivers, and outdoor rinks. Watching hockey was limited by the cold and the lack of spectator facilities. Communities that could afford it enclosed their natural ice rinks; yet even under these conditions games were cold for spectators, as well as dependent on weather. As Ken Dryden observes, for Prairie boys of the vintage of Max Bentley or the young

Gordie Howe, there was much less *organized* hockey than later became the norm.

The hockey culture that came to characterize the rural Prairies after the war couldn't fully develop until relative affluence and wartime construction techniques brought indoor arenas within the reach of smaller towns and villages. Better rural roads and increased ownership of pleasure vehicles also played their part by making an evening's travel to other communities more feasible. Together these developments meant that winter sports played indoors—curling as well as hockey—became the focal points of a gregarious intracommunity and intercommunity culture that, for the generation of Canadians who grew up between the 1940s and the 1960s, represented the friendliness and togetherness of small-town Canada. Small towns all over the country built "memorial" arenas, and along with bonspiels community hockey (at all age levels) became synonymous with small-town Canadian life.

In the 1990s, these post-war rinks, and even a later generation of "centennial" arenas, are becoming old and sometimes uninsurable. They need to be replaced, but with costs now running into the millions of dollars, new buildings are almost impossible for a hinterland town or village with an eroded municipal tax base. Yet without the arena one of the major centres of community life disappears. There is less "to do," and this makes it harder to attract the teachers and medical personnel who provide other contributions to the viability of rural communities. Without the arena, moreover, it also becomes more difficult to keep people "at home" on the weekends; they'd rather travel to the nearest big city. It is not surprising, then, that Dryden and MacGregor found that men they interviewed in Radisson, Saskatchewan, feared the loss of their arena as the beginning of the end for their village and way of life. As Dryden and McGregor conclude, "The arena that was a symbol of community development is becoming a symbol of community transformation and dissolution."[1]

It is worth underscoring the importance of hockey in the traditional life of small-town Canada. Even though many towns and villages only got indoor arenas in the postwar boom, there was a long tradition of competitive senior hockey in larger centres such as Trail and Penticton in British Columbia or Whitby and Belleville in Ontario. In the 1950s and 1960s all of these towns produced world championship teams with semi-professional players. While senior hockey has since withered away in most parts of Canada, junior hockey still thrives—and still matters—in places like Kamloops, Medicine Hat, and Swift Current in the West, or

Peterborough, Belleville, and Kitchener in Ontario. Moreover, senior hockey continues to hang on in parts of Saskatchewan and Atlantic Canada that remain relatively isolated from urban entertainment. Having the best team in the area still means something in places such as Kindersley, Saskatchewan, which has a population of about five thousand and is half a day's drive from the nearest big city. Senior teams like the Kindersley Clippers still play skilled hockey, and the players and fans who keep the senior game alive represent a powerful tradition in Canadian sport and community life. It is partly because of this tradition that saving the arena takes on such symbolic significance and has become a focus for urgent fundraising campaigns in many small communities.

There is much to honour in this tradition of community hockey. It is necessary, nonetheless, to understand the limits to hopes that community hockey can help preserve the small-town way of life. First, we shouldn't lose sight of the economic forces and the political decisions that are restructuring the face of rural Canada. Community hockey thrived in Canada when residents still looked primarily to their own communities for entertainment, shopping, and socializing. Today senior hockey is struggling in rural Saskatchewan because drought and debt combine to squeeze farm-belt incomes and because cable TV and satellite technology now bring much more NHL (National Hockey League) hockey, as well as other "major-league" entertainment, into local living rooms. In other areas, as mines and mills have closed or laid off workers in resource-extraction communities, families have moved away and the businesses that remain have struggled. These tendencies have made it increasingly difficult to raise money for any kind of community recreational activity.

It is difficult, but sometimes possible, for communities to resist the effects of closures by trying to reconstitute essential services themselves. A recent study of a rural community in transition conducted by sociologists Philip Hansen and Alicja Muszynski describes a Saskatchewan village that, over ten years, lost its rail line, its grain elevators, its co-op services (including grocery store, lumber yard, and garage), and a farm implement dealer whose franchisor switched to a dealer in a larger town nearby.[2] Not unlike the people of Radisson who Dryden and MacGregor describe in Home Game, the village people and surrounding farmers were determined to do whatever they could to save their community—so much so that local families now operate the garage, the grocery, and the lumber yard, while a young electrician has started up a new business. The village, as a result, continues as a viable service centre for surrounding farms.

Hansen and Muszynski indicate that economic survival is not by itself a sufficient condition (though it is certainly a necessary one) for the survival of a rural community. Community survival also requires a collective sense of identification and public spirit, which in turn requires the survival of other kinds of organizations and associations that can regularly renew social relationships. Recognizing this, people in the community were raising money for a curling and bowling facility that would serve as a multipurpose community centre. Indeed, Hansen and Muszynski note the popular sentiment that it "is the strength of these institutions of common life, and not just the strength of the local business community, which accounts for the survival of the village against the forces arrayed against it." Popular cultural practices, as well as the organizations and associations that promote them, have long helped to cultivate community attachments. Without curling, bowling, hockey, and the local café, many people believe that "the community, if it existed at all, would be very different and it is doubtful if local businesses would survive for very long."[3] One rural reeve cited in Hansen and Muszynski's study highlighted the plight of hockey as part of a set of connected processes of disintegration, noting a "decline in the number of committees dealing with local issues and the inability of the village to ice a youth hockey team, just ten years after a local squad had won a provincial championship." This was seen to be "part of a larger process in which people constructed ties to other areas and no longer concentrated on building a local community."[4]

The villagers in this study also realized that community spirit and good leisure facilities were not enough by themselves to keep their community viable. These things make a place "lively," and they provide reasons for families to stay and attractions for young professionals or business people to move in. However, rural towns and villages still need a critical mass of commercial services, and they also need the public services that are necessary to both business and community life. The most important public services are the school and the post office, and many villages see the potential loss of either of these as a continuing threat to their survival. Such threatened losses underline the vulnerability of peripheral communities across the country to political and economic decisions made elsewhere, exemplified in recent years by the federal government's decision to "rationalize" post and rail services in rural Canada. Here, we are brought face to face with the "limits of leisure" in accomplishing community renewal. Hockey has long been an important rallying point for community spirit across rural Canada; but when the economic viability of life in, say, rural Saskatchewan or northern Ontario is undermined, it is unrealistic to expect leisure practices, organizations, and associations to make more than a symbolic difference.

Boosterism, Urban Communities, and Professional Sport

Another important issue is whether the boosterism that is a feature of small-town life has the same meanings as in larger cities. In their discussions of both small-town Saskatchewan and the city of Saskatoon, Dryden and MacGregor positively equate boosterism with community spirit and with a commendable refusal to give up in the face of challenges. Boosterism combines a promoter's professional optimism with a competitiveness that is presented simply as an instinct for survival. "Things come to those who go out and get," and in the competitions for businesses and rail lines, as well as hospitals and schools, that have been part of the history of the West, boosterism has long been regarded as necessary.

Dryden and MacGregor emphasize the continuities between the history of small-town boosterism on the Prairies and the campaign waged by promoters to bring NHL hockey to Saskatoon (or, one might add, by extension, to bring the Olympics to Calgary or Toronto). In our view, however, this emphasis on what is common obscures a number of more significant differences. The small-town hockey arena today is largely a participatory recreation facility. Such facilities are usually simple and inexpensive in design, because providing a spectator "experience" is not a major part of the objective. The arenas are primarily community meeting places where local people gather to participate and socialize. And even in small communities with semi-professional teams, the teams and facilities have tended not to be run with profitmaking as their central purpose.

Conversely, "major-league" professional hockey teams have been part of an expansive world of commercial entertainments that help to constitute "modern" urban culture in the twentieth century. Civic "builders" from Montreal to Vancouver saw successful pro hockey teams and large arenas as assets that could attract continent-wide media attention to their cities and advertise them as dynamic, modern places, with local economies that invite investment. Urban professional sports teams were promoted, to use Carl Betke's phrase, as part of a broader "corporate-civic" project.[5] Betke's own analysis of this corporate civic project focuses on the case of Edmonton beginning in the first decade of the twentieth century. In Edmonton city politicians were sometimes even partners in specific sports promotions. More typical, though, was the networking of local business and political leaders on the board of the Edmonton Exhibition Association, a voluntary association whose purpose was to bring events and "attractions" to the city. The construction in 1913 of the enclosed Edmonton Stock Pavilion, which would provide an attractive venue for a variety of indoor events, was of great significance. The Pavilion was the pride and joy of local boosters. It had an arena floor "larger than that of Madison Square Garden in New York" and could seat six thousand spectators "as comfortably as in a modern theatre" for events as various as circuses, jumping and horse shows, theatrical productions, and hockey.[6]

The coalitions of business, political, and media leaders in Edmonton and Calgary have all been duplicated with minor variations in Vancouver, Toronto, and Montreal. However, it is worth noting the extent to which civic and *commercial* ambitions have combined in facilities ranging from the Edmonton Pavilion to the more recent construction of Olympic Stadium in Montreal, the Olympic Saddledome in Calgary, the SkyDome in Toronto, and B.C. Place in Vancouver. These commercial entertainment facilities have been built first and foremost to accommodate spectators, and often in a style that is itself intended to be part of the attraction. The promoters of professional sports have pushed for these grand facilities because they know their competition is with other forms of entertainment as much as it is with other teams. Such facilities are rarely appropriate for high levels of public participation, nor are they usually very cost effective.[7]

Nonetheless, largely because of the apparently "natural" connections between public entertainments and the promotion of "community," there is a long history of popular support for the civic provision of land for professional sports venues. Any opposition has seldom received the same kind of coverage in the local media as do the supporting views of local business leaders, politicians, and sport figures. Opponents of such projects have been repeatedly cast as carpers and naysayers, or as members of special interest groups who don't have the overall "community's needs" in mind. As a result their arguments have seldom received serious coverage.

One argument worth noting here is the suggestion that boosterism may well have quite different effects in big cities than in small towns. In smaller centres where cheap land has allowed widespread property ownership, growth-oriented "community" projects may well benefit a significant majority of community members. In larger centres, the ambitious projects of boosters have often absorbed civic resources, while much-needed public services remain underfunded. Meanwhile the "attractions" that such projects add to the life of the city often prove too expensive for the city's least affluent citizens.[8]

The promotion of spectator sport in large cities has sometimes brought together in common projects and aspirations people who would otherwise be strangers. Civic boosters in these cities have been able, certainly, to tap into this sense of collective identification. They have established a strong cultural link between popular desires to have high-profile sporting teams represent the city and a narrower set of corporate and/or civic interests. Popular expressions of pride and desires for entertaining spectacle have coincided with the financial interests of local business and the sometimes self-aggrandizing aspirations of local politicians. The irony is that the fortunes of professional teams featuring players from outside the community—and owned by private citizens or companies for the purpose of making a profit—gradually come to be seen as civic resources, as an integral part of the life of urban communities. So, even though the Canadiens are owned by Molson's, the Oilers by Peter Pocklington, or the Canucks by the Griffiths family, people in Montreal, Edmonton, and Vancouver still feel that the teams belong to them. These attachments to professional sports teams have been relatively easy to mobilize in support of land deals, zoning concessions, and public subsidies that clearly benefit private interests.

Communities, Popular Culture, and the Pleasures of Fandom

We don't mean to suggest that the widespread support for professional sport as a form of urban spectacle in Canada has only worked on behalf of narrow corporate or class interests. Since the early part of this century the sense of rivalry and the rooting for the home team that developed around professional sports have offered more than the experience of belonging to a particular city or community. It also afforded a sense of membership in a wider community of interest, as well as an entrée into the international world. It was, in part, through the construction of popular identifications with the progress of local representatives in national and continental competitions that many people who had been local or at most provincial in their horizons began to follow events in the world beyond. And if membership in the "wide world of sport" didn't necessarily turn sports fans into cosmopolitans, knowledge of results, techniques, and standards developed elsewhere at least gave some fans a broader frame of reference they could use to view local performances.

This kind of comparative knowledge has always been one of the pleasures of being a sports fan. It is also part of what it means to feel like you belong to broader imagined "communities" of enthusiasts and like-minded consumers. In the case of hockey the knowledge that has come from accumulated experiences of playing and watching the game at different levels has settled so deeply in the Canadian social memory that the very act of consuming the game has had a tendency to make people feel "Canadian." In this regard hockey's integration into consumer culture from the late nineteenth century to the present day has opened up important forms of communal experience and identity. For example, the consumers of commodities associated with hockey—sticks, sweaters, pads, playing cards, hockey books, as well as professional games—share names, legends, and histories that correspond with specific teams and brand-name products. Through their acts of consumption and the accompanying display of goods, players and fans from Victoria to St. John's have been able to feel a sense of having something in common. This sense of commonality has fixed itself in the Canadian collective memory to the point where it has helped to build a national popular culture.

We've already noted how this version of a national popular culture has never been quite what many advocates of a Canadian "national culture" had in mind. For one thing, it is a national popular culture that became consolidated as much through commercial as non-commercial activity. English-Canadian cultural leaders in the late nineteenth century tended to believe that Canadian culture could best be fashioned through widespread acceptance of the British ideal of the "amateur." By the 1940s that commitment to amateurism in the arts and in "cultural" organizations had broadened to include recognition of the importance of professional artists, authors, and other cultural producers. But the idea remained that an indigenous national culture was best pursued through public initiatives designed to make connections between "nation" and the idea of self-improvement. While organizers of amateur sport have sometimes suggested that sport has a place alongside more traditional cultural initiatives, this argument has never impressed many Canadian intellectuals. They have usually seen commercial sport as being even worse than amateur sport, and hockey's obvious success in helping to define a national popular culture partially explains the lingering resentment that people with highbrow inclinations frequently have for the game. "What kind of country," someone inevitably writes at playoff time, "postpones the national news for a hockey game?"

The note of condescension in this question has never played well in communities such as Trail, Timmins, Whitby, or Chicoutimi. Part of hockey's significance as a form of commercial spectacle is precisely the degree to which it has allowed Canadians to express themselves *outside* of the "socially improving" activities promoted by intellectual and political elites. Yet at the same time hockey has also contributed to a vision of Canadian culture that is resolutely masculine and white. Moreover, when it comes to defining the nature and meaning of hockey's place in Canadian culture, the prominence of the professional game has given an edge to commentators whose views of the "good of the game" have been virtually synonymous with the marketing ambitions of advertisers, media professionals, team owners, and corporate and civic boosters. Strangely, the continentalist nature of the hockey business created an immensely ironic situation where the doings of, say, the Detroit Red Wings, Pittsburgh Penguins, or Boston Bruins came to be seen as major "Canadian" events, the subject of much national interest and conversation.

Many would suggest that for adults hero-identification is properly a passing phase and that adolescent dreams ought to yield to a realism induced by jobs and families. There are, of course, some adult men who live most of their weeks in sport-related fantasies and never cope well with everyday life. But many adult fans who lead perfectly normal lives find that sports speak to their dreams and fantasies in positive ways. The problem is that civic boosters, team owners, and other corporate interests have exploited precisely this same set of needs in their efforts to sell projects that often only deliver more broken promises and unrealized dreams.

The fantasies that sport promotes among many adult fans are rooted in images from the past. Visiting arenas and ballparks, even watching sports on television or listening to the radio, can bring back visions of warmly remembered places and times, friends and families. In this remembering, people feel reconnected with parts of their lives that they may have lost touch with. These experiences of memory and connection may be especially important in understanding the appeal of sports among the mobile middle classes. The sports world, through the continuing involvements it offers with the teams, heroes, and memories of childhood, can provide threads of continuity (however apparently trivial) in lives otherwise lived in separate chapters: in different jobs, with different partners and sets of friends, in different cities. At another more collective level, team traditions like that of Les Canadiens or stirring comebacks like Team Canada's victory in the 1972 Challenge Series with the last-minute heroics of Paul Henderson's winning goal all become part of a collective popular memory which, in turn, can become the currency of identification among strangers.

In Canada today the class origins of these different spectatorial practices often seem little more than a distant memory, even though the French sociologist Pierre Bourdieu reminds us that the attitude of dispassionate connoisseurship in sports spectating is still regarded as "better" in the hierarchy of cultural distinctions associated with "taste" in Western societies.[9] What also needs to be recognized is that even the most partisan fan's way of watching is not undiscriminating. Cultural studies researchers have argued that throughout contemporary popular cultures discriminations and choices in cultural consumption are frequently made according to criteria of social relevance rather than abstract notions of quality. In sport this means that when people identify themselves as Bruins' fans or Canadiens' fans, or when they root for the underdog, they are "choosing sides" in ways that say something about their own social identifications. For example, even though the traditions of flair and style versus tough "lunch pail" hockey that the Canadiens and Bruins historically represented have become altered in the makeup of the present-day teams, the connotations live on and help to construct popular identifications. Similarly, when people identified with the Flyers in the 1970s, or with a Bob Probert or (in a different way) a Ron Duguay, they were celebrating various kinds of unruliness and expressing another kind of social identification.[10]

Through such identifications, fans "live" a side of themselves that may occasionally be expressed in more concrete and politically significant ways, but which for most people is normally repressed in the context of their rule-bound lives. Moreover, when people display their consumer choices with sweaters, caps, and jackets they participate in identifications among like-minded people. Through such choices they advertise their social allegiances and often experience a sense of community and a sense of collective fun that is quite different from the experience of the connoisseur. Fans become participants in the show, and, in the words of the British cultural theorist John Fiske, their "participation brings with it the pleasures of revelry and festivity, of self expression, and the expression and experience of solidarity with others."[11]

We should be wary of implying that these different ways of watching sport are mutually exclusive. Certainly, one of the features of any truly popular form is its capacity to mean different things to different people, to lend itself to many different readings and fantasies. This is arguably one explanation of sport's widespread appeal, as well as of what some would call its triviality. It may also be that watching sport involves "a kind of unspoken dialogue between the rational assessment of the strengths and tactics of each side, and a fierce loyalty to one of the two teams."[12] Some of the most committed fans are also among the most knowledgeable. What is almost certainly true is that this loyalty, and the sense of involvement that comes with it, together add another whole dimension, a feeling of community, to the appreciation of the connoisseur. It is through this involvement that the fan becomes a participant and a member of . . . something.

But what exactly is this something? What kinds of communities are communities of fans? Undoubtedly, professional sports teams have become important focal points of civic attention and pride in many North American cities, and it is clear that some pro teams—like the Toronto Blue Jays or the Los Angeles Raiders—develop a national and even continental following. Yet there is a clear difference between these communities of sporting enthusiasts and the idea of "community" as a group of people united by their common fate and by the need to make their community a humane and decent place to live and work. Spectators at professional sports contests, like those at other professional entertainments, know one another only accidentally. They are consumers of a collective entertainment experience, temporarily united by common passions and memories centred around a shared product preference, but not necessarily by anything else. To say this is not to deny the potential power of these experiences. It is only that "communities" formed around acts of consumption or product loyalties (whether to the Toronto Maple Leafs or Ford trucks) are not political communities in any meaningful sense of the word. If we confuse these different meanings of community on a continual basis, or if political communities are effectively remade into communities of consumption and lifestyle, then surely we lose something important about the meaning and practice of public life.

We want to follow Raymond Williams and suggest that today's ephemeral consumer identities are "radically reduced" identities, insofar as the act of pursuing our interests *first and foremost as consumers* may actively undermine the livelihood of the communities we live in and whose vitality we depend on in other parts of our lives. Another corollary of learning to identify ourselves primarily as consumers is that we come to be persuaded that our lives are most effectively enhanced by more consumer choices, in other words by the expansion of the market alone rather than through political activity or voluntary community activity.

This trend seems to translate, for many people, into an almost supernatural worship of the market and, coincidentally, into a belief that the best and most attractive communities are the ones that offer the most dynamic entrepreneurial environments as well as access to "world class" entertainment and shopping.

Notes

Originally published as "Communities, Civic Boosterism, and Fans," in *Hockey Night in Canada: Sport, Identities and Cultural Politics*, by Richard Gruneau and David Whitson. Copyright © Richard Gruneau and David Whitson 1994. Reprinted with permission of the authors.

1. Ken Dryden and Roy MacGregor, *Home Game: Hockey and Life in Canada* (Toronto: McClelland and Stewart, 1989), 23.

2. Philip Hansen and Alicja Muszynski, "Crisis in Rural Life and Crisis in Thinking: Directions for Critical Research," *Canadian Review of Sociology and Anthropology* 27.1 (1990).

3. Ibid., 17.

4. Ibid., 19 and note 8.

5. Carl Betke, "Sports Promotion in the Western Canadian City: The Example of Early Edmonton," *Urban History Review* 12.2 (1983): 47–56.

6. Ibid., 53.

7. For a useful discussion of this point see Chuck Reasons, " 'It's Just a Game': The 1988 Winter Olympics," in *Stampede City: Power and Politics in the West*, ed. Reasons (Toronto: Between the Lines, 1984).

8. Our discussion here is indebted to Paul Voisey, *Vulcan: The Making of a Prairie Community* (Toronto: University of Toronto Press, 1988), 240; and Alan Artibise, *Winnipeg: A Social History of Urban Growth, 1874–1914* (Montreal: McGill-Queen's University Press, 1975).

9. Pierre Bourdieu, *Distinction* (Cambridge, Mass.: Harvard University Press, 1984), 32–41.

10. Bob Probert and Ron Duguay were professional hockey players in the 1980s and 1990s. Probert was popular as an unmanageable hockey tough guy and general rule breaker. Duguay's "unruliness" stemmed from his unprecedented (for hockey) exploitation of his sex symbol looks, which included work as a model for a jeans company.—Eds.

11. John Fiske, *Understanding Popular Culture* (Boston: Unwin Hyman, 1989), 141.

12. Richard Holt, *Sport and the British* (New York: Oxford University Press, 1989), 162.

SERRA TINIC

Global Vistas and Local Reflections: Negotiating Place and Identity in Vancouver Television

Serra Tinic (b. 1965) completed her Ph.D. at Indiana University in 1999. She is currently an associate professor in the Department of Sociology at the University of Alberta. She is the author of *On Location: Canada's Television Industry in a Global Market* (2005).

In the 1980s the B.C. Ministry of Small Business, Tourism and Culture developed the "Supernatural British Columbia" campaign, which promoted travel to the province by extolling the beauty and variety of British Columbia's natural landscape in a series of advertisements directed at both the American and out-of-province Canadian markets. While "Supernatural B.C." remains the province's official tourism motto to this day, by the mid-1990s the designation of the term became more closely associated with the fact that Vancouver was the production home of nine of the top American "supernatural" television series including *The X-Files*, *Highlander*, *The Outer Limits*, *Poltergeist: The Series*, *Sliders*, *Strange Luck*, *Millennium*, *Stargate*, and *The Sentinel*.[1] The connection here is not meant to appear facetious. The rationale for producing these episodics in Vancouver is, in fact, largely due to the diversity of locations available in a coastal province that also contains a glacier mountain range and a dry, rugged interior region. The Lower Mainland's gray, rainy, and foggy winters also provide the natural light and settings that writer-producers and directors of photography (DOPs) relish in their efforts to establish the necessary atmosphere for such programs. And it is no coincidence that the B.C. Film Commission, the organization largely responsible for recruiting runaway American television and film production, works under the auspices of the Ministry of Small Business, Tourism and Culture.

The connection to small business is, however, misleading. In British

Columbia, film and television production and tourism are multi-million dollar industries that are integral components of the province's larger economic globalization strategy and goal to establish Vancouver as a "world-class," or global city. By 1997 the television and motion picture industry had spent directly an estimated $700 million dollars in Vancouver, an increase of $100 million from 1996. During that year, the B.C. Film Commission provided service to $2.7 billion worth of productions (one-third of the potential market) and confirmed Vancouver's status as the third-largest production center for American movies and television series.[2] In fact, of the over two hundred television programs and movies shot in the province between 1996 and 1997, only an estimated 20 percent were domestic Canadian productions.[3]

This integration of the Vancouver locations industry into the larger Hollywood production structure has led some people to argue that foreign production has not only displaced indigenous production in British Columbia but that it has also erased any sense of *place* by commodifying it or selling producers "an industrial setting (physical sites and services) rather than a cultural and historical site (a source of stories and characters)": "The B.C. example illustrates how the locations industry denies British Columbia its sociocultural specificity. It empties this place of its sociality, its status as community, and frames it simply as geographical space."[4] Gasher's indictment of American and other international productions in British Columbia is partially accurate. Foreign producers do not choose to bring their projects to Vancouver to tell Canadian stories or portray Canadian settings. In fact, much of their pre-production work consists of finding sites that can "stand-in" for other places, usually someplace in the United States, and then "dressing" it accordingly (which means removing any physical objects that could identify the location as Canadian in any way).

However, Gasher's argument, which is based primarily on archival analysis of industry promotional documents and production figures, misses the point in two very important respects. First, unlike other forms of international capital and resource/production flows, the "globally mobile" film and television industry does not merely "create and use up places for the purposes of production or consumption."[5] In other words, merely by filming projects in Vancouver, international producers do not first exhaust the labour, resources, or sites needed for indigenous production and then move on to the next "locations city," leaving Vancouver a depleted resource town. In fact, before British Columbia was able to attract runaway American production, local producers were dependent on the transitory whims of central Canadian broadcasters and policymakers to support and maintain any level of domestic television and film production in the province. The fact that there were far fewer domestic productions prior to Hollywood's arrival in British Columbia further contradicts Gasher's implication that the foreign television and film industry somehow supplants the domestic.

The second, and related, problematic assumption in Gasher's argument is that increased domestic production automatically guarantees the portrayal of British Columbia's "sociocultural specificity" as a place rather than as empty "geographical space." However, domestic producers also often disguise the culturally specific aspects of their stories and settings in order to sell them to international audiences and even, sometimes, to national broadcasters. Also missing from Gasher's analysis is any implication of what constitutes the sociocultural specificity of British Columbia that has been erased by the development of the Vancouver locations industry and what types of depiction of community and place experiences might potentially be developed by the domestic production industry.

This essay addresses some of the critiques of international, especially American, film and television production in Vancouver through a consideration of the development of British Columbia's locations industry within the context of the province's larger strategy of economic and cultural globalization. [The first part] examines the goals and rationale behind the provincial government's efforts to attract runaway American television and film production as a component of a larger plan to attract global capital. The [next part] moves away from the Vancouver-Hollywood production relationship and briefly examines how one broadcasting venue—community television—uniquely addresses discourses of culture and community within the global-local dynamic of Vancouver. Thus, while it is acknowledged that runaway American production does erase Vancouver (and Canada) as a *lived place*, it can be seen that alternative media provide the opportunity to sustain a televisual forum for various groups and individuals to negotiate the cultural contestations that are inextricably linked to the sociocultural specificities of the globalizing city.

"The British Columbia Shooting Gallery: We Can Give It to You for a Song"

The above title, from the B.C. Film Commission's centerpiece promotional brochure, is perhaps the best illustration of Gasher's argument that the locations industry commodifies Vancouver as geographical space to be sold to international television and film producers. The *Shooting Gallery* is a 30-page, glossy magazine that underscores the reasons why foreign producers have flocked to Vancouver over the past decade: the diversity of British Columbia's geography, the cheap Canadian dollar (at its 1990s' peak it was equivalent to 79 cents U.S. and it later fell to a new low of 69 cents in 2001), well-trained film crews, and, importantly, the proximity to Los Angeles, the center of the American industry. The discourse of commerce provides the subtext of the publication and uses a play on words and song titles to frame snapshots of Vancouver communities frozen into stage-set vignettes with generic locations identifications: "The Big City," "Urban Ethnic," "Deep Woods," "Industrial," "Residential," "The Mountains," "The Period Look," "The Railroads," "The Countryside," "The Farm," "The Wild West," "Small Towns," "High Tech," "Coastlines," "Ranch Country," and "Wilderness." Beginning with the subtitle, "We can give it to you for a song" the brochure tells foreign producers that "This land is your land" and that, for a fraction of the costs elsewhere, Vancouver can be made to look like anywhere in the world with the closing invitation to "Come and get it. . . ."[6]

Attracting and facilitating international production in Vancouver is, in fact, the central objective of the B.C. Film Commission. The Commission was created in 1978 by a provincial government that sought to diversify its resource-based economy by creating an industry that would not be subject to the exigencies of commodities markets. To this extent, the B.C. government's economic strategy exemplifies the patterns of post-Fordism in Canada during the late 1970s and 1980s. At the time, the provinces found themselves increasingly in conflict and competition in their efforts to restructure politically and economically in ways "which often implied abandoning efforts to protect the borders of the domestic economy" and favoured "accommodating new regimes of accumulation."[7] An important aspect of this process was the appeals made by provincial governments, using the neo-liberal discourse of globalization, to encourage "unions to participate in new kinds of tripartite bodies to design programs for restructuring industry and re-locating Canadian production in the new global economy."[8] The B.C. Film Commission's mandate exemplifies this strategy. The first step to developing the Vancouver locations and service industry was to negotiate a cooperative agreement with the B.C. film and television unions and thereby establish a conducive economic environment for American producers.

American producers are primarily interested in Vancouver as a *space* in which to invest capital in order to garner greater profit rather than a *place* about which to tell stories. To this end, they largely ignore the *place* of Vancouver as long as it does not interfere with capital accumulation. But the question then remains: What defines Vancouver as a place and what types of stories does it offer to domestic producers who are interested in telling them? The following section explores the sociocultural specificities of the place of Vancouver before turning to the second, related question: Does the growth of the *space* of "Hollywood North" somehow preclude the possibility of telling stories about the *place* of Vancouver?

A "Real" Sense of *Place*? The Case of Community Television

In 1994 the *Canadian Journal of Communication* devoted a special issue to the consideration of questions of media and cultural development within the context of global free trade zones and satellite communications, or what the editors referred to as the "open economy" for cultural production. The majority of articles argued for greater support of media that supported national cultural goals as a counterweight to the consumer model of media production that dominates the global cultural economy. Nevertheless, there was at least a tacit acknowledgement, among all contributors, that the lack of government commitment, internationally, to national public service broadcasting has perhaps permanently undermined the capability of such institutions to fulfill cultural development mandates. What was most notable, however, was that rather than arguing for an abandonment of the effort to sustain a sense of cultural community through broadcasting, some researchers advocated expanding public support to include traditionally overlooked media forms into the cultural development model. Of particular interest to these contributors was the relatively low investment and highly localized community broadcasting media.

[This] is something that community television programmers in Vancouver have long realized—namely, that they have been fulfilling the spirit of the C[anadian] B[roadcasting] C[orporation]'s regional mandate for local and regional community expression for decades at a fraction of the cost and with even less policy attention or support than that given to the national public broadcaster. This is not to say that community television should become a replacement for the CBC as it lacks the resources to execute the second component of the Corporation's regional mandate, which is to represent the local to the national community. What the case of community television does illustrate, nonetheless, is the capacity to convey the socio-cultural specificity of *place* through broadcasting to an audience who has, until recently, escaped the notice of market researchers.

Community television was never intended to fill a void left by the CBC but, instead, was developed to provide an alternative forum for local groups and issues that were underrepresented in both the commercial and national public broadcasting sectors. It was introduced in 1969 when the Canadian Radio-Telecommunications Commission (CRTC) required all cable companies to include a community channel within their service area as a public contribution in return for the benefit they would enjoy as a monopoly operation. As a part of their license, and depending on the number of subscribers, cable operators would be required to invest up to five percent of their profits annually in equipment and expenses for community television facilities.

What differentiates community television from both the private and public networks is that it is expected to be user-defined television that provides a forum for local community participation in both informational and entertainment programming. As Goldberg emphasizes, it is important not to confuse community television with the numerous "citizen access" stations that exist throughout North America.[9] While people living in the community are welcome to walk into their local station and suggest an idea or ask to participate in the production process, the community channel has become a semi-professional broadcasting endeavour with a highly developed training program administered by the parent cable company. Consequently, community television is best described as a "collectivist, pluralist, egalitarian concept embedded in a hierarchical, privately controlled, corporate structure."[10] Despite the apparent contradictions within this framework, community television in Vancouver provided an example of innovative local programming freed from the profit demands of commercial broadcasting. Indeed, Vancouver community programming thrived for two primary reasons—first, it was largely ignored by its parent company, Rogers Cable; and secondly, it drew on the resources of a large group of committed volunteer producers and crews within the community.

Aside from a small cadre of full-time program co-ordinators, community television is largely the domain of production volunteers whose interests in the station range from a part-time hobby to training for professional broadcasting careers to those who see their participation as a means to serve particular community needs and interests. When I first began the community television component of my study, the station was in an interesting state of transition. With advances in portable and lower-cost broadcasting technologies, the community station had reached broadcast quality and was beginning to "bicycle" its programs to larger educational and cultural channels such as Knowledge Network and Vision Television, as well as some specialty channels, including the Life Network. The increasingly professional "look" of the programming combined with the availability of a well-trained volunteer production crew thus made community television an attractive alternative for local independent producers who faced limited opportunities and avenues for domestic production.

For those producers who seek to develop ideas that draw upon the experiences of life in the place of Vancouver, community television does offer a structure and level of access that is particularly suited to the representation of the socio-cultural specificity of the city. Rogers community television was organized according to the particular cultural-geographic needs of the Lower Mainland. Within this structure, fourteen community television offices covered the region and four neighbourhood stations were given the specific task of programming for metropolitan Vancouver (Kitsilano-West side, Vancouver main office, Vancouver West End, Vancouver Eastside). Vancouver is very much a neighbourhood-oriented city and, in many ways, the neighbourhoods are more like towns to the extent that they differ culturally, economically and socially from one another. The capacity to produce programs from each neighbourhood and then air the variety of stories on a single channel allowed Vancouver community television to operate as an idealized and local microcosm of the original vision for the regional-national mandate of the CBC. In this respect, the emphasis given to the importance of Vancouver's cultural geography contributes to an exploration of *place* that is unique from the traditional broadcast networks in that members of the community identify and generate the programs that portray the everyday lived realities of life in Vancouver. Thus community television has often been at the vanguard in examining the new cultural formations and struggles that have evolved through the localization of global processes. Herein, the issues of immigration, economic disparity, and environmental/resource crises have been translated into regular television series on the community channel while appearing only as episodic news events on mainstream television.

The priority given to the *processes* of socio-political and cultural contestations within the *place* of Vancouver is a key distinguishing feature of community television. While documentary-style programs like *Silent*

Winter and *Fish Story* cover regional concerns and run approximately six episodes per year, neighbourhood productions such as *Eastside Story* and *Chinatown Today* are weekly series that explore the socio-cultural struggles that provide a symbolic televisual map of the city in the manner suggested by King's earlier depiction of life in the global city.[11] *Eastside Story*, another award-winning community television production, provides viewers throughout the city with a critical portrayal of everyday life in the country's poorest neighbourhood and relates the impact of the area's marginalization to the growing class struggles within metropolitan Vancouver. From a similar perspective, members of the Chinese Canadian community produce the only regular television series in British Columbia that addresses the quotidian experiences of life for the province's largest ethnic community: *Chinatown Today*.

It is this capacity for community television to incorporate grass-roots participation in the production process that has allowed this broadcasting voice to more fully explore and represent the lived culture of Vancouver than have the national public and private television networks. And it is not just isolated interest groups or ethnic communities who use the channel to give voice to their experiences and concerns. Community television in the Vancouver regional district generates over 3,000 hours of programming annually and the range in genres varies from documentary, informational series, cultural performances, to arts and entertainment and magazine shows. In fact, one producer I spoke with had even developed a children's program and a weekly locally inspired sitcom at the Vancouver studio. This individual had purposefully developed these ideas within the community channel because the levels of access and experimentation allowed there could not be found in any other broadcasting structure.

Community television is able to deal with alternative issues and experiment with innovative story ideas and styles because it is a non-profit medium. Put simply, community television can address marginalized voices because it does not have to concern itself with maximizing audiences and pitching content to a dominant construction of locality. In fact, as mentioned earlier, Vancouver community television's parent company Rogers Cable largely left the channel to its own devices because corporate executives assumed that no one watched the community channel anyway. A change in attitude, and control, was swift in coming when Rogers conducted its first audience survey in late 1996 and found that close to 600,000 viewers were tuning into the community channel every week. The timing of the Rogers survey coincided with CRTC hearings over the continued necessity for protecting community television into the next decade. In March 1997, the CRTC announced that new cable companies entering the market would no longer need to provide a community channel in their basic service package and that the national regulator would no longer protect existing community channels. Rogers Cable had apparently envisioned the CRTC's final decision and in January 1997 began a complete restructuring of its community channels across the country.

What became immediately evident in the case of Vancouver community programming was that Rogers was less concerned with "local reflection" than it was with the ability to use the channel to "promote a positive corporate image" for the company. With the knowledge that 600,000 people were watching the community channel, Rogers saw an opportunity to develop a standardized national schedule that would allow for promotion of the cable company and its related entertainment and communications services such as video rental chains across Canada. Consequently, Rogers closed five community television facilities in the Vancouver regional district, leaving one neighbourhood studio for metropolitan Vancouver.[12] Not only did Vancouver lose its essential neighbourhood focus but much of its regular programming was cancelled to make room for new standardized magazine shows that would appear across Canada with a local focus and an emphasis on marketing Rogers products and services. The flagship example of this type of program is the weekly talk show *Plugged In*, which currently appears across Canada as *Plugged In Vancouver*, *Plugged In Ottawa*, *Plugged In Toronto*, etc. In the midst of shuffling the schedule according to the company's national advertising needs there was talk of collapsing several multicultural programs into a weekly *South Asian* hour, which provided some interesting implications for impending struggles for content domination between the Indian and Southeast Asian communities. What appeared certain, however, was that the term "community" would no longer be solely defined at the local level.

Vancouver community television provides an interesting glimpse of the current moment in Canadian television broadcasting. Herein, the move away from regulatory support or commitment to a public service mandate for television, one which addresses the issues of culture and community, indicates that the move toward a global consumer model of broadcasting is not resulting in a "disappearance of the national" in television programming as much as it is in a "disappearance of the local."[13]

The Global Cultural Economy or Where is Here?

As the foregoing discussion indicates, it is no longer sufficient to talk in nostalgic terms about the representation of some neatly bounded and defined notion of a local or national community. The case of Vancouver illustrates how the local and the global are inextricably bound into a new form of community. However, what does remain at stake is the question of where and how the new cultural forms emanating from this particular global-local nexus will find representation in the current media environment. While Vancouver independent producers and CBC managers have had some time to adjust to the diminishing opportunities for developing local cultural expression within television programming, this is an entirely new experience for producers in community television who have always seen the local as their particular cultural terrain. And, although all of the producers I spoke with accept that the globalization of media culture is inevitable, almost all stated that the turn to international audiences is happening during a time when people most need to understand the changes they are facing directly within in their local and national communities. As one community television producer stated: "[Global culture] is like global capital. It *lives on the surface*—there's no commitment to the place, the people, the towns."[14] Perhaps it is because of their own commitment to working at the local level to describe global interconnections that volunteers at Vancouver community television were best able to articulate the perceived importance of a medium for local expression:

> VP 1: As everyone looks at the global less people are taking care of people at the local level. We have to put more effort and attention on them than ever before.[15]

> VP 2: We've got too little Canadian content as it is. Actually, forget Canadian content. How about Vancouver content? The local is a reality check: Look, here I am. I want to be in touch with who I am.[16]

It is this last comment—the perceived link between place and identity— that remains at the core of the debate within the cultural development model of Canadian broadcasting and communications policies. Implicit within this statement is that the turn to the global media environment somehow diminishes or erases this connection. The implications generated within the context of the Vancouver television case study suggest that identities tend to be most *dis-located* from *place* when national and international market motivations supersede cultural considerations in the global cultural economy.

Notes

Originally published as "Global Vistas and Local Reflection: Negotiating Place and Identity in Vancouver Television," in *Television and New Media* 7.2 (2006): 154–83. Copyright © Sage Publishers. Reprinted with permission of the publisher.

1. Not all of these programs remain in production in Vancouver today. *Sliders* and *Strange Luck* were both cancelled by Fox after their first seasons and *The X-Files* moved to Los Angeles in 1998 partially in response to lead actor David Duchovny's ongoing complaints about Vancouver's weather.

2. B.C. Film Commission, *Quick Facts about the B.C. Film Commission* (Vancouver, 1997).

3. Leo Rice-Barker, "Finance Extends Service Shelter," *Playback*, January 13, 1997, 3.

4. Mike Gasher, "The Audiovisual Locations Industry in Canada: Considering British Columbia as Hollywood North," *Canadian Journal of Communication* 20 (1995): 233, 239.

5. David Morley and Kevin Robins, *Spaces of Identity: Global Media, Electronic Landscapes and Cultural Boundaries* (London: Routledge, 1995), 31.

6. Perhaps the most problematic example of the commodification of culture in *The Shooting Gallery* is a photograph of a group of First Peoples dressed in traditional clothes and performing in a ceremonial dance, accompanied by text reading: "The tribes with legends and totems. Proud people willing to share their heritage with you."

7. Jane Jenson, "All the World's a Stage: Spaces and Times in Canadian Political Economy," in *Production, Space, Identity: Political Economy Faces the 21st Century*, ed. Jane Jenson, Rianne Mahon, and Manfred Bienefeld (Toronto: Canadian Scholars' Press, 1993), 159.

8. Jenson, "All the World's a Stage," 158.

9. Kim Goldberg, *The Barefoot Channel: Community Television as a Tool for Social Change* (Vancouver: New Star Books, 1990).

10. Goldberg, *The Barefoot Channel*, 38.

11. Anthony King, "Re-Presenting World Cities: Cultural Theory/Social Practice," in *World Cities in a World System*, ed. P. L. Knox and P. J. Taylor (Cambridge: Cambridge University Press, 1995), 215–31.

12. Volunteers at the Vancouver East community television station successfully negotiated an agreement with Rogers in which the cable company agreed to donate the studio's existing production equipment to the staff producers and to continue to pay their operating expenses until January 1997. At that point, the former Vancouver East community station officially became an independent, non-profit organization called Independent Community Television Co-operative (ICTV). The organization continues to produce the series *East Side Story* and is active in grassroots community movements within the neighborhood.

13. Rowland Lorimer, "Of Culture, the Economy, Cultural Production, and Cultural Producers: An Orientation," *Canadian Journal of Communication* 19 (1994): 259–89.

14. Unpublished interview, April 27, 1997, emphasis added.

15. Unpublished interview, June 18, 1997.

16. Unpublished interview, June 12, 1997.

III

Government Documents

PREFACE TO GOVERNMENT DOCUMENTS

This section includes excerpts from three documents produced by the Canadian federal government. The first two are reports from royal commissions instructed by the government to investigate specific issues through extensive public inquiry. Throughout its history, such commissions have been used in Canada (and other Commonwealth nations, such as the United Kingdom, Australia, and New Zealand) to explore issues of major public concern with the aim of generating policy recommendations that might address and ameliorate blind spots, problems, and limits in government policy. Royal commissions act at one remove from government; as a result, it is expected that they can generate recommendations both more intensive and extensive than might come out of the halls of government itself. Commissions are typically chaired by known public figures (after whom they are frequently popularly named), who are given considerable power, money, and time to conduct a detailed investigation and submit a major report.

Since Confederation in 1867, over two hundred commissions have been established in Canada. The impact of some of them has been negligible, with their findings and public policy recommendations lying unaddressed and becoming buried in government files. The expense and time taken up by such commissions has led to some criticisms of their continued utility or necessity. Nonetheless, and perhaps especially in the period following World War II, a number of royal commissions have played a significant role in both public and academic discussions of the direction and shape of Canadian social, cultural, and political life. Commissions such as the Royal Commission on the Status of Women (1967–70) and the Royal Commission on Aboriginal Peoples (1991–96), for example, have become touchstones for further explorations of the situation of women and aboriginal peoples in Canada—as much for what these commissions failed to address as for the substantive findings of their reports.

The reports issued by the Royal Commission on National Development in the Arts, Letters and Sciences (1949–51, usually better known as the Massey Commission after its chair, Vincent Massey) and the Royal Commission on Bilingualism and Biculturalism (1963–69, known colloquially as the "Bi and Bi Commission") have both had a significant impact on Canadian culture. (The final date in each case is when the commission's report was issued.) Unsurprisingly, given the topics they addressed, they have also attracted significant critical examination from many perspectives. The Massey Commission took up a topic that continues to haunt discussions of Canadian culture: the specific *Canadianness* of Canadian culture vis-à-vis the culture of the United States. The report's conceptualization of cultural and national difference, cultural protectionism, and the role of government agencies in supporting and promoting national culture continues to be of interest to those working in Canadian cultural studies. Just as important, the Bi and Bi Commission's investigation of the relationship between the "two founding nations," French and English, has had a lasting impact on discussions of language and culture in Canada. The Commission found that French Canadians were underrepresented in business and politics and that the French language was threatened in Canada. Among the outcomes of the Bi and Bi Commission was the Official Languages Act (1969), which made Canada an officially bilingual country, and the language rights provisions included in the Canadian Charter of Rights and Freedoms (1982).

The final document included here is an excerpt from a pamphlet produced by the federal government in 1978 to explain its multiculturalism policy and the activities of the "Multiculturalism Directorate." It includes a document tabled in the House of Commons by Prime Minister Trudeau in 1971 that provided an overview of government policies directed toward the promotion of multiculturalism. There has been sustained critical attention to and interrogation of multiculturalism as state policy over the intervening three and a half decades (examples of which can be found in this volume). Indeed, it may certainly be argued that multiculturalism has been one of the main issues in Canadian cultural studies.

As with the documents on Canadian culture and bilingualism, this early document on multiculturalism is intended to give context and background to the critical investigations of these issues in Canada. But the presence of these documents also draws attention to a crucial difference between cultural studies in Canada and in the United States and the United Kingdom. In Canada, government documents such as these have drawn sustained analysis far beyond what one finds in these other sites: in Canada, institutions, agencies, and government programs are not only as important as popular cultural artifacts and commodity culture, but perhaps more so. The documents provided here have played a central part in the development of cultural studies in Canada.

GOVERNMENT OF CANADA

From the *Report of the Royal Commission* on *National Development in the Arts, Letters and Sciences* (Massey Commission)

Chapter 1: The Nature of the Task

THE MANDATE

Our task has been neither modest in scope nor simple in character. The subjects with which we have dealt cover the entire field of letters, the arts and sciences within the jurisdiction of the federal state. But although numerous and varied they are all parts of one whole. Our concern throughout was with the needs and desires of the citizen in relation to science, literature, art, music, the drama, films, broadcasting. In accordance with our instructions we examined also research as related to the national welfare, and considered what the Federal Government might do in the development of the individual through scholarships and bursaries. Such an inquiry as we have been asked to make is probably unique; it is certainly unprecedented in Canada.

[...]

4. In the preamble to our Terms of Reference appears the following passage: "That it is desirable that the Canadian people should know as much as possible about their country, its history and traditions; and about their national life and common achievements; that it is in the national interest to give encouragement to institutions which express national feeling, promote common understanding and add to the variety and richness of Canadian life, rural as well as urban." There have been in the past many attempts to appraise our physical resources. Our study, however, is concerned with human assets, with what might be called in a

broad sense spiritual resources, which are less tangible but whose importance needs no emphasis.

5. The introductory passage quoted above suggests two basic assumptions which underlie our task. First, it clearly implies that there are important things in the life of a nation which cannot be weighed or measured. These intangible elements are not only essential in themselves; they may serve to inspire a nation's devotion and to prompt a people's action. When Mr. Churchill in 1940 called the British people to their supreme effort, he invoked the traditions of his country, and based his appeal on the common background from which had grown the character and the way of life of his fellow countrymen. In the spiritual heritage of Great Britain was found the quickening force to meet the menacing facts of that perilous hour. Nothing could have been more "practical" than that appeal to thought and emotion. We have had examples of this truth in our own history. The vitality of life in French-speaking Canada and its effective coherence as a living community have come of a loyalty to unseen factors, above all of fidelity to an historic tradition. When the United Empire Loyalists came to British North America they were carried as communities through the years of danger and hardship by their faithful adherence to a common set of beliefs. Canada became a national entity because of certain habits of mind and convictions which its people shared and would not surrender. Our country was sustained through difficult times by the power of this spiritual legacy. It will flourish in the future in proportion as we believe in ourselves. It is the intangibles which give a nation not only its essential character but its vitality as well. What may seem unimportant or even irrelevant under the pressure of daily life may well be the thing which endures, which may give a community its power to survive.

6. But tradition is always in the making and from this fact we draw a second assumption: the innumerable institutions, movements and individuals interested in the arts, letters and sciences throughout our country are now forming the national tradition of the future. Through all the complexities and diversities of race, religion, language and geography, the forces which have made Canada a nation and which alone can keep her one are being shaped. These are not to be found in the material sphere alone. Physical links are essential to the unifying process but true unity belongs to the realm of ideas. It is a matter for men's minds and hearts. Canadians realize this and are conscious of the importance of national tradition in the making.

From the *Report on the Arts, Letters and Sciences*   519

7. Our task was opportune by reason of certain characteristics of modern life. One of these is the increase in leisure. The work of artists, writers and musicians is now of importance to a far larger number of people than ever before. Most persons today have more leisure than had their parents; and this development, along with compulsory education and modern communications, enables them to enjoy those things which had previously been available only to a small minority. But leisure is something more than just spare time. Its activities can often bring the inner satisfaction which is denied by dull or routine work. This lends added import to an inquiry concerned with such matters as books, pictures, plays, films and the radio.

8. At the outset of the inquiry we were asked whether it was our purpose to try to "educate" the public in literature, music and the arts in the sense of declaring what was good for them to see or hear. We answered that nothing was further from our minds than the thought of suggesting standards in taste from some cultural stratosphere. A correspondent quoted by one witness complained that he was confronted by too much "cultural tripe" on the air. If his grievance was that he had no alternative to the serious programmes he found unpalatable he was a legitimate object of sympathy. Our hope is that there will be a widening opportunity for the Canadian public to enjoy works of genuine merit in all fields, but this must be a matter of their own free choice. We believe, however, that the appetite grows by eating. The best must be made available to those who wish it. The inquiry will have served one important purpose if it contributes to this end.

9. Today governments play a part not foreseen a generation ago, in the matters which we are required to review. In most modern states there are ministries of "fine arts" or of "cultural affairs." Some measure of official responsibility in this field is now accepted in all civilized countries whatever political philosophy may prevail. In Great Britain, to avoid the danger of bureaucratic control or of political interference, semi-independent bodies, referred to later in this Report, have been set up for the promotion of the arts and letters. We have given careful consideration to this experience as it may apply to Canada.

10. In this country we have two problems. One is common to all states, the other is peculiar to ourselves. First, how can government aid be given to projects in the field of the arts and letters without stifling efforts which must spring from the desires of the people themselves? Second, how can

this aid be given consistently with our federal structure and in harmony with our diversities? On these matters we have received many and varying views. The response of the general public reflects an acceptance of the usefulness of the inquiry and the assumption underlying it, that the Federal Government has some measure of responsibility in this field.

THE QUESTION OF EDUCATION

11. There is, however, one problem which has troubled a number of those presenting briefs to us. We feel it to be of sufficient importance to warrant attention at the beginning of this Report. Although the word culture does not appear in our Terms of Reference, the public with a natural desire to express in some general way the essential character of our inquiry immediately and instinctively called us the "Cultural Commission." We have listened to many interesting discussions on the significance of culture: "The greatest wealth of the nation," says a French-speaking group; of "equal importance" with bathtubs and automobiles observes a more cautious English-speaking counterpart.[1] Some witnesses have welcomed an investigation into our cultural life and its possibilities. Others, however, have shown some concern lest in occupying ourselves with our national cultures, we should encroach on the field of education obviously so closely related.

12. We feel that on the delicate and much disputed question of education there is a good deal of unnecessary confusion which can and should be cleared away. A more precise understanding of the word in its several implications may help to remove the atmosphere of tension which unnecessarily worries many serious people, including some who have presented briefs to us. "Education belongs exclusively to the provinces," say some. "But that," is the retort, "does not affect the right of the Federal Government to make such contributions to the cause of education as lie within its means." The conflict can be resolved very simply by a clarification of the issue. The whole misunderstanding arises from an imperfect grasp of the nature and the end, the kinds and the methods of education.

13. Education is the progressive development of the individual in all his faculties, physical and intellectual, aesthetic and moral. As a result of the disciplined growth of the entire personality, the educated man shows a balanced development of all his powers; he has fully realized his human possibilities. Modern society recognizes, apart from the common experience of life, two means of achieving this end: formal education in schools and universities, and general non-academic education through books,

periodicals, radio, films, museums, art galleries, lectures and study groups. These are instruments of education; when, as often happens, they are used by the school, they are a part of formal education. They are, however, more generally the means by which every individual benefits outside school hours, and much more after his school days are over.

14. This point brings us to the relation of culture to education. Culture is that part of education which enriches the mind and refines the taste. It is the development of the intelligence through the arts, letters and sciences. This development, of course, occurs in formal education. It is continued and it bears fruit during adult life largely through the instruments of general education; and general or adult education we are called upon to investigate.

15. The essential distinction between formal education and general non-academic education has been reflected in submissions made to us and in our public sessions. For example, the Canadian Catholic Conference, in its brief, says: "We feel it appropriate to observe that we could not properly deal here with the specific problems of formal education at its various levels. This is a matter which belongs entirely within the competence of the provinces. . . . It is our wish to speak in particular of this kind of education which is ordinarily referred to as 'adult education.' "[2] The delegation of the *Comité Permanent de la Survivance Française en Amérique* made the following further observation in giving evidence in Quebec City: " . . . The domain of formal education belongs to the provinces, but beside the domain of formal education is that of culture or general education; and this you have been instructed to review. In our view, culture should be a matter for federal and even for international interest."[3]

16. In a country which boasts of freedom based on law and inspired by Christian principles, it is perhaps unnecessary to say that education is not primarily a responsibility of the state at all, whether provincial or federal. Education is primarily a personal responsibility, as well as a fundamental right of the individual considered as a free and rational being. Naturally, however, the individual becomes entirely himself only as a member of society; and for his education he must depend first on his parents and then on various more or less formal social groups, including those controlled by Municipal, Provincial and Federal Governments. To maintain that education must always be primarily a personal and family responsibility is not to deny the supplementary but essential functions of these groups and their governments, nor their natural and permanent

interest in the education of the individual. These functions in each country are determined by law.

17. There is no general prohibition in Canadian law against any group, governmental or voluntary, contributing to the education of the individual in its broadest sense. Thus, the activities of the Federal Government and of other bodies in broadcasting, films, museums, libraries, research institutions and similar fields are not in conflict with any existing law. All civilized societies strive for a common good, including not only material but intellectual and moral elements. If the Federal Government is to renounce its right to associate itself with other social groups, public and private, in the general education of Canadian citizens, it denies its intellectual and moral purpose, the complete conception of the common good is lost, and Canada, as such, becomes a materialistic society.

18. In accordance with the principles just explained, we are convinced that our activities have in no way invaded the rights of the provinces but may rather have been helpful in suggesting means of co-operation. We are happy to have been confirmed in this belief by several provincial departments of education which, by presenting briefs and discussing freely with us those general aspects of education in which they and we have a common concern, have given us most valuable help and encouragement in our work.

Chapter II: The Forces of Geography

1. CANADIANS, with their customary optimism, may think that the fate of their civilization is in their own hands. So it is. But this young nation, struggling to be itseif [sic], must shape its course with an eye to three conditions so familiar that their significance can too easily be ignored. Canada has a small and scattered population in a vast area; this population is clustered along the rim of another country many times more populous and of far greater economic strength; a majority of Canadians share their mother tongue with that neighbour, which leads to peculiarly close and intimate relations. One or two of these conditions will be found in many modern countries. But Canada alone possesses all three. What is their effect, good or bad, on what we call Canadianism?

2. The vast resources of our country are obviously a material advantage although a somewhat perilous one in this age. The intangible qualities of our sprawling mass of territory also have their consequences. Canada's

scattered regions are dominated by the mysterious expanses of the Canadian Shield, with the still more mysterious Arctic beyond, pressing down and hemming in the areas of civilized life. No feeling person could be unaffected by the stark beauty of our hinterland. It has moved the artist as well as the prospector. Through the painters and poets who have interpreted their country with force and originality, Canadians have a quiet pride in what even in this overcrowded twentieth century world is still "the great lone land."

3. Along with attachment to the whole of the country with its receding distances goes the sturdy self-reliance of local communities. These are separated by both geography and history. In all our travels we were impressed by differences of tradition and atmosphere in regions such as the Atlantic Provinces, the Prairies and British Columbia. The very existence of these differences contributes vastly to "the variety and richness of Canadian life" and promises a healthy resistance to the standardization which is so great a peril of modern civilization. There is nothing in this antagonistic to a Canadian spirit. On the contrary, it has been as essential in the inspiration of artist and poet as has been the massive Canadian landscape. Canadian civilization is all the stronger for its sincere and unaffected regionalism.

4. On the other hand, the isolations of this vast country exact their price. "Art is a communication." Even in acknowledging what the artist has done to create a Canadian spirit, we are reminded that he must be able to reach his community, and that he must have some intercourse with colleagues and critics if he is to do good work. Moreover, he must have the material support which as a rule only a concentrated community can give. Canada has bound herself together with expensive links of physical communication, but these exact a tax which the artist can bear even less easily than can trade and industry. This problem was discussed before us at length especially by some representative groups on the Pacific Coast; there, as in the Maritimes, people understand the cost of isolation.

5. Even the everyday activities of civilized life suffer. In a country small in area and compact in population, national organizations of painting, letters, music, architecture, drama and of other such activities are relatively simple to create and maintain. In Canada all national gatherings for whatever purpose, are costly in time and money; yet our regionalism makes them doubly necessary. It would be easy to give many concrete instances of worthy organizations whose activities lack energy and co-

herence merely because they want the resources for a permanent secretary and for regular, well attended meetings. Commercial organizations realize the problem and pay the price. Voluntary societies realize the problem too, but without adequate resources they must resign themselves to a limited effectiveness.

6. This isolation imposed by the conditions of our life affects the work of government institutions also. In a country such as ours where many people are remote from the national capital and from other large centres of population, it is of obvious importance to extend to them as far as may be possible the services of the national institutions in Ottawa. This was a point freely admitted by all except a few metropolitan groups with strong urban preoccupations. Our national institutions operating on a restricted budget and preoccupied with their immediate task are sometimes in danger of confusing Canada with Ottawa. This danger, those who live at a distance and who know the need of national services, are quick to notice. "It was with considerable amusement," said a group from the Prairies, "that we read under the heading National Museum . . . that 'It is centrally located and readily reached by bus and street car.' . . . We ask if we can be expected to take this statement seriously?"[4] The good-natured joke was preliminary to a helpful discussion of what such a national institution could do for the rest of Canada. The responsibility is fully accepted. The difficulty is a measure of the cost of our size and shape.

7. But apart from these problems of dispersal we face, for the most part without any physical barriers, a vast and wealthy country to which we are linked not only by language but by many common traditions. Language and tradition link us also with two mother countries. But from these we are geographically isolated. On this continent, as we have observed, our population stretches in a narrow and not even continuous ribbon along our frontier—fourteen millions along a five thousand mile front. In meeting influences from across the border as pervasive as they are friendly, we have not even the advantages of what soldiers call defence in depth.

8. From these influences, pervasive and friendly as they are, much that is valuable has come to us, as we shall have occasion to observe repeatedly in this chapter and indeed throughout this entire survey: gifts of money spent in Canada, grants offered to Canadians for study abroad, the free enjoyment of all the facilities of many institutions which we cannot afford, and the importation of many valuable things which we could not

easily produce for ourselves. We have gained much. In this preliminary stock-taking of Canadian cultural life it may be fair to inquire whether we have gained a little too much.

9. We are thus deeply indebted to American generosity. Money has flowed across the border from such groups as the Carnegie Corporation, which has spent $7,346,188 in Canada since 1911 and the Rockefeller Foundation, to which we are indebted for the sum of $11,817,707 since 1914. There are other institutions from whose operations we benefit such as the Guggenheim Foundation and the American Association for the Advancement of Science. Through their generosity countless individuals have enjoyed opportunities for creative work or for further cultivation of their particular field of study. Applied with wisdom and imagination, these gifts have helped Canadians to live their own life and to develop a better Canadianism. Libraries given to remote rural areas or to poorly endowed educational institutions are another example of the great diversity of our neighbour's broad benevolence. Many institutions in Canada essential to the equipment of a modern nation could not have been established or maintained without money provided from the United States. In addition, the scholarships and fellowships awarded to Canadian students in American universities without any discrimination, represent an impressive contribution to the advanced training of our young men and women of promise.

10. Of American institutions we make the freest use, and we are encouraged to do so by the similarities in our ways of life and by the close and friendly personal relations between scholars as individuals and in groups. Not only American universities and graduate schools but specialized schools of all sorts (library schools, schools of art, of music and dramatics), great national institutions (libraries, museums, archives centres of science and learning)—all are freely placed at our disposal.[5] We use various American information services as if they were our own, and there are few Canadian scholars who do not belong to one or more American learned societies.

11. Finally, we benefit from vast importations of what might be familiarly called the American cultural output. We import newspapers, periodicals, books, maps and endless educational equipment. We also import artistic talent, either personally in the travelling artist or company, or on the screen, in recordings and over the air. Every Sunday, tens of thousands tacitly acknowledge their cultural indebtedness as they turn off the radio

at the close of the Sunday symphony from New York and settle down to the latest American Book of the Month.

12. Granted that most of these American donations are good in themselves, it does not follow that they have always been good for Canadians. We have not much right to be proud of our record as patrons of the arts. Is it possible that, beside the munificence of a Carnegie or a Rockefeller Canadian contributions look so small that it seems hardly worth while making them? Or have we learned, wrongly, from our neighbour an unnecessary dependence on the contributions of the rich? A similar unworthy reliance on others appears in another field. Canada sends a number of students abroad, many of them on fellowships provided by other countries; Canada offers very few of her own fellowships to non-Canadians, none at all until very recently. Perhaps we have been tempted by a too easy benevolence, but this leaves us in an undignified position, unworthy of our real power and prestige.

13. Canada has, moreover, paid a heavy price for this easy dependence on charity and especially on American charity. First, many of our best students, on completing their studies at American institutions, accept positions there and do not return. The United States wisely relaxes its rigid immigration laws for all members of "learned professions" and profits accordingly. Our neighbours, able to take their choice of the foreign students attracted to their universities by far-seeing generosity, naturally choose many Canadians, partly because they are there in such numbers, partly because they fit in more readily with American ways than do others.

14. In consideration of American generosity in educating her citizens Canada "sells down south" as many as 2,500 professional men and women in a year.[6] Moreover, Canada by her too great dependence on American fellowships for advanced study, particularly in the humanities and social studies, has starved her own universities which lack not only money but the community of scholarship essential to the best work. " . . . American generosity has blinded our eyes to our own necessities. Culturally we have feasted on the bounty of our neighbours, and then we ask plaintively what is wrong with our progress in the arts." So runs a comment in the brief [of the] Conference of Canadian Universities.[7]

15. This impoverishment of Canadian universities for want of effort to keep our scholars at home, brings us to the whole question of our dependence on the United States for the satisfaction of so many non-

material needs. Few Canadians realize the extent of this dependence. We know that if some disaster were to cut off our ready access to our neighbours, our whole economic life would be dislocated; but do we realize our lack of self-reliance in other matters?

16. Such a catastrophe for instance would no doubt hasten the establishment of the National Library so long overdue, but without many bibliographic aids now coming to us from the United States this would be very difficult, and the library would be deprived of countless invaluable Canadian books now available only in the United States. Moreover, it would be difficult to staff it properly without the facilities for advanced library training not found in Canada. The National Conference of Canadian Universities would no doubt make hasty plans for developing and expanding the few adequate schools of graduate studies which we now possess in view of the expense of sending large numbers of students to England or France. The development of many various specialized schools in the arts would be essential. Extensive provision would have to be made also for advanced study, research, and publication in the humanities and social studies as these are now almost wholly supported by American bounty. One Canadian body in this field indeed derives its entire support from the United States.

17. In this general picture of American influence on our cultural life it is perhaps permissible to mention that it extends to an extraordinary degree into an area beyond the limits of our inquiry, but closely related to it. Teachers from English-speaking Canada who wish to improve their talents or raise their professional status almost automatically make their pilgrimage to Teachers College at Columbia University or to one of half a dozen similar institutions. They return to occupy senior positions in elementary and high schools and to staff our normal schools and colleges of education. How many Canadians realize that over a large part of Canada the schools are accepting tacit direction from New York that they would not think of taking from Ottawa? On the quality of this direction it is not our place to pronounce, but we may make two general observations: first, Americans themselves are becoming restive under the regime; second, our use of American institutions, or our lazy, even abject imitation of them has caused an uncritical acceptance of ideas and assumptions which are alien to our tradition. But for American hospitality we might, in Canada, have been led to develop educational ideas and practices more in keeping with our own way of life.

18. It may be added that we should also have been forced to produce our own educational materials—books, maps, pictures and so forth. As it is, the dependence of English-speaking Canada on the United States for these publications is excessive. In the elementary schools and high schools the actual texts may be produced in Canada, but teachers complain that far too much of the supplementary material is American with an emphasis and direction appropriate for American children but unsuitable for Canadian. As an illustration of the unsuitability of even the best American material, the statement was made in one of our briefs that out of thirty-four children in a Grade VIII class in a Canadian school, nineteen knew all about the significance of July 4 and only seven could explain that of July 1.

19. In our universities the situation is very much more serious. The comparative smallness of the Canadian university population, and the accessibility of American publishing houses with their huge markets has resulted in an almost universal dependence on the American product. It is interesting that a vigorous complaint of American text books should come from a scientist: "Where personalities and priorities are in question, American writings are very much biased in favour of the American. This is not to suggest that the facts will be distorted, but by mentioning the American names and industries and omitting mention of any others, a very unbalanced picture can be given. To subject Canadian students year in and year out to these influences is not particularly good for the growth of a wholesome Canadianism."[8]

20. In other fields, the complaint may be not so much one of bias as of emphasis. In history, for example, dependence on the United States for source books and text books makes it difficult for history departments to plan any courses not generally taught in American universities. Junior courses in Canadian history present particular problems because American publishers do not find an adequate market for books and maps in that field. It must be emphasized that we have benefited greatly from many American productions; but because we have left the whole field to our neighbour our own special needs are not supplied.

21. Although in French-speaking Canada the difference in language offers some measure of protection, elsewhere in Canada the uncritical use of American training institutions, and therefore of American educational philosophy and what are referred to as teaching aids, has certainly tended to make our educational systems less Canadian, less suited to our

traditions, less appreciative of the resources of our two cultures. It has also meant—and this is a matter with which we have a direct concern—that a large number of our leading teachers who are not only teachers but community leaders have received the final and often the most influential part of their training in the United States. This training may be excellent in itself, but it is surely permissible to wish that men and women who are going to exercise such a powerful influence on Canadian life should meet and work in some institution which, however international its staff may be could put Canadian interests and problems in the first place.

22. The problem of text books just mentioned shows how American imports may harm as well as help us. But this is only part of the larger problem of vast cultural importations. Elsewhere in this Report we refer to concert tours in Canada organized beyond our borders. These are good insofar as they enable Canadians to hear artists eminent in the musical world. But, to hear the recognized artists, subscribers must also support many who are unknown and who, we are told, could not compete with Canadian talent if they were not supported by these powerful organizations. The unfortunate Canadian artist to get placed must go across the line, not the most happy solution for him or for his community.

23. Every intelligent Canadian acknowledges his debt to the United States for excellent films, radio programmes and periodicals. But the price may be excessive. Of films and radio we shall speak in more detail later but it may be noted in passing that our national radio which carries the Sunday symphony from New York also carries the soap-opera. In the periodical press we receive indeed many admirable American journals but also a flood of others much less admirable which, as we have been clearly told, is threatening to submerge completely our national product: "A Canadian culture with an English-French background," so runs the brief of the Société des Ecrivains Canadiens, "will never reach the level which we desire so long as suitable measures are not taken against the invasion of the Canadian press by one of the most detestable products of the American press, so long as thousands of pages Made in United States are slavishly reproduced by English language papers or translated for French-speaking readers, so long as pulp magazines and other works of the same nature enter or are distributed in Canada without any restriction, as is now the case."[9]

24. The Canadian Periodical Press Association tells the same tale. Although during the last generation our periodicals have maintained and

greatly strengthened their position, the competition they face has been almost overwhelming. Canadian magazines with much difficulty have achieved a circulation of nearly forty-two millions a year as against an American circulation in Canada of over eighty-six millions. "Canada. . . . is the only country of any size in the world," one of their members has observed, "whose people read more foreign periodicals than they do periodicals published in their own land, local newspapers excluded."[10] The Canadian periodical cannot in its turn invade the American market; for Americans, it seems, simply do not know enough about Canada to appreciate Canadian material. Our periodicals cannot hold their own except in their limited and unprotected market, nine million English-speaking readers. These must be set against the one hundred and sixty millions served by their competitors in the whole North American continent.[11]

25. The American invasion by film, radio and periodical is formidable. Much of what comes to us is good and of this we shall be speaking presently. It has, however, been represented to us that many of the radio programmes have in fact no particular application to Canada or to Canadian conditions and that some of them, including certain children's programmes of the "crime" and "horror" type, are positively harmful. News commentaries too, and even live broadcasts from American sources are designed for American ears and are almost certain to have an American slant and emphasis by reason of what they include or omit, as well as because of the opinions expressed. We think it permissible to record these comments on American radio since we observe that in the United States many radio programmes and American broadcasting in general have recently been severely criticized. It will, we think, be readily agreed that we in Canada should take measures to avoid in our radio, and in our television, at least those aspects of American broadcasting which have provoked in the United States the most out-spoken and the sharpest opposition.[12]

26. American influences on Canadian life to say the least are impressive. There should be no thought of interfering with the liberty of all Canadians to enjoy them. Cultural exchanges are excellent in themselves. They widen the choice of the consumer and provide stimulating competition for the producer. It cannot be denied, however, that a vast and disproportionate amount of material coming from a single alien source may stifle rather than stimulate our own creative effort; and, passively accepted without any standard of comparison, this may weaken critical faculties. We are now spending millions to maintain a national indepen-

From the *Report on the Arts, Letters and Sciences* 531

dence which would be nothing but an empty shell without a vigorous and distinctive cultural life. We have seen that we have its elements in our traditions and in our history; we have made important progress, often aided by American generosity. We must not be blind, however, to the very present danger of permanent dependence.

Notes

Originally published in the *Report of the Royal Commission on National Development*, by the Government of Canada. Copyright © National Library of Canada. Reprinted with permission of the National Library of Canada from *The Massey Commission Report* (1951).

1. Association Canadienne des Educateurs de Langue Française, Brief, 3 (original in French); Division of Adult Education, Department of Education, Province of Nova Scotia, Brief, 3.

2. Conférence Catholique Canadienne, Brief, 3 and 4 (original in French).

3. Comité Permanent de la Survivance Française en Amérique, Transcript of Evidence, 77 (original in French).

4. Saskatoon Archaeological Society, Brief, 1.

5. We are informed that there is in Canada no adequate advanced training in a number of important studies including: Town Planning, Industrial Design, Library Science, Dramatic Art, Ballet, Pictoral Arts, Journalism.

6. Private report from Dominion Bureau of Statistics based on figures supplied by United States Immigration Service.

7. National Conference of Canadian Universities, Brief, 12.

8. Professor J. W. T. Spinks, Dean of Graduate Studies, University of Saskatchewan, Special Study, *Scientific Research in Canada*, 48.

9. Société des Ecrivains Canadiens, Brief, 10 (original in French).

10. B. K Sandwell, Special Study, *Present Day Influences on Canadian Society*, 16.

11. Ibid., 17.

12. Cf. John Crosby, "Seven Deadly Sins of the Air," published in *Life* (New York), November 6, 1950, 147ff.

GOVERNMENT OF CANADA

From the *Report of the Royal Commission* on *Bilingualism and Biculturalism* (Bi and Bi Commission)

Preamble

Ten Canadians traveled through the country for months, met thousands of their fellow citizens, heard and read what they had to say. The ten do not now claim that they are relying on this as a scientific investigation, nor do they have solutions to propose at this stage. All they say is this: here's what we saw and heard, and here is the preliminary—but unanimous—conclusion we have drawn.

The members of the Commission feel the need to share with their fellow citizens the experience they have been through, and the lessons they have so far taken from it. This experience may be summarized very simply. The Commissioners, like all Canadians who read newspapers, fully expected to find themselves confronted by tensions and conflicts. They knew that there had been strains throughout the history of Confederation; and that difficulties can be expected in a country where cultures exist side by side. What the Commissioners have discovered little by little, however, is very different: they have been driven to the conclusion that Canada, without being fully conscious of the fact, is passing through the greatest crisis in its history.

The source of the crisis lies in the Province of Quebec; that fact could be established without an extensive inquiry. There are other secondary sources in the French-speaking minorities of the other provinces and in the "ethnic minorities"—although this does not mean in any way that to us such problems are in themselves secondary. But, although a provincial crisis at the outset, it has become a Canadian crisis, because of the size and strategic importance of Quebec, and because it has inevitably set off a series of chain reactions elsewhere.

What does this crisis spring from? Our inquiry is not far enough advanced to enable us to establish exactly its underlying causes and its extent. All we can do is describe it as we see it now: *it would appear from what is happening that the state of affairs established in 1867, and never since seriously challenged, is now for the first time being rejected by the French Canadians of Quebec.*

Who is right and who is wrong? We do not even ask ourselves that question; we simply record the existence of a crisis which we believe to be very serious. If it should persist and gather momentum it could destroy Canada. On the other hand, if it is overcome, it will have contributed to the rebirth of a richer and more dynamic Canada. But this will be possible only if we face the reality of the crisis and grapple with it in time.

That is why we believe it necessary to make this statement to Canadians.

We have to communicate an experience through which we have actually lived, and to show that simple realities of everyday life came to reveal the existence, the depth and the sharpness of the crisis.

Moreover, we are going to have to put our country's divisions on display, and we appreciate the dangers of doing so. But the feeling of the Commission is that at this point the danger of a clear and frank statement is less than the danger of silence; this type of disease cannot be cured by keeping it hidden indefinitely from the patient. Above all the Commissioners are convinced that they are demonstrating a supreme confidence in Canada; because to tell a people plainly, even bluntly, what you believe to be the truth, is to show your own conviction that it is strong enough to face the truth. It is in fact to say to the country that you have faith in it and in its future.

[. . .]

Chapter 3

29. It soon became apparent, as might have been expected, that conflicts in opinion were rooted in widely differing conceptions of the Canadian state and society. The image of his country that each Canadian had forged for himself inevitably determined his assessment of the present predicament and formed the background and basis of his participation in the discussions. At once striking contrasts emerged between French

and English-speaking Canadians, and even more between French-speaking Quebec and the rest of Canada, as each tried to relate the implications of the co-existence of two cultures to the Canada he recognized.

A. CONCEPTS OF DUALISM

30. French-speaking Canadians for the most part accepted without discussion the broad basic idea of "equal partnership" expressed in the Commission's terms of reference; they proceeded immediately to examine specific problem areas such as education, industry and the public sector. It must be noted, however, that some Quebec separatists and quasi-separatists[1] derided the whole idea of equal partnership, not so much because they opposed it in principle, as because they felt sure it was unattainable or that English-speaking Canadians would never allow it to be implemented; thus, from their viewpoint, since equality can never be fully realized, Quebec must separate, or at least obtain the largest possible measure of autonomy.

Similarly among English-speaking participants there were a number who at the outset vigorously denied the relevance for Canada of the equal partnership principle. However, many others viewed the idea sympathetically; but even among these, few appeared to understand all the implications of the concept.

Here then was one major contrast: with the exception of the separatists and the quasi-separatists, who consider the goal of equal partnership to be utopian, the French-speaking Canadians we met, when confronted with the idea, said: "It's a good idea. But it has not yet been implemented in this or that field and in the future it must be." Whereas English-speaking Canadians, except for the most negative group, would say: "But what is meant by equal partnership? Where does the idea come from? What historical and constitutional foundation does it have?"

31. Among French-speaking Canadians, the expression "two founding peoples" was quite frequently used. "Our rights and privileges in the Canadian Federation are not completely honoured, and we feel our group should have priority precisely because it is one of the founding races," stated a Franco-Ontarian in Windsor.

Typically enough, he was linking the concept of founding peoples to the idea of a contract between them, which established French Canada's rights at the time of Confederation. In the past, two major versions of the compact theory have been elaborated: a compact among provinces and a treaty between "races." Quebec's rights (and those of the other provinces) have been based on the first version; the rights of French Canadians throughout Canada on the second. We encountered protagonists for both ideas, and in each case resentment was strong. As another man at Windsor put it: "The grievance here is that the Canadian of French descent, according to the Confederation of 1867, is not getting the privileges he was granted."

Speakers rarely attempted to justify this sense of indignation by precise references to the text of the BNA Act. More often, the concept of a compact was simply advanced as a basic assumption of Canadian federalism. A concrete example of what respect for the treaty-between-races version of the contract idea entailed was often given, however, this was the treatment which the French-speaking majority in Quebec accorded to its English-speaking minority. As a man in Rimouski put it: "For its part Quebec would like to see the French minorities of the other provinces given the same treatment it accords its own English minority."[2]

French Canadian speakers from the Maritimes, Ontario and the West accepted this test, and in doing so they implied that their English-speaking compatriots had broken a solemn undertaking.

32. Many English-speaking participants, however, rejected the concept of two founding races. In Calgary, for example, we heard one man say: "Our Canada is no longer made of two founding races, or should I say floundering races, but through immigration is made up of numerous races, and our real problem is to blend them into one Canada, not two or more."

The BNA Act was often presented as "not a union of two nations but of four provinces, one of which happened to be French" (Moncton), or "an arrangement made nearly a hundred years ago whereby a certain territory in [this] new Canada was set aside where the French influence was to be on a parity" (Calgary). A citizen in Regina pointed out that the text of the BNA Act referred only to religious rights and to the distribution of powers between the federal and provincial levels of government, and he argued that the Act had no significance as a compact between two founding groups. A separatist in Quebec City also refused to recognize any evidence in the BNA Act of a special arrangement between the two peoples. He declared that, "The facts and the text of article 133 of the Constitution completely establish that it is absolutely not so and that Quebec is the only province where French is the official language."[3]

A lawyer from Calgary, in a letter to the Commission, expressed this whole point of view in very precise terms: "As to the matter of constitutional law, the Canadian Confederation is not based on an equal partnership of the two founding races. That idea originates in the so-called compact theory of Confederation which is neither historically nor legally correct. Confederation is based on the British North America Act, court decisions and various conventions which prescribe the relationship of the various provinces the one to the other and to the federal government. Partnership of races, much less equal partnership, is an unknown concept. . . ."

Not only was Canadian history frequently not interpreted in the same way by French-speaking and English-speaking participants, it was sometimes relegated to a secondary importance by the latter: "Canada's future is a lot more important than her past, so let's all work together to create a Canadianism in Canada" (Victoria). As one might expect, this was a view more often expressed in the younger provinces of Alberta and Saskatchewan; yet these sentiments found a kind of echo on occasion from Quebec separatists who attached no importance to the idea of two founding groups, but who were very much interested in the future—a future in which Quebec would be separate from the rest of Canada.

33. These notions and expressions—"equal partnership," "two founding groups," "a compact"—are traditional in French Canada. "Two nations" is a more recent and vivid way of expressing this desire for a recognition of the dual character of the country. French Canadians, who used to refer to themselves as "a race," or "a nationality," now more and more speak of themselves as "a nation." "How do you propose," asked one man in Sherbrooke, "with some scheme of bilingualism, to establish good will and understanding in Canada, unless you accept the existence of a French Canadian nation at the outset?"[4] This idea of a French Canadian nation, having a common language, territory, history and a common culture or way of life, was expressed in Quebec by many people who have no association with separatism. In their mind, it provides the foundation for the ideal of a partnership on equal terms. And when these Quebec French Canadians think of themselves as one nation, it is easy— if not logical—for them to lump all the others together as a nation. Thus concentrating on themselves, and on what we may call their own self-conquest, they view the rest of Canada as a single entity—"les Anglais"— the non-self. The expression "two nations" still rings in our ears, it was so often heard in Quebec meetings.

The matter looked very different to most English-speaking Canadians that we met. They might concede that there are uses of the word "nation" which are suited to the French Canadians in Quebec, but the same term, they felt, could not so easily be applied to all the non-French inhabitants of Canada taken as a whole. The non-French people are united only by their common citizenship in Canada, the bond that also links them with the Canadians living in Quebec. One man in Halifax did suggest that the powerful sense of cultural identity which French Canadians express by the word "nation" might develop in English-speaking Canada in the future. He hoped that, "If we have time, we in English Canada can perhaps define what our identity is and then, knowing that, perhaps we can work with those in Canada who already know what their cultural identity is." But most Canadians whose background was not French seemed to equate the word "nation" with Canada, and they thought of the country as a single nation-state.

Is this difference in the meaning assigned to the word "nation" merely a matter of semantics? Perhaps the French phrase "one country, two nations" may seem to mean almost the same as the English phrase "one nation, two cultures" or even "one nation, two languages." Yet one senses that this last expression in particular signifies much less. A discussion leader in Newfoundland put it this way: "The crux of the whole issue is that we have people looking on themselves as French Canadians, when they should be looking on themselves as Canadians who speak French."

Indeed it seemed that French-speaking participants used the term "nation" to emphasize their understanding of a bi-national Canada while English-speaking ones used it to insist on the necessity of "national unity" for the country. Even the difference in meaning and use of the term "national" illustrates the gap in understanding.

The explosive potential of this difference in perception was emphasized by a man in Saskatoon who registered his own concern that, "Unless the bi-national character of the Canadian state is recognized by the English as well as by the French, the future of this country is very much in doubt." But even with such a blunt statement of the problem, it seemed that the dualistic idea of a nation was still foreign to most of the participants in this meeting—and in many others.

34. Interestingly enough, the idea was also unacceptable to many French-speaking Canadians, especially those who advocated a new and distinct political status for Quebec. They gave to the word "nation" almost the same meaning as many English-speaking Canadians whom we heard. For them also, the nation and the state must coincide; there simply cannot be two "nations" in one state. But then, of course, this one "nation-state" must be a French Canadian state.

Such a coincidence of opposites was often evident: the language and way of thinking of many French-speaking Canadians anxious for a radical change—whatever specific new political arrangement they desired—was much closer to the language and way of thinking of those English-speaking Canadians who hold a unitary concept of Canada, than it was to the traditional language and thinking of other French-speaking Canadians. But of course their respective conclusions were in dramatic opposition: we mean by this, that those who openly promote the idea of a fully independent Quebec, and those who are in sympathy with this view, put the same maximum emphasis on unity as do many English-speaking Canadians. Both groups insist on the necessity of unity of language and culture within one country. In the light of this conviction, French Canadian separatists expressed before us their belief in the inevitability of a sovereign Quebec. To the slogans "One nation, Canada," or "One Canada, two nations," their answer is, "One nation, Quebec." Many times during our regional meetings, we felt that from a certain point of view, the very existence of Quebec separatism is a response to the unitary concept of Canada held by English-speaking Canadians: people who felt that, because of their cultural and linguistic differences they were being pushed into a reserve, concluded that the only way out was to build an independent state where they would be free.

35. A special problem brought into sharp relief by the concept of two founding peoples is of course the situation of the Canadian Indian and Eskimo. Their unique position was put most poignantly in Sudbury by an Indian woman who asked the evening meeting, "Why is the Indian always forgotten? This was the first culture and this was the first language in Canada. We are told that the BNA Act was between the French and English—where was the Indian during this time?" In Toronto, in the course of a conversation with the members of the Indian Advisory Committee of the Ontario Department of Public Welfare, the chiefs who were present after recalling that many Indians speak French, summed up their fate in this way: "If the French people think that they lost a lot of their rights since Confederation, what should the Indian say? They lost the whole land." One of the participants in the discussion protested about school textbooks: "Our children learn that Indians are all savages." Finally the increasing assimilation of the Indians who are forced to leave the reserves for economic reasons was the object of another statement: "As soon as an Indian wants to succeed in Canadian life he must assimilate. They [Canadians] call them non-Indian-Indians. . . . Furthermore,

close to 80 per cent of the Ontario young Indians are marrying other than Indians."

The Eskimo was not present at our "southern" meetings, so [a tour] of the Eastern Arctic was made by two Commissioners: there the problems of the written languages, the school system and the economic future were discussed with Eskimo Community Councils, government officials and missionaries.

We found great sympathy in "white" audiences for the plight in which Canada's two indigenous peoples find themselves, as the relentless march of North American industry and technology moves into territories once exclusively their own. We were impressed by this unanimity of views.

B. OBJECTIONS TO DUALITY: MULTICULTURALISM

36. *Dualistic concepts* of Canada variously expressed in the terms "equal partnership," "two founding races" and "two nations" encountered opposition, as we have said, from Canadians who wanted their country, however they define it, to be seen as a single entity. These unitary concepts will be treated more fully below.

However, the idea of Canada having a dual nature aroused fears among members of the other ethnic groups. The question was posed in Winnipeg: "Are we, west of the Ontario border, to be considered second-class citizens? We are a third of the population in this country . . . and should be considered equal citizens." "Is there some justification," asked a man in Sudbury, "for members of the other groups to be afraid of being caught in a power play, right in the centre [between the English and the French]?" Or, as stated in Kingston, is it true that "my freedoms are actually limited because my extraction is not from one of the so-called founding races?"

This fear that other ethnic groups might be forgotten in the developing dialogue between Canadians of French and British origin was coupled with a strong affirmation of their importance to Canada. On several occasions this was expressed by an over-estimation of their numbers, as by the Winnipeg speaker who said: "We are the third element of the population of this country, of which I think our proportion today is almost one-third."[5]

We were reminded of the prominent role which men and women from Germany, the Ukraine, the Scandinavian countries, Holland, Poland and elsewhere had played in the settlement of the West. In many communities, we were told, a vigorous sense of cultural identity persists.

A Saskatchewan lawyer wrote in a letter to the Commission: "the Dominion government . . . settled the different immigrant nationalities in little island groups with the result that we have large areas which are bilingual. They [the immigrant groups] speak the language of their respective fatherlands and English. Some of the older generations speak nothing but their native tongue."

This picture of non-French, non-British Canadians as pioneers contrasted sharply with the tendency of some participants at the regional meetings either to ignore them or to think of them only as recent immigrants. The term "New Canadian," which was used so often, did not satisfy the desire for distinctive recognition which was felt especially by Ukrainian Canadians, whose grandfathers had been among the first to plough the open lands of the Prairies. For those Canadians of German descent whose ancestors came to Nova Scotia or Ontario in the eighteenth century, the expression, "New Canadian" was even more inapplicable. The desire of these groups to be seen as a special element in Canadian life was strongest on the Prairies. Elsewhere solidarity with English or, in some cases, French Canada, was more often emphasized.

37. What image of Canada would do justice to the presence of these varied ethnic groups? This question preoccupied western participants especially, and the answer they often gave was "multiculturalism," or, more elaborately "the Canadian mosaic." They asked: If two cultures are accepted, why not many? Why should Canada not be a country in which a multitude of cultural groups live side by side yet distinct from one another, all contributing to a richly varied society? Certainly, it was stated, the mosaic idea was infinitely preferable to the "melting pot."

Sometimes, however, a vision emerged of the separate elements, which derived from countries other than Britain and France, being welded together into a new corporate entity. At the preliminary hearing in Ottawa it was said: "We respectfully acknowledge the fact that the problem is primarily with the two founding races, the French-speaking Canadians and the British Canadians, but over the years a third force, a vital force, has emerged and this force must be recognized." And sometimes this "force" was seen in relation to the two main groups, stabilizing, mediating, uniting. One spokesman declared: "The ethnic groups in Canada are, and will continue to be, a unifying force, a cementing force in the Confederation of Canada."

An attempt was made at some regional meetings to discover what unifying values are held in common by Canadians of German, Italian,

Chinese, Ukrainian and other ethnic extraction, but a full discussion didn't seem to follow, and this variant on the multicultural theme tended to blend with the mosaic idea. Indeed the notion of a "third force" had few supporters even among the "New Canadians."

38. Is there some way of reconciling the concepts of dualism and multiculturalism? A great deal of ingenuity and goodwill was sometimes devoted to the task, and we were struck by the fact that several speakers of Polish and Ukrainian origin made a point of expressing themselves in both English and French at our preliminary hearing in Ottawa in November 1963. Once the disquieting idea of "second-class citizenship" had been aired and the strongest possible protest lodged against it, an occasional participant would voice an opinion like that expressed in Kingston: "The demands of bilingualism are justified. We do not see any justification for the introduction of other official languages. We are opposed to any 'balkanization' and to the idea of the 'melting pot.' In the complex ethnic situation existing in Canada, the only kind of unity which can reasonably be striven for and achieved is unity in diversity: the harmonious co-operation of all ethnic groups in the Canadian country as a whole."

More frequently, however, speakers would turn to specific issues. It was suggested to us that there could be special recognition of languages other than French and English without these other languages being given official status. Others pointed out that the maintenance of religious groups is intimately linked with the preservation of language. Once or twice, indeed, it was proposed that the word "bilingualism" in the Commission's terms of reference should be interpreted to mean either French or English plus the mother tongue of the individual in question. The teaching of languages other than French and English as optional subjects in schools and universities; greater use of these languages on radio and television; public aid to cultural projects—these proposals were advanced most often in attempts to give solid substance to the abstract concept of a multicultural Canada.

C. "ONE CANADA"

39. Time and again, during our evening meetings outside Quebec, we could sense a growing unease in part of the audience when the discussion dwelt on differences between Canadians, and we could predict that before long a spokesman for the "One Canada" idea would rise and take the microphone. Sometimes he would express disquiet about regional-

ism and provincialism; sometimes it was the idea of divisions on the basis of language or culture. "Let's all be Canadians," we were told repeatedly, but the meaning of the phrase varied subtly from speaker to speaker.

The sense of regional or provincial identity that many English Canadians appear to possess usually came out in statements which began: "We Maritimers" or "We Westerners," or "Here in Ontario we think . . ." but what followed was never an attempt to reject wider loyalties. Indeed loyalty to the region or province was not seen as a substitute for loyalty to the country, as we sometimes found in Quebec. Rather, the participant would draw attention to factors in the history or geography, or in the economic and social life of his locality which, to him, were his first concerns and coloured his view of the whole Canadian situation. He by no means wished himself and his fellows to be lumped together indiscriminately with those Canadians who lived half a continent away. Yet even though the affirmation of uniqueness went no further than this, it was likely to provoke a response such as that of the speaker in Calgary who said, "I don't want to be identified as an Albertan, or as a Saskatchewanian, or an Ontarian; I wish to be considered a Canadian"; or the participant in Victoria, who said that it is "a matter of loyalty: if Canada is a country, and we are Canadians, then we should be as one in looking for the good of Canada."

40. The "One Canada" idea was often expressed even more vigorously. What effect would the recognition of multiculturalism have on education, asked a man in Port Arthur: "If 75 Ukrainian families wish to have Ukrainian taught in the high school then do 60 French families have the same right? 55 Finnish families? 30 Italian families? 20 Norwegians? Is there not a danger that the country will become balkanized?" This fear of "balkanization" led a number of participants to plumb for the American "melting pot" idea. Canadians of British origin were not the only ones to make this choice. Indeed it was a first generation immigrant from Europe to Winnipeg who called for the "development of a truly unique Canadian culture" as opposed to a "polycultural kind of nation."

What would this single Canadian culture, to which all should assimilate, be like? Usually the answer was clear and explicit. "If we want to have a nation," according to a Winnipeg man, "there is only one way and that's for all of us to look at each other and say we are Canadians regardless of ethnic origin and regardless of the language you speak in your home. You are a Canadian and if English is the predominating tongue in this country then that is what we will speak." And in New Brunswick a discussion leader reported that his group believed "Canada and New Brunswick should be unilingual, and if people want to stay in Canada, let them learn English." Again in Yarmouth, a participant expressed his distaste for "hyphenated Canadianism." He disliked "to hear people speaking about English Canada, French Canada or whatever it may be." This was an oft-repeated opinion among English Canadians, and it sometimes seemed that those who stated it felt that discarding the term "English Canada" was exactly equivalent to setting aside the phrase "French Canada." A man in London thought otherwise: "For an English Canadian to say that he is a Canadian without prefix involves no sacrifice," he said, "because Canada for him is an enlargement of what he knows as an Ontarian, as a Manitoban or as a Nova Scotian, but when we say that a French Canadian should be a Canadian really like us . . . we are asking him to make the supreme sacrifice."

41. Perhaps the reason why this last point was not more fully discussed among English Canadians was because of a widespread feeling, which cropped up persistently, that it was "unnatural" to speak anything but English in North America.

In St. John's, Nfld., we heard: "The standard process of history is for a minority to be assimilated or absorbed. What we are doing . . . here is to stand in the way of that process."

At the same place: "The feeling is that if this [assimilation] has happened to other ethnic groups, why hasn't it happened to French Canadians?"

In Windsor: "Canada is a melting pot. . . . French Canadians will inevitably be assimilated."

In Saskatoon: a discussion group wondered why assimilation has not already taken place and concluded that this is due to article 133 of the constitution; thus French Canada is the artificial, almost accidental result of a decision taken by politicians at the beginning of Confederation. In Victoria, during a private press meeting, we were asked in an aggressive tone of voice whether it is true that French Canadians are compelled to learn French "by the Roman Catholic Church, the Liberal Party and the Social Credit Party." The group of people around us seemed to attach great weight to this question.

When our public meetings were over and we met in conversation with local people, we were told stories which illustrated even more vividly the idea of the artificiality of non-English culture. For example: on the Prairies an English Canadian, upon hearing some people from Quebec speaking French among themselves, went up to them and, in a friendly way, asked them about different aspects of their life. Among other things he said: "Your children may learn French in class, but which language do they speak when they go out to play?" In other words: in class they are forced to listen to their instructors; but when they are allowed out don't they speak English like everyone else? In another part of the country, some ladies who had spent some time in Quebec showed their surprise at having heard very young children speaking French. How on earth, they seemed to be asking, do three-year olds and five-year olds manage to speak a language which adults [of a different culture] find so difficult to learn? This naïveté is not uncommon: the simplest and most natural of acts, that of speaking from infancy the language of one's parents, takes on the appearance of a veritable feat of genius to those who forget that this language is the children's own mother tongue.

42. Nothing could be more foreign to the thinking of the French Canadians we met than the idea that their language and their culture are an artificial fact in North America: to some it was even an insult. At one time a group of English Canadians were speaking with a certain detachment of the "French minority," when a French Canadian present suddenly flung at them: "Do you know, gentlemen, that French has been spoken in Quebec without a break since 1608!"[6] We felt that, moved by a feeling of hurt pride, that man was presenting his letters patent of nobility.

It was even implied at times that French Canadians are the only "true" Canadians. English-speaking Canadians were often referred to as "les Anglais" or as "les Anglo-Saxons," a term which English-speaking people of Scottish or Irish descent let alone German or Ukrainian, heard without pleasure but not without surprise. Sometimes it was meant as a term of opprobrium, but more often it was simply an everyday phrase used to describe English-speaking Canadians, just as the latter frequently refer to "the French," meaning French Canadians. At Chicoutimi one speaker remarked bitterly, "All we're doing here is making the English rich . . ."[7] But at Rimouski another participant talked about "our friends, the English."[8] Whatever the other overtones, such expressions seemed to carry with them the idea that English Canadians were not really rooted in Canada, [and] that they were recent arrivals linked still to another land. The real way, the natural way, to be Canadian was to be French Canadian.[9]

Though the expression "Québec d'abord"—"Quebec first"—was not often heard in our meetings in French Canada, the idea behind these words seemed to inspire many of the attitudes expressed. Most participants evidently took for granted the primary importance of Quebec as a society and especially as a political entity. This assumption seemed so strong and so clear that it was considered unnecessary to state it in so many words.

In their extreme formulations, the two expressions "One Canada" and "Québec d'abord"—appear to be in sharp contrast to each other. Those who held such different ideas were in agreement, however, in that they did not believe in equal partnership.

Notes

Originally published in the Report of the Commission on Bilingualism and Biculturalism, by the Government of Canada. Copyright © National Library of Canada. Reprinted with permission of the National Library of Canada from the Report of the Commission on Bilingualism and Biculturalism (1963).

1. By the term "quasi-separatism" we are trying to describe in an approximate way not an organized social movement but a state of mind that often manifested itself in the regional meetings held in the province of Quebec. Nobody claimed to belong to this group, and we are creating this classification somewhat arbitrarily. By quasi-separatism we mean a state of mind peculiar to those who, although they have not chosen separatism, could probably do so under certain circumstances—and this without causing them any great feeling of disruption—since they were already defining their position almost exclusively from a Quebec point of view. For more detailed study of their position see Chapter VI [of the report; not included in this selection.—Eds.].

2. "Le Québec, pour sa part, veut qu'on donne aux minorities françaises des autres parties du Canada ce que lui-même il accorde à la minorité anglaise chez lui" (Rimouski).

3. "Les faits et le texte de l'article 133 de la Constitution établissent bien que c'est absolument faux et que le Québec est la seule province où le français est la langue officielle" (Québec). Article 133 guarantees the use of the English and French languages in the laws, legislature and the courts of Quebec and in the Federal Parliament and the courts.

4. "Comment prétendez-vous . . . avec une question de bilinguisme établir la bonne entente au Canada, si on n'accepte meme pas au départ l'existence d'une nation canadienne- française" (Sherbrooke).

5. The 1961 Census of Canada establishes at 13.5 % those Canadians whose mother tongue is other than English or French, while those of non-French, non-British origin constitute 25.8 % of the population. Of course, this "third element" is composed of many different linguistic groups, the most important of which are listed in the Working Paper of Appendix IV [of this report; not included in this selection.—Eds.].

6. "Savez-vous, messieurs, que le français est parlé sans interruption à Québec depuis 1608?"

The Acadian branch is even four years older than the Quebec one: Acadia was already in existence in present day Nova Scotia in 1604. Thus the French have been established in North America for three and a half centuries and in two original homes: Quebec, numerically the most important, and Acadia, whose main centre has become New Brunswick. As a result of distance and the vagaries of history, the French in Quebec and those in Acadia have long lived quite separately and have developed what may be called two strong regional particularisms. However, the unifying factors are equally strong such as the possession of a common origin and language, the North American environment and the feeling of belonging to the same "French minority" within the country.

People from the two groups spread across Canada; we found descendants of the French from Quebec or from Acadia everywhere, from Halifax to Victoria. We heard the sentence mentioned above ("French has been spoken in Quebec without a break since 1608") from a middle-aged man in Manitoba, who did not forget to add that his own family had been established in Canada since the seventeenth century. This sort of remark heard in Nova Scotia and Prince Edward Island as well as in Ontario or British Colombia, led us to think that many members of the various French minority groups carried with them, even into the provinces most remote from Quebec, the consciousness of a historical continuity and a feeling of French solidarity.

7. "Nous sommes là pour enrichir les Anglais . . ." (Chicoutimi).

8. " . . . nos amis les Anglais" (Rimouski).

9. This is the reverse of the feeling among some English Canadians, noted above, that to be French-speaking in Canada is not quite normal. It is often forgotten in Quebec that English settlement ante-dates French in large areas of Canada, notably Hudson's Bay and the Arctic, in most of Ontario and the Prairies, and in British Colombia. Here the presence of the French appears as strange as the presence of the English in Chicoutimi or Beauce regions.

From *Multiculturalism and the Government of Canada* (Canadian Government Pamphlet)

in the beginning . . .

> "In (the new) Parliament there will be no question of race, nationality, religion or locality. . . . The basis of action adopted by the delegates to the Quebec Conference in preparing the resolutions, was to do justice to all—justice to all races, to all religions, to all nationalities and to all interests. . . ."
> (Hector L. Langevin—1865)

some years later . . .

> "For here (in Canada), I want the marble to remain the marble; the granite to remain the granite; the oak to remain the oak; and out of all of these elements I would build a nation great among the nations of the world."
> (Prime Minister Sir Wilfred Laurier—circa 1903)

in the sixties . . .

> "Canada is a garden . . . into which has been transplanted the hardiest and brightest flowers from many lands, each retaining in its new environment the best of the qualities for which it was loved and prized in its native land. . . ."
> (Prime Minister John Diefenbaker—1961)

> "What better way could we prepare for our centenary than by taking effective steps now to deepen and strengthen the reality and the hopes of Confederation so that all Canadians, without regard to race or language or cultural background may feel with confidence that within this nation they can realize, without discrimination and in full part-

nership, a good destiny for themselves and for those who follow them."
(Prime Minister Lester Pearson—1962)

in the seventies . . .

"A policy of multiculturalism within a bilingual framework commends itself to the Government as the most suitable means of assuring the cultural freedom of Canadians. . . . A vigorous policy of multiculturalism will help form . . . the base of a society which is based on fair play for all."
(Prime Minister Pierre E. Trudeau—1971)

"Our Multiculturalism Policy stems from a pragmatic base. We are not trying to create a multicultural society, we already live in one. We are simply recognizing the reality that exists. National unity requires that we understand all our people and have a mutual respect for one another. Multiculturalism helps create this climate of understanding in our society."
(Norman Cafik—1977)

In 1972, the Prime Minister appointed a minister responsible for the implementation of the multi-culturalism policy and for the furthering of this policy across the very broad spectrum of government programs and policies.

The Minister and his staff actively communicate with all sectors of government and the public to promote an awareness of the pluralistic nature of Canadian society. They seek to further through various avenues the acceptance of ethno-cultural groups and their members as full participants in Canadian society.

The Multiculturalism Directorate and Its Program

The Multiculturalism Directorate is responsible for the implementation of a variety of activities that support the multiculturalism policy as announced by the Prime Minister. The Directorate's main objective is "to encourage and assist, within the framework of Canada's Official Languages Policy and in the spirit of existing human rights codes, the full realization of the multicultural nature of Canadian society through programs which promote the preservation and sharing of cultural heritages and which facilitate mutual appreciation and understanding among all Canadians."

In working to achieve this objective the Directorate has two main lines of approach: one is directed specifically towards Canadian cultural groups and organizations to help them to articulate their needs and achieve their individual aspirations and the other is directed at society at large to increase awareness and appreciation of the bilingual and multicultural nature of our country.

A wide variety of activities is pursued by the Directorate with the aim of directly assisting the country's many cultural groups and communities in their efforts to maintain and develop their culture in the Canadian context. Activities or projects which are encouraged and supported may include conferences or seminars discussing current issues of concern to a particular group; ways and means of refining organizational skills; the collection and exhibition of art and craft works; the production of audio-visual or other resource material for use within a group or to be shared by other groups; the writing of creative literature and its publication in either of the official languages or in the ancestral languages; the development of the performing arts and many others. Special consideration is given to projects which promote the cultural integration of immigrants. All in all the emphasis is on projects which can be seen to be meaningful in the development of a given group and which contribute to the objectives of the Multiculturalism policy.

Beyond projects such as the ones listed above, which are initiated by members of the various cultural communities, the Directorate itself has initiated a number of projects also directed at the cultural development of communities. These include the provision of support for the teaching of ancestral languages in classroom settings but outside the formally organized school systems. Financial assistance is given not only towards the operating costs of the courses but also towards the cost of training instructors and developing language teaching-aids relevant to the Canadian context. Efforts are also made to encourage the growth of co-ordinating organizations, such as multicultural councils, which promote inter-cultural activities and stimulate creative encounters and interchange. Such interchange can contribute a great deal to the breaking down of barriers among Canadians and can play a significant part in creating a feeling for the uniqueness of this nation.

Conveying such a feeling of uniqueness to the rest of Canadian society is what the other aspect of the Directorate's program attempts to achieve. For this, close co-operation is established and continuous exchange of information carried on with cultural institutions and agencies that have programs dealing with cultural development such as the Canada Council, the National Library, the Public Archives, the National Museums, the National Film Board, folk arts councils and various national organizations of authors, artists, playwrights, publishers and educational resource developers. Multiculturalism is promoted also through a public relations program directed at the mass media, through information campaigns and through the encouragement of those projects which may have a particular impact on public opinion.

The following are some examples of more specific activities that are being undertaken in this area.

Support is provided for scholarly research and academic courses of study in the field of the humanities, social sciences and fine arts relating to important aspects of cultural pluralism in Canada. Not only is research supported and encouraged but provisions exist for arranging exchanges of professors and lecturers for academic sessions or just individual lectures. Research projects are evaluated by an advisory body, the Canadian Ethnic Studies Advisory Committee, which is composed of academics from a variety of disciplines.

A series of ethnic histories have been or are being commissioned in order to encourage an awareness of the integral part played by various minority groups in Canadian history. These histories are intended for the general public as well as educational institutions. A series of anthologies in the official languages is also being planned. This series would display and promote the creative literary contribution of Canada's many cultures. Translation into the official languages is encouraged as one way of reaching as many Canadians as possible. There are also a number of ongoing activities in the performing arts such as multicultural theatre and choir festivals, workshops and involvement in major national events.

In addition to these two well-defined aspects of the Directorate's work there is, naturally, a continuous process of becoming acquainted with the concerns and activities of cultural groups, and of keeping abreast of cultural events in Canada and abroad as well as of educational resources available and all other potentially useful information, so that the functions of the Directorate can be carried out in the most efficient and effective way possible.

A large part of this information gathering is accomplished through the Ethnic Press Analysis Service which analyses more than 200 ethnic newspapers and periodicals published in over 30 languages. This Service provides the government with information on and analyses of opinion trends and major events within ethno-cultural communities. This is being done through the publication of a monthly review of the ethnic press, special bulletins on specific topics, translations of individual articles, and written and verbal replies concerning reports on ethno-cultural groups, organizations and events which are made available to all federal government departments and federal agencies. The Service also carries on liaison activities with the Canadian Ethnic Press Federation and its four affiliated press clubs of ethnic newspapers as well as the *Canadian Scene*.

A very important element of the whole program is the part played by the officers who carry it out. To ensure maximum effectiveness, these officers carry out both national responsibilities from Ottawa and regional and local responsibilities from offices located across the country. Program officers develop and maintain meaningful contact with national and a multitude of local organizations. They provide information about assistance available from various sources, relay concerns to governments and private agencies and, in general, act as resource persons with respect to community development or as experts in certain disciplines or areas of culture. Both national and field representatives closely co-ordinate and co-operate in their work to ensure that communities, regardless of their national or regional character, are fully assisted in their endeavours to participate completely in Canada's pluralistic society.

Document Tabled in the House of Commons on October 8, 1971 by the Prime Minister.

The purpose of this document is to present a survey of the principal policies relating to the maintenance and development of multiculturalism throughout Canada and to provide a summary of Government decisions on the recommendations made in Book IV of the Royal Commission on Bilingualism and Biculturalism.

The document outlines in Part A the Federal Government's response in general to the recommendations of Book IV of the Royal Commission Report and gives some of the reasons for its belief in multiculturalism.

In Part B are outlined the Policy objectives which will serve to guide the Federal Government's programs in this area.

Part C contains a general description of the programs to be undertaken by the Federal Government and its agencies to implement and advance the policies resulting from acceptance of the recommendations of Book IV of the Royal Commission's Report.

PART A: FEDERAL RESPONSE IN GENERAL
Book IV of the Royal Commission on Bilingualism and Biculturalism contains 16 recommendations of which eight are addressed specifically to the Federal Government or its agencies.

Three deal with matters under exclusive provincial jurisdiction. One of the recommendations urges federal financial aid to linguistically handicapped children in public school. Another is concerned with conditions for citizenship, the right to vote, and the right to stand for election to public office, and thus is addressed to both the federal and the provincial governments. One appeals to agencies at all three levels of Government to provide support to cultural and research organizations. The remaining recommendations are addressed to Canadian universities.

The Government accepts and endorses the recommendations and spirit of Book IV of the Royal Commission on Bilingualism and Biculturalism. It believes the time is overdue for the people of Canada to become more aware of the rich tradition of the many cultures we have in Canada. Canada's citizens come from almost every country in the world, and bring with them every major world religion and language. This cultural diversity endows all Canadians with a great variety of human experience. The Government regards this as a heritage to treasure and believes that Canada would be poorer if we adopted assimilation programs forcing our citizen to forsake and forget the cultures they have brought to us.

The Federal Government hopes the provinces will also respond positively to those recommendations which the Commissioners addressed to them. The Prime Minister has written to each of the Provincial Premiers outlining the policies and programs which the Federal Government is initiating and asking for their co-operation. Some provinces have already taken the initiative and are responding to the recommendations directed at them.

The Government, while responding positively to the Commission's recommendations, wishes to go beyond them to the spirit of Book IV to ensure that Canada's cultural diversity continues.

Cultural diversity throughout the world is being eroded by the impact of industrial technology, mass communications and urbanization. Many writers have discussed this as the creation of a mass society—in which mass produced culture and entertainment and large impersonal institutions threaten to denature and depersonalize man. One of man's basic needs is a sense of belonging and a good deal of contemporary social unrest—in all age groups—exists because this need has not been met. Ethnic groups are certainly not the only way in which this need for belonging can be met, but they have been an important one in Canadian society. Ethnic pluralism can help us overcome or prevent the homogenization and depersonalization of mass society. Vibrant ethnic groups can give Canadians of the second, third, and subsequent generations a feeling that they are connected with tradition and with human experience in various parts of the world and different periods of time.

Two misconceptions often arise when cultural diversity is discussed.

(a) *Cultural Identity and National Allegiance.* The sense of identity developed by each citizen as a unique individual is distinct from his national allegiance. There is no reason to suppose that a citizen who identifies himself with pride as a Chinese-Canadian, who is deeply involved in the cultural activities of the Chinese community in Canada, will be less loyal or concerned with Canadian matters than a citizen of Scottish origin who takes part in a bagpipe band or a highland dancing group. Cultural identity is not the same thing as allegiance to a country. Each of us is born into a particular family with a distinct heritage: that is, everyone— French, English, Italian and Slav included—has an "ethnic" background. The more secure we feel in one particular social context, the more we are free to explore our identity beyond it. Ethnic groups provide people with a sense of belonging which can make them better able to cope with the rest of the society than they would as isolated individuals. Ethnic loyalties need not, and usually do not, detract from wider loyalties to community and country.

Canadian identity will not be undermined by multiculturalism. Indeed, we believe that cultural pluralism is the very essence of Canadian identity. Every ethnic group has the right to preserve and develop its own culture and values within the Canadian context. To say we have two official languages is not to say we have two official cultures, and no particular culture is more "official" than another. A policy of multiculturalism must be a policy for all Canadians.

(b) *Language and Culture.* The distinction between language and culture has never been clearly defined. The very name of the Royal Commission whose recommendations we now seek to implement tends to indicate that bilingualism and biculturalism are indivisible. But, biculturalism does not properly describe our society; multi-culturalism is more accurate. The Official Languages Act designated two languages, English and French, as the official languages of Canada for the purposes of all the institutions of the Parliament and Government of Canada; no reference was made to cultures, and this Act does not impinge upon the role of all languages as instruments of the various Canadian cultures. Nor, on the other hand, should the recognition of the cultural value of many languages weaken the position of Canada's two official languages. Their use by all of the citizens of Canada will continue to be promoted and encouraged.

PART B: POLICY OBJECTIVES IN THE FEDERAL SPHERE
The Government is concerned with preserving human rights, developing Canadian identity, strengthening citizenship participation, reinforcing Canadian unity and encouraging cultural diversification within a bilingual framework. These objectives can best be served through a policy of multiculturalism composed of four main elements.

> 1. The Government of Canada will support all of Canada's cultures and will seek to assist, resources permitting, the development of those cultural groups which have demonstrated a desire and effort to continue to develop, a capacity to grow and contribute to Canada, as well as a clear need for assistance.

The special role of the Government will be to support and encourage those cultures and cultural groups which Canadians wish to preserve.

The stronger and more populous cultural groups generally have the resources to be self-supporting and general cultural activities tend to be supportive of them. The two largest cultures, in areas where they exist in a minority situation, are already supported under the aegis of the Government's official language programs. New programs are proposed to give support to minority cultural groups in keeping with their needs and particular situations.

However, the Government cannot and should not take upon itself the responsibility for the continued viability of all ethnic groups. The objective of our policy is the cultural survival and development of groups to the degree that a given group exhibits a desire for this. Government aid to cultural groups must proceed on the basis of aid to self-effort. And in our concern for the preservation of ethnic identity, we should not forget that individuals in a democracy may choose not to be concerned about maintaining a strong sense of their ethnic identity.

> 2. The Government will assist members of all cultural groups to overcome cultural barriers to full participation in Canadian society.

The law can and will protect individuals from overt discrimination but there are more subtle barriers to entry into Canadian society. A sense of not belonging, or a feeling of inferiority, whatever its cause, cannot be legislated out of existence. Programs outlined in this document have been designed to foster confidence in one's individual cultural identity and in one's rightful place in Canadian life. Histories, films and museum exhibits showing the great contributions of Canada's various cultural groups will help achieve this objective. But, we must emphasize that every Canadian must help eliminate discrimination. Every Canadian must contribute to the sense of national acceptance and belonging.

3. The Government will promote creative encounters and interchange among all Canadian cultural groups in the interest of national unity.

As Canadians become more sensitive to their own ethnic identity and to the richness of this country, we will become more involved with one another and develop a greater acceptance of differences and a greater pride in our heritage. Cultural and intellectual creativity in almost all societies has been fostered by the interaction and creative relationship of different ethnic groups within that society. Government aid to multi-cultural centres, to specific projects of ethnic groups, and to displays of the performing and visual arts as well as the programs already mentioned, will promote cultural exchange. The Government has made it very clear that it does not plan on aiding individual groups to cut themselves off from the rest of society. The programs are designed to encourage cultural groups to share their heritage with all other Canadians and with other countries, and to make us all aware of our cultural diversity.

4. The Government will continue to assist immigrants to acquire at least one of Canada's official languages in order to become full participants in Canadians society.

The Federal Government, through the Manpower and Immigration Department and the Citizenship Branch of the Department of the Secretary of State, already assists the provinces in language training for adults, but new arrivals in Canada require additional help to adjust to and participate in Canadian life.

PART C: PROGRAMS OF IMPLEMENTATION

Six programs have been developed to implement the policy of the Federal Government. These programs will be carried out under the administration of the Citizenship Branch of the Department of the Secretary of State with the exception of those proposed by the federal cultural agencies which will be administered by the agencies concerned but co-ordinated through an Inter-Agency Co-ordinating Committee.

Program 1: Multicultural Grants—A grants program has been developed to meet specific recommendations in the Commission's Report and the demonstrated need of cultural groups. Grants will be made to activities which meet some or all of the four parts of the policy outlined in Part B.

Activities eligible for federal assistance will include multicultural encounters; organizational meetings for new cultural groups; citizenship preparation and immigrant orientation programs; conferences; youth activities; cultural exchanges between groups as well as other projects. Grants will also be made available for multicultural centres in areas where there is a demonstrated need and desire from the community for such a facility. Existing multicultural centres, like that in Winnipeg, have proved their value in providing services to help new immigrants adjust to Canadian life, and in promoting inter-ethnic activity on a continuous basis.

Program II: Culture Development Program.—A Culture Development Program will be instituted to produce much needed data on the precise relationship of language to cultural development. It will provide essential information on the extent and nature of the demands of individual cultural groups for language retention and cultural development. It will examine existing organizations and facilities, including educational institutions, the press, radio and television to determine the part they now play and their potential role in cultural development. The study will incorporate those recommendations directed to the Canadian Radio-Television and Telecommunications Commission for studies of the best means by which radio and television can contribute to the maintenance of language and cultures.

The program has been designed to produce results within one year. The data will serve as an information base for some of the other programs and for future long range planning by the Citizenship Branch, the cultural agencies, and other Government departments.

The Government is initiating steps to help provide textbooks for non-official language teaching, since Book IV of the Royal Commission's Report found there are almost no textbooks suitable for teaching a third language to children living in Canada. The acquisition of the ancestral language is an important part of the process of developing a cultural identity, and the Federal Government proposes to discuss this with the provinces to find a mutually satisfactory way to meet some of the costs of preparation and production of third language textbooks or audio-visual aids for language teaching.

Although the Commission made no formal recommendation regarding the ethnic press, aside from advocating the continuation of existing Government support in the form of advertising and information, the

Culture Development Program will also undertake a study of the ethnic press and other media which could be better utilized to carry essential information to those persons who use languages other than English or French. We recognize that the ethnic press plays an important part in bringing information to recent immigrants and elderly people who have difficulty reading Canada's official languages, as well as in helping to develop Canada's cultures.

Program *III: Ethnic Histories*—A clear need exists for the writing of objective, analytical, and readable histories of the ethnic groups in Canada, and for the distribution of these works to as wide a readership as possible. The Citizenship Branch will commission 20 histories specifically directed to the background, contributions and problems of various cultural groups in Canada. The program will offer visible, effective and valuable recognition of the contribution of our diverse ethnic groups to Canada. It will promote knowledge of and respect for the cultural heritage of the groups concerned, as well as providing invaluable resource material for students, writers and government agencies.

Program *IV: Canadian Ethnic Studies*—The need exists and was recognized by the Commission, for systematic and continuous study of Canada's multi-ethnic society. The Department of the Secretary of State will therefore undertake a detailed investigation of the problems concerned with the development of a Canadian Ethnic Studies Program or Centre(s) and will prepare a plan of implementation.

Program *V: Teaching of Official Languages*—The Federal Government already assists the provinces in the teaching of English and French to adult immigrants, and accepts in principle recommendation 4 of the Royal Commission relating to special instruction in the appropriate official language for children who enter the public school system without a knowledge of that language.

The Federal Government therefore proposes to undertake discussions with the provinces to find a mutually acceptable form of federal assistance towards the teaching of official languages to children.

Program *VI: Programs of the Federal Cultural Agencies*—The government asked the federal cultural agencies referred to in Book IV to respond to the recommendations of the Report. The programs they will be undertaking will enable all Canadians to gain an awareness of the cultural heritage of all of Canada's ethnic groups.

National Museum of Man. The Commission recommended "that the Museum receive additional funds to carry out its projects regarding the history, social organizations and folk arts of cultural groups other than the British and French." The Government concurs with this recommendation and will fund the following projects to be undertaken by the Museum:

(a) purchase of artifacts representing Canada's ethnic diversity
(b) research on the folk arts and music of the various ethnic communities in Canada
(c) other Museum extension and educational projects designed to reach the public at large.

National Film Board. For many years, the Board has been producing versions of some of its films in languages other than English or French for use abroad in co-operation with the Department of External Affairs. The Royal Commission recommended that the Board advertise that it has films in languages other than English and French and make these available for domestic consumption, and also expand its production of films that inform Canadians about one another, including films about the contributions and problems of all our various ethnic groups. The Board has indicated that it will not only respond positively to these recommendations, but that it will also survey the cultural communities in order to determine what types of film they would like produced in their ancestral languages.

National Library. Although many public libraries in Canada do have collections of books in non-official languages, the supply is well below the demand. The Canadian Library Association has studied the problem and has recommended the creation of a multicultural language and literature centre at the National Library. The Library will embark immediately on a preliminary study leading to the creation of this centre. The centre will administer a program designed to deposit in local libraries books in languages other than English and French. The Library will also acquire publications produced by and for non-English and non-French groups in Canada.

Public Archives. The Public Archives in Ottawa has relatively few holdings relating to Canada's various cultural groups or their activities. The same is true of most archives across the country. Such material should be collected, since the history of immigration and cultural groups is an integral part of the history of this country.

The Public Archives will be given funds to acquire the records and papers of all the various ethnic organizations and associations which are significant documents of Canadian history.

Note

Originally published in *Multiculturalism and the Government of Canada*, by the Government of Canada. Copyright © Department of Canadian Heritage. Reprinted with permission of the Minister of Public Works and Government Services Canada from *Multiculturalism and the Government of Canada* (1978).

Afterword

YVES LABERGE

Are Cultural Studies an Anglo-Saxon Paradigm? Reflections on Cultural Studies in Francophone Networks

Yves Laberge received his Ph.D. in sociology from Laval University in 1998. Laberge has contributed more than one hundred articles and entries to journals, edited volumes, encyclopedias, and reference books, including *Men and Masculinities: A Social, Cultural, and Historical Encyclopedia* (2004), *Encyclopedia of Capitalism* (2004), and *Encyclopedia of Twentieth-Century Photography* (2005). He served as a member of the advisory board for three encyclopedias: *France and the Americas: Culture, Politics, and History* (2005), *Germany and the Americas* (2005), and *Encyclopedia of the Blues* (2005).

Although difficult to define, Cultural Studies represents an interdisciplinary approach that analyzes texts, messages, signs, cultural icons, representations, films, television programs or news, in order to understand premises, stereotypes, attitudes, symbolic meanings, hidden ideologies—in other words, the shaping of culture and its social reproduction in various discourses. Here, culture is to be taken either as mass culture, popular culture, counterculture or culture at the margins, be it mainstream culture or within subcultures. Borrowing from sociology, media studies, ethnicity, revisiting Marxism and Antonio Gramsci's model of hegemony, scholars in cultural studies want to explain how social power shapes culture and therefore can institutionalize a hegemonic culture. Another aim is to observe how cultural identities are produced, especially in post-colonial contexts. This theoretical framework linked with the understanding of dominant forces and the marginalisation processes inevitably brings in issues related to class, race and gender.

—Yves Laberge, "Stuart Hall," *Encyclopedia of the World's Minorities*

Introduction

Cultural studies, gender studies, postcolonial studies: all of these familiar approaches for Canadian and U.S. scholars have not until lately found their way into scholarly work in France or Quebec, even though many francophone academics obviously think about issues related to culture, feminism, and the colonial era.[1] Even a discipline such as comparative literature does not find many adepts among French students nowadays, and the number of courses or programs in comparative studies is very limited in French networks. No label has yet been forged in the French language to pinpoint cultural studies as such: in France, most scholars still refer to cultural studies by using these two English words instead of saying "études culturelles."[2] Indeed, many academics would argue that cultural studies are not just studies about culture, as anglophones usually agree to say, adding that the "études culturelles" are much more complex than the mere understanding of culture.[3]

There is no doubt about the importance and institutional presence of cultural studies in the United Kingdom, North America, Australia, and elsewhere: there is a Spanish cultural studies tradition, as well as a Latin American cultural studies and a German cultural studies.[4] The number of books, articles, and actual courses available in these languages speaks for itself. But still, there is almost no cultural studies in France, and not much more in Quebec. If the expression "French cultural studies" has existed for some twenty years—and there is even a fine academic journal with this title—one has to admit that most of the users of the label are anglophone scholars, either language teachers or notable academics teaching French civilization.[5] This linguistic division between scholars is not a problem in and of itself, but it might confirm a kind of resistance or ignorance—or perhaps indifference?—among most French academics towards cultural studies. However, I am sure my colleagues who are not francophones will confirm they have also met with some perplexity in their own networks while trying to promote research in cultural studies.

As for postmodernist issues and postmodern theory, there were different intersections and borrowings between the British cultural studies and French modern thought, especially from the 1960s until the turn of the century. In many respects, the relationship between cultural studies and French thought was like a one-way street between the 1960s and the early twenty-first century, since cultural studies were seemingly nowhere in France until Armand Mattelart and Erik Neveu published the first French book exclusively dedicated to that topic, *Introduction aux Cultural*

Studies (2003).⁶ Prominent authors in cultural studies, such as Stuart Hall, owe much to some contemporary French thinkers, including Roland Barthes, Michel Foucault, and Louis Althusser. In his portrait of Stuart Hall, scholar Chris Rojek indicates that Hall's main influences around 1970 were Ferdinand de Saussure, Claude Lévi-Strauss, and Louis Althusser.⁷ It is necessary to question this disproportion of intellectual influences between England and France in the field of cultural studies: French authors clearly inspired British cultural studies, but there was no cultural studies breakthrough in France in the twentieth century.

This afterword mainly addresses the French presence in cultural studies. When I refer to French, it should be clear that I am also thinking of issues and debates in Quebec: this is why such questions and issues are included in an anthology about Canadian cultural studies. First, from a historical and epistemological perspective, I want to trace the theoretical contribution of some influential French authors who were often cited by some of the founders of cultural studies and their followers, especially in the United Kingdom. Second, I want to reflect on the way French scholars do research on mass culture and ideology in a fashion that could somehow be related to cultural studies. Finally, I want to end with a critique of "actually existing" Canadian cultural studies and raise a few issues related to overlooked francophone dimensions in cultural studies.

Why Were Cultural Studies not Invented by the French?

If French thought was so seminal in cultural studies, why did no French scholar ever "invent" this approach?

In the many definitions of cultural studies, scholars usually present three interlinked dimensions: the main topics (analysis of popular culture, the media, but also everyday life), the driving issues (power, gender, stereotyping, "otherness"), and finally the theoretical approaches used, all of which add up to questioning the hegemony that makes dominant institutions reproduce themselves. Take, for instance, Toby Miller's clear and generous description: "Cultural Studies is animated by subjectivity and power—how human subjects are formed and how they experience cultural and social space."⁸

In a fine chapter titled "The Political Economy of 'Studies'" (a title in which the author does not include the word "cultural"), Ruth Butterworth acknowledges the essential contribution of four French theorists. She points to the work of Louis Althusser, Michel Foucault, Jacques Derrida, and Jean-François Lyotard—whom she identifies as the "cultural studies gurus"—as the true inspirations for the field.[9] Using some of their work, she explains how these four French authors contributed to framing postmodern thought as well as the cultural studies approach.[10] The debt owed by Stuart Hall to these figures, especially toward Althusser, is confirmed here, but also by Douglas Kellner and by John Hartley in his *Short History of Cultural Studies*.[11]

We could certainly add to the list of French authors who are seen as essential in the making of cultural studies the names of theoreticians like Michel de Certeau, Roland Barthes, and Armand Mattelart. My point here is not to say: "Hey, look how important were some French scholars in the genesis of what we now do; you should like the French people and spend your next holiday in France!" (in the mode of some Canadians who take pride in claiming that famous writers like Marshall McLuhan and celebrities such as William Shatner happen to be Canadians).[12] Rather, I want to raise another, more fundamental question: why wasn't cultural studies invented by French academics sometime during the late 1960s? This question looms large when we think about the strength of the reflection on postmodernism that emerged in French and English theory circles almost simultaneously with the emergence of cultural studies, the latter occurring mostly in Great Britain and, later, in the United States, but nowhere in francophone circles.

One has to admit that various scholars in France did undertake core research about culture, domination, and ideology, just as they analyzed postmodernity, including Lyotard, Jean Baudrillard, and others. The most salient work was often quoted and reproduced in many anthologies and readers in cultural studies.[13] But it was mostly excerpts from articles or chapters that were used and then mixed with the work of other authors in a kind of collage that obscured the original context out of which this work arose.

Although many anthologies and readers in cultural studies included chapters or articles by celebrated French writers, very few of these writers paid tribute to those editors and publishers who made them even more famous in the English-speaking world. Even at the end of his life, Pierre Bourdieu did not like cultural studies and remained critical towards this approach. Although he was much quoted and praised in the United States for the "cultural" dimensions of his oeuvre, Bourdieu included a severe critique of cultural studies in one of his last books, *Science de la science et réflexivité* (2001),[14] claiming that it was too theoretical and contained too little empirical data. He describes cultural studies in no uncertain terms:

"cette région bâtarde où tous les sociologues sont philosophes et tous les philosophes sociologues, où se côtoient et se confondent les philosophes (français) qui s'occupent de sciences sociales et les adeptes indéterminés des nouvelles sciences, *cultural studies* ou *minority studies*, qui puisent à tort et à travers dans la philosophie (française) et les sciences sociales."[15]

Many French scholars who were working on culture created something quite different from what Anglo-Saxons did while founding cultural studies as an antidiscipline. Over four decades, Bourdieu did his own sociology of culture centered on processes of domination, and the Belgian sociologist Armand Mattelart also focused on the study of popular culture, for instance in Chile, studying (with Ariel Dorfman) the capitalist ideologies appearing in the translations of Disney's comic books during the Allende years in the early 1970s.[16]

There is at least one exception to the general invisibility of British cultural studies in France. In Armand and Michèle Mattelart's book, *Penser les médias* (1986), the authors suggest that the works of English colleagues such as Stuart Hall should be translated and used in French, describing the Centre for Contemporary Cultural Studies as an "irradiant school."[17] Simultaneously, the Mattelarts also acknowledged the debt owed by the Birmingham school to Althusser and Barthes.[18] In general, however, the work of Hall took time to be discovered in France; in fact, by the time it had begun to be read Hall had already officially retired. A special issue of a French peer-reviewed journal in media studies, *Réseaux*, was the first to translate Stuart Hall's classic article "Encoding, Decoding," and later dedicated a whole issue to cultural studies in 1996.[19] Among the contributors were Armand Mattelart and other younger French scholars in media studies. Before that, most studies of mass and popular culture by French academics were carried out in sociology or anthropology, without ever using the label cultural studies.[20]

Why Don't the French "Do" Cultural Studies?

When I look at Chris Barker's excellent reference book, *The Sage Dictionary of Cultural Studies* (2004), I am always amazed to see that about one-third of the entries for individual theorists are in fact dedicated to French authors: Barthes, Baudrillard, Bourdieu, Michel de Certeau, Gilles Deleuze, Jacques Derrida, Foucault, Julia Kristeva, Jacques Lacan, Lyotard, and Saussure.[21] It is true that all these authors were used in many ways in cultural studies, but none of them has ever used the expression "cultural studies" or identified himself or herself by this approach. I find myself asking: "How could these French authors be so influential in cultural studies without ever employing this expression anywhere in their works?"

It is often repeated that cultural studies are not merely studies about culture. One of the main ingredients that make this approach distinctive and relevant is its sharp critique of hegemony and its attention to the ways in which mass culture is always reproduced within the same general patterns. Political economy approaches to culture had demonstrated this earlier, and many scholars in cultural studies used authors like Antonio Gramsci, Baudrillard, and Althusser in order to introduce this critical element into their theoretical frameworks.[22] It seemed that cultural studies could not truly work without a Marxist perspective that was brought in through an appeal to these European authors. For instance, John Hartley, in his *Short History of Cultural Studies*, writes that the Birmingham centre focused essentially on Gramsci and Althusser: "The main theoretical achievement of the Centre and its intellectual allies was to produce sustained re-readings of Marx, especially via new interpretations of continental Marxist philosophy."[23] However, while Marxist approaches were blossoming on many U.K. and U.S. campuses in the 1970s, it was simultaneously declining in most French universities.

In some ways, francophone scholars *were* the first to use the original concepts that formed the basis of cultural studies. They had direct access to the original works by Foucault, Baudrillard, Bourdieu, and Althusser, without the filter of translation or recontextualization. These authors are not unknown in Quebec either; they are often quoted and still have an important influence. The real things to ask are: What did French scholars do with the works of such authors, so much praised in anglophone countries? Why didn't this mixture of ideas and theories lead them to do cultural studies? And why does there seem to be no research in cultural studies in Quebec, which could (theoretically) have drawn on research being undertaken in both French and English academic contexts?

To answer these questions, we would have to look again at various definitions of cultural studies, then try to understand the different theories and paradigms in use in contemporary social sciences within specific intellectual histories, traditions, and trajectories. Accessibility of materials and translation plays a major role: books written in English were not always easily accessible in French libraries and bookstores as they were in Quebec; this situation has only changed recently as a result of access to foreign books via the Internet. Even so, it remains surprising to see the small number of book reviews about English-language books in most social sciences journals published in France (just as we do not see many reviews of French books in most English journals). Innovative concepts have to be available directly to scholars if they are to be used in research and teaching. If there are no translations, new theories cannot easily become accessible to teachers or to their students.

There is no question about the importance of translations in bringing knowledge and new theoretical trends into a discipline. For instance, Roland Barthes's short chronicles on modern lifestyles first began to be published in 1952 in the French magazine *Le Nouvel Observateur*. These articles became a book in France in 1957 (*Mythologies*), but were translated in English much later, in 1973. By the time anglophone readers were taking up these ideas, for French scholars they had been replaced by Barthes's more recent works. The pace and order of translation were determinant in the diffusion of French ideas in anglophone circles, as they were in the opposite direction. For instance, Richard Hoggart's seminal book *The Uses of Literacy* (1957) was translated in French (*La culture du pauvre*) and published in 1970 by the Éditions de Minuit (which was on many occasions Bourdieu's publisher). It is important to remember that *La culture du pauvre* remained for three decades the only original book in cultural studies that was available in a French translation.

The particular moment when authors emerge in a foreign context can also determine the momentum and impact of their ideas. In some cases, French authors gained international recognition at the moment when interest in their ideas had already faded in their own country. For instance, Althusser was quite influential and quoted by francophone scholars during the 1960s and 1970s, when his most important books were initially released. By the 1980s, his influence in Quebec had all but disappeared.

Allow me to highlight the consequences of this by drawing on a personal anecdote. Back in 1991, I presented a paper on the media construction of environmental issues at a conference organized by the Université du Quebec à Montréal (UQAM), which was seen at the time as the most "leftist" institution in Canada—one that could be compared in political orientation to the Université de Paris–Vincennes in France. My theoretical framework was not based on cultural studies (I did not even mention it), but I relied on Althusser's famous conception of the ideological state apparatus. Only years later did I learn how much that theoretical interpretative model had influenced Stuart Hall.[24] I considered this framework as a "passage obligé" in my demonstration, a useful and well-known model, something everyone could agree upon before discussion of the main issues—in this case, the analysis of a clip from the TV news and an advertising message about pollution. However, after finishing my presentation, I received an unexpected comment. Much to my surprise, a respected scholar and social scientist from the Université de Montréal asked me a surprising question: "How can you validate your demonstration on such grounds as Louis Althusser's framework?" For this professor of political science, Althusser's theory was like a phantom from the past, a mistake we made long ago, an "erreur de jeunesse" that no longer had a place in the academy after the recent fall of the Soviet Empire. I was astonished. This was not just an isolated opinion, since many colleagues in the auditorium agreed that in this new era, neither Althusser nor Marx could bring a valuable framework to any rigorous analysis of media content because their ideas seemed *dépassé*. These scholars were not right-wing thinkers, but a group of leftist professors whose ideologies (or illusions) fell simultaneously with the Berlin Wall in 1989. As I reread my paper afterward, full of doubts, I still thought that Althusser's crucial concept of the "ideological state apparatus" was essential to my analysis and could not in any sense be replaced. It was just that I could not find similar theoretical tools in the writings of any other author. (I was not aware of the work of Gramsci or Lukács at that time.)[25]

This odd situation reminds me that when Althusser was discovered with enthusiasm in Anglo-Saxon cultural studies networks in the late 1970s, he was already seen as a figure of the past in France and Quebec. We could say the same thing about de Certeau or Barthes, who were influential in France during the 1970s, but were discovered only posthumously in the United States. Post-Marxist ideas were at their peak in Quebec during the 1960s. As Louis Balthazar argues in his fine article on Gilles Bourque's book *Question nationale et classes sociales au Québec* (1760–1840), Althusser and Henri Lefebvre were quite influential among sociologists and even among political scientists in Quebec.[26] More recently, I have been surprised to see numerous quotations by U.S. scholars of works by Baudrillard and Virilio—figures who have lost favor in most French academic circles. François Cusset has written a fascinating analysis of this situation in *French Theory: Foucault, Derrida, Deleuze & Cie et les mutations de la vie intellectuelle aux États-Unis* (2003). In this book, he claims that in many cases Anglo-Saxon reappropriations of selected elements of the French theory have been futile, fragmented, and superficial.[27] Cusset focuses on well-known French scholars such as Foucault, Baudrillard, Derrida, and de Certeau, exploring the problematic ways in which their ideas were understood and reappropriated in American universities.

This resistance toward theorists such as Gramsci, Baudrillard, and

Althusser in francophone academic circles during the late 1980s and in the 1990s can partly explain why the emergence of cultural studies did not occur in France and Quebec at this time. For instance, in the field of film studies, the main theoretical approaches between 1980 and 2000 were the study of narration, film semiotics, and feminist critique (without including the study of masculinities per se). These dominant paradigms excluded theoretical approaches related to sociology, economics, or politics. In other words, research was carried out on culture and related matters in Quebec, but within a completely different theoretical trajectory than developments taking place in English Canada over the same period.

How Did Scholars Study Culture in Quebec?

If scholars in Quebec studied culture without using cultural studies, what exactly did they do?

In recent decades, research on culture has been carried out in various ways in Quebec.[28] Among many social scientists, Fernand Dumont (1927–97) was seen as the foremost theoretician on culture in Canada.[29] Dumont was an academic, but also the founder of the Institut Québécois de Recherche sur la Culture (Quebecois Institute for Research on Culture, IQRC), which later was integrated into the Institut National de Recherche Scientifique (National Institute of Scientific Research, INRS). Throughout his career, Dumont focused on three main topics: culture, ideology, and the place of Quebec. In his celebrated book Le lieu de l'homme (1968), Dumont established his own theory of "culture première" and "culture seconde" in order to explain how culture changes over time.[30]

Almost twenty years after Le lieu de l'homme, in Le sort de la culture, Dumont explored again the many facets of culture, specifically the transformation of culture into "cultural" as a symptom of a society's problems.[31] A few years later, Dumont's Raisons communes (1995) offered a strong critique of the Canadian governmental policy on multiculturalism, which denied the concept of the two founding nations in order to promote the "noble idea" of multiculturalism. This new state ideology became dominant during the Trudeau years in the early 1970s. Dumont explained that the former notion of the two founding nations was the guiding principle of inclusion for the French population that formed a majority in Canada until the early nineteenth century.[32] Dumont argues that the reason for this shift to multiculturalism is neither "natural" nor demographic, but political, a consequence of the anglicization of new immigrants in Canada and the banning of French in schools in Manitoba and Ontario in the early twentieth century.

Dumont's work did not receive much critical attention in Canada outside Quebec, with the sole exception of Michael A. Weinstein's *Culture Critique: Fernand Dumont and New Quebec Sociology.*[33] Only one of Dumont's books has been translated into English: *The Vigil of Quebec* (1974), a collection of eighteen essays written between 1960 and 1970, which do not deal with culture, but with the place of Quebec in Canada, before and after the October 1970 crisis.[34] In the last part of *The Vigil of Quebec*, Dumont promoted the idea of a socialist, independent Quebec, not only explaining how it could be possible, but arguing that this was the only possibility for the survival of francophone citizens in Quebec following October 1970.

Oddly, no Canadian scholar has noticed the absence of research about francophone citizens in Canada from the perspective of cultural studies. If the status of minorities is often discussed since the Meech Lake Accord,[35] francophone citizens now seem to have become, if not a minority, then a marginalized community in Canada.[36] In many ways, the recognition of the Quebecois as a nation by the Canadian Parliament in November 2006 only confirmed the marginalization of the Quebecois, generating enormous debate and misunderstandings in Quebec and in Canada. The degree to which recent research about Canada excludes the francophone dimension is surprising, and is an issue to which I will return in the last part of this essay.[37]

The disappearance of the francophone minority in Canada was sometimes seen as a sign of progress by anglophone observers, from the British representative Lord Durham to U.S. president Franklin D. Roosevelt, who once suggested to Canadian prime minister William Lyon Mackenzie King that he use various propaganda methods to assimilate French-speaking Canadian citizens. According to Jean-François Lisée, Roosevelt even offered logistical help to Mackenzie King in this endeavor.[38] In his report to the queen a century earlier, Durham argued that the French citizens of Canada had no culture or history.[39] Despite the waning of research on Quebec/Canada cultural relations, it is obvious that identity politics in terms of English/French relations play a crucial role in understanding Canadian society—which brings us to ongoing debates about Canadian society and the place of Quebec.

Canadian Identity and Citizenship

The points of intersection between cultural studies and Canadian Studies remain largely unexplored. Central to both approaches is the touchy subject of Canadian identity. As Ien Ang formulates it, identity is "the way we represent and narrativize ourselves to ourselves and others."[40] Here I want to reflect on Canadian identity at a time when "Canadian" only meant a French-speaking citizen as opposed to the English.

The earliest analysis of the Canadian identity was not made by a Canadian sociologist, but rather by influential French author Alexis de Tocqueville (1805–59), who visited Montreal and Quebec City in August 1831. He was surprised to learn that in 1831 English speakers living in Canada called themselves "the English," while French-speaking citizens referred to themselves neither as "Français" nor as "French-Canadians," but only as "Canadiens."[41] In other words, the term "Canadien" was used exclusively by francophones; both communities tacitly agreed on this terminology up to Confederation in 1867, at which point "Canadien" or "Canadian" was imposed on all citizens living in Canada.

In a letter to his brother Édouard in November 1831, Tocqueville wrote that francophones living in Canada were like "foreigners in their own country."[42] In a sense, Tocqueville was the absolute opposite of Lord Durham. He saw francophone citizens as being at the heart of the American continent. A century later, U.S. sociologist Everett C. Hughes expressed the same generous attitude in his book *French Canada in Transition* (1944). Hughes had visited many villages in Quebec in order to understand the shifts in Canadian society and the quest for identity in traditional Quebec.[43]

From time to time, social shifts created debates, discussions, and analyses of French-Canadian identity, as exemplified by Jean Bouthillette's *Le Canadien français et son double* (1972). This remarkable work explains the identity shifts that occurred over the last two centuries in Canada, a period that saw francophone citizens define themselves as "Canadiens" before the 1867 Confederation, "Canadiens français" in the first half of the twentieth century, and "Québécois" from the 1960s onward in conjunction with the "Révolution tranquille" (Quiet Revolution).[44]

Other scholarly works in Quebec studied French-Canadian mass culture as early as the 1980s, without referring to the theories or approaches of cultural studies—for instance, the monumental study of weekly novels published in Montreal under the rubric of IXE-13, the Canadian equivalent of the U.S. detective and spy stories that were popular after World

War II. IXE-13 was the code name of a French-speaking secret agent who worked for the Canadian government, trying to chase communist foreigners and secret agents living in Canada. Almost a thousand weekly stories were written in total by Pierre Sorel (a pseudonym for actor Pierre Daignault), and millions of copies were sold in Quebec between 1947 and 1966. The study of these stories employed multiple theoretical frameworks, primarily drawn from the French intellectual tradition, including semiotics, gender studies, and ideological analyses. Though this study did not inspire similar group projects in turn, it was positively received by critics in Quebec when it first appeared.[45]

One member of this group of scholars, Marie-José des Rivières, wrote an original study of the popular Quebec women's magazine *Châtelaine*, conducting an analysis of the short stories in the magazine in a manner similar to cultural studies.[46] Other such studies include the work of Lucie Robert and Micheline Cambron, who analyzed Quebec popular culture and the construction of identity in their Ph.D. theses.[47] These three examples confirm that rigorous research on popular culture was being conducted in Quebec during the 1980s, even if it was being done outside of the framework of the broad set of studies being described as cultural studies in the anglophone world.

Other analyses of Quebec identity have appeared elsewhere, including outside of the academy, such as the film *Alias Will James*, by the novelist Jacques Godbout, which traced the true origins of Will James, the famous American author of cowboy stories. Often seen as an icon of the American West who became a posthumous member of the "Nevada Writers Hall of Fame," Will James never told anyone that he was in fact francophone—a Quebecois born in Saint-Nazaire with the name of Ernest Dufault (1892–1942).[48]

So how did scholars study culture in Quebec? They worked according to approaches and traditions coming from France, England, and Quebec, or forged their own concepts in order to understand mass culture. In these works, scholars from English Canada were usually not an inspiration and most of the time were not even minimally cited.

A Critique of Canadian Cultural Studies

Research in cultural studies took flight in Canada throughout the 1980s and 1990s. It was based almost entirely within anglophone universities (including McGill and Concordia, both located in Montreal), and supported both in Canadian academic journals such as the *Canadian Journal of*

Social and Political Thought, Topia: Canadian Journal of Cultural Studies, University of Toronto Quarterly, and Canadian Review of Comparative Literature and in international publications based in the United States, United Kingdom, and Australia.[49] With the exception of the anglophone universities in Quebec (McGill, Concordia, and Bishops), there are still no graduate or undergraduate programs in cultural studies in Quebec.

Although nothing is perfect in this odd world, I sometimes feel that scholars doing cultural studies in Canada miss the point by concentrating, for instance, on various minorities, while either failing to address issues related to francophone groups, or, even worse, contributing to already persistent stereotypes about Quebec in the current media. Cultural studies shares with sociology a strong consensus "on the unacceptability of racially structured patterns of social inequality."[50] Nonetheless, and to offer just a small sample of a larger trend, two recent books on Canadian cinema reinforce stereotypes about the Quebecois as dominant, abusive, and racist with respect to minorities in Quebec, while failing entirely to see the Quebecois as a distinct minority within the Canadian context.

The hefty North of Everything: English-Canadian Cinema since 1980 aims to be a comprehensive account of recent cinema in Canada, but draws a limit at "English-Canadian" films in order to sidestep criticisms that it does not address Quebec—a common enough tactic in much English Canadian writing about Canada. The absence of a chapter on Quebec cinema or francophone cinema outside Quebec is excused by Seth Feldman, who writes that "Quebec has been replaced here by a welcome emphasis on Native filmmaking."[51] In a chapter about the Native filmmaker Alanis Obomsawin written by one of the two editors of the book, Jerry White expresses his doubts about Quebec's policies toward Natives: "This is not the place to enter into a debate about the policy of Quebec towards Natives: suffice to say that the matter of Quebec's policies towards Natives seems a questionable line of inquiry, since these policy matters are, by nature of most relevant treaties, a federal matter." White simultaneously raises doubts about Quebec's treatment of Natives while suspending any detailed analsysis, writing that "this is not the place to enter into a history lesson."[52]

My second example is drawn from Christopher Gittings's passionate Canadian National Cinema (2002). As one axis of inquiry, Gittings seeks to find illustrations of racism in Canadian film history. Among the many examples he uses, he takes up one of Canada's most celebrated films, Mon Oncle Antoine.[53] Approaching this iconic film through the lens of cultural studies, Gittings writes that *Mon Oncle Antoine* is "constructing 'the people' of Quebec as an ethno-national group, Québécois, producing a *pure laine* Quebec, that . . . excludes First Nations, Anglophones and Quebeckers of colour."[54] The author does not seem to understand that this feature film depicts the class-based system of French Canadian society during the early 1940s, a specific sociocultural formation studied by numerous sociologists including Everett Hughes. The two anglophone characters seen in the film are much more powerful than all the others, since they are the foreman and the boss of the mine: they appear briefly, but impose both their English language and their rules on the francophone employees. They stand as allegorical illustrations of the dominance of the anglophone minority in Quebec in the mid-twentieth century.

For Jutra, this political vision is coherent with his whole oeuvre. As for the accusations of racism made by Gittings, one need only look to Jutra's previous feature film, *À tout prendre* (1963), which features as its main character an Afro-American woman of Haitian descent. Although this was an essential film in Canadian cinema, it is barely mentioned in Gittings's book; nor does he consider Gilles Groulx's beautiful film *Le chat dans le sac* (NFB, 1964), which shows cross-cultural relationships between a francophone young man and a young anglophone Jewish woman from Montreal. Issues about identity are brought in right from the beginning of the film, when the woman says directly to the camera: "I am Barbara and I am Jewish." Her boyfriend introduces himself in a different way: "My name is Claude; I am French-Canadian, therefore I seek myself." These are among the strongest pleas for an identity in the whole history of the Canadian cinema.

Lastly, it would be important to add that the many critics who write that Natives are absent from Quebec's films often neglect to mention Gilles Carle's *Red* (1970), or the twenty documentaries and feature films made by the director Arthur Lamothe from the 1960s to the 1990s about Natives living in Quebec. None of these important films is mentioned in Gittings's book, which is questionable (to say the least), given the confidence with which he proclaims Quebecois racism through his reading of Jutra's film.

My critique of the actually existing Canadian cultural studies—its failure to take up francophone and Quebecois issues except through unquestioned and limited cultural frameworks—should be seen by anglophone scholars as an invitation to discover and investigate the culture in Quebec in order to understand its dynamism and richness. One of the aims of Canadian cultural studies should be to understand the marginalization of French culture and its minimal presence in English Canada, in the media, bookstores, record stores, and elsewhere in the public sphere. One has to question the reasons for the progressive disappearance of French culture in the rest of Canada over the last two centuries. This seems to me to be as important as the study of the dynamics of minority and diaspora communities in Canada—indeed, it is only by understanding the fullness of what is "Canada" that such dynamics can be properly understood in the first place.

Conclusion

What are we to say about the differences between cultural studies as practiced, constructed, and negotiated in anglophone-dominant countries (United Kingdom, United States, Australia, and Canada) on one hand, and the research on culture carried out by academics in France and Quebec on the other? First, even without specific reference to cultural studies, it is clear there have been some similar approaches to culture by francophone scholars in Quebec, making use of theoretical frameworks from the sociology of the media or of literature. In some cases, these scholars have made direct use of theoretical resources that are also important in cultural studies, such as the works of Foucault, Barthes, and Bourdieu. One of the major differences has been the absence of a post-Marxist perspective in most French texts about culture from the 1980s, an element that has characterized much of anglophone cultural studies. The political contexts were obviously not the same in France and elsewhere. Post-Marxist ideology was at its peak in many French universities in the years immediately following May 1968; by the time the theoretical wave that started here crashed on the shores of anglophone campuses, the sea was once again smooth back in France by the late 1970s. As Brent Pickett puts it in his excellent book, "the Foucault of 1971 held the position that prisons should be abolished; the Foucault of a decade later specifically disavowed such a view although he supported some reforms."[55] In anglophone contexts, the shadow cast by the first Foucault is so large as to make it impossible to see the second.

If we agree that cultural studies can be seen as an interdisciplinary analysis of some aspects of everyday life from a critical point of view, including the study of the media and popular culture, we also have to insist that its main theoretical contribution lies in its critical, if not radical take on events. In other words, scholars in cultural studies try to understand the media and everyday life *with a sufficient dose* of neo-Marxism, be it from Gramsci, Althusser, the Frankfurt School, or even Bourdieu. French authors working on culture did not mix together theoretical elements in the same way their English colleagues did; French academics studied culture in other ways, using different approaches and methods more or less linked with a post-Marxist tradition, with the result belonging to the sociology of culture and the political economy of culture.[56] The promise of Canadian cultural studies lies in the possibilities that exist in navigating and bringing together both of these traditions—a combination of approaches that, while not without its problems and difficulties, also offers the possibility of a wholly original way to approach the drama of contemporary culture today.

Notes

1. See the numerous works of Edgar Morin, Marc Ferro, and countless feminist authors in Quebec. See also the special issue "Writers, Intellectuals and the Colonial Experience," *French Cultural Studies* 17.2 (2006).
2. See for instance "Les Cultural Studies," a special issue of the French journal *Réseaux: Communication technologie société* 80 (November–December, 1996).
3. See Jeff Lewis, "Defining Culture," in *Cultural Studies: The Basics* (London: Sage, 2002), 3–37.
4. See, among others: Rob Burns, ed., *German Cultural Studies. An Introduction* (London: Oxford University Press, 1995); the *Journal of Spanish Cultural Studies* and the *Journal of Latin American Cultural Studies* (both published by Routledge).
5. The academic journal *French Cultural Studies* is now published by Sage in England. The book *Contemporary French Cultural Studies* was edited by William Kidd and Sian Reynolds (New York: Arnold, 2000).
6. Armand Mattelart and Erik Neveu, *Introduction aux Cultural Studies* (Paris: Éditions La Découverte, 2003). This book offers a general overview and critique of cultural studies, and does not make major theoretical additions to the field.
7. Chris Rojek, *Stuart Hall* (London: Polity, 2003), 119.
8. Toby Miller, "What It Is and What It Isn't: Introducing . . . Cultural Studies," in *A Companion to Cultural Studies*, ed. Toby Miller (Oxford: Blackwell, 2001), 1.
9. See Ruth Butterworth, "The Political Economy of 'Studies,' " in *After the Disciplines: The Emergence of Cultural Studies*, ed. Michael Peters (Westport: Bergin and Garvey, 1999), 41.
10. Ibid.
11. See Douglas Kellner, "Cultural Studies and Philosophy: An Intervention," in *A Companion to Cultural Studies*, ed. Toby Miller (Oxford: Blackwell, 2001), 140; and John Hartley, *A Short History of Cultural Studies* (London: Sage, 2003).
12. See the entries on Mack Sennett and William Shatner, both born in Quebec, and other famous Canadians who engaged in most of their career outside of Canada, such as Dan Aykroyd, in *Take One's Essential Guide to Canadian Film*, ed. Wyndham Wise (Toronto: University of Toronto Press, 2001).

13. For example, these French authors are reunited in the two editions of one of the best-selling anthologies in the field: *The Cultural Studies Reader*, ed. Simon During (1993; London: Routledge, 1999).

14. Pierre Bourdieu, *Science of Science and Reflexivity*, trans. Richard Nice (Chicago: University of Chicago Press, 2004).—Eds.

15. "That artificial intersection where all sociologists become philosophers and all philosophers become sociologists, where (French) philosophers gather, mix up and work on social sciences, and where approximate adepts of some new sciences, such as cultural studies or minority studies, steal without shame in (French) philosophy and social sciences" (my translation). Pierre Bourdieu, *Science de la science et réflexivité. Cours au Collège de France 2000–2001* (Paris: Éditions Raisons d'agir, 2001), 22. See also Pierre Bourdieu and Loïc Wacquant, "On the Cunning of Imperialist Reason," *Theory, Culture and Society* 16.1 (1999): 51.

16. Armand Mattelart and Ariel Dorfman, *How to Read Donald Duck: Imperialist Ideology in the Disney Comic* (New York: I. G. Editions, 1975). This book has been translated into eight languages. The obscure, French version (*Donald l'imposteur*) has been out of print for thirty years. To my view, this analysis using a post-Marxist framework was written within the terms of the tradition of cultural studies, but without ever once making reference to this expression.

17. Armand Mattelart and Michèle Mattelart, *Rethinking Media Theory: Signposts and New Directions*, trans. James Cohen and Marina Urquidi (Minneapolis: University of Minnesota Press, 1992), 21.

18. See Armand Mattelart and Michèle Mattelart, *Penser les médias* (Paris: La Découverte, 1986), 21.

19. See the special issue "Les Cultural Studies," *Réseaux: Communication technologie société* 80 (1996). The very long article by Armand Mattelart and Erik Neveu in this issue became a part of their book, *Introduction aux Cultural Studies*. The French translation of Stuart Hall's classic article appeared in an earlier issue of *Réseaux*.

20. See, for instance, the numerous works of Edgar Morin, Georges Balandier, and Jean Baudrillard.

21. Chris Barker, *The Sage Dictionary of Cultural Studies* (London: Sage, 2004).

22. See Andrew Calabrese and Colin Sparks, *Toward a Political Economy of Culture: Capitalism and Communication in the Twenty-First Century* (Lanham, Md.: Rowman and Littlefield, 2004).

23. Hartley, *Short History*, 93.

24. Stuart Hall, "Cultural Studies and Its Theoretical Legacies," in *Without Guarantees: In Honour of Stuart Hall*, ed. Paul Gilroy, Lawrence Grossberg, and Angela McRobbie (London: Verso, 2000), 101.

25. I was introduced to Althusser's writings during an excellent seminar given by Marc Raboy, at that time a professor at Laval University, who was familiar with post-Marxist theories.

26. See Louis Balthazar's article on Gilles Bourque's book *Question nationale et classes sociales au Québec (1760–1840)*, in *Dictionnaire des oeuvres littéraires du Québec*, vol. 5, 1970–1975, ed. Maurice Lemire (Montreal: Fides, 1987), 753.

27. As a complement to this chapter, see my review essay on François Cusset's *French Theory: Foucault, Derrida, Deleuze et Cie et les mutations de la vie intellectuelle aux États-Unis,* in the *International Journal of Baudrillard Studies* 2.2 (2005), available at http://www.ubish ops.ca/BaudrillardStudies/vol2_2/laberge.htm.

28. See the many intellectual portraits gathered in *Monuments intellectuels québécois du XXe siècle,* ed. Claude Cordo (Sillery: Septentrion, 2006).

29. See Simon Langlois, "A Productive Decade in the Tradition of Canadian Sociology," *Canadian Journal of Sociology* 25.3 (Summer 2000), 391–97.

30. Dumont's book *Le lieu de l'homme* won the Governor General's Award in 1968. See my account of Fernand Dumont's theory of culture in "De la culture aux cultures. Délimitations d'un concept pluri-sémantique," *Laval théologique et philosophique* 52.3 (1996), 805–25.

31. Fernand Dumont, *Le sort de la culture* (Montreal: Hexagone-Typo, 1995), 61.

32. Fernand Dumont, *Raisons communes* (Montreal: Boréal, 1995), 41. Dumont offers an assessment of the Quebec Referendum of 1980 and criticizes Pierre Trudeau, with whom he used to work in the early 1960s at *Cité Libre.*

33. Michael A. Weinstein, *Culture Critique: Fernand Dumont and New Quebec Sociology* (Montreal: New World Perspectives, 1985; New York: St. Martin's, 1985).

34. Fernand Dumont, *The Vigil of Quebec* (Toronto: University of Toronto Press, 1974); see the French edition of *La vigile du Québec. Octobre 1970: l'impasse?* (Montreal: Hurtubise, 1971).

35. The Meech Lake Accord (1987) was a set of proposed amendments to the Canadian Constitution which were intended to negotiate a new relationship of the province of Quebec to the federal government and the other provinces. It was not ratified, which had many consequences, including an increase in support for Quebec separatism.—Eds.

36. See the study by the political scientist Josée Legault, *L'invention d'une Minorité. Les Anglo-Québécois* (Montreal: Boréal, 1992).

37. Examples of books about Canada and Canadian politics from the last decade that contain a minimal perspective on Quebec include Lisa Young and Keith Archer, *Regionalism and Party Politics in Canada* (Don Mills, Ont.: Oxford University Press, 2002); Janine Brodie and Linda Trimble, eds., *Reinventing Canada: Politics of the 21st Century* (New York: Prentice Hall, 2003); Janet L. Hiebert, *Limiting Rights: The Dilemma of Judicial Review* (Montreal: McGill-Queen's University Press, 1996); James Tully, *Strange Multiplicity: Constitutionalism in an Age of Diversity* (Cambridge: Cambridge University Press, 1995); Fen Osler Hampson, Norman Hillmer, and Maureen Appel Molot, eds., *Canada among Nations 2001: The Axworthy Legacy* (New York: Oxford University Press, 2001); Don Carmichael, Tom Pocklington, and Greg Pyrcz, *Democracy, Rights, and Well-Being in Canada* (Toronto: Harcourt Brace Canada, 2000); Martin Westmacott and Hugh Mellon, *Challenges to Canadian Federalism* (Toronto: Prentice-Hall Canada, 1998); Joel Bakan, *Just Words: Constitutional Rights and Social Wrongs* (Toronto: University of Toronto Press, 1997); and Harvey Lazar, ed., *Canada: The State of the Federation 1999/2000: Toward a New Mission Statement for Canadian Fiscal Federalism* (Kingston, Ont.: Institute of Inter-

governmental Relations, 2000); I wish to thank Professor François Rocher for directing me to these references.

38. Jean-François Lisée, *Dans l'oeil de l'aigle* (Montreal: Boréal, 1990).

39. An e-version of the controversial *Report of Lord Durham on the Affairs of British North America* (1839) can be found at http://www2.marianopolis.edu/quebechistory/docs/durham/.

40. Ien Ang, "Identity Blues," in *Without Guarantees: In Honour of Stuart Hall*, ed. Paul Gilroy, Lawrence Grossberg, and Angela McRobbie (London: Verso, 2000), 1.

41. Tocqueville wrote: "Les Anglais et les Français se fondent si peu que les seconds gardent exclusivement le nom de Canadiens, les autres continuant à s'appeler Anglais." Alexis de Tocqueville, *Regards sur le Bas-Canada*, ed. Claude Corbo (1831; Montreal: Typo, 2003), 163.

42. Elsewhere, Tocqueville also wrote in enthusiastic terms: "Je viens de voir dans le Canada un million de Français braves, intelligents, faits pour former un jour une grande nation française en Amérique, qui vivent en quelque sorte en étrangers dans leur pays." Ibid., 211.

43. Everett C. Hughes, *French Canada in Transition* (Chicago: University of Chicago Press, 1944).

44. Jean Bouthillette, *Le Canadien français et son double* (Montreal: Hexagone, 1972). On Canadian identity, see also Mikhaël Elbaz, Andrée Fortin, and Guy Laforest, eds., *Les frontières de l'identité. Modernité et postmodernisme* (Sainte-Foy: Presses de l'Université Laval, 1996).

45. Guy Bouchard et al., eds., *Le phénomène IXE-13* (Quebec: Presses de l'Université Laval, 1984). See my article on this collection: "Le phénomène IXE-13," *Dictionnaire des œuvres littéraires du Québec. 1981–1985* (Montreal: Fides, 2003), 716–17.

46. Marie-José des Rivières, *Châtelaine et la littérature (1960–1975): Essai* (Montreal: L'Hexagone, 1992); this work is adapted from her Ph.D. thesis in literature.

47. Although they do not refer by name to cultural studies, all three authors refer to the French version of Richard Hoggart, *The Uses of Literacy* (*La culture du pauvre* [Paris: Éditions de Minuit, 1970]). Micheline Cambron, *Une société, un récit. Discours culturel au Québec, 1967–1976. Essai* (Montreal: L'Hexagone, 1989); and Lucie Robert, *L'institution du littéraire au Québec* (Quebec: Presses de l'Université Laval, 1989).

48. Jacques Godbout, *Alias Will James* (Montreal: NFB, 1988).

49. For instance, Canadian scholar Rosemary Coombe contributed a chapter, "Is There a Cultural Studies of Law?," to *A Companion to Cultural Studies*, ed. Toby Miller (Oxford: Blackwell, 2001), 36–62.

50. Chris Shilling and Philip A Mellor, *The Sociological Ambition* (London: Sage, 2001), 147.

51. Seth Feldman, "Foreword," in *North of Everything: English-Canadian Cinema since 1980*, ed. William Beard and Jerry White (Edmonton: University of Alberta Press, 2002), xiii.

52. Jerry White, "Alanis Obomsawin, Documentary Form and the Canadian Nation(s)," in *North of Everything: English-Canadian Cinema since 1980*, ed. William Beard

and Jerry White (Edmonton: University of Alberta Press, 2002), 368. See my detailed analysis of this problematic chapter: Yves Laberge, "La diversité des cinémas canadiens. Les méthodes d'analyse du cinéma au Canada," *Etudes canadiennes/Canadian Studies. Revue interdisciplinaire des études canadiennes en France* 59 (2005): 77–91.

53. Claude Jutra, *Mon Oncle Antoine* (Montréal, National Film Board of Canada, DVD, 1971).

54. Christopher E. Gittings, *Canadian National Cinema* (London: Routledge, 2002), 117.

55. Brent Pickett, *On the Use and Abuse of Foucault for Politics* (Lanham, Md.: Lexington Books, 2005), 65.

56. For instance, Ginette Vinsonneau wrote a fine book on cultural identity in which nothing is said about cultural studies. The names of Stuart Hall and Raymond Williams are mentioned in just one endnote. See Ginette Vinsonneau, *L'identité culturelle* (Paris: Armand Colin, 2002). See my comments in the short review of that book, published in *Canadian Ethnic Studies* 36.2 (2004): 146–47.

CONTRIBUTORS

Ian Angus is a professor in the Department of Humanities at Simon Fraser University. He is the author of *Emergent Publics: An Essay on Social Movements and Democracy* (2001), *(Dis)figurations: Discourse/Critique/Ethics* (2000), and *A Border Within: National Identity, Cultural Plurality, and Wilderness* (1997), among other works.

Himani Bannerji is a professor of sociology at York University. She is the author of numerous books, including *Inventing Subjects: Studies in Hegemony, Patriarchy, and Colonialism* (2001) and *The Dark Side of the Nation: Essays on Multiculturalism, Nationalism and Gender* (2000).

Jody Berland is an associate professor of humanities at York University. She is the founding editor of *Topia: Canadian Journal of Cultural Studies*, which celebrated its tenth anniversary in 2007, and author of *North of Empire: Culture, Space, Technology* (forthcoming).

Paul-Émile Borduas (1905–60) was one of the most prominent Canadian artists of the twentieth century. A member of the prominent post–World War II group of Quebecois abstract artists known as Les Automatistes, Borduas's manifesto *Refus Global* (1948) has been described as the most important text in the history of Canadian art.

Harold Cardinal (1945–2005) was an influential Cree writer, political figure, and lawyer. In books such as *The Unjust Society* (1969) and *The Rebirth of Canada's Indians* (1977), he advocated for the rights of Canada's aboriginal community. In 2001 he received the National Aboriginal Lifetime Achievement Award.

Maurice Charland is a professor of communication studies at Concordia University. He is a coauthor (with Michael Dorland) of *Law, Rhetoric, and Irony in the Formation of Canadian Civil Culture* (2002).

Stephen Crocker is an associate professor of sociology at Memorial University. He conducts research and teaches in the areas of sociological theory, the philosophy and sociology of time, and globalization.

Ioan Davies (1936–2000) taught in the Department of Sociology at York University. He was one of the founders of *Border/Lines*, Canada's first cultural studies magazine, and the author of books including *Cultural Studies and Beyond: Fragments of Empire* (1995) and *Writers in Prison* (1990).

Fernand Dumont (1927–97) is one of the most important intellectuals to emerge from Quebec. A major figure in the field of sociology, Dumont published over twenty books during his career, including academic works, poetry, and memoirs. Dumont spent his career as a professor at Laval University; he was made an officer of the Order of Quebec in 1992.

Kristina Fagan is an assistant professor of English at the University of Saskatchewan. Her research focuses on autobiography and storytelling in Canadian aboriginal communities, and their impact on literary theory and criticism.

Gail Faurschou holds a Ph.D. from York University and has taught communication and political economy at York University and Simon Fraser University. She is a senior research associate at the University of Alberta for *Kolkata Wonderland*, a video project on the information technology industry in India. She is currently completing her book *Finance, Fetishism and Popular Culture*.

Len Findlay is a professor of English and director of the Humanities Research Unit at the University of Saskatchewan. He has published widely in cultural studies, contemporary theory, Canadian studies, and aboriginal studies. In 2004, he published a new edition of Marx and Engel's *The Communist Manifesto*.

Northrop Frye (1912–91) was one of the twentieth century's most important and influential literary critics and theorists. His numerous books include *Fearful Symmetry: A Study of William Blake* (1947), *Anatomy of Criticism: Four Essays* (1957), and *The Bush Garden: Essays on the Canadian Imagination* (1971).

George Grant (1918–88) was a philosopher and public intellectual, and the author of *Lament for a Nation: The Defeat of Canadian Nationalism* (1965) and *Technology and Empire: Perspectives on North America* (1969), among other works. He taught at Dalhousie University and at McMaster University.

Rick Gruneau is a professor in the School of Communication at Simon Fraser University. He is the author of *Class, Sports and Social Development* (1999) and coauthor of *The Missing News: Filters and Blind Spots in Canada's Press* (2000). He has also written numerous essays dealing with communications and cultural theory.

Harold Innis (1894–1952) was a major Canadian scholar whose work has had a significant impact on the fields of communication studies, political economy, and cultural studies. A professor of political economy at the University of Toronto, he wrote a series of classic studies, including *The Fur Trade in Canada* (1930) and *The Cod Fisheries: A History of an International Economy* (1940), as well as groundbreaking books in media and communications such as *Empire and Communication* (1950) and *The Bias of Communication* (1951).

Fredric Jameson is the William A. Lane Jr. Professor of Comparative Literature at Duke University. His recent works include *Archaeologies of the Future: The Desire Called Utopia and Other Science Fictions* (2005), *The Modernist Papers* (2007), and *Valences of the Dialectic* (2009).

Yves Laberge is a sociologist and consultant who has worked at the CNRS (Centre National de la Recherche Scientifique) in France. Among other duties, he has served recently as a member of the advisory board for three encyclopedias: *France and the Americas: Culture, Politics, and History* (2005), *Germany and the Americas* (2005), and *Encyclopedia of the Blues* (2005).

Jocelyn Létourneau is the Canada Research Chair in Contemporary Political History and Economy in Quebec at Laval University. He is the author most recently of *Que veulent vraiment les Québécois?* (2006), *Le Québec, les Québécois: un parcours historique* (2004), and *A History for the Future: Rewriting Memory and Identity in Quebec* (2004).

Eva Mackey is an associate professor in the School of Canadian Studies at Carleton University. She is author of *The House of Difference: Cultural Politics and National Identity in Canada* (1999).

Lee Maracle is a Canadian First Nations writer. The author of numerous novels and books of poetry, as well as works of nonfiction, she is currently the writer-in-residence for First Nations House at the University of Toronto.

Marshall McLuhan (1911–80), a globally important intellectual, wrote a series of pathbreaking books exploring the impact of new technologies on twentieth-century social and cultural life. His books include *The Mechanical Bride* (1951), *The Gutenberg Galaxy* (1962), and *Understanding Media* (1964). McLuhan taught at the University of Toronto, where he founded the Centre for Culture and Technology (1963).

Katharyne Mitchell is a professor of geography at the University of Washington. She is the author of *Crossing the Neoliberal Line: Pacific Rim Migration and the Metropolis* (2004), coauthor of *Neoliberal Subjects: Education, Multiculturalism and the New Exceptionalism* (2007), and coeditor of *A Companion Guide to Political Geography* (2007).

Sourayan Mookerjea is an associate professor of sociology at the University of Alberta. He is the author of *Crisis and Catachresis: Pedagogy at the Limits of Identity Politics* (1996) and conducts research related to globalization and contemporary social theory.

Kevin Pask is a professor in the Department of English at Concordia University. He is the author of *The Emergence of the English Author: Scripting the Life of the Poet in Early Modern England* (1996).

Rob Shields is the Henry Marshall Tory Chair in the Departments of Sociology and Art and Design at the University of Alberta. He is the founding editor of the journal *Space and Culture* and author of *The Virtual* (2003), *Lefebvre, Love, and Struggle: Spatial Dialectics* (1999), *Places on the Margin: Alternative Geographies of Modernity* (1991), and other works.

Will Straw is a professor in the Department of Art History and Communications at McGill University. Author of numerous essays on film, music, and cultural studies, he is the author of *Cyanide and Sin: Visualizing Crime in 50s America* (2006) and coeditor of *Accounting for Culture: Thinking Through Cultural Citizenship* (2005) and *The Cambridge Companion to Rock and Pop* (2001).

Imre Szeman is the Senator McMaster Chair of Globalization and Cultural Studies at McMaster University. He is the author of *Zones of Instability: Literature, Postcolonialism and the Nation* (2003), coauthor of *Popular Culture: A User's Guide* (2004), and coeditor of the *Johns Hopkins Guide to Literary Theory and Criticism* (2005).

Serra Tinic is an associate professor of sociology at the University of Alberta. She is the author of *On Location: Canada's Television Industry in a Global Market* (2005).

David Whitson is a professor in the Department of Political Science at the University of Alberta. He is a coauthor, with Rick Gruneau, of the widely acclaimed *Hockey Night in Canada: Sport, Identities, and Cultural Politics* (1993) and coeditor (with Gruneau) of *Artificial Ice: Hockey, Culture, and Commerce* (2006).

Anthony Wilden taught communication theory at the School of Communication at Simon Fraser University. *The Language of the Self* (1968, reprinted as *Speech and Language in Psychoanalysis*) translated and introduced the work of Jacques Lacan to English audiences. He is the author of *System and Structure: Essays in Communication and Exchange* (1972) and *The Imaginary Canadian* (1980), among other works.

INDEX OF NAMES

Adams, Howard, 392

Adams, John, 56–57

Adams, John Quincy, 58

Aird, John, 314

Alfred, Taiaiake, 390–91, 395–402

Althusser, Louis, 568

Anderson, Benedict, 290, 293, 298, 301, 329, 341 n. 5, 393

Ang, Ien, 571

Angus, Ian, 28, 231, 480

Appadurai, Arjun, 371, 430

Arrighi, Giovanni, 18, 20

Atsenhaienton, 398, 401

Atwood, Margaret, 75–76, 446

Auden, W. H., 78–79

Austin-Smith, Brenda, 374

Bailey, Alfred, 116

Balibar, Étienne, 3

Bannerji, Himani, 9, 10, 27, 327

Barthes, Roland, 567

Baxter, David, 357–58

Beattie, Munro, 123–24, 126

Beaulieu, Victor-Lévy, 253, 273 n. 17

Bell, Claudia, 393

Bellamy, Edward, 137

Benjamin, Walter, 444, 451

Bennett, J. G., 44

Bennett, Michael, 315–16

Bennett, Tony, 17, 459

Bentham, Jeremy, 45

Berger, Thomas, 287 n. 25

Bergson, Henri, 50, 437

Berland, Jody, 472

Berman, Marshall, 444

Bernanos, Georges, 177

Betke, Carl, 493

Bloch, Ernst, 425–26

Bloomfield, Morton, 74–75

Bonaparte, Napoleon, 92

Borduas, Paul-Émile, 11, 13, 100

Bouchard, Gérard, 248, 272 n. 15

Bouchard, Lucien, 292, 294, 297, 306 n. 22

Bourassa, Henri, 174, 199 n. 2

Bourdieu, Pierre, 15, 364 n. 32, 371, 498, 564–65

Bouthillette, Jean, 571

Breckenridge, Carol, 371

Brooke, Frances, 121

Brooks, Chris, 434

Bunyan, Paul, 76–77

Burke, Johnny, 437

Butterworth, Ruth, 563–64

Cafik, Norman, 549

Calvino, Italo, 444, 452

Camus, Albert, 138

Cantin, Serge, 260–61

Cardinal, Harold, 9, 11, 13, 26–27, 200–201

Carey, James, 466

Carothers, J. C., 94

Cartier, Georges Etienne, 311, 322 n. 8

Cayley, David, 377

Chaplin, Charlie, 72, 77

Charland, Maurice, 308

Cheetham, James, 68 n. 13
Chrétien, Jean, 25, 200, 202, 204, 474
Churchill, Winston, 63, 152, 519
Cleisthenes, 41
Clement, Wallace, 233
Coates, Kenneth, 280
Cogswell, Fred, 118, 120–21
Colombo, John Robert, 486 n. 4
Cook, Ramsay, 80, 279
Cooper, Fennimore, 414
Copps, Sheila, 478
Courchene, David, 207
Creighton, Donald, 79–80, 246 n. 18, 278
Crocker, Stephen, 425
Crombie, David, 355
Crosbie, Lynn, 453–54

Davies, Ioan, 441
Davis, Jefferson, 60
Davis, Mike, 444
Day, Richard, 16
de Champlain, Samuel, 5
de Gaulle, Charles, 158 n. 4
de Tocqueville, Alexis. See Tocqueville
Diefenbaker, John, 84, 236, 548
Disraeli, Benjamin, 55, 129
Donnelly, Ignatius, 122
Dorfman, Ariel, 283
Dorland, Michael, 31 n. 9, 463
Drache, Daniel, 237
Drainie, Bronwyn, 375–76
Dryden, Ken, 489–91, 493
Duane, William, 68 n. 13
Dumont, Fernand, 11–12, 26, 173, 248, 250, 256, 258, 261–62, 271 n. 11, 299, 569, 570
Dumont, Micheline, 24
Duncan, Chester, 77
Durham, Lord (John Lambton), 75, 289

Eagleton, Terry, 474–75
Elliot, T. S., 83
Emerson, Ralph Waldo, 118

Fagan, Kristina, 390
Fanon, Frantz, 217, 426, 429
Feldman, Seth, 573
Ferro, Marc, 270 n. 3
Findlay, Len, 28, 405
Fiske, John, 498
Flax, Jane, 368
Forster, E. M., 93–94
Fraser, Joyce, 337
Fritzsche, Peter, 451
Frye, Northrop, 11, 13, 26, 239, 278–79, 453, 480–82

Galloway, David, 114
Garneau, François-Xavier, 177
Gasher, Mike, 502–3
Gellner, Ernest, 291, 294, 298, 302–4
Gilroy, Paul, 375, 379
Gissing, George, 47
Gittings, Christopher, 573–74
Godbout, Jacques, 253–54, 572
Goldberg, Kim, 506
Goldberg, Michael, 346
Gombrich, E. H., 91
Gordon, Walter, 184
Gramsci, Antonio, 232, 333, 345
Granet, Marcel, 38
Grant, George, 3, 11, 13, 26, 145–46, 232–36, 246 nn. 9–10, 453
Grant, Ulysses S., 60
Green, Joyce, 401
Groulx, Abbé Lionel, 295, 298
Gruneau, Rick, 488
Guy, Ray, 428
Gwyn, Richard, 429

Halfe, Louise, 394
Haliburton, Thomas, 115–16
Hall, Stuart, xi, 2, 17–18, 25, 434, 563–65, 567
Hamilton, Alexander, 56–57
Hamilton, S. W., 358
Handler, Richard, 369
Hansen, Philip, 491–92

Hardy, Thomas, 129–30
Harper, Elijah, 337, 342 n. 21
Harris, Mike, 447
Hartley, John, 566
Hartman, Geoffrey, 28, 414–17
Hawthorne, Nathaniel, 76
Hayes, Rutherford B., 60–61
Hegel, Georg, 148
Hicks, Edward, 125–26
Hitler, Adolf, 46
Hoggart, Richard, 567
hooks, bell, 344
Huerta, Ricardo, 436–37
Hughes, Everett C., 571
Hughes, Sam, 152
Hulan, Renee, 391
Hume, David, 90, 149
Hurtig, Mel, 235, 237
Hutcheon, Linda, 427, 433

Innis, Harold, xii, 11, 26, 37, 77, 119,
    232–33, 236, 241, 278, 285 n. 6, 309,
    314, 320

Jackson, Andrew, 58
Jacobs, Jane, 299, 445–46
James, Henry, 76
James, William, 50
Jameson, Fredric, 2, 406, 454
Jefferson, Thomas, 57
Johnson, E. Pauline, 401–2
Jones, Andy, 437
Jung, C. G., 98
Jutra, Claude, 574
Jutras, Hélène, 260, 274, 301

Karatani, Kojin, 456 n. 22
Karp, Ivan, 371
Kenner, Hugh, 77–78
Keynes, John Maynard, 45, 48, 50
Kierkegaard, Sören, 267
Kilbourn, William, 114–15
King, Mackenzie, 151–52, 312–14
Klinck, Carl, 115, 120

Kosseleck, Rheinhart, 426
Kroetsch, Robert, 479–81
Kruhlak, Orest, 357

Lacoursière, Jacques, 248–49
Laferrière, Dany, 302
Laframboise, Donna, 377
Lalla, Harry, 374
Lamartine, Alphonse de, 44
Landry, Bernard, 272 n. 15, 294, 297, 300
Langevin, Hector L., 548
Lastman, Mel, 447
Latouche, Daniel, 292–93, 297–98, 301
Laurier, Wilfrid, 353, 548
Laurin, Camille, 291
Laxer, Jim, 236–37
Layton, Irving, 124
Leacock, Stephen, 75, 77
Lee, Dennis, 441–42, 446, 454
Legault, Josée, 251–52, 260, 272 n. 13
Lepage, Robert, 300–301
Lesage, Jean, 22, 289, 296
Létourneau, Jocelyn, 29, 248, 291
Lévesque, René, 273 n. 16, 290, 296–97
Lévinas, Emmanuel, 267
Lewis, Wyndham, 94–95, 131
Liebling, A. J., 98
Lincoln, Abraham, 59
Litt, Paul, 241
Locke, John, 150, 172 n. 1
Lorimer, Rowland, 240
Lumsden, Ian, 239
Lyons, Oren, 400
Lyotard, Jean-François, 292

MacDonald, John A., 201, 318
Mackey, Eva, 27, 366
MacLure, Millar, 122
Macpherson, C. B., 445–46, 453
Macpherson, Jay, 117
Madison, James, 57
Mann, Thomas, 435
Maracle, Brian, 396–97, 400
Maracle, Lee, 28, 383–89

Marchand, Jean, 23, 180
Marcuse, Herbert, 161, 167–68
Marx, Karl, 16, 129, 135, 383–84
Mathews, Robin, 238
Mattelart, Armand, 283, 562, 565
Mays, John Bentley, 452–54
McClung, Nellie, 334, 342 n. 13
McConaghy, Cathryn, 392
McKinley, W. J., 61
McLuhan, Marshall, xii, 3, 11, 25–26, 71, 119, 126, 139–40, 453, 464
McNaught, Kenneth, 81, 475
Mercer, Rick, 472–73, 475, 481
Michaud, Yves, 306 n. 22
Mill, John Stuart, 137
Mirabaud, Pierre, 348
Miron, Gaston, 291
Mitchell, Katharyne, 28, 344
Moltke, Helmuth von, 44
Monroe, James, 57–58
Monture-Angus, Patricia, 396, 400
Moodie, Susanna, 115, 117
Moodley, Kogila, 369
Moore, C. C., 76
Moore, Henry, 448
Moran, Raymond, 316
Morton, W. L., 277–78
Mulroney, Brian, 24, 293, 303, 355
Muszynski, Alicja, 491–92
Myrdal, Gunnar, 213

Naylor, R. T., 233
Neveu, Erik, 562
nichol, bp, 450–51, 453
Northcliffe, Lord, 43

Ondaatje, Michael, 446
Orwell, George, 142–43
Ostrogorski, Moisey, 67

Parizeau, Jacques, 290, 293, 295
Parkman, Francis, 412–14
Pask, Kevin, 289
Pearson, Lester B., 21–23, 442, 549

Philip, Marlene Nourbese, 372
Pickett, Brent, 575
Pius XII, 97
Pocius, Gerald, 436
Polanyi, Karl, 48, 136
Polk, J. K., 59
Porteous, J. B., 191–92
Porter, John, 445
Poulantzas, Nicos, 361
Prang, Margaret, 241, 317
Pratt, E. J., 119, 121, 123, 126
Proulx, E. Annie, 429
Pue, Wes, 200

Ramraj, Victor, 411
Rankin, Harry, 346
Resnick, Philip, 244, 479
Richardson, John, 286 n. 13
Ricouer, Paul, 183
Riel, Louis, 120
Rioux, Marcel, 12
Roach, Charles, 378
Rooney, Ellen, 459
Roosevelt, Franklin D., 46, 62–63, 65, 154
Roosevelt, Theodore, 44, 46, 61–62, 64
Rousseau, Jean-Jacques, 142
Ruggie, John Gerard, 301

Sansom, G. B., 96
Sarnoff, David, 90
Sartre, Jean-Paul, 157
Saul, John Ralston, 272 n. 15, 482
Scaliger, Joseph Justus, 38–39
Scargill, M. H., 115
Schecter, Stephen, 482
Schramm, Wilbur, 97
Scott, Duncan Campbell, 116, 128 n. 7
Seidel, Gill, 376
Seyle, Hans, 89–90
Shakespeare, William, 89, 113
Shields, Rob, 29, 276
Silvera, Makeda, 337
Simpson, Audra, 396

Simpson, John Hope, 428, 439 n. 6

Slack, Enid, 358–59

Slick, Sam, 125

Smallwood, Joey, 429–30, 434

Smith, Dorothy, 447–48, 453

Smith, Linda Tuhiwai, 407–8, 410

Snow, C. P., 95

Söderlind, Sylvia, 31 n. 10

Solzhenitsyn, Aleksandr, 282

Sorel, Pierre (Pierre Daignault), 572

Souster, Raymond, 123

Spengler, Oswald, 50–51, 141

Stead, W. T., 43

Steele, James, 238

Stoddard, Lothrop, 350

Straw, Will, 457

Swift, Jonathan, 149

Tacitus, 417

Tait, Michael, 118

Taylor, Charles, 27, 306 n. 29, 479

Taylor, Zachary, 59

Testa, Bart, 30–31 n. 9

Thévenaz, Pierre, 192–93

Thibault, Lise, 272 n. 15

Thom, Martin, 298–99

Thorton, Henry, 312

Tinic, Serra, 501

Tocqueville, Alexis de, 54, 81, 92–93, 571

Toynbee, Arnold, 96

Tremblay, Michel, 296, 300

Trudeau, Pierre Elliot, 9, 21, 23, 32–33
    n. 24, 200–204, 296, 353, 442, 477,
    549

Truman, Harry, 65

Turmel, André, 252, 260, 272 n. 14

Turner, Frederick J., 83

Vallières, Pierre, 296

van Buren, Martin, 59

Vickers, Jill, 23–24

Viger, Denis-Benjamin, 179

Villard, Oswald Garrison, 44

Wacquant, Loïc, 15

Wallerstein, Immanuel, 18, 20, 22

Warrior, Robert, 395

Washington, George, 55–56

Waterston, Elizabeth, 117

Watkins, Melville, 233, 235

Watt, Frank, 122–23

Weber, Max, 148, 178, 291

Wells, H. G., 141–42

Westerman, Floyd, 385

White, Jerry, 573

Whitman, Walt, 76

Whitson, David, 488

Wilden, Tony, 11, 27, 210

Williams, Raymond, 345, 499

Wilson, Woodrow, 62–63

Windsor, Kenneth, 115

Womack, Craig, 392

Worsley, Peter, 296

Yeats, W. B., 83

Zalm, Vander, 347

SOURAYAN MOOKERJEA is an associate
professor of sociology at the University of Alberta.

IMRE SZEMAN is the Senator McMaster Chair of
Globalization and Cultural Studies and a professor
of English and cultural studies at McMaster
University.

GAIL FAURSCHOU is a senior research associate
at the University of Alberta for *Kolkata Wonderland*,
a video project on the information technology
industry in India.

Library of Congress Cataloging-in-Publication Data
Canadian cultural studies : a reader / Sourayan Mookerjea, Imre Szeman,
and Gail Faurschou, eds. ; foreword by Fredric Jameson.
p. cm.
Includes bibliographical references and index.
ISBN 978-0-8223-4398-1 (cloth : alk. paper)
ISBN 978-0-8223-4416-2 (pbk. : alk. paper)
1. Culture—Study and teaching—Canada. 2. Canada—Civilization. 3. Canada—
Social life and customs. I. Mookerjea, Sourayan II. Szeman, Imre, 1968–
III. Faurschou, Gail
HM623.C35 2009
306.0971′07—dc22   2008055240